CORE-PLUS MATHEMATICS PROJECT

Course Part B 2

Contemporary Mathematics in Context

A Unified Approach

CORE-PLUS MATHEMATICS PROJECT

Course
Part B **2**

Contemporary Mathematics in Context

A Unified Approach

Arthur F. Coxford
James T. Fey
Christian R. Hirsch
Harold L. Schoen
Gail Burrill
Eric W. Hart
Ann E. Watkins
with
Mary Jo Messenger
Beth Ritsema

EVERYDAY LEARNING™

Chicago, Illinois

Photo Acknowledgements

Cover Images: Images © 1997 Photodisc, Inc.

Photo credits are given on page T565 and constitute a continuation of the copyright page.
Everyday Learning Corporation would like to thank the following for providing photographs of
Core-Plus students in their schools. Many of these photographs appear throughout the text.

Janice Lee, Midland Valley High School, Langley, SC
Steve Matheos, Firestone High School, Akron, OH
Ann Post, Traverse City West Junior High School, Traverse City, MI
Alex Rachita, Ellet High School, Akron, OH
Judy Slezak, Prairie High School, Cedar Rapids, IA
The Core-Plus Mathematics Project

Everyday Learning Development Staff
Editorial: Anna Belluomini, Eric Karnowski, Steve Mico, Michael Murphy
Production/Design: Fran Brown, Hector Cuadra, Jess Schaal, Norma Underwood, Marie Walz

Additional Credits
Gregory Oles, J•B Vision Graphics

 This project was supported, in part, by the National Science Foundation.
The opinions expressed are those of the authors and not necessarily those of the Foundation.

ISBN 1-57039-484-9 (Part A)
ISBN 1-57039-488-1 (Part B)

1 2 3 4 5 6 7 8 9 WC 02 01 00 99 98

About the Core-Plus Mathematics Project

The **Core-Plus Mathematics Project (CPMP)** is a multiyear project funded by the National Science Foundation to develop student and teacher materials for a complete high school mathematics curriculum. Courses 1–3 comprise a core curriculum appropriate for *all* students. The fourth-year course continues the preparation of students for college mathematics.

Development Team

Project Director

Christian R. Hirsch
Western Michigan University

Project Co-Directors

Arthur F. Coxford
University of Michigan

James T. Fey
University of Maryland

Harold L. Schoen
University of Iowa

Senior Curriculum Developers

Gail Burrill
University of Wisconsin-Madison

Eric W. Hart
Western Michigan University

Ann E. Watkins
California State University, Northridge

Professional Development Coordinator

Beth Ritsema
Western Michigan University

Advisory Board

Diane Briars
Pittsburgh Public Schools

Jeremy Kilpatrick
University of Georgia

Kenneth Ruthven
University of Cambridge

David A. Smith
Duke University

Edna Vasquez
Detroit Renaissance High School

Curriculum Development Consultants

Alverna Champion
Grand Valley State University

Cherie Cornick
Wayne County Alliance for Mathematics and Science

Edgar Edwards
(Formerly) Virginia State Department of Education

Richard Scheaffer
University of Florida

Martha Siegel
Towson University

Edward Silver
University of Pittsburgh

Lee Stiff
North Carolina State University

Technical Coordinator

Wendy Weaver
Western Michigan University

Evaluation Coordinator

Steve Ziebarth
University of Iowa

Collaborating Teachers

Emma Ames
Oakland Mills High School, Maryland

Laurie Eyre
Maharishi School, Iowa

Cheryl Girardot
Sitka High School, Alaska

Joel Goodman
North Cedar Community High School, Iowa

Michael J. Link
Central Academy, Iowa

Mary Jo Messenger
Howard County Public Schools, Maryland

Valerie Mills
Ann Arbor Public Schools, Michigan

Jacqueline Stewart
Okemos High School, Michigan

Michael Verkaik
Holland Christian High School, Michigan

Marcia Weinhold
Kalamazoo Area Mathematics and Science Center, Michigan

Graduate Assistants

Diane Bean
University of Iowa

Judy Flowers
University of Michigan

Chris Rasmussen
University of Maryland

Rebecca Walker
Western Michigan University

Production and Support Staff

James Laser

Michelle Magers

Cheryl Peters

Jennifer Rosenboom

Kathryn Wright
Western Michigan University

Software Developers

Jim Flanders
Colorado Springs, Colorado

Eric Kamischke
Interlochen, Michigan

Core-Plus Mathematics Project Field-Test Sites

Special thanks are extended to these teachers and their students who participated in the testing and evaluation of Course 2.

Ann Arbor Huron High School
Ann Arbor, Michigan
  Ginger Gajar
  Brenda Garr

Ann Arbor Pioneer High School
Ann Arbor, Michigan
  Jim Brink
  Tammy Schirmer

Arthur Hill High School
Saginaw, Michigan
  Virginia Abbott
  Felix Bosco
  David Kabobel

Battle Creek Central High School
Battle Creek, Michigan
  Teresa Ballard
  Steven Ohs

Bedford High School
Temperance, Michigan
  Ellen Bacon
  Linda Martin
  Lynn Parachek

Bloomfield Hills Andover High School
Bloomfield Hills, Michigan
  Jane Briskey
  Cathy King
  Ed Okuniewski
  Linda Robinson
  Roger Siwajek

Brookwood High School
Snellville, Georgia
  Ginny Hanley
  Linda Wyatt

Caledonia High School
Caledonia, Michigan
  Jenny Diekevers
  Kim Drefcenski
  Thomas Oster

Centaurus High School
Lafayette, Colorado
  Eilene Leach
  Gail Reichert

Clio High School
Clio, Michigan
  Bruce Hanson
  David Sherry
  Lee Sheridan

Davison High School
Davison, Michigan
  Evelyn Ailing
  Wayne Desjarlais
  Darlene Tomczak
  Dan Tomczak

Dexter High School
Dexter, Michigan
  Kris Chatas
  Widge Proctor

Ellet High School
Akron, Ohio
  Marcia Csipke
  Jim Fillmore
  Scott Slusser

Firestone High School
Akron, Ohio
  Barbara Adler
  Barbara Crucs
  Jennifer Walls

Flint Northern High School
Flint, Michigan
  Al Wojtowicz

Goodrich High School
Goodrich, Michigan
  Mike Coke
  John Doerr

Grand Blanc High School
Grand Blanc, Michigan
  Charles Carmody
  Linda Nielsen

Grass Lake Junior/Senior High School
Grass Lake, Michigan
  Larry Poertner

Gull Lake High School
Richland, Michigan
   Darlene Kohrman
   Dorothy Louden

Kalamazoo Central High School
Kalamazoo, Michigan
   Gloria Foster
   Bonnie Frye
   Amy Schwentor

Kelloggsville Public Schools
Wyoming, Michigan
   Jerry Czarnecki
   Steve Ramsey
   John Ritzler

Knott County Central High School
Hindman, Kentucky
   Teresa Combs
   P. Denise Gibson
   Brenda Mullins

Midland Valley High School
Langley, South Carolina
   Kim Huebner
   Janice Lee

Murray-Wright High School
Detroit, Michigan
   Jack Sada

North Lamar High School
Paris, Texas
   Tommy Eads
   Barbara Eatherly

Okemos High School
Okemos, Michigan
   Lisa Crites
   Jacqueline Stewart

Portage Northern High School
Portage, Michigan
   Pete Jarrad
   Scott Moore
   Jerry Swoboda

Prairie High School
Cedar Rapids, Iowa
   Dave LaGrange
   Judy Slezak

San Pasqual High School
Escondido, California
   Damon Blackman
   Gary Hanel
   Ron Peet
   Torril Purvis
   Becky Stephens

Sitka High School
Sitka, Alaska
   Mikolas Bekeris
   Cheryl Girardot
   Dan Langbauer
   Tom Smircich

Sturgis High School
Sturgis, Michigan
   Craig Evans
   Kathy Parkhurst
   Dale Rauh
   JoAnn Roe
   Kathy Roy

Sweetwater High School
National City, California
   Bill Bokesch
   Joe Pistone

Tecumseh High School
Tecumseh, Michigan
   Jennifer Keffer
   Elizabeth Lentz
   Carl Novak
   Eric Roberts

Traverse City High School
Traverse City, Michigan
   Diana Lyon-Schumacher
   Ken May

Vallivue High School
Caldwell, Idaho
   Scott Coulter
   Kathy Harris

Ypsilanti High School
Ypsilanti, Michigan
   Valerie Mills
   Don Peurach
   Kristen Stewart

Overview of Course 2
Part A

Unit 1 ▶ Matrix Models

Matrix Models extends student ability to use matrices and matrix operations to represent and solve problems from a variety of real-world settings while connecting important mathematical ideas from several strands.

Topics include matrix models in such areas as inventory control, social relations, archeology, recidivism, ecosystems, sports, tournament rankings, and Markov processes; matrix operations, including row sums, matrix addition, scalar multiplication, matrix multiplication, and matrix powers.

Lesson 1   *Building and Using Matrix Models*
Lesson 2   *Multiplying Matrices*
Lesson 3   *Matrices and Systems of Linear Equations*
Lesson 4   *Looking Back*

Unit 2 ▶ Patterns of Location, Shape, and Size

Patterns of Location, Shape, and Size develops student understanding of coordinate methods for representing and analyzing relations among geometric shapes, and for describing geometric change.

Topics include modeling situations with coordinates, including computer-generated graphics, distance in the coordinate plane, midpoint of a segment, slope, designing and programming algorithms, matrices, systems of equations, coordinate models of isometric transformations (reflections, rotations, translations, glide reflections) and of size transformations, and similarity.

Lesson 1   *Predicting from Data*
Lesson 2   *Coordinate Models of Transformations*
Lesson 3   *Transformations, Matrices, and Animation*
Lesson 4   *Looking Back*

Unit 3 ▶ Patterns of Association

Patterns of Association develops student understanding of the strength of association between two variables, how to measure the degree of the relation, and how to use this measure as a tool to create and interpret prediction lines for paired data.

Topics include rank correlation, Pearson's correlation coefficient, cause and effect related to correlation, impact of outliers on correlation, least squares linear models, the relation of correlation to linear models, and variability in prediction.

Lesson 1   *Seeing and Measuring Association*
Lesson 2   *Correlation*
Lesson 3   *Least Squares Regression*
Lesson 4   *Looking Back*

Unit 4 ▶ Power Models

Power Models develops student ability to recognize data patterns that involve both direct and inverse power variation, to construct and analyze those models and combinations such as quadratic functions, and to apply those models to a variety of practical and scientific questions.

Topics include basic power models with rules of the form $y = ax^b$ (b a positive or negative integer), combinations of power models with other simple models, and analysis of quadratic functions and equations from tabular, graphic, and symbolic viewpoints.

Lesson 1   *Same Shape, Different Size*
Lesson 2   *Inverse Variation*
Lesson 3   *Quadratic Models*
Lesson 4   *Radicals and Fractional Power Models*
Lesson 5   *Looking Back*

Overview of Course 2
Part B

Unit 5 ▶ Network Optimization

Network Optimization extends student ability to use vertex-edge graphs to represent and analyze real-world situations involving network optimization, including optimal spanning networks and shortest routes.

Topics include vertex-edge graph models, optimization, algorithmic problem solving, matrices, trees, minimal spanning trees, shortest paths, Hamiltonian circuits and paths, and Traveling Salesperson problems.

Lesson 1	*Finding the Best Networks*
Lesson 2	*Shortest Paths and Circuits*
Lesson 3	*Looking Back*

Unit 6 ▶ Geometric Form and Its Function

Geometric Form and Its Function develops student ability to model and analyze physical phenomena with triangles, quadrilaterals, and circles and to use these shapes to investigate trigonometric functions, angular velocity, and periodic change.

Topics include parallelogram linkages, pantographs, similarity, triangular linkages (with one side that can change length), sine, cosine, and tangent ratios, indirect measurement, angular velocity, transmission factor, linear velocity, periodic change, period, amplitude, and graphs of functions of the form $y = A \sin (Bx)$ or $y = A \cos (Bx)$.

Lesson 1	*Flexible Quadrilaterals*
Lesson 2	*Triangles and Trigonometric Ratios*
Lesson 3	*The Power of the Circle*
Lesson 4	*Looking Back*

Unit 7 ▶ Patterns in Chance

Patterns in Chance develops student ability to understand and visualize situations involving chance by using simulation and mathematical analysis to construct probability distributions.

Topics include probability distributions and their graphs, multiplication rule for independent events, geometric distribution, expected value, rare events, and an introduction to the binomial distribution.

Lesson 1	*Waiting Times*
Lesson 2	*The Multiplication Rule*
Lesson 3	*Probability Distributions*
Lesson 4	*Expected Value of a Probability Distribution*
Lesson 5	*Looking Back*

Capstone ▶ Looking Back at Course 2

Forests, the Environment, and Mathematics is a thematic, two-week project-oriented activity that enables students to pull together and apply the important modeling concepts and methods developed throughout the course.

Contents

Part B

Unit 5 ▶ Network Optimization

Unit 6 ▶ Geometric Form and Its Function

Correlation of Course 2 to NCTM Standards

The *Contemporary Mathematics in Context* curriculum and the instructional and assessment practices it promotes address the focal points of the National Council of Teachers of Mathematics *Curriculum Standards* for grades 9–12. By design, the **process standards** on Problem Solving, Reasoning, Communication, and Connections are an integral part of each lesson of every unit in the curriculum.

The chart below correlates Course 2 units with the **content standards** for grades 9–12 in terms of primary emphases (✓) and connections (+).

	NCTM Grades 9–12 Content Standards									
	Algebra	Functions	Geometry from a Synthetic Viewpoint	Geometry from an Algebraic Viewpoint	Trigonometry	Statistics	Probability	Discrete Mathematics	Conceptual Under-pinnings of Calculus	Mathematical Structure
Course 2 Units										
Matrix Models	✓	✓	+			+		✓		+
Patterns of Location, Shape, and Size	✓	✓	+	✓				✓		+
Patterns of Association	✓	✓		+		✓		+		
Power Models	✓	✓	+			✓		+	✓	
Network Optimization	✓		+					✓		
Geometric Form and Its Function	✓	✓	✓	✓	✓	+			+	
Patterns in Chance	✓	✓	+	+		✓	✓	+	✓	
Capstone — Forests, the Environment, and Mathematics	✓	✓	✓	✓	✓	✓	✓	✓	✓	

Curriculum Overview

▶Introduction

Contemporary Mathematics in Context Course 2 continues a four-year integrated mathematics program developed by the **Core-Plus Mathematics Project (CPMP).** The curriculum builds upon the theme of mathematics as sense-making. Investigations of real-life contexts lead to discovery of important mathematics that make sense to students and, in turn, enable them to make sense out of new situations and problems. The curriculum materials have the following features:

■ Multiple Connected Strands

Contemporary Mathematics in Context is a comprehensive mathematical sciences curriculum. Each year the curriculum features multiple ideas from four strands: algebra and functions, geometry and trigonometry, statistics and probability, and discrete mathematics. These strands are unified by fundamental themes, by common topics, and by habits of mind or ways of thinking.

■ Mathematical Modeling

The curriculum emphasizes mathematical modeling and modeling concepts including data collection, representation, interpretation, prediction, and simulation.

■ Access

The curriculum is designed so that core topics are accessible to all students. Differences in students' performance and interest can be accommodated by the depth and level of abstraction to which topics are pursued, by the nature and degree of difficulty of applications, and by providing opportunities for student choice of homework tasks and projects.

■ Graphics Calculators

Numerical, graphics, and programming/link capabilities of graphics calculators are assumed and capitalized on. This technology permits the curriculum and instruction to emphasize multiple representations (numerical, graphical, and symbolic) and to focus on goals in which mathematical thinking is central.

■ Active Learning

Instructional practices promote mathematical thinking through the use of rich problem situations that involve students, both in collaborative groups and individually, in investigating, conjecturing, verifying, applying, evaluating, and communicating mathematical ideas.

■ Multidimensional Assessment

Comprehensive assessment of student understanding and progress through both curriculum-embedded assessment opportunities and supplementary assessment tasks enables monitoring and evaluation of each student's performance in terms of mathematical processes, content, and dispositions.

This curriculum promises to make mathematics accessible to a diverse student population. Developing mathematics along multiple strands nurtures the differing strengths and talents of students and simultaneously helps them to develop diverse mathematical insights. Developing mathematics from a modeling perspective permits students to experience mathematics as a means of making sense of data and problems that arise in diverse contexts within and across cultures. Engaging students in collaborating on tasks in small groups develops their ability to both deal with, and find commonality in, diversity of ideas. Using calculators as a means for learning and doing mathematics enables students to develop versatile ways of dealing with realistic situations and reduces the manipulative skill filter that has prevented large numbers of students from continuing their study of significant mathematics.

▶ Unified Mathematics

Each year *Contemporary Mathematics in Context* features "strands" of algebra and functions, geometry and trigonometry, statistics and probability, and discrete mathematics. These strands are unified within units by fundamental ideas such as symmetry, function, matrices, data analysis, and curve-fitting. The strands also are connected across units by mathematical habits of mind such as visual thinking, recursive thinking, searching for and describing patterns, making and checking conjectures, reasoning with multiple representations, inventing mathematics, and providing convincing arguments. The strands are unified further by the fundamental themes of data, representation, shape, and change. Important mathematical ideas are continually revisited through this attention to connections within and across strands, enabling students to develop a robust understanding of mathematics.

■ Algebra and Functions

The algebra and functions strand develops students' ability to recognize, represent, and solve problems involving relations among quantitative variables. Central to the development is the use of functions as mathematical models. The key algebraic models in the curriculum are linear, exponential, power, and periodic functions and combinations of these basic types. Each algebraic model is investigated in at least three linked representations—graphic, numeric, and symbolic—with the aid of technology. Attention is also given to modeling with systems, both linear and nonlinear, and to symbolic reasoning.

■ Geometry and Trigonometry

The primary goal of the geometry and trigonometry strand is to develop visual thinking and students' ability to construct, reason with, interpret, and apply mathematical models of patterns in the visual world. Modeling visual patterns involves describing the patterns with regard to shape, size, and location; representing visual patterns with drawings, coordinates, or vectors; and predicting changes, and invariants in visual patterns when some force is applied or action occurs to an object. Drawing, constructing, manipulating, and analyzing models of visual patterns in two and three dimensions are emphasized.

■ Statistics and Probability

The primary role of the statistics and probability strand is to develop students' ability to analyze data intelligently, to recognize and measure variation, and to understand the patterns that underlie probabilistic situations. Graphical methods of data analysis, simulations, sampling, and experience with the collection and interpretation of real data are featured.

■ Discrete Mathematics

The discrete mathematics strand develops students' ability to model and solve problems involving sequential change, decision making in finite settings, and relationships among a finite number of elements. Topics include matrices, vertex-edge graphs, recursion, models of social decision making, and systematic counting methods. Key themes are existence (*Is there a solution?*), optimization (*What is the best solution?*), and algorithmic problem solving (*Can you efficiently construct a solution?*).

▶Instructional Model

The curriculum for Course 2 consists of seven units and a culminating capstone experience. Each of the units is comprised of four to five multiday lessons in which major ideas are developed through investigations of rich applied problems. Units vary in length from approximately four to six weeks. The final element of Course 2, the capstone, is a thematic two-week project-oriented activity that enables students to pull together and apply the important modeling concepts and methods developed in the entire course.

The manner in which students meet mathematical ideas within lessons can be as important as the mathematics contained in those lessons. Lessons in *Contemporary Mathematics in Context* are therefore designed around a specific cycle of instructional activities intended primarily for small-group work in the classroom and for individual work outside of the classroom.

In Class The four-phase cycle of classroom activities—*Launch, Explore, Share and Summarize*, and *Apply*—is designed to actively engage students in investigating and making sense of problem situations, in constructing important mathematical concepts and methods, and in communicating their thinking and the results of their efforts. The chart below describes these phases of classroom instruction.

In-Class Instruction

LAUNCH full-class discussion

Think About This Situation

The lesson begins with a full-class discussion of a problem situation and of related questions to **think about.** This discussion sets the context for the student work to follow and helps to generate student interest; it also provides an opportunity for the teacher to assess student knowledge and to clarify directions for the group activities. *Teacher is director and moderator.*

EXPLORE small-group investigation

INVESTIGATION ▶1

Classroom activity then shifts to having the students **investigate** focused problems and questions related to the launching situation by gathering data, looking for patterns, constructing models and meanings, and making and verifying conjectures. As students work cooperatively in small groups, the teacher circulates from group to group providing guidance and support, clarifying or asking questions, giving hints, providing encouragement, and drawing group members into the discussion to help groups work more cooperatively. The unit materials and related questions posed by students drive the learning. *Teacher is facilitator.*

Checkpoint

A full-class discussion (referred to as a *Checkpoint*) of concepts and methods developed by different small groups then provides an opportunity to **share** progress and thinking. This discussion leads to a class **summary** of important ideas or to further exploration of a topic if competing perspectives remain. Varying points of view and differing conclusions that can be justified should be encouraged. *Teacher is moderator.*

APPLY individual task

▶On Your Own

Finally, students are given a task to complete on their own to **reinforce** their initial understanding of a concept or method. The teacher circulates in the room assessing levels of understanding. *Teacher is intellectual coach.*

Out of Class In addition to the classroom investigations, *Contemporary Mathematics in Context* provides sets of MORE tasks, which are designed to engage students in *Modeling* with, *Organizing*, *Reflecting* on, and *Extending* their mathematical knowledge. MORE tasks are provided for each lesson in the CPMP materials and are central to the learning goals of each lesson. MORE tasks are intended primarily for individual work outside of class. Selection of MORE activities for use with a given class should be based on student performance and the availability of time and technology. Also, students should exercise some choice of tasks to pursue, and at times they should be given the opportunity to pose their own problems and questions to investigate. The chart below describes the types of tasks in a typical MORE set.

MORE: Out-of-Class Activities	
Modeling	*Modeling* tasks are related or new contexts to which students can apply the ideas and methods that they have developed in the lesson.
Organizing	*Organizing* tasks offer opportunities for integrating the formal mathematics underlying the mathematical models developed in the lesson and for making connections with other strands.
Reflecting	*Reflecting* tasks encourage thinking about thinking, about mathematical meanings, and about processes, and promote self-monitoring and evaluation of understanding.
Extending	*Extending* tasks permit further, deeper, or more formal study of the topics under investigation.

►Assessment

Assessing what students know and are able to do is an integral part of *Contemporary Mathematics in Context* and the instructional model. Initially, as students pursue the investigations that make up the curriculum, the teacher is able to informally assess student performance in terms of process, content, and disposition. Then at the end of each investigation the *Checkpoint* and class discussion provide an opportunity for teachers to assess the levels of understanding that the various groups of students have reached. Finally, *On Your Own* problem situations and tasks in the MORE sets provide further opportunities to assess the level of understanding of each individual student.

A much more detailed description of the CPMP assessment program is given in *Implementing the CPMP Curriculum.*

►Organization of the Text

The organization of the student text, like that for Course 1, differs in several other ways from traditional textbooks. There are no boxed-off definitions, "worked-out" examples, or content summaries. Students learn mathematics by doing mathematics. Concept images are developed as students complete investigations and later concept definitions may appear. Mathematical ideas are developed and then shared by groups of students at strategically placed Checkpoints in the lessons. This discussion leads to a class summary of shared understandings.

It is important that each student construct a Mathematics Toolkit consisting of mathematical concepts and methods as they are developed. By organizing important class-generated ideas from a unit, occasional summary Checkpoint responses, or a unit summary in the student's own words, the student will have a valuable set of tools that can be used throughout the course and in subsequent courses.

Implementing the Curriculum

▶Planning for Instruction

The *Contemporary Mathematics in Context* curriculum is not only changing what mathematics all students have the opportunity to learn, but also changing how that learning occurs and is assessed. Active learning is most effective when accompanied with active teaching. Just as the student text is designed to actively engage students in doing mathematics, the teacher's resource materials are designed to support teachers in planning for instruction; in observing, listening to, questioning, facilitating student work, and orchestrating classroom discussion; and in managing the classroom.

The *Teacher's Guide* provides suggestions, based on the experiences of field-test teachers, for implementing this exciting new curriculum in your classroom. You probably will find several new ideas that can be overwhelming. The developers highly recommend that teachers who are teaching *Contemporary Mathematics in Context* for the first time do so at least in pairs who share a common planning period.

Each of the items listed below is included in the *Teacher's Guide* for each unit.
- Unit Overview
- Unit Planning Guide listing objectives, suggested timeline, and materials needed
- Instructional notes and suggestions
- Suggested assignments for each MORE set
- Solutions for Investigations and MORE tasks
- Unit summary and a look ahead

Teaching Resources include blackline masters for creating transparencies and handouts. *Assessment Resources* include quizzes for individual lessons, end-of-unit exams, and take-home assessment activities. Special calculator software has been developed to support students' investigations and modeling applications. Software for the TI-82, TI-83, and (in some cases) TI-92 graphics calculators is available on disk for downloading from Macintosh and DOS- or Windows-based (PC) computers.

Each unit of *Contemporary Mathematics in Context* includes content that may be new to many teachers or new approaches to familiar content. Thus, a first step toward planning the teaching of a unit is to review the scope and sequence of the unit itself. This review provides an overall feel for the goals of the unit and how it holds together. Working through the student investigations, if possible with a colleague, provides help in thinking about and understanding mathematical ideas that may be unfamiliar.

In the *Teacher's Guide* you will find teaching notes for each lesson in Course 2, including instructional suggestions and sample student responses to investigations and MORE sets. Thinking about the range of possible responses and solutions to problems in a lesson proves to be very helpful in facilitating student work.

Although not stated, it is assumed that students have access to graphics calculators at all times for in-class work and ideally for out-of-class work as well. Downloading and becoming familiar with the specially designed calculator software will require advanced planning as will acquiring physical materials.

The developers recommend that the homework (MORE) assignment *not* be held off until the end of the lesson or the investigation just preceding the MORE set. Some teachers choose to post the MORE assignment at the beginning of a lesson along with the due date—usually a day or two following planned completion of the lesson. Other teachers prefer to assign particular Modeling and Reflecting tasks at appropriate points during the course of the multiday lesson and then assign the remaining tasks toward the end of the lesson. Note that all recommended assignments include provision for student choice of some tasks. This is but one of many ways in which this curriculum is designed to accommodate and support differences in students' interests and performance levels.

It is strongly recommended that student solutions to Organizing tasks be discussed in class. These tasks help students organize and formalize the mathematics developed in context and connect it to other mathematics they have studied. Structuring the underlying mathematics and building connections is best accomplished by comparing and discussing student work and synthesizing key ideas within the classroom.

▶ Orchestrating Lessons

The *Contemporary Mathematics in Context* materials are designed to engage students actively in a four-phase cycle of classroom activities. The activities often require both students and teachers to assume roles quite different than those in more traditional mathematics classrooms. Becoming accustomed to these new roles usually takes time, perhaps a semester or more, but field-test teachers report that the time and effort required are well worth it in terms of student learning and professional fulfillment. Although realistic problem solving and investigative work by students is the heart of the curriculum, how teachers orchestrate the launching of that activity and the sharing and summarizing of results is critical to successful implementation.

Students enter the classroom with markedly different backgrounds, experience, and knowledge. These differences can be viewed as assets. Engaging the class in a free-flowing give-and-take discussion of how they think about the launch situations serves to connect lessons with the informal understandings of data, shape, change, and chance that students bring to the classroom. Try to maximize the participation of students in these discussions by emphasizing that their ideas and possible approaches are valued and important and that definitive answers are not necessarily expected at this time.

Once launched, a lesson may involve students working together collaboratively in small groups for a period of days punctuated occasionally by brief, whole-class discussion of questions students have raised. In this setting, the lesson becomes driven primarily by the instructional materials themselves. Rather than orchestrating class discussion, the teacher shifts to circulating among the groups and observing, listening, and interacting with students by asking guiding or probing questions. These small-group investigations lead to (re)invention of important mathematics that makes sense to students. Sharing and agreeing as a class on the mathematical ideas that groups are developing is the purpose of the "Checkpoints" in the instructional materials.

Class discussions at "Checkpoints" are orchestrated somewhat differently than during the launch of a lesson. At this stage, mathematical ideas and methods still may be under development and may vary for individual groups. So class discussion should involve groups comparing their methods and results, analyzing their work, and arriving at conclusions agreed upon by the class.

The investigations deepen students' understanding of mathematical ideas and extend their mathematical language in contexts. Occasionally, there is a need to introduce conventional or more technical terminology and symbolism. This occurs in the student materials immediately following a "Checkpoint" and before the corresponding "On Your Own" task. These connections should be introduced by the teacher as a natural way of closing the class discussion summarizing the "Checkpoint."

Managing Classroom Activities

▶ Active Learning and Collaborative Work

The *Contemporary Mathematics in Context* curriculum materials are designed to promote active, collaborative learning and group work for two important reasons. First, collaborative learning is the most effective method for engaging all the students in a class in the learning process. Second, practice in cooperative learning in the classroom is practice for real life: students develop and exercise the same skills in the classroom that they need in their lives at home, in the community, and in the workplace.

Value of Individuals

Perhaps the most fundamental belief underlying the use of cooperative learning is that every student is viewed as a valuable resource and contributor. In other words, every student participates in group work and is given the opportunity and time to voice ideas and opinions. Implementing this concept is not easy. It does not happen automatically. In order to set a tone that will promote respect for individuals and their contributions, classroom rules should be established and agreed upon by the learning community. Students should be included in the process of formulating the rules. The teacher should initiate a discussion of group rules and then post them in the classroom. The teacher should model all of the rules correctly to show that "we" begins with "me." Those who do not adhere to the rules must accept the consequences in accordance with classroom or school disciplinary procedures.

Importance of Social Connections

Even in classrooms in which the rules for showing respect have been clearly established, experience has shown that students still cannot talk with one another about mathematics (or social studies, or literature, or any other subject) if they do not first have positive social connections.

One way to develop this kind of common base is through team-building activities. These short activities (five to ten minutes) may be used at the beginning of the year to help students get acquainted with the whole class and may be used during the year whenever new groups are formed to help groupmates know one another better. Team-building activities help students learn new and positive things about classmates with whom they may have attended classes for years but have not known in depth. The time taken for these quick team-builders pays off later in helping students feel comfortable enough to work with the members of their group.

Need for Teaching Social Skills

Experience also has shown that social skills are critical to the successful functioning of any small group. Because there is no guarantee that students of any particular age will have the social skills necessary for effective group work, it often is necessary to teach these skills to build a collaborative learning environment.

These social skills are specific skills, not general goals. Examples of specific social skills that the teacher can teach in the classroom include responding to ideas respectfully, keeping track of time, disagreeing in an agreeable way, involving everyone, and following directions. Though goals such as cooperating and listening are important, they are too general to teach and practice.

One method of teaching social skills is to begin by selecting a specific skill and then having the class brainstorm to develop a script for practicing that skill. Next, the students practice that skill during their group work. Finally, in what is called the processing, the students discuss within their groups how well they performed the assigned social skill. Effective teaching of social skills requires practicing and processing; merely describing a specific social skill is not enough. Actual practice and processing are necessary for students really to learn the skill and to increase the use of appropriate behaviors during group work and other times during class.

One of the premises of cooperative learning is that by developing the appropriate skills through practice, anyone in the class can learn to work in a group with anyone else. Learning to work in groups is a continuous process, however, and the process can be helped by decisions that the teacher makes. *Implementing the CPMP Curriculum* provides information and support to help teachers make decisions about group size, composition, method of selection, student reaction to working in groups, and the duration of groups. It also provides advice on dealing effectively with student absences.

The culture created within the classroom is crucial to the success of this curriculum. It is important to inculcate in students a sense of inquiry and responsibility for their own learning. Without this commitment, active, collaborative learning by students cannot be effective. In order for students to work collaboratively, they must be able to understand the value of working together. Some students seem satisfied with the rationale that it is important in the business world. Others may need to understand that the struggle of verbalizing their thinking, listening to others' thinking, questioning themselves and other group members, and coming to an agreement increases their understanding and retention of the mathematics as well as contributes to forming important thinking skills or habits of mind.

Issues of helping students to work collaboratively will become less pressing as both you and your students experience this type of learning. You may find it helpful to refer to *Implementing the CPMP Curriculum* and discuss effective cooperative groups with colleagues a few weeks into the semester.

▶Assessment

Throughout the *Contemporary Mathematics in Context* curriculum, the term "assessment" is meant to include all instances of gathering information about students' levels of understanding and their disposition toward mathematics for purposes of making decisions about instruction. You may want to consult the extended section on assessment in *Implementing the CPMP Curriculum*.

The dimensions of student performance that are assessed in this curriculum (see chart below) are consistent with the assessment recommendations of the National Council of Teachers of Mathematics *Curriculum and Evaluation Standards for School Mathematics* (NCTM, 1988) and the *Assessment Standards for School Mathematics* (NCTM, 1995). They are much broader than those of a typical testing program.

Assessment Dimensions

Process	Content	Attitude
Problem Solving	Concepts	Beliefs
Reasoning	Applications	Perseverance
Communication	Representational Strategies	Confidence
Connections	Procedures	Enthusiasm

Sources of Assessment Information

Several kinds of assessment are available to teachers using *Contemporary Mathematics in Context*. Some of these sources reside within the curriculum itself, some of them are student-generated, and some are supplementary materials designed specifically for assessment. Understanding the nature of these sources is a prerequisite for establishing guidelines on how to score assessments, making judgments about what students know and are able to do, and assigning grades.

Curriculum Sources

Two features of the curriculum, questioning and observation by the teacher, provide fundamental and particularly useful ways of gathering assessment information. The student text uses questions to facilitate student understanding regarding new concepts, how these concepts fit with earlier ideas and with one another, and how they can be applied in problem situations. Whether students are working individually or in groups, the teacher is given a window to watch how the students think about and apply mathematics as they attempt to answer the questions posed by the curriculum materials. In fact, by observing how students respond to the curriculum-embedded questions, the teacher can assess student performance across all process, content, and attitude dimensions described in the chart on page xix.

Specific features in the student material that focus on different ways students respond to questions are the "Checkpoint," "On Your Own," and MORE (*Modeling, Organizing, Reflecting,* and *Extending*) sets at the end of each investigation. "Checkpoint" features are intended to bring students together, usually after they have been working in small groups, so they may share and discuss the progress each group has made during a sequence of related activities. Each "Checkpoint " is intended to be a whole-class discussion, so it should provide an opportunity for teachers to assess, informally, the levels of understanding that the various groups of students have reached.

Following each "Checkpoint," the "On Your Own" tasks are meant to be completed by students working individually. Student responses to these tasks provide an opportunity for teachers to assess the level of understanding of each student.

Activities in the MORE sets serve many purposes, including post-investigation assessment. Modeling tasks help students demonstrate how well they understand and can apply the concepts and procedures developed in an investigation. Organizing activities demonstrate how well students understand connections between the content of an investigation and other mathematical and real-world ideas. In-class discussions based on Organizing tasks are a crucial step in assisting students' development of a full understanding of the mathematical content and connections. Reflecting activities provide insights into students' beliefs, attitudes, and judgments of their own competence. Extending tasks show how well students are able to extend the present content beyond the level addressed in an investigation. The performance of students or groups of students in each of these types of activity provides the teacher with further information to help assess applicability, connectedness, and depth of the students' evolving understanding of mathematics.

Finally, an opportunity for group self-assessment is provided in the last element of each unit, the "Looking Back" lesson. These activities help students pull together and demonstrate what they have learned in the unit and at the same time provide helpful review and confidence building for students.

Student-Generated Sources

Other possible sources of assessment information are writings and materials produced by the students in the form of student journals and portfolios. Student journals are notebooks in which students are encouraged to write (briefly, but frequently) their personal reflections concerning the class, the mathematics they are learning, and their progress. These journals are an excellent way for the teacher to gain insights into how individual students are feeling about the class, what they do and do not understand, and what some of their particular learning difficulties are. For many students, the journal is a nonthreatening way to communicate with the teacher about matters that may be too difficult or too time-consuming to talk about directly. Journals also encourage students to assess their own understanding of, and disposition toward, the mathematics they are studying. The teacher should collect, read, and respond to each journal at least once a month—more often if possible.

The *Contemporary Mathematics in Context* assessment program provides many items that would be appropriate for students' portfolios, including reports of individual and group projects, journal excerpts, teacher-completed observation checklists, end-of-unit assessments (especially the take-home activities), and the extended cumulative projects. One way students can develop a portfolio is to collect all their written work in a folder, sometimes called a working portfolio. Then at least once each semester, students go through their working portfolio and choose items that they think best represent their growth during this time period. After writing a paragraph or two explaining why each piece of work was chosen, each student puts the chosen items with the written rationales into a new folder that becomes the actual portfolio.

Assessment Resources

The *Contemporary Mathematics in Context* instructional materials include for each unit a third source of assessment information—*Assessment Resources*—which contains end-of-lesson quizzes and end-of-unit assessments in the form of an in-class unit exam and a take-home assessment. Calculators often are required and it is intended that they always are available to students. Since many rich opportunities for assessing students are embedded in the curriculum itself, you may choose not to use all the lesson quizzes for each unit.

End-of-Lesson Quizzes Two forms of a quiz covering the main ideas of each lesson are provided. These quizzes, which are the most traditional of all the assessment methods and instruments included with the *Contemporary Mathematics in Context* materials, are comprised of fairly straightforward problems meant to determine if students have developed understanding of the important concepts and procedures of each lesson. Thus, the quizzes focus on the content dimension of the Assessment Dimensions.

In-Class Exams Two forms of in-class exams are provided for each unit and are intended to be completed in a 50-minute class period by students working individually. Calculators are required in most cases and are intended to be available to students. It also is recommended that students have access to the textbook and to their journals and class notes. The two forms of each exam are *not* equivalent, although they assess essentially the same mathematical ideas. Teachers should preview the two versions carefully before making a choice, and they should feel free to revise or delete items and add new ones if necessary.

Take-Home Assessments Five possible take-home assessment activities are included for each unit. The students or the teacher should choose one or, at most, two of these activities. These assessments, some of which are best done by students working in pairs or small groups, provide students with the opportunity to organize the information from the completed unit, to extend the ideas of the unit into other areas of interest to them, to work with another student or group of students, and to avoid the time pressure often generated by in-class exams. Of the five activities in a take-home assessment package, the first three require a day or two for one or two students to complete. The last two activities of a take-home assessment package are extended projects that require up to a week for students, usually working in groups, to complete. It is recommended that, on one or two occasions during the time that students are working on extended projects, the teacher use some class time to check on students' progress and to give guidance and encouragement.

Extended Cumulative Projects Assessment traditionally has been based on evaluating work that students have completed in a very short time period and under restricted conditions. Some assessment, however, should involve work done over a longer time period—a week or more—and with the aid of resources. Thus, an extended assessment project is included with the Unit 3 assessments. These projects are investigations that make use of some of the main ideas encountered in the curriculum up to that time. The activities, which are intended to be completed by small groups of students in a week or more, are similar to the extended take-home assessment projects at the end of each unit, except that they require understanding of mathematical content from several units.

Scoring Assessments

High expectations of the quality of students' written work will encourage students to reach their potential. Assigning scores to open-ended assessments and to observations of students' performance requires more subjective judgment by the teacher than does grading short-answer or multiple-choice tests. It is therefore not possible to provide a complete set of explicit guidelines for scoring open-ended assessment items and written or oral reports. However, some general guidelines may be helpful. When scoring student work on open-ended assessment tasks, the goal is to reward in a fair and consistent way the kinds of thinking and understanding that the task is meant to measure. Preparing to score open-ended assessment tasks is best done using a three-step process. First, teachers should have a general rubric, or scoring scheme, with several response levels in mind. The general rubric is the foundation for scoring across a wide range of types of open-ended tasks. The following general rubric can be used for most assessment tasks provided with *Contemporary Mathematics in Context*.

General Scoring Rubric

4 points	Contains complete response with clear, coherent, and unambiguous explanation; includes clear and simple diagram, if appropriate; communicates effectively to identified audience; shows understanding of question's mathematical ideas and processes; identifies all important elements of question; includes examples and counterexamples; gives strong supporting arguments
3 points	Contains good solid response with some, but not all, of the characteristics above; explains less completely; may include minor error of execution but not of understanding
2 points	Contains complete response, but explanation is muddled; presents incomplete arguments; includes diagrams that are inappropriate or unclear, or fails to provide a diagram when it would be appropriate; indicates some understanding of mathematical ideas, but in an unclear way; shows clear evidence of understanding some important ideas while also making one or more fundamental, specific errors
1 point	Omits parts of question and response; has major errors; uses inappropriate strategies
0 points	No response; frivolous or irrelevant response

Assigning Grades

Because the *Contemporary Mathematics in Context* approach and materials provide a wide variety of assessment information, the teacher will be in a good position to assign a fair grade for student work. With such a wide choice for assessment, a word of caution is appropriate: *it is easy to overassess students, and care must be taken to avoid doing so.* A quiz need not be given after every lesson nor an in-class exam after every unit. The authors believe it is best to vary assessment methods from lesson to lesson and from unit to unit. If information on what students understand and are able to do is available from their homework and in-class work, it may not be necessary to take the time for a formal quiz after each lesson. Similarly, information from project work may replace an in-class exam.

Deciding exactly how to weigh the various kinds of assessment information is a decision that the teacher will need to make and communicate clearly to the students.

Maintaining Skills

The developers have identified a set of paper-and-pencil technical competencies that all students should acquire. To provide additional practice with these core competencies, a special maintenance feature is included in blackline master form in the *Teaching Resources*.

Beginning with Unit 4 of Course 1, Graph Models, and then continuing with each unit thereafter, a supplementary set of maintenance tasks provides periodic review and additional practice of basic skills. These skills will be continually revisited to ensure mastery by each student at some point in the curriculum.

Use of the maintenance material following the start of Lesson 2 of each unit will allow students time to simultaneously work on skills during the latter part of a unit without interrupting the flow of the unit. You may wish to allow a few minutes at the end of selected class periods to revisit these skills with various groups of students who need assistance while other groups choose an Extending task.

The maintenance material prepared for each unit spans technical competencies across each of the strands. In each case, the first presented task is a contextual problem, but the remaining tasks are not contextualized. Students should *not* use a calculator for these tasks unless so directed.

Additional Resources

The *Implementing the Core-Plus Mathematics Curriculum* contains expanded information in the scope and sequence of Courses 1, 2, and 3; on managing classroom activities; and on the assessment program. It also provides a list of colleges and universities to which students from pilot-test schools have been admitted. A section on communication with parents includes a template for a parent letter, which overviews this curriculum and intended instructional practices. You will find it useful to have the implementation guide available for reference throughout the school year.

Unit 5 ▶ Network Optimization

UNIT OVERVIEW In this unit students will continue to investigate graph models. In the "Graph Models" unit from Course 1, they explored Euler paths, vertex coloring, and critical paths. In "Matrix Models," they studied matrix representation of graphs. In "Network Optimization," they will study minimal spanning trees, shortest paths, Hamiltonian paths, and the Traveling Salesperson Problem. These graph models will give students powerful mathematical tools to make sense of situations involving relationships among a finite number of elements.

Three important themes in discrete mathematics are existence (*Does a solution exist?*), algorithmic problem solving (*Can you efficiently find a solution?*), and optimization (*What is the best solution?*). This unit continues the development of all three of these themes, with an emphasis on optimization and algorithmic problem solving. Students will optimize by looking for *minimal* spanning trees, *shortest* paths, and *shortest* Hamiltonian circuits. Students will further develop the skill of algorithmic problem solving as they carefully design, use, and analyze their own algorithms as well as given algorithms.

This unit from the discrete mathematics strand of the curriculum contains concepts that most students find interesting, relevant, and sensible. Students who may have been struggling with previous material can master the mathematics in this unit. Teachers indicate that this successful experience provides many students the impetus to tackle the remaining units of the year.

Unit 5 Objectives

- To gain experience in mathematical modeling by building and using vertex-edge graph models to solve problems in a variety of real-world settings
- To develop the skill of algorithmic problem solving by designing, using, and analyzing systematic procedures for solving problems
- To optimize networks in different ways and in different contexts by finding minimal spanning trees, shortest paths, Hamiltonian paths, and by analyzing the Traveling Salesperson Problem

▶ A Note on Vocabulary

This unit introduces additional graph models, but it is called "Network Optimization." The word *network* is used here for several reasons. First, the terms *graph* and *network* are used interchangeably in some mathematics sources. Second, *network* is a more intuitive descriptor for many of the contexts in this unit. Third, this unit is primarily about graphs with weights on the edges, and weighted graphs often are called networks. It is *not* important for students to differentiate technically between *graphs* and *networks*. Be sure that students do not get so focused on vocabulary that they miss the larger objectives of the unit as stated above.

Network Optimization

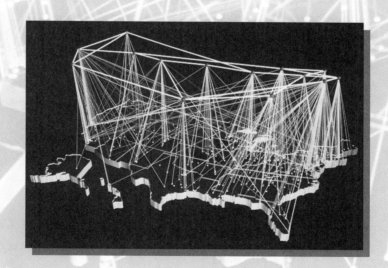

319

Assessing Student Understanding

In place of an in-class test or exam, you may wish to have students do a project that involves finding new contexts and problems that could be modeled with a graph. Students should be allowed to draw on their knowledge of Euler paths, critical paths, and vertex coloring from Course 1. But be sure they use also the graph models from this unit: minimal spanning trees, shortest paths, Hamiltonian circuits, and the Traveling Salesperson Problem. Student's choices of a graph model and what the vertices and edges represent will allow you to assess their understanding of representing and analyzing problem situations. The choice of an algorithm to apply to a graph model should be a sense-making process for students. Algorithms needn't be memorized, but students should understand, design, apply and, whenever reasonable, analyze algorithms.

Additional References

The following references may be useful if you would like more information about graph models and networks.

If you choose to use videos with your students, consider carefully the content of each video. It is important to keep the investigative nature of this unit intact. For example, some videos may present the main point of the investigation and so should be shown after, not before the investigation. However, some parts of some videos may serve well as part of a lesson launch.

COMAP, *For All Practical Purposes: Introduction to Contemporary Mathematics.* Fourth edition. New York: W.H. Freeman, 1997.

COMAP, *Principles and Practices of Mathematics.* New York: Springer, 1997.

Cozzens and Porter. *Problem Solving Using Graphs*, HiMAP Module 6. Lexington, Mass.: COMAP, 1987.

Crisler, Fisher, and Froelich. *Discrete Mathematics Through Applications.* New York: W.H. Freeman, 1994.

Dossey, et al. *Discrete Mathematics.* Third edition. New York: Addison-Wesley, 1997.

For All Practical Purposes Series. Annenberg/CPB, 1985. Video.

Geometry: New Tools for New Technologies. Lexington, Mass.: COMAP, 1992. Video.

Kenney and Hirsch (eds.). *Discrete Mathematics Across the Curriculum, K–12.* Reston, Va.: National Council of Teachers of Mathematics, 1991 NCTM Yearbook, 1991.

Malkevitch and Meyer. *Graphs, Models, and Finite Mathematics.* Englewood Cliffs, NJ: Prentice-Hall, 1974.

Ore, Oystein. *Graphs and Their Uses* (revised and updated by Robin Wilson). Washington, D.C.: Mathematical Association of America, New Mathematical Library 34, 1990.

ORSA promotional video. Operations Research Society of America, 1990. Video.

Patterns: Networks, Paths, and Knots. Sunburst, 1993. Video.

Tannenbaum and Arnold. *Excursions in Modern Mathematics.* Second edition. Englewood Cliffs, NJ: Prentice-Hall, 1995.

Wilson and Watkins. *Graphs: An Introductory Approach.* New York: John Wiley and Sons, 1990.

See Teaching Masters 117a–117d for Maintenance tasks that students can work on after Lesson 1.

Unit 5 Planning Guide

Lesson Objectives	MORE Assignments	Suggested Pacing	Materials
Lesson 1 *Finding the Best Networks* • To represent and analyze a variety of real-world situations using minimal spanning trees • To apply and analyze both given and student-generated algorithms for finding minimal spanning trees • To construct and interpret a distance matrix for a network	**After page 325** Students can begin Modeling Tasks 2–4; Organizing Task 1 or 3; or Reflecting Task 1 or 2 from p. 328. **page 328** **Modeling:** 1 and choice of one* **Organizing:** 1 and 3 **Reflecting:** 1 and choice of one* **Extending:** Choose one*	5 days	• Teaching Resources 118–121 • Assessment Resources 169–175
Lesson 2 *Shortest Paths and Circuits* • To represent and analyze a variety of real-world situations using shortest paths, Hamiltonian circuits, and the Traveling Salesperson Problem • To apply and analyze both given and student-generated algorithms, and brute-force methods for the Traveling Salesperson Problem • To understand the limitations of the computer as a brute-force tool for solving problems	**After page 345** Students can begin Modeling Task 3 from p. 352. **After page 348** Students can begin Modeling Task 2 or 5, and Organizing Task 1 from p. 352. **page 353** **Modeling:** 3 and choice of one* **Organizing:** 1 and 3 **Reflecting:** 5 **Extending:** 4 or 6*	6 days	• Teaching Resources 117a–117d, 122–127 • Assessment Resources 176–181 • Demonstration model of dodecahedron (See Master 125)
Lesson 3 *Looking Back* • To review the major objectives of the unit		2–3 days (includes testing)	• Teaching Resources 128a–129 • Assessment Resources 182–199

*When choice is indicated, it is important to leave the choice to the student.
Note: It is best if Organizing tasks are discussed by the whole class after they have been assigned as homework.

Lesson 1

Finding the Best Networks

Everywhere you look, you'll see people trying to get the best in life, whether it's "going for the gold" in the Olympics, getting the best education, or even something as ordinary as finding the best route from home to school. Of course, what is best depends on the situation. In your previous work in mathematics, you may have investigated situations in which finding the "best" meant finding the best-fitting line for a scatterplot of data, the best plan for controlling population growth, the most stable geometric shape, or the fairest ranking of a tournament. In the context of vertex-edge graph models, you may have found the length of a longest path through a project digraph, the fewest number of colors needed to color the vertices of a graph, or the most efficient circuit through a graph using

all the edges. In this unit, you will continue to "find the best" in the context of graph models. In particular, you will study shortest paths and networks.

In this information age, it is important to find the best way to stay informed. You need to have the right information at the right time in order to make the best decisions and take the most effective action. One way to keep informed is through computer networks. Many places, including businesses, schools, and libraries, have computers linked together in networks so that information can be shared among many users. In fact, there is a common saying that "the network *is* the computer."

Lesson 1 *Finding The Best Networks*

LESSON OVERVIEW In Lesson 1, the context of computer networks and road networks are used to develop student understanding of minimal spanning trees and distance matrices. Drawing on their ability to model situations with vertex-edge graphs, students investigate weighted graphs and look for shortest networks that include each vertex and have a minimum total length (minimal spanning trees). Matrices are used to present the weights of edges in an organized manner.

Algorithmic thinking is developed in Investigation 1 as well as throughout the unit. In Investigation 2, students explore matrices and graph models to optimize a road network. Students should realize that in order to understand these mathematical representations, they must not lose sight of the particular context of the representation. For example, matrix row sums may have a meaning in one context, but no meaning in another context.

Lesson Objectives

- To represent and analyze a variety of real-world situations using minimal spanning trees
- To apply and analyze both given and student-generated algorithms for finding minimal spanning trees
- To construct and interpret a distance matrix for a network

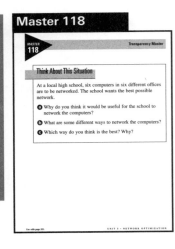

LAUNCH full-class discussion

Think About This Situation

See Teaching Master 118.

ⓐ If their computers are networked, the teachers and administrators can easily exchange files and records, share appropriate software, send e-mail, *etc.*

ⓑ Possible responses are that the computers could be networked with wires, modems and phone lines, via a server, simply by exchanging floppy disks (the so-called "sneaker network" since the floppies are shared by having someone, in sneakers, running the disks from one computer to the next). Students also might mention different technical methods of networking computers, like Ethernet or Appletalk.

ⓒ Students may propose many different interpretations of which is best, for example, the cheapest, fastest, easiest to set up, and easiest to use. All possibilities should be entertained at this point. The unit will focus on particular answers to "Which is best?" by looking at shortest paths, shortest circuits, and shortest spanning trees, where "shortest" is interpreted in many different ways.

EXPLORE small-group investigation

INVESTIGATION 1▸ Optimizing a Computer Network

Learning to design, use, and analyze algorithms is a major focus of the unit. Students have worked with algorithms on many occasions in the past. Some of those algorithms may not have made much sense to students, but they did work (for example, the algorithm to divide by a fraction: invert the divisor and multiply). This investigation provides opportunities for students to write and use algorithms that make sense to them and also to interpret algorithms that are provided to them.

It is important that students understand that computers can be connected directly or indirectly, as discussed in the investigation introduction.

1. **a.** Five meters of wire are needed to connect the computers at locations *C* and *E*.

   b. The amount of wire needed to connect the computers at locations *A* and *B* is the same as the amount needed to connect the computers at locations *B* and *A*.

   c. There is no number for the *D-D* entry because there is no need to connect the computer at location *D* to itself. The *D-B* entry is empty because, evidently, there is no way to connect the computers at locations *B* and *D*.

   d. The matrix is symmetric because the direction in which you put in the wire (from *A* to *B* or from *B* to *A*) doesn't matter. In a similar manner, if you cannot connect two computers, then the entries representing both orders of connection are empty.

It may have been some time since students used vertex-edge graphs. As students construct the graphs in Activities 2 and 3, it is very helpful to encourage them to talk about why the graphs of different groups might look different. For example, you might ask, "Since your graphs look different, can they both be correct models of the situation?" Some students may want to make the lengths of the graph edges proportional to the length of the wire represented although this is not necessary to the model. Some may want to complete a circuit even though it is not appropriate for these cases. As students compare graphs, all of these issues should be resolved.

Think About This Situation

At a local high school, six computers in six different offices are to be networked. The school wants the best possible network.

a Why do you think it would be useful for the school to network the computers?

b What are some different ways to network the computers?

c Which way do you think is the best? Why?

INVESTIGATION 1 Optimizing a Computer Network

Suppose the school decides to link all the computers to each other without any kind of separate *junction box* or *server*. One way to get the "best" network is to use the least amount of wire to link all the computers. Since electronic signals move so quickly, the connection between two computers is virtually as efficient whether they are linked directly or indirectly through another computer. The person in charge of setting up the network wants to answer the following question:

What is the minimum amount of wire needed to connect all six computers so that every computer is linked directly or indirectly to every other computer?

Because of the location of the offices and the computers, it is not possible to run wire directly between every pair of computers. The matrix below shows which computers can be linked directly as well as how much wire is needed. The computers are represented by letters and the distances are in meters.

	A	B	C	D	E	F
A	–	9	–	–	–	3
B	9	–	8	–	8	11
C	–	8	–	3	5	–
D	–	–	3	–	6	11
E	–	8	5	6	–	9
F	3	11	–	11	9	–

1. Examine the computer network matrix.

   a. What does the "5" in the *C* row mean?

   b. Why is the *A-B* entry the same as the *B-A* entry?

   c. Why isn't there a *D-D* entry? Why isn't there a *D-B* entry?

   d. Why does it make sense that the matrix is symmetric?

2. Working as a group, represent the information in the matrix with a vertex-edge graph. Recall that when building a graph model you must specify what the vertices and edges represent.

   a. What should the vertices of the graph represent?

   b. What should the edges represent?

   c. Compare your graph to that of another group. Resolve any differences.

3. Now, work in pairs to analyze the computer network problem.

   a. What is the least amount of wire needed to connect the computers so that every computer is linked directly or indirectly to every other computer?

   b. Make a copy of the graph you agreed on in Part c of Activity 2, and then darken the edges of a shortest network.

   c. Write a description of a method for finding a shortest network.

   d. Compare your shortest network and the minimum amount of wire needed to what the other members of your group found. Discuss and resolve any differences.

4. In Activity 3 Part c, you and your partner wrote a description of a method for finding a shortest network.

   a. Exchange written descriptions with another pair of members of your group. Make a new copy of the graph, and try to use their method to find a shortest network.

   b. Does each method work?

   c. Work together as a group to refine the methods, and then write down a step-by-step procedure—an **algorithm**—for each method that works.

5. Think about the properties of the shortest wiring networks you have been investigating. State whether each of the following statements is *true* or *false*. In each case, give a reason justifying your answer. Compare your answers to those of other groups and resolve any differences.

   a. There is only one correct answer possible for the minimum amount of wire needed to connect all six computers.

   b. There can be more than one shortest network for a given situation.

   c. There is more than one algorithm for finding a shortest network.

   d. A shortest network must be all in one piece; that is, the network must be **connected.**

   e. All vertices must be joined by the network.

   f. A shortest network cannot contain any circuits. (A **circuit** is a path that starts and ends at the same vertex and does not repeat any edges.)

2. **a.** Vertices represent computers.

    b. Edges represent connections.

    c. There probably will be many different-looking graphs. It is only important that each graph accurately represents the information in the table. The shape and size of the graphs are not important at all.

3. **This activity can be used as a think-pair-share activity. Each student could work through this on his or her own, so that each has some answers, graphs, and methods (algorithms) to discuss and compare when grouped in pairs. Then, in Part d, each pair of students can share results with another pair.**

    a. 28 meters is the minimum amount of wire needed to connect all six computers.

    b. Following are two shortest networks. There are others.

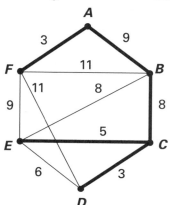 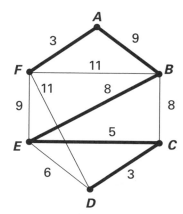

    c. Responses will vary. One possibility is given in Activity 8, page 323.

    d. Students should see that everyone gets the same number for the length of a shortest network, *but* there may be more than one network with this shortest length.

4. **Here students engage in the important activity of *algorithmic problem solving*. This activity is vital to all mathematics, but particularly to discrete mathematics. This may be a good time to draw the whole class together to ensure that everyone has solved the problem, and to give everyone a chance to use someone else's algorithm. One way to do this is to have a student read aloud his or her algorithm while you, or another student, attempt to execute the instructions exactly as they are spoken, without any extraneous judgment. Then the students can discuss, as a class, whether the instructions were clear and whether they accomplished the goal.**

5. All the statements are true, and all are important for the students to understand before they continue with this investigation. The computer-network problem they have been working on should have elicited all these statements.

    a. True. There is only one correct answer possible for the minimum amount of wire needed to connect all six computers. There cannot be two different minimums.

    b. True. There can be more than one shortest network for a given problem. The total lengths must be the same, but the edges might be different.

    c. Responses will vary, depending on the students' earlier work, but the statement is true. There is more than one algorithm for finding a shortest network. Students should justify their responses with good reasoning.

See additional Teaching Notes on page T366C.

Unit 5

6. a. A tree in nature is all in one piece; *i.e.*, connected. Also, the branches typically do not curve back into themselves and form loops; *i.e.*, there are no circuits. Thus, a tree in nature has the same two essential properties as trees in mathematics.

b. The definition of *minimal spanning tree* includes properties discussed in Activity 5. In that activity, students should have concluded that shortest networks are connected (Part d), have no circuits (Part f), include all vertices (Part e), and have minimum length. That is, they are trees of minimum length that include all vertices. Thus, they are minimal spanning trees. The term *minimal spanning tree* will be used for the rest of the unit.

You may wish to have students look up the verb "to span" in the dictionary and discuss why it is appropriate to use it in the context of graph theory.

7. a. In addition to the two spanning trees shown by the heavy edges in Activity 3, Part b (page T322), this algorithm can produce either of the following trees.

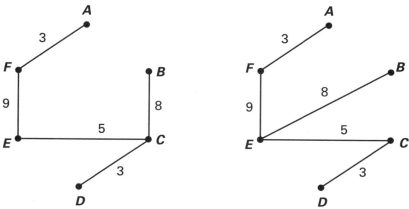

b. This algorithm could be called a best-edge algorithm, because the minimal spanning tree is constructed by adding the shortest (best) edge possible at each step.

c. The lengths of the two minimal spanning trees should be the same even if the spanning trees themselves are not identical.

NOTE: When Kruskal discovered his best-edge algorithm, he was not sure whether it was worthy of publication, but fortunately some friends convinced him to publish it!

---

8. a. There are four such minimal spanning trees. Each has length 260.

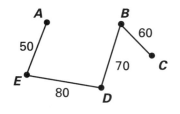 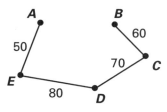 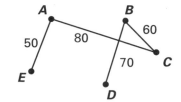 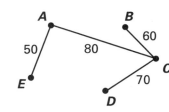

b. Since the second step of the algorithm includes the phrase, "If there is more than one such edge, choose any one," there is room for variation.

c. All minimal spanning trees produced by the algorithm are shown in Part a.

d. Responses may vary, depending on the algorithms students produced in Activity 4.

6. A connected graph that has no circuits is called a **tree**.

   a. Why does it make sense to call such a graph a tree?

   b. A **minimal spanning tree** in a connected graph is a tree that has minimum total length and *spans* the graph—that is, it includes every vertex. Explain why the shortest networks you have found in the computer network graph are minimal spanning trees.

7. As you may have concluded in Activity 5, Part c, there are several possible algorithms for finding a minimal spanning tree in a connected graph. Study the algorithm below.

   i. Draw all the vertices, but no edges.

   ii. Add the shortest edge that will not create a curcuit. If there is more than one such edge, choose any one. The edge you add does not have to be connected to previously-added edges, and you may use more than one edge of the same length.

   iii. Repeat Step ii until it is no longer possible to add an edge without creating a circuit.

   a. Follow the steps of this algorithm to construct a minimal spanning tree for the computer network graph.

   b. Explain why this algorithm could be called a *best-edge algorithm*.

   c. Compare the minimal spanning tree you get using this best-edge algorithm to the one you found in Activity 3. How do the lengths of the minimal spanning trees compare?

8. Examine the graph below.

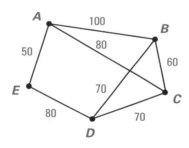

   a. Use the best-edge algorithm to find a minimal spanning tree for this graph. Calculate its length.

   b. Explain why the algorithm can produce different minimal spanning trees.

   c. Find all possible minimal spanning trees for the graph. Compare their lengths.

   d. How is the algorithm similar to or different from the algorithms you produced in Activity 4?

9. Students in one class claimed that the following algorithm will produce a minimal spanning tree in a given graph.

   i. Make a copy of the graph with the edges drawn lightly.

   ii. Choose a starting vertex.

   iii. From the vertex where you are, darken the shortest edge that will not create a circuit. (If there is more than one such edge, choose any one.) Then move to the end vertex of that edge.

   iv. Repeat Step iii until all vertices have been reached.

Complete Parts a–f to test this algorithm. First make four copies of the graph below.

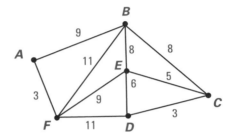

   a. Apply the algorithm to the graph starting with vertex *E*. What is the total length of the network you get?

   b. Explain why this algorithm could be called a *nearest-neighbor algorithm*.

   c. Apply the algorithm starting with vertex *C*. Record the length of the resulting network.

   d. Apply the algorithm starting with vertex *A*. What happens?

   e. Now use the best-edge algorithm described in Activity 7 to find a minimal spanning tree for this graph.

   f. Do you think the nearest-neighbor algorithm is a good algorithm for finding a minimal spanning tree? Write a brief justification of your answer.

10. How are the nearest-neighbor algorithm and the best-edge algorithm similar? How are they different?

11. Two important questions about any algorithm are "Does it always work?" and "Is it efficient?" You will continue to investigate these questions for different algorithms throughout this unit. For the best-edge algorithm described in Activity 7, mathematicians have proven that the answer to both questions is "yes." The best-edge algorithm will efficiently find a minimal spanning tree for any connected graph. What are your thoughts about these questions for the nearest-neighbor algorithm?

   a. Does it always work?

   b. Is it efficient?

9. **a.** Starting at *E*, this algorithm generates the route *E-C-D-F-A-B* for a total length of 31. See the diagram at the right.

   b. This algorithm could be called a nearest-neighbor because the tree is built by connecting a vertex to the vertex that is closest to it.

   c. Starting at *C*, this algorithm generates the route *C-D-E-B-A-F* for a total length of 29. See the diagram at the right.

   d. Starting at *A*, this algorithm generates the route *A-F-E-C-D*, and then gets stuck. In this case, the algorithm does not produce a spanning tree. See the diagram at the right.

   e. One minimal spanning tree produced by the best-edge algorithm is shown at the right. The length of this tree is 28.

   f. No. The nearest-neighbor algorithm might fail to generate a spanning tree, and even when it does produce a spanning tree, that tree may not be minimal. The best-edge algorithm applied to the example above generates a spanning tree with length 28, which is less than the lengths of the trees obtained by using the nearest-neighbor algorithm starting at vertex *E* or *C*.

10. Similarities: At each step, you choose the shortest edge that does not create a circuit. Differences: (1) In the best-edge algorithm, you choose the shortest edge from among all edges that have not yet been used, while in the nearest-neighbor algorithm, you choose the shortest edge from among only those edges that are connected to the vertex of your current location. (2) The best-edge algorithm seems always to produce a minimal spanning tree, while the nearest-neighbor algorithm does not. (See Activity 11 for a definitive statement about the correctness and efficiency of the best-edge algorithm.) (3) In the best-edge algorithm, the edges you add may not form a connected network until the end of the procedure, while in the nearest-neighbor algorithm, you create a successively longer connected path at each step.

11. **a.** No, the nearest-neighbor algorithm is not a guaranteed method for producing a minimal spanning tree. See, for example, Activity 9. (Also see the note following the Checkpoint for an explanation of why the nearest-neighbor algorithm is important even though it is not a guaranteed solution method.)

   b. Students will not be able to give a technical answer to this question. Such analysis is beyond the scope of this course. If "efficient" is limited to "ease of use," students may very well argue that it is efficient, since the steps are easy to carry out and it is similar to the best-edge algorithm, which is efficient. Efficiency of algorithms is an important issue to which students should be alerted. It is not possible to study it formally in this course, but the issue is dealt with again informally when brute-force methods are discussed in the next lesson. For more details on algorithm efficiency and problem complexity, see the solution to Reflecting Task 3 in Lesson 2 (page T357). A good introduction to these ideas is given in Chapter 6 of COMAP's *Principles and Practice of Mathematics* (New York: Springer, 1997).

Unit 5

9. **a.**
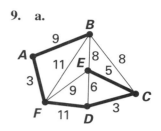

9. **c.**
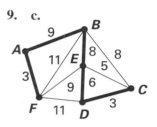

9. **d.**
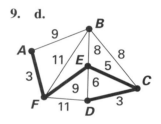

9. **e.**
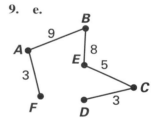

Master 119

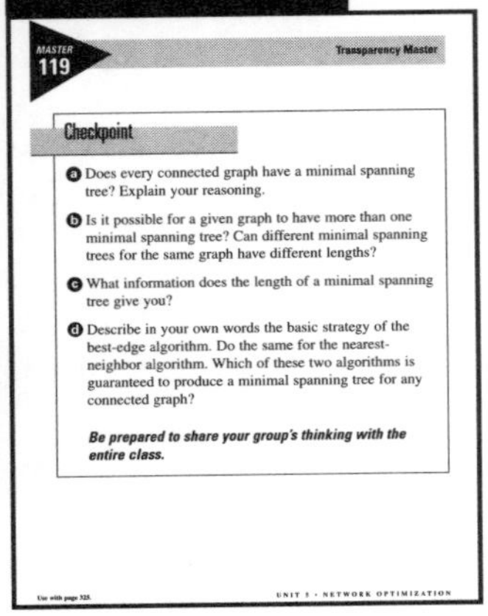

MASTER 119   Transparency Master

Checkpoint

ⓐ Does every connected graph have a minimal spanning tree? Explain your reasoning.

ⓑ Is it possible for a given graph to have more than one minimal spanning tree? Can different minimal spanning trees for the same graph have different lengths?

ⓒ What information does the length of a minimal spanning tree give you?

ⓓ Describe in your own words the basic strategy of the best-edge algorithm. Do the same for the nearest-neighbor algorithm. Which of these two algorithms is guaranteed to produce a minimal spanning tree for any connected graph?

Be prepared to share your group's thinking with the entire class.

Use with page 325.   UNIT 5 • NETWORK OPTIMIZATION

SHARE AND SUMMARIZE   full-class discussion

Checkpoint

See Teaching Master 119.

ⓐ Yes, every connected graph has a minimal spanning tree. This could be explained in several ways. One explanation simply involves constructing a minimal spanning tree with the best-edge algorithm. That is, every connected graph has a minimal spanning tree because the best-edge algorithm is guaranteed to produce one in any connected graph (see Activity 11). Another argument might be the following: Since the graph is connected, all vertices are spanned already. Remove edges that create circuits to get a tree (which will still span all vertices). Thus it is a spanning tree. There may be many ways to remove such edges, but there are only finitely many ways since there are finitely many edges. Among the lengths of the finitely many different possible spanning trees, there must be a minimum length. So there must be a minimal spanning tree.

ⓑ A graph can have more than one minimal spanning tree, but all the minimal spanning trees must have the same minimum length. (See, for example, Activity 8.)

ⓒ The specific information provided by the length of a minimal spanning tree depends on the context. For example, in the computer-network problem, the length of a minimal spanning tree is the minimum amount of wire needed to connect the computers so that every computer is linked directly or indirectly to every other computer. Generally, the length of a minimal spanning tree is the minimum distance needed to join all the vertices in the graph. (However, this is slightly vague; what is meant by *distance* varies.)

ⓓ Students should be encouraged to characterize the algorithms in a simple, sensible, and accurate way. For example, in the best-edge algorithm, you add the best edge possible at each step; in the nearest-neighbor algorithm, you move to the nearest neighbor at each step. Students' descriptions also may be more detailed: In the best-edge algorithm, you successively add shortest edges without creating circuits, and any edge you add does not have to be connected to a previously added edge. In the nearest-neighbor algorithm, you likewise successively add shortest edges without creating circuits, but you start at a certain vertex and only add edges that are connected to the vertex where you are.

Students need to be clear that although the nearest-neighbor algorithm does have an appeal, it is not a guaranteed method for finding a minimal spanning tree. The best-edge algorithm is a guaranteed method.

Since the nearest-neighbor algorithm is not a method that works very well, students may wonder why they are studying it. There are several good reasons. First, it is an algorithm that often comes up naturally in initial attempts to find minimal spanning trees (and in other graph problems), and therefore, it needs to be discussed and analyzed. Second, by comparing two different algorithms, students gain experience in the important skill of algorithmic problem solving, which involves designing, using, comparing, and analyzing algorithms. Third, although the algorithm does not generally work as an exact solution method, it is intuitive and easy to apply, and so it can have value for approximating solutions in other contexts. (For example, see the Traveling Salesperson Problem in the next lesson.) Fourth, students should understand there may be algorithms that seem reasonable for a given problem, and yet they do not work well. Finally, this algorithm optimizes at each step, and yet it does not optimize for the whole problem. This situation often occurs in optimization problems. We sometimes say that a *locally* optimal solution is not necessarily a *globally* optimal solution.

See additional Teaching Notes on page T366C.

CONSTRUCTING A MATH TOOLKIT: Students should record, in a manner that makes sense to them, the best-edge algorithm for finding a minimal spanning tree.

MORE

ASSIGNMENT *pp. 328–339*

Students can now begin Modeling Tasks 2–4; Organizing Task 1 or 3; or Reflecting Task 1 or 2 from MORE assignment following Investigation 2.

Checkpoint

a Does every connected graph have a minimal spanning tree? Explain your reasoning.

b Is it possible for a given graph to have more than one minimal spanning tree? Can different minimal spanning trees for the same graph have different lengths?

c What information does the length of a minimal spanning tree give you?

d Describe in your own words the basic strategy of the best-edge algorithm. Do the same for the nearest-neighbor algorithm. Which of these two algorithms is guaranteed to produce a minimal spanning tree for any connected graph?

Be prepared to share your group's thinking with the entire class.

The best-edge algorithm that you investigated in Activities 7 and 8 was first discovered by Joseph Kruskal, a mathematician at AT&T Bell Laboratories, and so it is also called *Kruskal's algorithm*. Kruskal made the discovery while still a graduate student in the 1950s.

▶On Your Own

A landscape architect has been contracted to design a sprinkler system for a large lawn. There will be six sprinkler heads that must be connected by a buried network of pipes to the main water source. The possible connections and distances in yards are shown in the diagram below. The main water source is represented by vertex *B*. What is the least amount of pipe needed to construct the sprinkler network? Draw a landscape plan showing the optimal sprinkler network.

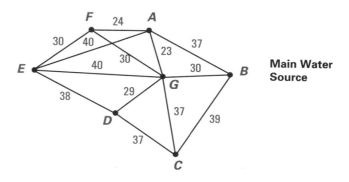

INVESTIGATION 2 Optimizing a Road Network

You can use graph models to optimize many different kinds of networks. For example, consider the following road network. There are seven small towns in Johnson County that are connected to each other by gravel roads, as in the following diagram. (The diagram is not drawn to scale and the roads often are curvy.) The distances are given in miles. The county, which has a limited budget, wants to pave some of the roads so that people can get from every town to every other town on paved roads, either directly or indirectly, and yet the total number of miles paved is the minimum possible.

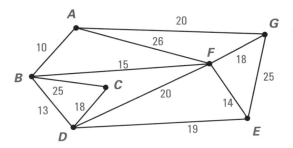

1. Find and draw a network of paved roads that will fulfill the county's requirements. Eliminate any unpaved roads from your drawing.

2. Construct a *distance matrix* for your paved-road network by completing a copy of the matrix below. The entries give the shortest distance between towns on the paved-road network you should have found, not on the original gravel-road network shown above.

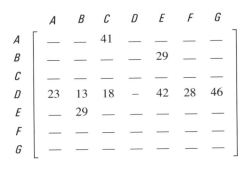

	A	B	C	D	E	F	G
A	—	—	41	—	—	—	—
B	—	—	—	—	29	—	—
C	—	—	—	—	—	—	—
D	23	13	18	—	42	28	46
E	—	29	—	—	—	—	—
F	—	—	—	—	—	—	—
G	—	—	—	—	—	—	—

a. Explain why the A-C entry is 41 and the D-E entry is 42.

b. Why is the B-E entry the same as the E-B entry?

c. Fill in all the entries of the matrix. Divide this job among your group.

d. Describe and explain any patterns you see in the matrix.

INVESTIGATION 2 Optimizing a Road Network

Discuss this situation with your students to be sure that they understand that, as far as the county government is concerned, an acceptable route from *A* to *C* might be very circuitous. The officials are not concerned with the shortest driving time. They are only interested in minimizing costs for the road.

You can help students be more effective with their graphs for Activity 1 by providing markers or colored pencils to color the edges that make the spanning tree or by suggesting that they make a tree that only shows the paved roads. Using Teaching Master 120a will help Activity 2 go smoothly.

Activity 4 is a good activity to include in a large-group summary discussion because it highlights the limitations of a mathematical model. Graphs and matrices are reasonable models for this situation and they provide a useful solution. However, as with all mathematical models, they do not capture every aspect of the situation. It is always a good idea to interpret a solution in terms of the original overall context.

1. The paved-road network will be a minimal spanning tree. Students may or may not use the best-edge algorithm. The minimal spanning tree shown below is unique.

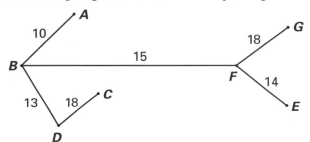

For now, it is best to have students draw (or redraw) their minimal spanning trees as above, without any other edges of the graph shown, rather than darkening the edges of the minimal spanning tree on the entire graph. This will avoid confusion when finding paths and working with distance matrices in the following activities.

2. **See Teaching Masters 120a and 120b.**

   It is important to note that the distances in the matrix are the shortest distances along the paved roads, not the shortest distance on any road.

   a. The 41 for the *A-C* entry represents the paved-road distance from *A* to *B* to *D* to *C* (10 + 13 + 18).

   The 42 for the *D-E* entry represents the paved-road distance from *D* to *B* to *F* to *E* (13 + 15 + 14).

   b. The distance from *E* to *B* is the same as the distance from *B* to *E*.

   c.

	A	*B*	*C*	*D*	*E*	*F*	*G*
A	–	10	41	23	39	25	43
B	10	–	31	13	29	15	33
C	41	31	–	18	60	46	64
D	23	13	18	–	42	28	46
E	39	29	60	42	–	14	32
F	25	15	46	28	14	–	18
G	43	33	64	46	32	18	–

   d. The matrix is symmetric about the main diagonal because the distance from any point *X* to any point *Y* is the same as the distance from *Y* to *X*.

Master 120a

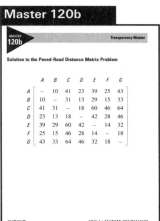

Master 120b

Unit 5

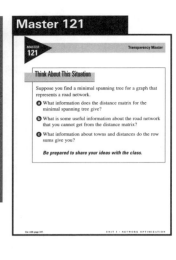

3. a. Towns *C* and *G* are farthest apart on the paved-road network. The *C*-*G* entry is the largest number of miles (64).

b.

Row	A	B	C	D	E	F	G
Row Sum	181	131	260	170	216	146	236

The row sum for a given town is the sum of all the distances from the town to all other towns. That is, if you were to take separate trips from the given town to each of the other towns, the sum of the distances of all the separate trips would be equal to the row sum. Since the matrix is symmetric, you can also think of a row sum as the sum of all the distances from all other towns to the town indicated by the row. That is, if there were to be a meeting in the town indicated by the row, the row sum would be the total travel distance for one person from each town to attend.

c. A larger row sum indicates that a town is farther away from the other towns; *i.e.*, it is relatively isolated. A smaller row sum indicates that there is less total distance to all other towns. Such a town would be centrally located. Thus, Town *C* is the most isolated and Town *B* is the most centrally located.

4. This is an important discussion. Mathematical models always simplify situations as they model them. In this case, there certainly are other factors that need to be considered when finding the "best" network. For example, it may be that the two most populous towns are connected only very indirectly, and so a different network would be better for more people. For almost any choice, the towns on the "fringes" of the minimal spanning tree probably would be dissatisfied. There may not *be* an absolute "best" answer.

SHARE AND SUMMARIZE   full-class discussion

Checkpoint

See Teaching Master 121.

ⓐ Each entry of the distance matrix indicates the shortest distance between each pair of towns on the minimal spanning tree network.

ⓑ The distance matrix does not tell whether the towns are directly or indirectly connected or whether there is a shorter route on unpaved roads.

ⓒ The row sum for a given town is the sum of the distances of separate trips from the given town to all other towns. Thus, it is a measure of how centrally located a town is on the minimal spanning tree network.

JOURNAL ENTRY: In this lesson students have encountered the new idea of a minimal spanning tree, which overlaps considerably with more familiar ideas about circuits and paths. They will benefit from a short reflection time. Here is a suggested prompt.

■ Draw a connected graph with 6 vertices and an Euler circuit. List in order the vertices in the circuit. Draw a connected graph with 6 vertices and an Euler path (noncircuit). List in order the vertices on the path. Draw a connected graph with 6 vertices and highlight the minimal spanning tree.

■ In each case above, describe an appropriate context and say what the edges and vertices represent.

■ How are circuits, paths, and trees alike? How are they different?

---

3. Use the distance matrix to analyze further the road network.

   a. Which two towns are farthest apart on the paved-road network?

   b. Compute the row sums of the distance matrix. What information do the row sums give about distances on the paved-road network?

   c. Which town seems to be most isolated on the paved-road network? Which town seems most centrally located? Explain how these questions can be answered by examining the distance matrix.

4. Which towns might be dissatisfied with this paved-road network? Why? What are some other considerations that might be taken into account when planning an optimal paved-road network?

Checkpoint

Suppose you find a minimal spanning tree for a graph that represents a road network.

a What information does the distance matrix for the minimal spanning tree give you?

b What is some useful information about the road network that you cannot get from the distance matrix?

c What information about towns and distances do the row sums give you?

Be prepared to share your ideas with the class.

LESSON 1 • FINDING THE BEST NETWORKS   327

On Your Own

In Investigation 1, you optimized a computer network by finding a network that used the least amount of wire. Another factor that you might want to optimize is cost. Consider the same six computers in the same six offices. The matrix below shows the *cost*, in dollars, to make each possible direct connection.

$$\begin{array}{c} \\ A \\ B \\ C \\ D \\ E \\ F \end{array} \begin{array}{cccccc} A & B & C & D & E & F \\ \left[\begin{array}{cccccc} - & 39 & - & - & - & 33 \\ 39 & - & 38 & - & 39 & 41 \\ - & 38 & - & 44 & 41 & - \\ - & - & 44 & - & 36 & 37 \\ - & 39 & 41 & 36 & - & 36 \\ 33 & 41 & - & 37 & 36 & - \end{array}\right] \end{array}$$

a. Represent the information in the matrix with a vertex-edge graph.

b. Use the best-edge algorithm to find a network that connects all six computers, either directly or indirectly, for the least total cost.

c. Construct the "distance" matrix for your minimal spanning tree (similar to the one you constructed for Activity 2 of Investigation 2). Note that in this case, the entries of the "distance" matrix actually show the *cost* of the connection between each pair of vertices on the least-cost network.

d. Do you think that the row sums of the "distance" matrix provide any relevant information about the least-cost network? Explain.

MORE
Modeling • Organizing • Reflecting • Extending

Modeling

1. The graph to the right shows a road network connecting six towns (not shown to scale). The distances shown are in miles. The Highway Department wants to plow enough roads after a snowstorm so that people can travel from any town to any other town on plowed roads. However, because of the time and cost involved, they want to plow as few miles of road as possible.

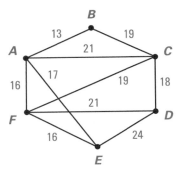

▶**On Your Own**

NOTE: Here students will take a different look at "Which is the best?" by optimizing *cost* instead of *distance*.

---

a.

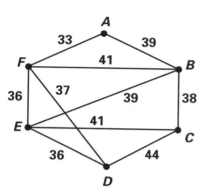

b. Students may connect *B* to *A* instead of *E*.

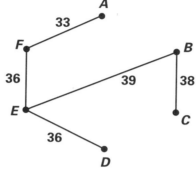

c. It is important for students to begin thinking of *distance, length,* and *shortest* as generic terms, rather than limiting themselves to the terms' literal meanings. In the next lesson, we begin using the standard graph-theoretic term *weight,* instead of *length.*

If *B* is connected directly to *E*, as shown in Part b, the distance matrix is shown on the left. If *B* is connected directly to *A*, the distance matrix is the one shown on the right.

	A	B	C	D	E	F			A	B	C	D	E	F
A	–	108	146	105	69	33		A	–	39	77	105	69	33
B	108	–	38	75	39	75		B	39	–	38	144	108	72
C	146	38	–	113	77	113		C	77	38	–	182	146	110
D	105	75	113	–	36	72		D	105	144	182	–	36	72
E	69	39	77	36	–	36		E	69	108	146	36	–	36
F	33	75	113	72	36	–		F	33	72	110	72	36	–

d. Students may come up with a variety of answers here. Accept any well-defended answer. Note, however, that the row sums are much more ambiguous and less clearly informative in this context than in the mileage context of a road network. An important point in Parts c and d is that mathematical constructions, such as distance matrices and row sums, may be more useful in one context than they are in another. In this case, the information that row sums provide for the cost context is not as relevant as for the mileage context. It doesn't make much sense to think of the sum of the separate costs of running wire from a given computer to each of the others.

Unit 5

Modeling: 1 and choice of one*
Organizing: 1 and 3
Reflecting: 1 and choice of one*
Extending: Choose one*

*When choice is indicated, it is important
to leave the choice to the student.
NOTE: *It is best if Organizing tasks are discussed as a whole class after they have
been assigned as homework.*

MORE   independent assignment

Modeling

1. a. As shown below, there are two minimal spanning trees: (1) *AB, AF, EF, CD, BC* and
(2) *AB, AF, EF, CD, CF*. The roads are listed in the order generated by the best-edge
algorithm. Both trees have a total length of 82 miles.

Tree 1   Tree 2

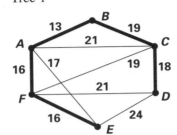   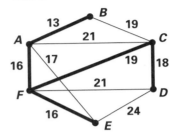

b. See Part a above.

c.   Tree 1   Tree 2

	A	B	C	D	E	F
A	–	13	32	50	32	16
B	13	–	19	37	45	29
C	32	19	–	18	64	48
D	50	37	18	–	82	66
E	32	45	64	82	–	16
F	16	29	48	66	16	–

	A	B	C	D	E	F
A	–	13	35	53	32	16
B	13	–	48	66	45	29
C	35	48	–	18	35	19
D	53	66	18	–	53	37
E	32	45	35	53	–	16
F	16	29	19	37	16	–

d. The row sums for Tree 1 are *A*: 143, *B*: 143, *C*: 181, *D*: 253, *E*: 239, *F*: 175. This
indicates that *A* and *B* are the most centrally located on this network.

   The row sums for Tree 2 are *A*: 149, *B*: 201, *C*: 155, *D*: 227, *E*: 181, *F*: 117. On
this network, *F* is the most centrally located.

e. Responses may vary. The primary effect of substituting *CF* for *BC* is to improve the
ED route at the expense of the *BC* route. Geometrically, this makes a more equitable
spanning tree. Also note that the sum of all row sums in the first matrix is more than
the sum of all row sums in the second matrix, which again leads one to prefer the second. In practice, however, one should gather more data on road usage before making
the decision.

2. a. The table presents the same information as a graph with vertices representing the
names and edges representing the costs of phoning. A spanning tree will have six
edges. Use Kruskal's algorithm directly on the table to select edges of minimal cost
and build a minimal spanning tree. The result is the network shown below and a total
network calling cost of $17.65.

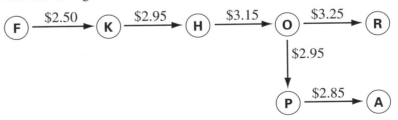

b. Felix calls Kit, Kit calls Hillary, Hillary calls Owen, Owen calls Pearl and Robin, and
Pearl calls Amy.

a. Find and draw a network that will meet the Highway Department's requirements. What is the total number of miles that must be plowed?

b. As you know from this lesson, there may be several networks that satisfy the Highway Department's requirements. Find all the plowed-road networks that will work. Check the total length of each such network and make sure that you get the same total mileage for each that you got in Part a.

c. Construct a distance matrix for each shortest network (that is, for each minimal spanning tree) that you found in Parts a and b.

d. For each plowed-road network, which town is most centrally located? On what quantitative (numerical) information did you base your decision?

e. Each plowed-road network that you found has the same total length. Despite this, do you think one is better than another? Justify your answer by using information from the graphs and the distance matrices.

2. A family with seven members in different parts of the country has a relative working overseas. The family wants to set up a telephone-calling network so everyone will know the latest news about the overseas relative, for the least total cost. The relative overseas will call Felix, and then Felix will start the message through the network. The table below shows the cost for a 15-minute phone call between each pair of family members.

Phone Call Costs

	Amy	Felix	Hillary	Kit	Owen	Pearl	Robin
Amy		$3.50	$4.75	$3.80	$4.10	$2.85	$5.10
Felix	$3.50		$3.75	$2.50	$4.50	$4.10	$3.40
Hillary	$4.75	$3.75		$2.95	$3.15	$4.40	$3.50
Kit	$3.80	$2.50	$2.95		$4.25	$3.30	$3.40
Owen	$4.10	$4.50	$3.15	$4.25		$2.95	$3.25
Pearl	$2.85	$4.10	$4.40	$3.30	$2.95		$3.60
Robin	$5.10	$3.40	$3.50	$3.40	$3.25	$3.60	

a. What is the total cost of the least expensive calling network they can set up?

b. Write a description of who should call whom in this least expensive calling network.

Modeling • Organizing • Reflecting • Extending

3. There are many situations in which it is useful to detect *clustering*. For example, health officials might want to know if outbreaks of the flu are spread randomly over the country or if there are geographic clusters where high percentages of people are sick. Geologists might want to know if the distribution of iron ore is spread evenly through an ore field or if high densities of ore are clustered in particular areas. Economists might want to know if small business start-ups are more common, that is, clustered, in some areas. There are several techniques that have been devised to detect clustering. A technique involving minimal spanning trees is illustrated in the following copper-ore mining context.

Great Lakes Mining Company would like to know if copper ore is evenly distributed throughout a particular region or if there are clusters of ore. The company drills a grid of nine test holes in each of two ore fields. The following diagrams show the grid of test holes in each ore field, along with the percentage of copper, expressed as a decimal, in the sample from each test hole.

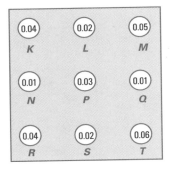

a. Construct a graph model for the grid in each ore field. Represent each test hole as a vertex, and connect two vertices with an edge if the test holes are next to each other (vertically, horizontally, or diagonally).

b. For each edge, compute the absolute value of the difference between the concentrations of copper at the two vertices on the edge. Label the edge with this number. For example, consider the grid on the left. Since the concentration at test hole A is 0.01 and the concentration at test hole E is 0.04, label the edge connecting A and E with $|0.01 - 0.04|$ or 0.03.

c. Find a minimal spanning tree for each of the two graphs. What is the total length of each minimal spanning tree? (Note that "total length" here refers to the sum of the concentration differences on each edge.)

3. a.

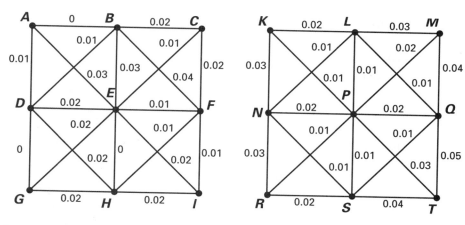

b. The weights of the edges are shown on the graph models above.

c. Minimal spanning trees may vary. The lengths of the minimal spanning trees are 0.06 and 0.11 for the left and right ore fields respectively. The following is an example of a minimal spanning tree for each. Other trees are possible.

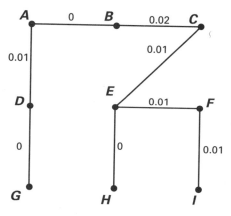
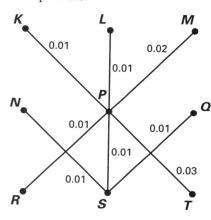

Unit 5

3. d. ■ If there is a cluster of test holes with similar concentrations of copper, the differences between the concentrations will be small, and so the numbers on the edges also will be small.

■ Clustering in an ore field leads to small differences between ore concentrations, which leads to many edges with small numbers on them, which in turn leads to a short minimal spanning tree. Thus, an ore field with more clustering than another will have a shorter minimal spanning tree.

■ The ore field on the left (page 330, Part c) has greater clustering. While the two fields have similar concentration levels, the minimal spanning tree of the one on the left has smaller total length.

NOTE: Minimal spanning trees are useful for helping to detect clustering when the fields being compared have similar levels of ore concentrations. They may be less useful if this is not the case. For example, an ore field with no clustering but low concentrations will have a short minimal spanning tree that could, in fact, be shorter than the minimal spanning tree for a field with lots of clustering and high concentrations.

---

4. a. The minimum amount of wire needed is 108 feet. The following is one possible minimal spanning tree:

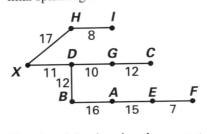

b. The electrician is using the nearest-neighbor algorithm.

c. Applying the algorithm starting at X yields: *X-D-G-C-B-A-E*(or *F*)-*F*(or *E*). It is not possible to continue at this point because the algorithm requires that we add edges without creating circuits; yet the only edge that now can be added is an edge back to A, which creates a circuit. But vertices *H* and *I* have not been reached. No spanning tree is found using this algorithm. (Note that even if we use the network produced by the algorithm and then wire in vertices *H* and *I*, the total amount of wire needed would be 112 feet, which is more than the minimum amount of 108 feet.)

d. Now consider the connection between the length of a minimal spanning tree and clusters of ore concentrations.

- In general, if there is a cluster of test holes with similar concentrations of copper, will the numbers on the edges in that cluster be large or small? Why?

- If there is more clustering in one of the ore fields, will the length of the minimal spanning tree for that ore field be larger or smaller than the other one? Why?

- Which of the two ore fields in this example has greater clustering of concentrations of copper? Explain in terms of minimal spanning trees.

4. A restaurant has opened an outdoor patio for evening dining. The owner wants to hang nine decorative light fixtures at designated locations on the overhead latticework. Because of the layout of the patio and the latticework, it is not possible to install wiring between every pair of lights. The matrix below shows the distances in feet between lights that can be linked directly. The main power supply from the restaurant building is at location X. The owner wants to use the minimum amount of wire to get all nine lights connected.

	X	A	B	C	D	E	F	G	H	I
X	–	18	–	–	11	–	–	13	17	–
A	18	–	16	–	–	15	15	–	–	–
B	–	16	–	16	12	–	–	–	–	–
C	–	–	16	–	–	–	–	12	–	–
D	11	–	12	–	–	–	–	10	–	–
E	–	15	–	–	–	–	7	–	–	–
F	–	15	–	–	–	7	–	–	–	–
G	13	–	–	12	10	–	–	–	18	–
H	17	–	–	–	–	–	–	18	–	8
I	–	–	–	–	–	–	–	–	8	–

a. What is the minimum amount of wire needed to connect all nine lights?

b. Suppose the electrician decides to start at the power supply, X, then go to the closest light, then go to the closest light from there, and so on. What algorithm does she seem to be using?

c. Apply the electrician's algorithm to the graph, starting at X. Describe what happens.

Organizing

1. In this lesson, you found shortest networks by finding minimal spanning trees. Graphs for problems involving minimal spanning trees always have numbers associated with their edges. Now consider graphs that do not have numbers on the edges. In these cases, you might be interested in finding a network that connects all the vertices of a graph and uses the fewest number of edges. Such a graph is called a **spanning tree**.

   a. Find a spanning tree for each graph below. Describe the method you used to find the spanning trees.

   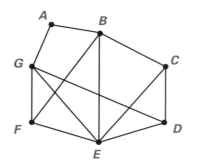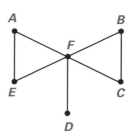

   b. Find three different spanning trees for the following graph.

   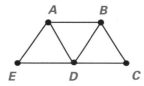

   c. Write a rule relating the number of vertices in a graph and the number of edges in a spanning tree for the graph.

2. Recall that a tree is a connected graph that has no circuits. In Course 1, you investigated vertex colorings of graphs. In this task, you will consider vertex colorings of trees.

   a. Draw three different trees, each having at least six vertices.

   b. What is the minimum number of colors needed to color the vertices of each tree so that any two vertices connected by an edge have different colors?

   c. What is the minimum number of colors needed to color the vertices of *any* tree so that two vertices connected by an edge have different colors? Explain your reasoning.

Organizing

1. **a.** Spanning trees may vary. One possibility for each graph is shown below. One method for finding a spanning tree is to systematically remove edges that form circuits.

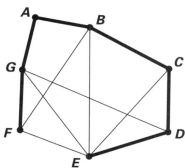 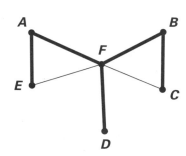

   b. There are many possible spanning trees. For example:

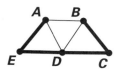 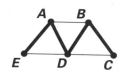 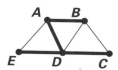

   c. The number of edges (E) in a spanning tree is always one less than the number of vertices (V) in the graph. $E = V - 1$

2. **a.** Responses may vary. Three possible trees are shown below.

  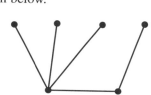

   b. For each of the three trees in Part a, you only need two colors.

   c. Every tree can be colored using only two colors. To do this, start anywhere and then alternate colors as you step from vertex to vertex. Only a circuit may need more than two colors (if it consists of an odd number of vertices). Since a tree has no circuits, you will not need a third color.

3. **a.** ■ Grid A is rigid; Grid B is not. Student explanations may vary. Students simply may notice fewer braces on Grid B, but it is hoped that they will notice that the first column and last row could collapse.

■ Three braces can be removed from Grid A. One possibility is shown below.

■ Two braces must be added to Grid B. One solution is shown below. See Part c on page T334 for a criterion for rigidity.

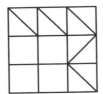

b. ■ There is a brace where the top row intersects the middle column.
■ There is no brace in the cell in the center of the grid.
■ Following is the graph for Grid B.

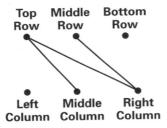

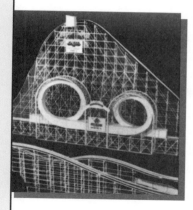

3. If you make a rectangular frame, like framing used for scaffolding, it is necessary to brace it with a diagonal strip. Without such a strip it can deform, as illustrated below.

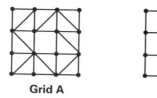 A shape like this  will deform under a load to a shape like this, unless it is braced like this.

Buildings and bridges often are constructed of rectangular steel grids, such as those shown below. To make grids rigid, you do not have to brace each cell with a diagonal, but you do have to brace some of them.

a. One of the two grids below is rigid and the other is not.

Grid A   **Grid B**

- Which is the rigid grid? Explain your choice.
- For the rigid grid, remove some of the braces without making the grid nonrigid. (You may want to make a physical model to help.)
- For the nonrigid grid, add some diagonal braces to make the grid rigid. (Again, you may find a physical model helpful.)

b. You can use vertex-edge graphs to help solve problems like those above. The first step is to model the grid with a graph. Let the vertices represent the rows and columns of the grid. Then draw an edge between a row-vertex and a column-vertex if the cell for that row and column is braced. The graph for Grid A is drawn below.

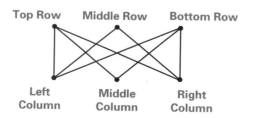

Top Row   Middle Row   Bottom Row

Left Column   Middle Column   Right Column

- Explain why there is an edge from the top-row vertex to the middle-column vertex.
- Explain why there is no edge from the middle-row vertex to the middle-column vertex.
- Construct the graph for Grid B.

LESSON 1 • FINDING THE BEST NETWORKS   333

c. Compare the graphs for Grid A and Grid B.

- Is the graph for Grid A connected? Is Grid A rigid?

- Is the graph for Grid B connected? Is Grid B rigid?

- Do you think connectedness of a graph model of a grid will ensure the corresponding grid is rigid? Draw another connected graph and another nonconnected graph, each of which could model a grid. What is true about the rigidity of their corresponding grids? Do these examples support your conjecture?

d. A rigid grid may have "extra" bracings. For example, in Part a you discovered that it was possible to remove some of the cell bracings of Grid A and still maintain the rigidity. Now investigate what this means in terms of the corresponding graph.

- On a copy of the graph for Grid A, eliminate "extra" edges, one at a time. Stop when you think that removing another edge will result in a graph that represents a nonrigid grid. How is your final "subgraph" related to the original graph?

- Draw a rigid grid that has the minimum number of bracings. Examine its corresponding vertex-edge graph representation. Is there anything special about this graph?

- What feature of a graph model of a rigid grid would indicate that the grid has the minimum number of bracings? Make a conjecture. Add the minimum number of bracings to Grid B to make it rigid, and then examine the corresponding graph. Does this example support your conjecture?

4. In Organizing Task 3, you discovered how to use graphs to analyze rigidity of rectangular grids. You probably found the following:

- A grid is rigid provided its graph is connected.

- The minimum number of bracings to make the grid rigid have been used only when its graph is a spanning tree.

Consider the grid shown at the right.

a. Draw the graph for this grid.

b. Is the grid rigid? How can you tell by looking at the graph?

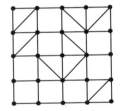

c. Have the minimum number of cells been braced? How can you tell by looking at the graph?

d. Remove "extra" bracings by removing edges that create circuits.

e. Draw the corresponding grid with a minimum number of bracings to make it rigid.

f. The key fact about grids and graphs is that a grid is rigid provided its graph is connected. Explain why this fact makes sense.

3. c. ■ Yes; yes.

   ■ No, the graph for Grid B consists of three pieces. No, Grid B is not rigid.

   ■ See student grids and graphs. If a graph corresponding to a grid is connected, then the grid is rigid.

d. ■ One subgraph is shown below. After eliminating all "extra" edges, the remaining edges should be a spanning tree for the graph.

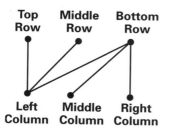

   ■ Grids and graphs will vary. If a grid has the minimum number of bracings, the corresponding vertex-edge graph will be a spanning tree for the vertices. See the notes to Activity 4, Part f (page T366D), for an explanation.

   ■ If the graph model is a spanning tree, it represents a rigid grid with the minimum number of bracings.

4. a.

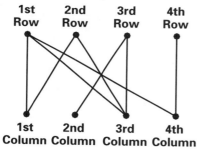

b. The grid is rigid since its graph is connected.

c. There is one extra brace. The graph contains one circuit, which is highlighted in the graph below.

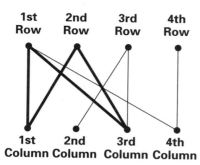

d. Any one brace from the circuit can be removed.

See additional Teaching Notes on page T366D.

Reflecting

1. **a.** If each edge has equal weight, the paths all would have total weight that is a multiple of the edge weights. To get a path with less weight, you would have to eliminate an edge—which is the same thing you do for unweighted graphs.

   b. This suggests that the results and algorithms created for graphs with numbers on their edges also should apply to graphs without numbers on their edges.

2. **a.** A connected graph can have many circuits. In terms of keeping the graph connected, the edges that form circuits are redundant. That is, you can remove edges that form circuits and the resulting graph is still connected. But once there are no circuits, it is impossible to remove edges without disconnecting the graph. Thus, a connected graph with no circuits (a tree) has the fewest number of edges possible to maintain connectivity. In this sense, a tree is a minimal, connected graph.

   b. Since a tree is connected, there is a path from any vertex to any other vertex. Thus, adding an edge between any two vertices in the graph will introduce a circuit. In this way, a tree is a maximal graph with no circuits.

3. **a.** Responses may vary. The graph suggests structural integration, lines, and angles rather than classical curves, continuous progress punctuated by angular passages, or strongly purposeful music with jagged inner content.

   b. Responses will vary. Students may suggest that Stravinsky chose a tree to emphasize that the themes in his music do not recur as was common in much of the classical music before his time.

4. Responses will vary. Situations should reflect the need to link a set of objects while minimizing cost, distance, or some other factor. One example that minimizes cost might be building underground tunnels to link important locations in a city. An example unlike any in the unit might be designing a network that minimizes the risk of having some type of communication overheard. In this situation, each vertex might be a person and the edges would be weighted with the number of people likely to overhear the communication between the people. In this case, the minimum spanning tree would give the most secure way to get the message to all people.

Reflecting

1. Refer back to Organizing Task 1 on page 332. Graphs without numbers on their edges can be considered graphs *with* numbers on the edges by using the same number on all the edges. For example, you could put a "1" on each edge. (The number on an edge is called its *weight*. You will investigate weighted graphs in Lesson 2.)

    a. Explain why putting the same number on each edge is like having no numbers on the edges.

    b. What does this suggest about the results and algorithms created for graphs with numbers on their edges?

2. Think about the characteristics of those graphs which are also trees.

    a. Explain why a tree can be considered a *minimal* connected graph.

    b. Explain why a tree can be considered a *maximal* graph with no circuits.

3. There is a story that when composer Igor Stravinsky (1882–1971) was asked how he would describe his music pictorially, he replied, "This is my music:"

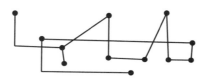

    a. What do you think Stravinsky meant?

    b. One of Stravinsky's most well-known compositions is *The Rite of Spring*. Listen to *The Rite of Spring*. Why do you think Stravinsky used a tree graph to describe his music? (Incidentally, because *The Rite of Spring* sounded so unexpectedly different and unusual, the premiere performance caused a riot in the audience.)

4. Think of a situation, different from any in this lesson, in which it would be helpful to find a minimal spanning tree. Describe the situation and explain how a minimal spanning tree could be used.

Extending

1. There is a popular solitaire game called *Clock Solitaire*. As with many games, there is a lot of mathematics underlying the game. In fact, with a little vertex-edge graph modeling, you can determine whether you will win the game before you actually start playing.

Here's how to play the game:

Start with a standard deck of 52 cards and make 13 piles of 4 cards each, with all cards face down. Place 12 of the piles in the positions of the numbers on a clock face, and place the 13th pile in the center of the clock. Turn over the top card of the center pile and slide it face-up under the pile whose number corresponds to the face value of the card. (Aces go to 1:00, jacks to 11:00, queens to 12:00, and kings go to the center pile. For example, if you turn over the top card of the center pile and it is a nine, then you would slide it face-up under the pile at 9:00.) Then turn over the top card on that pile, and place the new card where it indicates. You continue in this manner until it is no longer possible to turn up a card on the pile where you are. You win if you have turned up all 52 cards.

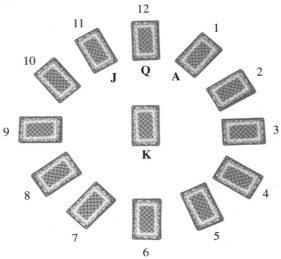

Get a deck of cards and play the game a few times. Then think about some patterns in the game.

a. After playing the game a few times, you will notice that the last play of the game is always on the center pile. Explain why this happens.

b. Set up another game of *Clock Solitaire,* but don't begin playing. Construct a graph model as follows, and call it the *total graph* for your game. Let the vertices be the positions of the piles. For each vertex, draw a directed edge from the vertex to each of the vertices indicated by the cards in the pile. So, for example, if the pile at 3:00 has a 9, 3, 2, and jack in it, then you would draw directed edges from the vertex at 3 to the vertices at 9, 3, 2, and 11. (The edge from 3 to 3 would be a loop.)

■ How many directed edges will be coming into each vertex? Why?

■ Explain why winning the game means that there is an Euler circuit in the total graph. (Recall that an Euler circuit is a circuit through a graph that uses each edge exactly once.)

Extending

1. a. For all piles *except the center pile* you add one card before you turn one over and proceed. Thus, for example, in the pile at the 3:00 position, you turn up a card each time a three is added:

First 3 added—turn over first card on the pile—proceed

Second 3 added—turn over the second card on the pile—proceed

... Fourth 3 added—turn over the fourth card—proceed

Thus, you never stop playing at a non-center pile—you always proceed. But since the center pile is where you start, the first card gets turned over without any card being added. Thus, for the center pile:

First king added—turn over the *second* card—proceed

... Fourth king added—no card to turn over—game ends.

b. ■ Allowing for loops, there are four edges directed toward each vertex because there are four cards of each type.

■ From Part a you know that every game starts and stops in the center, so every game is a circuit of the total graph. If you win, then you must have turned over every card. In this case, the circuit includes every edge and thus is an Euler circuit. (No edge can be repeated since no card is turned over more than once.)

1. c. ■ Graphs will vary depending on the game.

■ Yes. The last move is always a move to the center. If the last move is a winning move, it must come from the bottom of some pile. Thus, there must be an edge of the bottom-card graph coming into the center vertex.

d. ■ Students should win one game and lose the other.

■ Answers will vary. Here is one explanation. You must show that (1) if you win then the bottom-card graph is a tree, and (2) if the bottom-card graph is a tree, then you win.

(1) To show that the bottom-card graph is a tree, we must show that it is connected and has no circuits.

(i) We will first show that there is a directed path in the bottom-card graph from every vertex to the center, which makes the bottom-card graph connected. Since we win the game, the total-graph has a directed Euler circuit which starts and ends at the center and which, of course, includes all vertices. Start at any vertex, V. Suppose the bottom card in V points to W, that is, the last exit out of V is to W. Then the edge V-W is in the bottom-card graph. Take edge V-W from V to W. From W, follow the total-graph Euler circuit until you get back to the last exit out of W, which will be another edge on the bottom-card graph, say W-U. This gets you from V to W to U on the bottom-card graph. Continue in this way until you get to the center. (You know that you eventually will get to the center because the total-graph Euler circuit always gets there from any stage in this process.) Thus, there is a directed path in the bottom-card graph from every vertex to the center. Hence, the bottom-card graph is connected.

(ii) Now we will show that the bottom-card graph does not have any circuits. The center can't be part of any circuit in the bottom-card graph because there is no edge coming out it. A circuit without the center would mean that we take the last exit out of some noncenter vertex and then come back into it. But when we come back, there would be no way out since we already used the last exit. Thus, the game would stop before we got back to the center. This can't happen since we win the game and winning games always end up in the center. Thus, the bottom-card graph has no circuits.

Therefore, if we win, the bottom-card graph is connected and has no circuits, so it is a tree. (Note that the bottom-card graph is also a spanning tree.)

See additional Teaching Notes on page T366E.

c. The total graph is messy because it has so many edges. A simpler graph model, call it the *bottom-card graph*, is constructed as follows. Once again let the vertices be the positions of the piles. For every pile except the center pile, look at the *bottom* card and draw a directed edge from the vertex for that pile to the vertex indicated by the bottom card. For example, if the bottom card of the pile at 5:00 is a queen, then you would draw a directed edge from the vertex 5 to the vertex 12.

- Set up a game of *Clock Solitaire* and construct the bottom-card graph for the game.

- Because of the rules for how it is constructed, a bottom-card graph never has an edge coming out of the center vertex, where the kings go. If you win the game, will there be an edge going into the center vertex? Explain.

d. Here is an amazing fact: *You win the game exactly when the bottom-card graph is a tree*.

- Set up two games of *Clock Solitaire*, one with a bottom-card graph that is a tree and one with a graph that isn't. Play the games and see if you win one and lose the other.

- *Challenge*: Write a paragraph explaining why the amazing fact is true. **Hints:** Think of each edge on the bottom-card graph as representing the "last exit" out of the pile. Think of the bottom-card graph as part of the total graph.

2. The nearest-neighbor algorithm you investigated in Activity 9 on page 324 did not always produce a minimal spanning tree in a connected graph. Below is a modified version of that algorithm, called *Prim's algorithm*.

   i. Make a copy of the graph with the edges drawn lightly.

   ii. Choose a starting vertex. This is the beginning of the tree.

   iii. Find all edges that have one vertex in the tree constructed so far. Darken the shortest such edge that does not create a circuit. If there is more than one such edge, choose any one.

   iv. Repeat Step iii until all vertices have been reached.

a. Test Prim's algorithm using three copies of the following graph from Activity 9.

- Apply the algorithm starting at vertex *E*.

- Apply the algorithm starting at vertex *C*.

- Apply the algorithm starting at vertex *A*.

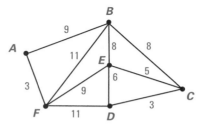

b. Compare Prim's algorithm with the nearest-neighbor algorithm in Activity 9 on page 324.

- How are they similar? How are they different?

- Compare the results in Part a above to those you got with the nearest-neighbor algorithm in Activity 9.

c. Explain why a tree is constructed at each stage of Prim's algorithm.

d. Do you think Prim's algorithm is a good procedure for finding a minimal spanning tree? Write a brief justification of your answer.

e. Compare Prim's algorithm with Kruskal's best-edge algorithm from Activity 7 on page 323.

- How are they similar? How are they different?

- Which algorithm would you prefer to use to find a minimal spanning tree? Why?

f. To find minimal spanning trees for large graphs, algorithms such as Prim's or Kruskal's must be implemented on a computer. Do you think it might be the case that the easier (preferred) algorithm for finding a minimal spanning tree for small graphs by hand is different from the best (most efficient) algorithm for large graphs by computer? Explain your reasoning.

Joseph Kruskal

3. To find a minimal spanning tree in a graph, you look for a network of existing edges that joins all the vertices and has minimum length. In some situations, you may want to create a minimal spanning network by adding new vertices and edges to the original graph. Such a network is called a **Steiner tree** (named after Jacob Steiner, a 19th century mathematician at the University of Berlin).

There is a way to use geometry to find Steiner trees. For this task, you should use a geometry software package that allows you to construct, measure, and move geometric figures.

a. Using a geometry software package, construct a triangle in which all the angles are less than 120°. (Actually, because of software limitations, it is best if all angles are less than 115°.) You can consider this triangle as a vertex-edge graph.

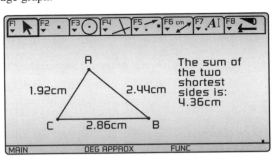

2. b. ■ This algorithm is similar to the nearest-neighbor algorithm in that at each step you add the shortest edge that does not create a circuit. The small but significant difference is that in the nearest-neighbor algorithm, the edge you add must be connected to the vertex where you are; while in Prim's algorithm, the edge you add must be connected to any vertex already reached. With this change, Prim's algorithm is guaranteed to find a minimal spanning tree.

■ Prim's algorithm produced three different minimal spanning trees for this graph while the nearest-neighbor algorithm from page 324 did not even guarantee a spanning trree or a minimal spanning tree.

c. At each step, the edge added must be connected to the existing tree such that no circuit is created. Thus, the tree grows at each step.

d. Prim's algorithm is efficient and effective. It always yields a minimal spanning tree. Look for a confident justification and evidence of understanding of both algorithms. (A technical answer is beyond the scope of this book, but students should at least comment that the algorithm worked on the example and seems efficient.)

e. ■ At each step, both algorithms add the shortest edge that does not create a circuit. However, the set of edges to choose from is different in the two algorithms. In Kruskal's algorithm, you choose from among all the edges, while in Prim's algorithm you consider only those edges adjacent to vertices already in the tree. Both algorithms are efficient and always produce a minimal spanning tree.

■ Responses will vary. Students should justify their choice of algorithms.

f. Yes. For example, it may be possible to find a minimal spanning tree for a small graph just by scanning the graph, checking out all possibilities, and choosing a minimal spanning tree. This kind of brute-force method can go very quickly for small graphs using the human eye and brain. However, programming a computer to use this procedure could be difficult and the algorithm might take a very long time to execute for large graphs. A computer would use a different algorithm, like Kruskal's best-edge algorithm or Prim's algorithm. In general, an algorithm that suits a computer may not suit a human, since humans and computers process information in different ways.

3. a. Students will construct diagrams using the geometry software.

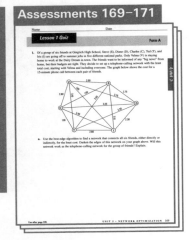
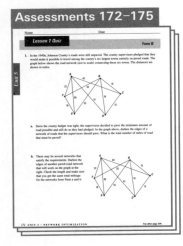
MORE *continued*

3. **b.** Responses will vary, depending on student-generated diagrams.

c. The length of this new network will be smaller than the minimal spanning tree length from Part b.

d. The triangle, its minimal spanning tree, and its Steiner tree will typically look something like the diagrams below. It always will be the case that the central angles surrounding the inside point will measure 120°.

| **Triangle** | **Minimal Spanning Tree** | **Steiner Tree** |

The Steiner tree problem with triangles is investigated further in the Capstone of Course 3. For another discussion of this problem see Chapter 7 in P. Tannenbaum and R. Arnold, *Excursions in Modern Mathematics*, Second Edition (Englewood Cliffs, NJ: Prentice-Hall, 1995). For a proof that the point surrounded with 120-degree angles gives the shortest network, see Exercise 45 on pages 254–255 in that text.

4. Programs will vary; following is an outline of a program.

This algorithm will give a minimal spanning tree for a graph G by adding edges of least weight whose addition does not create a circuit. At the end of the calculation, the minimal spanning tree is described by the edges in set T.

```
Begin program
    order the edges in G by increasing distance
Repeat loop until T is connected and contains all vertices of G
    IF next edge in order does not complete a circuit,
    THEN add that edge to T
End loop
End program
```

Following is another outline of a program. Here, E is the set of edges for G.

```
Begin program
    e = edge in E with smallest weight
    T = {e}
    E* = E − {e}
Repeat loop until E* is equal to the empty set
    e* = edge in E* with smallest weight
    T = T union {e*}
    E* = set of edges in E* − T whose addition to T does not create a circuit
End loop
End program
```

See Assessment Resources, pages 169–175.

Your goal in Parts b and c is to find a shortest network that joins all three of the triangle's vertices.

b. A minimal spanning tree for this triangular graph is just the network consisting of the two shortest sides. Find the sum of the lengths of the two shortest sides. Now you have the length of a minimal spanning tree.

c. Now consider a network where you are allowed to insert a new vertex and new edges. You will investigate whether this gives you a connected network that is shorter than the minimal spanning tree you found in Part b. Begin by using the software to perform the following construction:

- Insert a new point (vertex) inside the triangle.

- Construct segments from the inside point to each of the vertices of the triangle. (This gives you a network that connects all three of the triangle's vertices, but it uses a vertex and edges that are not part of the original triangle.)

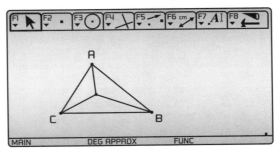

- Measure the length of this network by measuring each segment and adding the three lengths. (For best results, set the measurement precision of your geometry software so that lengths are measured in tenths of pixels.)

- Now use the software to grab the inside point and drag it around. Note that the network length changes as the point is moved. Drag the point around until the network length is as small as possible.

Is this length smaller than the minimal spanning tree length from Part b?

d. Find the measure of the three central angles that surround the inside point. (For best results, set the measurement precision of your geometry software to measure angles in whole-unit degrees.) Make a conjecture about the measures of these angles when the inside point is moved to a position giving the shortest connected network. Test your conjecture on some other triangles.

4. Write a calculator or computer program for the best-edge algorithm. Use your program to find a minimal spanning tree for the graphs in Modeling Task 1 on page 328 and Extending Task 2 on page 337.

Lesson 2 Shortest Paths and Circuits

In the last lesson, you investigated minimal spanning trees and their applications to finding shortest networks. The graphs you used to model situations had numbers associated with their edges. The numbers most often represented distance, but sometimes they represented other quantities like cost or concentration of copper ore. A graph with numbers on its edges is called a **weighted graph**, and the numbers, whatever they represent, are called **weights**.

In this lesson, you will investigate paths and circuits in weighted graphs. Problems of this type are common in the communications, shipping, and travel industries.

Think About This Situation

Rely on your common-sense notion of shortest paths and shortest circuits as you try to answer the following questions.

a What kinds of situations in the shipping or travel industry might involve shortest paths or shortest circuits?

b What kinds of situations in the communications industry might involve finding a shortest path or shortest circuit?

Shortest Paths and Circuits

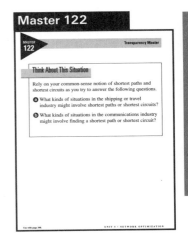

LESSON OVERVIEW In this lesson, students investigate contexts and questions that lead naturally to the need for shortest paths between two vertices and for shortest paths or circuits that include all vertices of a graph.

The standard graph-theoretic terms *weight* and *weighted graph* are introduced. This allows us to talk generally about all the different contexts that may arise, like mileage, cost, or time. In particular, the SHORTCUT software provided with this lesson uses these terms, as do virtually all references on graph theory.

Shortest circuits that visit every vertex can be characterized as minimal spanning circuits. Finding such a circuit is called the *Traveling Salesperson Problem*. When the edges are not weighted, and you are just trying to find a circuit that uses each vertex exactly once, it is called a *Hamiltonian circuit*.

Lesson Objectives

- To represent and analyze a variety of real-world situations using shortest paths, Hamiltonian circuits, and the Traveling Salesperson Problem
- To apply and analyze both given and student-generated algorithms, and brute-force methods for the Traveling Salesperson Problem
- To understand the limitations of the computer as a brute-force tool for solving problems

LAUNCH full-class discussion

The topics in this unit are quite interrelated. Similarities and differences in topics need to be discussed. At the same time, students should not complete this unit thinking that it is a unit on new vocabulary. At this point it might be helpful to provide students with a copy of the unit objectives and discuss their importance.

Think About This Situation

See Teaching Master 122.

ⓐ Responses will vary. Possible ideas include minimizing the total distance an airline passenger must fly when making a transcontinental flight if no direct flight is available, or finding the shortest distance a driver would have to travel in order to complete the delivery of several packages.

ⓑ Possibilities are determining how to most efficiently route phone calls or how to set up a local computer network for executives to communicate via electronic mail.

Students may need encouragement to think of additional situations or to ask adults with whom they are acquainted for additional contexts for networks. Some of these ideas may provide opportunities for a unit assessment project rather than the standard in-class test. (See "Assessing Student Understanding" on page T319A.)

INVESTIGATION 1 ► Shortest Routes

In this investigation, students explore another important graph theory concept. In Course 1, they studied Euler paths (paths that traverse each edge exactly once), and critical paths (a longest path through a graph). The last investigation explored minimal spanning trees (networks that connect each vertex using minimum total edge weight). Now they will study a shortest path from one given vertex to another, not necessarily connecting all vertices. The vocabulary and concepts in this unit overlap with those from the "Graph Models" unit in Course 1, and students need to talk about these ideas to each other and to explain their solutions in order to clarify the ideas.

1. **a.** In this context, "shortest path" means "cheapest airfare."
   b. The cheapest airfare between Minneapolis and Detroit is $379, the cost of flying from Minneapolis to St. Louis and St. Louis to Detroit. Between Kansas City and Grand Rapids, the cheapest airfare is $322, the result of flying through Chicago.
   c. Chicago and St. Louis have many cities to which they are directly connected. Because of this, the map shows many edges coming out of the vertices representing Chicago and St. Louis. These edges look like spokes of a wheel so, in turn, Chicago and St. Louis look like hubs.
   d. It's cheaper to go through St. Louis than Chicago.

INVESTIGATION 1 Shortest Routes

Shortest routes are important in many different contexts. Several are explored in this investigation.

Airfares Getting the least expensive airfare these days is not a simple matter. The fare you pay depends on many factors, such as how far in advance you buy your ticket or if you will stay over Saturday night. It even depends on the cities through which you fly to get to your final destination.

Kansas City, Kansas

Detroit

1. The diagram below shows sample airfares on a major airline for round-trip tickets, purchased two weeks in advance, with a Saturday night stay-over.

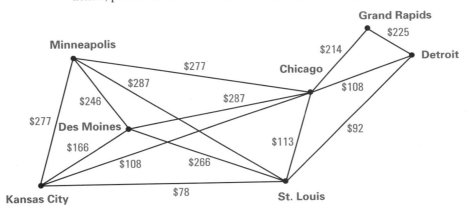

a. Thinking of this diagram as a weighted graph, what does the shortest path between two vertices tell you about airfare?

b. What is the cheapest airfare between Minneapolis and Detroit? Between Kansas City and Grand Rapids?

c. Why do you think Chicago and St. Louis are called major "hubs"?

d. If a friend was planning to travel from one of the three westernmost cities to Detroit, what advice would you give him or her?

Manufacturing Shortest paths also can be used to optimize a manufacturing process. Consider a toy company that makes a hand-crafted game which involves moving pegs around a wooden game board. In the following activity, you will analyze how the game board is made.

2. Three of the tasks required to make the game board are cutting the wood (*C*), drilling the holes (*H*), and stripping the wood (*S*). These three tasks can be done in any order, but the time required to do each task depends on when it is done. The manufacturer wants to answer the following question:

What is the most efficient order for doing the three tasks?

All the information about the tasks, their orders, and their times is given in the digraph below.

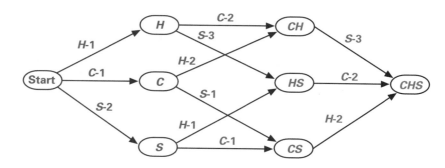

The vertices of this digraph represent stages of the manufacturing process. For example, "*S*" represents a piece of wood that has been stripped only; "*CS*" represents a piece of wood that has been cut and stripped but has not yet had holes drilled in it.

The labels on the edges tell which task will lead to the next stage and how many minutes that task will take. Remember that the time required for a task depends on when it is done. Thus, for example, the "*C-1*" label on the edge from *S* to *CS* means that it takes 1 minute to cut a piece of wood that has been stripped, while the "*C-2*" label on the edge from *H* to *CH* means that it takes 2 minutes to cut a piece of wood that has holes drilled in it.

a. Begin your analysis by practicing reading the digraph.

- Which vertex represents the stage in the manufacturing process where a piece of wood has been stripped and has holes drilled in it, but the wood has not yet been cut?

- What does the vertex "*CHS*" represent?

- How long does it take to strip a piece of wood that has been cut and has holes drilled into it?

- What does the label "*S-1*" on the edge from *C* to *CS* mean?

2.   a.   ■ Vertex *HS*

■ The wood has been cut and stripped and has had holes drilled in it.

■ 3 minutes

■ After the wood is cut, it takes 1 minute to strip the piece of wood.

2. **b.** ■ First strip, then cut, then drill holes. It will take 5 minutes.

   ■ The length of a path is the time it takes to process a piece of wood in the order indicated by the path.

   ■ There are 6 ways to order the letters *C, H,* and *S*; there are 6 paths through the graph. Students may just count without using formulas or specific techniques.

   c. ■ The most efficient order for doing the three tasks corresponds to the shortest path from Start to *CHS*. The shortest path is Start $\rightarrow C \rightarrow CS \rightarrow CHS$, so the most efficient order is cut, strip, drill holes.

   ■ The length of the process in the order given above is 4 minutes.

It is important for students to see the difference between shortest paths on the paved-road network from the last lesson and shortest paths on the entire network. The paved-road network was a minimal spanning tree, and there was only one path between any two towns (this is a property of trees), while there are many paths between any two towns for the entire network.

3. **a.** Three different paths from *A* to *E* are: *A-G-E, A-F-E,* and *A-B-D-E*. There are many other paths from *A* to *E*.

   b. The shortest path from *A* to *E* is *A-B-F-E*, with length 39. This has more legs than some other paths and "looks" longer on the graph, but when the weights are considered it is the shortest path.

   c. The shortest path from *F* to *A* is *F-B-A*, with length 25.

b. Now interpret paths in the digraph.

- What order of tasks is represented by the path: Start→S→CS→CHS? What is the length, in minutes, of this path?

- What does the length of a path tell you about the manufacturing process for the game board?

- How many different ways can you order the three tasks: C, H, and S? How does this relate to the number of different paths from Start to CHS?

c. Explain how to use paths in the digraph to answer these questions.

- What is the most efficient order for doing the three tasks?

- What is the total time required to manufacture the game board if the tasks are done in this optimal order?

Road Networks Reproduced below is the weighted graph representing the network of seven rural towns you investigated in Lesson 1. (The weights on the edges represent distances in miles). In that lesson, you found a minimal spanning tree that represented a paved-road network connecting all the towns. Only some roads were paved, and there was only one path from a given town to any other town on the paved-road network.

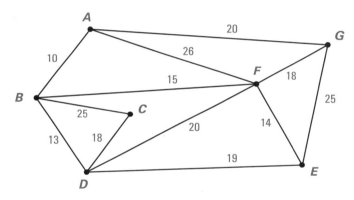

3. For this activity, assume that all the roads are paved and consider all the possible paths between each pair of towns.

a. Find three different paths from A to E. List the towns that make up each path.

b. What is the shortest path from A to E? What is the length of the shortest path?

c. What is the shortest path from F to A? What is its length?

d. A distance matrix shows the length of a *shortest* path between every two towns in a network. Finding all the shortest paths in this network is a lot of work since there are many paths between each pair of towns. An efficient algorithm for finding shortest paths is described in Extending Task 2, page 359, but it is very time-consuming to carry out by hand. The SHORTCUT software developed for your calculator, or similar computer software, can implement this algorithm for you. Use software to construct the distance matrix for the road network on the previous page.

e. Examine the distance matrix displayed by the software.

- Compare the matrix entry for the shortest distance between *A* and *E* with what you found in Part b.

- What is the farthest you would have to drive to get from one town to any other town?

- For each town, compare its row to its column. What pattern do you see? Explain why this pattern should be expected.

f. Now consider the row sums that the SHORTCUT program, or a similar program, computed.

- The row sum for vertex *F* is less than the row sum for vertex *G*. What does this mean in terms of towns and distances?

- Which town is the most isolated?

- Suppose a new county hospital to serve all seven towns is to be built in one of the towns. In which town should it be built? Why?

Checkpoint

a In this investigation, you studied shortest paths in three different contexts. What information did shortest paths give you in each of the contexts?

b In Lesson 1, you investigated minimal spanning trees. What is the difference between a minimal spanning tree and a shortest path? Describe a context different from those in Lessons 1 and 2 in which you would want to find a minimal spanning tree. Describe a new context in which you would want to find a shortest path.

Be prepared to share the results of your analyses with the class.

3. d. **If students are not using calculator or computer software, see Teaching Master 123 for a partially completed distance matrix for this activity.**

The SHORTCUT program uses Dijkstra's algorithm, which is investigated in Extending Task 2. Software for finding shortest paths and distances is important since it is so tedious to compute these things by hand in any but the simplest situations.

	A	B	C	D	E	F	G	Row Sum
A	–	10	35	23	39	25	20	152
B	10	–	25	13	29	15	30	122
C	35	25	–	18	37	38	55	208
D	23	13	18	–	19	20	38	131
E	39	29	37	19	–	14	25	163
F	25	15	38	20	14	–	18	130
G	20	30	55	38	25	18	–	186

e. ■ It is also 39.

■ 55 miles. The *C-G* entry is the largest.

■ The *n*th row of the distance matrix is the same as the *n*th column. This is true because for any two towns *X* and *Y*, the distance from *X* to *Y* is the same as the distance from *Y* to *X*. Thus, it makes sense that the distance matrix is symmetric.

f. ■ The total distance from *F* to each of the other towns is smaller than the total distance from *G* to each of the other towns. In some sense, *F* is more centrally located than *G*.

■ The town with the largest row sum is the most isolated. In this case, that is town *C*, with row sum 208.

■ *B* is the town with the smallest row sum, a total of 122. Hence, *B* seems to be most centrally located and would perhaps be the best choice for the hospital site. Other considerations such as population also should be taken into account.

SHARE AND SUMMARIZE full-class discussion

Checkpoint

See Teaching Master 124.

a Shortest paths in the three different contexts gave information about cheapest airfares, the optimum manufacturing process, and the shortest route between towns.

b A minimal spanning tree is a network of shortest total length (*i.e.*, smallest total weight) that joins all the vertices in a graph. A shortest path is simply the shortest route between two vertices. Thus, a minimal spanning tree is like a shortest tree instead of a shortest path. Also, a minimal spanning tree includes all vertices, and a shortest path generally does not include all vertices.

Contexts will vary. When laying out duct for a heating or cooling system, you might be interested in the minimal spanning tree. You might be interested in the shortest path from your house to your friend's house.

CONSTRUCTING A MATH TOOLKIT: Students should record in their Math Toolkits how a shortest path may differ from a minimal spanning tree.

JOURNAL ENTRY: You might go back to the original question on page 343 about a minimal distance paved-road network, adding the condition that *C* and *G* are the most populous cities and planners agreed to connect them with a shortest path. Ask students to recommend a paved-road network that meets the two conditions. This activity encourages students to make sense out of a new situation rather than simply apply previously-introduced algorithms.

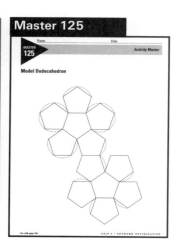

Master 125

Model Dodecahedron

MORE
ASSIGNMENT   *pp. 352–362*

Students now can begin
Modeling Task 3 from the
MORE Assignment following
Investigation 3.

APPLY   individual task

▶On Your Own

a. This activity asks students to find a minimal spanning tree. The only such tree is shown below. The length of this tree is 44.

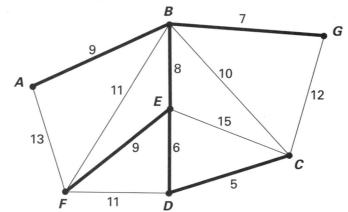

b. The shortest distance from *A* to *F* on the plowed road network above is 26 miles.

c. The shortest distance from *A* to *F* when roads are clear is 13 miles, since you can travel there directly. The point here is that shortest paths and distances depend on the network being used—in this case, the plowed-road network or the original, entire network.

EXPLORE   small-group investigation

INVESTIGATION 2   Graph Games

See Teaching Master 125.

In this investigation, students explore the final graph model for this unit, a Hamiltonian circuit (visit every vertex exactly once and return to start). Since a Hamiltonian circuit is different from an Euler circuit (which traverses every *edge* exactly once), students will have to take care to specify what kind of circuit they are considering.

A game is used in Activity 1 to motivate the idea of a circuit that visits each vertex. Notice that not every edge need be traversed. To help students understand the game, a demonstration dodecahedron would be useful. If you do not have such a model, you can construct one from Teaching Master 125. If you copy these onto cover stock, students can cut them out and tape them together. Push pins make adequate markers for the vertices, and students can try the game by winding thread from vertex to vertex. Students will have to visualize this arrangement of edges and vertices in two dimensions, which is a challenge for many. Once students have drawn the two-dimensional graph and have found a Hamiltonian circuit, you might ask them if they recall the rule for when an Euler circuit was possible (when each vertex has even degree). Then you can ask them if they think there might be a similar rule for identifying which graphs have a Hamiltonian circuit. (Later they will find out that there is not.)

See additional Teaching Notes on page T366F.

▶ **On Your Own**

Consider the road network below, where distances are shown in miles.

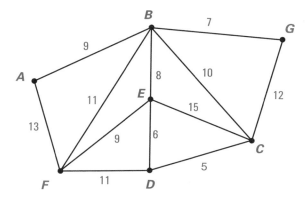

a. Suppose some of the roads need to be plowed after a snowstorm. Find the shortest possible network of plowed roads that will allow cars to drive from every town to every other town on plowed roads.

b. What is the shortest distance from A to F on the plowed-road network?

c. When there's no snow, all the roads can be used. Find the shortest distance from A to F when the roads are clear.

INVESTIGATION 2 ▶ Graph Games

Graphs are not only helpful in solving practical problems, they are also great for games. Described below are two classic games based on the same graph model.

1. Sir William Rowan Hamilton, a famous Irish mathematician, invented a game in 1857 based on a dodecahedron. Recall that a dodecahedron has 20 vertices and 12 faces, which are regular pentagons. The *Traveler's Dodecahedron* was a game consisting of a wooden dodecahedron with a peg at each vertex, and some string. The vertices were labeled with the names of cities from around the world, like Canton, New Delhi, and Zanzibar. The object of the game was to start at one city, visit the other 19 cities *only once*, and end back where you started. The string was wound around the pegs to keep track of the journey.

Since the dodecahedron was difficult to carry around, Hamilton made another version of the game, called the *Icosian Game*. The Icosian Game was made by "flattening" the dodecahedron into a vertex-edge graph with 20 vertices and 11 pentagonal regions.

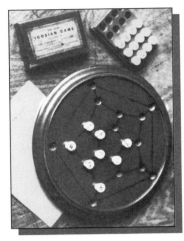

a. Draw a vertex-edge graph representing the Icosian Game.

b. Instead of using string, use your pencil to trace a path that will win the game.

c. Does it matter where you start? Explain why or why not.

A path like the one you traced to win the Icosian Game is called a Hamiltonian circuit. A **Hamiltonian circuit** is a circuit through a graph that starts at one vertex, visits all the other vertices *exactly once,* and finishes where it started. (By the way, Hamilton's games were interesting mathematically, but they were commercial disasters.)

2. A well-known game among chess players is called the *Knight's Tour Problem*. In one version of this game, you start with a knight on any square of a chessboard and try to visit each of the other squares exactly once by successively moving the knight. You must finish the knight's tour where you began.

A knight moves in an L-shaped pattern. For example, four sample moves of a knight are illustrated below. Any such L-shaped move is a legitimate move.

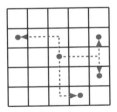

a. Explain how to model and solve this game using a graph and a Hamiltonian circuit. Don't solve the game yet, just explain how you could solve it using a Hamiltonian circuit.

1. **a.** Students should be able to draw the vertex-edge graph from the picture in the student text. Their graphs should be isomorphic to the one below. (That is, their visual placement of vertices and edges may be different, but all vertices should connect in exactly the same way.)

This is a good exercise in geometric visualization. Students may struggle a bit, but by using the picture and a model of a dodecahedron they should be able to do it. In particular, this is an opportunity for the more visual students to help their classmates.

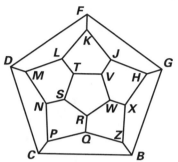

A diagram like this is sometimes called a Schlegel diagram.

b. Paths may vary. A suggested path is indicated by the numbers in the graph below; start at 1 and move through numerical order to 20, then back to 1.

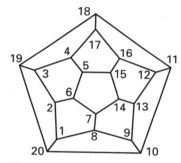

c. Since there is a circuit that includes all vertices, it doesn't matter where you start.

A technicality here is that Hamiltonian circuits cannot have repeated edges. This is automatically covered by the condition that no vertices are repeated, except in the case of two vertices and one edge (shown below).

A •——————————• B

In this case we do not want to call A-B-A a Hamiltonian circuit. This is covered by the definition of circuit on page 322, where it is stated that edges cannot be repeated. All these subtle points should not be discussed unless questions arise. Keep students focused on the basic ideas that Euler circuits refer to edges (use each edge exactly once) and Hamiltonian circuits refer to vertices (use each vertex exactly once).

2. **a.** Build a graph model by letting the vertices be the squares on the chessboard and connecting two vertices with an edge if it is possible to move between the corresponding squares with one move of a knight. Then a Hamiltonian circuit would correspond to a knight's tour, because each vertex (square) is visited (landed on by the touring knight) exactly once, and you begin and end at the same place.

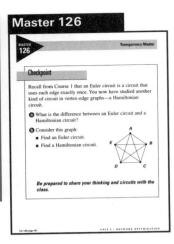

EXPLORE *continued*

2. b. If students get sidetracked about why the modified chessboard is shaped the way it is, you might tell them it is simply an interesting shape and refocus them on the questions.

The graph model for this "chessboard" is a graph with 8 vertices, representing the 8 squares on which you can land. See the graph at the right. This graph has a Hamiltonian circuit. (In fact, in this case the Hamiltonian circuit is also an Euler circuit.) Thus, one knight's tour would be *A-E-F-B-H-D-C-G-A.* You could start the knight's tour at any vertex.

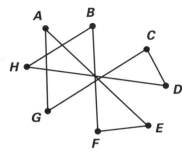

c. A graph model for this activity is at the right. It can be constructed by adding vertices *I, J,* and *K* and the necessary edges to the chessboard's graph in Part b. There is no Hamiltonian circuit and thus no knight's tour. In particular, vertices *I* and *K* prevent a Hamiltonian circuit because they each have degree 1. Thus, once you go to *I* or *K* you have nowhere to go next except back to the vertex you just visited. Visiting a vertex twice is not allowed in a Hamiltonian circuit.

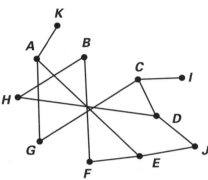

3. Recall that there is a necessary and sufficient condition for Euler circuits. That is, a connected graph has an Euler circuit if and only if it has no odd vertices. There are no known necessary and sufficient criteria for Hamiltonian circuits, although there are necessary conditions and (different) sufficient conditions.

An example of a necessary condition that students identify based on Activity 2, part c, is the following: If a graph has a Hamiltonian circuit, then there cannot be any vertices of degree 1. Thus, a property of a graph that guarantees it will not have a Hamiltonian circuit is the property of having a vertex of degree 1. (An example of a sufficient condition is the following: If *G* is a graph with *n* vertices, where $n > 2$, and if each vertex has degree at least $\frac{n}{2}$, then *G* has a Hamiltonian circuit.)

SHARE AND SUMMARIZE full-class discussion

Checkpoint

See Teaching Master 126.

ⓐ An Euler circuit uses each *edge* exactly once; a Hamiltonian circuit uses each *vertex* exactly once. A Hamiltonian circuit may miss some edges, and thus, is not an Euler circuit. An Euler circuit may revisit some vertices, and thus, is not a Hamiltonian circuit.

ⓑ ■ A possibility for an Euler circuit is found by first tracing the "pentagon" on the outside of the graph, then tracing the "star" inside the pentagon. (*A-B-C-D-E-A-C-E-B-D-A*) Each edge is used exactly once, and the circuit ends where it began.

■ One possibility for a Hamiltonian circuit is found by tracing the outside pentagon. (*A-B-C-D-E-A*) The circuit ends where it began and uses each vertex exactly once. Another possibility is to trace only the star.

b. Consider the modified chessboard below. The square with a cross in it is part of the chessboard; you can cross it, but you cannot land on it.

A	B	C
D	✕	E
F	G	H

Construct a graph model for the knight's tour problem on this modified chessboard. (Put lots of space between vertices so that the graph will be easy to read.) Solve the problem by finding a Hamiltonian circuit if possible. Explain your solution.

c. Use a Hamiltonian circuit to find a knight's tour on the "chessboard" below, if possible.

I	J	K
A	B	C
D	✕	E
F	G	H

3. Some graphs have Hamiltonian circuits and some do not. Unlike the case of Euler circuits, no one has yet found a simple test for determining whether or not a graph has a Hamiltonian circuit. Can you think of a property of a graph that will guarantee that it does *not* have a Hamiltonian circuit? Make a conjecture and defend it.

Checkpoint

Recall from Course 1 that an Euler circuit is a circuit that uses each edge exactly once. You now have studied another kind of circuit in vertex-edge graphs—a Hamiltonian circuit.

ⓐ What is the difference between an Euler circuit and a Hamiltonian circuit?

ⓑ Consider this graph:

- Find an Euler circuit.
- Find a Hamiltonian circuit.

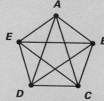

Be prepared to share your thinking and circuits with the entire class.

▶ On Your Own

The Checkpoint on page 347 gives an example of a graph that has both an Euler circuit and a Hamiltonian circuit. Draw the following graphs (if possible).

a. The graph does not have an Euler circuit or a Hamiltonian circuit.

b. The graph does not have an Euler circuit but does have a Hamiltonian circuit.

c. The graph has an Euler circuit but does not have a Hamiltonian circuit.

INVESTIGATION 3 The Traveling Salesperson Problem

The *Traveling Salesperson Problem* is one of the most famous problems in mathematics. It can be thought of as another game, but, as you will see, it also has many important applications. Here's the problem:

> *A sales representative wants to visit several different cities, each exactly once, and then return home. Among the possible routes, which one will minimize the total distance traveled?*

1. Consider the Traveling Salesperson Problem in the context of this airfare graph.

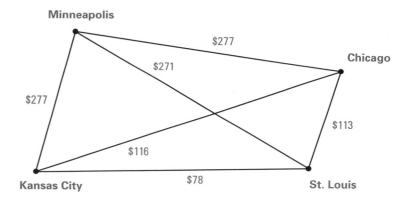

a. Without help from others in your group or class, solve the Traveling Salesperson Problem for this weighted graph. That is, find a circuit that visits each of the cities exactly once and has the minimum total weight. What does "weight" represent in this case?

b. Compare your solution to those of other members of your group. Resolve any differences.

APPLY individual task

▶On Your Own

Graphs may vary. Examples are given.

a.   b.   c.

MORE
ASSIGNMENT *pp. 352–362*

Students now can begin
Modeling Task 2 or 5, and
Organizing Task 1 from the
MORE assignment following
Investigation 3.

EXPLORE small-group investigation

INVESTIGATION ▶ 3 The Traveling Salesperson Problem

There are three key aspects to this investigation. The Traveling Salesperson Problem is a famous unsolved problem in mathematics. It is unsolved in the sense that no one knows an efficient algorithm that will find a solution to the Traveling Salesperson Problem for any graph. Students find it interesting that they can understand and work on a problem that mathematicians are still trying to solve completely. Many students enjoy the feeling of being on a frontier. Also, it may give students a new view of mathematics as a growing field, rather than a dry and dusty collection of facts that have been known for centuries.

The notion of "efficiency" is important in this investigation. Students will see that there is a so-called brute-force solution to the Traveling Salesperson Problem, but it is so inefficient that even the world's fastest computer would take years to solve even a small version by checking all possibilities. This should give students an important perspective on the limitations of computers.

Once again students will see the power of graph models as they investigate applications of the Traveling Salesperson Problem.

1. **a.** There are only three possible circuits. (See Part e.) The one with minimum total weight is M-C-K-S-M. In this case "weight" represents cost. This route would cost $742.

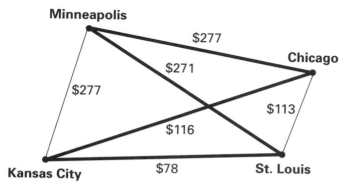

b. See student work.

1. c. There is no known efficient algorithm for solving the Traveling Salesperson Problem, so for students to be sure they have the minimum, they would need to have checked all possible circuits. However, there are a variety of reasonable methods (algorithms) that students should be encouraged to describe. In Activities 3 and 4, and in Extending Task 4 (page 360), they explore possible algorithms.

d. Since all possible circuits have been examined, there cannot exist a shorter one.

e. If we needed to specify a starting point or direction of travel, then there are a lot of "different" circuits. Since our only concern is total cost, then there are just three different circuits as shown below.

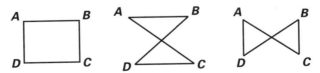

f. Many students may be unfamiliar with the word *contiguous*. You may need to clarify for them. Responses will vary. Students should discuss whether their method will work in a 48-vertex graph and if it will be efficient. This discussion sets the stage for subsequent activities. It is extremely unlikely that the method described in Part c will be generalizable to a graph with 48 vertices in a way that will guarantee the optimal circuit. (See the paragraphs after the Checkpoint on page 351.)

At this point you may wish to bring to students' attention that the unit and lesson objectives emphasize *representing, finding,* and *analyzing*—not *memorizing*—the vocabulary or algorithms.

2. a. A solution to the Traveling Salesperson Problem is a minimum weight Hamiltonian circuit, that is, a shortest Hamiltonian circuit.

b. A solution to the Traveling Salesperson Problem is like a minimal spanning tree because it spans all the vertices and has minimum weight. It is different because it is a circuit rather than a tree.

c. A solution to the Traveling Salesperson Problem is a type of shortest circuit—it is a shortest circuit that includes each vertex once, i.e., a shortest spanning circuit.

3. a. ■ If you create a partial circuit that does not include all vertices, then the final circuit that does include all the vertices would have to visit some vertex more than once.

■ Any vertex that is touched by three edges must be visited more than once.

b. Applying this algorithm to the airfare graph in Activity 1 yields the circuit shown below, which is not the shortest circuit. So this algorithm does not produce a solution to the Traveling Salesperson Problem.

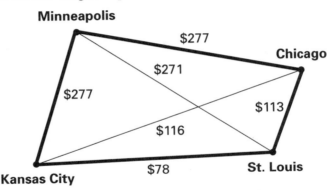

c. As a group, write a description of a method for finding the optimal circuit.

d. How do you know that there is no circuit less expensive?

e. How many different Hamiltonian circuits are there in this graph? For the purpose of finding the total cost of circuits, two circuits are different only if they have different edges. It doesn't matter where you start or which direction you go around the circuit.

f. Could you generalize your method in Part c to find the optimal circuit for the capitals of all 48 contiguous states? Explain your reasoning.

2. Compare solving the Traveling Salesperson Problem to some of the other problems you have solved in this unit.

a. What is the relationship between a Hamiltonian circuit and a solution to the Traveling Salesperson Problem?

b. Describe how a solution to the Traveling Salesperson Problem is similar to, and yet different from, a minimal spanning tree.

c. This investigation is part of a lesson entitled "Shortest Paths and Circuits." Explain how a solution to the Traveling Salesperson Problem is a shortest path or circuit.

3. In Lesson 1, you used Kruskal's best-edge algorithm to find a minimal spanning tree. One group of students devised the following best-edge algorithm for the Traveling Salesperson Problem. They claim it will solve the Traveling Salesperson Problem.

i. Make a copy of the graph with the edges drawn lightly.

ii. Darken the shortest edge not yet used, provided that:

- you do not create a circuit of darkened edges, unless all the vertices are included;

- no vertex is touched by three darkened edges.

(The edge you darken does not have to be connected to previously darkened edges.)

iii. Repeat Step ii as long as it is possible to do so.

a. Analyze this algorithm.

- Why do you think this algorithm requires that you do not create a circuit of darkened edges, unless all the vertices are included?

- Why do you think this algorithm requires that no vertex is touched by three darkened edges?

b. Apply the algorithm to the airfare graph in Activity 1, page 348. Does this algorithm produce a solution to the Traveling Salesperson Problem?

4. One method that certainly will work to solve the Traveling Salesperson Problem is to list all possible circuits, compute the length of each one, and choose the shortest. This approach of checking all possibilities is sometimes called a **brute force method**. With computers available to do all the calculations, you might think this is the way to proceed.

   However, think about how long it will take a computer to use the brute force method to solve the Traveling Salesperson Problem for the 26 cities shown in the following map. Assume each city is connected directly to all the others, and the tour starts at Atlanta.

   a. Starting from Atlanta, how many cities could be the first stop?

   b. Once you choose a city for this first stop, how many cities could be the second stop in the circuit? Remember that every city is connected directly to every other city, and each city is visited exactly once.

   c. How many different first-stop/second-stop combinations are there? Justify your answer.

   d. How many cities could be the third stop of the circuit? How many different combinations of first-stop/second-stop/third-stop are there?

   e. How many different circuits are possible using all the cities?

   f. Suppose a computer program can compute the length of one billion circuits per second. How many seconds will it take to compute the length of all the circuits? How many years?

   g. Under what conditions do you think the brute force method is a practical way to solve the Traveling Salesperson Problem?

4. a. Starting from Atlanta, 25 cities could be the first stop.

   b. Once you choose a city for this first stop, 24 cities could be the second stop in the circuit.

   c. There are 25×24 or 600 different first-stop/second-stop combinations.

   d. Any of 23 cities could be the third stop of the circuit. There are $25 \times 24 \times 23$ or 13,800 different first-stop/second-stop/third-stop combinations.

   e. It seems that $25 \times 24 \times 23 \times 22 \times 21 \times 20 \times \ldots \times 1$ or approximately 1.55×10^{25} different circuits are possible using all the cities. For the purposes of this problem, such an answer is appropriate. However, often traveling through a circuit in the reverse order is considered the same circuit, so the true answer is actually half that.

   f. Since traversing a circuit in either direction will give the same length, the computer only needs to find the lengths of half of the 25! circuits.

   It will take $\left(\frac{25!}{2}\right)\left(\frac{1}{1,000,000,000}\right)$ or approximately 7.7556×10^{15} seconds. Divide that by the number of seconds in a year (31,536,000) to get about 245,928,622 years.

   g. The brute-force method is a practical way to solve the Traveling Salesperson Problem only when there are very few vertices in the graph.

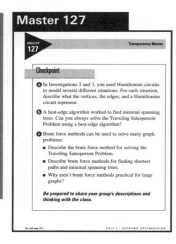

Checkpoint

See Teaching Master 127.

a For the Icosian game, the vertices are the cities or pegs, the edges are the edges of the dodecahedron, and a Hamiltonian circuit represents winning the game. For the knight's tour, the vertices are the squares of a chessboard, two vertices are connected by an edge if you can get from one square to the other by one move of a knight, and a Hamiltonian circuit corresponds to winning the game. In the airfare graph, the vertices are the cities, the edges correspond to direct air routes between cities, and a shortest Hamiltonian circuit corresponds to solving the Traveling Salesperson Problem for the graph.

b The best-edge algorithm worked for finding a minimal spanning tree, but it does not work for solving the Traveling Salesperson Problem. The point here is that the same type of algorithm can work in one setting, but not another.

c ■ The brute-force method for solving the Traveling Salesperson Problem would require that you find the total weight of all Hamiltonian circuits in the graph and then choose the one with the smallest total weight.

■ Brute-force methods for finding shortest paths and minimal spanning trees would require that you find all the lengths of paths between two points or the total weights of all spanning trees and then choose the one with the smallest weight.

■ Brute-force methods are not practical for large graphs because there are so many possibilities to check that even the fastest computer could take many years to check them all.

Following are two interesting articles about the Traveling Salesperson Problem.

Kolata, Gina. "Math Problem, Long Baffling, Slowly Yields." *The New York Times*, 12 March 1991.

Zimmer, Carl. "And One for the Road." *Discover*, January 1993, pp. 91–92.

Checkpoint

a In Investigations 2 and 3, you used Hamiltonian circuits to model several different situations. For each situation, describe what the vertices, the edges, and a Hamiltonian circuit represent.

b A best-edge algorithm worked to find minimal spanning trees. Can you always solve the Traveling Salesperson Problem using a best-edge algorithm?

c Brute force methods can be used to solve many graph problems.

■ Describe the brute force method for solving the Traveling Salesperson Problem.

■ Describe brute force methods for finding shortest paths and minimal spanning trees.

■ Why aren't brute force methods practical for large graphs?

Be prepared to share your group's descriptions and thinking with the class.

In this lesson, you have explored two famous problems in mathematics: the general Traveling Salesperson Problem and characterizing graphs that have a Hamiltonian circuit. Both of these problems are currently unsolved! New applications and new mathematics have been developed as researchers continue to work on these problems.

For the Traveling Salesperson Problem, the goal is to find an efficient solution that will work in all situations. You have seen one method, the best-edge algorithm, that is efficient but does not guarantee a solution. You have seen another method, the brute force method, that guarantees a solution but is not efficient. No one knows a method that is both efficient and works in all situations.

Since solving the Traveling Salesperson Problem has applications for so many different kinds of networks, like telephone and transportation networks, mathematicians are always looking for better algorithms that will solve the problem for larger graphs. In 1986, the Traveling Salesperson Problem was solved efficiently for a graph with 532 vertices, and by 1994 the record was 7,397 vertices. More recently, mathematicians have found methods that are guaranteed to find a circuit that is less than one percent longer than the shortest possible circuit, even for graphs with several hundred thousand vertices.

On Your Own

The matrix below shows the mileage between four cities.

$$
\begin{array}{c c c c c}
 & A & B & C & D \\
A & - & 20 & 25 & 40 \\
B & 20 & - & 35 & 45 \\
C & 25 & 35 & - & 30 \\
D & 40 & 45 & 30 & - \\
\end{array}
$$

a. Represent the information in the matrix with a weighted graph.

b. Trace all the different Hamiltonian circuits starting at *A*. List the vertices in each circuit.

c. Record the total length of each circuit.

d. Would you get different answers in Part c if the starting vertex was *B?*

e. Is there a difference between circuit *A-B-C-D-A* and circuit *A-D-C-B-A?* Explain your reasoning.

f. What is the solution to the Traveling Salesperson Problem for this graph?

MORE
Modeling • Organizing • Reflecting • Extending

Modeling

1. Integrated circuit boards are used in a variety of electronic devices, including modern kitchen appliances, video games, automobile ignition systems, and the guidance systems in commercial airliners. To manufacture a circuit board, a laser must drill as many as several million holes on a single board. This usually is done with a laser in a fixed position; the circuit board is turned to the positions that must be drilled. For maximum efficiency, the board must end up in its original position, no hole should pass under the laser more than once, and the total distance that the board is moved should be as small as possible.

On Your Own

a. See the graph at the right.

b–c. *A-B-C-D-A*, length 125
A-B-D-C-A, length 120
A-D-B-C-A, length 145

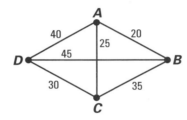

If students choose to include the reverse order circuits, there will be six circuits. Students may indicate that reverse order circuits are the same or that they are different. They certainly are different in that the cities are visited in a different order, but they are the same in that they use the same undirected path through the graph. If you were finding and computing all circuits (*i.e.*, using a brute-force method), you would not bother computing the reverse order circuit once you have the original. So, in terms of enumerating and checking all possible circuits, there are only three. In fact, when counting all possible circuits that need to be checked using brute force in the general case of a complete graph with n vertices, there are really only $\frac{(n-1)!}{2}$ circuits to check. In this case students should see that there are only $\frac{(4-1)!}{2}$, or three "patterns," that is, if the cities are put in a rectangular pattern, then the three "different" patterns look like:

 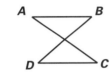

d. No. You will get the same answer for the total length of a circuit no matter where you start the circuit.

e. Responses may vary. There is no difference between these two circuits other than they are listed in reverse order.

f. The solution is *A-B-D-C-A* with length of 120 miles. (You may start at any vertex.)

Unit 5

MORE independent assignment

Modeling

1. **a.**

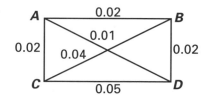

   b. In the drilling problem, we have to visit each position once and return to the original position. In effect, the drill moves over the positions as if it were a traveling salesperson.

   c. The minimal Hamiltonian circuit is *A-D-B-C-A*, with length 0.09. One can start at any point and go around in either direction.

2. **a.** The three properties can be verified by inspection.

   b. 000, 001, 010, 011, 100, 101, 110, 111

   c.

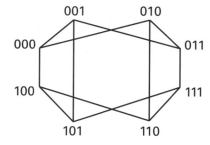

To see how this problem is solved using graphs, consider a simple situation in which there are just four holes to be drilled. The distance, in millimeters, that the board must be moved from one hole to another is given in the matrix below.

$$\begin{array}{c c c c c}
 & A & B & C & D \\
A & \begin{bmatrix} - \\ 0.02 \\ 0.02 \\ 0.01 \end{bmatrix} & \begin{matrix} 0.02 \\ - \\ 0.04 \\ 0.02 \end{matrix} & \begin{matrix} 0.02 \\ 0.04 \\ - \\ 0.05 \end{matrix} & \begin{matrix} 0.01 \\ 0.02 \\ 0.05 \\ - \end{matrix} \end{array}$$

a. Represent the information in the matrix with a weighted graph.

b. Explain why solving the circuit board problem is the same as solving the Traveling Salesperson Problem for this graph.

c. Find the order for drilling the holes that will minimize the total distance that the board has to be moved.

2. Information is transmitted between computers by converting the information into strings of 1s and 0s and then sending these strings as electronic signals from one computer to another. The method used to translate the information into 1s and 0s is called a *code*. The computers that send and receive the information know how to create and interpret the code.

One commonly used code is called a *Gray Code*. A Gray Code is a list of 0-1 strings with the following properties:

- Every string of a given length is in the list.
- Each string in the list differs from the preceding one in exactly one position.
- The first and last strings in the list differ in exactly one position.

a. Here is a Gray Code using strings of length two:

10   00   01   11

Verify that the three properties of a Gray Code are satisfied.

When the strings are short and there are so few of them, it is possible to find a Gray Code by trial and error. Using Hamiltonian circuits is one way to find Gray Codes with longer strings. Consider strings of length three.

b. A string of length three has a 1 or a 0 in each of the three positions. For example, 100 and 011 are 0-1 strings of length three. List all eight 0-1 strings of length three.

c. Build a graph model by letting the vertices be the eight 0-1 strings and connecting two vertices with an edge if the two strings differ in exactly one position.

Cray Supercomputer

d. Find a Hamiltonian circuit in the graph and then list all the vertices in the circuit in order.

e. Is the list you made in Part d a Gray Code? Why or why not?

f. Find another Gray Code using strings of length three.

3. A company is expanding into a new region of the country. It will set up offices in five cities in the region. The airfare (in dollars) for direct flights between each pair of cities is shown in the matrix below.

$$
\begin{array}{c c c c c c}
 & A & B & C & D & E \\
A & - & 500 & 400 & 250 & 100 \\
B & 500 & - & 200 & 900 & 250 \\
C & 400 & 200 & - & 100 & 250 \\
D & 250 & 900 & 100 & - & 550 \\
E & 100 & 250 & 250 & 550 & -
\end{array}
$$

One of the five cities will be the regional headquarters, at which regular meetings will be held. The president of the company asks you to use the information in the matrix to recommend one city to be the regional headquarters. Make a recommendation and defend your choice.

4. Three different features appear in a local newspaper every day. The features are scheduled to be printed in three jobs, all on the same printing press. After each job, the press must be cleaned and reset for the next job. After the last job, the press is reset for the first job to be run the next morning. The time, in minutes, needed to set up the press between each pair of jobs is shown in the matrix below.

$$
\begin{array}{c c c c}
 & A & B & C \\
A & - & 25 & 15 \\
B & 30 & - & 25 \\
C & 20 & 20 & -
\end{array}
$$

The newspaper production manager wants to schedule the jobs so that the total set-up time is minimal.

a. Model this situation with a *weighted digraph.*

b. Show how a solution to the Traveling Salesperson Problem will tell you how to schedule the jobs so that the total set-up time is minimal.

c. In what order should the jobs be scheduled and what is the minimum total set-up time?

2. d. One possibility is 000, 001, 011, 111, 101, 100, 110, 010.

 e. Yes, the list is a Gray Code: all eight possible strings are included; each string in the sequence differs from its predecessor in one place only; and the last string differs from the first in one place only.

 f. Another possibility is 100, 000, 010, 110, 111, 011, 001, 101.

3. Student responses may vary. Any proposed solution that is well justified should be considered acceptable. However, the most natural analysis using ideas from this unit involves shortest paths and the distance matrix. Note that the entries of the distance matrix give the length of the shortest path (*i.e.*, the cheapest airfare) between cities while the matrix in the student text gives information for *direct* flights. The row sum (or column sum) for a given city in the distance matrix is the total of the cheapest airfares for flying from every city to the given city. Thus, the city with the smallest row sum would yield the cheapest total airfare for people coming in for a meeting. Such a city is a good candidate for the regional headquarters. Using this reasoning, *C* would be the choice for the regional headquarters. See the distance matrix below, which students could generate using the SHORT-CUT software.

	A	B	C	D	E	Row Sum
A	–	350	350	250	100	1050
B	350	–	200	300	250	1100
C	350	200	–	100	250	900
D	250	300	100	–	350	1000
E	100	250	250	350	–	950

4. a. In the digraph below, the numbers represent the time required to set up the press between jobs. For example, after Job *A*, 25 minutes are needed to set up for Job *B*.

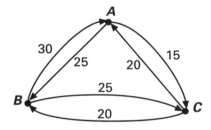

 b. A solution to the Traveling Salesperson Problem will give us a sequence of jobs in which each job is done exactly once and the sum of the set-up times between jobs is minimized.

 c. There are only two circuits which visit every vertex exactly once, the outer one and the inner one. The outer one is shorter with length 65 minutes. The optimum schedule for the jobs has them in the order *A-C-B-A*. It does not matter which job is first. The minimum total set-up time is 65 minutes.

5. a. There are several Hamiltonian circuits. One is shown below.

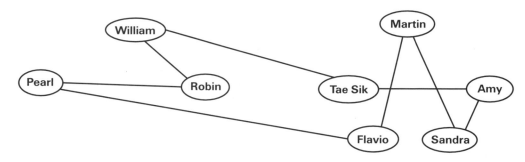

b. Simply wrap the Hamiltonian circuit around the table and then adjacent people will know each other. The seating chart that corresponds to the Hamiltonian circuit from Part a is shown here.

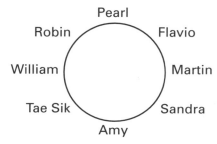

Organizing

1. a.

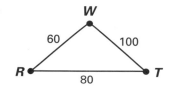

b.

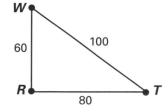

c. Responses may vary. For example, what kind of angle is formed by the line segments representing the road from *R* to *W* and the road from *R* to *T*?

d. Responses may vary. For example, which two cities are closest to one another?

5. Pearl has invited seven of her friends, who do not all know each other, for dinner. All eight people will be seated at a round table and Pearl wants to seat them so that each guest will know the persons sitting on each side of him or her. In the graph below, two people who know each other are connected by an edge.

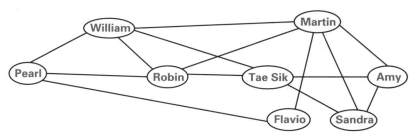

a. Show how you can use a Hamiltonian circuit to decide how to seat the people according to Pearl's requirement.

b. Sketch a diagram of the round table and show how the people should be seated.

Organizing

1. A key characteristic of vertex-edge graphs is that the position of the vertices and the actual geometric length of the edges does not matter. All that matters is the way in which the edges connect the vertices. So, for example, when drawing a graph that represents a distance matrix, the graph does not have to be drawn to scale. In geometry, on the other hand, position and length are important factors. To appreciate this important difference between geometry and graph theory, consider the following shortest distance matrix. Each entry shows the shortest distance, in miles, between the two corresponding towns.

$$
\begin{array}{c}
\\
\text{Woebegone (W)} \\
\text{Rivendell (R)} \\
\text{Troy (T)}
\end{array}
\begin{array}{ccc}
W & R & T \\
\left[\begin{array}{ccc}
- & 60 & 100 \\
60 & - & 80 \\
100 & 80 & -
\end{array}\right]
\end{array}
$$

a. Draw a vertex-edge graph that represents the information in the matrix.

b. Use a compass and ruler to draw a scale diagram showing the distances between the three towns. Assume straight-line roads between the towns.

c. State a question involving these three towns that is best answered using a geometric model.

d. State a question that could be answered using either model.

Modeling • Organizing • Reflecting • Extending

2. A **Hamiltonian path** is a path that visits each vertex of a graph exactly once. Thus, a Hamiltonian circuit is a special type of Hamiltonion path: one which starts and ends at the same vertex. Hamiltonian paths can be used to analyze tournament rankings.

   Consider a round-robin tennis tournament involving four players. The matrix below shows the results of the tournament. Recall that the matrix is read from row to column, with a "1" indicating a win. For example, the "1" in the Flavio-Simon entry means that Flavio beat Simon.

   ### Tournament Results

	J	S	F	B
Josh (J)	0	0	0	1
Simon (S)	1	0	0	1
Flavio (F)	1	1	0	1
Bill (B)	0	0	0	0

   a. Draw a digraph representing the information in the matrix.

   b. Find all the Hamiltonian paths in the graph.

   c. Use the Hamiltonian path to rank the players in the tournament. Explain the connection between your ranking and the Hamiltonian path.

   d. In the "Matrix Models" unit of Part A of this course, you used row sums and powers of matrices to rank tournaments. Rank the tournament as you did in that unit and compare your ranking to that in Part c above.

3. Recall from the "Matrix Models" unit how you used powers of an adjacency matrix for a graph to get information about the number of paths of certain lengths in the graph. You also can use powers of an adjacency matrix to find the shortest path length between vertices. Consider the digraph at the right.

   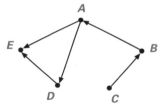

   a. Construct an adjacency matrix M for this digraph. List the vertices in alphabetical order. Find M^2, M^3, and M^4.

   b. Consider paths from C to E.

   ■ What is the shortest path length from C to E? (Since there are no weights on the edges, the length of a path is the number of edges in the path.)

   ■ Examine the C-E entry in M, M^2, M^3, and M^4. What is the relationship between these entries and the shortest path length from C to E?

   c. Explain how you can determine the lengths of shortest paths between vertices in the digraph by examining the powers of the adjacency matrix.

2. a.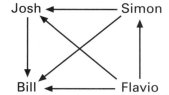

b. The only Hamiltonian path is *F-S-J-B*.

c. The Hamiltonian path provides a sequence of players in which each player beats the next. Thus, the Hamiltonian path *F-S-J-B* also serves as a ranking.

d. The ranking *F-S-J-B* determined by the Hamiltonian path corresponds to the ranking determined by the row sums of the tournament matrix.

3. a. The adjacency matrix is:

$$
\begin{array}{c c}
 & \begin{array}{ccccc} A & B & C & D & E \end{array} \\
\begin{array}{c} A \\ B \\ C \\ D \\ E \end{array} &
\left[\begin{array}{ccccc}
0 & 0 & 0 & 1 & 1 \\
1 & 0 & 0 & 0 & 0 \\
0 & 1 & 0 & 0 & 0 \\
0 & 0 & 0 & 0 & 1 \\
0 & 0 & 0 & 0 & 0
\end{array}\right]
\end{array}
$$

The values of M^2, M^3, and M^4 are as follows:

$$
M^2 = \begin{bmatrix}
0 & 0 & 0 & 0 & 1 \\
0 & 0 & 0 & 1 & 1 \\
1 & 0 & 0 & 0 & 0 \\
0 & 0 & 0 & 0 & 0 \\
0 & 0 & 0 & 0 & 0
\end{bmatrix}
\quad
M^3 = \begin{bmatrix}
0 & 0 & 0 & 0 & 0 \\
0 & 0 & 0 & 0 & 1 \\
0 & 0 & 0 & 1 & 1 \\
0 & 0 & 0 & 0 & 0 \\
0 & 0 & 0 & 0 & 0
\end{bmatrix}
\quad
M^4 = \begin{bmatrix}
0 & 0 & 0 & 0 & 0 \\
0 & 0 & 0 & 0 & 0 \\
0 & 0 & 0 & 0 & 1 \\
0 & 0 & 0 & 0 & 0 \\
0 & 0 & 0 & 0 & 0
\end{bmatrix}
$$

b. ■ The shortest path length from *C* to *E* is 3.

■ The *C-E* entries of *M* and M^2 are zero, but the *C-E* entries of M^3 and M^4 are 1. The shortest path from *C* to *E* is 3, which is the power of the matrix that first shows a 1 in the *C-E* entry.

c. The length of the shortest path from a vertex *X* to a vertex *Y* will be the smallest exponent *n* such that the *X-Y* entry in M^n is nonzero.

Unit 5

4. **a.** A tree cannot have a Hamiltonian path unless it is a chain; *i.e.*, it has a trunk but no branches. Another way to say this is that a tree does not have a Hamiltonian path if it has any vertices of degree greater than two.

   b. All complete graphs have Hamiltonian circuits; for example, just go around the "outside." See the complete graph on five vertices below.

   c. ■ The graph on the right has a Hamiltonian circuit.
   ■ If there are the same number of vertices in each set, and this number is greater than one, then there is a Hamiltonian circuit. This is because in a bipartite graph you can only go back and forth between the two sets; there are no edges between vertices in the same set. So, when trying to find a Hamiltonian circuit, you start in one set, go over to the other, back to the first, and so on. This over-and-back movement implies that if you have the same number of vertices in each set, then you will be able to go over and back through all the vertices and end up where you started. Thus, there is a Hamiltonian circuit.

Reflecting

1. Responses may vary. Perhaps there are too few amateur mathematicians, or maybe the games were too easy.

2. Students may view mathematical knowledge as nothing new; it is all old knowledge, especially since they may not have studied much recent mathematics. They probably will be surprised at how fast mathematical knowledge is growing today. It is hoped that the current, and unsolved, problems they encountered in this unit will begin to change those students' views of mathematics from seeing it as old and dull to seeing it as modern and vital.

3. Students should reflect on the limitations of using computers to solve problems. For example, they have already seen that even seemingly simple problems, like the 25-vertex Traveling Salesperson Problem, can involve so many possibilities that even with the fastest computer, checking them all is unrealistic.

   When thinking about using computers and algorithms to solve problems, there are two fundamental questions that need to be answered:
   ■ Is there a solution algorithm?
   ■ If there is a solution algorithm, is it efficient; that is, can it be executed in a reasonable amount of time?

   Depending on the answers to these questions, problems may fall into one of four categories:
   ■ problems for which no solution algorithm exists, for example, a safe, general computer virus-checking program (algorithm) is impossible;

See additional Teaching Notes on page T366F.

4. In this task, you will investigate Hamiltonian paths and circuits in particular types of graphs.

a. A **Hamiltonian path** is a path that visits each vertex of a graph exactly once. Thus, a Hamiltonian path is like a Hamiltonian circuit, except the path is not required to start and end at the same vertex. Is it possible for a tree to have a Hamiltonian path? Why or why not?

b. A **complete graph** is a graph in which every pair of vertices is joined by exactly one edge. Does a complete graph have a Hamiltonian circuit? Illustrate your answer with a complete graph that has five vertices.

c. A **bipartite graph** is a graph whose vertices can be split into two sets, such that every edge of the graph joins a vertex from one set to a vertex of the other set. A **complete bipartite graph** is a bipartite graph in which every vertex of one set is joined to every vertex in the other set by exactly one edge. For example, here are two complete bipartite graphs:

■ Which of these two complete bipartite graphs has a Hamiltonian circuit?

■ Make a conjecture about the kinds of complete bipartite graphs that have Hamiltonian circuits. Defend your conjecture.

Reflecting

1. Why do you think Hamilton's *Traveler's Dodecahedron* and *Icosian* games were not commercially successful?

2. It is estimated that more new mathematics have been developed in the last 20 years than in all the past history of mathematics. In fact, most of the mathematics you have investigated in this unit were developed in the last few decades, or even more recently. For example, Kruskal's algorithm for minimal spanning trees was developed in the 1950s, and new results related to the Traveling Salesperson Problem are discovered almost every year. Based upon your experience in this unit and additional research, write a short essay on your view of mathematics as a modern, active field.

3. With the rapid development of more and more powerful computers, do you think that any problem eventually can be solved with a brute force method, by having a computer check all possibilities? Or do you think that there is some fundamental limitation to the ability of computers to solve problems? Explain your thinking.

4. The graph models you have studied in the *Contemporary Mathematics in Context* courses include Euler circuits, Hamiltonian circuits, shortest paths, critical paths, minimal spanning trees, vertex coloring, and the Traveling Salesperson Problem.

a. What kinds of problems do vertex-edge graph models help you to solve?

b. Which graph models were easiest to learn? To apply?

c. Of all the vertex-edge graph models you have studied, which is your favorite? Why?

5. The title of this lesson is "Shortest Paths and Circuits," while the title of the unit is "Network Optimization." *Optimize* means to find the best.

a. Give an example in which the shortest path is not the best path. (Your example does not have to be from this unit.)

b. A solution to the Traveling Salesperson Problem is a shortest circuit. The brute force method is a guaranteed way to find a shortest circuit. Despite all this, a group of students claims that finding a shortest circuit is not necessarily the best solution to the Traveling Salesperson Problem. Explain what they might mean.

c. Explain why the best solution method for a small graph may not be the best solution method for a large graph. Give an example.

Extending

1. In Modeling Task 2, page 353, you found Gray Codes by finding Hamiltonian circuits in a graph in which the vertices are 0-1 strings and the edges connect strings that differ in exactly one position.

a. Redraw the graph you constructed in Modeling Task 2 (for strings of length three) so that it looks like a cube.

b. It turns out that all Gray Codes can be represented using graphs that look like "cubes" in different dimensions. Draw a graph that can be used to find Gray Codes for strings of length two that looks like a two-dimensional "cube," that is, a square.

c. For strings of length four, the graph will look like a four-dimensional "cube." Try to draw such a "cube."

d. Label the vertices of the four-dimensional cube with all the 0-1 strings of length four so two vertices are connected by an edge if the two strings differ in exactly one position. Find a Gray Code by finding a Hamiltonian circuit through the graph.

4. **a.** Responses may vary. Many types of problems can be modeled by vertex-edge graphs: routes, scheduling, shortest paths or circuits, networks for telecommunications, clustering, *etc.*

   b. Responses will vary, according to student opinion.

   c. Responses will vary. These responses provide a good basis for a full-class discussion.

5. **a.** There are many "informal" examples that students might give. The best path for a walk home with your best friend might be the longest path possible. The best path for an informative but not boring tour through a museum is neither the longest or shortest path, but something between those. An example of a more technical example is the idea of a critical path, from Course 1. The "best" path in a project digraph is a critical path, which is a longest path through the digraph. For another example, see Part b below.

   b. In solving the Traveling Salesperson Problem for a large graph, the best path may not be the shortest path, because it might take years or centuries to find a shortest path. In this situation, which arises often in the world of work, the best solution is some reasonably short path that does not take too long to compute.

   c. In general, the brute-force method will solve a given problem, but it will be too inefficient to use for large graphs. For example, see Part b above. Another example relates to the "eye-ball" method, that is, just finding a solution by looking (with perhaps a few mental calculations) and seeing what you want. This method can be very effective for small graphs but clearly is not efficient for larger graphs. The need for algorithms emerges when you work with large graphs.

Extending

1. **a.** Answers may vary. The cube below comes from the answer given in Modeling Task 2, Part c.

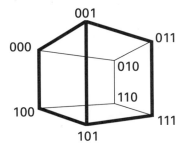

   b. Here, the graph is unique. Only reflections and rotations of the one shown are valid.

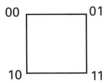

See additional Teaching Notes on page T366G.

2.

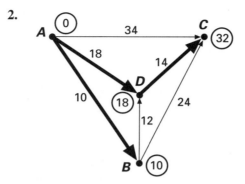

2. The SHORTCUT software finds shortest paths by using a method called *Dijkstra's algorithm*, named after E. W. Dijkstra, a Dutch mathematician who discovered the algorithm in 1959. Although you must work through the steps of the algorithm very carefully, the basic idea is simple. First, you choose a starting vertex, and you find the vertex closest to the start. Then, you find the next closest vertex to the start, and so on until you have accounted for every vertex. You darken edges and keep track of distances as you go. At the end, you have a shortest path from the start to every other vertex in the graph.

E.W. Dijkstra

Here are the steps of Dijkstra's algorithm:

i. Choose and circle a starting vertex. Since it is the start, write the number 0 next to it, indicating length 0, and circle the number.

ii. Examine *all* edges from the starting vertex. Choose the shortest one (break ties arbitrarily) and darken it. Circle the vertex reached by the shortest edge. Write the length of the edge next to the vertex and circle the number. This number is the length of the shortest path from the start to that vertex.

iii. Examine *all* edges that go from any circled vertex to an uncircled vertex. For each such edge, do the following computation and write the sum on the edge:

$$(length\ of\ edge) + \begin{pmatrix} circled\ number\ next\ to\ circled\ vertex \\ out\ of\ which\ the\ edge\ comes \end{pmatrix}$$

Darken the edge that yields the smallest sum, and circle the vertex at the end of that edge. Write the computed sum for the edge next to the vertex and circle the number. This number is the shortest distance from the start to that vertex. Erase all the other sums you computed.

iv. Repeat Step iii until there are no more edges from a circled vertex to an uncircled vertex. The circled numbers next to each vertex show the shortest path length from the start to that vertex. The darkened edges show a shortest path from the start to each vertex.

Follow the steps of Dijkstra's algorithm to find a shortest path and the shortest path length from vertex *A* to each of the other vertices in the digraph at the right.

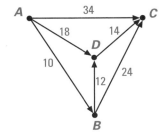

3. The SHORTCUT software uses Dijkstra's algorithm (see Extending Task 2) to find shortest paths. In this task, you will see why Dijkstra's algorithm is sometimes called a "tree-growing" algorithm. Consider the digraph below.

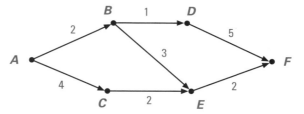

a. Implement Dijkstra's algorithm, either by hand or by using the SHORTCUT program, to find a shortest path and the shortest path length from *A* to each of the other vertices in the digraph.

b. Darken the edges of a shortest path from *A* to each of the other vertices in the graph.

c. Describe the graph consisting of the darkened edges.

■ Is it a tree?

■ Is it a spanning tree?

■ Is it a minimal spanning tree?

4. The nearest-neighbor algorithm you investigated in Activity 9 of Lesson 1 (page 324) did not always produce a minimal spanning tree. A similar algorithm can be applied to the Traveling Salesperson Problem.

a. Look back at the nearest-neighbor algorithm for minimal spanning trees. By slightly modifying that algorithm, write the steps of a nearest-neighbor algorithm for the Traveling Salesperson Problem.

b. Apply your modified algorithm to try to find a solution to the Traveling Salesperson Problem for the weighted graph below.

■ Starting at *A*

■ Starting at *B*

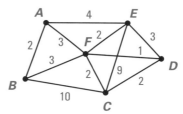

c. What is the shortest possible circuit? Can the shortest possible circuit be obtained by your algorithm using any starting point?

d. Do you think the nearest-neighbor algorithm is a good algorithm for solving the Traveling Salesperson Problem? Explain your reasoning.

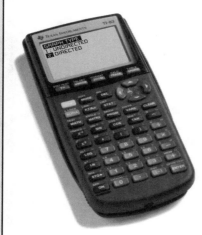

3. **a.** Dijkstra's algorithm determines the sequence of shortest paths $AB = 2$, $ABD = 3$, $AC = 4$, $ABE = 5$, and $ABEF = 7$.

b.

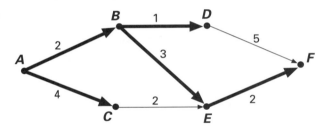

c. ■ Yes. Dijkstra's algorithm specifically avoids making circuits by only looking at edges that link circled and uncircled vertices. Also, it only adds edges to vertices that are circled, so the growing subgraph stays connected.

■ Yes, Dijkstra's tree is a spanning tree. It continues to grow until it has connected all the vertices.

■ No, it is not minimal. It has length 12, and the minimal spanning tree consisting of AB, BD, AC, CE, and EF has length 11. Dijkstra's algorithm solves the shortest path problem, not the minimal spanning tree problem.

4. **a.** **i.** Make a copy of the graph with the edges drawn lightly.

ii. Choose a starting vertex.

iii. Darken the shortest edge that connects to the vertex where you are, as long as it does not create a circuit. (If there is more than one such edge, choose any such one.) Move to the end vertex of that edge.

iv. Repeat Step iii until all vertices have been reached. Then if possible, return to the starting vertex.

b. ■ The path starting at A is A-B-F-D-C-E-A with length 21.

■ The path starting at B hits a dead end at E.

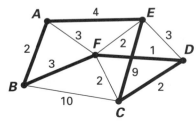 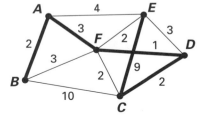

c. By inspection, the shortest circuit is A-B-F-C-D-E-A with length 16. (The circuit can begin at any vertex.) This circuit cannot be found using the algorithm.

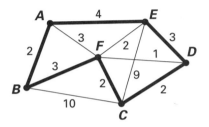

See additional Teaching Notes on page T366H.

Unit 5

5. **a.** The Hamiltonian path is *F-B-E-G-A-D-C*.

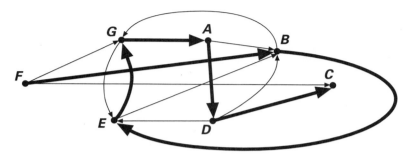

   b. Responses will vary.

5. You have seen in this lesson that there is no known efficient method for solving the Traveling Salesperson Problem. The same is true for finding Hamiltonian circuits and paths. Most experts believe that efficient solutions for these problems will never be found, at least not by using traditional electronic computers. In 1994, computer scientist Leonard M. Adleman of the University of Southern California in Los Angeles opened up the possibility of using nature as the computer to solve these problems. Dr. Adleman successfully carried out a laboratory experiment in which he used DNA to do the computations needed to solve a Hamiltonian path problem. Dr. Adleman stated, "This is the first example, I think, of an actual computation carried out at the molecular level." This method has not been shown to solve all Hamiltonian problems, and the particular problem solved was quite small, but it opens up some amazing possibilities for mathematics and computer science.

a. Below is the graph that Dr. Adleman used in his experiment. All the information in the graph was encoded using strands of DNA, and then the computations needed to find a Hamiltonian path were carried out by biochemical processes. Of course, this graph is small enough that the Hamiltonian path also can be found without gene splicing or conventional computers. Find the Hamiltonian path.

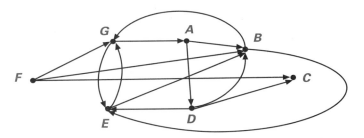

b. Find out more about this groundbreaking experiment in "molecular computation" by reading some of the articles below. Write a short report incorporating your findings.

- Adleman, Leonard M. Molecular Computation of Solutions to Combinatorial Problems. *Science*, November 11, 1994.

- Delvin, Keith. Test Tube Computing with DNA. *Math Horizons*, April, 1995.

- Kolata, Gina. Scientist At Work: Leonard Adleman: Hitting the High Spots of Computer Theory. *The New York Times*, Late Edition, December 15, 1994.

LESSON 2 • SHORTEST PATHS AND CIRCUITS   **361**

Fan Chung

6. Vertex-edge graphs are part of an area of mathematics called discrete mathematics. A leading contemporary researcher in discrete mathematics is Fan Chung, a mathematician who earned her doctorate in 1974 and has worked at Bell Labs, Harvard University, and the University of Pennsylvania. Although many of the problems that Dr. Chung works on look like games, often they have important applications in areas like communication networks and design of computer hardware and software.

Consider one such problem. In the graph below, suppose a person is standing at each vertex. The first letter of each vertex label is the name of the vertex; the second letter is the destination that each person must reach by walking along edges of the graph. The goal is for all the people to walk to their destinations without overusing any edge. By trying to solve a problem like this, you can find out how accessible a network is—that is, if it has any "bottlenecks" where there is excessive traffic.

a. Assume that an edge is "overused" if it is used more than twice. Find routes for all walkers so that everyone reaches their destination but no edge is overused. Are other routes possible?

b. Describe the strategy you used to find the routes.

c. State, and try to solve, at least one other problem related to this situation.

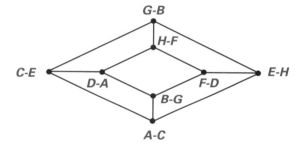

MORE *continued*

6. **a.** There is more than one solution. In the solution below, the path used for each vertex label is shown. For example, label *B-G* means that the person at vertex *B*, which is the bottom vertex of the inside diamond, must walk to vertex *G*, which is the top-most vertex of the graph. A path for doing so is shown by listing the vertices in the path, *B–D–C–G*.

A-C: A–C
C-E: C–G–E
E-H: E–F–H
H-F: H–F
F-D: F–B–D
D-A: D–C–A
B-G: B–D–C–G
G-B: G–E–F–B

b. Students should describe the strategy they used to find the routes in Part a. The descriptions could be specific algorithms, or they could be a statement of general guidelines. The more detailed the description, the better. Sample responses are given below.

■ Trial and error

■ Always taking the shortest path, start with some vertex and go to its destination; then proceed from that vertex to its destination. Continue in this way until you cannot proceed further. Then start with a new vertex and repeat the process. Continue until all people at all vertices have moved to their destination.

■ Order the vertices in some manner, say alphabetically, and try to find paths for each vertex in the order in which it appears in the list.

■ Whenever you have a choice, always choose a path that does not use an edge twice. That is, traverse an edge for the second time only as a last resort.

c. Some related problems are the following.

■ What is the fewest number of repeated edges that must be used?

■ Can you find routes if each edge can only be used once?

See Assessment Resources, pages 176–181.

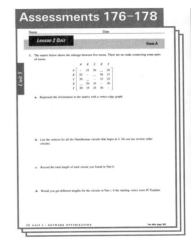

Lesson 3 *Looking Back*

In this unit, students have investigated several new graph models: trees, minimal spanning trees, shortest paths, Hamiltonian circuits, and Traveling Salesperson Problems. In order to use these models effectively to solve problems, students need to know what they are, how to use them, and when to use them.

As students work solutions for these problems, you may want to ask them why they chose a particular strategy or model. For example, you might ask, "What was it in the situation that suggested a particular model?" Student answers to this question are particularly helpful for other students to hear. Listening to them promotes the ideas that there may be more than one solution and that good problem solvers take time to think about the situation, trying to get beneath the surface issues to the underlying problem.

Activity 2 is purposely open-ended. Students should be given the opportunity to synthesize and apply their knowledge by solving a less structured problem. After at least one group presents their solution you might then ask other questions not brought up by students that bring closure to the discussion.

1. **a.** Consider the graph representing the cities and routes connecting them. This problem is a Traveling Salesperson Problem. (Remember there is no efficient general algorithm for solving problems of this type.)

   b. To find the shortest route from Scottsville to Rockbridge, a network of all cities and possible routes could be created and represented as a graph. The desired route then could be found by considering the shortest path connecting the vertices representing Scottsville and Rockbridge.

   c. To solve this, use an algorithm to find a minimal spanning tree.

Lesson 3

Looking Back

In this unit, you have investigated the Traveling Salesperson Problem and many new vertex-edge graph models: trees, minimal spanning trees, shortest paths, and Hamiltonian circuits. In order to effectively use these models to solve problems, you need to know what they are, when to use them, and how to use them.

1. Consider the map below of a region of Kentucky.

For each of the following questions, state which graph model could be used to model the situation. You do not need to answer the questions, just state which graph model applies. Explain your choice of models.

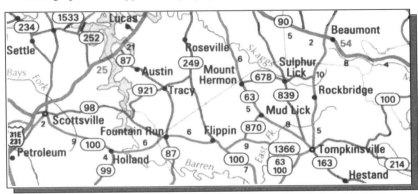

Map © 1997 by Rand McNally, R.L. 97-S-79

a. Suppose a truck driver must visit each town in the region to deliver packages, beginning and ending at Tompkinsville. What is the minimum number of miles the driver would have to drive?

b. What is the shortest route from Scottsville to Rockbridge?

c. Since snowstorms are uncommon in Kentucky, the transportation departments do not have a lot of snowplows standing by. So when it does snow, they need to have an efficient plan for plowing the roads. Suppose the goal is to plow just enough roads so that there is a way to get from every town to every other town on plowed roads. What is the minimum number of miles that must be plowed in order to achieve this goal?

2. The influence one person exerts over another is an important question that sociologists study. Consider a group of five associates in an architectural firm.

    A sociologist asks each person to fill out a questionnaire identifying the one person in the group whose opinion they value the most. If person X values person Y's opinion, then it is assumed that person X is influenced by person Y. The sociologist wants to find out which person has the most influence on the group. The results of the questionnaire are tabulated below.

Results of Influence Study

Member of the Group	Person Whose Opinion Is Valued Most
A	D
B	A
C	B
D	B
E	D

Working together with your group members, use these data and some kind of network optimization to determine who is the most influential person in the group. Justify your conclusion.

It is important for students to develop and use the skill of mathematical modeling. In Activity 2 students work on an open-ended problem that asks them to analyze influence in terms of graph models. They may even use the methods from "Matrix Models" and rank using powers of matrices and row sums. Whatever method they use, they should explain what they are trying to optimize and why their model is appropriate. You may wish to have groups present their models and solutions following the Checkpoint.

2. ■ Students may build a graph model where the edges represent influence as shown on the right.

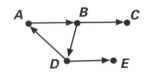

If students have difficulty beginning, suggest they consider a graph model and a way to model "influence." Students' conclusions should include consideration of path length and distance matrices. You might ask the following questions. "Does a shorter or longer path indicate more influence?" (shorter) "Would a distance matrix be helpful?" "How is direct and indirect influence shown in the graph? " Student responses should be similar to those below.

■ A has more influence over B; A's influence over B is direct because B values A's opinion most, but A's influence over E is indirect because it must depend on the support of B and D.

■ The numbers in the distance matrix below are the number of edges in the shortest directed path from the row index to the column index. For example, the shortest directed path from A to E has length 3. Each X indicates that there is no path for the indicated vertices.

$$
\begin{array}{c c c c c c}
 & A & B & C & D & E \\
A & - & 1 & 2 & 2 & 3 \\
B & 2 & - & 1 & 1 & 2 \\
C & X & X & - & X & X \\
D & 1 & 2 & 3 & - & 1 \\
E & X & X & X & X & -
\end{array}
$$

Notice that the distance matrix is not symmetrical because the edges are directed. The row sums are A: 8, B: 6, D: 7. The lowest row sum indicates the most direct influence on the group. B appears to be the most influential member of the group because B's row sum is smallest. This implies that B's influence on the other members of the group is more immediate than anyone else's.

■ The rows with an X are ignored because an X means no path, which means no influence. Since larger path lengths mean less influence, it would make sense to replace each X with a large number, like 100. Then we could find and compare all row sums. The very large row sums for the rows that formerly contained an X would indicate very little influence.

■ Students compare their solutions.

■ The solution involved networks through the graph model and optimization because we found the person with the most influence by finding the smallest row sum.

3. a. Here is a possible list of concepts from this unit:
- minimal spanning tree
- Traveling Salesperson Problem
- best-edge algorithm
- Hamiltonian circuit
- shortest path
- tree
- distance matrix
- brute-force method

b.
- There is an edge from "best-edge algorithm" to "minimal spanning tree" because the best-edge algorithm will generate a minimal spanning tree.
- There should not be an edge from "best-edge algorithm" to "Traveling Salesperson Problem" because the algorithm does not provide a solution to the Traveling Salesperson Problem.
- The edge between "Traveling Salesperson Problem" and "minimal spanning tree" is labeled "tree vs. circuit" because a solution to the Traveling Salesperson Problem can be described as a minimal spanning *circuit* as opposed to a minimal spanning *tree*.

c. One possible concept map is shown below. Students may have trouble articulating some of the connections, but they should be encouraged to try.

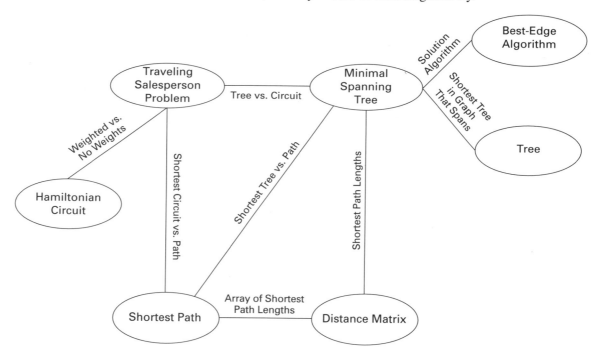

3. You have used vertex-edge graphs to model a variety of situations. You also can use graphs to represent and analyze relationships among the new concepts that you are learning. This is done using a type of graph called a *concept map*. In a concept map, the vertices represent ideas or concepts, and edges illustrate how the concepts are connected. The edges may or may not have labels. The first step in building a concept map for some area of study is to list all the concepts you can think of. Here is the beginning of such a list for this unit on network optimization:

- minimal spanning tree
- Traveling Salesperson Problem
- best-edge algorithm

a. Add to this list. Include all the concepts from this unit that you can recall.

The next step in building a concept map is to let the concepts in the list be the vertices of a graph, and then draw edges between vertices to show connections between concepts. The edges should be labeled to show *how* the vertex concepts are connected. There are many different concept maps that can be drawn. The beginning of one concept map for this unit is drawn below.

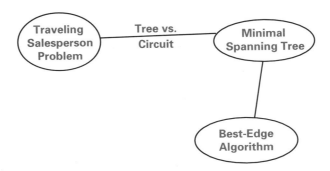

b. Interpret the sample concept map above.

- Why is there an edge from *best-edge algorithm* to *minimal spanning tree?*
- Why shouldn't an edge be drawn from *best-edge algorithm* to *Traveling Salesperson Problem?*
- The edge between *Traveling Salesperson Problem* and *minimal spanning tree* is labeled *tree vs. circuit.* Explain why a solution to the Traveling Salesperson Problem can be described as a minimal spanning circuit, and then explain why the edge is labeled *tree vs. circuit.*

c. Complete the concept map by adding all the concepts (vertices) that you listed in Part a along with appropriate edges that show connections among the concepts.

Checkpoint

In this unit, you have studied many concepts and methods related to network optimization.

ⓐ Compare your group's concept map from Activity 3 with another group's map. Discuss similarities and differences.

ⓑ Optimization or "finding the best" is an important theme throughout this unit. Describe three problem situations from the unit in which you "found the best." In each case, explain how you used a graph model to solve the problem.

ⓒ Describe one similarity between minimal spanning trees and shortest paths. Describe one difference.

ⓓ Describe one similarity between minimal spanning tree problems and the Traveling Salesperson Problem. Describe one difference.

ⓔ Describe one similarity between the Traveling Salesperson Problem and shortest path problems. Describe one difference.

ⓕ In this unit, you explored a variety of algorithms and methods for solving network optimization problems, including best-edge algorithms and brute force methods. For each of these two solution procedures, do the following.

- Describe the basic strategy.
- Give some examples of problems that can be solved using the procedure.
- List some advantages and disadvantages of the procedure.

Be prepared to share your group's examples and descriptions with the entire class.

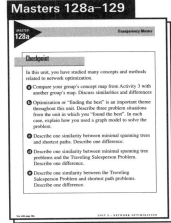

SHARE AND SUMMARIZE full-class discussion

Checkpoint

See Teaching Masters 128a–128b.

Some students may well have obtained the objectives of the unit and yet find it difficult to keep some of the vocabulary straight. It is not necessary to press them for mastery of the vocabulary.

ⓐ Students should discuss their concept maps.

ⓑ Possible examples:

Best	Graph Model Type
Cheapest airfare	Shortest Path
Least amount of wire	Minimal Spanning Tree
Shortest route between two cities	Shortest Path
Shortest circuit through a network of cities	Traveling Salesperson Problem or Minimal Hamiltonian Circuit
Phone network	Minimal Spanning Tree
Detecting clustering	Minimal Spanning Tree
Traveler's Dodecahedron	Hamiltonian circuit

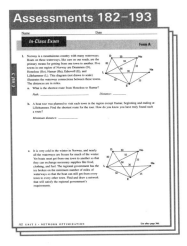

ⓒ Minimal spanning trees and shortest paths are both the "shortest" in some sense. But a minimal spanning tree is a shortest *tree* that includes all vertices as opposed to a shortest *path* that generally does not include all vertices.

ⓓ In both minimal spanning tree problems and the Traveling Salesperson Problem, you are looking for something that is minimal and spanning. In one case, you want a minimal spanning *tree*, and in the other, you want a minimal spanning *circuit*.

ⓔ In both the Traveling Salesperson Problem and shortest path problems, you are looking for the "shortest"—but in the one case, it is a shortest *circuit* that includes all the vertices; in the other, it is a shortest *path* that generally does not include all the vertices.

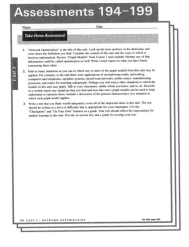

ⓕ ■ Best-edge algorithm: Add the best possible edge at each step.
Brute-force method: Find all possibilities, check them all, and choose the best.

■ The best-edge algorithm will find a minimal spanning tree. It will not solve the Traveling Salesperson Problem. It was not discussed for shortest path problems.
The brute-force method will work, in theory, for any finite problem.

■ Some advantages of the best-edge algorithm that students might suggest are that it is easy to understand and apply, it will find minimal spanning trees, and it seems efficient. (In fact, it has been proven to be efficient.) A possible disadvantage is that it does not work for the Traveling Salesperson Problem.

Some advantages for the brute-force method are that it is easy to understand, and it works for any problem with a finite number of possibilities. Disadvantages are that it can be difficult and time consuming to apply for large problems. Thus, the brute force method, while providing a solution in theory, is often not practical.

You may wish to use Teaching Master 129 to promote a class discussion about mathematical habits of mind. Reflection and discussion will assist students in recognizing the valuable mathematical thinking skills they are cultivating.

NOTE: If minimal spanning trees are roughly characterized as "shortest trees," then this unit is primarily about shortest trees, paths, and circuits.

See Assessment Resources, 182–199.

Looking Back, Looking Ahead

▶Reflecting on Mathematical Content

This unit continued the development of vertex-edge graphs as mathematical models. In the Course 1 unit "Graph Models," students explored applications of Euler circuits and paths, vertex coloring, and critical paths. "Graph Models" also introduced matrix representation of graphs. In "Matrix Models," students used matrix representations to analyze situations involving paths of certain lengths in graphs, such as contamination paths in a predator-prey food web. In the present unit, "Network Optimization," students investigated minimal spanning trees, shortest paths, Hamiltonian paths, and the Traveling Salesperson Problem. In total, these graph models, along with others studied in the MORE sets, have given students a powerful set of tools that they can use to make sense of situations involving relationships among a finite number of elements.

The tables below summarize what students have learned about vertex-edge graphs at this point in the curriculum. Vertex-edge graphs model relationships among a finite number of elements. The elements are represented by the vertices and the edges are used to represent the relationships. The *Contemporary Mathematics in Context* curriculum focuses on three fundamental types of problems in graph theory: optimal paths and circuits, optimal spanning circuits, and vertex coloring.

Optimal Paths and Circuits

Graph Model	Description	Sample Application
Euler paths	use each edge exactly once	determine snowplow routes
Hamiltonian paths	visit each vertex exactly once	rank tournaments
Shortest paths	shortest path from here to there	measure degree of influence
Critical paths	longest path/critical tasks	schedule large projects

Optimal Spanning Networks

Graph Model	Description	Sample Application
Minimal spanning trees	join all vertices, no circuits, minimum total weight	optimal computer or road networks
Traveling Salesperson Problems	visit all vertices, start = end, minimum total weight	manufacture integrated circuit boards

Graph Coloring

Graph Model	Description	Sample Applications
Vertex coloring	Adjacent vertices get different colors, use fewest number of colors	manage conflicts (radio frequencies, meeting schedules, chemical storage)

Unit 5 Assessment

Teaching Notes *continued*

Notes continued from page T322

5. **d.** True. A shortest network must be connected. It must be possible to get from any vertex (computer) to any other vertex (computer), directly or indirectly. The definition of *connected* given here is intuitive and accurate. It just means that there are no isolated vertices or other separate pieces of the graph.

e. True. All vertices (computers) must be in the network. Another way to say this, using the formal language introduced in Activity 6, is that the network *spans* all the vertices.

f. True. This is an important point since it is the key to most algorithms. If there were a circuit, then there would be more than one way to move between vertices. This means there would be unnecessary edges, which would make the network longer than it needs to be.

Notes continued from page T325

| **APPLY** | individual task |

▶ On Your Own

Applying Kruskal's algorithm to the graph yields a minimum of 173 yards of pipe needed to construct the sprinkler network.

The two minimal spanning trees are shown below.

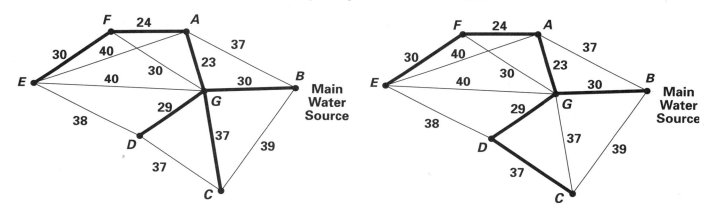

Teaching Notes *continued*

Notes continued
from page T334

4. e. If the brace in the 2nd row, 3rd column is removed, the following graph and grid are produced.

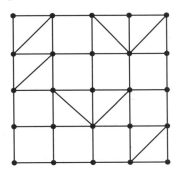
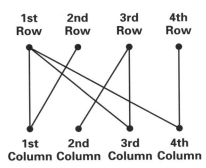

f. This explanation may be difficult for students to verbalize. You may wish to suggest the terminology *posts* for vertical segments of the grid and *beams* for horizontal segments. One possible explanation follows.

  Assume that the grid is positioned so that the upper left post is, in fact, vertical. For any grid, braced or not, all posts in a given row are parallel, and all beams in a given column are parallel, since the cells are rhombuses. A brace in square (i, j) of the grid forces the posts and beams in that cell to be perpendicular, and thus all the posts in row i are forced to be perpendicular to all the beams in column j.

  Now, if the graph is connected, then there is a path between every pair of vertices. Every edge in a path corresponds to a brace in a cell, which forces a perpendicular post-beam relation. Thus, since there is a path from the top-row vertex to all other row vertices, the posts in all rows are parallel. For example, suppose the top-row vertex is connected to the right-column vertex, which is connected to the bottom-row vertex. Then the top-row posts are perpendicular to the right-column beams, which are perpendicular to the bottom-row posts. So the top-row posts must be parallel to the bottom-row posts.

  Similarly, since there is a path from the top-row vertex to all the column vertices, the beams in every column are perpendicular to the posts in every row. Thus, every cell is forced to be a square and the grid is rigid.

Notes continued from page T337

1. d. (2) Now we must show that if the bottom-card graph is a tree, then we win the game. The game ends when all four kings have been turned over, and we win the game if all the cards have been turned over. So, we will show that when all the kings have been turned over, all the cards will in fact have been turned over. Consider the following argument.

(i) We are assuming that the bottom-card graph is a tree. Start at any non-center vertex and follow the path of bottom-card edges that starts from that vertex. (This is a path of "last exits.") Since there is exactly one edge out of every vertex except the center, this path must either create a circuit or end at the center. Since the bottom-card graph is a tree, it cannot contain circuits. Thus there is a directed path in the bottom-card graph from every noncenter vertex to the center vertex.

(ii) Now think about what needs to happen to get the kings turned over. By Step i, there is a directed path in the bottom-card graph from every non-center vertex to the center (king) vertex K. Thus, there is a bottom-card edge from some vertex V to K. That is, there is a king at the bottom of pile V. To get to this king, all cards in pile V must be turned over. If there is an edge W-V, then there is a V card at the bottom of the W pile, which means that all the W cards must be turned over. Continuing in this way, we see that if X is on a path in the bottom-card graph leading to the center vertex, then all cards in X must be turned over. But by Step i, all vertices are part of a path to the center. So all cards at all vertices must be turned over. Thus, the game is won.

2. a. Responses may vary because Step ii allows for choice between edges of the same length. One set of solutions is shown below.

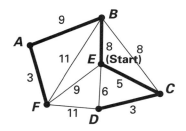
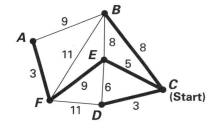
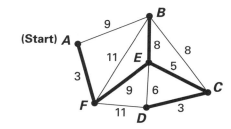

Teaching Notes *continued*

Notes continued
from page T345

Because this investigation involves a lot of visualization, you may find that students who have found symbolic investigations difficult now can excel. You also may find that groups work at very different rates from each other. If a group finishes early, you might have other challenges ready for the students. For example, you might ask them to draw a graph that has a Hamiltonian circuit but not an Euler circuit, or an Euler circuit but not a Hamiltonian circuit, or a Hamiltonian circuit but not an Euler path. Or you might have copies of Teaching Master 125 available for students to create the dodecahedron.

Notes continued
from page T357

- problems that have a solution algorithm but no efficient algorithm, thus no computer, no matter how fast, could solve these problems in a reasonable amount of time;
- problems that have efficient solution algorithms, like the minimal spanning tree problem; and
- problems which are believed to have no efficient solution algorithm, but no one knows for sure, like the Traveling Salesperson Problem.

Notes continued from page T358

1. c.

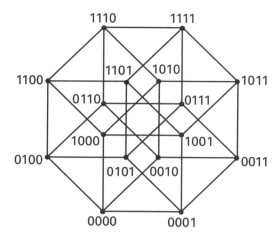

Listed below are some resources on four-dimensional cubes.

Abbott, Edwin. *Flatland.* New York: Dover Publications, 1952.

Geometry Center, The (University of Minnesota). The Topological Zoo. http://www.geom.umn.edu/zoo.

Peterson, Ivars. *The Mathematical Tourist.* New York, W. H. Freeman, 1988, pp. 85–91.

Watkins, John, and Bobin Wilson. *Graphs: An Introductory Approach.* New York, Wiley and Sons, 1990.

d. There are many possibilities. One Gray Code is: 0000, 0001, 0011, 1011, 1001, 1000, 1010, 0010, 0110, 0111, 0101, 1101, 1111, 1110, 1100, 0100.

Teaching Notes *continued*

Notes continued
from page T360

4. d. Responses may vary. Actually, there is no effective algorithm for solving this problem: for big graphs, the brute force approach takes too long. It is useful, therefore, to have algorithms that generate approximate solutions, and algorithms that refine guesses. Frequently, the nearest-neighbor algorithm, however, may not even approximate adequately.

In general, the algorithm might give a shortest circuit for some starting points, but it will not guarantee a shortest circuit. In fact, sometimes it won't even give a circuit at all, because it results in a dead end. This example is one where it never gives the shortest circuit. The main advantage to the nearest-neighbor algorithm is that it is very simple to implement.

Unit 6

Geometric Form and Its Function

UNIT OVERVIEW Many everyday objects are made in a particular form because that form or geometric shape is essential to the function of the object. An absurd, but illustrative, example is the wheel. Think of automobile tires that are square. They certainly would try an engineer's ingenuity to produce a smooth-riding automobile! Examples such as this make it clear that function and shape are often closely related.

In this unit, three basic shapes (quadrilaterals, triangles, and circles) are studied. Each has characteristics that make it particularly important for engineers, architects, and other designers. Quadrilaterals with hinged or pivoting vertices have many mechanical applications, and they can be used to create similar figures. Triangles also have applications related to similarity, in addition to applications that make use of their rigidity and other characteristics. Circles are particularly useful in situations involving periodic change, including smooth, repetitive motions.

Unit 6 Objectives

- ■ To investigate the characteristics of quadrilaterals and the mechanical uses of quadrilateral linkages
- ■ To investigate ways that triangles are used to maintain rigidity in structures with one side of variable length
- ■ To explore properties and applications of the sine, cosine, and tangent ratios for the length of sides of right triangles
- ■ To explore the characteristics of circles and relate circles to rotating objects, angular velocity, and the graphs of trigonometric functions

Geometric Form and Its Function

Unit **6**

Unit 6

367

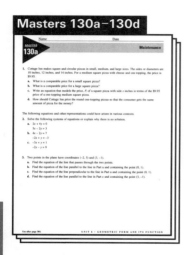

▶Use of the Three Basic Shapes Throughout the Unit

As the unit begins, students study quadrilaterals and their uses when they have hinged or pivoting vertices. (Polygons with hinged vertices that allow angles to move are called *linkages*.) Mechanical applications of 4-bar linkages are the first context for this investigation. Then students use pantographs as another application of a quadrilateral linkage, namely, to produce an instrument that will copy shapes but increase or decrease their size. Thus they can see how quadrilateral linkages are related to similarity through size transformations. Since this is the third unit in Course 2 in which students build an understanding of the concept of similarity, students should quickly progress through Investigation 2 of Lesson 1.

In the second lesson, students explore uses of triangles, beginning by examining triangular linkages with one side that can vary in length. This form is a valuable tool in the design of many objects because it combines rigidity with controlled change. In the second investigation, students apply the concept of similarity to triangles and begin their study of the trigonometric ratios sine, cosine, and tangent. These ratios are important and unique because they allow us to relate angle measures with linear measures. Students use trigonometric ratios in Investigation 3 for indirect measurement problems.

The last lesson in this unit focuses student attention on circles. As in the previous two lessons, the first investigation is strongly contextualized and hands-on in style. With models of pulleys and sprockets, students examine the transmission factor for pairs of pulleys that form the basis for both bicycle gears and block and tackle. Next, students investigate angle measure in terms of revolutions, degrees, and radians. In the final two investigations, Ferris wheels are used to model periodic change from which the graphs of sine and cosine functions are developed.

See Teaching Masters 130a–130d for Maintenance tasks that students can work on after Lesson 1.

Unit 6 Planning Guide

Lesson Objectives	MORE Assignments	Suggested Pacing	Materials
Lesson 1 *Flexible Quadrilaterals* • To recognize the use of quadrilaterals in the construction of common manufactured objects • To describe similar plane shapes, determine if plane shapes are similar, and use the relationship among lengths, angles, and areas of similar shapes • To construct a pantograph to be used to generate a specific scale factor	**after page 372** Students can begin Modeling Task 1, 3, or 5; or Reflecting Task 2 or 4 from p. 377. **page 377** **Modeling:** 1, choice of 3 or 5* **Organizing:** 1 or 2, and 3* **Reflecting:** 1, and choice of one* **Extending:** 5	6 days	• Each group: Linkage strips (plastic or cardboard), paper fasteners, metric rulers, protractors, large sheets of plain paper (12"x18"), scissors, single-hole paper punch • Optional: Simple drawing such as a comic strip cell • Teaching Resources 131–135 • Assessment Resources 200–203
Lesson 2 *Triangles and Trigonometric Ratios* • To recognize the use of triangles with a variable-length side in manufactured goods, and to analyze effects of the variability on angles and heights in those goods • To determine the sine, cosine, and tangent of an angle in a right triangle • To solve indirect measurement problems	**page 389** **Modeling:** Choose one* **Organizing:** 2 and 4 **Reflecting:** Choose one* **Extending:** 1 or 3* **after page 399** Students can begin Organizing Task 2 or 3; Reflecting Task 1 or 2; or Extending Task 1 from p. 406. **page 406** **Modeling:** 1, and 3 or 4* **Organizing:** 2, 3, and 5 **Reflecting:** 1, and choice of one* **Extending:** 1	12 days	• Each group: Linkage strips, paper fasteners (8), metric rulers, protractors, scissors • Teaching Resources 130a–130d, 136–140 • Assessment Resources 204–209
Lesson 3 *The Power of the Circle* • To analyze a situation involving pulleys or sprockets to determine transmission factors, angular velocity, and linear velocity • To sketch the graphs of the sine and the cosine functions • To determine the period and amplitude of $A \sin Bx$ or $A \cos Bx$ • To use sines and cosines to model periodic phenomena • To use radian and degree measures with trigonometric functions	**after page 417** Students can begin Reflecting Task 1 or 3 from p. 424 **after page 419** Students can begin Modeling Task 3 (or any other Modeling task); Organizing Task 2 or 3, or Extending Task 1 or 5 from p. 424. **page 424** **Modeling:** 3 and choice of one* **Organizing:** 2 and 3 **Reflecting:** 1 and 4 **Extending:** 1 or 5* **after page 435** Students can begin Organizing Task 3 or 4 or Reflecting Task 2 from p. 442. **page 442** **Modeling:** 1 and 2 **Organizing:** 3 and 4 **Reflecting:** 2 **Extending:** Choose one*	13 days	• Spools of thread of various diameters (with or without thread) or round containers, such as oatmeal boxes; string; rubber bands or elastic; dowels, straws, or chopsticks; protractors, rulers, and compasses; manila file folders • Teaching Resources 141–146 • Assessment Resources 210–215
Lesson 4 *Looking Back* • To review the major objectives of the unit		2–3 days (includes testing)	• Teaching Resources 147a–147b • Assessment Resources 216–231

* When choice is indicated, it is important to leave the choice to the student.
Note: It is best if Organizing tasks are discussed as a whole class after they have been assigned as homework.

Lesson 1

Flexible Quadrilaterals

The geometric form of an object often is influenced by its function, whether the object is naturally occurring or engineered. Because bee honeycombs are hexagonal prisms, the individual cells not only hold honey, but they also fit together with no gaps. Thus, the particular geometric form serves two functions. The designs of objects by architects and engineers are similarly influenced by the objects' functions. For example, buildings and bridges must be rigid. Motors and bicycles involve circular motion. The suspension system of an automobile helps control motion of the vehicle.

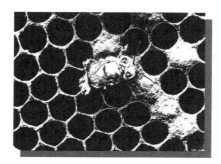

Lesson 1 *Flexible Quadrilaterals*

LESSON OVERVIEW The important idea in this lesson is that some geometric shapes are well suited to the particular functions they fulfill. You may want to ask students to be on the lookout for examples of devices and/or structures that utilize flexible quadrilaterals, triangles, and circles in their everyday lives and to keep a record of their observations during this unit of study.

Lesson Objectives

- To recognize the use of quadrilaterals in the construction of common manufactured objects
- To describe similar plane shapes; determine if plane shapes are similar; and use the relationship among lengths, angles, and areas of similar shapes
- To construct a pantograph to be used to generate a specific scale factor

LAUNCH full-class discussion

A good way to begin a class discussion is by referring to the pictures on page 368 and asking, "What shapes do you see? Why are these shapes well suited to their purpose?" You also might ask students to name other familiar objects in which form and function are related.

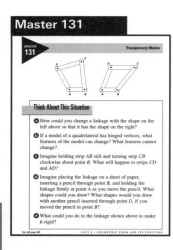

Think About This Situation

See Teaching Master 131.

It would be helpful, but is not essential, to have one or more ready-made linkages available at this stage. (Not everyone can visualize well from a two-dimensional sketch.) One could be used as a demonstration model; each group might have one to share as the students discuss the questions. This also would be a good time to demonstrate that if all the linkages are not connected carefully, they may not have full range of movement. See the note on page T370. (In an ideal world, students could meet this problem and overcome it, but in the practical world of the classroom, time is at a premium. It might be better just to deal with this problem up front and save precious time for more momentous discoveries.)

The questions are designed to prompt students to reflect *briefly* on how a flexible quadrilateral will move and transform itself. Students will spend more time examining the mechanical workings of a 4-bar linkage in the first investigation.

NOTE: Students are only visualizing this situation at this time. The models they construct in Lesson 1 will allow them to explore these ideas more fully.

ⓐ Keep *A* fixed and pull *C* to the right and down slightly.

ⓑ The angle measures, and thus shape, can change, but the lengths of the sides remain the same.

ⓒ As point *C* rotates about point *B*, point *D* will rotate about *A*. Strip *AD* will spin in a circle about *A*, but strip *CD*'s motion is difficult to describe. The demonstration model is particularly helpful here.

ⓓ Let students make conjectures at this stage without making a final decision. Students may suggest (correctly) that a pencil in *B* would produce an arc or a circle with center at *A* and radius of length *AB*. A pencil in *D* would produce an arc or a circle with center at *A* and radius of length *AD*.

ⓔ To make the linkage rigid, you could add a support connecting *A* to *C* or *B* to *D*.

Triangles, quadrilaterals, and circles are geometric shapes commonly used by designers. A triangle is rigid; a circle turns easily about its center; and the appearance of a quadrilateral can be changed by changing the measures of its interior angles, without changing the length of any side.

Shown below is a simple linkage made from plastic strips joined with brass paper fasteners. Imagine the various ways you could change the shape of this linkage. The diagrams below show two possible shapes for the linkage.

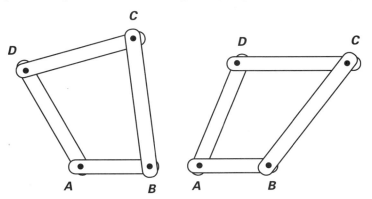

Think About This Situation

a How could you change a linkage with the shape on the left above so that it has the shape on the right?

b If a model of a quadrilateral has hinged vertices, what features of the model can change? What features cannot change?

c Imagine holding strip *AB* still and turning strip *CB* clockwise about point *B*. What will happen to strips *CD* and *AD*?

d Imagine placing the linkage on a sheet of paper, inserting a pencil through point *B*, and holding the linkage firmly at point *A* as you move the pencil. What shapes could you draw? What shapes would you draw with another pencil inserted through point *D*, if you moved the pencil in point *B*?

e What could you do to the linkage shown above to make it rigid?

In this unit, you will explore some of the ways in which triangular, quadrilateral, and circular shapes are used to perform everyday activities and help solve problems. You will become more aware of how function and geometric form are related.

INVESTIGATION 1 ▶ Using Quadrilaterals in Linkages

Quadrilaterals are rigid when *triangulated*, but when they have no diagonal, they change shape readily. Mechanical engineers use the nonrigidity of quadrilaterals to their advantage in the design of linkages. A **quadrilateral**, or **4-bar, linkage** like the one shown below can change shape by pivoting about its vertices. At the same time, the linkage retains some of the characteristics of the original shape.

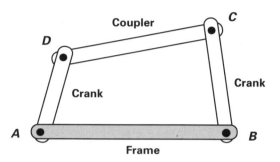

When 4-bar, or quadrilateral, linkages are used in mechanical contexts, one of the four sides is fixed so it does not move. It is called the *frame*. The two sides attached to the frame are called *cranks*; one is called the *driver* and the other is called the *follower*. The driver is the crank most directly affected by the user of the linkage. The cranks are connected by the *coupler*.

1. These features of a quadrilateral linkage can be seen in handcars like the one shown below. Make a cardboard model of this handcar. Use paper fasteners to put it together.

   a. What are the cranks? Where are these shown in the diagram? Describe their motions.

   b. What are the endpoints of the coupler?

   c. What points determine the frame?

   d. Does the driver crank cause the follower crank to rotate?

In 1883, a mathematician named Grashof suggested the following general principle for quadrilateral linkages:

   If the sum of the lengths of the shortest and longest sides is less than or equal to the sum of the lengths of the remaining two sides, then the shortest side can rotate completely.

2. Obtain some plastic or cardboard strips and paper fasteners. Working with a partner, make a model to investigate the truth of Grashof's principle for the situation described on the following page.

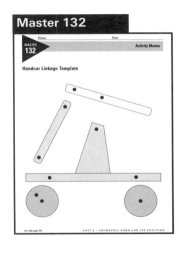

EXPLORE   small-group investigation

INVESTIGATION 1 ▶ Using Quadrilaterals in Linkages

During this investigation, students will experiment with simple examples of 4-bar linkages to gain first-hand information about how such linkages function and to determine the characteristics of geometric shapes that explain how these various mechanical devices function.

This is a "hands-on" investigation. Students are expected to build and examine several examples of linkages. Students in each group will need to have *linkage strips* with holes and paper fasteners to make the models. Plastic strips are available for purchase through Everyday Learning Corporation. An alternative is to create the strips from stiff paper such as file folders.

NOTE: There are a variety of ways to attach the strips together, many of which may interfere with student explorations. If students create a linkage such as the one shown in the diagram, with the bottom strip under both sides and the top strip attached under one side and over the other side, only the crank *BC* will rotate completely. Strip *AD* cannot get past *AB* for a complete rotation. Have students attach strips as indicated in the diagram in the student text, page 370. Thereafter, any time students note a problem with incomplete rotations, they should determine if the problem is only with the placement of the strips. In some cases, the shortest side may rotate completely in one direction and not in the other direction.

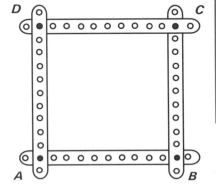

1. **See Teaching Master 132.**

    In Activity 1, the quadrilateral is not obvious because one side is not visible. For this activity, a full-class introduction works best. You can begin by asking a series of questions: "Where is the crank?" (Segment *WX*) "When you move side *WX*, what also moves?" (Side *WV* and side *VU*) "What does not move?" (Students may point out that side *UZ* does not change, nor does the support for *X*. It may take them a few minutes to realize that "side" *UX* does not change. So side *UX* is another side of the quadrilateral—actually the frame.) After the introduction, students should work in pairs to complete Activity 1. Students could make a working model of this out of 4 strips, or they could make a more complete model that

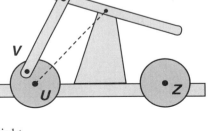

    is more realistic. The 4-strip model would look like the one shown to the right. You might want to provide pieces for students to cut out and assemble into a complete model. See Teaching Master 132 for a template of the necessary pieces.

    a. The cranks are side *WX* and side *UV*. The driver crank, *WX*, should cause the follower crank, *UV*, to rotate completely about point *U*.

    b. Points *V* and *W* are the endpoints of the coupler.

    c. Points *X* and *U* determine the frame even though there is no physical object directly connecting them. They are the two immobile points.

    d. Side *XW* is the driver crank. It oscillates up and down, pivoting about *X* and causing the wheel to turn. Side *UV* is the follower crank. It rotates about *U*.

    See additional Teaching Notes on page T453C.

2. In this activity, students test their understanding of the Grashof principle. They try to construct appropriate 4-bar linkages and then check that the shortest side can rotate completely for their model as well as the models created by other pairs of students.

   a. Lengths will vary.

      You may wish to have some students display their models to the entire class so that the class can see a variety of models. If all pairs of students construct models that closely match the diagram in the text, ask students who finish the investigation quickly this question: "Must the shortest side and the longest side be adjacent in order for Grashof's principle to hold?" (No.)

   b. Yes, strip *AD* should rotate completely about point *A*.

   c. Point *C* moves along an arc and will not rotate completely about point *B*. Strip *BC* sweeps out a sector of a circle with radius *BC*. As you facilitate the work, ask students to describe the size of the sector that their model makes.

   d. The handcar linkage is the same except that the oscillation of side *WX* causes the wheel in the model to turn.

   e. Turn *AD* circularly and extend *BC* beyond *C* to be the oscillating stirrer. The same idea can be used to make the windshield wiper. If students cannot visualize the stirring motion at this point, come back to this item at the end of the investigation.

   f. Comparing responses at this time will help students develop vocabulary for describing these types of situations.

3. a. Students should mention that one pair of opposite sides are the same length and parallel, or that both pairs of opposite sides are the same length.

   b. The figure changes from a long thin parallelogram (or a segment if collapsed completely) to a thicker parallelogram (at its thickest, it is a rectangle) and back to a long thin parallelogram. The angles change size as the vertex is moved left and right. Two properties that do not change are the lengths of the sides and the parallelism of the opposite sides.

   NOTE: Students should be moving the coupler right and left. If instead students completely rotate the crank (which moves the coupler), they still should respond correctly to these items.

   ---

   c. Each vertex follows a circular path up to a 180° arc (or full circle if the student is rotating the crank). The centers are the points where the frame and cranks for each vertex intersect and the radius of the circle is the length of the crank.

   d. One endpoint on a moving side is fixed with the other endpoint a fixed distance from it. The moving point follows a circular path with the fixed point as the center of the circle and the radius equal to the length of the moving side.

   e. The chosen point also moves along a circular path. Imagine adding another point on the frame in the same relative position as the chosen point. Then these points form another parallelogram. As the coupler moves, the chosen point rotates about the new frame point with the circle the vertex creates.

See additional Teaching Notes on page T453C.

a. Design your quadrilateral linkage *ABCD* so that strip *AB* is the longest side, strip *AD* is the shortest side, and $AB + AD < BC + CD$. What are the lengths of the sides of your model?

b. Does strip *AD* rotate completely?

c. Describe the motion of strip *BC*. Through what part of a circle does it move?

d. How is your model of the handcar in Activity 1 related to this linkage?

e. How could this linkage be used to make a stirring mechanism? To make a windshield wiper work?

f. Compare your responses with those of another pair of students.

3. Next, work with a partner to make a model of a *parallelogram linkage* using plastic or cardboard strips and paper fasteners to connect the sides.

a. Explain how you know your model is a parallelogram.

b. Choose a side to be the frame and hold it fixed on your desk as the base of the quadrilateral. Move one of the vertices on the opposite side (the coupler) to the right and then to the left. As the vertex moves, the shape of the linkage changes. Describe the changes you see. What properties of the shape, if any, do *not* change?

c. Move the coupler back and forth in small increments. With each move, mark the location of each vertex of the coupler. What patterns do these points follow?

d. Write an explanation that will convince other members of your group that your pattern in Part c is actually the correct path each vertex follows.

e. Choose a point (but not a vertex) on the side opposite the frame. Move that side. What path does the chosen point follow? Explain why the point moves along the path it does.

4. The diagram below depicts a windshield wiper mechanism as found on buses and tractor-trailers. The wiper blade is attached to the mechanism in a fixed position.

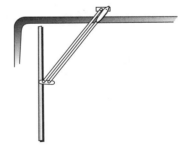

a. Make a sketch of this mechanism. Label the frame, cranks, and coupler.

b. Explain why this is a parallelogram linkage.

c. As the linkage moves, what paths do the ends of the wiper blade follow?

Unit 6

d. If the wiper blade is vertical (as shown) when the mechanism is at the beginning of a cycle, describe the positions of the blade when the mechanism is one quarter of the way through its cycle and when the mechanism is halfway through its cycle.

e. Sketch the region of the windshield that the blade keeps clean when in use.

Checkpoint

ⓐ Describe a quadrilateral linkage in which both the driver and follower cranks may make complete revolutions.

ⓑ List as many characteristics of a parallelogram linkage as you can. Which of these characteristics make it useful in mechanical devices?

Be prepared to share your group's descriptions and thinking with the entire class.

▶ On Your Own

Understanding the body mechanics involved in various physical activities is important to sports physicians and trainers. The diagram below shows a person pedaling a bicycle. Key points in the pedaling motion are labeled.

a. What kind of linkage is represented by *ABCD*?

b. Identify the frame, the coupler, the driver crank, and the follower crank.

c. What modifications to the situation would allow it to be modeled by a parallelogram linkage? Should a sports trainer recommend these modifications? Explain your reasoning.

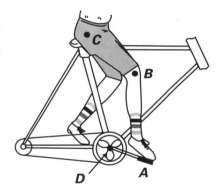

4. d. When the wiper blade is one-quarter of the way through its cycle, the blade will be vertical and the bottom end of the wiper will be the lowest point of its arc. When the wiper blade is halfway through its cycle, it will still be vertical, and the bottom end will be at a high point of its arc, possibly at a height equal to its starting point.

e. See shaded area on the sketch in Part a on page T453C.

SHARE AND SUMMARIZE full-class discussion

Checkpoint

See Teaching Master 133.

ⓐ In order for both the driver and follower cranks to make complete revolutions, the linkage must be a parallelogram linkage. If students are not able to explain why this is true, ask them to consider a trapezoid as indicated in the following explanation.

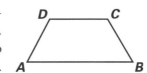

Both the driver and the follower cranks would need to be the shortest side, and thus they must be congruent. Since they are opposite sides of the quadrilateral, this forces the other two sides to be congruent for Grashof's principle to hold. This can be reasoned by thinking about an isosceles trapezoid with the legs as the shortest sides and the base AB as the longest side. Since $AB + AD$ must be less than or equal to $BC + CD$ and $AD = BC$, AB must be less than or equal to DC. Since AB is the longest side, DC cannot be longer and so must be equal to AB. Thus, we have a parallelogram because opposite sides are congruent.

ⓑ Both pairs of opposite sides are parallel and of equal length. Both pairs of opposite angles are equal in measure.

The parallelogram is a flexible polygon. Because the sum of the shortest side and longest side is always equal to the sum of the other two sides for any parallelogram, both the driver and follower cranks are able to make complete revolutions. This process changes back-and-forth motion into circular motion, making either a full circle or a partial arc (as with the wiper blade).

APPLY individual task

▶On Your Own

a. Quadrilateral linkage

b. Side CD is the frame, side AB is the coupler, side CB is the driver crank, and DA is the follower crank.

c. CD could be shortened to equal AB and the pedal DA extended to equal CB. A sports trainer would not recommend this adjustment. The pedal would not completely rotate since a person's thigh cannot completely rotate. As is, a person's thigh only needs to make a small arc to continue the pedaling.

MORE

ASSIGNMENT *pp. 377–383*

Students can now begin Modeling Tasks 1, 3, or 5; or Reflecting Tasks 2 or 4 from the MORE set following Investigation 2.

INVESTIGATION 2 Linkages and Similarity

In this investigation, students will create their own pantographs and then use them to explore and create similar shapes in the plane. They will measure the shapes, compare corresponding parts (angles and segments or sides), and deepen their understanding of the multiplicative relationship between the lengths of an image segment and its pre-image. Recall that this relationship (similarity) was presented in "Patterns of Location, Shape, and Size" by defining it as a constant ratio of corresponding lengths under a size transformation. It was revisited in "Power Models" as a context for square and cubic functions.

This investigation works well if you conceive of it as 2 parts: Activities 1–3 in which students learn to set up the pantograph and use it to have point *H* follow the motion of point *G*, but twice as far from the fixed point; and Activities 4–7 in which students investigate the changes in lengths and areas caused by specific scale factors. Activities 1–3 are likely to be a little frustrating and clumsy, as students get acquainted with the mechanism. It helps if you encourage students to express the relationship between △*FDG* and △*FBH* as a size transformation with fixed point *F*. (See Activity 2.) Making careful models (which is easier if you are using commercial plastic strips rather than homemade cardboard strips) and taking time now to experiment will save time later.

It is best if students work in pairs to complete Activities 1–3, and then share their procedures and results for these activities with the entire class. Then students can work in their small groups to complete Activities 4–7 and the Checkpoint that follows.

When possible, using commercial materials to make the pantographs will save class time, but pantographs made of cardboard will work. If students are making their own pantographs, it is very important that they measure the distance between holes very accurately. The model suggested here is made so that the lengths of 2, 4, 6, 8, ..., 24 cm are possible to represent. This choice limits the multipliers available if you are going to use the complete 24-cm length of segment *BH*. The possible scale factors are 24 divided by 2, 4, 6, 8, 10, ..., 22. The pantograph is a simple tool that can be used to generate a vast array of scale factors. For example, fixing *FD* = 8, *FB* = 24, *GD* = 8, *GE* = 16, and *BE* = 8 will give a pantograph for scale factor 3 because 3 × *FD* = *FB*. In the investigation, we have used only those multipliers available using *FB* = 24. It is possible for your students to create others if they understand how to manipulate and set up the pantograph.

1. If students make their own strips, they should cut out four 26-centimeter strips of tagboard or cardboard about 1.5 cm wide. They should punch holes whose centers are 1 cm from each end and additional holes every 2 cm along the strips. Accuracy is very important. The handmade strips must work the same as the manufactured ones.

   a. Quadrilateral *BDGE* is an equilateral parallelogram, or a rhombus, because all sides are equal in length.

See additional Teaching Notes on page T453C.

INVESTIGATION 2 Linkages and Similarity

Some quadrilateral linkages can change "back-and-forth" motion into rotary motion and vice versa. In a parallelogram linkage, both cranks can rotate completely. In addition to being used in mechanical devices, the parallelogram linkage serves as the basis for a linkage called a *pantograph*. The following pantograph is held firm at point *F*; the rods are hinged at *B*, *D*, *E*, and *G* so that *BDGE* is always a parallelogram. The other dots are holes that can be used to change the size of parallelogram *BDGE*.

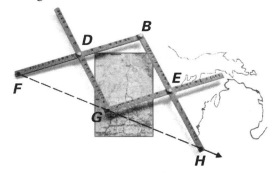

A pantograph can be used to enlarge or reduce the size of a map, a picture, or other figure while retaining its shape. In the following activities, you will explore how a pantograph works and why a figure and its pantograph image are *similar*.

1. Working with a partner, construct a model of a pantograph like the one shown below. Connect four linkage strips at pivot points *B*, *D*, *G*, and *E* with paper fasteners.

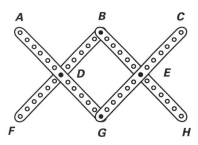

   a. What kind of parallelogram is *BDGE*? Explain your reasoning.

   b. Experiment to see if you can figure how to use a pantograph.

   c. What changes and what remains the same for quadrilateral *BDGE* as the pantograph is used?

   d. Compare your responses to Parts a and c with the responses of other group members.

2. Using a copy of the pantograph drawing in Activity 1, with points *B*, *D*, *E*, *F*, *G*, and *H* labeled, complete the activities below.

a. Outline △*FDG*. Then use a different colored pen or pencil to outline △*FBH*.

b. Compare △*FDG* and △*FBH*. How are their sides related? Their angles? How are the two triangles related?

3. Again working with your partner, use your model to explore the following questions. Compare your findings with other members of your group.

a. Draw a line across a sheet of paper and fix point *F* near one end. Place point *G* somewhere else on the line. Where is point *H* in relation to the line? If point *G* moves along the line, what path does point *H* follow? From your observations, how do you think points *F*, *G*, and *H* are related? Is this relation always true for other locations of points *F*, *G*, and *H*?

b. Adjust the pantograph so that *FG* is 6 centimeters. How long is $\overline{FH}$? How does length *FH* compare to length *FG*?

c. If *FG* is 9 centimeters, predict the length of $\overline{FH}$. Check your prediction using the pantograph.

d. In general, for this setup of the pantograph, what will be the relation between the lengths *FG* and *FH*? Write this relation in equation form: *FH* = ————.

4. Next, mark a point *F* on a large sheet of paper. Then position and hold your pantograph on the paper so that the points *F* on the pantograph and on the paper are aligned. Using the drawing below as a guide, mark points *P* and *Q* on your paper. Insert a pencil through the hole at point *H*.

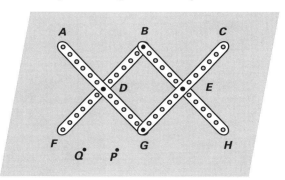

a. Find the image of *P* by placing *G* over *P* and marking the location of *H*. Label your mark to be the image point *P′*. What is true about *F*, *P*, and *P′*?

b. Find the image of *Q* in the same manner. Label it *Q′*. What is true about *F*, *Q*, and *Q′*?

c. Compare the distances *PQ* and *P′Q′*. How does this relationship compare with your observations in Part b of Activity 2, about the corresponding sides of △*FDG* and △*FBH*?

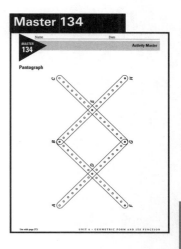

2. **See Teaching Master 134 for an enlarged copy of the labeled pantograph.**
   a. See student diagrams.
   b. The length of the sides of △*FBH* are twice the length of the sides of △*FDG*. The corresponding angles are the same measure. The triangles are similar.

3. Following this activity, it may help ensure consistent, accurate results if students share the techniques they used to measure the line segments. For example, it is helpful to measure from center point to center point of the paper fastener and to check that the three points along the base of the pantograph (*F*, *G*, and *H*) are aligned carefully. You may want to let students know that this activity is intended to give them their first experience using a pantograph to enlarge segments and shapes.
   a. Point *H* is farther to the right on the line. As point *G* moves along the line, point *H* also does. Points *F*, *G*, and *H* will always be collinear.
   b. *FH* = 12 cm when *FG* = 6 cm. The length *FH* is twice the length *FG*.
   c. *FH* = 18 cm when *FG* = 9 cm.
   d. $FH = 2 \cdot FG$

   NOTE: Students will need large sheets of construction paper or newsprint for Activities 4–7.

   ---

4. a. *F*, *P*, and *P′* are collinear.
   b. *F*, *Q*, and *Q′* are collinear.
   c. $2 \cdot PQ = P'Q'$
      When comparing the lengths of corresponding line segments, we see that both situations have a scale factor of 2.

4. **d.** This part provides students with an opportunity to work with the pantograph and to see another example.

   e. $2 \cdot PQ = P'Q'$

   Regardless of the line segment created by students, the image segment should be twice the length of the pre-image segment. A line segment from $\triangle FBH$ is twice the length of a corresponding line segment from $\triangle FDG$. Help students focus on the size transformation with fixed point F.

   In Activities 5–7, students explore other scale factors and the construction of plane shapes under a size transformation. *Caution students* to think through the positioning on their paper of the points, line segments, or triangles and the fixed point of the pantograph before they begin an activity to ensure that they will have sufficient room to complete the activity. You also might want to suggest that students use small triangles. Activity 5 uses a scale factor of 3, and Activity 6 revisits the idea of area of similar triangles. Finally, in Activity 7, the students are asked to set up a pantograph so that it produces a given scale factor.

5. **a.** Line segments in $\triangle FBH$ are three times the length of corresponding segments in $\triangle FDG$. The corresponding angles of the two triangles are congruent. The triangles are similar. The scale factor is 3.

   b. $P'Q'$ will be 3 times 5 cm in length, or 15 cm. Distances GF and HF are corresponding sides of similar triangles FDG and FBH with scale factor of 3.

   c. ■ The pantograph will increase distances by a factor of 3.
   ■ The pantograph will change distances by a factor of k.

6. **a.** See student diagrams. Since points F, G, and H are always collinear, when you move G along a straight line, H must move along the same line. Thus it is sufficient to find the images of the three vertices and then connect them to get the image triangle.

   b. The lengths of the corresponding sides of the image triangle are three times the lengths of the sides of the original triangle. The two triangles are similar.

   c. The area of the original triangle is 20 cm². The area of the image triangle is 180 cm². The image triangle has area 9 times the area of the original triangle. (The multiplier is the square of the scale factor.)

   d. See student diagrams. The pantograph should be set as shown in the diagram in Activity 4.

   e. The sides of the image triangle have lengths twice the lengths of the sides of the original triangle. The area of the image triangle is 4 times the area of the original triangle.

   f. The corresponding angles are the same size.

d. Choose two new locations for points *P* and *Q* and repeat the process described in Parts a–c.

e. In general, how is the distance between any two points *P* and *Q* related to the distance between the image points *P′* and *Q′*? Explain how this relationship also can be seen in the relationship between corresponding sides of △*FDG* and △*FBH*.

5. Now reassemble your pantograph as illustrated in the diagram below.

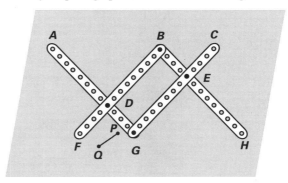

a. Compare △*FDG* and △*FBH*. How are their sides related? Their angles? How are the two triangles related? What is the scale factor?

b. Draw a segment, $\overline{PQ}$, that is 5 cm long, and predict the length of the image $\overline{P′Q′}$. Check your prediction using the pantograph. Explain why the distances *GF* and *HF* are similarly related.

c. How will the pantograph affect distances if it is assembled so that:
- $BF = 3 \cdot DF$?
- $BF = k \cdot DF$?

6. On a large sheet of paper, draw a right triangle with legs 5 and 8 centimeters. Position the triangle so that there is room to create an enlargement of it using your pantograph.

a. Using your pantograph as assembled in Activity 5, find the image of the right triangle. Is it sufficient to find the images of the three vertices and then connect them to get the image triangle? Explain your reasoning.

b. How are the corresponding sides of the original triangle and the image triangle related? How are the two triangles related?

c. What is the area of the original triangle? The image triangle? Describe the relationship between these areas.

d. Reset your pantograph so that it multiplies distances by 2. Use it to find another image of the original right triangle you drew.

e. How are corresponding sides of the original and image triangles related? How are the areas of the two triangles related?

f. Explain how the size of an angle in a figure and the size of the corresponding angle in its pantograph image are related.

7. Consider how you would assemble your pantograph so that it multiplies distances by 4.

    a. Draw a triangle with area 10 cm². Predict the area of the image triangle made with this pantograph.

    b. Compare your predictions with those of another group. Resolve any differences.

Checkpoint

Suppose a pantograph is to be used to make an enlargement of a shape using a scale factor of k.

ⓐ How would you assemble the pantograph?

ⓑ How will the two shapes be related?

ⓒ How will corresponding lengths found in the two shapes be related? How will measures of corresponding angles be related? How will areas of corresponding regions be related?

Be prepared to share your responses and explain your reasoning.

▶ On Your Own

Suppose a pantograph is assembled to enlarge this cartoon by a scale factor of 6. Assume points on the pantograph are labeled as in Activity 1.

    a. What are the lengths of the sides of △*FDG*? Of △*FBH*?

    b. How are the angles of △*FDG* and △*FBH* related?

    c. Compare the areas of △*FDG* and △*FBH*.

    d. What will be true about the shape and size of the pyramid in the enlarged image of the cartoon?

"We had a little problem with the decimal point"

©1995; Reprinted courtesy of Bunny Hoest and Parade Magazine.

7. Some students may have trouble making the specific scale in this activity. They may compare the lengths of the segments *FD* and *DB*, instead of comparing the part FD to the whole FB. This goes back to the idea of comparing the triangles *FDG* and *FBH* in Activity 2. As you circulate among the groups and see how they set up the pantograph, you may want to talk with them about how the scale is calculated. You might ask them again about the sides of the triangles, for example: "So you have this set so that *FD* is *x* in length. Show me where the scale 1:4 appears in your pantograph. Have you thought about making the sides of △*FDG* 4 times smaller? Larger? Where is the new triangle with sides 4 times bigger in your model?"

For some students the confusion is over the basic principle, which is that *the distances from the fixed point are enlarged by a certain factor.* If your students seem to be focused on comparing the distances *FG* and *GH* rather than *FG* and *FH*, they may be thinking in terms of producing a larger figure, without ever realizing that the figure is larger because all the distances from *F* have been multiplied by the scale factor.

Students should be familiar with the idea of a scale factor from previous work, and most will find it fairly straightforward to track comparisons of lengths of corresponding sides. Some students might not, however, make the connection that a scale factor of 3, for example, makes the area increase by a factor of 3^2. Engage them in conversation on this point. "I thought you said the scale factor was 3. Why is the area of the new triangle not 3 times bigger also? Did the base get bigger? Did the height get bigger? Why does it make sense that the area of the image triangle is 9 times bigger?"

To multiply distances by 4, the pantograph should be assembled as shown. The length *FB* should be four times the length *FD*.

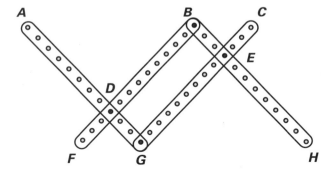

a. The area of the image triangle will be 10 cm^2 · 4^2 or 160 cm^2.

b. Groups should compare work.

SHARE AND SUMMARIZE full-class discussion

Checkpoint

See Teaching Master 135.

a The scale factor of the larger triangle to the smaller triangle must be *k*. Thus the length of a side of the large triangle divided by the length of the corresponding side of the smaller triangle must equal *k*. Using the labels used throughout the investigation, the pantograph should have $FB = k \cdot FD$, $GE = BD$, $DG = BE = FD$, and $BH = BF$.

See additional Teaching Notes on page T453D.

CONSTRUCTING A MATH TOOLKIT: Have students look back to the geometry section of their Math Toolkits for entries on the concept of similarity. Students should refine (if necessary) and extend their notes to include a summary of how a particular pantograph is used to create similar figures.

Modeling: 1, and choice of
3 or 5*

Organizing: 1 or 2, and 3*

Reflecting: 1, and choice of one*

Extending: 5

*When choice is indicated, it is important
to leave the choice to the student.
NOTE: *It is best if Organizing tasks are discussed as a whole class after they have
been assigned as homework.*

Modeling

1. **a.** Quadrilateral *BDEC* is one parallelogram linkage; quadrilateral *ACGF* is another.

   b. The height of the light shade will change, but it will keep its tilt relative to *BDEC*.

   c. Changing *BDEC* moves the light shade back and forth, and up and down, but its angle to the horizontal remains unchanged.

   d. Once the angle of the light to the horizontal is set, it remains unchanged by adjusting the lamp.

2. **a.** Yes, the trays remain horizontal because the linkages are parallelograms (implying that the opposite sides will remain parallel). The trays' positions are determined by the "frame" side of the linkage, which is fixed in a horizontal position.

MORE

Modeling • Organizing • Reflecting • Extending

Modeling

1. A common adjustable desk lamp is shown in the diagram below. The pivots at the labeled points are snug, but they will allow pivoting to adjust the lamp position.

   a. Identify the parallelogram linkages that are used in this lamp.

   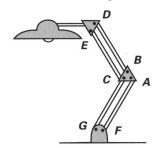

   b. Describe how the position of the light shade changes as you make *AFGC* vertical.

   c. Keeping *AFGC* in one position, how does changing the position of *BDEC* change the position of the light shade?

   d. Make a cardboard model of this lamp linkage. Investigate the angle the light shade makes with the horizontal for various positions of the parallelogram linkages.

2. Trays in sewing boxes, tool boxes, and tackle boxes often use a linkage system to make accessible two or more trays by lifting only the top one. When this is done, the linkage allows them to close and fit nicely inside the box. Examine the two boxes shown below.

   a. For each box, do the trays remain horizontal when opening them? When they are completely opened? Explain your reasoning.

b. Make a sketch of a two-dimensional side view of each box showing how the linkage works.

c. Sketch a side view of a linkage system for a four-tray box.

3. Sketch a pantograph assembled from strips that are 30 cm from the center of one endhole to the center of the other endhole. Additional holes are punched, each 1 cm from its neighbors. Label the pantograph in the same way as the pantograph on page 373.

a. What whole-number scale factors are designed into this pantograph? Describe the lengths of $\overline{FD}$ and $\overline{FB}$ in each case.

b. How would you set up the pantograph to get a scale factor of $\frac{3}{2}$?

c. How would you set up the pantograph to get a scale factor of 2.5?

d. Suppose you have two shapes, and Shape II is the image of Shape I using the pantograph in Part c.

- If a segment in Shape I measures 3 cm, what is the measure of the corresponding segment in Shape II?

- If a segment in Shape II measures 9 cm, what is the measure of the corresponding segment in Shape I?

- If the area of Shape I is 80 cm^2, what is the area of Shape II?

- If the area of Shape II is 100 cm^2, what is the area of Shape I?

4. A common method of designing a pop-up page or greeting card is based on a parallelogram. Tabs attached to facing pages form two consecutive faces of a prism with a parallelogram base. The other two faces are attached to the tabs and serve as props for the picture. As a page or card is turned, the prism unfolds and the picture pops up.

Compass Productions, Long Beach, CA

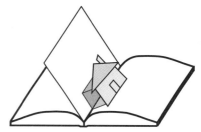

The dark gray shaded area indicates the pop-up tab that pulls the picture off the page as the page is turned.

a. Use this method to construct a paper model of a pop-up picture. Use a piece of paper folded in the middle as consecutive pages of a book. A second piece of paper is needed to carry the picture. Make your model carefully. Test it. Modify it until it works well.

b. Why does the picture in your model lie flat when the book is closed?

c. Why does the picture in your model lie flat when the book is wide open?

d. When will the picture be positioned perpendicular to the right-hand page?

e. When will the picture make a 120° angle with the right-hand page?

f. Could the parallelogram base of the prism be replaced by any other quadrilateral? If so, which ones? If not, explain your reasoning.

2. b.

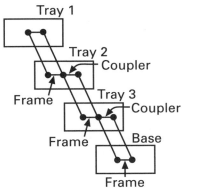

c.

3. a. Scale factors from 2 to 30 are designed into this pantograph. The following table gives possible lengths for *FD* and *FB* to produce each scale factor. If students assume that *FB* must be 30, the only scale factors that they get are 2, 3, 5, 6, 10, 15, and 30. If they make this assumption, you may wish to challenge it by asking if the length *FB* must be 30.

FD	*FB*	Scale Factor	*FD*	*FB*	Scale Factor
15	30	2	1	16	16
10	30	3	1	17	17
7	28	4	1	18	18
6	30	5	1	19	19
5	30	6	1	20	20
4	28	7	1	21	21
3	24	8	1	22	22
3	27	9	1	23	23
3	30	10	1	24	24
2	22	11	1	25	25
2	24	12	1	26	26
2	26	13	1	27	27
2	28	14	1	28	28
2	30	15	1	29	29
			1	30	30

b. One possibility is to let *FD* = 20 and *FB* = 30. Then the scale factor is $\frac{FB}{FD}$ or 1.5.

c. One possibility is to let *FD* = 12 and *FB* = 30. Then the scale factor is $\frac{30}{12}$ or 2.5.

d. ■ The segment in Shape II measures $2.5 \cdot 3$ or 7.5 cm.
■ The segment in Shape I measures $9 \cdot \frac{1}{2.5}$ or 3.6 cm.
■ Area of Shape II = $(2.5)^2 \cdot 80 = 6.25 \cdot 80$ or 500 cm^2
■ Area of Shape I = $100 \cdot \frac{1}{2.5^2} = 16$ cm^2

See additional Teaching Notes on page T453D.

Unit 6

5. **a–b.**

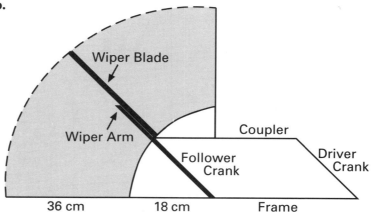

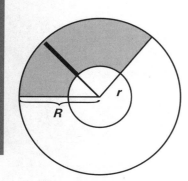

c. Answers will vary depending on the model students develop. Using the sketch above, a student might list the following differences: the wiper blade is an extension of one side of the linkage rather than an attached segment, and the frame is a long side of the quadrilateral rather than a short side. Note that the quadrilateral linkage does not have to be a parallelogram linkage.

d. Answers may vary depending on the student's model. For the sketch above, Area $= [(\pi \cdot R^2) - (\pi \cdot r^2)] \cdot \frac{100}{360}$, where $R = 36 + 18$ cm and $r = 18$ cm. Therefore the area swept clean by the wiper blades is about 2,262 cm^2.

Organizing

1. **a.** $(6, 9)$

b. Points chosen will vary. The coordinates of the pre-image point are multiplied by 3 to get the coordinates of the corresponding image points.

c. The actual points on the scatterplots will vary, but they should be modeled well by a line through the origin with a slope of 3.

d. The algebraic model for the scatterplot is a line with equation $y = 3x$. If the pre-image has an x-coordinate of 18, the image has an x-coordinate of 54.

2. **a.** $(-6, -12)$

b. Points chosen will vary. In each case, the coordinates of the image points are -2 times the coordinates of the pre-image points. (Students may expect to multiply by 3 since the scale factor was set to be 3.)

c. Scatterplots will vary. The points should be on a line that passes through the origin and decreases with a slope of about -2.

d. $y = -2x$

The y-coordinate of the image point will be 48.

e. The scale factor is -2.

5. A windshield wiper on an ordinary automobile oscillates back and forth to remove water.

a. Make a sketch of a linkage that could be used to perform this function.

b. In your sketch, identify the frame, cranks (driver and follower), and coupler.

c. How does this type of mechanism differ from the wiper mechanism for a tractor-trailer, described in Activity 4 of Investigation 1 (page 371)?

d. Suppose a 36-cm wiper blade is attached at its midpoint to the end of a 36-cm wiper arm and oscillates through a 100° angle. Find the area of the windshield swept clean by this wiper.

Organizing

1. Imagine a pantograph (labeled as in Investigation 2) set to have a scale factor of 3. Imagine point *F* fixed at the origin of a coordinate system.

a. If you place *G* over the point (2, 3) on the coordinate system, what are the coordinates of the corresponding point at *H*?

b. Answer the question asked in Part a for several additional points as well. What pattern do you see relating the coordinates of the points at *G* and their images at *H*?

c. Make a scatterplot of (*x-coordinate of pre-image point, x-coordinate of image point*) data.

d. Find an algebraic model that best summarizes the pattern in the scatterplot. Use your model to predict the *x*-coordinate of an image point whose pre-image has an *x*-coordinate of 18.

2. Imagine a pantograph (labeled as in Investigation 2) assembled with a scale factor of 3. Imagine point *G* fixed at the origin of a coordinate system.

a. If you place *F* over the point (3, 6) on the coordinate system, what are the coordinates of the corresponding point at *H*?

b. Consider placing *F* over several additional points in all four quadrants and find their images as you did in Part a. What pattern do you see relating the coordinates of the points and their images?

c. Make a scatterplot of (*y-coordinate of pre-image point, y-coordinate of image point*) data. What kind of relation do you observe?

d. Write an equation describing the relation you observed in Part c. Use your equation to predict the *y*-coordinate of an image point whose pre-image has a *y*-coordinate of –24.

e. What is the scale factor in using a pantograph in this way?

3. In the "Patterns of Location, Shape, and Size" unit, you investigated size transformations in a coordinate plane. Recall that a size transformation with magnitude 3 was described by the following rule:

$$\begin{array}{ccc} \text{pre-image} & & \text{image} \\ (x, y) & \rightarrow & (3x, 3y) \end{array}$$

  a. On a coordinate grid, graph the following points and their images under the size transformation above.

  $A(1, 3)$ $\qquad$ $B(2, -3)$ $\qquad$ $C(-2, -1)$ $\qquad$ $D(-2, 4)$

  b. How is quadrilateral *ABCD* related to its size transformation image?

  c. How could you achieve the same enlargement of quadrilateral *ABCD* using a pantograph?

4. Think about finding the image of a shape using a pantograph with scale factor 2, and then finding the image of that image with a scale factor 3 pantograph.

  a. How are the original shape and the final image related with respect to lengths? With respect to areas?

  b. If you wished to accomplish this enlargement using a single pantograph, what scale factor would be needed? Explain your reasoning.

  c. Suppose you used a combination of pantographs with scale factors *h* and *k*. How should the scale factor of a single pantograph be set to accomplish the same magnification?

Reflecting

1. What did you find most challenging in your work with parallelogram and quadrilateral linkages and pantographs? What suggestions would you offer to others who are just beginning this lesson?

2. Talk with someone who enjoys model railroads, or visit a local hobby shop in preparation for answering the following questions.

  a. How is a parallelogram linkage used on models of old train locomotives?

  b. How is this use different from the other uses of linkages with which you are familiar?

3. a.

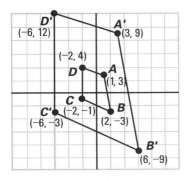

b. The two quadrilaterals are similar. Each segment of the image is three times as long as the corresponding segment of the pre-image.

c. Shapes that are related by a size transformation with magnitude 3 are similar, so a pantograph set for a factor of 3 would produce the same result. Often the size transformation is used to define similar shapes.

4. a. Lengths are multiplied by 6. Areas are multiplied by 6^2 or 36.

b. A scale factor of 6. If the first image is 2 times the original when that image is enlarged three times, the result is $2 \cdot 3$ or 6 times the original. Hence a scale factor of 6 would create the same transformation as the pair of transformations.

c. The pantograph should be set to have a scale factor of $h \cdot k$.

Reflecting

1. Responses will vary. This is an opportunity for students to reflect on their learning and to think about what they could have done to make the lesson go more smoothly.

2. Responses will vary. A general response follows.

a. The bar connects the wheels so that turning one turns the other. The parallelogram linkage is found in the wheel centers and the pivots for the bar.

b. In this example, the pivots travel around a circle. Most of the other examples used an arc.

MORE *continued*

3. You could count (or measure) to determine the length of each segment, and then calculate the scale factor by finding the ratio of *FB* to *FD*.

4. Examples will vary. Some examples include venetian blinds, casement windows (often found in porches), and some heavy machinery.

Extending

1. **a.** Strip *CD* moves up and left when strip *AF* moves down and right, but it always remains parallel to strips *AF* and *BE*. Also, *CD* moves twice as far as *AF*. The scale factor is –2.

   b. Strip *CD* moves in the same direction as strip *BE* but 3 times as far. Again, strips *AF*, *BE*, and *CD* remain parallel.

   c. The points between *B* and *C* remain on a line. Each particular point *P* moves along an arc of a circle centered at *A* with radius *AP*. These points move in the same direction as strip *BE*. This is also true of points between *A* and *B*. The points between *D* and *C* move on a circular arc with center on strip *AF* and radius of length *AC*.

   d. No movement occurs. Strip *BF* triangulates the linkage, and it becomes a rigid shape.

2. **a.** In each case, *F* is fixed, the shape is placed at *G*, and the image is drawn at *H*.

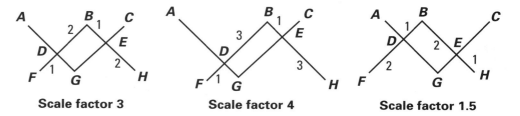

Scale factor 3 Scale factor 4 Scale factor 1.5

Unit 6

3. Explain how you can determine the scale factor of a pantograph using a diagram similar to those found in Investigation 2 (pages 373–375).

4. Find an example of a parallelogram linkage different from the examples in this lesson. Write a paragraph describing its purpose and how it works.

Extending

1. Make the linkage shown below, in which $AF = BE = CD$, $BC = ED = 2AB$, and $AB = FE$. Note that there is only one strip (shown horizontal) connecting points D, E, and F. Similarly, there is only one connecting A, B, and C.

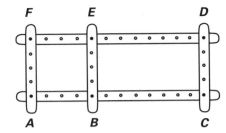

a. Hold strip EB fixed and move strip AF. Describe the motion of strip CD.

b. Hold strip AF fixed and move strip BE. Describe how strip CD moves compared to strip BE.

c. When strip AF is fixed and strip BE moves, what can you say about the movement of points on the linkage that lie between points B and C? Between points A and B? Between points D and C?

d. Fix a strip between points F and B and move strip CD. What happens? Explain why this occurs.

2. Expandable safety gates, such as the one shown in the diagram below, are based on parallelogram linkages. Pivots are placed at each intersection point so that the gate will close and open.

a. Place a sheet of paper over the diagram and then trace out linkages that would have scale factors of 3, 4, and 1.5 if they were pantographs.

b. The gate network can be used to design linkages like a pantograph that will enlarge (or reduce) shapes. For example, the two-rhombus linkage below, with point *F* fixed, enlarges a shape at *G* to a shape at *H*, with scale factor 3. Model this linkage to check that it enlarges with scale factor 3.

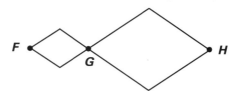

c. Draw two additional linkages based on the safety gate that have a scale factor of 3. How must the three points *F*, *G*, and *H* be related in each case?

3. Connect three strips *DA*, *AB*, and *BC* (with *DA* = *BC*) with paper fasteners at *A* and *B*. Fasten ends *C* and *D* to a card so that *DC* = *AB*. Hold the card perpendicular to the floor and adjust the fasteners to allow strip *AB* to swing easily back and forth.

a. Hold $\overline{CD}$ horizontal and swing strip *AB* back and forth. Does strip *AB* remain horizontal as it swings? Why or why not?

b. What path does a point on strip *AD* or strip *BC* follow as strip *AB* swings back and forth?

c. Investigate the paths of points *A*, *B*, and additional points on strip *AB* as the strip swings back and forth. (Marking positions on paper will help.)

d. Explain how this linkage could be used to design a child's toy.

4. The linkage shown below is made up of three rhombuses. The longer bars such as *PQ* are three times the lengths of the shorter bars such as *XP*.

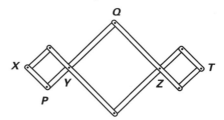

a. Suppose you hold the linkage fixed at *X* and copy a shape at *Y* with pencils inserted at both *Z* and *T*. What are the scale factors?

b. Suppose you fix *X* and copy a shape at *Z* with pencils at both *Y* and *T*. What are the scale factors?

c. How can the linkage be used to produce similar shapes with each scale factor below?

  ■ $\dfrac{1}{4}$ ■ $\dfrac{3}{4}$ ■ $\dfrac{3}{2}$ ■ $\dfrac{2}{3}$

d. Make a model of the linkage to check your conclusions in Parts a–c.

e. Design three different linkages that are capable of making a copy similar to the original with scale factor 4.

2. b. Students should make a model.

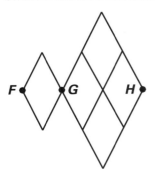

c. Points *F, G,* and *H* must be on a line and $\frac{FH}{FG} = 3$. Two possible examples follow:

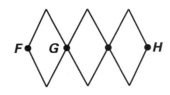

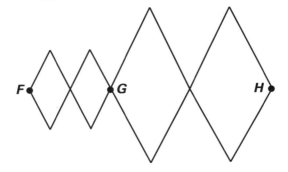

3. a. Yes, it remains parallel to segment *CD*, and segment *CD* is horizontal.

b. The point follows an arc of a circle centered at point *D* or *C*.

c. *A, B,* and all other points on *AB* move in circular arcs centered at a point on strip *DC* and with radius *CB*.

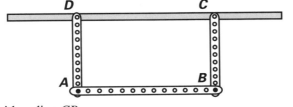

d. Responses will vary. One answer is that it could be used to design a swing that would keep the rider level.

4. a. The size of the image at *Z* will be 3 times the size of the shape at *Y*. The size of the image at *T* will be 4 times the size of the shape at *Y*.

b. The size of the image at *Y* will be $\frac{1}{3}$ the size of the shape at *Z*. The size of the image at *T* will be $\frac{4}{3}$ the size of the shape at *Z*.

c. ■ Shape at *T*, copy at *Y* with *X* fixed
   ■ Shape at *T*, copy at *Z* with *X* fixed
   ■ Shape at *Z*, copy at *T* with *Y* fixed
   ■ Shape at *T*, copy at *Z* with *Y* fixed

d. See student models and drawings.

See additional Teaching Notes on page T453E.

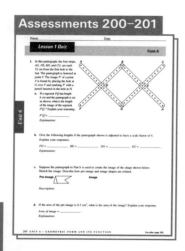
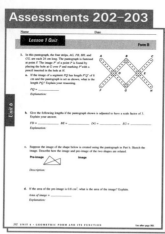
MORE *continued*

5. **a.** They are similar.

    b. The scale factor is $\frac{1}{2}$.

    c. First set up the pantograph so that it normally multiplies by three. One possibility is to let $FB = 24$ and $FD = 8$. To change to a scale factor of $\frac{1}{3}$, place the shape at H. Then the image will be at G when the fixed point is F.

    d. Students might enjoy reducing their school logo or other simple drawing, but any geometric figure will work to let them verify that pantographs also can be used to reduce.

    e. Etching by hand cannot be done accurately when the lettering is very small.

    f. The company might computerize the movement for standard letter etching. They might be sure the fittings for the pantographs are tight.

See Assessment Resources, pages 200–203.

5. Assemble a pantograph with scale factor 2, labeled as in Investigation 2.

a. If you fasten the pantograph at vertex F, trace a shape using vertex H, and draw the image with a pencil inserted through the hole at G, how are the two shapes related?

b. What is the scale factor for this arrangement?

c. Set up your pantograph so that a reduction by a scale factor of $\frac{1}{3}$ can be accomplished. What point is fixed? Where do you place the shape to be copied?

d. How can you check that your model in Part c is properly assembled?

e. Companies that make very small letter etchings use reducing pantographs. In terms of our pantograph labeling, they have model letters that are traced at H while the etched letters are produced at G. What are some reasons such a procedure might be used rather than etching the small letters directly?

f. How might the etching company control the variation in their etchings?

Unit 6

Lesson 2

Triangles and Trigonometric Ratios

Quadrilaterals, especially parallelograms, have many uses because they can pivot about their vertices to change shape without changing the length of any sides. Triangular shapes, whether their vertices can pivot or not, are rigid once the lengths of the sides are specified.

The rigidity of triangles is often used to make more complex structures rigid. In contrast, the truck crane shown below operates by adjusting the length of a side of a triangular structure. As the hydraulic cylinder lengthens, the boom rises.

Think About This Situation

Examine the design of the truck crane shown.

a About what point does the boom pivot?

b Why is the boom structure rigid?

c Under what conditions could the boom be raised so that it is perpendicular to the truck bed? What kind of triangle would be formed?

d Describe other situations in which adjusting the length of one side of a triangular shape serves a useful function.

Lesson 2 Triangles and Trigonometric Ratios

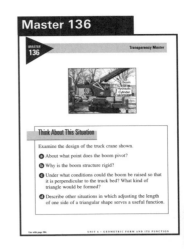

LESSON OVERVIEW This lesson focuses on triangles and the invariances and changes that occur when one side changes in length or when one triangle is similar to another. Students will have an opportunity to review and extend their understandings of similar shapes. The initial investigation explores triangles with a variable side. The second investigation looks at conditions that guarantee two triangles are similar and then introduces sine, cosine, and tangent functions in right triangles. In the third investigation, students will use the triangular ratios to make indirect measurements in several different contexts.

Students will need to know how to use protractors to measure the angles of a triangle (how to orient the protractor and the triangle to measure each angle) and to create an angle of given measure at the endpoint of a line segment.

Lesson Objectives

- To recognize the use of triangles with a variable-length side in manufactured goods, and to analyze effects of the variability on angles and heights in those goods
- To determine the sine, cosine, and tangent of an angle in a right triangle
- To solve indirect measurement problems

LAUNCH full-class discussion

As a launch to Lesson 2, students should examine the truck crane and try to explain how it might work. The questions in the "Think About This Situation" will help generate more discussion and other ideas. You also might ask students to contrast the rigidity of triangular shapes with the variability of linkages that have four sides. Students initially may find it difficult to identify real-world applications of triangles for themselves, since most students do not recognize such uses until they begin to look for them. The discussion should be brief. The idea is to help students begin to focus on the triangle and the mathematics that surround it.

Think About This Situation

See Teaching Master 136.

a The boom pivots about the axle on its leftmost endpoint.

b The boom will be rigid because it is a side of a triangle formed by the elevating cylinder and a part of the truck.

c The boom could be raised so that it was vertical if the elevating cylinder was long enough and could pivot to the left. A right triangle would be formed.

d Responses will vary. Some examples are a lawn chair, a nutcracker, and a car jack.

Unit 6

INVESTIGATION ▶ 1 Triangles with a Variable-Length Side

In this investigation, students explore patterns observed in the measures of angles and altitudes of a triangle with a variable-length side. Since the three side lengths of a triangle uniquely determine its characteristics, changing the length of one side of a triangle changes nearly all its aspects. Thus the measures of all angles change as does the altitude to the changing side (and all other altitudes). It is these two changing aspects that make this triangular structure useful. As the investigation proceeds, students will make models of objects and use those models to examine the changes that occur.

This is a hands-on investigation. Students will need to have sufficient materials to construct each of four models and the tools needed to measure lengths and angles on those models. You might display an actual car jack for Activity 3 or 4. This investigation is fun. Students are required to use construction and measurement skills developed in the previous investigation in addition to the skills needed to make scatterplots and look for rate-of-change patterns in those plots.

It helps to start this investigation with a full-class discussion of the construction techniques that helped students build models that could be measured accurately from the previous lesson. Accurate angle and altitude measurements are critical to the success of this investigation, and therefore it will be important to lay preliminary ground work that will maximize the uniformity and stability of the student models. Because this investigation requires many angle measurements, students may find it helpful to draw a line down the center of each strip that will aid in consistent angle measurement. Some students may want to trace their triangles in order to measure the angles and distances.

Before students begin the actual construction of the model in Activity 1, you might ask them how the model relates to the truck crane. They should see that this model could be used to simulate the action of the truck crane, and they should be able to match corresponding parts. You also might ask them what would be some useful information about the truck crane that they could find from this model. Possible answers are how the angle sizes change as the side *AC* is altered; the maximum height of the top of the crane, that is, the altitude from *B*; the path that *B* moves through; the rate at which *B* rises for each unit change in *AC*; and the particular length for side *AC* (or particular angle size for the angle at *C*) needed to create a particular height for *B*. When students realize the complexity of the interrelationships and the usefulness of the model, they can proceed to the actual model making.

1. Students should be prepared to share their results and methods with the entire class. You may wish to have students demonstrate their models. Students should also compare the results of angle and altitude measurements and speculate on the causes of any variations in the results.

   a. The maximum length needed for strip *AD* from first hole to last hole is
      10 + 16 or 26 cm.

   b. When the length *AC* is changed, the three angles and the altitude from *B* change in measure.

See additional Teaching Notes on page T453E.

INVESTIGATION 1 Triangles with a Variable-Length Side

In the first investigation of this lesson, you will explore uses of adjustable triangular shapes, with a side that can vary in length.

1. Make a model of a triangle with a variable-length side as illustrated below. Make strip *AB* 10 cm long and strip *BC* 16 cm long from endhole to endhole.

   a. What is the maximum length needed for strip *AD*? Make strip *AD* with holes 2 cm apart (or draw a segment, $\overline{AD}$, on your paper and mark points 2 cm apart).

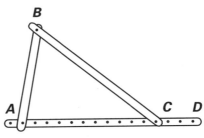

   b. Use strip *AD* to form △*ABC* with a variable side *AC*. When you change the length *AC*, what else changes?

   c. Adjust the length of $\overline{AC}$ in equal step sizes. At each step, use a ruler and protractor to obtain and record the measurements indicated in the table below. Share the workload among members of your group.

Length *AC*	Measure of ∠*A*	Measure of ∠*B*	Measure of ∠*C*	Perpendicular Distance From Point *B* to $\overline{AD}$
___	___	___	___	___
___	___	___	___	___

   d. Using the lengths of $\overline{AC}$ on the horizontal axis, make individual scatterplots of the following data pairs. Describe any patterns you see.

   ■ *(length AC, measure of ∠A)*

   ■ *(length AC, measure of ∠B)*

   ■ *(length AC, measure of ∠C)*

   ■ *(length AC, perpendicular distance from point B to $\overline{AD}$)*

   e. Describe how each of the other variables changes as length *AC* changes in equal amounts.

   f. Compare the scatterplot of *(length AC, measure of ∠A)* with that of *(length AC, measure of ∠B)*.

   g. Compare the scatterplot of *(length AC, measure of ∠C)* with that of *(length AC, perpendicular distance from point B to $\overline{AD}$)*.

As one side of a triangle changes, the height and all the angles of the triangle change. These corresponding changes are used in the world around you to serve various functions. Consider first how changing the length of a side *AC* changes the angles at *A* and at *B*.

2. Side views of two reclining lawn chairs are shown below.

   a. Examine the first design at the right.

   ▪ How many seating positions does this chair have?

   ▪ Identify the three vertices of a variable-sided triangle.

   ▪ Explain how this chair works in terms of a variable-sided triangle.

   b. Here is another way to design a reclining chair. The arms can hook the legs at point *C*. The front leg is attached to the seat at *F*; the back leg hits a rod at the back of the seat (*E*), which keeps that leg from collapsing.

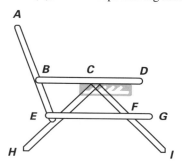

   ▪ Identify the three vertices of a variable-sided triangle.

   ▪ How many positions does this chair have?

   c. Make a sketch or a two-dimensional side-view model of a variable-sided triangle like the one used in the chair in Part b. In your model or with your sketch, find the maximum reclining angle. Find the smallest reclining angle.

In Activity 2, the angle of recline of the chairs varied as the length of a variable side of a triangle changed. In other applications of a triangle *ABC* with variable side *AC*, the height of point *B* above side *AC* is important, rather than the size of an angle.

It is best if the full class discusses the results and processes in Activity 1. Following this discussion, students should work in small groups to complete Activities 2–4 and the Checkpoint. They should especially note unexpected discoveries they observe while working on each model. As always, they should be prepared to share their results with the entire class.

2. In this activity, the way an angle changes is the most important characteristic—you can recline by making an angle larger. Students will not need to spend much time on this activity. The central idea here is simply that variable-sided triangles are used in a number of very common applications.

   a. ■ There are four seating positions for this chair.
      ■ The back brace is one side of the triangle. The back is another side, and the back leg with notches is the variable side.
      ■ As the back brace is moved higher up the leg of the chair (which makes one side of the triangle shorter) the chair back makes a greater angle with the horizontal. This makes you sit up straighter.

   b. ■ The vertices are the point E where the seat and back attach; the point B where the arm and back attach; and the adjustable point C along the arm where the legs attach.
      ■ There are four seating positions, or six positions if you include the fold-up position and the nearly flat position.

   c. Responses will depend on student models. Students should measure $\angle BEG$ from their model when the chair is in the two positions.

In Activities 3 and 4, the perpendicular distances to the horizontal base are the important and useful characteristic. However, the jacks in both activities also produce straight-line motion, and so they provide an opportunity to examine rates of change.

3. This type of automobile jack is common today. It may be quicker and more effective to use the real thing in class rather than having students build a model.

    a. Students build the model.

    b. The linkage is rigid because rod *AC* divides rhombus *ABCD* into two triangles.

    c. △*ABC* has variable side *AC*; △*ACD* also has variable side *AC*.

    d. The jack could be stored with *B* and *D* close to each other. In this case, side *AC* would need to be somewhat longer than the sum of the lengths of sides *AD* and *DC* if it is to remain threaded when stored.

    e. Point *B* moves straight upward. It follows a line that is perpendicular to side *AC*.

    f. When the jack is fully extended, the height of *B* is approximately equal to the sum of the lengths of sides *AB* and *AD*. In reality, the jack loses stability when *A* and *C* get close, so the usable height will be somewhat less than this sum.

4. Some groups may prefer to make successive drawings with a compass and straightedge as a replacement for the cardboard or strip model. This is an alternative approach that will work just as well. If students create an actual model, they will find it very helpful to tape the model to a piece of graph paper, thus stabilizing the model so that the movement of the arm *DC* is not confused with inadvertent movement of the model during the experiment. It also will help to align the strip *AE* with a line on the graph paper.

    a. Students should build and experiment with the model.

    b. See the diagram below. Point *D* follows a straight line perpendicular to segment *AC* from point *A*. A jack must lift a car straight upward or the car might slip off the jack.

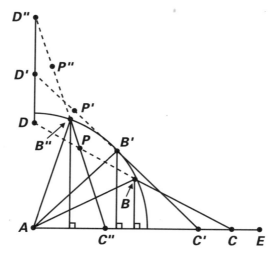

3. An automobile jack that comes with some makes of automobiles is shown below. Points *A* and *C* are connected by a long threaded rod.

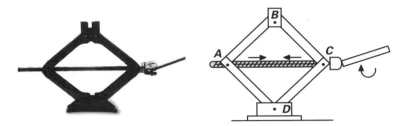

   a. Model this jack using plastic strips. You can simulate the threaded rod by cutting a slit in a strip of cardboard and using that strip for the rod *AC*. Washers at *A* and *C* may make the model work more smoothly.

   b. Examine your model. Is this linkage rigid? Explain why or why not.

   c. Identify the triangles that have a side that may be adjusted in length.

   d. How could this linkage be stored in a car? About how long would the threaded rod need to be?

   e. As the threaded rod connecting points *A* and *C* is turned at a constant speed, *A* and *C* approach each other at a constant rate. What path does point *B* follow if the base of the jack *D* is in a fixed position?

   f. Approximately how high is point *B* when the model jack is fully extended?

4. Another kind of automobile jack, shown in the following diagram, is used on racetracks and in garages that do quick tire changes. The jack has wheels to move it around. Bar *BD* has one end that can be moved toward and away from point *A* by turning a threaded rod. In the diagram, the bar ends at point *C*, but it can be moved as far as point *E*.

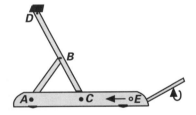

   a. Make a model of this jack using plastic strips or stiff cardboard. The length of line segment *AE* should be 20 cm. The lengths *AB*, *BC*, and *BD* should be 10 cm each. Fix point *A* and let point *C* slide along a slot *AE*. Experiment with your model to see how it works.

   b. As point *C* moves toward point *A*, what path does point *D* follow? Why is your observation important to the safe use of the automobile jack?

c. As point C moves toward point A, what path does point B follow?

   d. Choose a point between points D and B and trace its path as point C moves toward point A.

   e. Collect data relating the distance AC to the distance AD for different positions of point C. Describe the rate of change in AD as AC decreases in unit increments.

5. Now adjust your model from Activity 4 so that the measure of $\angle C$ is 45°.

   a. Find the height of point D.

   b. What is the length of base AC?

   c. What kind of triangle is $\triangle DAC$?

Checkpoint

Triangular shapes often are useful because they are rigid. But designing triangular shapes to permit one side to vary in length makes them even more useful.

a Describe the characteristics of a variable-sided triangle that make it useful in the design of everyday objects.

b Suppose $\triangle ABC$ has an adjustable side AC. How would the measure of $\angle C$ and the height of $\triangle ABC$ (from vertex B to side AC) be affected as the adjustable side changes in length?

Be prepared to share your conclusions and reasoning with the class.

On Your Own

Architects sometimes use large tables that can be tilted forward, as shown in the photo at the right. How could you use a variable-sided triangle to make such a table that has three tilt positions? In your design, what is the size of the angle formed by the stand and the variable side when the table top is horizontal? When the top is at a 45° angle to the horizontal?

   c.   Point *B* moves along a circular arc centered at point *A*.

   d.   A point *P* between points *D* and *B* moves on a curved path toward line *AD*. (It theoretically reaches the line *AD* when *C* reaches *A*.)

   e.   The resulting data is in the table at the right.

       As *AC* decreases, the length *AD* increases very quickly at first, then its rate of increase decreases as point *C* gets closer to point *A*.

5. Approximate measurements follow.

   a.   Point *D* is about 14 cm above point *A*.

   b.   *AC* is about 14 cm also.

   c.   *DAC* is an isosceles right triangle.

AC (cm)	*AD* (cm)	*AC* (cm)	*AD* (cm)
20	0	10	17.3
19	6.2	9	17.9
18	8.7	8	18.3
17	10.5	7	18.7
16	12.0	6	19.1
15	13.2	5	19.4
14	14.3	4	19.6
13	15.2	3	19.8
12	16.0	2	19.9
11	16.7	1	20.0

Unit 6

SHARE AND SUMMARIZE   full-class discussion

Before proceeding to the Checkpoint, review Investigation 1 briefly by having each group explain what they discovered about a particular model. Groups can recount selected pieces of each activity, or comment on their model. Ask the whole class to comment on similarities and differences that they see in the functions of the various devices. (In all cases, altering one side of a triangle alters the height of some significant part of the model. In all cases except one, the variable side was horizontal. In some cases, the highest point was elevated vertically, and in other cases, the highest point followed a curved path as it was raised.)

Checkpoint

See Teaching Master 137.

  ⓐ Triangles are rigid shapes, the height of the triangle will change as the variable side is adjusted, and the angles all change as the variable side is adjusted.

  ⓑ Assuming the triangle starts with maximum length for *AC*, as *AC* decreases, both ∠*C* and the height initially will increase rapidly. As the angle at *A* nears 90°, the rate of change of ∠*C* and the height will slow. If angle *A* can become obtuse, both the measure of ∠*C* and the height will begin to decrease. The rate of decrease will be slow at first, but it will increase as side *AC* reaches its minimum.

JOURNAL ENTRY: Having considered four applications of an adjustable triangle, think of other applications of triangle mechanics in the world around you and then sketch and record them in your journal.

APPLY   individual task

▶On Your Own

There are a variety of ways to do this. One would be to attach a prop about midway between the front and back on each side edge and make notches in the bottom near the back that would hold the top in position. Students' angle measures will depend on their designs.

Modeling: Choose one*
Organizing: 2 and 4
Reflecting: Choose one*
Extending: 1 or 3*

*When choice is indicated, it is important to leave the choice to the student.
NOTE: It is best if Organizing tasks are discussed as a whole class after they have been assigned as homework.

Angle	Notch Distance from Hinged Edge
10°	69 cm or 10 cm
20°	64 cm or 11 cm
30°	57 cm or 12 cm
40°	46 cm or 15 cm

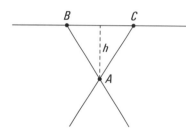

Modeling

1. **Students will need to construct a model of the cold frame to answer all of the questions. They should use a trial-and-error method, measuring the various angles and lengths, to complete this task. Many different answers are possible, but students should be encouraged to use a triangle with a variable-length side in their solutions.**

   a. There are many designs that will work. One would be to attach a prop on the lid, about 40 cm from the 120-cm edge, and to construct a prop and notches in the base of the cold frame that will give the angles desired. Students will need to build a working model or make a scale drawing.

   b. Responses will vary, depending on the students' models. If the prop is attached on the lid 40 cm from the hinged edge and the prop is 30 cm long, the notch distances from the hinged edge are shown in the table. These numbers may be obtained from measuring. Some students will notice two locations to put the notches in the frame.

   c. For the model in Part b, the new notch would be either 61 cm or about 11.5 cm from the hinged edge.

   d. The height of the edge opposite the hinge is $80 \sin 20°$ or about 27 cm.

2. a. Students should build the model.

   b. For this example, assume that the legs are attached to each other with hinges at their midpoints (other assumptions are possible). Then we will attach one leg (the rear one, for example) to the board with hinges. The front leg will fit in notches so that the working heights are attained.

   c. A variable-sided triangle is formed by the ironing board and the top half of the two legs.

   d. A working height of 90 cm means that there is a distance of 45 cm from the floor to the midpoint joint and another 45 cm from there to the ironing board. The latter distance is the measure of the altitude of the variable-sided triangle. This altitude is one leg of a right triangle, and the other leg is along the board with length x. (The distance between the hinge and the place where the board leg must be attached is $2x$.) The hypotenuse of the right triangle is 55 cm, half the length of the board legs. These numbers may be obtained by measurement or by use of the Pythagorean Theorem. Students must measure to find the angle measurements.

Working Height (cm)	Lengths *AB* and *AC* (cm)	Height, *h* (cm)	Distance *BC* (cm)	∠*A*	∠*B* and ∠*C*
90	55	45	63.2	70°	55°
85	55	42.5	69.8	79°	50.5°
80	55	40	75.5	87°	46.5°
75	55	37.5	80.5	94°	43°
70	55	35	84.9	101°	39.5°

MORE

Modeling • Organizing • Reflecting • Extending

Modeling

1. A cold frame is a box used to grow young plants in the spring. Traditionally, the top of the box is made of glass to let in light. The top can be propped open so the plants become accustomed to actual weather conditions before they are transplanted outside the box. One cold frame has a top measuring 120 cm by 80 cm, hinged along the 120-cm edge. It can be opened to a 10°, 20°, 30°, or 40° angle.

   a. Design a system that will accomplish the desired openings using only one bar to prop open the top.

   b. Describe the measurements needed in your propping system.

   c. If you wanted to add to your design a 25° opening, where would the prop be placed?

   d. How high above the horizontal frame is the front of the lid when the angle is 20°?

2. Most ironing boards can be adjusted to different heights. One ironing board, designed similar to the one shown here, has legs that are each 110 cm. Possible working heights are 90 cm, 85 cm, 80 cm, 75 cm, and 70 cm.

   a. Make a scale model of the board described above.

   b. Describe how the legs should be attached to the board.

   c. How is a variable-sided triangle used in the design?

   d. For each working height, give the side and angle measurements of the adjustable triangles.

3. A carnival ride consists of six small airplanes attached to a vertical pole. (See the diagram below.) As the pole rotates, the planes fly around the pole. A rider can control the height of the plane by changing the length of the hydraulic cylinder attached at point C. In a typical design, $BD = 4$ m, $BA = 1.5$ m, $BC = 1.5$ m, $BE = 1.5$ m, and AC varies between 1.5 and 2.2 m.

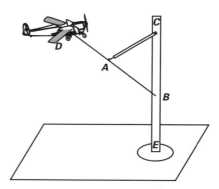

   a. Make a model of this carnival ride.

   b. What is the smallest measure of $\angle ABC$? How far above the ground is the plane for that smallest angle?

   c. If the hydraulic cylinder is fully extended, what is the measure of $\angle ABC$?

   d. What variation does the height of the airplane have as $\angle ABC$ changes from its minimum to its maximum size?

   e. How should the hydraulic cylinder be adjusted so that the plane will fly 2.5 meters above the ground?

Organizing

1. If necessary, re-enter the (*length AC, measure of* $\angle A$) and (*length AC, measure of* $\angle B$) data you collected for Activity 1 of Investigation 1 (page 385) into the data lists of your graphing calculator or computer software.

   a. Compare the scatterplots of (*length AC, measure of* $\angle A$) and (*length AC, measure of* $\angle B$).

   b. For each plot, investigate modeling the pattern in the data with different types of functions: linear, exponential, and power. Are any of these models a good fit for the data? Explain the reasons for your conclusions.

3. **a.** Students should build the model.

   b. Since ∠*ABC* is smallest when *AC* is a minimum, the minimum measure of ∠*ABC* is 60° when all sides of △*ABC* are 1.5 m. At this point, the plane is 3.5 meters above the ground.

   c. The measure of △*ABC* is about 94°.

   d. It can go as high as about 0.5 meter above the top attachment on the pole, and it can go to about 0.3 meter below point *B*. So the height of the plane ranges from 1.2 meters to 3.5 meters above the ground.

   e. The cylinder would need to be expanded to about 1.8 meters to fly the plane 2.5 meters above the ground.

Organizing

1. **a.** The graphs appear to be reflections about a vertical line through *AC* ≈ 18.

   b. Even though a linear regression would give a high correlation value, the plots do *not* appear to be linear. The pattern in the data points below and above the regression line indicate that a linear model is not a good choice. The quadratic regression also gives an equation that shows a pattern in the data points above and below the quadratic model. Both the power regression model and the exponential regression model (when the data point (28, 0) is removed) indicate similar tendencies. The curved nature of the graphs may lead some students to try a cubic regression, which produces a fairly good fit. The cubic regression rounded to hundredths *(for length AC, measure of ∠A)* is $y = -0.05x^3 + 2.92x^2 - 58.98x + 485.72$.

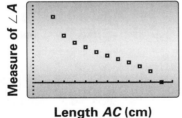

Measure of ∠*A* / Length *AC* (cm)

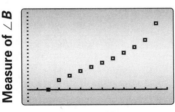

Measure of ∠*B* / Length *AC* (cm)

Unit 6

NOTE: The word "altitude" here refers to the distance from *B* to *AD*.

1. c. Students may try to model the (*measure of ∠A, measure of ∠B*) data by a line. However, as you can see in the second graph below, these data do have a slight curvature.

A visual inspection of the scatterplot confirmed by the correlation coefficient indicates that the (*measure of ∠C, altitude*) data can be modeled by a line. The least squares linear regression equation is $y = 0.294x + 0.089$. The slope of 0.294 gives the altitude change in centimeters for each increase of 1° in measure of ∠C. The *y*-intercept should represent the altitude when m∠C is 0°. The altitude is approximately zero, indicating that no such triangle could exist.

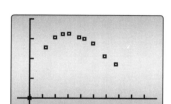

(*measure of ∠A, measure of ∠B*)

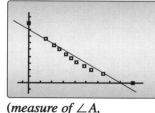

(*measure of ∠A, measure of ∠B*) with linear regression line

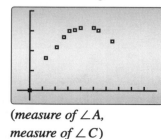

(*measure of ∠A, measure of ∠C*)

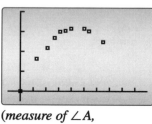

(*measure of ∠A, altitude*)

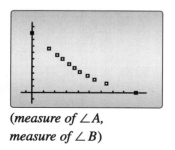

(*measure of ∠B, measure of ∠C*)

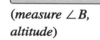

(*measure ∠B, altitude*)

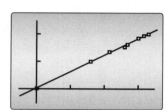

(*measure of ∠C, altitude*)

(*measure of ∠C, altitude*) with linear regression line

d. Except for the two mentioned in Part c, the data pairs all show a pattern of increasing and then decreasing. The (*measure of ∠B, measure of ∠C*) data and (measure of ∠B, altitude) data increase quickly, then decrease slowly. The (*measure of ∠A, measure of ∠C*) data and (*measure of ∠A, altitude*) data are more symmetrical. The (*measure of ∠A, measure of ∠B*) data are always decreasing, but not at a constant rate.

2. a. Tell students that they will need 7 or 8 data points to analyze the (*x, y*) relationship correctly. Actual measurements will vary based on the size of the rhombus and the position of the linkage.

b. The data should show that as *x* increases, *y* decreases. The scatterplot appears to be a quarter circle.

c. ■ The points do not show constant change, so the pattern of change is not linear.
■ The *y* values do not appear to be decreasing by a constant multiple, so the change is not exponential.
■ No, the pattern of change does not match that of a power function or that of a quadratic function. However, some students may see part of a parabola (quadratic). Remind students that a power rule is only of the form $y = ax^n$.

See additional Teaching Notes on page T453G.

Unit 6

c. Examine the scatterplots of other pairs of the measures you collected for Activity 1 of Investigation 1. Which of these plots are modeled well by a line? Find an equation of each such line and explain what the slope and *y*-intercept of the model mean.

d. What can you say about the other data patterns in Part c?

2. Make a linkage in the shape of a rhombus.

a. Experiment by changing the rhombus linkage from short (vertically) to tall. Using small changes, collect data on the lengths *x* and *y* of the diagonals.

b. Make a scatterplot of the (*x*, *y*) data. Describe any patterns you see.

c. Analyze the pattern of change.

■ Does the pattern of change appear to be linear? Explain.

■ Does the pattern of change appear to be exponential? Explain.

■ Does the pattern of change appear to be that of a power or a quadratic rule? Explain.

3. Place the model of the jack you constructed for Activity 4 of Investigation 1 (page 387) on a coordinate system. Fix point *A* at the origin and position side *AE* along the positive *x*-axis. Collect data on the coordinates of points *C* and *B* as point *C* moves away from point *A* along the *x*-axis.

a. As point *C* moves, what is the relationship between the *x*-coordinate of point *C* and the *x*-coordinate of point *B*?

b. What is the relationship between the *y*-coordinate of point *D* and the *y*-coordinate of point *B*, for each position of point *C*? Explain your reasoning.

c. Make a scatterplot of the (*x-coordinate of C*, *y-coordinate of B*) data. What pattern do you see? Does a linear, exponential, or power model seem to fit these data?

d. Make a scatterplot of the (*x-coordinate of B*, *y-coordinate of B*) data. What pattern do you see? Does a linear, exponential, or power model seem to fit these data?

4. Ramps often provide alternate routes for people who are not able to use stairs. The design of a ramp is not based solely on the smoothness of its surface.

a. The maximum *gradient* of ramps for handicap access is 8.33%. (That is, the slope is 0.0833 or $\frac{5}{60}$.) The maximum ground distance allowed for a single ramp at the maximum gradient is 30 feet. Design two different accesses to a door which has its sill 3.5 feet from the ground surface.

b. The *mechanical advantage* of a single ramp is the ratio $\frac{\text{effort distance}}{\text{resistance distance}}$, that is, $\frac{\text{height of ramp}}{\text{length of ramp}}$. Which single ramp in your response to Part a has the best (lowest) mechanical advantage?

c. What is the minimum length ramp that can be used in this situation? What is the mechanical advantage of that ramp?

Reflecting

1. People who travel often need an easy way to move their luggage. The cart below will fold up to a small size for storage.

BEST CARRY-ON LUGGAGE CART

This cart was ranked best against other models tested by a panel of our customers for its superior stability, design features and overall performance. Exceptionally versatile, its four-wheeled design means that you can push or pull up to 225 pounds of luggage with remarkable stability and without putting any weight-strain on your arms.

Source: Hammacher Schlemmer Catalog, Spring 1994.

a. Explain how a triangle with a variable-length side is used in this cart's design.

b. Design your own carry-on luggage cart that does not make use of a triangle with a variable-length side. Illustrate your design with a sketch and compare its functionality to the cart in the photo.

2. Choose one of the following items and explain how it makes use of a triangle with a side of adjustable length.

a. Umbrella   **b.** Music stand

c. Window-opening apparatus   **d.** Slide projector (adjustable)

e. Backhoe   **f.** Metal folding chair

g. Pruning shears

4. a. The gradient for a ramp of maximum ground length (30 feet) is $\frac{3.5}{30}$ or approximately 12%, so the gradient is too great for a single ramp. Using the maximum gradient of 8.33% or $\frac{5}{60}$, and a ramp 30 feet long, we can get the maximum rise x. $\frac{x}{30} = \frac{5}{60}$ so, $x = 2.5$ feet. A two-part ramp could be used to provide access to the door 3.5 feet off the ground. Two possible configurations follow.

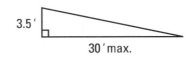

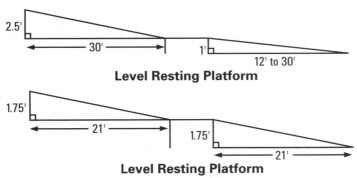

Level Resting Platform

Level Resting Platform

b. Students may need to be reminded that the length of the ramp (distance the person travels) is longer than the ground length used in Part a. They must use the Pythagorean Theorem to calculate that distance. The mechanical advantage of the 30-foot ramp is $\frac{2.5}{\sqrt{2.5^2 + 30^2}}$ or approximately 8.3%. The ramp that accomplishes the one-foot change could have length from 12 feet to 30 feet. At 12 feet, the mechanical advantage is $\frac{1}{\sqrt{1 + 12^2}}$ or approximately 8.3%; for 30 feet, it is $\frac{1}{\sqrt{1 + 30^2}}$ or approximately 3.3%. Each part of the second design has mechanical advantage $\frac{1.75}{\sqrt{1.75^2 + 21^2}}$ or approximately 8.3%. The two choices have equal mechanical advantage if the 12-foot length is used for the first design.

c. The minimum length of the two parts of the ramp (not including the flat part) for either design is 42 feet. This corresponds to a mechanical advantage of 8.3%.

Reflecting

1. a. The brace attaching the small wheels to the frame folds out to make a triangular support.

b. Student designs will vary. A cart could simply have two wheels and be balanced by tipping it toward the person pulling it.

2. a–g. Responses will vary.

MORE *continued*

3. Responses may vary. The triangular shapes are probably more useful since they allow support while the shape changes. Much heavy machinery and everyday objects make use of the triangle with variable side.

4. Much of the shape of a mechanical part depends on what purpose the part will serve. Engineers cannot consider only how something will look. They must also consider its function.

Extending

1. **Teaching Master 138 may help students organize their work for Part b of this task.**

    a. The cable running from C to A is the variable side of $\triangle ABC$.

    b. Students do not have trigonometric ratios and laws at this point. They will need to build a model and make measurements.

    When AB is in the horizontal position, the length of AC is $\sqrt{450}$ or approximately 21.2 meters. It takes 84.8 seconds, 63.6 seconds, and 42.4 seconds for AB to reach the vertical position at the rates of $\frac{1}{4}$ meter per second, $\frac{1}{3}$ meter per second, and $\frac{1}{2}$ meter per second respectively. Graphs of the (*time, angle of elevation*) data for each rate are shown on the left. Student graphs should be linear as shown below.

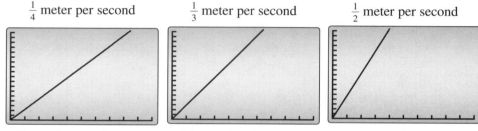

$\frac{1}{4}$ meter per second $\frac{1}{3}$ meter per second $\frac{1}{2}$ meter per second

For each rate, the measure of the angle of elevation increases at an approximately constant rate. The rate of change of the angle measure is the fastest for the fastest rate ($\frac{1}{2}$ mps) and slowest for the slowest rate ($\frac{1}{4}$ mps).

c. Students should use their models to measure the distance from A to the horizontal dashed line. Using Part b, they can position the model so that the value of x is correct for different times and rates, and then they can measure the corresponding distances. Using 10-second intervals, they should get answers close to those in the following table.

For each rate the distance is increasing, but at a decreasing rate. The distance increases fairly quickly at first, but as x approaches 90° the rate of change is very small.

Distances from A to Horizontal

Time (in seconds)	Rate: 1/4 meter per second	Rate: 1/3 meter per second	Rate: 1/2 meter per second
10	3.3 m	4.3 m	6.2 m
20	6.2 m	7.9 m	10.8 m
30	8.7 m	10.8 m	13.7 m
40	10.8 m	12.9 m	15.0 m
50	12.5 m	14.3 m	
60	13.7 m	15.0 m	
70	14.5 m		
80	15.0 m		

See additional Teaching Notes on page T453H.

$\frac{1}{4}$ meter per second

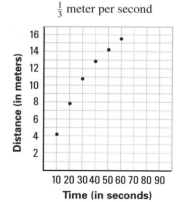

Distance (in meters) / Time (in seconds)

$\frac{1}{3}$ meter per second

Distance (in meters) / Time (in seconds)

$\frac{1}{2}$ meter per second

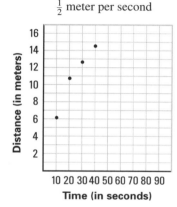

Distance (in meters) / Time (in seconds)

3. Parallelogram linkages and variable-sided triangle linkages each have a number of uses. Which of the two linkages do you consider to be the most useful? Why?

4. Listening to engineers, you may hear the statement, "form follows function." What do you think they mean by this statement? To what extent do you agree with it?

Extending

1. A large hoisting derrick has a boom *AB* that is 15 meters long. It is raised by a cable which may be shortened using a winch at three rates: $\frac{1}{4}$ meter per second, $\frac{1}{3}$ meter per second, or $\frac{1}{2}$ meter per second.

   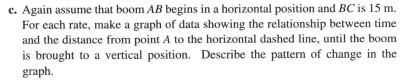

   a. What is the variable side in this situation?

   b. Assume the boom *AB* begins in a horizontal position and *BC* is 15 meters. For each rate, make a graph showing the relationship between time and the measure of the *angle of elevation x*, until the boom is brought to a vertical position. Describe the pattern of change.

   c. Again assume that boom *AB* begins in a horizontal position and *BC* is 15 m. For each rate, make a graph of data showing the relationship between time and the distance from point *A* to the horizontal dashed line, until the boom is brought to a vertical position. Describe the pattern of change in the graph.

2. Suppose a cold frame (see Modeling Task 1) has been designed to be held open by a prop 30 cm long, attached to the top 50 cm from the hinged end. The free end of the prop rests in one of several notches, spaced equally apart, on the side of the cold frame. Imagine or sketch the prop placed in any notch on the side.

   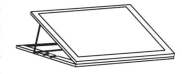

   a. If the free end of the prop is moved to a notch *farther* from the hinged end of the frame, what happens to the measure of the angle at the hinged end? Is the size of the change constant as the prop is moved *out* to each notch?

LESSON 2 • TRIANGLES AND TRIGONOMETRIC RATIOS   393

b. If the free end is returned to its starting position and then moved to a notch *closer* to the hinged end of the box, what happens to the measure of the angle at the hinge? Is the size of the change constant as the prop is moved *in* to each notch?

c. To make the largest opening for this cold frame, where should the designer position the notch? With this largest opening, what is the angle formed by the prop where it meets the side of the cold frame?

d. For what kind of hinged structure might you want to design a prop that attaches near the hinged end, rather than in the middle of the structure? Which attachment place do you think works best for the cold frame?

e. Now experiment with either the length of the prop or where it is attached to the raised lid. Under what conditions will there be two possible ways to place the prop to get a desired opening size? Under what conditions will there be only one way to get a desired opening size?

3. A ramp is an example of an *inclined plane*. By adjusting the height of an incline you can investigate basic scientific principles.

a. Imagine placing a skateboard on a ramp and allowing it to roll with no initial push. What do you think is the relationship between the height of the ramp and the elapsed time for the skateboard to roll down it?

b. Design and conduct an experiment to investigate the relationship between height of an inclined plane and time for an object to roll down the plane. (The science department in your school may have materials to help in the design of your experiment.)

c. Find a rule that you believe fits the pattern in the (*height, elapsed time*) data that you have collected.

d. Write a report summarizing your experiment's design, methods, and results. Describe any limitations of your modeling rule.

4. Refer to the inclined-plane experiment in Task 3. Design and conduct an experiment to investigate how the weight of the object rolled down the ramp affects the pattern of change in the corresponding (*height, elapsed time*) data. How is the effect of weight seen in the scatterplots of the data? In the corresponding modeling equations?

2. **b.** If the initial position is greater than 40 cm from the hinged side, the angle increases as the prop is moved toward the hinge, until it reaches 40 cm from the hinge. As it moves closer than 40 cm from the hinge, the angle decreases. The size change depends on the spacing of the notches. (See Part a.)

    c. The largest angle is formed when the prop is in a notch 40 cm from the hinged side, and the angle formed by the prop and the box side is 90°.

    d. Opinions will vary. Students may benefit from looking again at the truck crane photo on page 384 and noting the angle at the boom and piston junction. The cold frame may be more stable in the wind with the notches more than 40 cm from the hinge.

    e. When the desired opening is achieved by a prop that is perpendicular to the frame at the notch, there is only one way to have that opening. However, the same opening could be achieved in two prop locations if you move the prop's attachment point on the lid closer to the hinge or make the prop longer.

3. **a.** The higher the ramp is, the faster the skateboard will roll down it; however, if it is rolling farther down, the time may be the same. Friction may also be a factor.

    b. The hardest part of designing an experiment will be finding a way to measure the time interval accurately. Students may need to consider reaction time if using a stopwatch.

    c. The rule will depend on the data they collect. There is no "correct" relationship since it will depend on the accuracy of their timing method. In general, the steeper the incline, the larger the component of the gravitational force on the rolling object, so the faster it will go. If the length of the path it rolls stays the same, elapsed time will decrease as steepness of the incline increases. The relationship probably will not be linear.

    d. Limitations should include a discussion of the accuracy of the timing method.

4. Galileo showed weight alone has no effect on the acceleration of an object in free fall, although air resistance and friction do. Students may find some variation since they can control neither air resistance nor friction. Modeling equations will vary.

Unit 6

INVESTIGATION 2 What's the Angle?

In this investigation, students begin exploring the conditions that guarantee that two triangles are similar. Next they explore special cases of similar right triangles, thus developing an understanding of trigonometric ratios. In Investigation 3, the trigonometric ratios are used for indirect measurement problems.

It helps to begin the investigation with a full-class discussion and brief review of similarity and scale factor. The discussion should remind students that when you know two shapes are similar, you know a great deal about the angles and sides. You can ask questions such as the following about any two similar plane shapes. Students may find that creating examples is helpful in answering these questions.

■ What can you say about two corresponding angles?

■ If the measure of ∠ C is 43°, what is the measure of its corresponding angle?

■ How could you estimate the scale factor using measurement techniques?

■ How can you use the scale factor to find lengths?

Students should work in pairs to complete Activity 1. If you follow with a full-class discussion of the activity, you can check that students are able to identify the conditions needed to guarantee that two triangles are similar. You also may want to point out the use of the congruent symbol in the introduction to the investigation.

You may want students to record in their Math Toolkits the rule they have found in Activity 1: If two angles of one triangle are congruent to two angles of another triangle then the triangles are similar. Some students may believe that they have proved this because they drew triangles and checked the scale factors by measuring, and they were convinced that corresponding sides were proportional copies. However, they did not really prove this; what they have at this stage is a very plausible conjecture. Some may feel that this is a subtle point, but it is one worth pointing out to your students. Students will deal more carefully with the concept of proof in Course 3.

Finally, students should work in small groups to complete the investigation and the Checkpoint. You may want to remind students that accurate measurements and careful drawings will be very important as they look once again for patterns in the data. Note that Part d of the "On Your Own" is a new question for students. They should use a guess-and-check method rather than the $\sin^{-1}$ function, which is introduced in Investigation 3.

1. The purpose of this activity is for students to conclude that two triangles are similar if they have two (and therefore three) corresponding angles congruent.
    a. ■ The remaining angle measure is 70°.
       ■ Yes, the triangles are similar. All the corresponding angles are congruent, and if you multiply any of the sides of one triangle (*A*) by the particular scale factor, *s,* for these triangles, then you will get the measure of the corresponding side of the second triangle (*B*). Students should be able to find the scale factor for their triangles by calculating the ratio of the measure of one side of triangle *B* to the measure of its corresponding side in triangle *A*. Since measurement has error, the common multiplier may be approximate only.
    b. ■ The remaining angle measure is 20°.
       ■ Yes, the triangles are similar. The angles are congruent in pairs. Students can measure corresponding sides and see if there is a common multiplier from the corresponding sides of one triangle to the sides of the other.

INVESTIGATION 2 ▸ What's the Angle?

In the previous investigation, you learned that when the rigidity property of triangles is combined with the ability to adjust the length of a side, the opportunities for useful application expand greatly. You probably noticed that the methods used to determine lengths and angle measures involved measuring the models you made. In this investigation, you will use right triangles and similarity to explore other ways in which lengths and angle measures can be determined.

Recall that if two figures are *similar* with a scale factor of *s*, then corresponding angles are congruent (≅) and lengths of the corresponding sides are related by the multiplier *s*. The two school crossing signs shown below are similar.

Here pentagon *ABCDE* is similar to *A'B'C'D'E'* (*ABCDE* ~ *A'B'C'D'E'*) with a scale factor of 2. ∠*B* corresponds to ∠*B'*, so ∠*B* ≅ ∠*B'*. (∠*B* is congruent to ∠*B'*.) Segment *ED* corresponds to segment *E'D'*, so 2 · *ED* = *E'D'* or, equivalently, $ED = \frac{E'D'}{2}$.

1. Imagine that you and a classmate each draw a triangle with three angles of one triangle congruent to three angles of the other triangle. Do you think the two triangles will be similar? Make a conjecture.

   a. Now conduct the following experiment. Have each member of your group draw a segment (no two with the same length). Use a protractor to draw a 50° angle at one end of the segment. Then draw a 60° angle at the other end of the segment to form a triangle.

   ■ What should be the measure of the third angle? Check your answer.

   ■ Are these triangles similar to one another? What evidence can you give to support your view?

   b. Repeat Part a with angles measuring 40° and 120°. Are these triangles similar? Give evidence to support your claim.

c. Which, if any, of the following statements do you think are always true? Justify your response with reasons or a counterexample.

- If one triangle has three angles congruent to three corresponding angles on another triangle, then the triangles are similar.

- If one triangle has two angles congruent to two corresponding angles on another triangle, then the triangles are similar.

- If one triangle has one angle congruent to one angle on another triangle, then the triangles are similar.

2. Now apply your discoveries in Activity 1 to the special case of right triangles.

a. Each group member should draw a segment *AC* (each a different length). Using your segment *AC* as a side, draw △*ABC* with ∠*A* measuring 35° and a right angle at *C*. It is important to draw your triangle very carefully. What is the measure of the other angle (∠*B*)?

b. Are the triangles your group members drew similar? Explain.

c. Choose the smallest triangle drawn in Part a. Determine the approximate scale factors relating this triangle to the others drawn by group members.

For a right triangle *ABC*, it is standard procedure to label the right angle with the capital letter *C* and to label the sides opposite the three angles lower case *a*, *b*, and *c* as shown. Complete a labeling of your triangle in this way. (Additional ways to refer to the sides of a right triangle are

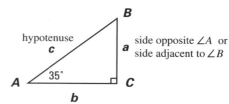

also included in the diagram. The **hypotenuse** is always the side opposite the right angle, but the designation of the other sides depends on which angle is considered.)

3. A diagram of a right △*ABC* is given below. Give the measures of the following angles or sides:

a. ∠*C*

b. ∠*B*

c. Side opposite ∠*A*

d. Side (leg) adjacent to ∠*B*

e. Side (leg) adjacent to ∠*A*

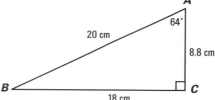

1. c. ■ True, because the triangles will be related by a scale factor.

■ True, because the third angles also will be congruent.

■ False, because fixing only one of the angles in a triangle will not guarantee that the other two angles will be congruent.

2. Although the application to right triangles seems to suggest only one angle is needed, students should recognize that because the triangle is a right triangle, the second angle is always 90°.

a. The measure of $\angle B$ is 55°.

b. Yes, the triangles are similar, because all corresponding angles are congruent.

c. Responses will vary depending on the students' triangles. In general, the scale factor is $\dfrac{\text{length } BC \text{ (other triangle)}}{\text{length } BC \text{ (smallest triangle)}}$.

3. a. 90°

   b. 26°

   c. 18 cm

   d. 18 cm

   e. 8.8 cm

Unit 6

4. This activity is designed to help students discover the trigonometric ratios for themselves. The patterns should be fairly evident when listed in table form. If larger differences occur, ask students to remeasure to verify accuracy.

   a. Answers may vary slightly, due to measurement error.

      The ratio $\frac{a}{c}$ is always about 0.57.

      The ratio $\frac{b}{c}$ is always about 0.82.

      The ratio $\frac{a}{b}$ is always about 0.70.

   b. The pattern should be the same for each group.

   c. The value of each ratio is independent of the triangle; they depend only upon the triangles having an acute angle of 35°.

   d. $\dfrac{a}{c} = \dfrac{\text{length of side opposite } \angle A}{\text{length of hypotenuse}}$; $\dfrac{b}{c} = \dfrac{\text{length of side adjacent to } \angle A}{\text{length of hypotenuse}}$;

      $\dfrac{a}{b} = \dfrac{\text{length of side opposite } \angle A}{\text{length of side adjacent to } \angle A}$

      $\dfrac{a}{c} = \dfrac{\text{length of side adjacent to } \angle B}{\text{length of hypotenuse}}$; $\dfrac{b}{c} = \dfrac{\text{length of side opposite } \angle B}{\text{length of hypotenuse}}$;

      $\dfrac{a}{b} = \dfrac{\text{length of side adjacent to } \angle B}{\text{length of side opposite } \angle B}$

   e. The three ratios in the table will be identical for any right triangle *ABC* with a 35° angle at *A*.

   f. A right triangle *ABC* with an angle of 55° will have ratios identical to those in the table if the 55° angle is at *B*.

5. a. $\frac{a}{c} \approx 0.64$; $\frac{b}{c} \approx 0.77$; $\frac{a}{b} \approx 0.84$

   b. Regardless of which right triangle with $\angle A = 40°$ is used to compute the ratios, the values for each ratio are the same.

   c. Each of the ratios $\frac{a}{c}$, $\frac{b}{c}$, and $\frac{a}{b}$ are the same for each of the similar triangles in which the measure of $\angle A$ was 40°. This pattern also exists for the similar triangles in which the measure of $\angle A$ was 35°. However, the ratios were not equal for triangles from Activities 4 and 5. The two sets of triangles were not similar to one another.

   d. The important variable is the measure of one acute angle of the right triangle.

      You may want to discuss with the whole class the summarizing and terminology explanation that follows Activity 5. Here students may need help in understanding "side opposite," "side adjacent," and "hypotenuse." Since the trigonometric functions are ratios of linear measures, the values of the functions have no units. The argument of the function has units of degrees in these activities.

4. Refer to the right triangles your group drew for Activity 2.

a. Make a table like the one below. Each group member should choose a unit of measure. Carefully measure and calculate the indicated ratios for the triangle you drew. Express the ratios to the nearest 0.01. Investigate patterns in the three ratios for your group's triangles.

Triangle Side Ratios

Ratio	Student 1	Student 2	Student 3	Student 4
$\dfrac{a}{c}$				
$\dfrac{b}{c}$				
$\dfrac{a}{b}$				

b. Compare the ratios from your group with those of other groups.

c. On the basis of Parts a and b, make a conjecture about the three ratios in the table for any right $\triangle ABC$ with a 35° angle at A.

d. How could the three ratios be described in terms of the hypotenuse and the sides opposite and adjacent to $\angle A$? In terms of the hypotenuse and the sides opposite and adjacent to $\angle B$?

e. Make a conjecture about the three ratios in the table for any right triangle with a 35° angle.

f. Make a conjecture about the three ratios for any right triangle with a 55° angle.

5. As a group, draw several examples of a right $\triangle ABC$ in which $\angle A$ has a measure of 40° and $\angle C$ has a measure of 90°.

a. Compute the three ratios $\dfrac{a}{c}$, $\dfrac{b}{c}$, and $\dfrac{a}{b}$. Record the ratios in a table like the one in Activity 4.

b. What pattern do you see in these ratios?

c. How is the pattern for these ratios similar to the pattern for the ratios in Activity 4? How is it different?

d. What seems to cause the differences in the results from the two activities? Test your conjecture by experimenting with another set of similar right triangles and inspecting the ratios.

You have observed that as the measure of an acute angle changes in a right triangle, ratios of the lengths of the sides also change. In fact, each ratio is a function of the size of the angle. These relationships are important because they relate measures of angles (in degrees) to ratios of linear measures (in centimeters, miles, and so on). The relationships or functions have special names. For a right triangle ABC with sides a, b, and c, the **sine**, **cosine**, and **tangent** ratios for $\angle A$ are defined as follows:

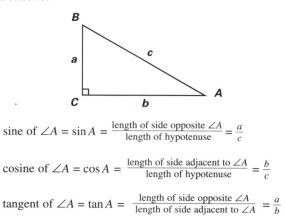

$$\text{sine of } \angle A = \sin A = \frac{\text{length of side opposite } \angle A}{\text{length of hypotenuse}} = \frac{a}{c}$$

$$\text{cosine of } \angle A = \cos A = \frac{\text{length of side adjacent to } \angle A}{\text{length of hypotenuse}} = \frac{b}{c}$$

$$\text{tangent of } \angle A = \tan A = \frac{\text{length of side opposite } \angle A}{\text{length of side adjacent to } \angle A} = \frac{a}{b}$$

These ratios are called **trigonometric ratios**.

Sine B, cosine B, and tangent B are similarly defined by forming the ratios using the sides opposite and adjacent to $\angle B$. The abbreviations are $\sin B$, $\cos B$, and $\tan B$.

6. Refer to the triangles you drew for Activity 5. Write the definitions for $\sin B$, $\cos B$, and $\tan B$, and then find $\sin 50°$, $\cos 50°$, and $\tan 50°$.

7. Suppose you have a right triangle with an acute angle of $27.5°$. One way you could find the sine, cosine, and tangent of $27.5°$ would be to make a very accurate right triangle and measure. Another way is to use your calculator.

   a. To calculate a trigonometric ratio for an angle measured in degrees, first be sure your calculator is set in *degree* mode. Then simply press the keys corresponding to the ratio desired. For example, to calculate $\sin 27.5°$ on most calculators, press $\boxed{\text{SIN}}$ 27.5 $\boxed{\text{ENTER}}$. Try it. Then calculate $\cos 27.5°$ and $\tan 27.5°$.

   b. Compare $\sin 27.4°$ and $\sin 27.6°$ to your value for $\sin 27.5°$. How many decimal places should you include to show that the angle whose sine you are finding was measured to the nearest $0.1°$?

   c. How many decimal places should you report for $\sin 66.5°$ to indicate that the angle was measured to the nearest $0.1°$?

   d. Use your calculator to find the sine, cosine, and tangent of $35°$ and of $50°$. Compare these results with those you obtained by measuring in Activities 4 and 5.

6. sine of $\angle B = \sin B = \frac{b}{c}$ $\sin 50° \approx 0.76$

cosine of $\angle B = \cos B = \frac{a}{c}$ $\cos 50° \approx 0.64$

tangent of $\angle B = \tan B = \frac{b}{a}$ $\tan 50° \approx 1.19$

7. **a.** Students should set their calculators to the degree mode. However, some calculators offer another option. Label the angles with the degree symbol and the calculator will interpret it as degrees regardless of the mode. For the TI-82 and 83, the needed degree symbol can be found under the times menu (2nd MATRIX).

$\sin 27.5° \approx 0.4617$
$\cos 27.5° \approx 0.8870$
$\tan 27.5° \approx 0.5206$

b. $\sin 27.4° \approx 0.4602$, $\sin 27.6° \approx 0.4633$, so we must include at least three decimal places to show the difference between 27.5° and 27.6°.

c. Because the rate of change of the sine function is lower near 66.5° than 27.5°, $\sin 66.5°$ requires four decimal places to differentiate it from $\sin 66.6°$.

d. Results should be close to the ratios calculated in Activities 4 and 5.

SHARE AND SUMMARIZE full-class discussion

Before proceeding to the Checkpoint questions, you might introduce the paragraph above the Checkpoint by asking questions such as the following:

■ If I want to know what sin 42° is, what kind of answer can I expect? What is the unit of measure? (Many students will have noticed that the sine of any angle has been less than 1. Since the sine of an angle is a ratio of lengths, there is no unit of measure.)

■ Could you find an estimate of this value without using your calculator? Does your process explain why the answers are all less than 1 for sine ratios? (You can draw a right triangle with 42° as one of its angles, measure the opposite side and the hypotenuse, and find the ratio of these lengths. The hypotenuse is always the longest side.)

■ Will someone else get the same answer if they draw a different right triangle with a 42° angle? Explain. (Yes, except for measurement error.)

■ So if all the estimates will be approximately the same, could we split up the work and find the sine of every angle from 0° to 180°? (If we concentrate on whole numbers this is possible, but a tedious task.)

■ Since sin 42° is the same every time you find it, it makes sense to write it down in a table. What would be a more convenient way? (Use your calculator.)

At this point you might show students an old book of trigonometric tables. Students usually enjoy the idea that they have a way of finding values of the trigonometric ratios that is "superior" to the "old-fashioned" way that their teacher may have used when he or she was a student. You may find that students are curious about how the calculator is producing these values. Encourage student conjecture and research to answer this question.

Unit 6

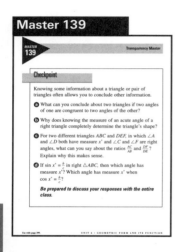

Checkpoint

See Teaching Master 139.

ⓐ The two triangles are similar. This is usually summarized in the angle-angle similarity theorem.

ⓑ Since a right triangle always has a 90° angle, fixing an acute angle gives you two fixed angles, making all such triangles similar.

ⓒ Student answers will focus either on the name of the ratio or on the fact that the ratio will always have the same value. They may say that $\frac{ac}{ab}$ is the cosine of angle A, or cos $(x°)$. Or they may say that since two right triangles with an angle size $x°$ are similar, then the ratio $\frac{b}{c}$ in one triangle will be transformed to become $\frac{sb}{sc}$ in the other triangle.

ⓓ Angle B has measure x for sin $x° = \frac{b}{c}$.
Angle A has measure x for cos $x°$.

CONSTRUCTING A MATH TOOLKIT: Ask students to summarize the conditions or cases that guarantee that two triangles will be similar and record their thoughts in their Math Toolkits. Students should include at least the four following cases and may speculate on others.

- Three angles of one triangle are congruent to three angles of another triangle.
- Two angles of one triangle are congruent to two angles of another triangle.
- The acute angles of two right triangles are congruent.
- Three pairs of sides of two triangles have the same scale factor.

Students also should record definitions and sketches for the congruent symbol and the three right triangle ratios: sine, cosine, and tangent for an angle in their Math Toolkits.

APPLY   individual task

▶On Your Own

Students probably will try a guess-and-check or table refinement method for Part d. You may want to prompt students to insert sin x and cos x in the "$y =$" menu so they can examine both tables simultaneously. After working individually, students may compare methods.

a. Side RQ is opposite $\angle P$; side RQ is adjacent to $\angle R$; side PR is the hypotenuse.

b. $RQ^2 + PQ^2 = PR^2$
$\quad 7^2 + PQ^2 = 25^2$
$\qquad\quad PQ^2 = 625 - 49$
$\qquad\quad PQ = 24$

c. $\sin P = \frac{7}{25} = 0.280 \qquad \tan P = \frac{7}{24} \approx 0.292$
$\sin R = \frac{24}{25} = 0.960 \qquad \cos R = \frac{7}{25} = 0.280$

d. The measure of $\angle R$ is between 73.7° and 73.8°; sin 73.8° and sin 73.7° both round to 0.960. Tables giving sine and cosine values for angles from 73.7° to 73.8°, in steps of 0.01°, shows that 73.74 is the only value that gives sin $R = 0.960$ and cos $R = 0.280$, so to the nearest 0.1°, the angle is 73.7°.

MORE
ASSIGNMENT   *pp. 406–411*

Students can now begin Organizing Task 2 or 3, Reflecting Task 1 or 2; or Extending Task 1 from the MORE set following Investigation 3.

You can use your calculator to compute values for sine, cosine, and tangent of any angle. Several hundred years ago mathematicians spent years calculating these ratios by hand to several decimal places so that they could be used in surveying and astronomy. Until recently, before scientific and graphing calculators became common, people usually looked up the ratio values from a large table. Now that a calculator replaces this tedious work, you can concentrate on understanding trigonometric ratios and their uses.

Checkpoint

Knowing some information about a triangle or pair of triangles often allows you to conclude other information.

a What can you conclude about two triangles if two angles of one are congruent to two angles of the other?

b Why does knowing the measure of an acute angle of a right triangle completely determine the triangle's shape?

c For two different triangles ABC and DEF, in which $\angle A$ and $\angle D$ both have measure $x°$ and $\angle C$ and $\angle F$ are right angles, what can you say about the ratios $\frac{AC}{AB}$ and $\frac{DF}{DE}$? Explain why this makes sense.

d If $\sin x° = \frac{b}{c}$ in right $\triangle ABC$, then which angle has measure $x°$? Which angle has measure $x°$ when $\cos x° = \frac{b}{c}$?

Be prepared to discuss your responses with the entire class.

On Your Own

Refer to the drawing of $\triangle PQR$ below.

a. Which is the side opposite $\angle P$? The side adjacent to $\angle R$? The hypotenuse?

b. Use the Pythagorean Theorem to find the length of side PQ.

c. Find the following trigonometric ratios:
- $\sin P$
- $\sin R$
- $\tan P$
- $\cos R$

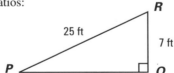

d. Valerie measured $\angle R$ and found it to be almost 74°. Use a calculator and your results from Part c to estimate the measure of $\angle R$ to the nearest 0.1°.

LESSON 2 • TRIANGLES AND TRIGONOMETRIC RATIOS   399

INVESTIGATION 3 Measuring Without Measuring

Shown below is Chicago's *Bat Column*, a sculpture by Claes Oldenburg.

1. **a.** In your group, brainstorm about possible ways to determine the height of the sculpture.

   b. Choose one method and write a detailed plan.

   c. Trade plans with another group and compare the two plans.

   d. What assumptions did the other group make in devising its plan?

   e. Which plan seems easier to carry out? Why?

Your class probably thought of several plans to determine the height of *Bat Column*. For example, one could use an extension ladder on a fire truck to climb to the top and drop a weighted and measured cord to the ground. This would be a *direct measurement* procedure. An *indirect* way to measure the height would be to use a right triangle and a trigonometric ratio.

2. **a.** In the situation depicted below, what lengths and angles could you determine easily by direct measurement (and without using high-powered equipment)?

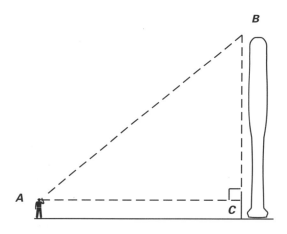

INVESTIGATION 3 ▶ Measuring Without Measuring

In this investigation, students are asked to solve a variety of indirect measurement problems using trigonometric ratios. Trigonometric functions and inverse trigonometric functions are used to help find the unknown sizes of angles and sides.

One way to begin this investigation is to ask students to speculate on the differences between direct and indirect measurement. Use Activity 1 to motivate a class discussion of the differences between indirect and direct measurement and how a person might measure indirectly. Students may need to be encouraged to think of ways to measure the *Bat Column* if they were in Chicago, looking at it! Such a discussion will allow you to assess informally how students are thinking. You may see some students making plans that utilize the trigonometric ratios and others who make use of pairs of similar triangles. In any case, the discussion can give you information useful in decision making as you progress through the lesson. As you end the discussion, you might let students know that during this investigation they will explore a variety of ways to use the trigonometric ratios, which they learned about in the previous investigation, to find needed measurements without actually measuring, that is, by indirect measurement.

Next, students should work in small groups to complete Activity 2. There are many difficult ideas and skills presented in this activity, so you may find it worthwhile to take some time in another full-class discussion. You may want to urge students to be prepared to share their solutions. Students should be able to set up an appropriate trigonometric ratio and equation to find the length of the unknown side. They also should realize that there is frequently more than one equation possible.

Activity 3 can be mystifying for some students. There are two levels that cause difficulty: the conceptual level of setting up the equation and the technical skill level involved in solving it. It is worth taking time with this activity so that students can use successfully all the powerful ideas they have just learned about trigonometric ratios. Rather than assigning the class to work on Activity 3 in small groups, you may find it helpful to let students try the first few items as a whole group, with student volunteers working the problems at the board or overhead projector, taking advice from the class, and getting prompts as necessary. For example, with a correctly labeled triangle in Activity 3, Part a, some students may suggest writing $\sin 52° = \frac{b}{c}$. Even if there is a long silence, let the students realize on their own that this suggestion doesn't help because there are too many variables. If no one suggests a way to start, then consider suggesting this unproductive beginning, because it is important for students to think about which ratios are useful. Avoid a demonstration of a technique, since this robs students of the opportunity of seeing for themselves that there are unproductive beginnings and more than one path to take when solving a problem. Once the whole class has completed two problems, ask someone to summarize the strategies they are using.

Students should return to their small groups to complete the remaining activities in this investigation and the Checkpoint.

See additional Teaching Notes on page T453H.

2. **b.** Sine and tangent both include *BC*. Tangent includes *AC*, which is measurable.

c. Cosine and tangent both include *BC*. The measure of ∠*B* will be 90° − m∠*A*.

d. ∠*B* = 35°

e. It may be helpful for students to answer Parts e and f orally, rather than trying to write the explanations. While answers will vary, the following are possible responses.

■ D'wan wants to know what number divided by 20 will equal 1.43. He works backwards to undo the division, that is, he multiplies 1.43 by 20 to see what the original number must have been.

■ Krista also was working backwards to solve her equation. She first thinks, if 20 divided by *BC* will equal 0.7, then 0.7 times *BC* should equal 20. Next, she can undo the multiplication to get *BC* by dividing 20 by 0.7.

■ Their answers are not correct. They have found the length *BC* but not the height of the sculpture. Their calculations of *BC* are correct, however. Through different relationships they arrived at the same answer. In each case, they used sound reasoning and made no errors.

f. All that remains is to add 28.6 m and the distance from point *C* to the bottom of the sculpture, or 28.6 and the height of the person measuring the angle of elevation.

b. Which trigonometric ratios of $\angle A$ involve side BC? Of these, which also involve a measurable length?

c. Which of the trigonometric ratios of $\angle B$ involve side BC and a measurable length? If you know the size of $\angle A$, how can you find the measure of $\angle B$?

d. Krista and D'wan decided to find the height of *Bat Column* themselves. First Krista chose a spot to be point A, 20 meters from the sculpture (point C). D'wan used a *clinometer*, like the one shown at the right, to estimate the measure of $\angle A$ (the *angle of elevation* from the horizontal to the top of the bat). He measured $\angle A$ to be 55°. What is the measure of $\angle B$?

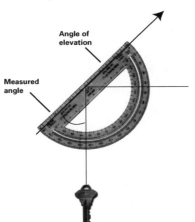

Angle of elevation

Measured angle

e. Krista and D'wan proceeded to find the height of the bat independently as shown below.

D'wan

I need to find BC so that
$$\frac{BC}{AC} = \tan 55°.$$
But $\tan 55° = 1.43$ and $AC = 20$ m.
So I need to solve
$$\frac{BC}{20} = 1.43.$$
If I multiply the equation by 20, I get
$$BC = 1.43 \cdot 20$$
$$BC = 28.6 \text{ m}$$

Krista

$$\tan 35° = \frac{AC}{BC}$$
$$0.7 = \frac{20}{BC}$$
Multiplying the equation by BC, I get
$$0.7 \cdot BC = 20.$$
Dividing by 0.7, I get
$$BC = \frac{20}{0.7} \quad \text{or } 28.6 \text{ m.}$$

■ Analyze D'wan's thinking. Why did he multiply by 20?

■ Analyze Krista's thinking. Why did she multiply by BC? Why did she divide by 0.7?

■ Are the answers correct? Explain your response.

f. How could you use Krista's and D'wan's work to help estimate the height of *Bat Column*?

Unit 6

g. Kim said he could find the length AB (the line of sight distance) by solving $\cos 55° = \frac{AC}{AB}$. Analyze Kim's thinking shown here.

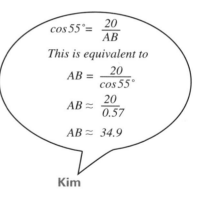

$\cos 55° = \dfrac{20}{AB}$

This is equivalent to

$AB = \dfrac{20}{\cos 55°}$.

$AB \approx \dfrac{20}{0.57}$

$AB \approx 34.9$

Kim

- Explain Kim's thinking.
- Is Kim correct?
- What is another way Kim could have found AB using trigonometric ratios?
- Could you find AB without using trigonometric ratios? Explain your reasoning.

3. Each Part below gives data for right $\triangle ABC$. Sketch a model triangle and then, using your calculator, find the lengths of the remaining two sides.

   a. $\angle B = 52°$, $a = 5$ m   **b.** $\angle A = 78°$, $a = 5$ mi

   c. $\angle A = 21°$, $b = 8$ in.   **d.** $\angle B = 8°$, $b = 8$ ft

   e. $\angle B = 37°$, $c = 42$ yd   **f.** $\angle A = 82°$, $c = 14$ cm

4. Terri is flying a kite and has let out 500 feet of string. Her end of the string is 3 feet off the ground.

   a. If $\angle KIT$ has a measure of 40°, approximately how high off the ground is the kite?

   b. As the wind picks up, Terri is able to fly the kite at a 56° angle with the horizontal. Approximately how high is the kite?

   c. What is the highest Terri could fly the kite on 500 feet of string? What would be the measure of $\angle KIT$ then?

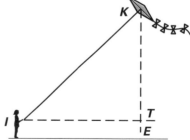

   d. Experiment with your calculator to estimate the measure of $\angle KIT$ needed to fly the kite at a height of 425 feet.

In the previous situations, you used trigonometric ratios to determine an unknown or inaccessible distance. In Activity 4 Part d, you probably found a way to find the measure of an angle when you know the lengths of two sides in a right triangle.

2. g. ■ He used the cosine relationship and then worked to rearrange the equation until he could solve for *AB*.

■ Yes, Kim is correct.

■ There are several other ways to set up equations to find *AB* by using trigonometric ratios. They are cos 35°, sin 55°, and cos 55°.

■ You could use the Pythagorean Theorem to find the missing third side of the right triangle. However, this assumes you know the height of the sculpture, which we found using trigonometric ratios. Students may argue that the answer is no, you cannot find the length without the ratios.

3. Encourage students to sketch each of the right triangles. Solutions follow, but students could calculate the other acute angle and then use different ratios to calculate the unknown lengths. See page T400 for additional suggestions in the investigation overview.

a. $\tan 52° = \frac{b}{5}$

$b = 5 \tan 52°$

$b \approx 6.40 \text{ m}$

$\cos 52° = \frac{5}{c}$

$c = \frac{5}{\cos 52°}$

$c \approx 8.12 \text{ m}$

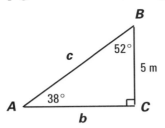

b. $\tan 78° = \frac{5}{b}$

$b \tan 78° = 5$

$b = \frac{5}{\tan 78°}$

$b \approx 1.06 \text{ mi}$

$\sin 78° = \frac{5}{c}$

$c = \frac{5}{\sin 78°}$

$c \approx 5.11 \text{ mi}$

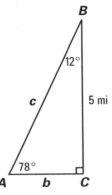

c. $\tan 21° = \frac{a}{8}$

$a = 8 \tan 21°$

$a \approx 3.07 \text{ in}$

$\cos 21° = \frac{8}{c}$

$c = \frac{8}{\cos 21°}$

$c \approx 8.57 \text{ in}$

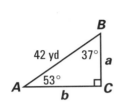

d. $\tan 82° = \frac{a}{8}$

$a = 8 \tan 82°$

$a \approx 56.92 \text{ ft}$

$\cos 82° = \frac{8}{c}$

$c = \frac{8}{\cos 82°}$

$c \approx 57.48 \text{ ft}$

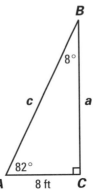

e. $\cos 37° = \frac{a}{42}$

$a = 42 \cos 37°$

$a \approx 33.54 \text{ yd}$

$\sin 37° = \frac{b}{42}$

$b = 42 \sin 37°$

$b \approx 25.28 \text{ yd}$

f. $\sin 82° = \frac{a}{14}$

$a = 14 \sin 82°$

$a \approx 13.86 \text{ cm}$

$\cos 82° = \frac{b}{14}$

$b = 14 \cos 82°$

$b \approx 1.95 \text{ cm}$

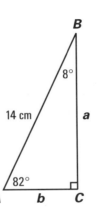

See additional Teaching Notes on page T453H.

Unit 6

5. This activity introduces the inverse use of the trigonometric ratios and should be done as a draw-and-measure (guess-and-check) activity so that students will see that the ratios actually do determine the angles.

    a. About 36° or 37°

    b. 60°

    c. About 38° or 39°

    d. Responses will vary depending on students' approaches.

6. The calculator inverse trig functions are introduced in this activity. No attempt is made to talk about "inverses" formally. The idea is simply that the calculator will identify the correct angle (such as those students constructed in Activity 5) when the ratio is known. The calculator will display the inverse trig function names ($\cos^{-1}$, $\sin^{-1}$, etc.), but this symbolism is not necessary for all students to understand. Rather, if the issue comes up, you simply can say $\cos^{-1}\left(\frac{2}{3}\right)$ means the "angle whose cosine is $\frac{2}{3}$."

    a. Be sure students know how to use the $\sin^{-1}$ to find $\sin^{-1} 0.8 \approx 53.13$. Most calculators have the $\sin^{-1}$ function as $\boxed{\text{2nd}}$ $\boxed{\text{SIN}}$ or some equivalent.

    b. $\sin 53.13010235° = 0.8$

    c. $\sin 36.86989765° \approx \frac{3}{5}$

    $\cos 60° = \frac{1}{2}$

    $\tan 38.65980825° \approx \frac{4}{5}$

    d. ■ The measure of $\angle B$ is approximately 61.477°.
    ■ The measure of $\angle A$ is approximately 58.430°.
    ■ The measure of $\angle B$ is approximately 77.702°.

7. This is another application for groups to sketch, analyze, and solve using the trigonometric ratios. The activity uses the ideas of angle of elevation and angle of depression, but those ideas are not named or stressed in any way. Rather, the situation is described, and it is up to the group members to make a sketch with appropriate angles. The technical terms are presented in the text following the Checkpoint.

    a. The diagram below is not drawn to scale.

    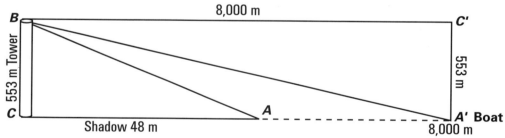

    b. Using $\triangle ABC$:

    $\tan A = \frac{553}{48}$

    $\tan A \approx 11.52083$

    $A \approx 85°$

5. Estimate (to the nearest degree) the measure of acute angle B for each of the following trigonometric ratios of $\angle B$. Check your estimate in each case by drawing a model right $\triangle ABC$, using sides whose lengths give the appropriate ratio, and then measuring $\angle B$.

   a. $\sin B = \frac{3}{5}$

   b. $\cos B = \frac{1}{2}$

   c. $\tan B = \frac{4}{5}$

   d. Consider how you found the measure of an acute angle when you knew a trigonometric ratio for a right triangle with that angle measure. Compare your group's approach with the approaches of other groups.

6. You know how to use a calculator to produce a trigonometric ratio when you know the measure of an angle. You also can use a calculator to produce the angle when you know a trigonometric ratio as in Activity 5.

   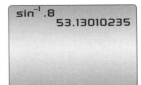

   a. Suppose you know $\sin A = \frac{4}{5} = 0.8$. Use the "$\sin^{-1}$" function of your calculator to compute the angle whose sine is 0.8. (Make certain your calculator is set in degree mode.)

   b. What would you get if you calculated the sine of the angle in the calculator display above?

   c. Use your calculator to find the measure of $\angle B$ that corresponds to each of the ratios given in Activity 5. Compare these values to the values you obtained in that activity.

   d. Use your calculator to find the measure of each angle.

   - $\tan B = 1.84$
   - $\sin A = 0.852$
   - $\cos B = 0.213$

7. The Canadian National Tower in Toronto, Ontario, is approximately 553 meters tall. This tower is the tallest free-standing structure in the world.

   a. Sketch the tower and add the features described in Parts b, c, and d as you work to answer each part.

   b. At some time on a sunny day, the sun makes the tower cast a 48-meter shadow. What is the measure of the angle formed by a sun ray and the ground at the tip of the shadow?

c. From the top of the Canadian National Tower, a boat is observed in Lake Ontario, approximately 8,000 meters away from the base of the tower. Assume the base of the tower is approximately level with the lake surface. What angle below the horizontal must the observer look to see the boat?

d. Estimate the line of sight distance from the observer to the boat in Part c. Find this distance using trigonometric ratios and without using them.

8. Lakeshia is about 1.7 meters tall. When standing 5 meters from her school building, her angle of sight to the top of the building is 75°.

   a. Estimate the height of the building.

   b. Suppose Lakeshia moves to a position 10 meters from the building. What is the angle of her new line of sight to the top of the building?

   c. Marcio, who is also about 1.7 meters tall, is standing on top of the building. He sees Lakeshia standing 15 meters from the building. At what angle below the horizontal is his line of sight to Lakeshia?

Checkpoint

Trigonometric ratios are useful to calculate lengths and angles in right-triangle models. Refer to the right triangle shown below in summarizing your thinking about how to use trigonometric ratios.

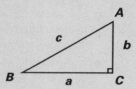

ⓐ If you knew a and the measure of $\angle B$, how would you find b? What calculator keystroke sequence would you use?

ⓑ If you knew b and c, how would you find the measure of $\angle A$? What calculator keystroke sequence would you use?

ⓒ If you knew b and the measure of $\angle B$, how would you find c? What calculator keystroke sequence would you use?

Be prepared to explain your methods to the whole class.

---

7. c. Using $\triangle A'BC'$:

$$\tan B = \frac{553}{8000}$$
$$\tan B = 0.069125$$
$$B \approx 4°$$

d. 8,019 meters is the distance for the line of sight. It can be found by using the Pythagorean Relation: $8{,}000^2 + 553^2 = (distance)^2$. Trigonometric ratios may be used also.

8. a. Use $\triangle ABC$:

$$\tan 75° = \frac{BC}{5}$$
$$3.732 \cdot 5 \approx BC$$
$$18.66 \text{ m} \approx BC$$
$$\text{school height} \approx BC + 1.7 \text{ m}$$
$$= 20.36 \text{ m}$$

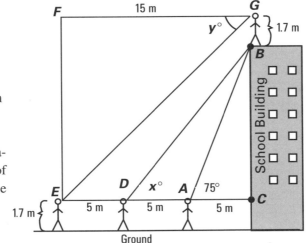

b. Use $\triangle BCD$; let x be the measure of the angle the line of sight makes above the horizontal:

$$\tan x = \frac{18.66}{10}$$
$$\tan x = 1.866$$
$$x \approx 62°$$

c. Use $\triangle GEF$; let y be the measure of the angle the line of sight makes below the horizontal. Since Lakeshia and Marcio are the same height, the distance FE will be the same as the height of the school building.

$$\tan y = \frac{18.66 + 1.7}{15}$$
$$\tan y \approx 1.357$$
$$y \approx 54°$$

SHARE AND SUMMARIZE   full-class discussion

Checkpoint

See Teaching Master 140.

ⓐ $\tan B = \frac{b}{a}$ therefore $b = \tan B \cdot a$

One calculator keystroke sequence is

a `TAN` B `ENTER` , where a and B are numbers.

ⓑ $\cos A = \frac{b}{c}$ So one keystroke sequence is:

`2nd` `COS` `(` b `÷` c `)` `ENTER` , where b and c are numbers.

ⓒ $\sin B = \frac{b}{c}$, so $c \cdot \sin B = b$ and $c = \frac{b}{\sin B}$

One keystroke sequence is:

b `÷` `SIN` B `ENTER` where b and B are numbers.

CONSTRUCTING A MATH TOOLKIT: Ask students to summarize the information sets that they would need to find a missing side or a missing angle of a given right triangle. They should also write illustrated definitions for an angle of elevation and angle of depression in their Math Toolkits.

APPLY individual task

On Your Own

a. You can find the vertical distance from the observer's eye level to the top of the rig (the height of the triangle), the distance from the observer to the center of the platform (the base of the triangle), and the line-of-sight distance from the observer to the top of the drill rig (the hypotenuse of the triangle).

The vertical distance to the top of the rig is 130 + 15 or 145 meters.

The distance to the platform is $\frac{145}{\tan 21°}$ or approximately 378 meters.

The line-of-sight distance is $\frac{145}{\sin 21°}$ or approximately 405 meters.

b.
$$\tan A = \frac{145}{200}$$
$$A \approx 36°$$

Unit 6

The **angle of elevation** to the top of an object is the angle formed by the horizontal and the line of sight to the top of the object. In the diagram below, ∠ACD is the angle of elevation. The **angle of depression** to an object is the angle formed by the horizontal and the line of sight to the object below. In the diagram, ∠BAC is the angle of depression.

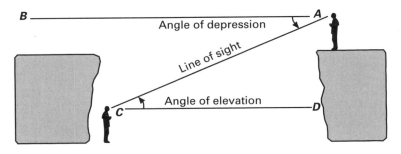

On Your Own

A person on an oil-drilling ship in the Gulf of Mexico sees a semi-submersible platform with a tower on top of it. The tower stands 130 meters above the platform floor.

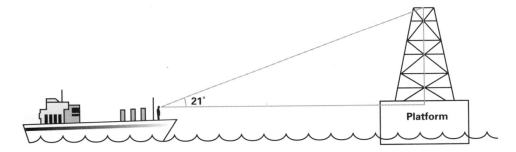

a. If the observer's position on the boat is 15 meters under the floor of the platform and the angle of elevation to the top of the rig is 21°, what three distances can you find? Find them.

b. The boat moves so that it is 200 meters from the center of the oil rig. What is the angle of elevation now?

MORE

Modeling • Organizing • Reflecting • Extending

Modeling

1. At places along the south bank of the Kalamazoo River, the river is substantially below the level of the ground. The land slopes downward at an angle of approximately 63° from the horizontal. The best way to get to the water is to go directly down the slope to the water's edge, a distance of approximately 123 meters.

   a. Make a sketch of this situation showing distances and angles.

   b. How far, horizontally, is the edge of the water from the edge of the bank, just where the land begins to slope?

   c. How far above the surface of the Kalamazoo River is the land on the south bank?

2. Commercial aircraft usually fly at an altitude between 9 and 11 kilometers (29,000 to 36,000 feet). When landing, their gradual descent to an airport runway occurs over a long distance.

   a. Suppose a commercial airliner begins its descent from an altitude of 9 km with an angle of descent of 2.5°. At what distance from the runway should the descent begin?

   b. Suppose a commercial airliner flying at an altitude of 11 km begins its descent at a horizontal distance 270 km from the runway. What is its angle of descent?

   c. The *cockpit cutoff angle* of an airliner is the angle from the horizontal to the line of sight between the pilot and the nose of the plane. Suppose a pilot is flying an aircraft with a cockpit cutoff angle of 14° at an altitude of 1.5 km. How far from the near edge of a lake, measuring along her line of sight, will she be when she is last able to see that edge of the lake?

   d. What is the horizontal distance to the lake when the pilot in Part c is last able to see the edge of the lake?

Cockpit cutoff angle

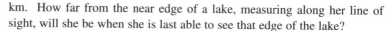

Modeling

MORE
ASSIGNMENT *pp. 406–411*

Modeling: 1, and 3 or 4*
Organizing: 2, 3, and 5
Reflecting: 1, and choice of one*
Extending: 1

When choice is indicated, it is important to leave the choice to the student.
NOTE: *It is best if Organizing tasks are discussed as a whole class after they have been assigned as homework.*

1. a.

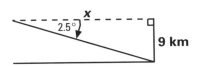

(Diagram: points A and C on top line, $63°$ angle at A, 123 m along line AB, point B on river, right angle at C.)

b. $\cos 63° = \frac{AC}{123}$ $AC = 123 \cdot \cos 63°$
                                   $AC \approx 55.8$ m or about 56 m

c. $\sin 63° = \frac{BC}{123}$ $BC = 123 \sin 63°$
                                   $BC \approx 109.6$ m or about 110 m

2. a. $\tan 2.5° = \frac{9}{x}$ so $x = \frac{9}{\tan 2.5°}$ and $x \approx 206$ km.
The descent should begin about 206 km (horizontally) from the runway.

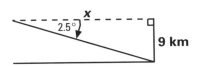

b. $\tan x = \frac{11}{270}$; $x \approx 2.33°$

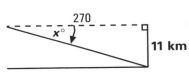

c. Since $-x$ is the distance along her line of sight,
$\sin 14° = \frac{1.5}{x}$
$x = \frac{1.5}{\sin 14°} \approx 6.2$ km
The plane is about 6.2 km from the lake.

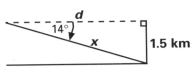

d. At the time she last sees the edge of the lake, the horizontal distance d is $\frac{1.5}{\tan 14°}$ or approximately 6 km.

Unit 6

3. a.

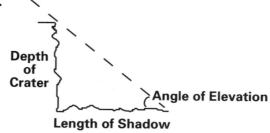

Depth of Crater

Angle of Elevation

Length of Shadow

b. Use the tangent for the angle of elevation:

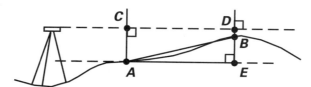

tan (*angle of elevation*) = $\frac{crater\ depth}{shadow\ length}$

c. tan 24° = $\frac{crater\ depth}{315}$ *crater depth* = 315 · tan 24°

crater depth ≈ 140.25 m

d. tan 28° = $\frac{crater\ depth}{264}$ *crater depth* = 264 · tan 28°

crater depth ≈ 140.37 m

Parts c and d are similar values, so the first value is an acceptable estimate.

4. a.

3. Astronomers use the length of shadows in craters on the moon's surface to determine the depth of the craters. Since they can determine the position of the sun and moon rather precisely, they can compute the angle of elevation of the sun from the crater floor.

  a. Sketch a side view of a crater, floor, and shadow.

  b. What trigonometric ratio can be used to estimate the height of the crater wall?

  c. The shadow in one crater is 315 meters when the angle of elevation to the sun is 24°. Estimate the height of the crater wall.

  d. To check the results of Part c, astronomers identified a shadow of 264 meters when the angle of elevation was 28°. Is this consistent with the data in Part c?

4. The *grade* of a road is the ratio of the vertical distance traveled to the horizontal distance traveled. The angle of incline is the angle between the horizontal and the roadbed.

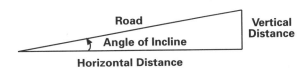

  a. To find the grade of a roadbed, two extendible rods are placed in the ground so they stand completely vertical. A level sighting instrument is used to help adjust the rods until their upper tips are on the horizontal line of sight.

    Make a sketch of the terrain shown below, and then sketch in the rods AC and BD so that $\overline{CD}$ is horizontal.

b. What measures in the diagram of Part a would you need to know to determine the grade of the roadbed?

c. Suppose the rod at A is 2.5 meters, the rod at B is 1.2 meters, and the distance from C to D is 54 meters. Find the grade.

d. Find the angle of incline for the situation in Part c. What trigonometric ratio did you use?

e. Suppose the road grade is 7%. What is the angle of incline?

f. An exit ramp for interstate highway I-94 is to be built with a 4.34% grade to an overpass that is 11 meters above the road surface. How far from the overpass should the engineers plan to begin the ramp?

g. How much could the ramp be shortened if a 5% grade were used?

Organizing

1. Two right triangles, ABC and $A'B'C'$, with right angles at C and C', are similar with a scale factor of k. The lengths of the sides of $\triangle ABC$ are a, b, and c.

   a. Write expressions for the lengths of the sides of $\triangle A'B'C'$.

   b. Write expressions for $\sin A$, $\sin A'$, $\tan A$, and $\tan A'$. What do you notice?

   c. On the basis of your observations in Parts a and b, write an argument demonstrating that $\cos A = \cos A'$ for any two similar right triangles ABC and $A'B'C'$.

2. Enter the numbers 0 through 90, in steps of 5, into List 1 of your calculator or computer software. If you are using a graphing calculator, make certain it is set in degree mode. If you are using computer software, find out how to make certain the software uses angle measurements expressed in degrees.

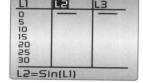

   a. Fill List 2 with the sine of the angle measurements in List 1.
   (That is, $L_2 = \sin L_1$.)

   ■ As the measure of an angle increases from 0° to 90°, how does the sine ratio change?

   ■ Examine a scatterplot of this data. How does this plot compare with those of linear, exponential, power, and quadratic models?

   b. Repeat Part a, filling List 3 with the cosine of the angle measurements in List 1.

   c. Delete the 90 from List 1 and repeat Part a, filling List 4 with the tangent of the angle measurements in List 1.

4. b. You would need to know *CD* and *BE* (the difference in the lengths of *AC* and *BD*).

c. The grade is $\frac{2.5 - 1.2}{54}$ which is $\frac{1.3}{54}$ or approximately 0.024.

d. The angle is about 1.4°. This is computed by solving for *A* in the tangent ratio:

$\tan A = \frac{1.3}{54}$

e. If the grade is 7%, $\left(\text{or } \frac{7}{100}\right)$, then $\tan A = \frac{7}{100}$ and so $A \approx 4°$.

f. Let *d* represent the distance from the overpass.

$0.0434 = \frac{11}{d}$

$d = \frac{11}{0.0434} \approx 253.5$

Engineers should plan to begin about 254 meters from the overpass.

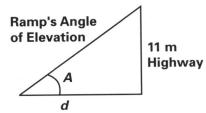

Ramp's Angle of Elevation

11 m Highway

A

d

g. For a 5% grade, $d = \frac{11}{0.05} = 220$ meters.

A savings of about 34 meters could be realized.

Organizing

1. a. The lengths of the sides of *A'B'C'* are *ka*, *kb*, and *kc*.

b. $\sin A = \frac{a}{c}$ $\sin A' = \frac{ka}{kc}$

$\tan A = \frac{a}{b}$ $\tan A' = \frac{ka}{kb}$

The pairs of ratios are equal.

$\frac{ka}{kc} = \frac{a}{c}$ and $\frac{ka}{kb} = \frac{a}{b}$

This means that $\sin A = \sin A'$ and $\tan A = \tan A'$

c. Let the sides of *ABC* be *a*, *b*, and *c*; let *r* be the scale factor so the sides of *A'B'C'* are

$a' = ra$, $b' = rb$ and $c' = rc$.

$\cos A = \frac{b}{c}$ and $\cos A' = \frac{b'}{c'} = \frac{rb}{rc} = \frac{b}{c}$

$\cos A = \cos A'$

(Triangle diagram with vertices *A*, *B*, *C*; side *c* from *A* to *B*, side *a* from *B* to *C*, side *b* from *A* to *C*, right angle at *C*.)

2. In Lesson 3, students will investigate the graphs of the trigonometric functions. You may wish to revisit this task at that time.

a. ■ As the measure of an angle increases from 0° to 90°, the sine ratio increases from 0 to 1. Note that these increases are not constant, however.

■ The plot is clearly not linear. It is not exponential since it goes through the point (0, 0). In this window, however, the graph superficially appears as though it could be modeled by a quadratic function. A power model must contain (0, 0), so students may suggest a power model with exponent less than 1.

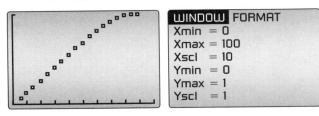

```
WINDOW FORMAT
Xmin = 0
Xmax = 100
Xscl = 10
Ymin = 0
Ymax = 1
Yscl = 1
```

See additional Teaching Notes on page T453I.

3. The entries in List 2 will be such that $L_2 = 90 - L_1$.

   a. One approach would be to see that $L_3 = \sin L_1$ and $L_4 = \cos L_2$ are identical, therefore $\sin A = \cos B$.

   b. Here students may simply say that as one set increases, the other decreases, or that both lists contain the same numbers. If they remember the definitions from a triangle, $\tan A = \frac{a}{b}$, and $\tan B = \frac{b}{a}$, they may recognize that tan A is the reciprocal of tan B. This could be verified in the lists by using $L_4 = \tan L_1$, $L_5 = \tan L_2$, and then noting that $L_6 = \frac{1}{L_4}$ is identical to L_5.

   c. The list $L_2 = \frac{\sin L_1}{\cos L_2}$ is identical to the list $L_3 = \tan L_1$.

      Another approach is to note: $\frac{\sin A}{\cos A} = \frac{\frac{a}{c}}{\frac{b}{c}} = \frac{a}{b} = \tan A$

   d. Using lists, students can see that $(\sin A)^2$ and $(\cos A)^2$ have corresponding elements 0.25 and 0.75, 0.5 and 0.5, 0.75 and 0.25. If they add the two lists, the new list will be all 1s.

      Using the triangle definitions of the ratios:

      $(\sin A)^2 = \frac{a^2}{c^2}$ and $(\cos A)^2 = \frac{b^2}{c^2}$

      $(\sin A)^2 = \frac{a^2}{c^2} + \frac{b^2}{c^2} = \frac{a^2 + b^2}{c^2}$

      since $a^2 + b^2 = c^2$ in a right triangle, $\frac{a^2 + b^2}{c^2} = \frac{c^2}{c^2} = 1$

      thus $(\sin A)^2 + (\cos A)^2 = 1$ for all angles A.

4. In Part c of Organizing Task 3, students found that $\frac{\sin A}{\cos A} = \tan A$.

   This is true for any acute angle A in a right triangle, by the definitions of sine, cosine, and tangent.

   $$\frac{\sin A}{\cos A} = \frac{\frac{\text{length of side opposite } \angle A}{\text{hypotenuse}}}{\frac{\text{length of side adjacent to } \angle A}{\text{hypotenuse}}} = \frac{\text{length of side opposite } \angle A}{\text{length of side adjacent to } \angle A} = \tan A$$

   In Part d, students discovered that $(\sin A)^2 + (\cos A)^2 = 1$. Again we will use the definitions of sine and cosine to show this is true for any acute angle of a right triangle.

   $$(\sin A)^2 + (\cos A)^2 = \left(\frac{\text{length of side opposite } \angle A}{\text{hypotenuse}}\right)^2 + \left(\frac{\text{length of side adjacent to } \angle A}{\text{hypotenuse}}\right)^2$$

   $$= \frac{(\text{length of side opposite } \angle A)^2 + (\text{length of side adjacent to } \angle A)^2}{\text{hypotenuse}^2}$$

   $$= \frac{\text{hypotenuse}^2}{\text{hypotenuse}^2} \text{ (by Pythagorean Theorem)}$$

   $$= 1$$

5. a. See diagram in margin.

51.8°
115
115
230
51.8°

> **See additional Teaching Notes on page T453I.**

3. Systematically vary the acute angles of a right $\triangle ABC$ with $\angle C$ a right angle, and investigate possible patterns relating the trigonometric ratios given below in Parts a–d. It may help to modify the method outlined in Organizing Task 2, with numbers 5 through 85, in steps of 5, in List 1. The entries in List 1 would be possible degree measures for $\angle A$, and you can place in List 2 the corresponding degree measures of $\angle B$.

   a. $\sin A$ and $\cos B$

   b. $\tan A$ and $\tan B$

   c. $\frac{\sin A}{\cos A}$ and $\tan A$

   d. $(\sin A)^2$ and $(\cos A)^2$

4. Use the definitions of the trigonometric ratios to explain why the patterns you observed in Parts c and d of Organizing Task 3 will be true for any acute angle A in a right triangle.

5. The Pyramid of Cheops in Egypt is a right square pyramid. The base edge measures about 230 meters and each face makes an angle with the horizontal desert floor of 51.8°.

   a. Make a model or a sketch of the Pyramid of Cheops. (Use coffee-stirrers or other manipulatives for your model.)

   b. Determine the height of the pyramid.

   c. If you were climbing the pyramid, what would be the shortest route to the top? What is the length of this route?

   d. What is the *grade* of a pyramid face? (See Modeling Task 4 on page 407 for a definition of *grade*.)

   e. Determine the dimensions of the faces of the pyramid.

   f. Determine the volume of the Pyramid of Cheops using the formula $V = \frac{1}{3}Bh$, where B is the area of the base and h is the height of the pyramid.

Unit 6

Reflecting

1. In this lesson, as well as in previous units, you have engaged in important kinds of mathematical thinking. From time to time, it is helpful to examine the kinds of thinking that are broadly useful in doing mathematics. Look over the three investigations and the MORE tasks you completed in this lesson, and consider some of the mathematical thinking you have done. Describe examples in which you did each of the following:

   a. Experimented

   b. Used a variety of representations, like tables, graphs, equations, or verbal descriptions

   c. Searched for patterns

   d. Formulated or found a mathematical model

   e. Visualized

   f. Made and checked conjectures

2. For a right $\triangle ABC$ with $\angle C$ a right angle, if the sides are measured in feet, what is the unit of measure for $\cos A$? Explain your reasoning. What if one side is measured in inches and the other two sides are measured in feet?

3. Consult resources on the history of mathematics to determine the origin of the words sine, cosine, and tangent.

4. a. How is the slope of a line $y = ax$, where $a > 0$, related to the tangent of the angle formed by the line and the positive x-axis?

   b. Write an equation of the line through the origin that forms a 60° angle with the positive x-axis.

5. Find the tallest object on your school campus that cannot easily be measured directly. Prepare a plan to determine the height of the object. Carry out your plan, if it is reasonably possible. (See Extending Task 4 for a way to determine angles, if needed.)

Extending

1. In $\triangle ABC$ shown here, $\overline{BD}$ is an altitude.

   a. Write expressions to represent $\sin A$ and $\sin C$.

   b. Use the results of Part a to write a single equation involving $\sin A$, $\sin C$, a, and c.

   c. Repeat Parts a and b for the altitude from C to $\overline{AB}$, using $\angle A$ and $\angle B$.

   d. What can you conclude about $\frac{\sin A}{a}$, $\frac{\sin B}{b}$, and $\frac{\sin C}{c}$?

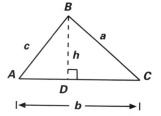

Reflecting

1. Responses will vary. An example of each is given below.
   a. *Experimented:* The automobile jacks of Investigation 1, Activities 3 and 4 are two examples of experimentation.
   b. *Varied Representation:* Varied representations were used as students studied the angles and altitudes of variable-sided triangles in Investigation 1.
   c. *Searched for Patterns:* Pattern search occurred in Investigation 1 dealing with the jacks and in the study of the ratios of sides of triangles in Investigation 2.
   d. *Math Model:* One mathematical model found is the linear motion of the automobile jacks. Another is the development of the trigonometric ratios, which are the models of the relations among sides of similar triangles.
   e. *Visualized:* Visualization was called for in many indirect measurement situations. Also the motion of the auto jacks called for visualization of the path of the jack.
   f. *Conjectures:* The development of the trigonometric functions called for conjectures about patterns.

2. Regardless of what unit is used in measuring the sides of a right triangle, the cosine of A is simply a number. That is, $\cos A$ is the ratio of the length of the side adjacent to $\angle A$ divided by the length of the hypotenuse. Thus the unit used for the length of the sides is immaterial. Of course, all three sides must be measured in the same units.

3. The following information is from *National Council of Teachers of Mathematics Yearbook 31* (Reston, VA: NCTM, 1969), and from Carl Boyer and Uta Merzback, *A History of Mathematics* Second Edition (John Wiley and Sons, Inc.: New York, 1989).

   Sine: Around A.D. 500, the Hindu computed half chords (sines) and used the name *jya*. Later Arabs transliterated this to *jyb*, which was later incorrectly read as *jayb* by Gherardo of Cremona (c. 1150). Gherardo used the Latin equivalent *sinus*, which we now use in the form *sine*.

   Cosine: Cosine, meaning sine of the complement of the angle, began in 1620 with Edmund Gunter who suggested *co.sinus*, which was modified to *consinus* and anglicized to *cosine*.

   Tangent: In 1551, Rheticus explicitly defined the ratio we know as tangent, but it wasn't until 1853 that Thomas Finche contributed the name *tangent*.

4. a. For $a > 0$, the tangent of the angle formed by the line $y = ax$ and the positive x-axis is exactly a, the slope of the given line. One way students can see this is to draw a set of coordinate axes and a line segment in the first quadrant with positive slope. This line segment represents the line $y = ax$, and may be considered the hypotenuse of a right triangle formed by the line segment, the positive x-axis, and a vertical line intersecting both the segment and the x-axis.

   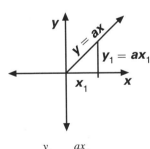

   The slope of a line is defined as the change in y divided by the change in x. This is exactly the length of the vertical line segment divided by the length of the segment of the x-axis used in the triangle, or the tangent of the angle formed by the line $y = ax$ and the x-axis.

   $$\frac{y_1}{x_1} = \frac{ax_1}{x_1} = a$$

   b. From Part a, we know the slope of the desired line is $\tan 60°$ or approximately 1.73. Thus the line $y = 1.73x$ forms a $60°$ angle with the x-axis.

See additional Teaching Notes on page T453J.

Unit 6

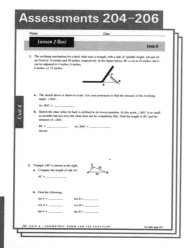

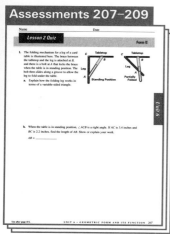

Assessments 204–206

Assessments 207–209

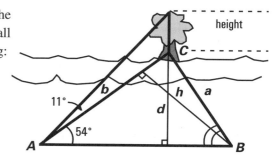

2. Notice that, by definition, $\sin C = \frac{h}{a}$ so $h = a \sin C$.

   Area of $ABC = \frac{1}{2} bh = \frac{1}{2} ba \sin C = \frac{1}{2} ab \sin C$.

3. The measure of angle C is 52°. Draw the altitude from vertex B to side AC, and call its length h. Then we have the following:

   $\sin 54° = \dfrac{h}{50}$

   $h = 50 \sin 54° \approx 40.5$

   $\sin 52° = \dfrac{40.5}{a}$

   $a = \dfrac{40.5}{\sin 52°} \approx 51.3$

   Now draw the altitude from vertex C to side AB, and call its length d. Then we have the following:

   $\sin 74° = \dfrac{d}{51.3}$

   $d = 51.3 \sin 74° \approx 49.3$

   $\sin 54° = \dfrac{49.3}{b}$

   $b = \dfrac{49.3}{\sin 54°} \approx 61.0$

   Use $\tan 11°$ to compute the height.

   $\tan 11° = \dfrac{\text{height}}{61}$

   height $= 61 \tan 11° \approx 11.9$ meters

   Maria is correct.

4. **a.** A clinometer is a large protractor; you align the elevated line along the clinometer's 0° line and note the angle determined by a plumb bob hanging from the zero point. The complement of this angle gives the angle of elevation.

   b. See student work.

   c. Responses will vary.

5. At a maximum slant of 75°, the ladder will reach 20 sin 75° or approximately 19.3 feet. At this angle, the vertical height lost by standing on a rung 2 feet down from the top of the ladder is 2 sin 75° or approximately 1.9 feet, putting the person's feet at 19.3 – 1.9 or 17.4 feet off the ground. The 7.5-foot reach with one arm places the maximum height at 17.4 + 7.5 or 24.9 feet. Students also may use 18 sin 75° + 7.5, which is approximately 24.9 feet.

6. Data will vary, but the general pattern should be as follows: The farther from the landmark, the lower the angle, so as paces increase, the angle decreases.

See Assessment Resources, pages 204–209.

2. Refer to the diagram for Extending Task 1. Explain why the following is true.

$$\text{Area of } \triangle ABC = \tfrac{1}{2}\, ab \cdot \sin C$$

3. While camping by the Merced River in Yosemite Valley, a group of friends were admiring a particular tree on the opposite bank. Maria said that the height of the tree could be determined from their side of the river by the following method:

  ■ Measure a 50-meter segment, $\overline{AB}$, on this shore.

  ■ Considering the tree to be located at point C, measure $\angle BAC$ and $\angle ABC$.

  ■ From A, measure the angle of elevation to the top of the tree.

  ■ Use the measurements above with some trigonometric ratios to calculate the height.

  The friends measured $\angle BAC$ to be 54° and $\angle ABC$ to be 74°. The angle of elevation from point A to the treetop was 11°.

  Draw a sketch of this situation and determine whether Maria was correct. If she was, compute the height; if she was not, explain why not.

4. A *clinometer* (see page 401) is an instrument used to measure angles of elevation.

  a. Consult references in the library to learn how a clinometer works.

  b. Build a wooden or stiff cardboard model of a clinometer.

  c. Use your model to estimate the height of a landmark in your community. Check your estimate against whatever information might be recorded in the community.

5. It is unfortunate, but custodians for public buildings often need to clean graffiti off walls. Mr. Pyper, the custodian at Downhill High School, has a 20-foot ladder. According to information on the ladder, it is safe at angles of 75° or less. If Mr. Pyper can stand on the rung 2 feet below the top of the ladder and reach $7\frac{1}{2}$ feet with one arm, what is the maximum height he can reach with the ladder?

6. Use the clinometer you designed in Extending Task 4. Choose a landmark in your community. Move to a location 100 paces from the landmark, then measure and record the angle of elevation. Move two paces closer to the landmark and repeat the procedure. Complete a table of data pairs (*paces from landmark, angle of elevation*) for 30 measurements. What patterns do you see in the data? Describe the patterns you see in the rate of change in the angles. Make a scatterplot of the (*paces from landmark, angle of elevation*) pairs and describe the graph.

Lesson 3

The Power of the Circle

Quadrilaterals and triangles are used to make everyday things work. Right triangles are the basis for trigonometric ratios relating angle measures to ratios of lengths of sides. Another family of shapes that is broadly useful is the circle and its three-dimensional relatives, such as spheres, cylinders, and circular cones.

An important characteristic of a circle is that it has rotational symmetry about its center. For example, the hub of an automobile wheel is at the center of a circle. As the car moves, it travels smoothly because the circular tire keeps the hub a constant distance from the pavement.

Motors often rotate a cylindrical drive shaft. The more energy output, the faster the drive shaft turns. On an automobile engine, for example, a belt connects three pulleys, one on the crankshaft, one which drives the fan, and another which drives the alternator. When the engine is running, the fan cools the radiator while the alternator generates electrical current.

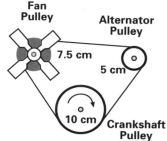

Think About This Situation

The diameter measurements given in the diagram above are for a particular four-cylinder sports car.

a How does the speed of the crankshaft affect the speed of the fan? Of the alternator?

b The idle speed of the crankshaft of a four-cylinder sports car is about 850 rpm (revolutions per minute).

 ■ How far, in centimeters, would a point on the edge of the fan pulley travel in one minute?

 ■ Do you think a similar point on the connected alternator pulley would travel the same distance in one minute? Why or why not?

c Describe another situation in which turning one pulley (or other circular object) turns another.

The Power of the Circle

Master 141

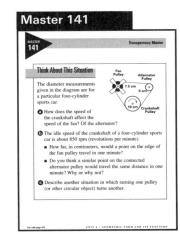

LESSON OVERVIEW

In the previous two lessons, characteristics of the quadrilateral and triangle were studied from points of view that supported particular applications. Uses of those shapes may not be obvious to the untrained eye. In the case of the circle, many of its uses are more evident because its shape is hard to hide in another shape, but, for example, a triangle can hide in a quadrilateral.

This lesson introduces many of the important ideas about circles and their characteristics. It begins with a study of pulleys and sprockets, moves to linear and angular velocity, and ends with the study of the graphs of the trigonometric functions and modeling periodic motion.

Lesson Objectives

■ To analyze a situation involving pulleys or sprockets to determine transmission factors, angular velocity, and linear velocity
■ To sketch the graphs of the sine and cosine functions
■ To determine the period and amplitude of $A \sin Bx$ or $A \cos Bx$
■ To use sines and cosines to model periodic phenomena
■ To use radian and degree measures with trigonometric functions

LAUNCH   full-class discussion

This lesson could be launched with a two-minute brainstorming session, in which groups write as many uses of circular objects (including cross sections that are circular) as they can. Once the group lists are made, you might make a composite list on the board. It is best if you take no more than one or two from a group before moving to the next so that all groups can contribute. For several of the uses identified, you might ask students to describe the characteristics of the circle that are central to each use. Most of these characteristics probably will relate to the complete rotational symmetry of the circle. Let students know that they will study the circle to see how that symmetry plays an important part in so many different applications.

Following the discussion on the applications of circles, students should consider the crankshaft-pulley/alternator-pulley/fan-pulley setup pictured on the opening page. Ask students to speculate on how turning one pulley will affect the other pulleys. This discussion will help you introduce the experiments with linked spools in the first part of Investigation 1.

See additional Teaching Notes on page T453J.

INVESTIGATION 1 Follow That Driver!

In this investigation students work with models of pulleys and sprockets and collect data that can be used to determine the transmission factor from one pulley to another. Students also investigate angular velocity and, using the transmission factor, determine associated angular and linear velocities.

This investigation is written in two sections. In the first section, students get an initial look at angular velocity given in revolutions per unit of time for a system of linked circles or cylinders. Here students explore pulley systems and develop an understanding of the transmission factor that relates a variety of linked pulley systems. The second section asks students to make the transition from revolutions per unit of time to understanding and determining linear velocity.

When Investigation 1 has been completed, the students should understand and be able to apply the concept of transmission factor, in its various forms, to several mechanical situations. The transmission factor from circle A to circle B is given by any of the following ratios:

$$\frac{\text{radius } A}{\text{radius } B} = \frac{\text{diameter } A}{\text{diameter } B} = \frac{\text{circumference } A}{\text{circumference } B} = \frac{\text{angle turned in } B}{\text{angle turned in } A}$$

Thus, if A is turning 3 revolutions per minute, B would turn $3 \times \left(\frac{\text{radius } A}{\text{radius } B}\right)$ revolutions per minute.

Activities 1–3 require students to work in pairs or groups of three. The extra hands are needed because distances and angles will need to be measured while the pulley system is being suspended. The linear data is easier to collect if students wrap a string around the spool (or use the thread on the spool itself) and measure how much comes off as the spool turns. Angles can be measured fairly easily if a baseline is marked on the spool. Setting this baseline to be either vertical or horizontal will simplify the angle measurement problem. For the best results, students should use spools that differ significantly in size.

NOTE: Any cylindrical shape such as oatmeal boxes or nut cans can be used with elastic bands as belts. Dowels inserted through the center of the cylinders will allow for easy turning.

1. **a.** The follower spool turns in the same direction.
   b. The follower spool turns more than one complete revolution when the driver spool has a larger radius than the follower spool. The two spools turn the same amount when they have equal radii. The follower spool turns less than one complete revolution when the follower radius is larger than the driver radius.
   c. The rubber band advances $2\pi r$ units; r is the radius of the driver spool.
   d. Students should make a table and look for a pattern. The pattern should be modeled by: $turn\ of\ follower\ spool = \frac{radius\ of\ driver \cdot turn\ of\ driver\ spool}{radius\ of\ follower}$. This may not be apparent if students' measurements are inaccurate. It will be clearer when students use the data in Part g or in Activity 3.
   e. This is a linear relationship and should appear so when plotted. Students should be able to find a symbolic model to fit, such as $F = 2.5D$ or $y = 2.5x$. At this stage, they may not see the connection with the radii. Some may see that the slope is $\frac{r_d}{r_f}$; where r_d and r_f are the radii of the driver and the follower, respectively.
   f. This part should generate discussion of measurement errors and differing transmission.

INVESTIGATION 1 ▶ Follow That Driver!

In this investigation, you will explore how rotating circular objects that are connected can serve useful purposes. A simple way to investigate how the turning of one circle (the *driver*) is related to the turning of another (the *follower*) is to experiment with thread spools and rubber bands. The spools model the pulleys, sprockets, or gears; the rubber bands model the belts or chains connecting the circular objects. Complete the first two activities working in pairs.

1. Use two thread spools of different sizes. If you use spools that still have thread be certain the thread is securely fastened.

   Put each spool on a shaft, such as a pencil, which permits the spool to turn freely. Make a *driver/follower* mechanism by slipping a rubber band over the two spools and spreading the spools apart so the rubber band is taut enough to reduce slippage. Choose one spool as the driver.

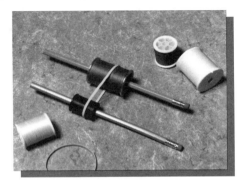

   a. Turn the driver spool. Describe what happens to the follower spool.

   b. Turn the driver spool one complete revolution. Does the follower spool make one complete revolution, or does it make more or fewer turns?

   c. Turn the driver spool one complete revolution. How far does the rubber band advance?

   d. Design and carry out an experiment that gives you information about how turning the driver spool affects the amount of turn of the follower spool, when the spools have different *radii*. Use whole number and fractional turns of the driver. Organize your (*driver turn amount*, *follower turn amount*) data in a table.

   e. Plot your (*driver turn amount*, *follower turn amount*) data. Find an algebraic model that fits the data.

   f. Compare your scatterplot and model with those of other pairs of students.

   - How are they the same? How are they different?

   - What might explain the differences?

Unit 6

g. Examine the driver/follower spool data below.

- What pattern would you expect to see in a plot of these data?
- What algebraic model do you suspect would fit these data?

Driver/Follower Data Set 1

Driver Radius: 2.5 cm	Follower Radius: 2 cm
Driver Turn Amount (in revolutions)	**Follower Turn Amount (in revolutions)**
0.5	0.6
1	1.3
2	2.5
3	3.8
5	6.2
8	10.0
10	12.5
12	15.0

Driver/Follower Data Set 2

Driver Radius: 1 cm	Follower Radius: 1.5 cm
Driver Turn Amount (in revolutions)	**Follower Turn Amount (in revolutions)**
0	0.0
1	0.7
3	2.0
5	3.4
7	4.6
9	6.0
12	8.0
15	10.0

2. Reverse the driver/follower roles of the two spools. How does turning the driver affect the follower now?

3. Suppose the driver spool has a radius of 2 cm and the follower spool has a 1-cm radius.

a. If the driver spool turns through 90 degrees, through how many degrees will the follower spool turn? Support your position experimentally or logically.

b. In general, how will turning the driver spool affect the follower spool? Provide evidence that your conjecture is true, using data or reasoning about the situation.

c. How do the lengths of the radii of the spools affect the driver/follower relation? Answer as precisely as possible.

d. The number by which the turn or speed of the driver is multiplied to get the turn or speed of the follower is often called the **transmission factor** from driver to follower. What is the transmission factor for a driver with a 4-cm radius and a follower with a 2-cm radius? If you reverse the roles, what is the transmission factor?

e. List two sets of driver/follower spool radii so that each set will have a transmission factor of 3. Do the same for transmission factors of $\frac{3}{2}$ and $\frac{4}{5}$.

f. If the driver has radius r_1 and the follower has radius r_2, what is the transmission factor?

1. **g.** ■ Students should expect a linear pattern in a plot of this data.

   ■ In both cases, the algebraic model $y = \dfrac{r_d}{r_f} \cdot x$ fits the data. Students may just suggest a linear model.

2. The effect is just the opposite. If the original follower turned further than the original driver, the new follower will now turn less than the new driver. Some students should be able to give numerical examples, such as "The first follower used to turn about 3 times as far, the new one turns about $\frac{1}{3}$ as far." In fact the transmission factor from B to A is the reciprocal of that from A to B, but students probably do not know this vocabulary yet.

3. **a.** 180°

   Support statements will vary. Students may argue that the follower will turn twice as far as the driver, so if the driver makes a $\frac{1}{4}$ turn the follower makes a $\frac{1}{2}$ turn.

   b. The follower will always travel twice as far. The circumference of the driver spool is twice that of the follower spool, so the follower spool will go around twice for each single turn of the driver spool.

   c. The follower always travels $\dfrac{r_d}{r_f}$ times as far.

   d. $\frac{4}{2}$ or 2, $\frac{2}{4}$ or $\frac{1}{2}$

   e.

Factor	Driver 1	Follower 1	Driver 2	Follower 2
3	3	1	6	2
$\frac{3}{2}$	3	2	6	4
$\frac{4}{5}$	4	5	8	10

   f. The transmission factor is $\dfrac{r_1}{r_2}$.

   A full-class discussion of insights gained in Activities 1–3 would benefit many students. Some will have achieved basic insights, such as that the follower spool turns farther than the driver spool if the driver spool is larger, but might not have related "further" to the ratio of the radii. Some will understand that the radii are the key but not be able to complete the connection. Some will neatly connect this ratio to the transmission factor, but even with accurate graphs, they might not see any connection between slope and the ratio of the radii. Whatever stage they have reached, a class discussion will be helpful to bring out all these ideas. Since the vocabulary *transmission factor* is not introduced until Activity 3, the discussion should give students their first opportunity to describe what they found in their experiments and graphs in Activity 1, using the new vocabulary. To be sure they understand the concept, you might ask, "What if the driver was 3 times as big as the follower? For one turn of the driver, how far would the follower turn? What would the graph look like? If the graph had a slope of 4, what does that tell you about the spools? If the graph had a slope of 0.5? If the transmission factor is 3, what does that tell you about the spools? About the graphs?"

Unit 6

4. a.

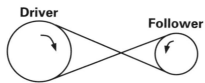

b. If both driver and follower turn counterclockwise, there would be no other differences.

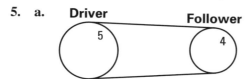

c. The magnitude of the effect is the same as for the model in Part a, but the follower turns in the opposite direction. Thus, the transmission factor could be $\frac{-r_1}{r_2}$, where the minus sign indicates that the wheels are turning in opposite directions. That difference is the only one necessary.

5. a.

Driver **Follower**

5   4

Driver-to-follower transmission factor is $\frac{5}{4}$ or 1.25.

b. $C_d = 2\pi r = 2\pi \cdot 5 = 10\pi$

$C_f = 2\pi \cdot 4 = 8\pi$

Transmission factor: $\dfrac{C_d}{C_f} = \dfrac{2\pi r_d}{2\pi r_f} = \dfrac{2\pi \cdot 5}{2\pi \cdot 4} = \dfrac{10\pi}{8\pi} = \dfrac{5}{4}$

Since the pulleys are attached by a belt, when the driver makes a full turn, it moves the belt a distance equal to its circumference. The belt then turns the follower that same distance, which is $\dfrac{C_d}{C_f}$ times the follower's circumference.

c. Since a point on the circle travels the complete circumference in each revolution it travels, the distance is 10π or approximately 31.4 inches.

d. The point moves 50 times the circumference of the driver.
$50 \cdot C \approx 1570 \, \frac{\text{inches}}{\text{min}}$

e. The transmission factor is 1.25. Therefore, the follower rotates at 1.25 times the rate of the driver.

$$1.25 \cdot 50 = 62.5 \text{ rpm}$$

Some students may calculate as follows: $\dfrac{1{,}570 \, \frac{\text{in}}{\text{min}}}{2\pi \cdot 4 \, \frac{\text{in}}{\text{rev}}} = 62.5 \text{ rpm}$

f. $C \cdot (\text{revolutions in one minute}) = (2\pi \cdot 4) \cdot 62.5 \approx 1{,}571 \text{ inches}$
The same distance is covered by both pulleys. The driver has a larger circumference but rotates more slowly than the follower. The follower has a smaller circumference but rotates more quickly than the driver.

4. In addition to designing a transmission factor into a pulley system, you must also consider the directions in which the pulleys turn.

a. In the spool/rubber band systems you made, did the driver and follower turn in the same direction? Sketch a spool/rubber band system in which turning the driver clockwise turns the follower clockwise also. Label the driver and follower. How would this system look if both the driver and follower were to turn counterclockwise?

b. Sketch a spool/rubber band system in which turning the driver spool clockwise turns the follower counterclockwise. Make a physical model to check your thinking.

c. Suggest a way to describe the transmission factor for the system in Part b. Should the transmission factor differ from a system using the same spools turning in the same direction? If so, how? If not, why not?

5. A clockwise driver/follower system has a driver with a 5-inch radius and a follower with a 4-inch radius.

a. Sketch the system. What is the transmission factor for this system?

b. What are the circumferences of the two pulleys? How could you use the lengths of the circumferences to determine the transmission factor of the system? Explain why this is reasonable.

c. How far does a point on the edge of the driver travel in one revolution of the driver?

d. If the driver is rotating 50 revolutions per minute (rpm), how far does the point in Part c travel in 1 minute?

e. If the driver is turning at 50 rpm, how fast is the follower turning?

f. In one minute, how far does a point on the circumference of the follower travel? Compare this result with that in Part d and explain your findings.

6. Wanda is riding her mountain bicycle using the crankset (also called the pedal sprocket) with 42 teeth of equal size. The rear-wheel sprocket being used has 14 teeth of a size equal to the crankset teeth.

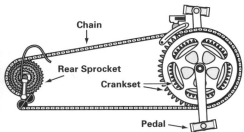

a. What does the "teeth per sprocket" information tell you about the circumferences of the two sprockets? Translate the information about teeth per sprocket into a transmission factor.

b. Wanda is pedaling at 80 revolutions per minute.

- What is the rate at which the rear sprocket is turning? Explain.
- What is the rate at which the rear wheel is turning? Explain.

c. The wheel on Wanda's mountain bike has a radius of about 33 cm.

- How far does the bicycle travel for each complete revolution of the 14-tooth rear sprocket?
- How far does the bicycle travel for each complete revolution of the front sprocket?
- If Wanda pedals 80 rpm, how far will she travel in one minute?

d. How long will Wanda need to pedal at 80 rpm to travel 2 kilometers?

Checkpoint

a What is the significance of the transmission factor in the design of rotating objects that are connected?

b How can you use information about the radii of two connected pulleys, spools, or sprockets to determine the transmission factor?

c Describe the similarities and differences for two belt-drive systems that have transmission factors of $\frac{2}{3}$ and $-\frac{2}{3}$.

d If you know how fast a pulley is turning, how can you determine how far a point on its circumference travels in a given amount of time?

Be prepared to share your descriptions and thinking with the entire class.

As you have seen, the transmission factor for rotating circular objects is positive when the two circular objects turn in the same direction. When they turn in opposite directions, the transmission factor is expressed as a negative value. Using negative numbers to indicate the direction opposite of an accepted standard direction is common in mathematics and science.

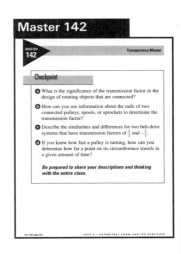

6. This activity is an example in which the transmission factor is used to determine rates for attached sprockets given pedaling rates, and vice versa. Students also look at how rotations per minute relates to distance traveled. Students may have a difficult time understanding that the revolutions per minute for the inside and outside of a wheel will be the same (Part b). You might suggest that students simulate this situation or observe a bike wheel at home to verify for themselves that this is the case.

   a. Since the teeth are equally spaced, the ratio of the teeth of the sprockets is proportional to the ratio of the circumferences of the sprockets, which we know is proportional to the ratio of the radii of the sprockets. Thus we can use teeth per sprocket just as if they were the radii for purposes of finding the transmission factor. The transmission factor is $\frac{42}{14} = 3$.

   b. ■ Rear sprocket rate $= 3 \cdot$ crankset rate $= 3 \cdot 80 = 240$ rpm

      The transmission factor gives the relation between the turning rates. Thus, multiplying by the 3 gives the rear turning rate.

      ■ The rear wheel turns at 240 rpm also since it is attached to the rear sprocket.

   c. ■ Distance $= 2 \cdot \pi \cdot 33 = 66\pi$ cm ≈ 207 cm

      ■ Distance $= 3 \cdot$ (distance traveled with one revolution of the back wheel)
         $= 3 \cdot 66\pi$ cm $= 198\,\pi$ cm ≈ 622 cm

      ■ Distance $= 80 \cdot$ (distance in one revolution)
         $= 80 \cdot 198\,\pi$ cm $= 15{,}840\pi$ cm $\approx 49{,}762.8$ cm or about 498 meters

   d. 2 kilometers $= 2{,}000$ meters. Since Wanda pedals 498 meters in 1 minute, she will need to pedal for $\dfrac{2{,}000 \text{ m}}{498 \text{ m/min}}$ or approximately 4.02 minutes.

SHARE AND SUMMARIZE full-class discussion

Checkpoint

See Teaching Master 142.

ⓐ The transmission factor describes the relationship between the driver and the follower. A transmission factor of b means that a single turn of the driver will cause b turns in the follower.

ⓑ If the driver is A with radius r_A and the follower is B with radius r_B, the transmission factor from A to B is $\dfrac{r_A}{r_B}$.

ⓒ The radii of the pulleys are in the same ratio $\left(\frac{2}{3}\right)$ and the magnification effect of the setup is the same. The difference is that for $\frac{2}{3}$, the pulleys turn in the same direction, while for $-\frac{2}{3}$, they turn in opposite directions.

ⓓ Explanations may vary. The distance traveled by a point on the circumference depends on two variables: R, the number of revolutions per minute, and r, the radius of the pulley. Some students may respond that the revolutions per minute alone do not allow you to determine distance since the revolutions per minute on the inside and outside of a disk are the same. Without knowing r, you cannot say exactly how far the point moves around the circumference. Other students may explain in algebraic language that the radius is needed. If the pulley has radius r, it rolls $2\pi r$ for each revolution. If it makes R revolutions per minute, it rolls $R \cdot 2\pi r$ units. Try to elicit both explanations from the class.

CONSTRUCTING A MATH TOOLKIT: Ask students to summarize the concepts in the first portion of this investigation. Students should include how to find and use a transmission factor, and how the rate at which a pulley is turning can be used to determine how far a point on the edge of the pulley is turning.

MORE

Students can begin Reflecting Task 1 or 3 from the MORE assignment following Investigation 2.

Unit 6

APPLY   individual task

▶**On Your Own**

a. The transmission factor is $\frac{42}{28}$ or $\frac{3}{2}$.

b. The rear sprocket turns at $40 \cdot \frac{3}{2}$ or 60 rpm.

c. 60 rpm $\cdot 2\pi \cdot 32$ cm $\approx 12{,}063.7$ cm

≈ 120.6 m

EXPLORE   small-group investigation

In the remainder of this investigation, students will continue to develop understanding of angular and linear velocity. Angular velocity is most commonly expressed in revolutions per minute, but students also will express it in degrees per minute.

Students will need a clear understanding of the similarities and differences between angular and linear velocity. If you have difficulty assessing students' understanding of the two rates while monitoring group interactions, you may wish to interrupt the group work after Activity 7 to assess with an informal mini-Checkpoint. Asking students to illustrate with a drawing or model may be especially helpful for students who have had little experience with mechanical models. Students should be able to articulate that these rates measure different things. *Angular* velocity quantifies the amount of turning (revolutions) that a circle or cylinder does in a given unit of time, while *linear* velocity quantifies the distance a point on the rim of the circle or cylinder will travel in a given unit of time. Note that both are rates and therefore are given in (a measurement) per unit of time.

7. a. 2,100 rotations per minute · 360 degrees per rotation = 756,000 degrees per minute

b. $\frac{360{,}000 \text{ deg/min}}{360 \text{ deg/rev}} = 1{,}000$ rpm

c. ■ 1 rpm = 360 degrees per minute

■ 1 degree per minute = $\frac{1}{360}$ rpm

► On Your Own

Wanda's mountain bike has 21 speeds. To get started, she shifts gears so the chain connects the 42-tooth crankset with a 28-tooth rear-wheel sprocket.

a. What is the transmission factor for this system?

b. If Wanda pedals at 40 rpm, at what rate do the rear sprocket and wheel turn?

c. If Wanda pedals at 40 rpm, how far will she travel in one minute if her bike has tires with 64-cm diameters?

The rate (usually in revolutions per minute) at which an object such as a pulley, sprocket, or drive shaft turns is called its **angular velocity**. When Wanda pedaled her bike at 80 rpm, the angular velocity was 80 revolutions per minute. Since one complete revolution turns through 360 degrees, an angular velocity of 80 rpm is also $80 \cdot 360°$ per minute or 28,800° per minute. The distance that a point on a revolving circle moves in a unit of time is called its **linear velocity**.

In Activity 6 Part c, you found the linear velocity in cm/min of a point on a bike's tire. In Activities 7 and 8, you will explore more fully the idea of angular and linear velocity and how they are affected in systems in which one sprocket or pulley drives another.

7. a. The Ford Explorer has a tachometer on its instrument panel that gives revolutions per minute (rpm) of the engine. When the car is driven steadily at about 60 mph in overdrive, the tachometer reads about 2,100 rpm. What is the equivalent angular velocity in degrees per minute?

b. The idle speed of the engine is about 360,000° per minute. What is the reading (in rpm) of the tachometer?

c. Complete each statement

- 1 rpm = _____ degrees per minute
- 1 degree per minute = _____ rpm

8. A new 21-speed mountain bike has a crankset of 3 sprockets with 48, 40, and 30 teeth; the bike has 7 sprockets for the rear wheel with 30, 27, 24, 21, 18, 15, and 12 teeth.

a. What is the largest transmission factor available for this bicycle? What is the smallest?

b. Suppose in cross-country riding you can maintain an angular velocity of 70 rpm for the crankset. How fast can you make the rear wheel turn?

c. The radius of a mountain bike tire is about 34 cm. What is the linear velocity of the rear wheel when the crankset turns at 70 rpm and the transmission factor is greatest? When the crankset turns at 70 rpm and the transmission factor is least?

9. The crankshaft of a particular automobile engine has an angular velocity of 1,500 rpm at 30 mph. The crankshaft pulley has a diameter of 10 cm, and it is attached to an air conditioner compressor pulley with a 7-cm diameter and an alternator pulley with a 5-cm diameter.

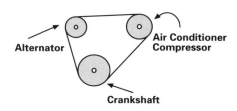

a. At what angular velocities do the compressor and alternator turn?

b. The three pulleys are connected by a 60-cm belt. At a crankshaft rate of 1,500 rpm, how many times will the belt revolve through its 60-cm length in one minute?

c. Most belts do not show significant wear until each point of the belt has traveled about 20,000 kilometers. How long can the engine run at 1,500 rpm before the fan belt typically would show wear?

Checkpoint

ⓐ How is *degrees per unit of time* related to *revolutions per unit of time*?

ⓑ In what units may the angular velocity and the linear velocity of a point in circular motion be measured? Give a rationale for each unit chosen.

ⓒ Explain the relations among the radii, the circumferences, and the transmission factor of two connected circular pulleys.

Be prepared to explain your group's responses to the whole class.

Master 143

8. a. The largest transmission factor available is $\frac{48}{12}$ or 4. The smallest transmission factor available is $\frac{30}{30}$ or 1.

b. The highest transmission factor is 4, so the rear wheel can turn at $4 \cdot 70$ revolutions per minute or 280 rpm.

c. Using the greatest transmission which is 4, the crankset speed of 70 rpm and a wheel radius of 34 cm:

Linear velocity = distance traveled by a point on the circumference per minute

$$= 280 \cdot \text{length of circumference per minute}$$
$$= 280(2\pi \cdot 34) \text{ centimeters per minute}$$
$$= 19,040 \cdot \pi \text{ cm per minute}$$
$$\approx 598.2 \text{ meters per minute}$$

The lowest transmission factor is 1. Thus the 70 rpm translates into 70 rpm angular velocity of the rear wheel.

$$70 \cdot 2\pi \cdot 34 = 4,760\pi \text{ cm per minute}$$
$$\approx 14,954 \text{ cm per minute or } 149.5 \text{ meters per minute}$$

9. a. The 10-cm pulley turns at 1,500 rpm since it is attached to the crankshaft. The transmission factor to the compressor pulley is $\frac{10}{7}$, so this pulley has angular velocity equal to $\frac{10}{7} \cdot 1,500$ rpm or approximately 2,142.9 rpm.
The alternator pulley turns at $2 \cdot 1,500$ or 3,000 rpm.

b. $1,500 \cdot 5 \cdot 2 \cdot \pi = 15,000\pi$ cm per minute
To find the number of times the 60-cm belt revolves, divide:

$$\frac{15,000\pi}{60} = 250\pi \approx 785 \text{ times}$$

c. 1,500 rpm translates into $1,500 \cdot 2\pi \cdot 5$ cm per minute linear velocity. This is $15,000\pi$ cm each minute. To change this to kilometers per minute, first divide by 100 to change to meters and then by 1,000 to change to kilometers. Therefore, $15,000\pi$ cm per minute $= 0.15\pi$ kilometers per minute.

To change to kilometers per hour, multiply by 60 min/hr. Therefore, 0.15π kilometers per minute $= 9\pi$ kilometers per hour. (The belt travels 9π kilometers each hour of continuous running.)

To determine the hours needed to reach 20,000 km, divide 20,000 by 9π:

$$\frac{20,000}{9\pi} \approx 707.4 \text{ hours}$$

This is approximately 29.5 days of nonstop driving. (At 30 mph, you will travel about 21,220 miles.)

SHARE AND SUMMARIZE full-class discussion

Checkpoint

See Teaching Master 143.

a Degrees per unit of time equals 360 deg/rev times revolutions per unit of time, since each revolution has 360 degrees.

See additional Teaching Notes on page T453K.

CONSTRUCTING A MATH TOOLKIT: Ask students to write illustrated definitions for each of the new terms in this investigation including *angular velocity* and *linear velocity*. If students have been identifying other mechanical applications of pulley systems, you may wish to have them use their applications to illustrate the concepts.

MORE

ASSIGNMENT   *pp. 424–431*

Students can now begin
Modeling Task 3 and their
choice of another Modeling
Task, Organizing Task 2 or 3, or
Extending Task 1 or 5 from the
MORE assignment following
Investigation 2.

APPLY individual task

▶**On Your Own**

a.   ■ The transmission factor is $\frac{30}{5}$ or 6. Therefore, if the driver moves at 1 revolution per second, the sewing machine pulley turns at 6 revolutions per second (or 6 stitches per second). Thus the sewing machine makes 10 minutes · 60 seconds/minute · 6 stitches/second or 3,600 stitches in 10 minutes.

   ■ The belt travels one complete rotation of the driver or 30π cm each second. Therefore, it travels $30\pi \frac{cm}{sec}$ · 10 min · 60 $\frac{sec}{min}$ or approximately 56,549 cm in 10 minutes.

b.   The 5-cm sewing pulley must make 6 revolutions per second. Thus $\frac{1.5}{5} \cdot x$ rps = 6 rps; x is the angular velocity of the motor. Solving for x gives 20 revolutions per second, or 7,200 degrees per second.

EXPLORE small-group investigation

INVESTIGATION ▶2▶ Radian Measure

In this investigation, radian measure of angles is introduced. Students first review the two familiar ways in which they measured angles, namely, revolutions and degrees. These are modeled by examining the angle swept by a rotating object. Students are introduced to radian measure through an experiment in which they discover that the size of the central angle of a circle, determined by an arc equal in length to the radius of the circle, remains the same for all circles.

Compasses, protractors, and string or dental floss are necessary for this investigation.

Students should proceed through the early activities quite rapidly. It is especially important that groups work together on Activity 3 to avoid stalling the investigation at that point. You may wish to bring the class together, briefly, after Activity 3. See the notes on page T420.

Students may find the notion of a radian difficult to grasp. This may be because the vocabulary word is close to "radius" or because students have confused ideas about what an angle measure is. Some students become distracted by the sector of the circle, and they may see a radian as a geometric shape rather than a measurement unit. Activity 3 encourages students to make the logical connection that if it takes 2π radii to wrap around the circumference of any circle, then it also will take 2π times the measure of the angle created at the center, subtended by an arc with length equal to one radius, to complete one revolution. It is important that students see that this is true for all circles; you may wish to draw several circles for students, thereby avoiding the time necessary to organize the distribution and use of compasses.

▶ On Your Own

Although they are no longer used in the United States, foot-operated sewing machines are used in developing countries where electricity either is not available or is too expensive. The foot-operated sewing machine shown below has a driver pulley which is 30 cm in diameter and is attached by a belt to a sewing pulley with a 5-cm diameter. The sewing machine makes one stitch for each revolution of its sewing pulley.

a. The driver pulley is turned easily at one revolution per second.

- How many stitches does the machine make in 10 minutes?
- How far would the belt travel in 10 minutes?

b. If the foot pedal (driver) was replaced by an electric motor with a pulley of diameter 1.5 cm, how fast would it need to turn to duplicate the same sewing rate? Give your answer in two ways, revolutions/second and degrees/second.

INVESTIGATION 2 Radian Measure

Angular velocity can be modeled with two strips attached to a cardboard disk as shown below. One strip (in this case, strip *OB*) is fixed like the frame in a linkage and the other strip can turn about the center of the circle. As strip *OA* rotates about *O* in a counterclockwise direction, the angle *AOB* sweeps through measures from 0° to 360°.

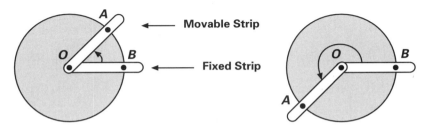

G. 2/31

1. Imagine the starting position for strip *OA* has point *A* coinciding with point *B* in the diagram on the previous page. Then imagine that strip *OA* rotates through the angles indicated in Parts a–f. Describe the location of point *A* at the end of each rotation.

   a. 1 revolution

   b. 360°

   c. $\frac{1}{2}$ revolution

   d. 180°

   e. $2\frac{1}{2}$ revolutions

   f. 45°

2. Now think about the relationship between circular revolutions and degrees.

   a. How many degrees are swept through when strip *OA* rotates $\frac{3}{4}$ revolution? $1\frac{1}{2}$ revolutions? *n* revolutions?

   b. How many revolutions are swept through when strip *OA* rotates 60°? 480°? *n*°?

   c. Complete the following:

   1 revolution = _____ degrees

   1 degree = _____ revolutions

Revolutions and degrees are two units by which you can measure ∠*AOB*. In the next activity you will investigate another unit of angle measure.

3. Working in a group of at least four students, conduct the following experiment. Share the workload among your group members.

   a. With a compass, draw 8 circles with radii varying from 3 cm to 10 cm in increments of 1 cm. For each circle, let *O* be the center of the circle and let *B* be a point on the circle. Use a pipe cleaner, dental floss, or string to locate a new point *A* on the circle so that the length of the arc *AB* is equal to the radius of the circle. Draw ∠*AOB* and measure it, using degrees as your unit. For each circle, record both its radius and the measure of ∠*AOB*. (A shorter way of writing "the measure of ∠*AOB*" is **m∠*AOB*.**)

   b. Examine the numerical data. Describe any patterns you observe. Make and describe the scatterplot of (*radius, measure of* ∠*AOB*) data.

   c. What size angle would be determined by a 13-cm arc in a circle with a radius of 13 cm? Explain your thinking.

   d. Suppose a circle with center *O* has radius *r*. What will the measure of ∠*AOB* be if the arc *AB* is *r* units long?

1. **a–b.** Point *A* returns to its original location.

    c–e. Point *A* is directly opposite its original location.

    f. Point *A* is halfway between its original location and due north on the circle.

2. **a.** $\frac{3}{4} \cdot 360° = 270°$, $1.5 \cdot 360° = 540°$, $n \cdot 360°$

    b. $\frac{60}{360} = \frac{1}{6}$ revolution, $\frac{480}{360} = \frac{4}{3}$ revolutions, $\frac{n}{360}$ revolutions

    c. 1 revolution = 360 degrees, 1 degree $= \frac{1}{360}$ revolution

3. **a.** Data should be recorded in a table. Theoretically each angle measure should be approximately 57°. The actual angle measures may vary somewhat due to imprecise measuring of the string or the angles.

    b. Students should observe that the measures of the angles are clustered around 57°. The scatterplot should show the points clustered around a horizontal line.

    c. Based on the pattern observed in Part b, the angle should be approximately 57°.

    d. $m\angle AOB \approx 57°$

Students may find it helpful if you draw the whole class together for a discussion about the results from Activity 3. Be sure to ask why it is reasonable to expect that the angle measure always will be the same size; this draws on students' understanding of similarity and of what they already know about the circumference of a circle. (All sectors created by this process are similar; they are all "wedges" of a circle; you need 2π wedges to complete each circle.)

You also might ask students why they find degrees easy to understand. What is logical about using 360 units to divide up a revolution? A very short conversation should bring out that students are only comfortable with this system because of long familiarity and that they have probably never wondered why "360." (It is an ancient unit of measurement and seems related to the distance thought to have been traveled by the sun, around the earth, in one day.) Ask them to think of other examples of something that can be measured with two different systems. (Heights in centimeters and in inches, etc.) Finally ask them to draw any angle and measure it in degrees and in radians. (They can use their protractors to measure the angle in degrees, but they will have to create new benchmarks on their protractors to measure the angle in radians. The answer will have to be very approximate, such as "about $1\frac{1}{4}$ radians.")

For other ideas, see "Using Technology to Introduce Radian Measure," *The Mathematics Teacher*, **Vol. 90, No. 2, Feb. 1997.**

Unit 6

4. **a.** 1 radian $<$ 1 revolution

1 radian $>$ 1 degree

b. The measure of $\angle AOB$ is 2 radians since the arc intercepted is 2 times the radius.

c. The measure of $\angle AOB$ is $\frac{22}{4}$ or 5.5 radians since 22 inches is 5.5 times the radius.

d. ■ The length of the intercepted arc is half the circumference, $\frac{2\pi r}{2}$ or πr. The radian measure of $\angle AOB$ is $\frac{\text{arc length}}{\text{radius}}$ or $\frac{\pi r}{r}$, which is equal to π.

■ Since there are $2\pi r$ linear units in a circumference and 1 radian $= r$, there are $\frac{2\pi r}{r}$ or 2π radians in the entire circle.

e. These are both 1 revolution, so they are identical in size.

A **radian** is the measure of an angle determined by joining the center of a circle to the endpoints of an arc equal in length to the radius of the circle. (See the diagram below.)

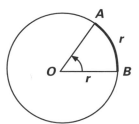

length arc _AB_ = _r_ = radius
m∠_AOB_ = 1 radian

4. Think about how you could measure angles in radians.

   a. Is 1 radian larger or smaller than 1 revolution? Than 1 degree?

   b. Draw a sketch of a circle with center _O_, radius 8 cm, and a *central angle AOB* which intercepts an arc _AB_ of length 16 cm. What is the radian measure of ∠_AOB_? Explain your reasoning.

   c. Draw a sketch of a circle with center _O_, radius 4 inches, and central angle _AOB_ which intercepts an arc _AB_ of length 22 inches. What is the radian measure of ∠_AOB_? Explain your reasoning.

   d. Reproduced below is the rotating strip model from the beginning of this investigation.

   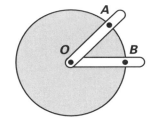

   ■ Imagine strip _OA_ making $\frac{1}{2}$ revolution from a starting point coinciding with strip _OB_. What would be the length of the *intercepted arc AB*? What would be the radian measure of the central angle _AOB_?

   ■ Imagine strip _OA_ making a complete revolution. What would be the radian measure of the angle it sweeps?

   e. Explain why an angle with measure 2π radians is congruent to an angle of 360˚.

The degree is the unit of angle measure used in some practical applications, such as surveying, navigation, and industrial design. In scientific work and in advanced work in mathematics, it is usually more convenient to use radian measure. In the next two activities, you will explore how to convert between degree and radian measures.

5. Analyze how Anna and Steve used the fact that 2π radians = 360° to find the radian measure equivalent to 120°.

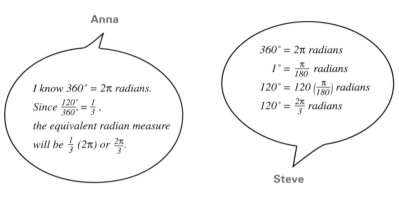

Anna

I know 360° = 2π radians.
Since $\frac{120°}{360°} = \frac{1}{3}$,
the equivalent radian measure
will be $\frac{1}{3}(2\pi)$ or $\frac{2\pi}{3}$.

$360° = 2\pi$ *radians*
$1° = \frac{\pi}{180}$ *radians*
$120° = 120\left(\frac{\pi}{180}\right)$ *radians*
$120° = \frac{2\pi}{3}$ *radians*

Steve

   a. How do you think Anna would find the radian measure equivalent to 30°?

   b. How do you think Steve would find the radian measure equivalent to 30°?

   c. Which method, Anna's or Steve's, do you find easiest to use?

   d. How do you think Anna would reason to find the degree measure equivalent to $\frac{\pi}{3}$ radians?

   e. How do you think Steve would reason to find the degree measure equivalent to $\frac{\pi}{3}$ radians?

6. Use any method you prefer to determine the equivalent angle measures in Parts a–c.

   a. Determine the radian measures equivalent to the following degree measures.

   ■ 45°   ■ 30°   ■ 150°   ■ 210°

   b. Determine the degree measures equivalent to the following radian measures.

   ■ $\frac{\pi}{6}$ ■ $\frac{\pi}{3}$ ■ $\frac{3\pi}{2}$ ■ $\frac{11\pi}{6}$

   c. Complete a copy of this table of degree/radian measure equivalents. Save your completed table to use later.

Degree/Radian Equivalents

Degrees	0	30	45	?	90	?	135	150	?	210	?	240	270	300	315	?	360
Radians	?	?	?	$\frac{\pi}{3}$	?	$\frac{2\pi}{3}$	?	?	π	?	$\frac{5\pi}{4}$	?	?	?	?	$\frac{11\pi}{6}$	?

5. a. Anna would use $360° = 2\pi$, $\frac{30°}{360°} = \frac{1}{12}$, and $\frac{1}{12}(2\pi) = \frac{\pi}{6}$ radians.

   b. Steve would use $1° = \frac{\pi}{180}$ radians, so $30° = 30\left(\frac{\pi}{180}\right) = \frac{\pi}{6}$ radians.

   c. Opinions will differ.

   d. Anna might reason $\frac{\pi}{3}$ is $\frac{2\pi}{6}$, which is $\frac{1}{6}$ of 2π, and $\frac{1}{6}$ of $360°$ is $60°$.

   e. Steve might reason $360° = 2\pi$ radians, so 1 radian $= \frac{180}{\pi}$ degrees.
   Then $\frac{\pi}{3}$ radians $\cdot \frac{180 \text{ degrees}}{\pi \text{ radians}} = 60°$.

6. a. ■ $45° = \frac{\pi}{4}$ radians   ■ $30° = \frac{\pi}{6}$ radians

   ■ $150° = \frac{5\pi}{6}$ radians   ■ $210° = \frac{7\pi}{6}$ radians

   b. ■ $\frac{\pi}{6} = 30°$ ■ $\frac{\pi}{3} = 60°$

   ■ $\frac{3\pi}{2} = 270°$ ■ $\frac{11\pi}{6} = 330°$

   c. Degree/Radian Equivalents

Degrees	0	30	45	60	90	120	135	150	180	210	225	240	270	300	315	330	360
Radians	0	$\frac{\pi}{6}$	$\frac{\pi}{4}$	$\frac{\pi}{3}$	$\frac{\pi}{2}$	$\frac{2\pi}{3}$	$\frac{3\pi}{4}$	$\frac{5\pi}{6}$	π	$\frac{7\pi}{6}$	$\frac{5\pi}{4}$	$\frac{4\pi}{3}$	$\frac{3\pi}{2}$	$\frac{5\pi}{3}$	$\frac{7\pi}{4}$	$\frac{11\pi}{6}$	2π

Unit 6

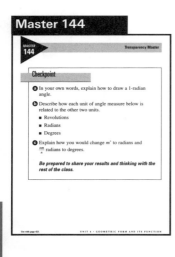

EXPLORE *continued*

7. a. 2,100 rpm $= 360 \cdot 2,100 = 756,000°$ per minute

2,100 rpm $= 2\pi \cdot 2,100 = 4,200\pi$ radians per minute

$\approx 13,195$ radians per minute

b. 1,000 rpm $= 2\pi \cdot 1,000 = 2,000\pi$ radians per minute

$\approx 6,283$ radians per minute

c. $6,000\pi$ radians per minute $= \dfrac{6,000\pi}{2\pi} = 3,000$ rpm

3,000 rpm $= 360 \cdot 3,000 = 1,080,000$ degrees per minute

SHARE AND SUMMARIZE full-class discussion

Checkpoint

See Teaching Master 144.

ⓐ Responses may vary, but students should describe an arc equal in length to the radius and indicate that the angle at the center of the circle determined by that arc has measure 1 radian.

ⓑ 1 revolution $= 2\pi$ radians $= 360$ degrees

ⓒ To change $m°$ to radians, multiply by $\dfrac{\pi}{180}$. $m° = \dfrac{m\pi}{180}$ radians. Since 2π radians $= 360°$, π radians $= 180°$. Thus, substitution of $180°$ for π in $\dfrac{m\pi}{n}$ will convert it to degrees: $\dfrac{m\pi}{n}$ radians $= \dfrac{180m}{n}$ degrees. (Students may prefer to multiply by $\dfrac{180}{\pi}$.)

CONSTRUCTING A MATH TOOLKIT: Ask students to write a description and draw a diagram showing the concept of radian measure. Also have them make a table (or circle diagram as in Investigation 3) of equivalent measures for angles using radians, expressed as fractions of π and degrees. (See Activity 6 Part c in Investigation 2.) This resource should be available for reference until the radian measures become familiar.

APPLY individual task

▶ On Your Own

a. 8π radians per second

b. 48π radians per second

c. $\dfrac{100\pi}{6}$ radians per second

7. Consider once again the information provided by a vehicle's tachometer.

   a. A tachometer of a Ford Explorer reads 2,100 rpm at 60 mph. Find the equivalent angular velocity in degrees per minute and in radians per minute.

   b. The idle speed of a Ford Explorer is 1,000 rpm. Find the angular velocity in radians per minute.

   c. What rpm reading would the tachometer show for an angular velocity of the engine at $6,000\pi$ radians per minute? What would be the degrees per minute equivalent of that angular velocity?

Checkpoint

a In your own words, explain how to draw a 1-radian angle.

b Describe how each unit of angle measure below is related to the other two units.
   ▪ Revolutions
   ▪ Radians
   ▪ Degrees

c Explain how you would change $m°$ to radians and $\frac{m\pi}{n}$ radians to degrees.

Be prepared to share your results and thinking with the rest of the class.

▶On Your Own

The driver pulley of the foot-operated sewing machine in the "On Your Own" on page 419 turns at 4 revolutions per second.

a. What is its angular velocity in radians per second?

b. The driver pulley (30-cm diameter) turns a sewing pulley with a 5-cm diameter. What is the angular velocity of the sewing pulley in radians per second?

c. A tailor wants the sewing pulley to turn at a rate of 100π radians per second. How fast, in radians per second, must the driver pulley turn to accomplish this rate?

Modeling • Organizing • Reflecting • Extending

Modeling

1. Some bikes used by racing cyclists have 7 sprockets of different sizes connected to the rear wheel and three different-sized sprockets in the crankset attached to the pedals. Typically, the 7 sprockets at the rear have 15, 17, 19, 21, 23, 25, and 27 teeth. The crankset sprockets have 28, 38, and 48 teeth.

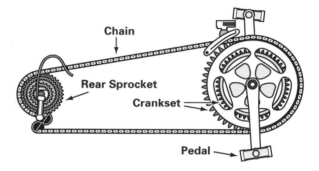

Chain
Rear Sprocket
Crankset
Pedal

a. What are the two largest crankset-to-rear-sprocket transmission factors? What are the two smallest?

b. One racing bike's wheels have a diameter of about 68 cm. For each of the four arrangements of sprockets in Part a, determine how far a wheel rolls for one revolution of the crankset.

c. In the level-ground touring mode, cyclists may turn the crankset at a rate of 80 times per minute. How fast will the rear wheel turn for the two smallest rear-wheel sprockets connected to the largest crankset sprocket?

d. When cyclists go downhill, sometimes they let the bike "free wheel"—that is, they stop pedaling. Why?

e. Assume the best crankset-to-rear-sprocket advantage and a pedaling rate of 80 rpm. When traveling downhill, what rear-wheel angular velocity would make continued pedaling not useful?

Modeling

1. **a.** $\frac{48}{15}$ or 3.2 is the largest transmission factor. $\frac{48}{17}$ or approximately 2.8 is the second largest transmission factor.

   $\frac{28}{27}$ or approximately 1.0 is the smallest transmission factor. $\frac{28}{25}$ or approximately 1.1 is the second smallest transmission factor.

   b. $\frac{48}{15} \cdot \pi \cdot 68 \approx 683.6$ cm

   $\frac{48}{17} \cdot \pi \cdot 68 \approx 603.2$ cm

   $\frac{28}{25} \cdot \pi \cdot 68 \approx 239.3$ cm

   $\frac{28}{27} \cdot \pi \cdot 68 \approx 221.5$ cm

   c. 80 rpm $\cdot \frac{48}{15} = 256$ rpm

   and 80 rpm $\cdot \frac{48}{17} = \frac{3,840}{17}$ rpm ≈ 225.9 rpm

   d. If the downward direction propels the bike at a rate that causes the rear wheel to turn more rapidly than the steady pedaling rate, then the pedaling would slow you down or have no effect.

   e. 80 rpm $\cdot \frac{48}{15} = 256$ rpm

   When the rear wheel turns at about 256 rpm or greater, pedaling at 80 rpm will have no effect.

MORE
ASSIGNMENT   *pp. 424–431*

Modeling: 3 and choice of one*
Organizing: 2 and 3
Reflecting: 1 and 4
Extending: 1 or 5*

*When choice is indicated, it is important to leave the choice to the student.
NOTE: *It is best if Organizing tasks are discussed as a whole class after they have been assigned as homework.*

Unit 6

2. This task is useful for helping students understand units of measure.

    a. $0.5 \frac{mi}{hr} \cdot 5,280 \frac{ft}{mi} \cdot \frac{1\ hr}{60\ min} = 44 \frac{ft}{min}$

        $1.2 \frac{mi}{hr} \cdot 5,280 \frac{ft}{mi} \cdot \frac{1\ hr}{60\ min} = 105.6 \frac{ft}{min}$

    b. At low speed: $\frac{146\ rpm}{44\ ft/min} \approx 3.3$ tilling cycles per foot

        At high speed: $\frac{146\ rpm}{105.6\ ft/min} = 1.4$ tilling cycles per foot

    c. Since the circumference of the wheels in feet is approximately 1.167π, the angular velocities of the wheels are $\frac{44\ ft/min}{1.167\pi\ ft/rev}$ or approximately 12.0 rpm and $\frac{105.6\ ft/min}{1.167\pi\ ft/rev}$ or approximately 28.8 rpm.

    d. Since the engine drive shaft rotates at 3,000 rpm and the follower (the wheels) turns at 12 rpm and 28.8 rpm, we have the following:

        velocity of driver · transmission factor = velocity of follower

        3,000 rpm $\cdot\ x = 12$ rpm $\rightarrow x = 0.004$

        3,000 rpm $\cdot\ x = 28.8$ rpm $\rightarrow x = 0.0096$

        The transmission factors are 0.004 and 0.0096.

3. **a.** For driver of 10 and follower of 4, the transmission factor is $\frac{10}{4}$ or 2.5. For the 8 to 2, the transmission factor is $\frac{8}{2}$ or 4. Since the 4 and 8 turn together, the rate that is transmitted to the 4 occurs at the 8 as well (like a rear wheel and sprocket). Thus, the transmission factor from *A* to *B* is $\frac{10}{4} \cdot \frac{8}{2}$ or 10.

    b. $\frac{x}{2} = 10$

        Therefore, if the radius of the single pulley were 20, it would do the job. A single pulley has only one belt to check, while a double pulley saves space by having smaller radii.

2. The Horse model of the Troy-Bilt Roto Tiller has two forward speeds when the engine drive shaft has angular velocity of 3,000 rpm. The speeds are 0.5 and 1.2 mph.

   a. In feet per minute, how fast does the tiller move at each speed?

   b. The tiller assembly turns at 146 revolutions per minute at both speeds. How many tilling cycles (revolutions) occur in each foot of a garden at each speed?

   c. The wheels on the tiller are 14 inches in diameter. What is the angular velocity of the wheels at each speed?

   d. What is the transmission factor from engine drive shaft to wheels at each speed?

3. Recall that a large driver pulley provides a smaller pulley with greater angular velocity than the driver itself has. For example, a transmission factor of 20 is attained by driving a 4-cm pulley with an 80-cm one. However, physical size constraints often limit the radii of the drivers. To avoid large driver pulleys, two or more pulley-belt systems may be hooked together so that the follower in one directly turns the driver of the second.

   a. Determine by experiment or reasoning the transmission factor from pulley A to pulley B in the diagram below. Two pulleys on the same shaft, as in the middle of the diagram, turn together and therefore have the same angular velocity.

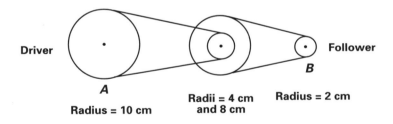

   b. What radius would the driver pulley need to be to produce the same transmission factor found in Part a if the intermediate double pulley were not there? What are the advantages of each setup?

c. Determine the transmission factor from *A* to *B* for each pulley/sprocket set up below. The numbers on the pulleys are their radii in centimeters.

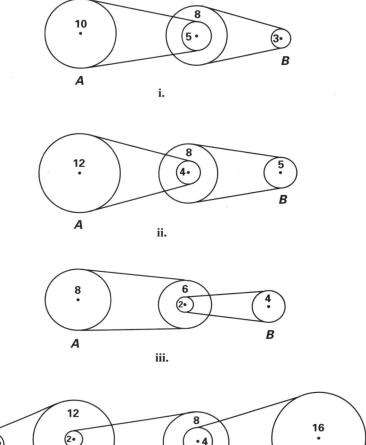

i.

ii.

iii.

iv.

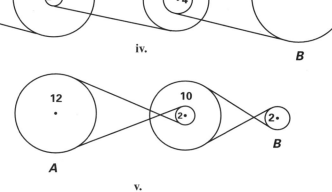

v.

3. c.   **i.** $\frac{10}{5} \cdot \frac{8}{3} = \frac{80}{15} \approx 5.3$

        ii. $\frac{12}{4} \cdot \frac{8}{5} = \frac{96}{20} = 4.8$

       iii. $\frac{8}{6} \cdot \frac{2}{4} = \frac{16}{24} = \frac{2}{3}$

       iv. $\frac{3}{12} \cdot \frac{2}{8} \cdot \frac{4}{16} = \frac{24}{12 \cdot 8 \cdot 16} = \frac{1}{64}$

        v. $\frac{-12}{2} \cdot \frac{-10}{2} = 30$

Unit 6

4. **a.** A sketch with a 7-cm and a 10-cm sprocket follows.

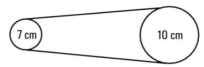

    b. ■ Angular velocity of rear axle $= \frac{7}{10} \cdot 1{,}620$ rpm $= 1{,}134$ rpm

        ■ Diameter (in km) $= 0.00028$ km

          Circumference (in km) $= 0.00028\pi$ km

          Speed $= 1{,}134$ rpm $\cdot 0.00028\pi$ km/revolution

                ≈ 0.998 km/min $\cdot 60$ min/hr

                ≈ 59.9 km/hr

    c. For a speed of 30 km/hr:

        x rpm $\cdot 0.00028\pi \, \frac{\text{km}}{\text{rev}} \cdot 60 \, \frac{\text{min}}{\text{hr}} = 30 \, \frac{\text{km}}{\text{hr}}$

        x rpm ≈ 568.4 rpm for the wheel

        Multiply by $\frac{10}{7}$ to get the engine speed of approximately 812 rpm.

Organizing

1. **a.** The maximum is $8 \div 5$ or 1.6.

        The minimum is $4 \div 10$ or 0.4.

4. In go-carts, the engine-driven sprocket is attached to the rear axle by a belt. These sprockets can have many different numbers of teeth depending upon course demands and safety.

a. Sketch the situation in which an engine sprocket with a 7-cm diameter drives a rear-axle sprocket with a 10-cm diameter.

b. The engine is turning at 1,620 rpm.

   ■ Find the angular velocity of the rear axle.

   ■ Find the go-cart's speed, in km per hour, if the rear wheels have a diameter of 28 cm.

c. When rounding corners, a speed of 30 km per hour or less is needed to reduce lateral sliding. What engine speed, in rpm, is desirable?

Organizing

1. Some automobile manufacturers are researching an automatic, continuously variable gear based on segments of cones. A simplified model is shown below. It consists of two 10-centimeter segments of right cones. The diameters of the circular ends are given. These partial cones form the basis for a *variable-drive* system, in which either partial cone can be moved laterally (left and right) along a shaft. (Cone-shaped drinking cups can be used to model this situation.)

   a. If the upper shape is the driver, what are the maximum and minimum transmission factors?

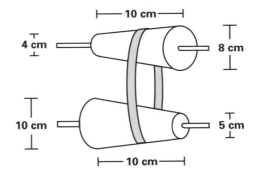

LESSON 3 • THE POWER OF THE CIRCLE   427

b. Suppose the belt is halfway between the two circular ends of the upper shape. If the lower shape is permitted to move laterally, what range of transmission factors is possible?

c. Describe a position of the belt for which the transmission factor is 1.

2. The transmission factor for pulley (or sprocket) A to pulley (or sprocket) B can be denoted **tf(AB)**. Assume A has radius r_1 and B has radius r_2.

a. What does tf(BA) represent?

b. Express tf(AB) in terms of the radii of A and B. Similarly, express tf(BA).

c. If the circumference of A is C_1 and the circumference of B is C_2, express tf(AB) in terms of C_1 and C_2.

d. Using the formula for the circumference of a circle, rewrite your expression in Part c to one involving only radii (r_1 or r_2). Is this result consistent with Part b? Why or why not?

e. Suppose B turns through an angle of $b°$ whenever A turns through an angle of $a°$. Express tf(AB) in terms of a and b.

3. A line that touches a circle in exactly one point is a **tangent** to the circle. As a belt leaves a pulley, the last point that touches the pulley is a point of tangency. The tangent has a unique relationship to the radius drawn to the tangency point.

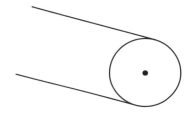

a. Investigate the suggested relationship. First, draw several circles with a compass. For each circle, draw a line that just touches the circle, and measure the angle determined by the radius and the tangent line at that point. What seems to be true in each case? Test your conjecture with another drawing.

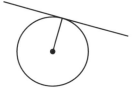

1. **b.** At a position halfway between a 4-cm radius circle and an 8-cm radius circle, the cross section is a 6-cm radius circle. Thus the driver pulley has a radius of 6 cm. Moving the lower partial cone gives radii from 5 to 10 cm. The transmission factors, therefore, range from $\frac{6}{5}$ to $\frac{6}{10}$.

   c. The transmission factor is 1 when the belt runs between locations on both pulleys that have equal radii. If the upper cone has the belt halfway between the ends, the radius is 6. The lower cone has a radius of 6 cm when the belt is $\frac{1}{5}$ the distance from the 5-cm end. Many other answers are possible.

2. This notation is similar to function notation, which will be introduced formally in the unit "Families of Functions" in Course 3.

   a. $tf(BA)$ represents the transmission factor from pulley B to pulley A.

   b. $tf(AB) = \frac{r_1}{r_2}$ $tf(BA) = \frac{r_2}{r_1}$

   c. $tf(AB) = \frac{C_1}{C_2}$

   d. $\frac{C_1}{C_2} = \frac{2\pi r_1}{2\pi r_2} = \frac{r_1}{r_2}$

   It is consistent. Since the circumference of circles are proportional to the radii, the ratios are the same.

   e. $tf(AB) = \frac{a}{b}$

3. **This item connects back to the Pythagorean Theorem and transformation concepts.**

   a. Students should find that the radius to the point of tangency is perpendicular to the tangent line.

Unit 6

3. **b.** Use the Pythagorean Theorem:

$$AC^2 + BC^2 = AB^2$$
$$AB^2 - AC^2 = BC^2$$
$$15^2 - 5^2 = BC^2$$
$$225 - 25 = BC^2$$
$$BC = \sqrt{200} \approx 14.1 \text{ cm}$$

c. $C'B$ is tangent to the circle at C' because the circle is its own image when reflected in any line containing the center. Thus C' is on the circle. Since all image angles have the same measures as their pre-images, m $\angle AC'B = 90°$ and $C'B$ is tangent to the circle at C'.

d. Two tangents to a circle from an external point are congruent, so their lengths are equal.

4. **a.** The arc length is $(p \cdot r)$ centimeters.

b. The linear velocity, l, is pr cm/min.

c. $l = 10 \frac{\text{cm}}{\text{radian}} \cdot 80 \frac{\text{radians}}{\text{sec}} = 800 \text{ cm/sec}$

d. The angular velocity is $\frac{30\pi}{10}$ or 3π radians/sec

e. $l = v \cdot r$ units of distance per unit of time

Reflecting

1. Student responses will vary but should include these ideas:
- *angular velocity · circumference = linear velocity*;
- since the points are moving at the same number of revolutions per minute (which is angular velocity) and the circumference of an inner circle will be less than the circumference of an outer circle, it must be that the linear velocity of a point on the smaller circle will be less than the linear velocity of a point on the larger circle.

b. In the diagram below, the circle has a radius of 5 cm. The length of $\overline{AB}$ is 15 cm. Segment BC is tangent to the circle at C. How long is $\overline{BC}$?

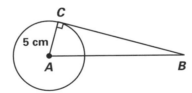

c. Make a copy of the diagram in Part b, above. Then, reflect $\triangle ABC$ across side AB. Let C' be the reflection image of C. Is $\overline{C'B}$ tangent to the circle at C'? Explain your reasoning.

d. Compare the lengths of the two lines from point B, tangent to the circle. What do you observe?

4. A circle of radius r centimeters has a circumference of $2\pi r$ centimeters.

   a. Suppose a point on the circle rotates through an angle of p radians. What is the length of the arc traversed by the point?

   b. Suppose a point rotates at p radians per minute. Find the linear velocity of the point.

   c. Suppose a circle with radius 10 cm has an angular velocity of 80 radians per second. Find the linear velocity of a point on the circle.

   d. Suppose a point on a circle with radius 10 cm has linear velocity of 30π cm per second. Find the angular velocity of the point.

   e. Explain how to convert an angular velocity v (in radians) for a circle of radius r into the linear velocity of a point on the circle.

Reflecting

1. Read the cartoon below. Using mathematical ideas you developed in Investigation 2, write a paragraph explaining to Calvin how two points on a record can move at two different speeds.

CALVIN AND HOBBES © 1990 Watterson. Dist. by UNIVERSAL PRESS SYNDICATE. Reprinted with permission. All rights reserved.

2. The *gear* of a bicycle is the product of the transmission factor and the diameter of the rear wheel, commonly 27 inches or 68 cm. What are the gears for the 21-speed mountain bike described in Activity 8 on page 418? How is "gearing" related to linear velocity?

3. The transmission factor of a pulley or sprocket set can be expressed in various ways: in terms of the radii, the diameters, the turning angles, the circumferences, or the numbers of teeth. How are these descriptions related? For you, which representations seem easiest to understand? Why?

4. Refer to the diagram at the right in answering the following questions.

  a. How would you express the radian measure of $\angle AOB$?

  b. In what sense does the radian measure count the number of radii?

  c. Suppose $\angle AOB$ were one third of a complete revolution and r were 4 cm. What would be the radian measure of $\angle AOB$? What would be the degree measure of $\angle AOB$?

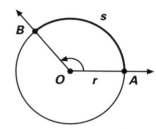

Extending

1. In 1985, John Howard, age 37, of Encinitas, California, rode a specially designed bicycle at the speed of 152.284 mph. Investigate this accomplishment to determine the special conditions of the ride. How did Howard make use of transmission factors?

2. Two pulleys have centers A and B which are p centimeters apart. The radii of circles A and B are r_1 and r_2 respectively, with $r_1 > r_2$.

  a. Find a general expression that can be used to determine the amount of belt in contact with pulley A in a direct-drive pulley system.

  b. Repeat Part a for an opposite-drive system (that is, when the belt is crossed).

3. A record player turntable can rotate at $33\frac{1}{3}$ rpm. On one particular player, the needle arm turns about a pivot point 19 cm from the turntable center. It is 18 cm from pivot to needle. One long-play record has a 15-cm radius with recording beginning at 14.5 cm and ending at 7 cm from the center.

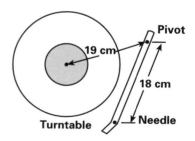

2. Gear = $tf(AB)$ · diameter of B

The gears are:

$\frac{48}{30}$ · diameter = 1.6(68 cm) = 108.8 cm $\frac{40}{30}$ · diameter ≈ 1.33(68 cm) ≈ 90.7 cm

$\frac{48}{27}$ · diameter ≈ 1.78(68 cm) ≈ 120.9 cm $\frac{40}{27}$ · diameter ≈ 1.48(68 cm) ≈ 100.7 cm

$\frac{48}{24}$ · diameter = 2(68 cm) = 136 cm $\frac{40}{24}$ · diameter ≈ 1.67(68 cm) ≈ 113.3 cm

$\frac{48}{21}$ · diameter ≈ 2.29(68 cm) ≈ 155.4 cm $\frac{40}{21}$ · diameter ≈ 1.90(68 cm) ≈ 129.5 cm

$\frac{48}{18}$ · diameter ≈ 2.67(68 cm) ≈ 181.3 cm $\frac{40}{18}$ · diameter ≈ 2.22(68 cm) ≈ 151.1 cm

$\frac{48}{15}$ · diameter = 3.2(68 cm) = 217.6 cm $\frac{40}{15}$ · diameter ≈ 2.67(68 cm) ≈ 181.3 cm

$\frac{48}{12}$ · diameter = 4(68 cm) = 272 cm $\frac{40}{12}$ · diameter ≈ 3.33(68 cm) ≈ 226.7 cm

$\frac{30}{30}$ · diameter = 1(68 cm) = 68 cm

$\frac{30}{27}$ · diameter ≈ 1.11(68 cm) ≈ 75.6 cm

$\frac{30}{24}$ · diameter = 1.25(68 cm) = 85 cm

$\frac{30}{21}$ · diameter ≈ 1.43(68 cm) ≈ 97.1 cm

$\frac{30}{18}$ · diameter ≈ 1.67(68 cm) ≈ 113.3 cm

$\frac{30}{15}$ · diameter = 2(68 cm) = 136 cm

$\frac{30}{12}$ · diameter = 2.5(68 cm) = 170 cm

NOTE: There are not 21 different gears on this bike!

Gear · π = linear velocity since

linear velocity = tf(AB) · π · diameter = Gear · π.

---

3. They are all related in that they are each proportional to the circumference, and it is the change in circumference length that translates into change in linear velocity for a fixed angular velocity. The hardest to understand seems to be the relation expressed in angular terms. The others often will be chosen equally as easiest to understand. Explanations will vary.

4. **a.** $m\angle AOB = \frac{s}{r}$

   b. An angle with measure 1 radian has an intercepted arc of length equal to the radius. So as an angle sweeps through each radian, the intercepted arc grows by one radius length.

   c. Radian measure: $\frac{2\pi}{3}$; degree measure: 120°

NOTE: You may also wish to ask students who are doing Reflecting Task 4 to find an *approximate* length for the arc cut off by ∠AOB in part c (Approximately 8 cm).

Extending

1. Howard added a second sprocket between the crankset and the rear wheel. This second sprocket allowed a transmission factor much larger than ordinary bicycles. See *Guinness Book of Records* for details.

See additional Teaching Notes on page T453K.

Unit 6

3. **a.** The needle follows an arc of the circle with center at the pivot and radius of 18 cm.

b. The chord of the arc through which the needle moves is 14.5 − 7 or 7.5 cm (our model simplifies the situation by assuming that the chord is 7.5 cm even though it would be slightly larger). Thus, from beginning to end, the needle arm forms an isosceles triangle with 18 cm sides and 7.5 cm base. Use this isosceles triangle to create a right triangle with hypotenuse 18 cm and one leg of 3.75 cm (one-half of 7.5 cm). Call the angle opposite that leg, angle A.

$\sin A = \frac{3.75}{18}$, so $A \approx 12.02°$

Double A to get the vertex angle of the isosceles triangle, 24.04°. Therefore, the arc length is $\frac{24.04°}{360°} \cdot 2\pi \cdot 18$ or 7.55 cm.

c. $33\frac{1}{3} \cdot 2\pi \cdot 14.5 \approx 3{,}036.9$ cm; $33\frac{1}{3} \cdot 2\pi \cdot 7 \approx 1{,}466.1$ cm

The linear velocities are approximately 3,037 cm per minute and 1,466 cm per minute.

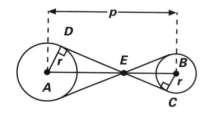

4. **a.** This situation is identical to the general situation from Extending Task 2, Part a (page 430). Here, we have the following measurements.

$AD = r_1 = 9$ $\qquad$ $ED = 3$
$BC = r_2 = 6$ $\qquad$ $CE = 25$
$AB = p = 25$

Since $\triangle CED$ is a right triangle, we have the following:

$CD^2 = CE^2 − ED^2 = 25^2 − 3^2 = 625 − 9 = 616$

$CD = \sqrt{616} \approx 24.82$

Using the reasoning found in Extending Task 2, we find the angle through which the belt touches pulley A to be $360° − 2\cos^{-1}\left(\frac{9-6}{25}\right)$ or approximately 193.8°. The corresponding belt length is $\frac{193.8°}{360°} \cdot 2\pi \cdot 9$ cm or approximately 30.44 cm. The analogous angle measure for pulley B is $2\cos^{-1}\left(\frac{9-6}{25}\right)$ or approximately 166.2°; and so the length is $\left(\frac{166.2°}{360°}\right) \cdot 2\pi \cdot 6$ cm or approximately 17.41 cm.

All together the belt must be 24.82 + 24.82 + 17.41 + 30.44 cm or 97.49 cm.

b. Again, this is a specific case of the situation in Extending Task 2 Part b. The measurements here are as follows:

$AD = r_1 = 9$ $\qquad$ $AE + EB = p = 25$
$BC = r_2 = 6$

The scale factor from $\triangle ADE$ to $\triangle BCE$ is $\frac{2}{3}$. Therefore, $\frac{BE}{AE} = \frac{2}{3}$ or $BE = \frac{2AE}{3}$. Since

$AE + EB = 25$, we know $AE + \frac{2AE}{3} = 25$ or $\frac{5AE}{3} = 25$. Thus $AE = 15$ and

$BE = 10$.

Therefore, $CE^2 = BE^2 − BC^2 = 100 − 36 = 64$ and

$DE^2 = AE^2 − AD^2 = 225 − 81 = 144$.

So, $CE = 8$ and $DE = 12$.

See additional Teaching Notes on page T453L.

Unit 6

a. If the record is played from start to finish, what path would you see the needle follow?

b. How far does the needle actually move?

c. How far does a point on the outermost (recorded) groove travel in one minute? On the innermost (recorded) groove? What are the linear velocities?

4. A pair of pulleys with 6-cm and 9-cm radii are used to make a belt drive system. They are set 25 cm apart, from center to center.

a. Suppose the pulleys are to turn in the same direction. Find the length of belt needed.

b. Suppose the pulleys are to turn in opposite directions. Find the length of belt needed.

c. Give a mathematical argument supporting the following observation: If two circles have tangents that cross between the circles, then the point of intersection of the two tangents lies on the line containing the centers of the circles. (**Hint:** Think about the symmetry of the situation.)

5. In this task, you will explore a shape that is different in form from a circle but can serve a similar design function.

a. Make a cardboard model of this shape as follows:

■ Construct an equilateral triangle of side length 6 cm.

■ At each vertex, draw (with a compass) a circle with radius 6 cm, darkening only the small arc between the other two vertices.

■ Carefully cut out the shape formed by the darkened arcs.

b. Draw a pair of parallel lines 6 cm apart. Place your model between the lines and roll it along one line. Note any unusual occurrences.

c. Conduct library research on the Wankel engine. How is it related to your model?

d. Investigate the concept of *shapes of constant width*. What are two other examples of such shapes?

INVESTIGATION 3 Modeling Circular Motion

You have seen many examples of circular motion in the previous investigations and in your everyday activities. The motion is so common and used in so many ways that it is important to have mathematical models of circular motion.

The Ferris wheel common to carnivals and fairs is a good example of how circular forms can be used to provide enjoyment to young and old. It provides a good context in which to study the nature of circular motion, especially that of a point on a circle such as a seat on the Ferris wheel.

1. Make a cardboard model of a Ferris wheel by drawing a circle with center *C* and radius 5 cm. Draw lines to divide circle *C* into twelve 30° angles, each with vertex *C*, and then cut out the circle.

   Punch a hole in the center of the circle and, using a paper fastener, attach it to a large piece of paper as shown below. (Be sure your circle can turn freely.) On the paper, draw line *PQ* as a horizontal axis through center *C*. Align two of the radii you drew with line *PQ*, then label the measure of each of the angles in degrees and radians as shown.

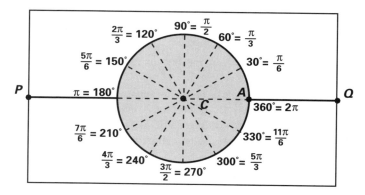

   Mark point *A* on your circle. Imagine your seat is at *A* and the Ferris wheel begins to turn. Let your circle model the side of the wheel where *A* moves counterclockwise.

   a. Describe how your distance from line *PQ* changes as the wheel turns.

   b. Measure the distance of point *A* above or below line *PQ* for each of the angles in your wheel. Represent the distance from point *A* to line *PQ* by a negative number when it is below line *PQ* and by a positive number when it is above line *PQ*. Enter these *directed distances* in a table similar to the one started below, with 30° increments.

   Note: Leave space for three additional rows to be added to your table later.

Measure of ∠ACQ	0°	30°	60°	90°	...	360°
Distance from Point *A* to Line *PQ*	0	2.5	?	?	...	?

   c. Make a scatterplot of your (*measure of ∠ACQ, distance from point A to line PQ*) data.

   d. The position of point *A* is a function of the size of ∠ACQ. For what size angles is point *A* above line *PQ*? How is this shown in the plot?

The introduction for this investigation is on page T453M.

1. **a.** Point A begins on the line PQ; it then moves above the line rather rapidly and continues to move farther above the line, but at a slower rate, until it reaches its maximum of 5 cm above line PQ. Then the process reverses until point A is on the line again but on the opposite side of circle C. Then Point A moves below line PQ. The distance below the line increases rapidly at first and then moves slowly as Point A nears the maximum distance of 5 below line PQ (the minimum value of -5). Point A then continues up to its original position. As the wheel continues to rotate, the pattern of the distance from line PQ (above and below) repeats. This is periodic change.

   b. Student responses will be measurements.

$m\angle ACQ$	0°	30°	60°	90°	120°	150°	180°	210°	240°	270°	300°	330°	360°
Measured Distance from A to $\overline{PQ}$	0	2.5	4.3	5	4.3	2.5	0	−2.5	−4.3	−5	−4.3	−2.5	0

   c. The sketch should be a set of discrete points showing the wave pattern, but it is likely that many students will show the continuous extension of the scatterplot-like graph. The graph should approximate $y = 5 \sin x$, but students do not know that at this point.

   d. Point A is above line PQ for angles with measures between 0° and 180°. The points are above the horizontal axis.

Unit 6

1. **e.** Point A is below line PQ for angles with measures between 180° and 360°. The points are below the horizontal axis.

   f. The maximum occurs at 90°; the minimum at 270°; zero at 0°, 180°, and 360°.

   g. Students will estimate from the graph or table. Approximate calculated values are:

   $5 \sin 45° \approx 3.5$ $5 \sin 195° \approx -1.3$ $5 \sin 110° \approx 4.7$

   $5 \sin 370° \approx 0.9$ $5 \sin 135° \approx 3.5$

2. **a.**

m∠ACQ	0°	30°	60°	90°	120°	150°	180°	210°	240°	270°	300°	330°	360°
Measured Distance from A to $\overline{ST}$	5	4.3	2.5	0	−2.5	−4.3	−5	−4.3	−2.5	0	2.5	4.3	5

   b. The change is again periodic. The periodic change occurs since the circle is symmetric about its center. Thus the same distances arise over and over again as the wheel turns since the 30° increments are factors of the 360° rotation.

   c. The sketch should be a set of discrete points showing the wave pattern, but it is likely that many students will show the continuous extension of the scatterplot-like graph. The graph should approximate $y = 5 \cos x$, but students do not know that at this point.

   d. The graph continues by repeating itself. The values on the horizontal axis should be 390°, 420°, etc.

   e. Students will estimate from the table or graph. Approximate calculated values are:

   $5 \cos 45° \approx 3.5$ $5 \cos 195° \approx -4.8$ $5 \cos 110° \approx -1.7$

   $5 \cos 370° \approx 4.9$ $5 \cos 135° \approx -3.5$

3. **If students have difficulty with Activity 3, Part a, try not to help right away. The question does not offer much of a clue about what kind of a connection between the design of the model and a trigonometric ratio is required. It is worth letting students spend a little time drawing the model, tinkering, and trying to recall the different trigonometric ratios they know. If no student finds a connection, then you might consider drawing a sequence of triangles on the board and asking if that helps:**

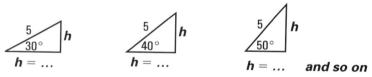

$h = \ldots$ $h = \ldots$ $h = \ldots$ *and so on*

   a. The distance from A to $\overline{PQ}$ after a 30° turn is AD, as shown in the diagram on page 433.

   Now $\sin 30° = \dfrac{AD}{AC} = \dfrac{AD}{5 \text{ cm}}$, so $AD = 5 \sin 30°$.

   Notice that as point A moves around the circle, Point D moves to the left on the x-axis, maintaining its position as the intersection of the x-axis and a vertical line drawn through A. For a 60° turn, $AD = 5 \sin 60°$.

   b–c.

m∠ACQ	0°	30°	60°	90°	120°	150°	180°	210°	240°	270°	300°	330°	360°
Calculated Distance from A to $\overline{PQ}$	0°	2.5	4.3	5	4.3	2.5	0	−2.5	−4.3	−5	−4.3	−2.5	0

e. For what angles is point *A* below line *PQ*? How is this shown in the plot?

f. For what angles is the directed distance of point *A* from line *PQ* a maximum? A minimum? Zero?

g. Use the pattern in the plot to predict the position of point *A* when the measure of ∠*ACQ* is 45°, 195°, 110°, 370°, and 135°.

2. Now draw a vertical line *ST* on the paper through the center *C* of the circle.

a. Use your physical model of the Ferris wheel to determine the distances from point *A* to this vertical line, as the wheel turns. Add a new row to your table labeled "Distance From Point *A* to Line *ST*." Record your measures. Use negative numbers when *A* is to the left of the line.

b. What patterns do you see in the directed distances?

c. Plot your (*measure of ∠ACQ, distance from point A to line ST*) data using the same scales on the coordinate axes as in Activity 1 Part c.

d. Suppose the Ferris wheel continues to turn. Continue the pattern in the plot to show the distance from point *A* to the vertical line *ST*. What additional values should you put on the horizontal axis?

e. Use the plot to predict the position of point *A* relative to the vertical line *ST* for angles of 45°, 195°, 110°, 370°, and 135°.

In Activities 1 and 2, you modeled important features of a Ferris wheel using a physical model, and you represented those features with tables and graphs. In the next activity, you will explore the possibility of describing the patterns of circular motion with an equation.

3. The figure at the right represents your physical model.

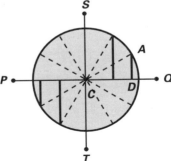

a. Using information about the design of your model and a trigonometric ratio, write an expression to calculate the distance from *A* to *PQ* after a 30° counterclockwise turn from the horizontal. Do the same for a 60° counterclockwise turn.

b. Make sure your calculator is in degree mode. Calculate the two distances in Part a. Add a row to the bottom of the table you started in Part b of Activity 1 and enter this new information in the table.

c. Determine the directed distances *AD* for the remaining angles 90°, 120°, 150°, …, up to 360°. Data lists might be helpful for this. Enter these data in the table.

d. Compare the distances *AD* that you determined by measuring (Activity 1 Part b) and by using the trigonometric ratio.

e. Write an equation that describes the directed distance (*AD*) from point *A* to the horizontal after the wheel turns $x°$ from the horizontal.

f. Produce a graph of your equation. How well does this equation model the data in Activity 1?

4. In this activity, you will investigate a similar relation between the angle of rotation of the Ferris wheel model and the horizontal distance a point is from the line *ST*.

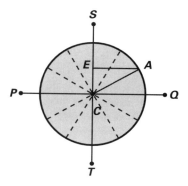

a. Refer to the figure above. Use an appropriate trigonometric ratio to calculate the distance, *AE*, from point *A* to the line *ST* after a counterclockwise 30° rotation. Add another row to the bottom of your table and record this information.

b. Use your calculator to determine the directed horizontal distance *AE* for the remaining angles 60°, 90°, 120°, …, up to 360°. Enter these data in the table.

c. Compare the distances *AE* that you determined by measuring (Activity 2 Part a) and by using the trigonometric ratio.

d. Write an equation that describes the directed distance *AE* that point *A* is from line *ST* after the wheel turns counterclockwise $x°$ from the horizontal.

e. Produce a graph of your equation. How well does this equation model the data in Activity 2?

5. Now, working in pairs and dividing the workload, make scatterplots that correspond to the following when the measure of $\angle ACQ$ is in radians: $\frac{\pi}{6}$, $\frac{\pi}{3}$, $\frac{\pi}{2}$, $\frac{2\pi}{3}$, $\frac{5\pi}{6}$, π, $\frac{7\pi}{6}$, $\frac{4\pi}{3}$, $\frac{3\pi}{2}$, $\frac{5\pi}{3}$, $\frac{11\pi}{6}$, and 2π.

i. (*measure of $\angle ACQ$, distance from point A to line PQ*) data

ii. (*measure of $\angle ACQ$, distance from point A to line ST*) data

a. How well does the equation you wrote for Activity 3 Part e model the data in Part i above? Make sure your calculator is in radian mode.

b. How well does the equation you wrote for Activity 4 Part d model the data in Part ii above?

3. d. Measured and calculated distances should be close if not exact.

   e. *Height of rider* $= 5 \sin x°$

   f. The graphs will be similar but probably not identical due to measurement errors. Note also that the graph of $y = 5 \sin x$ is continuous, not a discrete set of points like the original scatterplot in Activity 1.

4. a. $\cos 30° = \dfrac{AE}{5 \text{ cm}}$, $AE = 4.33$ cm

   b.

m∠*ACQ*	0°	30°	60°	90°	120°	150°	180°	210°	240°	270°	300°	330°	360°
Measured Distance from *A* to $\overline{PQ}$	0	2.5	4.3	5	4.3	2.5	0	–2.5	–4.3	–5	–4.3	–2.5	0
Measured Distance from *A* to $\overline{ST}$	5	4.3	2.5	0	–2.5	–4.3	–5	–4.3	–2.5	0	2.5	4.3	5
Calculated Distance from *A* to $\overline{PQ}$	0	2.5	4.3	5	4.3	2.5	0	–2.5	–4.3	–5	–4.3	–2.5	0
Calculated Distance from *A* to $\overline{ST}$	5°	4.3	2.5	0	–2.5	–4.3	–5	–4.3	–2.5	0	2.5	4.3	5

   c. They should be close if not exact.

   d. $AE = 5 \cos x°$

   e. They both should follow $y = 5 \cos x$.

5. To make the scatterplots, some students will enter the radian values individually into a data list. (You may want to be sure they know where to find π.) Others may want to use their skill of converting degrees to radians, filling one list with degree measures from 0 to 360 and converting those to radians. In either case, students should be prepared to see decimal equivalents of the radian measures.

   Besides remembering to change to radian mode, students also will have to change the values of Xmin and Xmax for their window. They can enter $-2π$ and $2π$ though the calculator probably will return decimal equivalents.

   a. If window and mode are properly adjusted and degrees are changed to radians, then the same model will fit the data again.

   b. Again, the model will fit the data.

Unit 6

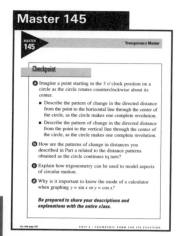

MASTER
145   Transparency Master

Checkpoint

ⓐ Imagine a point starting in the 3 o'clock position on a circle as the circle rotates counterclockwise about its center.
  ■ Describe the pattern of change in the directed distance from the point to the horizontal line through the center of the circle, as the circle makes one complete revolution.
  ■ Describe the pattern of change in the directed distance from the point to the vertical line through the center of the circle, as the circle makes one complete revolution.
ⓑ How are the patterns of change in distances you described in Part a related to the distance patterns obtained as the circle continues tq turn?
ⓒ Explain how trigonometry can be used to model aspects of circular motion.
ⓓ Why is it important to know the mode of a calculator when graphing $y = \sin x$ or $y = \cos x$?

Be prepared to share your descriptions and explanations with the entire class.

Use with page 435.   UNIT 6 • GEOMETRIC FORM AND ITS FUNCTION

SHARE AND SUMMARIZE full-class discussion

Checkpoint

See Teaching Master 145.

ⓐ ■ Initially, vertical distance increases rapidly starting at 0 and then continues to increase but at a slower rate until it reaches its maximum of 5 directly above the center of the circle (90°). Then the process reverses until it is 0 at 180°. Next, the distance increases rapidly again and then more slowly as the point nears the maximum distance of 5 (the minimum value of –5); the distance then continues back towards 0, its original value.

■ Initially, horizontal distance begins at its maximum of 5, drops slowly, then drops faster until it reaches 0 at 90°. From 0 the distances increase negatively, rapidly at first, then more slowly until the distance is 5 (the minimum value of –5) at 180°. Then the process reverses itself, increasing back to a distance of 0 and again finally to 5.

ⓑ The patterns are the same.

ⓒ $r \cdot \sin x = $ *distance from horizontal (vertical distance)*
$r \cdot \cos x = $ *distance from vertical (horizontal distance)*

ⓓ Sin x, takes on different values when x is in radians or degrees. The same is true for cos x. To be able to set the window correctly, you need to know whether radians or degrees are being used.

> CONSTRUCTING A MATH TOOLKIT: Ask students to write a general explanation of how trigonometric ratios can be used to locate vertical and horizontal distances on a circle if you know the radius of the circle and the measure of the angle. Illustrate the explanation using the right triangle modeled in the Ferris wheel application.

APPLY individual task

▶On Your Own

a. When Amanuel is halfway to the top, he has revolved 90°; his position is on the horizontal line and 15 meters from the vertical line.

b. Distance from horizontal: $15 \cdot \sin 56° \approx 15 \cdot 0.829 \approx 12.44\,\text{m}$
Distance from vertical: $15 \cdot \cos 56° \approx 15 \cdot 0.559 \approx 8.39\,\text{m}$

c. $r \cdot \sin x° = $ *distance from horizontal*
$r \cdot \cos x° = $ *distance from vertical*

d. In 50 seconds, he will rotate $\frac{50}{60}$ or $\frac{5}{6}$ of a full 360°. Therefore, he will rotate $\frac{5}{6} \cdot 360°$ or 300°. Thus his position is 15 cos 300° and 15 sin 300°. He is 15 cos 300° or 7.5 meters from the vertical and 15 sin 300 or approximately –12.99 meters below the horizontal.

MORE
ASSIGNMENT *pp. 442–449*

Students can now begin Organizing Tasks 3 or 4, or Reflecting Task 2 from the MORE assignment following Investigation 4.

Checkpoint

a Imagine a point starting in the 3 o'clock position on a circle, as the circle rotates counterclockwise about its center.

■ Describe the pattern of change in the directed distance from the point to the horizontal line through the center of the circle, as the circle makes one complete revolution.

■ Describe the pattern of change in the directed distance from the point to the vertical line through the center of the circle, as the circle makes one complete revolution.

b How are the patterns of change in distances you described in Part a related to the distance patterns obtained as the circle continues to turn?

c Explain how trigonometry can be used to model aspects of circular motion.

d Why is it important to know the mode of a calculator when graphing $y = \sin x$ or $y = \cos x$?

Be prepared to share your descriptions and explanations with the entire class.

On Your Own

At the Chelsea Community Fair, there is a Ferris wheel with a 15-meter radius. Amanuel is on a seat halfway to the highest point of the ride.

a. Make a sketch of Amanuel's position relative to the horizontal and vertical lines through the center of the wheel.

b. Find Amanuel's distance from the lines after the wheel has rotated counterclockwise through an angle of 56°.

c. Write equations that model Amanuel's position relative to the horizontal and vertical lines for any angle $x°$ from his starting point halfway up.

d. Suppose the wheel turns at one revolution every minute. In relation to his starting point, where will Amanuel be at the end of 50 seconds?

INVESTIGATION 4 Patterns of Periodic Change

Many everyday phenomena recur in patterns that are similar year after year. The plot below shows the pattern of change in the number of hours of daylight in Boston over a one-year period, in increments of 10 days. Find the points you think correspond with days in June and days in December.

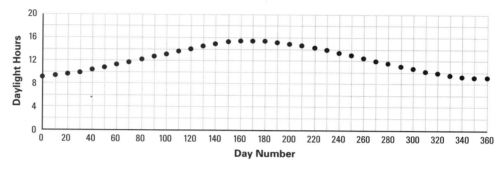

The recurring pattern in length of day is an example of **periodic change**. The complete pattern or *cycle* is seen each year. In fact, it is this cycle that determines the length of a year!

1. **a.** Working as a group, identify and describe three or four other real situations that exhibit periodic change.

   b. What is the length of the interval over which one complete cycle occurs for your situations?

   c. For each of your situations, make a sketch of the periodic pattern of change on a coordinate system of your choice. Label the axes clearly.

   d. Compare your situations and graphical representations with those of other groups.

2. Consider the functions you graphed in the previous investigation: $y = \sin x$ and $y = \cos x$. Set your calculator or graphing software in radian mode.

   a. Graph $y = \cos x$ on the interval $0 \leq x \leq 6\pi$. Make a sketch of this graph.

   b. Is this graph periodic? What is the length of one complete cycle? How many cycles are shown in your sketch?

   c. What are the maximum and minimum values attained by this function? At what values of x do they occur? At what values of x does the graph intersect the x-axis?

   d. Graph $y = \sin x$ on the interval $-2\pi \leq x \leq 4\pi$. Make a sketch of this graph.

   e. Is this graph periodic? What is the length of one complete cycle? How many cycles are shown in your sketch?

   f. What are the maximum and minimum values attained by this function? At what values of x do they occur? At what values of x does the graph intersect the x-axis?

INVESTIGATION 4 Patterns of Periodic Change

Now that students have a general idea about the shape of circular functions, they will investigate both $y = A \sin Bx$ and $y = A \cos Bx$ in greater detail. Students will look at how changes in amplitude and frequency express themselves in the equations and graphs of sine and cosine curves. Students also will extend the domain of these functions to include negative and larger, positive angle measures.

Start a discussion designed to get students thinking about the many situations in the world around them that can be modeled using circular functions. Draw attention to the daylight hours scatterplot at the beginning of this investigation. After the class has discussed the daylight hours graph, ask students how this graph might be different or similar if it were for daylight hours in Alaska or in Australia. Next ask students to compare the daylight hours graph with the graphs for sine and cosine they created in the previous investigation. Ask students what they think "periodic change" means.

Students should work on Activity 1 in small groups, and they can personalize the idea with a situation of their choice. You could provide each group with acetate and pens to sketch their graphs and then have each group share their graph with the entire class. Try to use the discussion to alert students to the distinguishing characteristics of the circular functions such as maximum/minimum, x- and y-intercepts, period, and general shapes.

As the groups go on to Activities 2–9, you might let them know that the purpose of the rest of this investigation is to explore this new class of functions in detail. As you circulate among groups, urge students to articulate verbally the changes and patterns that they discover.

1. **a.** There are many situations exhibiting periodic change such as level of the tides over time, a person's position as he or she rocks in a rocking chair, the position of a pendulum as it swings, the position of the hour (minute, second) hand of a clock, and average monthly temperatures.
   b. Responses will vary and will be unique to the context chosen by students.
   c. Sketches will vary, but all should show some sort of periodic or repeating pattern.
   d. Student work.
2. **a.** See the first two calculator screens on the right.
   b. The graph is periodic. 2π is the length of a cycle. The sketch shows 3 cycles.
   c. The maximum is 1, the minimum is −1. The maximum occurs at $x = 0, 2\pi, 4\pi, 6\pi$, etc. The minimum occurs at $\pi, 3\pi, 5\pi$, etc. The graph intersects x-axis at $\frac{\pi}{2}, \frac{3\pi}{2}, \frac{5\pi}{2}$, etc.
   d. See the last two calculator screens on the right.
   e. The graph is periodic. 2π is the length of a cycle. The sketch shows 3 cycles.
   f. The maximum is 1, the minimum is −1. The maximum occurs at $x = \frac{-3\pi}{2}, \frac{\pi}{2}, \frac{5\pi}{2}$, etc. The minimum occurs at $\frac{-\pi}{2}, \frac{3\pi}{2}, \frac{7\pi}{2}$, etc. Intercepts are $x = -2\pi, -\pi, 0, \pi, 2\pi, 3\pi, 4\pi$, etc.

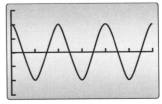

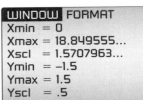

WINDOW FORMAT
Xmin = 0
Xmax = 18.849555...
Xscl = 1.5707963...
Ymin = −1.5
Ymax = 1.5
Yscl = .5

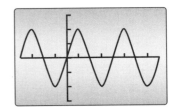

WINDOW FORMAT
Xmin = −6.283185...
Xmax = 12.566370...
Xscl = 1.5707963...
Ymin = −1.5
Ymax = 1.5
Yscl = .5

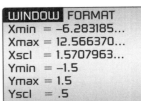

Unit 6

3. **a.** 5 cos x and cos x intersect the x-axis at the same points, reach their maximum and minimum values at the same x values, have cycles of equal lengths, and are the same shape. They differ in the maximum and minimum values. The same can be said for 5 sin x and sin x.

   b. For the distance from a point to the horizontal line, the sine ratio was used, with the radius r of the circle as the hypotenuse and the height y as the side opposite the central angle x, giving a ratio of $\sin x = \frac{y}{r}$. Simplified, $y = r \sin x$; with a radius of 5, the equation became $y = 5 \sin x$.

   Similarly, for the distance from the point to the vertical line, the cosine ratio was used, with the radius r of the circle as the hypotenuse and the horizontal distance y as the side adjacent to the central angle x, giving a ratio of $\cos x = \frac{y}{r}$. Simplified, $y = r \cos x$; with a radius of 5, the equation became $y = 5 \cos x$.
   For a radius of 8, the equations would become $y = 8 \sin x$ and $y = 8 \cos x$.

   c. Responses for degrees are given. Radian measures can be substituted. The TI-82 and TI-83 calculators have a standard trigonometric window from $-352.5°$ to $352.5°$. Responses are given for that interval.
   - Maximum value is at $(0°, 5)$.
     Minimum values are at $(-180°, -5)$ and $(180°, -5)$.
   - Calculator window is $-352.5 \leq x \leq 352.5$, however, if students use the trace feature and the screen scrolls left or right, they may have different values. All real numbers may be used for x.
   - $(-270°, 0)$, $(-90°, 0)$, $(90°, 0)$, and $(270°, 0)$ for this window.
   - Reflective symmetry across the y-axis
     Translational symmetry (Slide the portion between $0°$ and $360°$ either left or right $360°$, and it will map onto itself.)
     $180°$ rotational symmetry at any x-intercept
     Glide reflection (Slide the portion between $-90°$ and $90°$ to the right or left $180°$ and then flip over the x-axis, and it will map onto itself.)
   - Responses will vary. However, students should notice that the graph is a continuously repeating wave pattern going both left and right. Half of each complete cycle of the pattern is above the x-axis and half is below.

   d. You could interpret the negative x values as clockwise rotation of the Ferris wheel beginning at the 3 o'clock position.

   e. Nearly 2 complete cycles are shown on the display.

4. **a.** The maximum and minimum heights of the wave are reduced to 3 and -3, but it still crosses the x-axis at the same places.

   b. Again the maximum and minimum heights of the wave change, this time they are larger, 7 and -7. The wave pattern remains the same and the x-intercepts remain the same. We would expect $y = 4 \cos x$ to have the same wave pattern, but with maximum/minimum values of $4/-4$ because all the y values of $y = \sin x$ have been multiplied by 4.

Circular motion can generate patterns of periodic change, as you observed in the analysis of the position of a rider on a rotating Ferris wheel in the previous investigation. Now that you have constructed the trigonometric models describing these patterns, you are ready to examine, more carefully, properties of the trigonometric models themselves. That is, you will examine the symbolic forms, graphs, and tables of $y = \sin x$, $y = \cos x$, and variations of those equations.

As you work on the following activities, think of x as the measure of an angle with its vertex at the origin and one side on the positive x-axis. Be certain to set the mode of your calculator to "degree" if you want to work in degrees or to "radian" if you want to work in radians.

3. Your analysis of the Ferris wheel model led to two equations, $y = 5 \sin x$ and $y = 5 \cos x$, which described the position of a point on a circle in terms of distance from a horizontal and a vertical line respectively. Graph each of these equations using a graphing calculator or computer software. Use the automatic scaling feature for trigonometric functions (if there is one) to set the initial viewing window. Adjust the range of the y-axis to see a complete graph.

   a. Compare the graphs of $y = 5 \cos x$ and $y = \cos x$. Do the same for $y = \sin x$ and $y = 5 \sin x$. How are the graphs in each pair similar and how are they different?

   b. In terms of the Ferris wheel model, why are $\cos x$ and $\sin x$ multiplied by 5 in the rules $y = 5 \cos x$ and $y = 5 \sin x$? What multiplier would you expect if the Ferris wheel had a radius of 8? Why?

   c. Now carefully analyze the graph of $y = 5 \cos x$. Use the trace feature to help you. In your analysis, comment on each of the following features.

      ■ What are the maximum and minimum y values? What are the corresponding x values?

      ■ What are the possible input values for x?

      ■ For what values of x does the graph cross the x-axis?

      ■ Describe any symmetries you see in the graph.

      ■ Describe the overall appearance of the graph.

   d. How could you interpret negative input values for x in terms of the Ferris wheel model?

   e. How many cycles of the graph are shown in the calculator display?

4. Next, investigate the effect of the multiplier A in variations of the cosine function, $y = A \cos x$.

   a. Using your calculator or computer software, graph $y = 3 \cos x$ while the graph of $y = 5 \cos x$ is displayed. What is the effect of changing the 5 to 3?

   b. Produce the graph of $y = 7 \cos x$. How is this graph different from the graph of $y = 5 \cos x$? How is it similar? What would you expect for the graph of $y = 4 \cos x$? Why?

c. Now graph $y = \cos x$ and $y = 0.5\cos x$ using your calculator or computer software. Compare the two graphs.

d. How would you modify the graph of the basic function $y = \cos x$ to obtain the graph of $y = A\cos x$ when:

- A is a positive number greater than 1?
- A is a positive number between 0 and 1?

e. Investigate the effect of the multiplier A in $y = A\cos x$ when A is a negative number. Explain how it affects the graph for values less than -1 and also for values between -1 and 0.

f. How is the graph of $y = -A\cos x$ related to the graph of $y = A\cos x$?

g. What effect, if any, does multiplying the cosine function by a constant have on the number of cycles the graph makes for x between $-360°$ and $360°$ or between -2π and 2π?

5. Investigate the patterns in graphs of variations of the sine function, $y = A\sin x$. Again, use the automatic scaling feature (if there is one) of your calculator or computer software to set the initial viewing window. Adjust the range on the y-axis, if necessary, as you complete this activity.

a. Use the trace feature to help analyze the graph of $y = 5\sin x$. In your analysis, comment on each of the following features.

- What are the maximum and minimum y values? What are the corresponding x values?
- What are the possible input values for x?
- For what values of x does the graph cross the x-axis?
- Describe any symmetries you see in the graph.
- Describe the overall appearance of the graph.

b. How could you interpret negative input values for x in terms of the Ferris wheel model?

c. How many cycles of the graph are shown in your graph?

d. Investigate the effects of changing the multiplier A in $y = A\sin x$, as was done in Activity 3 for the cosine function. Based on your investigation, describe the effect of the multiplier A in $y = A\sin x$ when A is positive and when A is negative.

6. Compare the graphs of $y = \cos x$ and $y = \sin x$ on the interval $-720° \leq x \leq 720°$ or $-4\pi \leq x \leq 4\pi$.

a. Are there values of x for which $\sin x = \cos x$? If so, list them.

- Describe how you could find any such points using graphs and using tables.
- How could you interpret these x values in terms of a Ferris wheel model?

4. c. The wave pattern holds, but the maximum and minimum heights are reduced to 1 and −1 for $y = \cos x$ and to 0.5 and −0.5 for $y = 0.5 \cos x$. The x-intercepts are the same for both graphs.

d. In both cases, the wave pattern will remain constant, only the maximum and minimum values will change.

- If $A > 1$, then the graph of $y = A \cos x$ will have maximum and minimum values that are outside the fundamental graph of $y = \cos x$.
- If $0 < A < 1$, then the graph of $y = A \cos x$ will have maximum and minimum values that are within the fundamental graph of $y = \cos x$.

e. The negative sign, regardless of the size of A, will reflect or flip the wave over the x-axis. Other changes in the graph for $A < -1$ and $-1 < A < 0$ will be the same as the changes noted for $A > 1$ and $0 < A < 1$, respectively.

f. The graph of $y = -A \cos x$ is the reflection of the graph of $y = A \cos x$ over the x-axis.

g. Multiplying the cosine function by a constant has no effect on the number of cycles that function will have in a specified range.

5. a.
- Maximum values are at $(-270°, 5)$ and $(90°, 5)$ for the standard window. Minimum values are at $(-90°, -5)$ and $(270°, 5)$.
- Calculator window is $-352.5 \leq x \leq 352.5$.
- $-180°$, $0°$, and $180°$
- Translational symmetry (Slide the portion between $0°$ and $360°$ either left or right $360°$, and it will map onto itself.)
  180° rotational symmetry, about any x-intercept.
  Glide reflection (Slide the portion between $0°$ and $180°$ to the right or left $180°$ and then flip over the x-axis, and it will map onto itself.)
- Responses will vary. However, students should notice that the graph is a continuously repeating wave pattern going both left and right. Half of each complete cycle of the pattern is above the x-axis and half is below.

b. You could interpret the negative x values as clockwise rotation of the Ferris wheel beginning at the 3 o'clock position.

c. Nearly two complete cycles are shown on the display.

d. Students should use values for A that are greater than 5 and less than 5. Students should also select values for A that are negative.

As with the cosine function, changing values of A will not change the general shape of the wave pattern or the points at which it crosses the x-axis. It will change the height of the wave. Negative values for A will reflect or flip the wave over the x-axis.

6. a. Yes, $\sin x = \cos x$ for $x = -675°, -495°, -315°, -135°, 45°, 225°, 405°,$ and $585°$.

- On the graphs, you could trace to the approximate intersection and zoom in or use the graphical solving capabilities of the calculator. (On the TI-82 and TI-83 calculators, select the "intersect" option from the CALC menu, 2nd TRACE .) On side-by-side tables, you could look for the same y values, zooming in where necessary.
- On the Ferris wheel, $\sin x = \cos x$ wherever the rider is the same *directed* distance from the horizontal and vertical axes.

6. b. ■ On the given interval, $y = \sin x$ has maximum value at $-630°$, $-270°$, $90°$, and $450°$; the minimum value occurs at $-450°$, $-90°$, $270°$, and $630°$.

■ On the given interval, $y = \cos x$ has maximum value at $-720°$, $-360°$, $0°$, $360°$, and $720°$; the minimum value occurs at $-540°$, $-180°$, $180°$, and $540°$.

c. Translate the sine wave $90°$ or $\frac{\pi}{2}$ radians to the left, or $270°$ or $\frac{3\pi}{2}$ radians to the right to get the graph of the cosine function.

7. a. At 1 rpm, the wheel will have moved through x. Then at 2 rpm, the wheel will have moved through $2x$, and at 0.5 rpm, the wheel will have moved through $0.5x$.

b. For the 2 rpm rate, $y = r \sin 2x$ for the distance from the horizontal, where r is the radius of the Ferris wheel, so $y = 16 \sin 2x$.

$y = r \cos 2x$ for the distance from the vertical, where r is the radius of the Ferris wheel, so $y = 16 \cos 2x$.

For the $\frac{1}{2}$ rpm rate, $y = 16 \sin 0.5x$ for the distance from the horizontal and $y = 16 \cos 0.5x$ for the distance from the vertical.

c. The waves are the same shape, and they cross the y-axis at the same point as the parent function, but they complete one cycle in a different number of degrees. (They are also different heights due to the 16, as students should expect from Activities 3–5.) $y = 16 \sin 2x$ completes 2 cycles for every one cycle completed by $y = 16 \sin x$, but $y = 16 \sin 0.5x$ completes only $\frac{1}{2}$ cycle for every one cycle completed by $y = 16 \sin x$.

d. Doubling the angular velocity to 2 rpm causes the wave to complete 2 cycles in $360°$ or twice as many as at 1 rpm. At 0.5 rpm, half the angular velocity, the wave completes only half of its cycle in $360°$ or half as many as at 1 rpm.

e. At the end of one cycle, $\sin x = 0$ again for $x = 360°$.
At the end of one cycle, $\sin 2x = 0$ again for $x = 180°$.

f. At the end of one cycle, $\sin x = 0$ again for $x = 2\pi$.
At the end of one cycle, $\sin 2x = 0$ again for $x = \pi$.

b. The graphs of $y = \sin x$ and $y = \cos x$ have a maximum value of 1 and a minimum value of -1.

- In the interval $-720° \leq x \leq 720°$ or $-4\pi \leq x \leq 4\pi$, what values of x correspond to the maximum value of $y = \sin x$? To the minimum value of $y = \sin x$?

- In the interval $-720° \leq x \leq 720°$ or $-4\pi \leq x \leq 4\pi$, what values of x correspond to the maximum value of $y = \cos x$? To the minimum value of $y = \cos x$?

c. Describe how you could use a transformation of the graph of the sine function to get the graph of the cosine function.

7. A Ferris wheel operator can manipulate the speed at which the Ferris wheel turns. Consider speeds of 1 rpm (the original speed), 2 rpm, and $\frac{1}{2}$ rpm for a wheel 16 meters in diameter. Let the starting position for the measurement of angles be the 3 o'clock position. Measure the angles counterclockwise from the horizontal line through the center of the wheel.

a. Suppose a seat at the 3 o'clock position rotates through an angle with measure x in a given amount of time when the wheel is turning at 1 rpm. Through what angle will the same seat rotate in the same amount of time when the wheel turns at 2 rpm? At $\frac{1}{2}$ rpm?

b. For the 2 rpm rate, write an equation that models the height of the seat from the horizontal line through the center of the wheel, using the independent variable x as given in Part a. Write a second equation that models the directed distance of the seat from the vertical line through the center. Write corresponding rules for the $\frac{1}{2}$ rpm rate.

c. Graph each of the functions from Part b and compare them to the graphs of the basic functions, $y = \cos x$ and $y = \sin x$.

d. Compare the cycles of the graphs for $\frac{1}{2}$ rpm and 2 rpm with the cycle for 1 rpm. What effect does doubling the angular velocity of the Ferris wheel have on the cycle of the associated sine and cosine functions? What effect does halving the angular velocity have on the same functions?

e. When working in degrees, $\sin 0° = 0$. At the end of one cycle, $\sin x = 0$ again for what value of x? At the end of one cycle of $y = \sin 2x$, what is the value of x?

f. When working in radians, $\sin 0 = 0$. At the end of one cycle, $\sin x = 0$ again for what value of x? At the end of one cycle of $y = \sin 2x$, what is the value of x?

8. Reproduced below is the graph showing the patterns of change in the number of hours of daylight in Boston over a one-year period. Day 0 is January 1, and the year shown is not a leap year.

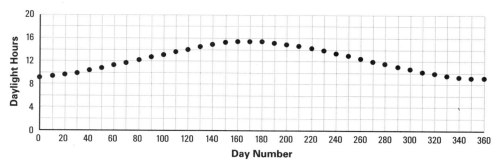

a. If you were to model this situation with a trigonometric function, what would be the independent (input) variable? The dependent variable?

b. Shown below are graphs of $y = \cos x$ and $y = -\cos x$ for $0 \le x \le 2\pi$.

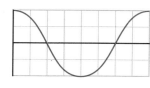

$y = \cos x$ $\qquad\qquad$ $y = -\cos x$

■ Which graph has a shape that approximates the graph of the number of hours of daylight in Boston over a one-year period?

■ Describe geometrically how you would transform the graph of the chosen trigonometric function so that it more closely matches the hours of daylight graph. (Customizing rules for trigonometric functions to match patterns of periodic change will be looked at more closely in Course 3.)

■ Some calculators and computer software have the capability to find the equation of a best-fitting trigonometric model. The trigonometric regression feature of the TI-83 calculator gives a model using the sine function for these data. An equivalent model that involves the cosine function is $y = -3.03 \cos(0.017x) + 12.31$. Does this model look like it would be a good fit for the data? What input values for x make sense in this situation?

8. **a.** The independent variable is *Day Number*, and the dependent variable is *Daylight Hours*.

  b. ■ $y = -\cos x$ has the right shape if we shift the whole graph up by about 12.

  ■ We would let the cycle be 360 days instead of 360°, and we would have to shift the whole graph up by about 12. Then we also need to stretch it vertically so the maximum and minimum values are more like 6 units apart instead of 2. If we try the graph of $y = -3\cos x + 12$, the graph looks like it might fit the data. (The equation $y = -3.03\cos(0.017x) + 12.31$ gives a very good fit, where x is in radians.)

  ■ Input values $0 \le x \le 360$ make sense.

Unit 6

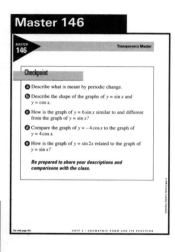

EXPLORE *continued*

8. c.   ■ May 1 is day 121 of the year. For $x = 121$, the model indicates there is approximately 13.73 hours of daylight.

■ Boston has 15 or more hours of daylight in the period from 160 to 210 days, or from June 9 to July 29. The summer solstice is June 22, which would be the longest day of the year. The model has its maximum of approximately 15.34 hours of daylight at day 185, July 4.

■ The model indicates that Boston has 12 or more hours of daylight from day 86 to day 283, or March 27 to October 10. (These data roughly correspond to the spring and fall equinoxes.)

9. a.   Responses will vary according to each group's examples.

b.   Only situations that deal with rotation in degrees would use the unit *degrees* for the independent variable.

SHARE AND SUMMARIZE   full-class discussion

Checkpoint

See Teaching Master 146.

If students respond superficially to Parts b–e, you might ask them for more specific comparisons of intercepts, maximums, and minimums.

ⓐ   Periodic change refers to a pattern of change in the y values of a function that repeats itself over every x-interval of a given length.

ⓑ   The graph of $y = \sin x$ is wave-like, beginning at 0 for $x = 0°$ and increasing to 1 at $x = 90°$, decreasing to 0 at $x = 180°$ and to –1 at $x = 270°$, then increasing to 0 again at 360°. This pattern is repeated over successive intervals of 360°. On this graph, the x-axis represents the central angle, and the y-axis is the distance from a point on the circle to the x-axis.

The graph of $y = \cos x$ is similar except that at $x = 0°$, it begins at 1, decreases to 0 at $x = 90°$ and to –1 at $x = 180°$, then it increases to 0 at 270° and to 1 at 360°. $y = \cos x$ is also periodic. On this graph, the x-axis represents the central angle, and the y-axis is the distance from a point on the circle to a vertical line through the center of the circle.

Another approach, which may be helpful for some students, is to examine tables of values for $y = \sin x$ and $y = \cos x$ on calculators. Ask students to compare these tables with the graphs of the functions: "Can you see the cycling of the functions on the tables? Can you find the maximum and minimum values? What changes in the table values will you see if the amplitude of the equation (the diameter of the Ferris wheel) changes and how will this compare to changes in the graphs due to amplitude changes?"

ⓒ $y = 6 \sin x$ and $y = \sin x$ are both wave-like with the high and low points occurring at the same values of x. They differ only in that the y values are 6 times as large for $y = 6 \sin x$ as the corresponding values for $y = \sin x$. This means that the maximum y value of $y = 6 \sin x$ is 6 and its minimum y value is –6, while $y = \sin x$ has a maximum y value of 1 and a minimum y value of –1.

> **See additional Teaching Notes on page T453N.**

c. Recall that the radian measure of an angle whose vertex is the center of a circle is the ratio $\frac{s}{r}$, where s is the length of the arc on the circle that the angle intercepts, and r is the radius of the circle. Since s and r are measured in the same unit, the ratio $\frac{s}{r}$ is a unit-free real number. Thus, radians can be used to model periodic situations in which the independent variable represents a real number, rather than an angle measure. Using radian mode and the modeling equation given in the last section of Part b, estimate:

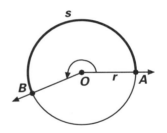

- the hours of daylight in Boston on May 1;
- the days when Boston has the most daylight hours; and
- the days when Boston has more than 12 hours of daylight.

9. Refer back to Activity 1 on page 436, and the situations your group identified as having periodic change.

   a. For each of the situations, describe the independent variable and the dependent variable.

   b. For each situation, was the independent variable a degree measure or a real number?

Checkpoint

ⓐ Describe what is meant by periodic change.

ⓑ Describe the shape of the graphs of $y = \sin x$ and $y = \cos x$.

ⓒ How is the graph of $y = 6 \sin x$ similar to and different from the graph of $y = \sin x$?

ⓓ Compare the graph of $y = -4 \cos x$ to the graph of $y = 4 \cos x$.

ⓔ How is the graph of $y = \sin 2x$ related to the graph of $y = \sin x$?

Be prepared to share your descriptions and comparisons with the class.

A graph that repeats itself over and over again is called a **periodic graph**. The **period** is the length of the smallest interval which contains a cycle of the graph. The period of a graph of $y = \cos Bx$ or $y = \sin Bx$ is determined by the value of B. Often, periodic graphs have a maximum and a minimum in one cycle. When they do, half the difference *maximum value – minimum value* is called the **amplitude**. The amplitude of $y = A \sin x$ or $y = A \cos x$ is $|A|$.

Unit 6

LESSON 3 • THE POWER OF THE CIRCLE   **441**

▶**On Your Own**

Portions of periodic graphs are shown below with windows $-720° \leq x \leq 720°$ or $-4\pi \leq x \leq 4\pi$ and $-6 \leq y \leq 6$. Without using a calculator or computer software, match each graph with one of the given rules. In each case, explain the reason for your choice.

- $y = 3\sin x$
- $y = 3\cos x$
- $y = 3 + \sin x$
- $y = -3\sin x$
- $y = -3\cos x$
- $y = \sin 3x$

a.

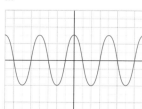

b.

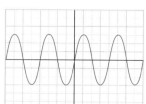

c.

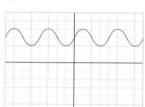

d.

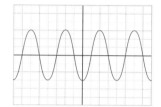

MORE
Modeling • Organizing • Reflecting • Extending

Modeling

1. The center of a Ferris wheel in an amusement park is 7 meters above the ground and the Ferris wheel itself is 12 meters across.

   a. Sketch the Ferris wheel.

   b. Ashley and her friend enter their seat when it is directly below the center. The wheel takes 20 seconds to make one complete revolution. Sketch a graph by hand showing their height above the ground during 1 minute of this ride.

▶**On Your Own**

a. $y = 3 \cos x$ The amplitude is 3, and the graph looks much like $y = \cos x$.

b. $y = 3 \sin x$ The amplitude is 3, and the graph looks much like $y = \sin x$.

c. $y = 3 + \sin x$ The graph is simply $y = \sin x$ shifted up 3 units.

d. $y = -3 \cos x$ The graph looks like the graph in Part a reflected across the x-axis.

MORE   **independent assignment**

Modeling

1. a.

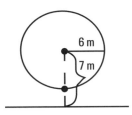

b.

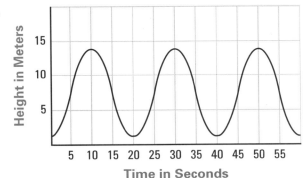

MORE
ASSIGNMENT   *pp. 442–449*

Modeling: 1 and 2
Organizing: 3 and 4
Reflecting: 2
Extending: Choose one*

*When choice is indicated, it is important to leave the choice to the student.
NOTE: *It is best if Organizing tasks are discussed as a whole class after they have been assigned as homework.*

1. c. Starting at the 3 o'clock position, the distance to the vertical line is a maximum.

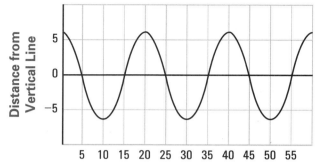

Time in Seconds

(y-axis label: Distance from Vertical Line)

d. Responses may vary. Three possible responses follow. The viewing window must be set correctly to see the expected graph.

i. $y = 6 \cos \dfrac{360°}{\text{rev}} x$, or $y = 6 \cos \dfrac{2\pi}{\text{rev}} x$

(Here x is measured in revolutions. Since 1 revolution is a period, the x values for the viewing window are 0 to 3.)

ii. $y = 6 \cos [(3 \text{ periods} \cdot 360° \text{ per period})x] = 6 \cos (1{,}080x)$ or
$y = 6 \cos [(3 \text{ periods} \cdot 2\pi \text{ per period})x] = 6 \cos (6\pi x)$

(Here x is time in minutes. The angular velocity is 1,080 degrees or 6π radians per minute, so there is $\frac{1}{3}$ of a minute in one period. The x values for the viewing window are 0 to 1.)

iii. $y = 6 \cos \left[\left(\dfrac{1 \text{ period}}{20 \text{ seconds}}\right) \cdot \left(\dfrac{360°}{1 \text{ period}}\right)\right] x = 6 \cos (18x)$ or

$y = 6 \cos \left[\left(\dfrac{1 \text{ period}}{20 \text{ seconds}}\right) \cdot \left(\dfrac{2\pi}{1 \text{ period}}\right)\right] x = 6 \cos \left(\dfrac{\pi}{10} x\right)$

(Here x is time in seconds. The angular velocity is 18 degrees or $\frac{\pi}{10}$ radians per second, so 20 seconds is one period. The viewing window has x values representing 0 to 60 seconds.)

2. a. Using 5-second increments, the table would be as follows:

x	0	5	10	15	20	25	30	35	40	45	50	55	60
y	1	7	13	7	1	7	13	7	1	7	13	7	1

b.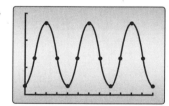

```
WINDOW FORMAT
Xmin =0
Xmax =60
Xscl =5
Ymin =0
Ymax =15
Yscl =5
```

c. The graph is periodic. The period is 20 seconds, which is $\frac{1}{3}$ minute or 1 revolution.

d. The last two equations model the data. For testing, the mode must be set correctly.

See additional Teaching Notes on page T453N.

Unit 6

c. Consider the seat that was at the 3 o'clock position when Ashley entered her seat. Sketch a graph by hand showing the directed distance between that seat and the vertical line through the center of the wheel, as the wheel makes 3 revolutions.

d. Write an equation modeling the periodic motion described in Part c.

2. Refer back to the Ferris wheel ride described in Part b of Modeling Task 1.

   a. Make a table of values for the time x and the height y of Ashley's seat above the *ground* during the first minute of the ride. Recall that it takes 20 seconds to make one complete revolution.

   b. Use the data pairs in Part a to sketch a graph of the height y as a function of the time x.

   c. Is this graph periodic? If so, what is its period?

   d. Here are several equations that were predicted to be models of the plot in Part b. Test each to determine if any are good models of these data.

   ■ $y = 6 \sin 18x + 7$ where 18 is angular velocity in degrees per second, x is time in seconds, and y is height in meters.

   ■ $y = -6 \cos 18x$ where 18 is angular velocity in degrees per second, x is time in seconds, and y is height in meters.

   ■ $y = -6 \cos 18x + 7$ where 18 is angular velocity in degrees per second, x is time in seconds, and y is height in meters.

   ■ $y = -6 \cos \frac{\pi x}{10} + 7$ where $\frac{\pi x}{10}$ is angular velocity in radians per second, x is time in seconds, and y is height in meters.

3. An amusement park is planning a new roller coaster. Part of it is to have the shape of the cosine function. The high and low points of this part differ by 24 meters and cover a horizontal distance of 40 meters from the high point to the low point. The low point is 6 meters below ground in a tunnel. Let y represent the number of meters the track is above or below ground, and let x represent the number of meters the track is horizontally from the high point.

   a. Sketch this situation.

   b. The equation $y = 12 \cos(4.5x) + 6$ models the situation when x and y are in meters and 4.5 is in degrees per meter. Rewrite $y = 12 \cos(4.5x) + 6$ as an equation for which the coefficient of x is in radians per meter.

c. What is the length of a vertical support girder at the high point? At a distance of 6 meters horizontally from the high point? At a distance of 20 meters horizontally from the high point?

d. Measured horizontally, how far from the high point does the roller coaster enter the tunnel?

```
WINDOW
Tmin=0
Tmax=360
Tstep=5
Xmin=-9
Xmax=9
Xscl=1
↓Ymin=-6
```

4. In Investigation 4, you modeled the distance from a point on a circle to a vertical line through the circle's center by the rule $y = 5 \cos x$. Similarly, you modeled the distance from the point to the horizontal line through the circle's center with the equation $y = 5 \sin x$. Another way to model this situation (which will be developed more fully in Course 4) is to use *parametric equations*. Parametric equations determine a graph using separate equations for the x- and y-coordinates for each point. Both equations are functions of another *parameter*, usually denoted T. Set your calculator or computer software to parametric mode, using degrees. (You may need to consult your manual.)

Set the viewing window so that T varies from 0 to 360 in steps of 5, x varies from –9 to 9, and y varies from –6 to 6. Then, in the functions list, enter $X_T = 5 \cos T$ and $Y_T = 5 \sin T$ as the first pair of equations.

a. Graph and trace values for $T = 30, 60, 90$, and so on.

b. What physical quantity is represented by X_T? By Y_T?

c. What measurement does T represent? What are the units of T?

d. How much does T change in one revolution?

e. If one revolution of the circle takes 20 seconds, what is the angular velocity of a point on the circle in units of T per second?

f. What is the linear velocity of a point in meters per second if the circle's radius is 5 centimeters?

g. What equations would model circular motion with a radius of 4 centimeters? Enter them as the second pair of parametric equations in your functions list.

h. Graph at the same time the equations for circles with the radii of 4 and 5 centimeters. (On some calculators, you need to set the mode for simultaneous graphs.) Watch carefully. If the circles both turn at the same angular velocity, on which circle does a point have the greater linear velocity? What is the linear velocity of the slower point?

3. **c.** The vertical support at the high point is 18 meters.

   The point 6 meters away has a height of $12 \cos (4.5 \cdot 6) + 6$ or approximately 16.7 meters. Students can get this value using the graph or a table.

   The point 20 meters away has a height of $12 \cos (4.5 \cdot 20) + 6$ or 6 meters.

   d. The horizontal distance x is about 26.7 meters when the vertical distance y is 0. Students can find this by using the graph or a table, by solving $0 = 12 \cos 4.5x + 6$ for x, or by using a calculator or computer software to find the zero of the function.

4. **a.** The graph is a circle. The values for x and y follow:

T	30°	60°	90°	120°	150°	180°	210°	240°	270°	300°	330°	360°
x	4.3	2.5	0	−2.5	−4.3	−5	−4.3	−2.5	0	2.5	4.3	5
y	2.5	4.3	5	4.3	2.5	0	−2.5	−4.3	−5	−4.3	−2.5	0

   b. x_T represents a point's distance from the vertical line going through the center of the wheel. y_T represents a point's distance from the horizontal line going through the center of the wheel.

   c. T represents the measure of the angle in degrees measured counterclockwise from the 3 o'clock position.

   d. T goes from 0° to 360° in one revolution.

   e. $\dfrac{360°}{1 \text{ rev}} \cdot \dfrac{1 \text{ rev}}{20 \text{ sec}} = \dfrac{360°}{20 \text{ sec}} = 18°$ per sec

   f. linear velocity $= \dfrac{\text{circumference of 1 rev}}{\text{time for 1 rev}} = \dfrac{5 \cdot 2\pi \text{ m}}{20 \text{ sec}} \approx \dfrac{10\pi \text{ m}}{20 \text{ sec}} \approx 1.57$ m/sec

   g. $x_T = 4 \cos T$

   $y_T = 4 \sin T$

   h. The point on the 5-centimeter radius wheel has the greater linear velocity. The slower point has linear velocity of $\dfrac{4 \cdot 2\pi \text{ m}}{20 \text{ sec}}$ or approximately 1.26 m/sec.

Unit 6

Organizing

1. **a.** If point A has coordinates (x, y), then $x = \cos t$, where t is the angle formed by the x-axis and the line from the origin to A. Similarly $y = \sin t$.

   b. The line is $y = mx$. The slope of the line is $m = \frac{\sin t}{\cos t}$.

   c. $\tan t = \frac{y}{x}$, which is also the slope or $\frac{\sin t}{\cos t}$

   d. The conjecture should be that $\tan t = \frac{\sin t}{\cos t}$, which is also the slope of line OA.

2. **a.** For both tables and graphs of models of the form $y = A \sin x$, $y = 0$ when x is any multiple of $180°$, including $0°$. The y values of $y = A \sin x$ are $A \cdot (y$ values of $y = \sin x)$. The period is $360°$, and the shapes of the graphs are all waves.

   b. ■ The graph of $y = -\cos x$ is a reflection of the graph of $y = \cos x$ across the x-axis.
   ■ The graph of $y = A \sin x$ may be obtained from $y = \sin x$ by stretching the amplitude from 1 to A.
   ■ If $A < 0$, the graph of $y = A \cos x$ may be obtained from $y = \cos x$ by first reflecting $\cos x$ across the x-axis and then stretching the amplitude from 1 to $|A|$.

   c. The graph of $y = \sin 2x$ achieves the same maximum and minimum (1 and -1 respectively) as $y = \sin x$ does, but it has a period of $180°$ instead of $360°$ (π instead of 2π). Similarly, the graph of $y = \cos 10x$ has the same amplitude as $y = \cos x$, but it has a period of $36°$ instead of $360°$ ($\frac{\pi}{5}$ instead of 2π).

   d. In general multiplying x by B will change the period of either function to $\frac{360°}{B}$ or $\frac{2\pi}{B}$.

3. **a.** ■ $0° < x < 90°$, the second side lies in quadrant I.
   ■ $90° < x < 180°$, the second side lies in quadrant II.
   ■ $180° < x < 270°$, the second side lies in quadrant III.
   ■ $270° < x < 360°$, the second side lies in quadrant IV.

   b. In each case, the trigonometric functions are obtained correctly by considering the length of the side of the triangle to be negative when it is horizontal and to the left of the y-axis or when it is vertical and below the x-axis. Thus, the change needed in that distance can be negative.

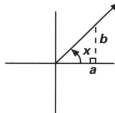
$0° < x < 90°$

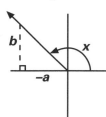
$90° < x < 180°$

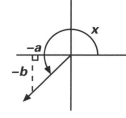
$180° < x < 270°$

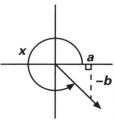
$270° < x < 360°$

   c. ■ $0 < x < \frac{\pi}{2}$
   ■ $\frac{\pi}{2} < x < \pi$
   ■ $\pi < x < \frac{3\pi}{2}$
   ■ $\frac{3\pi}{2} < x < 2\pi$

Organizing

1. Draw a circle with radius 1 unit, centered at the origin O of the coordinate plane. Choose any point $A(x, y)$ on that circle.

   a. Express the coordinates of A in terms of the sine and cosine of an angle at the center of the circle.

   b. Write an equation for the line containing the origin and point A. What is its slope?

   c. Find the tangent of the angle formed by line OA and the positive x-axis (measure counterclockwise).

   d. Compare your results in Parts b and c. What conjecture can you make?

2. In Investigation 4, you used trigonometric models of the form $y = A \sin x$ and $y = A \cos x$ to describe patterns of change associated with a rotating Ferris wheel.

   a. What do tables and graphs of models of the form $y = A \sin x$ have in common?

   b. Use the ideas of geometric transformations to describe how:

   ■ The graph of $y = -\cos x$ is related to the graph of $y = \cos x$.

   ■ The graph of $y = A \sin x$, where $A > 0$, is related to the graph of $y = \sin x$.

   ■ The graph of $y = A \cos x$, where $A < 0$, is related to the graph of $y = \cos x$.

   c. How is the graph of $y = \sin 2x$ related to the graph of $y = \sin x$? How is the graph of $y = \cos 10x$ related to the graph of $y = \cos x$?

   d. In general, when comparing the graphs of $y = \sin x$ and $y = \sin Bx$ or the graphs of $y = \cos x$ and $y = \cos Bx$, what seems to be the effect of the value of B when $B > 0$?

3. The trigonometric functions (sine, cosine, and tangent) are evaluated by the calculator for all angles whose degree measure x is between 0° and 360°.

   a. If one side of the angle lies along the positive x-axis, describe in which quadrant the other side of the angle lies for each range of values.

   ■ $0° < x < 90°$

   ■ $90° < x < 180°$

   ■ $180° < x < 270°$

   ■ $270° < x < 360°$

   b. For each of the angle ranges in Part a, draw a representative angle. Show how a right triangle can be drawn for each such angle so that the sides of the triangle give the expected trigonometric ratios. What modification in your usual idea of distance needs to be made in order for the ratios to agree in sign (positive or negative) with the calculated function values?

   c. Express each range of values from Part a in radian measure.

4. Reproduced below are some of the strip patterns from the "Patterns in Space and Visualization" unit in Course 1.

   a. How are the graphs of periodic models related to these strip patterns?

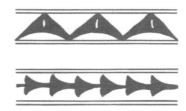

   b. What is the shortest distance you could translate the graph of $y = \sin x$ so that it would map onto itself?

   c. What symmetries, other than translational symmetry, do the graphs of $y = \sin x$ and $y = \cos x$ have? Describe any lines and any centers and angles of rotation involved in each.

5. Draw a circle with center at the origin O and radius 4.

   a. Let $A(x, y)$ be a point on the circle. Consider the angle formed by $\overline{OA}$ and the positive x-axis ($\angle O$). Express the coordinates x and y in terms of the sine and cosine of this angle.

   b. Use the distance formula to express the distance from A to O in terms of the sine and cosine of the angle at the origin. What can you conclude about $(\sin O)^2 + (\cos O)^2$? Do you think this conclusion applies to any angle? Provide evidence to support your answer.

Reflecting

1. Think about the graphs of $y = \sin x$ and $y = \cos x$.

   a. Describe a method you could use to make a quick sketch of each of these graphs.

   b. How is the graph of $y = \cos x$ related to the graph of $y = \sin x$?

2. Karen wishes to evaluate sin 25° using her calculator. She presses [SIN] 25 and [ENTER]. The calculator displays the screen at the right. What is wrong? What indicates an error?

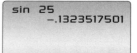

4. a. Both strip patterns and periodic graphs show translational symmetry. If you translate a periodic graph by a distance equal to the length of its period, the graph appears unmoved; that is, it maps onto itself.

   b. $360°$ or 2π

   c. $y = \sin x$ and $y = \cos x$ have $180°$ rotational symmetry about any point common to the graph and x-axis. They also have glide reflection symmetry: translate $180°$ or π radians parallel to the x-axis and then reflect across the x-axis.

5. a. $x = 4 \cos m\angle O$, $y = 4 \sin m\angle O$

   b. $\sqrt{(4 \cos m\angle O)^2 + (4 \sin m\angle O)^2} = \sqrt{16(\cos m\angle O)^2 + 16(\sin m\angle O)^2}$
   $= \sqrt{16[(\cos m\angle O)^2 + (\sin m\angle O)^2]}$
   $= 4\sqrt{(\cos m\angle O)^2 + (\sin m\angle O)^2}$

   This distance must be 4 since point A is on the circle with radius 4; thus, $(\cos m\angle O)^2 + (\sin m\angle O)^2 = 1$.

   This is a fundamental identity relating sine and cosine of any angle.

Reflecting

1. a. To see one complete period of $\sin x$, you could sketch a set of axes and label the x-axis with hash marks representing $0°$, $180°$, and $360°$, and label the y-axis with hash marks representing -1 and 1. Then mark values:
   $$\sin 0° = \sin 180° = \sin 360° = 0.$$
   The maximum value (1) of sine is at $x = 90°$; and the minimum value (-1) is at $x = 270°$. Connect these values with a wave-like graph.

   To sketch $\cos x$, draw similar hash marks, except $\cos 0° = 1$, the minimum value (-1) is at $x = 180°$, and $\cos 90° = \cos 270° = 0$.

   b. You may obtain a graph of $\cos x$ by shifting $\sin x$ $90°$ to the left on the x-axis.

2. The value given by the calculator cannot be correct, because $25°$ is located in quadrant I, and the values of sine in that quadrant are all positive. The calculator is probably in radian mode instead of degree mode.

3. a.

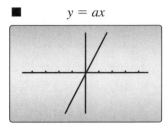
$y = ax$

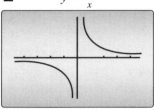
$y = \dfrac{a}{x}$

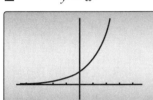
$y = a^x$

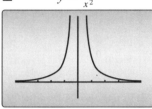
$y = \dfrac{a}{x^2}$

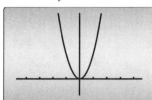
$y = ax^2$

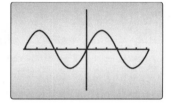
$y = a \sin x$

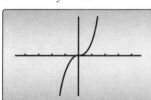
$y = ax^3$

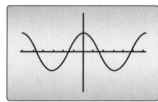
$y = a \cos x$

b. ■ $y = ax$ is the only linear function.

■ $y = a^x$ is asymptotic to the x-axis for $x < 0$ and increases rapidly for $x > 0$.

■ $y = ax^2$ is a parabola opening upward.

■ $y = ax^3$ is an increasing, non-linear function, passing through $(0, 0)$.

■ $y = \dfrac{a}{x}$ is asymptotic to both the x- and y-axes and has values only in quadrants I and III.

■ $y = \dfrac{a}{x^2}$ is asymptotic to both axes and has values only in quadrants I and II.

■ $y = a \sin x$ is a periodic function passing through the origin.

■ $y = a \cos x$ is a periodic function passing through $(0, a)$.

See additional Teaching Notes on page T4530.

3. In *Contemporary Mathematics in Context*, you have studied various patterns of change and how those patterns could be modeled using linear, exponential, power, and trigonometric functions. It is helpful to think about each "family" of functions in terms of basic symbolic rules and their corresponding graphs.

   a. Make and label a general sketch of the graph of each function rule below. In each case, $a > 1$.

   - $y = ax$ - $y = \dfrac{a}{x}$
   - $y = a^x$ - $y = \dfrac{a}{x^2}$
   - $y = ax^2$ - $y = a \sin x$
   - $y = ax^3$ - $y = a \cos x$

   b. Describe one characteristic of the graph of each function that sets it apart from the graphs of the other functions.

   c. Without sketching, explain how the graphs you drew in Part a would be different if $0 < a < 1$ and if $a < 0$.

4. Look back at the graph on page 440 of daylight hours for Boston over a one-year period. How would this graph be different if the number of daylight hours was obtained in Fairbanks, Alaska? At the equator?

Extending

1. Consider a circle of radius 6 with center at the origin.

   a. Lines with slopes 1 and –1 each intersect the circle in two points. Find the coordinates of these points.

   b. If you know one of the points of intersection in Part a, how can you use the symmetry of the circle to determine the remaining three?

   c. The line $y = \dfrac{\sqrt{3}}{3} x$ intersects the circle in two points. Find the coordinates of those points. Find the coordinates of the points on the circle that are symmetric to these points with respect to the x-axis. Then find the equation of the line containing these new points.

   d. What angle does $y = \dfrac{\sqrt{3}}{3} x$ make with the x-axis?

2. Investigate the effect that adding a constant to x has on the graph of $y = \sin x$.

   a. Start by graphing $y = \sin x$ and $y = \sin (x + 180°)$. How do the two graphs seem to be related?

   b. Experiment by adding different constants to x and then comparing graphs.

   c. Describe the relation between the graphs of $y = \sin x$ and $y = \sin (x + b)°$, where b is a constant.

3. Like the various situations you've seen in this lesson, electricity and sound are periodic phenomena that can be modeled by trigonometric equations. A steady electrical current can be created by rotating a rod with copper wire coiled around it through a magnetic field at a constant angular velocity.

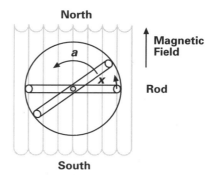

The electricity E created is measured in volts. It turns out that E is a function of the distance from the tip of the rotating rod to the horizontal. That is, E is a sine function. The equation is $E = E_0 \sin ax$, where a is the angular velocity in revolutions per second and $x \geq 0$ is time in seconds. For this activity, assume $E_0 = 100$ volts and that the angular velocity is 60 revolutions per second.

a. Write an equation for the voltage E in which the angular velocity a is expressed in degrees per second.

b. Graph the function over the interval from 0 to 2 seconds. What viewing window did you use? Do you think a different interval would give more or better information? Explain.

c. Try graphing the function for time intervals from 0 to:

- 1 second
- 0.5 second
- 0.1 second
- 0.05 second

Do any of these intervals give a clearer picture of the graph? If so, which ones?

d. Describe how many cycles of the graph you see in Part c when the interval is $0 \leq x \leq 0.1$. Why are there this many cycles?

e. Over what interval would you graph the function to show just one cycle of the graph? Test your conjecture by graphing the function over your interval. What interval would you use to show 10 cycles?

f. How can you use 60 revolutions per second to determine the period or length of one cycle?

3. a. $E = 100 \sin 21{,}600x$ or $E = 100 \sin 120\pi x$

  60 revolutions per second converts to 21,600 degrees/sec or 120π radians/sec.

b. Viewing windows should have Xmin = 0 and Xmax = 2. For the *y*-axis, the maximum should be at least 100, and the minimum should be at least –100. With this window, the graph seems to be several clumps of points and lines. A different window would be better. (Some calculators may show an interesting but misleading pattern to the graph; for example, the maximum values may seem to change from cycle to cycle.)

c. ■ Interval 0 to 1: Still unsatisfactory; there are still too many cycles displayed in too small a space.

  ■ Interval 0 to 0.5: Still unsatisfactory.

  ■ Interval 0 to 0.1: Finally, we can see individual cycles. There are now six cycles visible.

  ■ Interval 0 to 0.05: This shows three cycles and is clearly a "sine wave."

d. You see 6 cycles. Since the bar is rotating at 60 revolutions per second, the bar would rotate completely 6 times in $\frac{1}{10}$ second. Thus you will see the 6 cycles of the sine graph, one cycle for each revolution.

e. One cycle occurs for one revolution. Since there are 60 rps, you would need a graph over $\frac{1}{60}$ of a second. Entering $1 \div 60$ for Xmax and displaying the graph will show this. You would show 10 cycles by setting the scale so that 10 revolutions would occur. Thus, set Xmax at $\frac{1}{6}$.

f. The length of a cycle is the time needed for one revolution, that is, seconds per revolution. So the period is the reciprocal of the speed in rps or $\frac{1}{60}$ sec.

Unit 6

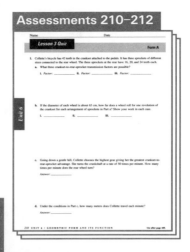
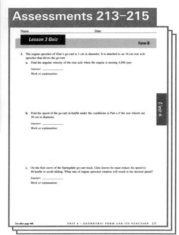
MORE *continued*

4. Students who have completed this task might be intrigued by the following questions: "What can you see when you look at the graphs of the models for middle C, low C, and the C two octaves above middle C? What would be the frequency for the C one octave above middle C?" (The periods of all the C graphs are multiples of each other. The frequency of the C one octave above middle C is 528 cycles per second.)

   a. 264 cycles per second = $264 \cdot 2\pi = 528\pi$ radians per second

   b. $y = 1 \cdot \sin (264$ cycles/sec $\cdot 2\pi$ radians per cycle$)x = \sin 528\pi x$, where x is in seconds.

   c. One cycle will occur in $\frac{1}{264}$ seconds. Windows may vary. For example, to show five cycles, use Xmax $= \frac{5}{264}$, Xmin $= 0$, Ymax $= 1.5$, and Ymin $= 1.5$.

   d. Xmax $= \frac{4}{264} = 0.01515...$

   e. The period is $\frac{1}{264}$ seconds. The period is the reciprocal of the frequency.

   f. $y = \sin (1{,}056$ cycles/sec $\cdot 2\pi$ radians/cycle $\cdot x) = \sin (2{,}112\pi x)$, where x is in seconds. The period is $\frac{1}{1056}$ seconds.

   g. $y = \sin (132$ cycles/sec $\cdot 2\pi$ radians/cycle $x) = \sin (264\pi x)$
   To show four cycles, use Xmax $= \frac{4}{132}$, Xmin $= 0$.

   h. Since middle C shows 4 cycles on this segment and one octave below middle C shows 2 cycles, it seems reasonable that one octave above will show 8 cycles. Since the frequency of middle C is 264 cycles per second and one octave above shows twice the cycles in the same interval, the frequency of one octave above should be 528 cycles per second.

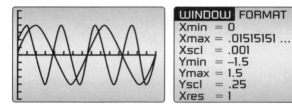

```
WINDOW FORMAT
Xmin = 0
Xmax = .01515151 ...
Xscl = .001
Ymin = −1.5
Ymax = 1.5
Yscl = .25
Xres = 1
```

See Assessment Resources, pages 210–215.

4. Simple sounds, such as those you can view on an oscilloscope, are modeled by trigonometric equations such as $y = A \sin Bx$ or $y = A \cos Bx$, where B is expressed in radians per second and x is time in seconds. The amplitude A represents loudness. A good example of a simple sound is the sound produced by a piano tuning fork.

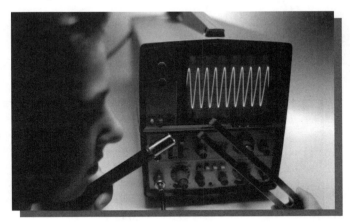

   a. The middle C tuning fork oscillates at 264 cycles per second. This is called its frequency. How many radians per second is this?

   b. Write a model for middle C sound when A is 1.

   c. Graph your model. What window should you use to display the graph well?

   d. Show four cycles of your model on the graphics screen. If you use 0 for the minimum x value, what should you use for the maximum value?

   e. What is the period of your model? How is it related to the frequency of 264 cycles per second?

   f. The C note two octaves above middle C has a frequency of 1,056 cycles per second. Model this sound with an equation. What is the period?

   g. The C note that is one octave below middle C has a frequency of 132 cycles per second. Model this sound with an equation. Graph your model.

   h. Graph your models for Parts b and g in the same viewing window. What do you think is the frequency of the C note one octave above middle C?

Unit 6

Looking Back

As you complete this unit, you may be wondering whether you have been studying mathematics or principles of engineering. That should not be surprising. In many applications of geometric shapes and principles, form and function are intertwined. You have seen that linkages and circular shapes, while simple in design, are useful in many different situations. Their usefulness is directly tied to their geometric properties. This final lesson will help you review and apply the major ideas in this unit.

1. Examine this 4-bar linkage with bars of the given lengths. Bar *AB* is the fixed frame.

   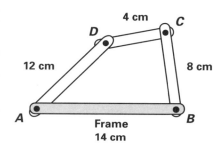

   a. Will either bar *AD* or bar *BC* make complete rotations about point *A* or point *B*? Explain.

   b. Using a scale drawing or a model, determine the largest angle that bar *AD* can make with bar *AB* (∠*DAB*).

   c. Find the smallest measure of ∠*DAB*.

   d. What is the angle through which bar *AD* rotates as bar *BC* is moved?

2. Indy-cars are special race cars that use a parallelogram linkage in the front suspension. The wheel is attached to the coupler, and the frame is attached to the car so that the frame is perpendicular to the ground. The linkage can pivot freely at points *A*, *B*, *C*, and *D*. When the car is not moving, the full width of the tire is in contact with the pavement.

   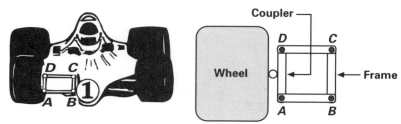

Lesson 4 *Looking Back*

1. **a.** No, bar *DC* is the shortest side, and it will rotate, but bars *AD* or *BC* will not.
   b. Close to 55° (actually, approximately 54.3°).
   c. Close to 15° (actually, approximately 15.4°).
   d. From about 15° to 55°

2. **a.** As the linkage moves up and down, the tire is free to move up and down but will remain parallel to the frame and level relative to the ground.

   b. It will remain parallel to the coupler.

   c. Because the frame is fixed perpendicular to the road, the coupler and the attached tire will remain perpendicular to the road.

3. **a.** The transmission factor is $\frac{15}{2}$ or 7.5. The bobbin would rotate at 1,125 rpm.

   b. The four-bar linkage is *CBAD*. The driver is *CB*; the follower is *AD*; the frame is *DC*.

   c. $y = 3 \sin x$ will model the distance from *A* to the horizontal as *AD* rotates about *D*.

   d. $y = 30 + 3 \sin x$ would model the height of *A* from the floor.

Unit 6

a. Describe the motion of the tire as the entire suspension linkage moves up and down.

b. If the tire is parallel to the coupler when the car is not moving, how is it related to the coupler when the car is in motion?

c. At the speeds that Indy-cars travel, it is important that they "grip" the road by having as great tire-to-pavement contact as possible. How does this suspension linkage design accomplish this goal?

3. Early spinning wheels were run by a *foot treadle* and a *flywheel*. The operator pushed the flywheel to start it turning, then kept it spinning by pressing the foot treadle at appropriate times. The spinning wheel on the left below has a flywheel with radius 15 inches. It is attached to a 2-inch radius pulley, called a *bobbin*, on which the yarn accumulates.

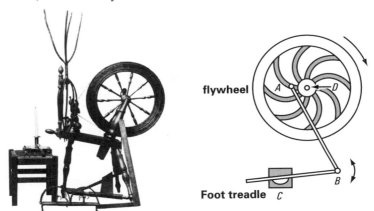

a. What is the transmission factor from the flywheel to the bobbin? An accomplished artisan can make the flywheel turn at 150 rpm. How fast will the bobbin rotate?

b. The diagram on the right above illustrates how the foot treadle turns the flywheel. Identify the 4-bar linkage that makes the spinning wheel work. What is the driver of this linkage? The follower? The frame?

c. If the length of $\overline{AD}$ is 3 inches, describe what is modeled by the equation $y = 3 \sin x$ where x is the degree measure of the angle that $\overline{AD}$ makes with the horizontal through point D.

d. If the center of the flywheel is 30 inches above the floor, how should the equation in Part c be modified to give the height of point A from the floor?

4. Depth sounders such as the one shown on the next page are used on pleasure and fishing boats. The sounder *transducer* sends out a signal that returns information to the boat. The screen will display the shape of the bottom of the lake or river, the depth of the water, and any fish that happen to be in the path of the signal. Sport fishers on inland, fresh-water lakes use the depth sounder to examine the characteristics of the bottom and to locate fish.

The transducer on one depth sounder sends out two signals. Each is in the shape of a right circular cone. One has a vertex angle of 16°, the other is 53°.

a. Make a sketch showing the depth sounder cones for both angles.

- The promotional material for this depth sounder claims the 16° angle signal identifies fish directly under a 14-foot boat that is about 5 feet wide. Is this a reasonable claim if fish are marked at a depth of 20 feet? Explain.

- How large is the radius of the 16° angle-signal cone when fish are marked at 10 feet? At 30 feet? At 50 feet?

b. The narrow-angle and wide-angle signals from the transducer are sent out at the same time. Fish in the wide-angle signal are shown differently on the display screen than those in the narrow-angle signal. Suppose a fish is spotted at 30 feet in the wide-angle cone. Other than the fact that the fish is at 30 feet, what else can you say about the location of the fish?

- What is the radius of the wide-angle cone when fish are spotted at 10 feet? At 20 feet? At 50 feet?

- How are the radii of the two signal cones related at the same depth?

- When the radius of the narrow cone is about 5 feet, what is the radius of the wide-angle cone at the same depth? What is that approximate depth?

c. How may trigonometric models be used to determine the radius of the circular field of the 16° signal at a depth of 100 feet? Of the 53° signal at a depth of 100 feet?

5. Suppose that you are trying to model the motion of a clock pendulum that moves as far as 5 inches to the right of vertical and swings with a period of 2 seconds.

a. Experiment with variations of the rule $y = \cos x$ to find:

- a function whose values range from –5 to 5 and has a period of 2π;

- a function that has period 2 and whose values range from –1 to 1; and

- a function that has a period of 2 and whose values range from –5 to 5.

4. a.

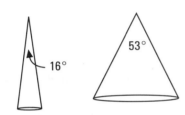

■ $\tan 8° = \frac{r}{20}$
   $r = 20 \tan 8°$
   $r \approx 2.8$ feet

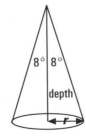

At 20 feet, the circular cross section of the cone has a radius of about 2.8 feet. Thus the circle has a diameter of about 5.6 feet.

■ $y = x \tan 8°$

Depth in Feet	Radius in Feet
10	1.4
30	4.2
50	7

b. ■ $\tan 26.5° = \frac{r}{30}$
   $r = 30 \tan 26.5°$
   $r \approx 15$ feet

The fish is located within a circle whose radius is about 15 feet, centered at the transducer.

In general, $r = d \tan 26.5°$ where d is the depth.

Depth in Feet	Radius in Feet
10	5
20	10
50	25

■ The exact relation is $\frac{\tan 8°}{\tan 26.5°}$ or approximately 0.28. Thus the radius of the 16° cone is about 0.3 times the radius of the 53° cone. (Since the radius of the 53° cone is about one-half the depth, this is easy to calculate in your head.)

■ The radius of the wide cone is approximately $\frac{5}{0.28}$ or 17.9 ft. If students use the 0.3 relation, the radius is approximately 16.7 ft.

The depth is approximately 35.6 feet since $\tan 8° = \frac{5}{\text{depth}}$.

See additional Teaching Notes on page T453Q.

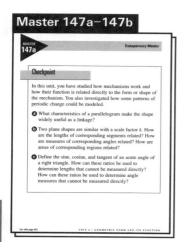

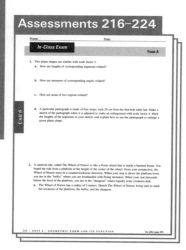

Assessments 216–224

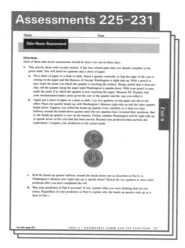

Assessments 225–231

SHARE AND SUMMARIZE full-class discussion

Checkpoint

See Teaching Masters 147a–147b.

ⓐ Responses will vary, but two very important concepts are that a parallelogram is not rigid and that opposite sides of a parallelogram are congruent and parallel. Congruence and parallel sides are maintained regardless of how the parallelogram is flexed. This allows for complete rotation as in train wheels or complete rotation of one side for partial rotation of the opposite side.

ⓑ The lengths of the segments of the second plane shape are k times the lengths of the segments of the first plane shape. Measures of corresponding angles are equal. The areas are related by a factor of k^2.

ⓒ Given a right triangle with acute angle C,

$$\sin C = \frac{\text{length of leg opposite } \angle C}{\text{length of hypotenuse}}$$

$$\cos C = \frac{\text{length of leg adjacent to } \angle C}{\text{length of hypotenuse}}$$

$$\tan C = \frac{\text{length of leg opposite } \angle C}{\text{length of leg adjacent to } \angle C}$$

These functions are useful for indirect measurement of lengths when an angle measure and the length of one side of a triangle are known or can be measured.

ⓓ ■ When the radii are equal, the angular velocity of the second circle is equal to that of the first.

■ When $r_1 > r_2$, the angular velocity of the second circle is increased by a factor of $\frac{r_1}{r_2}$.

■ When $r_2 > r_1$, the angular velocity of the second circle is decreased by a factor of $\frac{r_1}{r_2}$.

ⓔ If an angle has radian measure 2, then for a circle drawn with the angle vertex at its center and radius r, the arc determined by where the sides of the angle intersect the circle is $2r$ units long. Radians are used when measuring angular velocity because the numbers for radians per second will be smaller than the numbers for degrees per second, which makes the values easier to judge.

ⓕ Periodic motion is change of position that follows a repetitive pattern. $y = a \sin bx$ and $y = a \cos bx$ are used to model periodic motion because they themselves are periodic. The value of a is the measure of the maximum displacement of the motion being modeled from its middle position. The value of b represents the angular velocity of a rotating object if x is a measure of time. In other applications, b is the quotient of one revolution (2π or $360°$) divided by the period of the motion.

CONSTRUCTING A MATH TOOLKIT: Following a class discussion of the Checkpoint, students should reexamine their Math Toolkit entries for this unit to determine whether they need to augment their entries for the main ideas from this Checkpoint.

See Assessment Resources, pages 216-231.

b. How are the numbers in the final symbolic rule from Part a related to the motion of the pendulum you are modeling?

c. Graph the function that models the motion of the clock pendulum. Identify the coordinates of the *x*-intercepts and minimum and maximum points of the graph.

Checkpoint

In this unit you have studied how mechanisms work and how their function is related directly to the form or shape of the mechanism. You also investigated how some patterns of periodic change could be modeled.

ⓐ What characteristics of a parallelogram make the shape widely useful as a linkage?

ⓑ Two plane shapes are similar with a scale factor *k*. How are the lengths of corresponding segments related? How are measures of corresponding angles related? How are areas of corresponding regions related?

ⓒ Define the sine, cosine, and tangent of an acute angle of a right triangle. How can these ratios be used to determine lengths that cannot be measured directly? How can these ratios be used to determine angle measures that cannot be measured directly?

ⓓ How does the angular velocity of one rotating pulley or gear affect the angular velocity of a second pulley or gear connected to it by a belt, if the radii are r_1 and r_2 and the following is true:

- $r_1 = r_2$
- $r_1 > r_2$
- $r_1 < r_2$

ⓔ Although often measured in degrees, angles also can be measured in radians. Describe what it means to say an angle has radian measure 2. Describe another use for radians.

ⓕ Why are variations of trigonometric rules such as $y = a \sin bx$ or $y = a \cos bx$ often used to model periodic change? What does the value of *a* tell you about the situation being modeled? What does the value of *b* tell you?

Be prepared to explain your responses to the entire class.

Looking Back, Looking Ahead

▶Reflecting on Mathematical Content

The geometry/trigonometry strand of *Contemporary Mathematics in Context* began in Course 1 with a close examination of shapes in two- and three-dimensional space. It focused on the complementary skills of visualization and representation, on methods for characterizing figures by shape and by size, and on properties of shapes and their applications. The strand progressed in Course 2 through the use of coordinates to describe locations in a plane, to analyze properties of shapes, and to build models of isometries and size transformations. In the present unit, students have seen again the importance of shapes and shape properties in determining how things work. Students have seen how quadrilaterals form linkages, and how those linkages make things possible in the world from moving wiper blades to opening tackle or sewing boxes. Students studied how triangles and circles play central roles in rigid structures and in the world of motion. In addition, trigonometric ratios were introduced as a consequent of the invariance of the measures of angles in similar triangles. These trigonometric ratios were used to help analyze and represent circular motion. The result was the introduction of two new function rules to be added to those already developed in the functions/algebra strand.

Further properties of the trigonometric functions will be developed in the "Families of Functions" unit in Course 3. Concepts such as period, amplitude, and phase shift are developed further, and related, where appropriate, to the geometric transformations such as translation and one-way stretch. The trigonometry is extended further by introducing formally the ideas of the Law of Sines and the Law of Cosines. Each of these statements of a fundamental relation among the sides and angles of a triangle involves four variables. When three of these variables have given values, the fourth one is determined (with the exception of the ambiguous case for the Law of Sines). This situation is exploited to prove the familiar similarity and congruence theorems for triangles in the Course 3 unit "Shapes and Geometric Reasoning." In addition, the properties associated with parallel lines and transversals, parallelograms, and other quadrilaterals also are organized logically, and many familiar and unfamiliar characteristics of these shapes are proved by students. Thus the geometry/trigonometry strand began in Course 1 with a visual and descriptive look at shapes and their characteristics, progressed through the introduction of coordinate models, exploited properties of shapes to analyze linkages and "driver-follower" relations, and returns to shapes and their properties from a more logical and deductive point of view in Course 3. While this treatment will complete the core content for the geometry/trigonometry strand, it will be extended further for college-bound students in the Course 4 materials.

Unit 6 Assessment

Unit 6

Teaching Notes *continued*

Notes continued from page T370

After students complete Activity 1 of the investigation, they should read the Grashof principle given before Activity 2. It would be helpful to draw the full class back together to discuss the statement of Grashof's principle. You might ask, "How does the principle apply to the model you made in Activity 1?" ($VU + UX < VW + WX$, so *VU* can rotate completely.) You may need to have students actually measure line segments from center to center of the paper fasteners (not end to end of the strips) on their models.

When you are sure that everyone understands how to put together and use linkages and understands the Grashof principle, then students can continue on to Activities 2–4. A class discussion of these activities along with the Checkpoint items will help ensure that students are able to discuss ideas about 4-bar linkages.

Notes continued from page T371

4. Some students may be unable to visualize how the windshield wiper works, and they may benefit from constructing a model of it out of linkage strips.

   a.

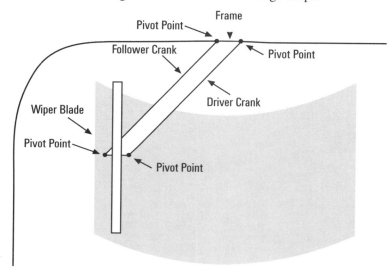

   b. Both pairs of opposite sides are congruent or parallel.

   c. The ends of the wiper blade follow circular paths.

Notes continued from page T373

1. b. Students might not figure out how to use the pantograph by experimentation. However, experimenting at this point will help make them more comfortable with the pantograph. As they work through the rest of the investigation, they will learn how a pantograph works.

   c. The length of each side is constant and the opposite sides remain parallel as the pantograph is opened and closed. The measures of angles change as the pantograph is moved. The lengths of the diagonals also change.

   d. Group comparisons provide students with an opportunity to discuss their observations further.

Teaching Notes *continued*

Notes continued
from page T376

b The shapes will be similar because the pantograph's effect is a size transformation.

c Corresponding lengths will be related by the scale factor *k*. Corresponding angles will have the same measure. The areas of corresponding regions will be related by the square of the scale factor.

APPLY   individual task

▶On Your Own

a. The lengths may vary some, but the lengths of sides in $\triangle FBH$ must be 6 times the corresponding lengths in $\triangle FDG$. Also, $FD = DG$ and $FB = BH$.

b. All pairs of corresponding angles have the same measure.

c. Area $(\triangle FBH) = (6)^2 \cdot$ Area $(\triangle FDG)$
$= 36 \cdot$ Area $(\triangle FDG)$

d. The lengths of the sides of the pyramid will be six times the lengths of the corresponding sides in the cartoon in the text. The shape will be the same, but the surface area will be 36 times the surface area of the original.

Notes continued
from page T376

4. a. It may help students to see a sample pop-up book as they create their own.

b. It lies flat because the left and upper sides of the parallelogram cross section are equal in length to the other two sides.

c. The picture lies flat for the same reason as in Part b above, except it is the upper and right sides that are equal to the lower (fixed) and left sides.

d. The picture is perpendicular to its page when the turning page is perpendicular to the right-hand page.

e. The picture makes a 120° angle with the right-hand or previous page when the turning page makes a 60° angle with the left-hand or following page.

f. The parallelogram is the only quadrilateral that can be used. A formal way to show this is to let the four sides (bottom, left, top, and right) be denoted *b, l, t,* and *r.* Then from Parts *b* and *c*, $b + 1 - t - r$ and $b + r = t + l$. This implies by subtraction that $l - r = r - l$. If a number and its additive inverse are equal, that number must be 0, and so the difference between l and r is 0, or $l = r$. If $l = r$, then $t = b$, and this is true only in a parallelogram. Informally, the argument can be made that the bottom, which is fixed, must add to the left and to the right to get the same number as when the top is added to the right and left respectively. This leads to the same conclusion.

Teaching Notes continued

**Notes continued
from page T382**

e. Linkages will vary. Possibilities include the following:

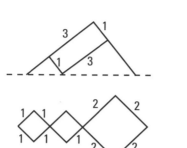 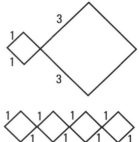

**Notes continued
from page T385**

1. c. The following measures are calculated values, rounded to nearest degree or tenth of a centimeter. Student measurements should be relatively close to these values. You may want to stress that data collection needs to be done with care to ensure meaningful output.

Length of AC (cm)	m∠ A	m∠ B	m∠ C	Distance From B to AD (cm)
26	0°	180°	0°	0
24	29°	133°	18°	4.8
22	42°	114°	25°	6.7
20	52°	98°	30°	7.9
18	62°	84°	34°	8.8
16	72°	72°	36°	9.5
14	82°	60°	38°	9.9
12	93°	49°	39°	10.0
10	106°	37°	37°	9.6
8	125°	24°	31°	8.2
6	180°	0°	0°	0

Page T385 Teaching Notes are continued on the next page.

Unit 6

Teaching Notes *continued*

Notes continued from page T385

1. d. Groups should collect, organize, and then analyze the data as suggested in the student text. It may be useful for comparing among the groups if students sketch their scatterplots. Note that the windows on these graphs are not all the same. The calculated ZoomStat feature produced these windows.

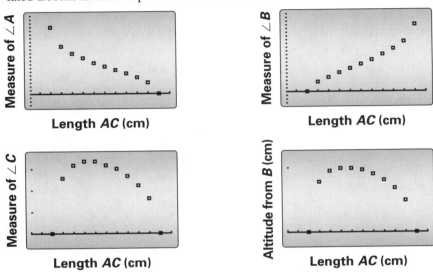

As length *AC* increases, the measure of ∠*A* is always decreasing and the measure of ∠*B* is always increasing. Neither of these measures changes at a constant rate. The measure of ∠*C* and the length of the altitude both increase and then decrease as the length of *AC* increases.

e. For some students, you may need to ask explicitly that they consider the rate of change found in the angle measures. All the variables change rapidly for large and small values of *AC* while in the mid-range the changes are more regular (less pronounced). The measure of ∠*A* decreases. The measure of ∠*B* increases. The measure of ∠*C* increases and then decreases. The length of the altitude increases and then decreases.

f. They appear to be reflections of each other or close to it.

g. If you use different scales, the scatterplots are very similar. (See Part d.) If you use the same scale for the *y*-axis, the scatterplot of the altitudes will be smaller but similar in shape to the measure of ∠*C* scatterplot.

Unit 6

Teaching Notes *continued*

**Notes continued
from page T391**

3. a. The *x*-coordinate of point *B* is always half the *x*-coordinate of point *C*.

b. The *y*-coordinate of point *B* is always half the *y*-coordinate of point *D*. This is true since point *D* moves in a vertical line as point *C* moves toward point *A*, and △*ABD* is an isosceles triangle. Thus the altitude from point *B* to side *AD* divides △ *ABD* into two congruent right triangles.

c. A table of values rounded to the nearest tenth and matching scatterplot are shown below.

x-coordinate of *C*	*y*-coordinate of *B*
2	10.0
4	9.8
6	9.5
8	9.2
10	8.7
12	8.0
14	7.1
16	6.0
18	4.4

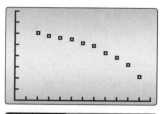

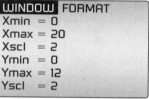

These data do not appear to fit a linear, exponential, or power model.

d.

x-coordinate of *B*	*y*-coordinate of *B*
1	10.0
2	9.8
3	9.5
4	9.2
5	8.7
6	8.0
7	7.1
8	6.0
9	4.4

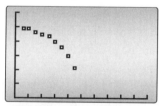

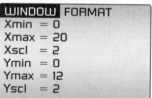

Again, none of the listed models seem to fit this data, but the graph looks like a quarter circle, with radius about 10.

NOTE: You may wish to focus students on the similarities in responses for Parts c and d. Ask students to compare the *x* and *y* values. How are the two graphs related? The graph in Part d is a horizontal size transformation or scale change of 0.5 of the graph in Part c.

Teaching Notes continued

2. a. Students may want to build a model or draw a diagram. If the initial prop position was greater than or equal to 40 cm from the hinged side, the angle decreases as the prop is moved away from the hinge; otherwise it increases. The change in size depends on the spacing of the notches. However, if the notches are evenly spaced, the angle's rate of change is not constant.

▸ **Notes continued from page T393**

---

1. a. There are several possible answers, for example: Drop a rope from top to ground, then measure the rope. Set up a similar triangle situation and use it to estimate the height. Compare the height of the *Bat Column* to the height of another object with a known height.

▸ **Notes continued from page T400**

 b–e. Responses will vary depending on the methods discussed in Part a and the groups' choices of methods.

2. This activity introduces the use of trigonometric ratios to make indirect measurements. Students should be encouraged to make sketches of all situations so that the correct trigonometric ratio is used. Individuals can work on these and compare results within their groups. Then the group can make corrections as needed and clarify any misunderstandings.

 a. You could measure AC and $\angle C$ and $\angle A$. Students may need help in seeing that $\angle A$ can be measured by "sighting" along a straight rod whose angle to the horizontal can be determined by using a protractor.

---

4. a. Since $\sin 40° = \dfrac{KT}{500 \text{ feet}}$, $KT = 500 \text{ feet} \cdot \sin 40°$ or approximately 321 feet. Thus the kite is approximately $321 + 3$ or 324 feet off the ground.

▸ **Notes continued from page T402**

 b. This time $\sin 56° = \dfrac{KT}{500 \text{ feet}}$, so $KT = 500 \text{ feet} \cdot \sin 56°$ or approximately 414.5 feet. The kite is approximately 417.5 feet off the ground.

 c. On 500 feet of string, with the string end 3 feet above the ground, 503 feet is the maximum that can be achieved. This would require the measure of $\angle KIT$ to be 90°.

 d. As a result of Part b, students will probably try values larger than 56° for the angle. Making a table of $\sin x$ starting at 56° will be very efficient. A good approximation for $\angle KIT$ is 57.5° or 57.6°.

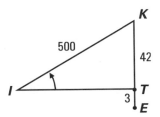

Teaching Notes *continued*

Notes continued from page T408

2. b. ■ As the measure of an angle increases from 0° to 90°, the cosine ratio decreases from 1 to 0.

■ Again, the plot is not linear and cannot be exponential since when $x = 90°$, $\cos x = 0$ and any base taken to the 0 power is 1. A power model must contain $(0, 0)$. A quadratic model seems to be the only likely possibility.

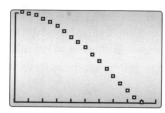
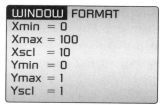

```
WINDOW  FORMAT
Xmin = 0
Xmax = 100
Xscl = 10
Ymin = 0
Ymax = 1
Yscl = 1
```

c. ■ As the measure of an angle increases from 0° to 85°, the tangent ratio increases from 0 to 11.43.

■ This plot is not linear, exponential, or a power relationship.

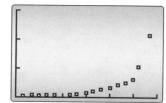

```
WINDOW  FORMAT
Xmin = 0
Xmax = 89
Xscl = 15
Ymin = 0
Ymax = 15
Yscl = 5
```

Notes continued from page T409

5. b. Since the base edge is 230 m, the center of the square base is 115 m from each side and directly below the vertex of the pyramid. The right triangle in the diagram has one leg of 115 m and acute angle of 51.8°. The height is the other leg.

$$\tan 51.8° = \frac{h}{115}$$
$$h = 115 \cdot \tan 51.8° \approx 146 \text{ m}$$

c. The shortest distance is straight up the center of a wall. That distance is the hypotenuse of the triangle in Part b.

$$d^2 = 115^2 + 146^2$$
$$d^2 = 34541$$
$$d \approx 186 \text{ m}$$

d. The grade is the tangent of the angle of inclination. In this case, the grade is $\tan 51.8°$, which is approximately 1.27 or 127%. This is quite steep.

e. Each face is an isosceles triangle with a base of 230 meters and the altitude approximately 186 meters. Since the altitude bisects the base, the length of the other two sides of the faces can be found by solving for d:

$$d^2 = 115^2 + 186^2$$
$$d^2 = 47821$$
$$d \approx 219 \text{ m}$$

Each face is a triangle with sides of 230 m, 219 m, and 219 m.

f. The volume is $\frac{1}{3} \cdot (230)^2 \cdot 146$ or approximately 2,574,000 m^3.

Teaching Notes *continued*

Notes continued from page T410

5. Responses will vary.

Extending

1. a. $\sin A = \dfrac{h}{c}$; $\sin C = \dfrac{h}{a}$

   b. $h = c \sin A$ and $h = a \sin C$, therefore $c \sin A = a \sin C$ or $\dfrac{\sin A}{a} = \dfrac{\sin C}{c}$.

   c. $\dfrac{\sin A}{a} = \dfrac{\sin B}{b}$

   d. The three ratios are equal: $\dfrac{\sin A}{a} = \dfrac{\sin B}{b} = \dfrac{\sin C}{c}$.

Think About This Situation

Notes continued from page T412

See Teaching Master 141.

These questions will help you assess the informal knowledge that students bring to this lesson. Student conjectures for Parts a and b should be left open so that students confirm or reject their conjectures while completing Investigation 1. You might want to ask students to look for additional pulley situations over the next week.

ⓐ As the crankshaft speed increases, the speed of the fan and alternator pulleys also increase. The fan will turn faster than the crankshaft because it is smaller. The speed of the alternator pulley would be fastest because its diameter is smallest.

ⓑ ■ A point on the edge of the crankshaft pulley would roll 850 times its circumference, which is $850 \cdot 10\pi$ or approximately 26,704 centimeters. The fan pulley point would travel the same distance.

   ■ Yes, the alternator pulley would roll the same distance because it is attached to the fan pulley by a belt.

ⓒ Examples may include a clothesline on pulleys; a watch mechanism; a cassette player; sets for a drama production; conveyors; and any belt-driven appliance such as a washer, dryer, snowblower, or lawn mower.

Unit 6

Teaching Notes *continued*

Notes continued from page T418

ⓑ Angular velocity may be measured in revolutions or degrees per unit of time. Linear velocity is measured in linear units (such as centimeters or feet) per unit of time because it is a distance per unit of time.

Revolutions per unit of time commonly is used in cars and other manufactured goods. It is easy to understand and interpret results in the smaller numbers. The degree is easily understood but leads to large numbers.

ⓒ $\dfrac{C_{driver}}{C_{follower}} = \dfrac{2\pi r_d}{2\pi r_f} = \dfrac{r_d}{r_f}$ = transmission factor; C represents circumference and r represents radius.

Notes continued from page T430

2. a. Draw line *CD* tangent to the circles as shown below. Also draw *CE* parallel to segment *AB*.

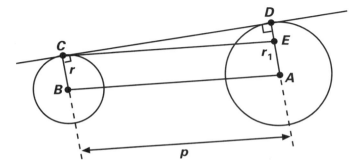

Segments *AD* and *BC* are parallel because they are both perpendicular to line *CD*. Thus *ABCE* is a parallelogram. That means $CE = p$ and $DE = r_1 - r_2$. Therefore, $\cos\angle DEC = \dfrac{r_1 - r_2}{p}$ and $m\angle DEC = \cos^{-1}\dfrac{r_1 - r_2}{p}$. Also, $m\angle DEC = m\angle DAB$.

NOTE: Students will need to deduce $m\angle DEC = m\angle DAB$ using their knowledge that opposite angles of a parallelogram are congruent. Properties of parallel lines are studied in Course 3.

The portion of circle *A* which the belt touches is the arc clockwise from point *D* to point *D'*, where *D'* is the reflection of point *D* across line *AB*. Double $m\angle DAB$ and subtract the result from 360° to determine the proportion of circle *A* that the belt touches, so our general expression follows:

$$required\ angle = 360° - 2\cos^{-1}\left(\dfrac{r_1 - r_2}{p}\right)$$

Use this angle to calculate the length of belt in contact with circle *A*. (The analogous portion for circle *B* can be found by observing that $m\angle ABC = 180° - m\angle DAB$. So $360° - 2m\angle ABC = 360° - 2(180° - m\angle DAB) = 2m\angle DAB$.)

Page T430 Teaching Notes are continued on the next page.

Teaching Notes *continued*

▶ **Notes continued from page T430**

2. **b.** $AE + EB = p$ or $EB = p - AE$

$\triangle ADE$ is similar to $\triangle BCE$.

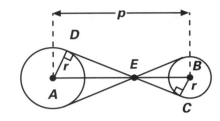

$\dfrac{r_2}{r_1} = \dfrac{EB}{AE} = \dfrac{p - AE}{AE} = \dfrac{p}{AE} = -1$, thus

$\dfrac{r_2}{r_1} = \dfrac{P}{AE} - 1$ and

$\dfrac{P}{AE} = \dfrac{r_2}{r_1} + 1$ or

$\dfrac{P}{AE} = \dfrac{r_2 + r_1}{r_1}$

$p = \left(\dfrac{r_2 + r_1}{r_1}\right) AE$

$AE = \dfrac{pr_1}{r_2 + r_1}$

$\cos \angle DAE = \dfrac{r_1}{\frac{pr_1}{r_2 + r_1}} = \dfrac{r_2 + r_1}{p}$

$m\angle DAE = \cos^{-1}\left(\dfrac{r_2 + r_1}{p}\right)$

As in Part a, use double the measure of $\angle DAE$ and subtract from 360°. Pulleys A and B have the same proportions touched by the belt.

▶ **Notes continued from page T431**

4. **c.** Think about two circles with centers A and B and the line containing their centers. Draw one tangent to the two circles that crosses line AB, as was done in Extending Task 2 Part b (page 430). Since it is a tangent, it is perpendicular to the radii to the points of tangency in each circle. Reflect the tangent and the radii through line AB. The resulting line is tangent to both circles. Furthermore, since the original tangent met line AB in a point, the image line does also and it is the same point. Therefore, the line AB contains the points of intersection of two tangents to two circles. (The same argument holds for two tangents that meet beyond the smaller circle.)

5. **a.** Students should construct a model similar to the Reuleaux Triangle shown here.
   b. The shape touches both lines as it rolls along.
   c. The Wankel engine is based on the shape shown here.
   d. The *NCTM 1979 Yearbook*, Chapter 18 Applications of Curves of Constant Width is a good resource for students. A circle and a five-sided shape similar to the Reuleaux Triangle are two other curves of constant width.

Page T431 Teaching Notes are continued on the next page.

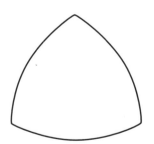

Reuleaux triangle

Unit 6

Teaching Notes continued

Notes continued
from page T431

EXPLORE small-group investigation

INVESTIGATION 3 Modeling Circular Motion

During this investigation, students will be working with physical models from which the graphs of sine and cosine will emerge as aspects of circular motion. They will investigate the periodic nature of the graphs and extend informally the domains of $y = A \sin x$ and $y = A \cos x$ to negative numbers and larger positive numbers. While creating and examining the graphs, the students will have the opportunity to develop a sense about the general shape of these curves and begin to explore the ideas of maximum and minimum values, amplitude, period, and cycle. Students should make the connection between the triangle ratios of sine and cosine and circular motion.

A good way to launch the investigation is to let students know that they will be extending their work with circles and trigonometric ratios to see how they might be related. A quick oral review of the sine and cosine triangle ratios and the parts of a right triangle will be helpful as they work through this investigation. You might also let them know that they will be looking at equations that have very different graphs and properties than they have seen before. The context of a Ferris wheel is used to help students make their first sketches of sine and cosine.

Students will need materials to cut out circular disks with a 5-cm radius as they begin Activity 1. When most students have created their models and have completed Activity 3, it would be helpful if you bring the class together for a mini-Checkpoint. Ask students to share their tables and graphs. Check to be sure that students understand the connections between their models, the values in their tables, and the points on their graphs. Students also should be able to read their graphs; that is, they should be able to use their graphs to estimate the y values (distances) for $x = 370°$ back through $x = 10°$.

Activities 3 and 4 are designed to help students connect their graphs in Activities 2 and 3 with the equations for the graphs $y = 5 \sin x$ and $y = 5 \cos x$. As you circulate among groups, you can check to be sure that students have made this crucial connection.

The final activity for this investigation helps students become familiar with trigonometric functions using radian measure.

Teaching Notes continued

Notes continued from page T441

d $y = -4 \cos x$ and $y = 4 \cos x$ are both wave-like, but $y = -4 \cos x$ is the reflection image of $y = 4 \cos x$ across the x-axis. Thus while they have the same maximum and minimum values (4 and −4), these occur at different values of x. The maximum of $y = 4 \cos x$ occurs at $x = 0°$, and the minimum of $y = 4 \cos x$ occurs at $180°$; the maximum of $y = -4 \cos x$ occurs at $x = 180°$, and the minimum occurs at $x = 0°$. These graphs reverse the intervals over which they are increasing and decreasing and where they are positive and negative as well. They both cross the x-axis at the same points.

e $y = \sin 2x$ and $y = \sin x$ have waves that are the same shape, they have the same maximum and minimum values, and they cross the y-axis at the same point; but they complete one cycle in a different number of degrees. $y = \sin 2x$ completes 2 cycles in $360°$ or 1 cycle in $180°$.

CONSTRUCTING A MATH TOOLKIT: Ask students to record in their Math Toolkits a sketch of the graph of $y = A \sin x$ for $-360° \leq x \leq 360°$ or $-2\pi \leq x \leq 2\pi$ along with a sketch of the triangle relationship modeled by the Ferris wheel. Students should label the two sketches and summarize the features of the graph for various amplitudes. Ask them to do the same with the graph of $y = A \cos x$ over the same interval.

You also might ask students to compare and contrast the graphs of these trigonometric functions with the graphs of other families such as linear and exponential functions.

Notes continued from page T443

3. a. Shape of Roller Coaster Section

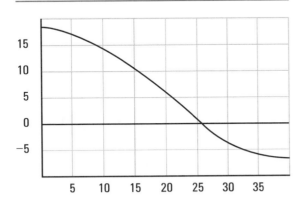

b. 4.5 degrees/meter $\cdot \dfrac{\pi \text{ radians}}{180 \text{ degrees}} = \dfrac{\pi}{40}$ radians/meter. The new equation is

$y = 12 \cos \left(\dfrac{\pi x}{40}\right) + 6$.

Teaching Notes continued

Notes continued from page T447

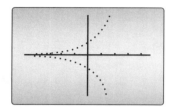

3. **c.** $0 < a < 1$:

- $y = ax$ would still be linear but with smaller (still positive) slope.
- $y = a^x$ would be a decreasing function asymptotic to the *x*-axis for $x > 0$.
- $y = ax^2$ would increase less rapidly as *x* increased.
- $y = ax^3$ would increase less rapidly and look "wider" ("flatter") as it crossed the *x*-axis.
- $y = \frac{a}{x}$ would look much the same but would decrease more quickly, making the curves go closer to the origin before turning.
- $y = \frac{a}{x^2}$ also goes closer to the origin before turning.
- $y = a \sin x$ would have a smaller amplitude.
- $y = a \cos x$ also would have a smaller amplitude.

$a < 0$: All of the functions would be reflected across the *x*-axis with the exception of $y = a^x$. Students should indicate that if $a < -1$, the graphs (except $y - a^x$) would resemble the graphs in Part a reflected across the *x*-axis. If $-1 < a < 0$, the graphs from Part c would be reflected across the *x*-axis. If $y = a^x$ were changed to $y = -a^x$, that is, $y = -(a^x)$, then it too would be reflected across the *x*-axis. However, if $a < 0$, the new function would be $y = (-b)^x$ (where *b* is the absolute value of *a*), which is defined only when *x* is an integer.

A graph for $a < -1$ is shown on the left:

4. If the daylight hours data had been gathered in Fairbanks, Alaska, the amplitude of the sinusoidal model would be much greater since in December and January, Fairbanks has almost no daylight, and in June and July, it has almost 24 hours of daylight.

At the equator, on the other hand, the amount of daylight does not change. There are 12 hours of daylight and 12 hours of darkness all year round, so the graph would be a straight line.

Extending

1. **a.** $x = 6 \cos t$ and $y = 6 \sin t$. Points on $y = x$ have equal *x* and *y* coordinates, since we have $\cos t = \sin t$, which is true only for $t = 45°$ or $t = 225°$ $\left(t = \frac{\pi}{4} \text{ or } t = \frac{5\pi}{4} \right)$. In quadrant I, $x = 6 \cos 45° \approx 4.24$ and $y = 6 \sin 45° \approx 4.24$. In quadrant III, $x = 6 \cos 225° \approx -4.24$ and $y = 6 \sin 225° \approx -4.24$.

Similarly, points on $y = -x$ have *x* and *y* coordinates that are opposites of each other, so $\cos t = -\sin t$. This is true for $t = 135°$ or $t = 315°$ $\left(t = \frac{3\pi}{4} \text{ or } t = \frac{7\pi}{4} \right)$. Thus the other points are $(-4.24, 4.24)$ and $4.24, -4.24)$.

Page T447 Teaching Notes are continued on the next page.

Teaching Notes *continued*

Notes continued from page T447

1. **a.** An alternative method:

    $x^2 + y^2 = 36$ and points on $y = x$ have equal coordinates, so $x^2 + x^2 = 36$. Solving for x and y, we have $x \approx 4.24$ and $y \approx 4.24$ or $x = -4.24$ and $y = -4.24$.

    b. Suppose you knew A (4.24, 4.24) is one of the points. Then reflection in the x-axis gives $A'(4.24, -4.24)$, reflection in the y-axis gives $A''(-4.24, 4.24)$, and a half turn about the origin gives $A'''(-4.24, -4.24)$.

    c. $x = 6 \cos t$ and $y = 6 \sin t$, so $6 \sin t = \frac{\sqrt{3}}{3} (6 \cos t)$. The two functions intersect at 30° and 210° (which can be found by using graph or table or by using technology to solve the equation), so $x = 6 \cos 30° \approx 5.2$ when $y = 6 \sin 30° = 3$, and $x = 6 \cos 210° \approx -5.2$ when $y = 6 \sin 210° \approx -3$.

    As in Part a, these values can be found algebraically. The equation should be

    $$x^2 + \left(\frac{\sqrt{3}}{3}x\right)^2 = 36$$

    The points symmetrically placed are $(3\sqrt{3}, -3)$ and $(-3\sqrt{3}, 3)$.

    The slope is $\frac{3 - (-3)}{-3\sqrt{3} - 3\sqrt{3}}$ or $\frac{-\sqrt{3}}{3}$.

    The equation of the line is $y = \frac{-\sqrt{3}}{3}x$.

    d. $\tan A = \frac{\sqrt{3}}{3}$, therefore, $A = \tan^{-1}\left(\frac{\sqrt{3}}{3}\right) = 30°$.

2. **a.** One possible answer is that $\sin (x + 180°)$ is the reflection of $\sin x$ in the x-axis. However, for this problem, it is more appropriately interpreted as a shift of the graph of $\sin x$, 180° to be left.

    b. Student work.

    c. The graph of $y = \sin (x + b)$ is the graph of $y = \sin x$, shifted so that the value at $x = 0$ is $\sin b$ rather than $\sin 0$. This means it is translated $|b|$ units to the right if b is negative and to the left if b is positive.

Unit 6

Notes continued from page T452

4. **c.** $\tan 8° = \frac{r}{100}$ in the right triangle formed by the altitude of the cone with the radius of the base r. Therefore, $r = 100 \tan 8°$, or, in the case of the 53° cone, $r = 100 \tan 26.5°$.

5. **a.** ■ $y = 5 \cos x$
   ■ $y = \cos (\pi x)$
   ■ $y = 5 \cos (\pi x)$

   b. The pendulum bob follows a path that begins 5 inches from the vertical, so we want the initial value of the function to be 5. Since cos 0° is 1, 5 cos 0° is 5. The two-second period requires the pendulum to stop and reverse direction every second, so we want the value of cos (Bx) to be zero whenever x is a positive integer. This is accomplished when $B = \pi$, or 180°. So the desired model for the motion of the pendulum is $y = 5 \cos (\pi x)$.

   c. The graph follows:

   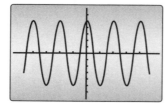
   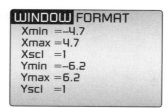

   The coordinates of the x-intercepts on the interval shown are (−4.5, 0), (−3.5, 0), (−2.5, 0), (−1.5, 0), (−0.5, 0), (0.5, 0), (1.5, 0), (2.5, 0), (3.5, 0), and (4.5, 0).
   The maximum value of the function is 5, and the coordinates for the maximum points are (−4, 5), (−2, 5), (0, 5), (2, 5), and (4, 5).
   The minimum value of the function is −5, and the coordinates of the minimum points are (−3, −5), (−1, −5), (1, −5), and (3, −5).

Teaching Notes *continued*

Your notes here:

Unit 7

Patterns in Chance

UNIT OVERVIEW This unit introduces students to probability distributions and to the Multiplication Rule for independent events: $P(A \text{ and } B) = P(A) \cdot P(B)$. The distribution studied is the geometric, or waiting-time distribution. Students learn how to construct this distribution both theoretically and by simulation; then they discover how to find the average waiting time. The specific problem that motivates the unit and is studied throughout is that of rolling two dice until doubles appears. This situation occurs, for example, in the game of Monopoly when a player is sent to "jail."

Specific topics explored in this unit include:

- Independent trials

  Is a person more likely to roll doubles after trying unsuccessfully many times than a person who is trying to roll doubles for the first time?

- Multiplication Rule for independent events

  What is the probability it will take a person exactly two rolls to get doubles for the first time?

- Mathematical expectation

  If 36 people each roll a pair of dice, how many would we expect to roll doubles?

- Probability distribution

  If many people try to roll doubles, what percentage do we expect to roll doubles on their nth try?

- Fair price and expected value

  On the average, how many rolls does it take before getting doubles?

- Rare events

  If it takes someone 10 rolls to get doubles for the first time, has the person been unusually unlucky?

In addition, probability distribution and infinite series are introduced in Extending tasks.

Unit 7 Objectives

- To construct a probability distribution by simulation and use it to understand and analyze the probabilistic situation
- To explore in depth the geometric, or waiting-time distribution
- To understand some fundamental ideas of probability: independent events, the Multiplication Rule, the expected value of a probability distribution, and rare events

Patterns in Chance

455

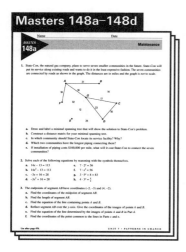
Histograms Throughout the Unit

Throughout this unit, it is helpful if you emphasize to students that they will understand a probability problem if they can construct a histogram of its probability distribution. That histogram can be constructed either theoretically or by simulation. As usual, students should take care with the labels on all histograms, so they know what the distribution tells them.

Misconceptions about Probability

People tend to have incorrect intuitions when it comes to many probabilistic events. Many students, and adults as well, believe that a person who has rolled a pair of dice several times without getting doubles is more likely to roll doubles on the next roll. (The person is "due" to get doubles.) Such misconceptions are confronted in this unit. One of the most important lessons we can teach students about probability is that they should be suspicious of their first impulse when analyzing random events.

The following references are good introductions to the research that documents students' misconceptions about probability.

Garfield, Joan, and Andrew Ahlgren. "Difficulties in Learning Basic Concepts in Probability and Statistics: Implications for Research." *Journal for Research in Mathematics Education*, 19 (1988): 44–63.

Hope, J. A., and I. W. Kelly. "Common Difficulties with Probabilistic Reasoning." *The Mathematics Teacher*, 76 (1983): 565–570.

Shaughnessy, J. Michael. "Misconceptions of Probability: From Systematic Errors to Systematic Experiments and Decisions." In *Teaching Statistics and Probability*, 1981 NCTM Yearbook. Reston, Virginia: National Council of Teachers of Mathematics, 1981.

"Probability and Statistics." *The Mathematics Teacher,* 86 (1993): 244–248.

"Research in Probability and Statistics: Reflections and Direction." In *Handbook of Research on Mathematics Teaching and Learning*, edited by Douglas Grouws. New York: Macmillan, 1992.

The Importance of Simulation

Simulation is the modeling of a probabilistic situation using random devices such as coins, spinners, random digit tables, and calculators or computers. Simulation is extremely helpful throughout any unit on probability. Setting up a simulation helps students clarify their assumptions about such things as whether trials are independent. Simulation also helps develop students' intuitions about probabilistic events. And, perhaps most importantly, students who have been introduced to simulation have real mathematical power for working with probabilistic situations. They know that they can get the answer to any probability problem that arises. Thus, students studying this unit should have completed the "Simulations Models" unit from Course 1. You may want to use Teaching Master 149, "Steps in a Simulation," at the beginning of Investigation 1 in Lesson 1 to facilitate a review of setting up simulations.

See Teaching Masters 148a–148d for Maintenance tasks that students can work on after Lesson 1.

Unit 7 Planning Guide

Lesson Objectives	MORE Assignments	Suggested Pacing	Materials
Lesson 1 *Waiting Times* • To use simulation to construct frequency distributions for waiting-time situations when trials are independent, and to recognize the shape as skewed right • To identify when trials are independent • To recognize rare events • To review finding the mean of a frequency distribution • To review finding the probabilities of events associated with rolling a pair of dice	**after page 459** Students can begin Modeling Task 4; Organizing Task 1 or 4; or Extending Task 2 or 3 from p. 466. **after page 461** Students can begin Modeling Task 1; Reflecting Task 1, 2, or 3; or Extending Task 1 from p. 466. **page 466** **Modeling:** 3, and 1 or 4* **Organizing:** 1 and 4 **Reflecting:** Choose one* **Extending:** Choose one*	5 days	• Pair of dice (for each student or pair of students if necessary) • Bag of markers or candy of two colors • Deck of cards • Teaching Resources 149–156 • Assessment Resources 232–237 • Optional: Monopoly game
Lesson 2 *The Multiplication Rule* • To use an area model to find the probability that two independent events both occur • To use the Multiplication Rule to find the probability that two independent events both occur • To decide if two events are independent	**page 477** **Modeling:** 2 and 3 **Organizing:** 1 and 2 **Reflecting:** 2 or 3* **Extending:** 2 and choice of one*	4 days	• Teaching Resources 148a–148d, 157–159 • Assessment Resources 238–243 • Optional: Dice, Monopoly game, game of Life
Lesson 3 *Probability Distributions* • To construct the theoretical frequency distribution for a waiting-time situation • To construct the probability distribution for a waiting-time situation • To understand how the word *expect* is used in probability	**page 489** **Modeling:** 1, 3, and choice of one* **Organizing:** 1 and 4 **Reflecting:** Choose two* **Extending:** 2 and 4 **after page 501** Students can begin Modeling Task 3; or Extending Task 2 or 3 from p. 503 **page 503** **Modeling:** 1 and 3 **Organizing:** 1, 2, and 3 **Reflecting:** 2 **Extending:** 1 and choice of one*	6 days	• Pair of dice for each student, or pair of students if necessary • Bag of beads or candy, two colors • Teaching Resources 160–168 • Assessment Resources 244–251 • Optional: Dice with 4, 8, 12, 20 sides; box of cereal with one of several prizes; Backgammon game, Monopoly game; Parcheesi game; blank dice with stickers for new numbers
Lesson 4 *Expected Value of a Probability Distribution* • To compute the fair price (expected value) of insurance and games of chance • To compute the expected value of a probability distribution • To estimate the expected value of a waiting-time distribution from the probability distribution table • To discover the simple formula for the expected value of a waiting-time distribution • To understand that some infinite series have a finite sum	**after page 513** Students can begin Modeling Task 1, Organizing Task 4, or Reflecting Task 3 or 4 from p. 516. **page 516** **Modeling:** 1, 3, and 4 **Organizing:** 3, and 2 or 4* **Reflecting:** Choose two* **Extending:** 3 **page 524** **Modeling:** 1 and 2 **Organizing:** 1, 2, and 4 **Reflecting:** Choose two* **Extending:** 2	7 days	• Teaching Resources 169–174 • Assessment Resources 252–257 • Optional: Picture of a roulette wheel, game of Life
Lesson 5 *Looking Back* • To review the major objectives of the Unit		3 days (includes testing)	• Teaching Resource 175 • Assessment Resources 258–277

When choice is indicated, it is important to leave the choice to the student.
Note: It is best if Organizing tasks are discussed as a whole class after they have been assigned as homework.

Waiting Times

Monopoly® is a board game that can be played by several players. Movement around the board is determined by rolling a pair of dice. Winning is based on a combination of chance and a sense for making smart real estate deals. While playing Monopoly, Anita draws the card shown below. She must go directly to the "jail" space on the board.

Anita may get out of jail by rolling doubles with a pair of dice on one of her next three turns. Doubles means that both dice show the same number on the top. If she does not roll doubles on any of the three turns, Anita must pay a $50 fine to get out of jail. Anita takes her first turn and doesn't roll doubles. On her second turn, she doesn't roll doubles again. On her third and final try, Anita doesn't roll doubles yet again. She grudgingly pays the $50 to get out of jail. Anita is feeling very unlucky.

Lesson 1 *Waiting Times*

LESSON OVERVIEW One of the most common probabilistic situations is waiting for a specific event to occur: waiting for red to come up in roulette, waiting for doubles to appear in backgammon or Monopoly, waiting for a day of rain on days when the weather forecaster says there is a 20 percent chance of rain, *etc*. In this lesson, students will be introduced to the idea of a *waiting-time distribution* (also called the *geometric distribution*). They will construct frequency distributions and histograms of waiting-time distributions and discover that all have the same basic shape.

In a standard waiting-time situation, the probability of a success on each trial is assumed to be the same, no matter what happened on previous trials. Students will explore situations in which this assumption is true (the trials are independent) and in which it is not.

Lesson Objectives

- To use simulation to construct frequency distributions for waiting-time situations when trials are independent, and to recognize the shape as skewed to the right
- To identify when trials are independent
- To recognize rare events
- To review finding the mean of a frequency distribution
- To review finding the probabilities of events associated with rolling a pair of dice

LAUNCH full-class discussion

You might want to begin this lesson by bringing in a Monopoly game and explaining the rules about how to get out of jail by rolling doubles. Present the situation on page 456 and let your students discuss it, using the "Think About This Situation" questions to facilitate the discussion. This will give you an opportunity to assess how much your students know about probability.

You may want to record, in a corner of a blackboard that you can leave untouched, for example, student guesses about what is likely and unlikely: "We think it is likely that Anita will get doubles in _____ or less. We think it is very unlikely she will have to wait more than _____."

Unit 7

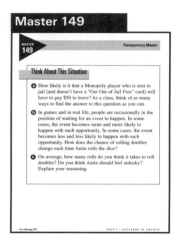

Master 149

Master 150

Master 151

LAUNCH *continued*

Think About This Situation

See Teaching Master 149.

ⓐ You might make a list of the ways students suggest to get the answer to this question. Some students surely will suggest trying the experiment of rolling dice. You also might let the class pursue one of these ideas if they want. At this stage, students aren't expected to know how to do this problem theoretically, and many may not know that the probability of rolling doubles on one roll of a pair of dice is $\frac{1}{6}$.

ⓑ Although your students may know that Anita's chance of rolling doubles remains the same each time she rolls the dice (because that is what they have been told), many of them won't really believe it. If you are interested in the psychology of learning probability and want to test this, take a coin and try the following experiment with your students. If you don't discuss the correct answer at this time, you can come back to this scenario while discussing the final unit checkpoint. Students should be able to answer the questions correctly at that time.

> Ask, "If I flip a coin ten times, how many heads do I expect to get, on the average?" (Most students will answer five. Be sure that they understand that, on the average, half of the flips of a fair coin will be heads.)

> Flip the coin and announce that you got a head. Flip it again and announce that you got another head. This shouldn't seem strange to the class. Now ask them, "When I have finished the ten flips, how many heads do you expect me to have?"

> Almost every student will answer five. This answer indicates that the students expect the coin to "balance out" the first two flips of heads. In other words, they believe that tails are due and now have a probability greater than $\frac{1}{2}$. There are eight flips left and they expect only three of them to be heads.

> The correct answer is six. You have eight flips left and, with a fair coin, you expect four of them to be heads and four to be tails. With the first two flips of heads, that means you expect six heads for the ten flips.

ⓒ Again, students may suggest trying an experiment. They won't know that the theoretical answer is 6, but you don't need to tell them yet. If the class pursued one of the suggestions in Part a, students might want to look back and see how those results might help them decide whether or not Anita should feel unlucky.

EXPLORE small-group investigation

INVESTIGATION ▶1 Waiting for Doubles

See Teaching Master 150.

By the end of this investigation, students will have constructed their first probability distribution, used it to give some estimates of probabilities, and calculated some theoretical answers for related questions. As you circulate among the groups, encourage them to describe what they are doing and to talk about the differences between finding experimental (Activity 2) and theoretical (Activity 3) probabilities. You also might remind them of the initial question, "On average, how many rolls does it take to get doubles?"

> **See additional Teaching Notes on page T533C.**

a How likely is it that a Monopoly player who is sent to jail (and doesn't have a "Get Out of Jail Free" card) will have to pay $50 to leave? As a class, think of as many ways to find the answer to this question as you can.

b In games and in real life, people are occasionally in the position of waiting for an *event* to happen. In some cases, the event becomes more and more likely to happen with each opportunity. In some cases, the event becomes less and less likely to happen with each opportunity. Does the chance of rolling doubles change each time Anita rolls the dice?

c On average, how many rolls do you think it takes to roll doubles? Do you think Anita should feel unlucky? Explain your reasoning.

INVESTIGATION 1 Waiting for Doubles

In this investigation, you will explore several aspects of Anita's situation. For this investigation, we will change the rules of Monopoly so that a player must stay in jail until he or she rolls doubles. A player cannot pay $50 to get out of jail in this version of the game, and there is no "Get Out of Jail Free" card.

1. Now suppose you are playing Monopoly under this new rule and have just been sent to jail. Take your first turn and roll a pair of dice. Did you roll doubles and get out of jail? If so, stop. If not, roll again. Did you roll doubles and get out of jail on your second turn? If so, stop. If not, roll again. Did you roll doubles and get out of jail on your third turn? If so, stop. If not, keep rolling until you get doubles.

   a. Copy the frequency table below and put a tally mark in the frequency column next to the event that happened to you. Add rows as needed.

Rolling Doubles

Event	Number of Rolls	Frequency
Rolled doubles on first try	1	
Rolled doubles on second try	2	
Rolled doubles on third try	3	
Rolled doubles on fourth try	4	
⋮	⋮	
Total		100

b. With other members of your class, perform this experiment a total of 100 times. Record the results in your frequency table.

c. Do the events in the frequency table appear to be **equally likely**? That is, does each of the events have the same chance of happening?

d. Use your frequency table to estimate the probability that Anita will have to pay $50, or use a "Get Out of Jail Free" card, to get out of jail when playing a standard version of Monopoly. Compare this estimate with your original estimate in Part a of the "Think About This Situation" on page 457.

e. Make a histogram of the data in your frequency table. Describe the shape of this histogram.

f. Explain why the frequencies in your table are decreasing even though the probability of rolling doubles on each attempt does not change.

2. Later in this unit, you will analyze Anita's situation theoretically. That is, you will use mathematical principles to find the probability she has to pay $50. As a first step, in this activity you will explore how to find the probability of various events when two dice are rolled.

a. Suppose a red die and a green die are rolled at the same time. Make a copy of the matrix-like chart below.

Rolling Two Dice

		Number on Green Die				
	1	2	3	4	5	6
1	1, 1					
2						
3		3, 2				
4					4, 5	
5						
6						

(Number on Red Die — row labels)

- What does the entry "3, 2" mean?
- Complete the chart, showing all possible outcomes when the two dice are rolled.
- How many outcomes are possible?
- Are these outcomes equally likely? Why or why not?

1. **c.** The events in the table are not equally likely. The probability of rolling doubles for the first time on that roll decreases with each roll. This is reflected in the table through the decreasing frequencies.

   d. Probabilities will vary based on the results of the experiment. Using the sample frequency table from Part b, students will find that the estimated probability that Anita will get out of jail in the first three rolls is $\frac{17 + 14 + 12}{100}$ or 0.43. Thus the estimated probability she will have to pay \$50 is $1 - 0.43$ or 0.57. (The theoretical probability is 0.58, as students will learn later.) Comparisons will depend on the students' original estimate.

   e. Histograms will vary. A sample histogram follows; most histograms won't be this smooth, and they usually will continue on to the right.

   ### Rolling Doubles

   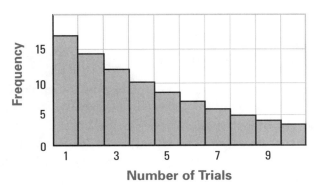

   The histogram is skewed right. The bars decrease in height. Each bar is about $\frac{5}{6}$ of the height of the bar to its left.

   f. There will be fewer people who will roll doubles for the first time on their second roll than who will roll doubles for the first time on their first roll. One way to picture this is to imagine all 100 people taking their first roll simultaneously. Those who get doubles on this roll (about $\frac{1}{6}$ of the 100 people) leave the room. Everyone who remains then tries a second time to get doubles. About $\frac{1}{6}$ will succeed. This isn't $\frac{1}{6}$ of 100, but $\frac{1}{6}$ of a smaller number.

2. **See Teaching Masters 152a–152b.**

   a. ■ The "3, 2" entry means that when the dice are rolled, there is a 3 on the red die and a 2 on the green die.

See additional Teaching Notes on page T533C.

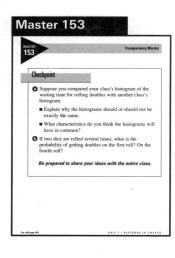

2. **b.** Students should use the table they just constructed to compute these figures.

■ $\frac{6}{36}$

■ $\frac{6}{36}$

■ $\frac{2}{36}$

■ $\frac{8}{36}$

■ $\frac{12}{36}$

It may be helpful if you point out that it is not always the best policy to write fractions in the lowest terms when computing probabilities. For example, it's much easier to compare the probability of rolling a sum of 7 with that of rolling a sum of 11 if both probabilities have a denominator of 36.

c. Yes, the probabilities are the same. The color simply helps organize the table of all possible outcomes.

d. Each has a $\frac{1}{6}$ chance of rolling doubles on her next turn.

SHARE AND SUMMARIZE   full-class discussion

If your students are not sure of the response to Part b of the Checkpoint on page 459, you may wish to have them carry out the following experiment. The workload should be divided among groups of students.

■ One group of students will represent Conchita trying to roll doubles on her first roll of the dice. That group will roll the dice many times, for example, 400 times, each time a "first try," and count the number of doubles. This group now has an approximation of the probability of rolling doubles on the first try.

■ The second group, representing Anita, would roll the dice until they did not get doubles twice in a row. The group would then try to get doubles on the third roll. Counting only the times the group tried a third roll, they should repeat this process 400 times (not doubles, not doubles, try to roll doubles). This group now has an approximation of the probability of rolling doubles on the third try, given that doubles didn't happen on the first or second try.

The two groups probably won't get exactly the same probability. Before the experiment, discuss with the class how close the relative frequencies will have to be so that they believe the theoretical probabilities are the same and how far apart the relative frequencies will have to be so that they believe the theoretical probabilities are different. (With 400 repetitions, there is a 95 percent chance that the probabilities will be within 0.05 of each other.)

One of the difficulties of simulation is the large number of trials needed to convince students that two probabilities are the same. If, for example, one student flips a nickel 100 times and another flips a penny 100 times, there is a very good chance that there will be a difference of 0.10 or more in the proportion of heads with the nickel and with the penny. One of the students could easily get 45 heads out of 100 and the other get 56 out of 100, for a difference of 0.11. Very roughly, if each experiment is repeated n times, there is a 95 percent chance that the two estimates will be no farther apart than $\frac{\sqrt{2}}{\sqrt{n}}$.

See additional Teaching Notes on page T533D.

b. If two dice are rolled, what is the probability of getting each of the following events?

- Doubles
- A sum of 7
- A sum of 11
- A sum of 7 or a sum of 11
- Either a 2 on one or both dice or a sum of 2

c. Is the probability of rolling doubles the same if both dice are the same color? Explain your reasoning.

d. Suppose that in playing the modified Monopoly game, Anita is still in jail after trying twice to roll doubles. Conchita has just been sent to jail. Does Anita or Conchita have a better chance of rolling doubles on her next turn? Compare your answer with that of other groups. Resolve any differences.

Checkpoint

ⓐ Suppose you compared your class's histogram of the waiting time for rolling doubles with another class's histogram.

- Explain why the histograms should or should not be exactly the same.
- What characteristics do you think the histograms will have in common?

ⓑ If two dice are rolled several times, what is the probability of getting doubles on the first roll? On the fourth roll?

Be prepared to share your ideas with the entire class.

▶On Your Own

Change the rules of Monopoly so that a player must flip a coin and get heads in order to get out of jail.

a. Play this version 24 times, either with a coin or by simulating the situation. Put your results in a table like the one in Activity 1 of Investigation 1. Then make a histogram of your results.

b. Is it harder or easier to get out of jail with this new rule instead of by rolling doubles? Explain your reasoning.

c. What is your estimate of the probability that a player will get out of jail in three flips or fewer?

INVESTIGATION 2 Independent Trials

In some situations, the probability of getting a particular event is the same on every opportunity (called a **trial**), no matter what happened on previous trials. In these cases, the trials are said to be **independent**. In other situations, the probability of getting a particular event changes depending on what has happened on previous trials. In these cases, the trials are called **dependent**.

1. In the previous investigation, you explored probabilities associated with rolling two dice. Are the rolls of dice independent or dependent? Explain your reasoning.

2. Think about the question of independent or dependent trials as you examine the following games of chance. To play these games, you will need a bag with one red and one yellow marker or token in it. You will also need some extra red and yellow markers. In each game, the goal is to draw a red marker. When that happens, the game stops and the player's score is the number of draws required. Each player starts his or her turn with one red and one yellow marker in the bag.

   a. First, analyze each of these games. Which game would you choose to play if you get a prize for having the smallest score?

   Game A: Draw until you get a red marker. Replace the marker after each draw. In addition, each time you draw a yellow marker, you must add another yellow marker to the bag before drawing again.

   Game B: Draw until you get a red marker. Replace the marker after each draw. In addition, each time you draw a yellow marker, you must add a red marker to the bag before drawing again.

   Game C: Draw until you get a red marker. Replace the marker after each draw, but don't add any other markers to the bag. (There are always the original two markers in the bag.)

   b. Now, play each game ten times and complete a frequency table like the one below, showing the number of draws required until a red marker appears. Share the work by having different members of your group play and record results for different games.

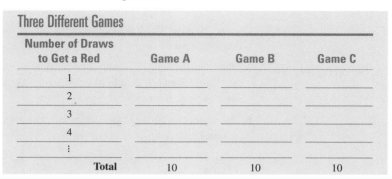

Three Different Games

Number of Draws to Get a Red	Game A	Game B	Game C
1			
2			
3			
4			
⋮			
Total	10	10	10

INVESTIGATION 2 Independent Trials

You may wish to launch this investigation by revisiting Part b of the Checkpoint on page 459. See the experiment suggested on page T459.

1. The rolls of the dice are independent. The probability of rolling doubles is the same on each roll, no matter what has happened before. If students still argue that rolls of dice are not independent, ask them how the dice have changed because of the results of the previous rolls.

2. **See Teaching Master 154.**

   The point of this activity is to show students a simple example of trials that are not independent. The probability of drawing a red marker is not the same for each trial in Games A and B.

   a. The best game to play is Game B, but the students may not understand that yet.

   b. A typical completed table might look like the following one. You may want to suggest a maximum number of tries after which the students should stop, especially for Game A.

Three Different Games

Number of Draws to Get a Red	Game A	Game B	Game C
1	5	5	5
2	2	3	2
3	1	2	2
4			1
5 or more	2		
Total	10	10	10

2. c. Game B

d. Game A

e. Game C

f. Responses should now be Game B.

3. a. The trials are independent. The probability remains $\frac{1}{2}$, no matter what has happened on previous flips.

b. The trials are independent. The probability should be the same for each ticket, no matter what has happened on previous weeks.

c. The trials are not independent. The probability that your name is called on a draw increases with each draw (provided it wasn't drawn already). For example, if there are 30 students in the class, the probability that your name is drawn on the first draw is $\frac{1}{30}$. Since the first slip of paper isn't replaced, the probability that your name is drawn on the second draw is $\frac{1}{29}$. Once your name is drawn, the probability drops to 0.

d. The trials are not independent. The probability increases with each bowl of cereal. Suppose there are 15 bowls of cereal in the box. The probability of getting the prize the first morning is $\frac{1}{15}$. If the prize is still in the box, the probability of getting it the second morning is $\frac{1}{14}$, etc. Once the prize appears, the probability drops to 0.

e. The trials are independent. The probability that a baby will be a girl is the same with each birth, no matter what gender the previous babies have been.

SHARE AND SUMMARIZE   full-class discussion

Checkpoint

See Teaching Master 155.

Responses will vary. Examples are given.

ⓐ The event is catching a fish. A trial is fishing for five minutes. If you have just caught a fish, your chances of catching another in the same spot probably go down since there is one less hungry fish and noise from the first catch may have scared away other fish.

  The event is finding a family member who can curl his or her tongue from the sides. A trial is checking a family member. There is some percentage of the population who can curl their tongues, and that percentage would be the probability the first family member you check could do this. But if you find one family member who can curl his or her tongue, the chances that the next family member can do this increases, as this trait tends to run in families.

ⓑ The event is a particular professional basketball player making a free throw. A trial is a free throw. (Contrary to what most people believe, statisticians don't believe that sports professionals have "streaks" and "slumps" that are longer than would be expected by chance. That is, if the player is an 80% free throw shooter, the probability is 80% on each free throw, no matter what has happened before in that game.)

APPLY   individual task

▶On Your Own

a. Yes, the probability of getting heads, $\frac{1}{2}$, is the same on each flip of the coin, no matter what has happened before.

b. No. The trials are not independent. On your first trip, the chances are high that you will see a species you have never seen before. After many trips to the park, it gets harder to spot a new species.

CONSTRUCTING A MATH TOOLKIT: Students should explain how to determine whether or not two trials are independent.

JOURNAL ENTRY: You might choose Reflecting Task 1, 2, or 4 as a journal entry.

MORE

ASSIGNMENT   *pp. 466–470*

Students now can begin Modeling Task 1; Reflecting Task 1, 2, or 3; or Extending Task 1 from the MORE assignment following Investigation 3.

c. In which game does the probability of drawing a red marker get larger with each trial?

d. In which game does the probability of drawing a red marker get smaller with each trial?

e. In which game are the trials independent?

f. Do you want to change your answer to Part a? Why or why not?

3. In each of the following situations, imagine you are waiting for an event to occur. In each case, decide if the trials are independent. Give reasons for your answers.

a. The event is getting heads. A trial is flipping a coin.

b. The event is winning a weekly lottery. A trial is buying one lottery ticket each week.

c. Ten students from your class will be selected at random. The name of each student is written on a slip of paper and the slips are placed in a box. One slip of paper is drawn at a time and not replaced before the next name is drawn. The event you are waiting for is to hear your name called. A trial is one name being drawn.

d. The event is getting the prize in a box of cereal that has been mixed well. The prize can be anywhere in the box, not just at the bottom or top. A trial is pouring and eating a bowl of cereal from the box. The trials continue each morning until you get the prize.

e. The event is having a daughter. A trial is having a baby.

Checkpoint

Think about situations involving chance that are different from those in this investigation.

ⓐ Give an example of trials that are dependent.

ⓑ Give an example of trials that are independent.

Be prepared to explain your examples to the class.

▶On Your Own

a. The modified version of Monopoly in the "On Your Own" on page 459 required the player to flip a coin and get heads in order to get out of jail. Are the trials independent in that version of Monopoly? Explain.

b. Suppose the event is seeing a species of bird that you have never seen before. A trial is going to the park to watch birds. Are the trials independent? Give a reason for your answer.

INVESTIGATION 3 The Distribution of Waiting Times

According to the company that makes them, "M&M's"® Chocolate Candies are put randomly into bags from a large vat in which all the colors have been mixed. This means we can assume that a bag of these candies is a random sample. It also means that the probability of getting a brown candy is almost exactly the same each time you draw a candy out of any bag.

1. Suppose each of five students took "M&M's"® Chocolate Candy at a time out of a large bag until he or she got a brown one. Marcia's fifth candy was her first brown one. The list below gives the number of draws that each student needed to get a brown candy.

Marcia	5
Jenny	10
David	3
Whitney	1
Simon	3

   a. What was the average (mean) number of candies that had to be taken out of the bag in order to get a brown one?

   b. The answer to Part a isn't a whole number, so it isn't really possible to make that number of draws. Give an example of another situation in which the average is not one of the possible events.

2. You may remember discovering, in Course 1, an easy method for calculating the mean of a frequency table. That method can be summarized by the following formula.

$$\bar{x} = \frac{\sum xf}{n}$$

Here, x is a data value, f is the frequency of that value, and n is the sum of the frequencies. The $\sum$ stands for "sum." When you use this formula, it is often efficient to add a third column, xf, to the frequency table.

   a. Use this formula to find the mean of the frequency table below.

x	f
0	9
1	5
2	6
3	4

   b. Explain how you could use (or did use) the list features of a graphing calculator or computer software to find the mean of this frequency table.

INVESTIGATION 3 ▸ The Distribution of Waiting Times

Before starting this investigation, students must understand how bags of "M&M's"® Chocolate Candies are filled. The company makes huge numbers of plain candies and then pours them into large vats in the following proportions:

30% brown	10% green
20% red	10% blue
20% yellow	10% orange

The candies are mixed and then poured into bags. It's possible, but very unlikely, that someday you will open a bag and find it contains only red candy.

This means that bags of "M&M's"® Chocolate Candies can be used like dice or a spinner in which the probability of a given event is the same on every trial. Be sure that students are not replacing the drawn candies back into the bag, even if small bags of candies are used. Each bag is a random sample from all candies.

Before beginning the investigation, you may want to perform the following experiment in class:

Give each student a small bag of candy or other way of simulating an event with probability 0.30. Each time a student draws a candy from a bag, the probability it is brown is 0.30. Alternatively, students could use a calculator or a random digit table with the digits 0, 1, 2 representing a brown candy, for example, and the other digits representing other colors.

First ask students how many students they expect to get a brown candy on the first try. Then have the students look at their first candy. Those students who draw a brown candy on the first try should go stand one behind the other at the side of the room.

Ask students how many of the remaining students they expect to get a brown candy on this try. Then have those students look at their second candy. Students who draw a brown candy on this second try should go stand one behind the other to the right of the first group.

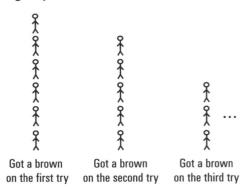

Got a brown   Got a brown   Got a brown
on the first try   on the second try   on the third try

Repeat this procedure until the class has formed a living histogram. (You may want to bring your camera!) Ask students why the lines keep getting shorter. (Because there are fewer students still trying to get a brown candy each time.) Ask students what proportion the length of each line is to the length of the preceding line. (Approximately 0.70.)

> **See additional Teaching Notes on page T533E.**

Unit 7

3. **a.** 644 students

    b. $\frac{644}{1,000} = 0.644$

    c. $\frac{177}{1,000} = 0.177$

3. Suppose each student in a group of 1,000 drew "M&M's"® Chocolate Candies one at a time out of individual bags until he or she got a brown one. A trial is taking a candy out of the bag. Each student counted the number of trials until a brown candy was drawn. A typical frequency distribution of the number of draws to get a brown candy appears below. The frequency distribution for this experiment is an example of a **waiting-time** (or **geometric**) **distribution**. (Waiting for doubles when playing Monopoly also has a waiting-time distribution.)

Drawing Candies

Number of Draws to Get First Brown (Event)	Number of Students (Frequency)
1	284
2	197
3	163
4	91
5	88
6	52
7	39
8	30
9	15
10	14
11	13
12	5
13	6
14	1
15	1
16	0
17	0
18	1
Total	1,000

a. How many students got their first brown candy in three draws or fewer?

b. Make an estimate of the probability that the first brown candy will appear on or before the third draw when a person draws candies out of a bag.

c. Make an estimate of the probability that the first brown candy will not appear until the sixth draw or later.

d. Examine the histogram of the distribution shown below.

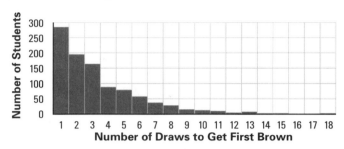

- Describe the histogram's basic shape.
- Estimate the average (mean) number of draws it takes to get the first brown candy by estimating the point where this histogram "balances."
- Why are the heights of the bars in the histogram decreasing?

e. Now calculate the average number of draws to get the first brown candy. Compare the calculated value with your estimate in Part d.

f. How can you use the table to estimate the percentage of candies that are brown? What is your estimate of this percentage?

g. Estimate the probability of drawing 11 candies or more before getting a brown one.

h. Marty is amazed that it took him so many draws to get his first brown candy. He noticed that 95% of the students got a brown candy before he did. How many candies did Marty draw?

Marty's result fell in the upper 5% of the waiting-time distribution for drawing a brown candy. When they have to wait so much longer than almost everyone else, lots of people begin to feel that something very unusual has happened. Thus, we will define a **rare event** as an event that falls in the upper 5% of a waiting-time distribution.

i. Is having to draw 11 candies a rare event? What about having to draw 8?

Checkpoint

Look over the situations with waiting-time distributions you have seen so far.

a How are the histograms similar?

b How can you estimate the average waiting time using a histogram? Using a frequency table?

c How can you determine if a specific event in a waiting-time distribution is a rare event?

Be prepared to share your ideas and methods with the entire class.

EXPLORE *continued*

3. d. ■ The histogram is skewed right.

■ The histogram appears to balance at about 3 or 4 candies. That is, the average student draws 3 or 4 candies to get the first brown one.

■ One way to see why the heights of the bars are decreasing is to imagine all 1,000 students standing up. Each takes a candy, and those who draw a brown candy are recorded in the first bar and sit down. About 30% or 300 of the students will sit. Now there are only about 700 students standing. About 30% or 210 of them will get their first brown candy on the second draw. The number of students is fewer than before because there were fewer students still standing on the second try.

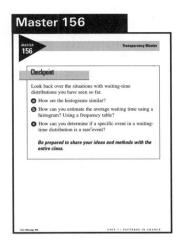

e. Drawing Candies

Number of Draws to Get First Brown Candy	Number of Students	Total Number of Candies Drawn to Get a Brown
1	284	284
2	197	394
3	163	489
4	91	364
5	88	440
6	52	312
7	39	273
8	30	240
9	15	135
10	14	140
11	13	143
12	5	60
13	6	78
14	1	14
15	1	15
16	0	0
17	0	0
18	1	18
Total	1,000	3,399

The average number of candies drawn until the first brown one appears is $\frac{3,399}{1,000}$ or 3.399. Students can compute this by entering the first two columns of the table above into their calculators and creating a third column, the product of the first two. They can use the calculators to find the sum of the third list and divide that sum by 1,000.

Students might say that x is the number of candies drawn before a brown and f is the number of students who had to draw this many, so xf is the total number of candies drawn for each group of students. Summing these totals gives the total candies drawn by *all* students, and then dividing by n gives the average number of candies drawn by any one student.

See additional Teaching Notes on page T533F.

▶**On Your Own**

a. A good estimate would be about 3. This is because the average number of candies was approximately 3.4 in Activity 3 Part e, when the probability was about 0.30. Here, the probability is a bit higher, $\frac{1}{3}$, so the average waiting time should be a bit less than 3.4.

b. The simulation may involve picking one of the digits 1, 2, or 3 at random. The number 1 might represent the Patrick Ewing poster. Students would pick digits until they picked a number 1. Other variations are possible.

c. Results of student simulations will vary.

d. Here is a frequency table that is close to the theoretical table.

Cereal Posters

Number of Boxes	Frequency
1	33
2	22
3	15
4	10
5	7
6	4
7	3
8	2
9	1
10	1
11	1
12	1
Total	100

e. The histogram for the Cereal Posters table follows. The basic shape is skewed right. Each bar is about $\frac{2}{3}$ the height of the one to the left.

Cereal Posters

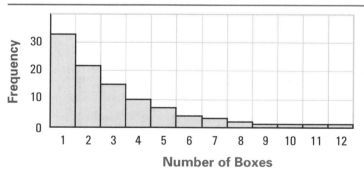

f. Student answers will depend on the results of their simulations. Students should use the formula $\bar{x} = \frac{\sum xf}{n}$. The theoretical answer is 3.

g. Estimates will depend on the results of the simulation but should be about 0.02. In the table in Part d, for example, $\frac{2}{100} = 0.02$ required more than 10 boxes.

h. The upper 5% of the distribution includes one 8 and all larger numbers. So 6 boxes is not a rare event.

►On Your Own

Cereal manufacturers often place small prizes in their cereal boxes as a marketing scheme. Boxes of one brand of cereal recently contained one of three basketball-player posters: Patrick Ewing, Alonzo Mourning, and Shawn Kemp. Suppose that equal numbers of these posters are placed randomly into the boxes. Patrick would like to get a Patrick Ewing poster.

a. On the average, how many boxes do you think Patrick would have to buy before getting a Patrick Ewing poster?

b. Designing simulations was an important part of the "Simulation Models" unit in Course 1. Design a simulation so that you can better estimate how many boxes of this cereal Patrick might have to buy before he gets a Patrick Ewing poster.

c. Repeat your simulation five times.

d. How many boxes did Patrick have to buy each time? Add your results to the frequency table below so that there is a total of 100 trials.

Getting a Patrick Ewing Poster

Number of Boxes	Frequency	Number of Boxes	Frequency
1	31	7	3
2	20	8	2
3	15	9	1
4	10	10	1
5	6	11	1
6	4	12	1
		Total	

e. Make a histogram of the results in the completed frequency table and describe its basic shape.

f. Use the completed frequency table to estimate how many boxes a person would have to buy to get a Patrick Ewing poster.

g. Estimate the chance that a person would have to buy more than 10 boxes to get a Ewing poster.

h. Is having to buy 6 boxes a rare event?

Modeling • Organizing • Reflecting • Extending

Modeling

1. Suppose you are trying to draw a heart from a regular deck of 52 cards.

   a. After each draw, you *do not* replace that card before you draw again.

   - What is the smallest number of cards you might have to draw in order to get a heart?

   - What is the largest number of cards you might have to draw in order to get a heart?

   - Are the draws independent? Explain.

   b. After each draw, you *do* replace that card (and reshuffle) before you draw again.

   - What is the smallest number of cards you might have to draw in order to get a heart?

   - What is the largest number of cards you might have to draw in order to get a heart?

   - Are the draws independent? Explain.

   c. Should you replace the card or not, if you want to get a heart in the least number of draws? Why does this make sense?

2. Describe a simulation using random digits to estimate the number of draws from a regular deck of cards needed to get a heart, if the card is replaced after each draw. Repeat your simulation 10 times.

   a. Based on your simulation, what is the average number of draws needed to get a heart?

   b. How would you modify your simulation model, if the card is *not* replaced after each draw?

3. Boxes of Kellogg's® Cocoa Krispies® cereal once contained one of four endangered animal stickers: bird of paradise, tiger, African elephant, and crocodile. Suppose that these stickers were placed randomly into the boxes and that there was an equal number of each kind of animal sticker.

   a. Polly likes birds and wanted the bird of paradise sticker. Describe a simulation to estimate the average number of boxes of Kellogg's® Cocoa Krispies® cereal that Polly would have had to buy before she got a bird sticker.

©1993 Kellogg Company

Modeling

MORE
ASSIGNMENT *pp. 466–470*

Modeling: 3, and 1 or 4*
Organizing: 1 and 4
Reflecting: Choose one*
Extending: Choose one*

*When choice is indicated, it is important to leave the choice to the student.
NOTE: It is best if Organizing tasks are discussed as a whole class after they have been assigned as homework.

1. Some students may not be very familiar with a deck of cards. Before assigning this problem, you may want to discuss how many and what kinds of cards make up a standard deck of 52 cards.

   a. ■ 1

      ■ 40. You might draw all 39 of the diamonds, clubs, and spades before drawing a heart.

      ■ No. The probability of getting a heart increases after each unsuccessful draw.

   b. ■ 1

      ■ You might draw forever.

      ■ Yes. The probability of getting a heart on each draw is $\frac{13}{52}$, or $\frac{1}{4}$.

   c. Do not replace the card. This makes sense because if you don't replace the card, the probability of getting a heart increases on the next draw.

2. Simulations may vary. For example, a simulation might use a calculator to generate integers 1 through 52 (through a command such as int 52 rand + 1). Let the integers 1 though 13 represent hearts. Count the number of integers until an integer in the interval 1 through 13 appears.

   Students also could use the random digit table and let 1 represent a heart. Digits 2, 3, and 4 could represent the other suits, and then students can ignore all other digits. Start at a random place on the table and count the number of digits (1 to 4) until a 1 appears.

   a. Responses will vary. The theoretical average is 4.

   b. If students used only 4 digits, they would have to redesign their simulation. The first simulation described above is easier to modify. The simulation will have to use one fewer random digit each time it is run. But the integers 1 through 13 will always represent a heart. So, the second draw will be simulated using int 51 rand + 1, the third draw will be simulated using int 50 rand + 1, and so on.

3. a. Responses may vary. One possible simulation is described here. Use a random digit table. Let the digit 1 represent a bird of paradise, 2 represent a tiger, 3 represent an African elephant, and 4 represent a crocodile. Ignore all other digits. Start at a random place on the table and count the number of digits (1 to 4) until a 1 appears.

3. **b.** Responses will vary according to student simulations.

c. A typical histogram will look like the following. The histogram is skewed right with the first bar being the tallest and the bars generally decreasing in height.

Bird of Paradise Sticker

d. The average number of boxes should be about 4, which is the theoretical average.

e. Responses will vary according to the students' completed histograms. From the preceding histogram, the estimated probability of having to buy more than 10 boxes is equal to $\frac{9}{100}$ or 0.09.

f. No. The upper 5% of the number of boxes will depend on the outcomes of the simulations. However, since more than 5% of the trials required more than 10 boxes, we know that having to buy 10 boxes is not a rare event.

4. **a.** $\frac{14}{36}$

You could roll (1, 2), (2, 1), (1, 1), (3, X), or (X, 3). The latter two together account for 11 possible rolls of the dice. Roll (3, 3) occurs in both (3, X) and (X, 3).

b. $\frac{15}{36}$

You could roll (5, X), (X, 5), (2, 3), (3, 2), (4, 1), or (1, 4).
Again, roll (5, 5) occurs in both (5, X) and (X, 5).

c. $\frac{3}{36}$

You could roll (6, 6), (3, 3), or (4, 4).

b. Repeat your simulation five times. Add your results to those in the frequency table below so that there is a total of 100 trials. Add additional rows if you need to.

Getting a Bird Sticker

Number of Boxes	Frequency	Number of Boxes	Frequency	Number of Boxes	Frequency
1	19	10	1	19	1
2	14	11	1	20	0
3	15	12	3	21	0
4	13	13	0	22	0
5	11	14	0	23	0
6	6	15	0	24	0
7	4	16	2	25	0
8	2	17	1	26	1
9	1	18	0	**Total**	

c. Make a histogram from the completed frequency table and describe its shape.

d. Use the completed frequency table to estimate the average number of boxes a person would have to buy to get a bird of paradise sticker.

e. Estimate the chance that a person would need to buy more than 10 boxes.

f. Is having to buy 10 boxes a rare event?

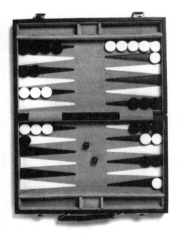

4. Backgammon is one of the oldest games in recorded history. It may have originated before 3000 B.C. in Mesopotamia (present-day Iraq). Today, it is played all over the world. In Backgammon, as in Monopoly, the number of spaces you can move a stone is determined by rolling two dice. In the game of Backgammon, if you "hit" another player's single stone exactly, that stone must go back to the beginning and start again.

To hit a stone that is three spaces ahead of you, you must roll a three. The three may be on one die or the three may be the sum of both dice. If you roll double 1s, you also can hit the stone because on doubles a player gets to move the numbers that show on the die twice each. So a player who rolls double ones could move 1+1+1, hit the stone, and then move the final 1.

a. What is the probability of being able to hit the stone of a player who is three spaces ahead of you?

b. What is the probability of being able to hit the stone of a player who is five spaces ahead of you?

c. What is the probability of being able to hit the stone of a player who is twelve spaces ahead of you?

Organizing

1. Refer to the frequency table your class prepared for Activity 1, Investigation 1 (page 458).

   a. Make a scatterplot of the (*number of rolls required, frequency*) data.

   b. If *NOW* is the number of people who got doubles on a roll and *NEXT* is the number of people who got doubles on the next roll, write an equation that approximates the relation between *NOW* and *NEXT*. Explain why your equation is reasonable in the context of rolling doubles.

   c. Is a linear model or an exponential model a better fit to the scatterplot? Why?

2. Recall that there are five regular polyhedra: tetrahedron (4 faces), hexahedron or cube (6 faces), octahedron (8 faces), dodecahedron (12 faces), and icosahedron (20 faces). Find or imagine pairs of dice in the shape of these polyhedra. Rolling each tetrahedral die generates numbers from 1 to 4, rolling each octahedral die generates numbers from 1 to 8, and so on.

   a. Make a chart like the one in Activity 2 of Investigation 1 (page 458) for a pair of tetrahedral dice. What is the probability of getting doubles?

   b. Repeat Part a in the case of a pair of octahedral dice.

   c. By looking for patterns in your work, find the probability of rolling doubles with the following pairs of dice:
   - Dodecahedral dice
   - Icosahedral dice

   d. For which pair of dice is the probability of getting doubles the greatest?

   e. If the number of faces on each of a pair of regular polyhedral dice is *n*, what is the probability of rolling doubles with that pair of dice?

3. Describe how you could use a calculator to simulate rolling an icosahedral die.

4. In "Network Optimization," you explored ways in which special vertex-edge graphs called trees could be used to model situations. Think of a way to use a tree graph to represent rolling two dice. Illustrate how you could use the tree graph to answer the questions in Activity 2 Part b, from Investigation 1 (page 459).

Tetrahedron

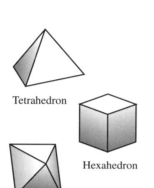

Hexahedron

Octahedron

Dodecahedron

Icosahedron

Reflecting

1. Suppose someone in your class is unsure about whether the probability of rolling doubles with one red die and one green die is the same as if both dice were red. Describe an experiment you could do to convince them.

Organizing

1. **a.** Scatterplots will vary according to the frequency table from Investigation 1, Activity 1.

   b. $NEXT = \frac{5}{6} \times NOW$

   When rolling dice, we expect approximately $\frac{1}{6}$ of the people to roll doubles. Say there are x people to start. Then $NOW = \frac{1}{6}x$. On the next roll, there are $\frac{5}{6}x$ people still trying to get doubles. Approximately $\frac{1}{6}$ of them will get doubles. So,

   $NEXT = \frac{1}{6}\left(\frac{5}{6}x\right) = \frac{5}{6}\left(\frac{1}{6}x\right) = \frac{5}{6}\,NOW.$

   c. The better algebraic model will probably be an exponential model. Later, students will learn that the theoretical equation for this distribution is $y = 100\left(\frac{1}{6}\right)\left(\frac{5}{6}\right)^x$.

2. **a.** Tetrahedral dice (four-sided):

1, 1	1, 2	1, 3	1, 4
2, 1	2, 2	2, 3	2, 4
3, 1	3, 2	3, 3	3, 4
4, 1	4, 2	4, 3	4, 4

   The probability of getting doubles is $\frac{4}{16}$, which is $\frac{1}{4}$ or 0.25.

   b. Octahedral dice (eight-sided):

1, 1	1, 2	1, 3	1, 4	1, 5	1, 6	1, 7	1, 8
2, 1	2, 2	2, 3	2, 4	2, 5	2, 6	2, 7	2, 8
3, 1	3, 2	3, 3	3, 4	3, 5	3, 6	3, 7	3, 8
4, 1	4, 2	4, 3	4, 4	4, 5	4, 6	4, 7	4, 8
5, 1	5, 2	5, 3	5, 4	5, 5	5, 6	5, 7	5, 8
6, 1	6, 2	6, 3	6, 4	6, 5	6, 6	6, 7	6, 8
7, 1	7, 2	7, 3	7, 4	7, 5	7, 6	7, 7	7, 8
8, 1	8, 2	8, 3	8, 4	8, 5	8, 6	8, 7	8, 8

   The probability of rolling doubles is $\frac{8}{64}$, which is $\frac{1}{8}$ or 0.125.

   c. ■ The probability of rolling doubles with a pair of dodecahedral dice is $\frac{1}{12}$.

   ■ The probability of rolling doubles with a pair of icosahedral dice is $\frac{1}{20}$.

   d. The probability is greatest for the tetrahedral dice.

   e. $\frac{1}{n}$

3. Calculator commands such as **int 20 rand + 1** will simulate rolling an icosahedral die. (Exact syntax will depend on the calculator model.)

See additional Teaching Notes on page T533G.

Unit 7

2. Most people, after a run of bad luck in a game, think that luck is "due" to change. This may be because they have some sense that a long string of bad luck is unlikely. For example, suppose you are about to flip a coin 6 times and are hoping for heads. People realize the probability of 6 tails in a row is rather small. They tend to use this same probability when they have already gotten 5 tails in a row. They may think that the chance of getting another tails is very small because the chance of getting 6 tails in a row is very small.

3. Questions will vary.

4. Responses may vary. For example, you are right that the probability of rolling doubles is still $\frac{1}{6}$, no matter how many times you have tried before. But remember that some people achieved doubles on their first try, so there was a smaller number of people still trying to get doubles on a second roll. About $\frac{1}{6}$ of the original group of people got doubles on their first try, and about $\frac{1}{6}$ of the people who were left got doubles on their second try.

Extending

1. The tires on cars actually rotate almost independently. Encourage your students to check this by using chalk on the tires of cars they can observe.

   A possible simulation would be to have two spinners with clock faces on them, one for the front tire and one for the back tire. Students would spin both spinners and note how often they **both** end up where they started.

   Most students think the man should have been found guilty. There is less than one chance in a hundred that both tires would end up in the same position after driving the car. The probability is exactly $\left(\frac{1}{12}\right)\left(\frac{1}{12}\right)$ or $\frac{1}{144}$. However, the judge said that 1 chance in 144 was reasonable doubt, and the man was acquitted.

2. Take a survey of your friends and family. Tell them about the problem of getting out of jail in Monopoly and then ask them to answer this question:

A player has tried twice to get out of jail. She has had no luck. Before her third try she says, "I have missed getting out of jail twice, so I'm due for doubles. My chances of rolling doubles are greater this time than on my first two tries." Is she correct?

Are you surprised at their answers? Why do some people believe that the chances of success increase after there have been several failures?

3. If you have not previously played Monopoly, learn how to play. Make a list of three probability questions that arose during your game. Find the answer to one of your questions by using a simulation.

4. Suppose a friend looks at the table in Activity 1 of Investigation 1 (page 458) and says, "I don't understand why the frequency for 'Rolled doubles on second try' is smaller than 'Rolled doubles on first try.' They should be equal because the probability of rolling doubles is the same, $\frac{1}{6}$, on each try." What would you say to this friend?

Extending

1. In a famous trial in Sweden, a parking officer had noted the position of the valve stems on the tires on one side of a car; upon returning later, the officer noted that the valve stems were still in the same position. The officer noted the position of the valve stems to the nearest "hour." For example, in the following picture, the valve stems are at 3:00 and at 10:00. The officer issued a ticket for overtime parking. However, the owner of the car claimed he had moved the car and returned to the same parking place.

Design a simulation to estimate the probability that if a car is moved, the valve stems return to the same position they had before the car was moved. You must make an assumption about how tires rotate. Try to find out whether this assumption is true or not before doing your simulation. Do you think the car owner should have been found guilty or innocent of the parking violation? Explain.

2. In the game of Backgammon, if you want to have the best chance of hitting an opponent's stone with a particular stone of your own on the next roll of dice, how many spaces away should your stone be? (The rules of Backgammon are explained in Modeling Task 4 on page 467.)

3. Shown below are labeled nets for special dice. Darnell selects one of the special dice and then Joy selects one of the remaining two.

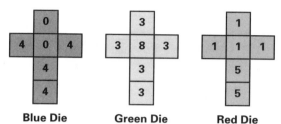

Blue Die   **Green Die**   **Red Die**

Each rolls his or her die. The person with the larger number wins. To help you decide if it is better to use, for example, the blue die or the green die, you might want to complete a table like the following:

Number on Green Die

		3	3	3	3	3	8
0	Green Die Wins						
0	Green Die Wins						
4	Blue Die Wins						
4							
4							
4							

(Number on Blue Die)

Which die should Darnell choose? Which should Joy choose? What is the surprise here? Can you find a different set of dice that has the same property?

4. Put two red and two yellow markers or tokens in a bag. Without looking, draw one. Replace it with a marker of the other color. Continue this process until all the markers in the bag are the same color.

   a. How many draws did it take until all markers in the bag were the same color?

   b. Make a frequency table and put your result in the table.

   c. Repeat this experiment 19 more times and place your results in the table. (You may want to combine your results with those of several classmates.)

   d. Make a histogram from your frequency table.

   e. Does this experiment generate a waiting-time distribution? Explain.

   f. Estimate the average number of draws needed until all the markers are the same color.

   g. Design a simulation that uses a random device instead of a bag of markers.

MORE *continued*

2. This table gives the probability that, on one roll of the dice, you will hit a player's stone the given number of spaces ahead of your stone (provided all the necessary spaces in between are legal landing spaces).

Spaces Ahead	Probability Will Hit		Spaces Ahead	Probability Will Hit
1	$\frac{11}{36}$		13	0
2	$\frac{12}{36}$		14	0
3	$\frac{14}{36}$		15	$\frac{1}{36}$
4	$\frac{15}{36}$		16	$\frac{1}{36}$
5	$\frac{15}{36}$		17	0
6	$\frac{17}{36}$		18	$\frac{1}{36}$
7	$\frac{6}{36}$		19	0
8	$\frac{6}{36}$		20	$\frac{1}{36}$
9	$\frac{5}{36}$		21	0
10	$\frac{3}{36}$		22	0
11	$\frac{2}{36}$		23	0
12	$\frac{3}{36}$		24	$\frac{1}{36}$

The best chance occurs when the player is 6 spaces ahead of you.

You may want to discuss why the sum of these probabilities is greater than $\frac{36}{36}$ or 1. The reason is that this is not a probability distribution table that shows all possible outcomes of some experiment. The same roll (2, 3), for example, can hit a player 2 spaces, 3 spaces, and 5 spaces ahead. So this single roll is represented three times in the chart above.

3. These are Efron dice, named after Bradley Efron, the Stanford statistician who discovered them. The blue die tends to beat the green die, the green die tends to beat the red die, and the red die tends to beat the blue die. For this reason, the dice are called *nontransitive*. No matter which die Darnell selects, Joy can select another that will have a greater probability of winning. To see that, for example, the blue die tends to beat the green die, we can construct this table. The entry in the table gives the winner on that particular roll.

Number on Green Die

		3	3	3	3	3	8
	0	Green Die Wins	Green	Green	Green	Green	Green
	0	Green Die Wins	Green	Green	Green	Green	Green
Number on Blue Die	4	Blue Die Wins	Blue	Blue	Blue	Blue	Green
	4	Blue	Blue	Blue	Blue	Blue	Green
	4	Blue	Blue	Blue	Blue	Blue	Green
	4	Blue	Blue	Blue	Blue	Blue	Green

The probability that the person with the blue die will win is $\frac{20}{36}$.

Many other sets of three dice have this property. A trivial way to construct a new set is to add 2 to each number on these three dice.

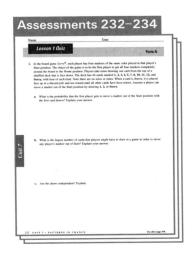

Assessments 232–234

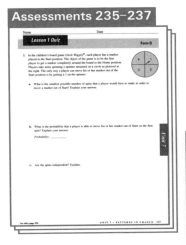

Assessments 235–237

See additional Teaching Notes on page T533H.

Unit 7

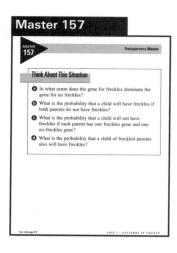

Lesson 2 *The Multiplication Rule*

LESSON OVERVIEW This lesson introduces students to the Multiplication Rule for independent events: $P(A \text{ and } B) = P(A) \cdot P(B)$.

This lesson has one investigation in three parts. In Activities 1–4, the use of an area model is developed. The concept is based on the idea that the total probability of all possible events is 100%, and this is modeled by the whole rectangular area. Each dimension of the rectangle can be subdivided to model the probability of each event. This, in turn, subdivides the internal area proportionally to represent the probability that one or the other or both events occur. In Activity 5, the Multiplication Rule $P(A \text{ and } B) = P(A) \cdot P(B)$ is introduced formally. The Multiplication Rule is used in Activities 6–8. Students also are expected to extend their understanding of the Multiplication Rule to situations in which there are more than two events. The third part of the Investigation, Activities 9 and 10, consider cases with which the Multiplication Rule should not be used even though the word *and* appears in the probability statement. Students need to reflect on when the Multiplication Rule works and when it does not. You may want them to write their thoughts about this.

Lesson Objectives

- To use an area model to find the probability that two independent events both occur
- To use the Multiplication Rule to find the probability that two independent events both occur
- To decide if two events are independent

LAUNCH   full-class discussion

The genetic model presented here somewhat oversimplifies the real situation. A biology teacher at your school can provide additional information about this basic Mendelian genetics model. If students have not had biology, they may not be familiar with the Punnett squares presented in Parts c and d. If the students don't bring them up at this point in time, it is not necessary to introduce them. They will be explored further in the investigation.

Think About This Situation

See Teaching Master 157.

ⓐ If a person has both a freckles gene and a no-freckles gene, then the freckles gene will dominate and the person will have freckles.

ⓑ The probability that the child of parents without freckles will have freckles is 0. Each parent has two no-freckles genes, and so the child must inherit a no-freckles gene from each parent.

See additional Teaching Notes on page T533I.

Unit 7

The Multiplication Rule

Some physical characteristics, such as freckles, eyelash length, and the ability to roll one's tongue up from the sides, are determined in a simple manner by genes inherited from one's parents. Each person has two genes that determine whether or not he or she will have freckles, one inherited from the father and one from the mother. If a child gets a "freckles" gene from either parent or from both parents, the child has freckles. In order not to have freckles, the child must inherit a "no-freckles" gene from both parents. This explains why the gene for freckles is called *dominant* and the gene for no-freckles is called *recessive*. A parent with two freckles genes must pass on a freckles gene to the child; a parent with two no-freckles genes must pass on a no-freckles gene. If a parent has one of each, the probability is $\frac{1}{2}$ that he or she will pass on the freckles gene and $\frac{1}{2}$ that he or she will pass on the no-freckles gene.

Think About This Situation

a In what sense does the gene for freckles dominate the gene for no freckles?

b What is the probability that a child will have freckles if both parents do not have freckles?

c What is the probability that a child will not have freckles if each parent has one freckles gene and one no-freckles gene?

d What is the probability that a child of freckled parents also will have freckles?

INVESTIGATION 1 Multiplying Probabilities

You have found that graphical representations of data can reveal important under-lying patterns and that making a "picture" of a mathematical situation can help you understand that situation better. In this investigation, you will use an *area model* to explore patterns in chance situations.

1. About half of all U.S. residents are female. According to a survey published in *USA Today*, one-third of TV viewers in the United States usually watch a commercial when it comes on.

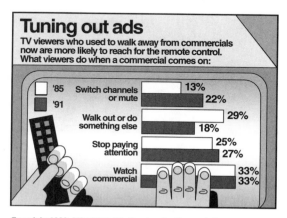

Copyright 1993, USA TODAY. Reprinted with permission.

a. Suppose a person from the United States is selected at random. From the information above, what do you think would be the probability that the person is a female who watches commercials?

b. Now examine the situation using the area model shown to the right. Explain why there are two rows labeled "No" for "Watches Commercial" and only one labeled "Yes." What assumption does this model make about commercial viewing habits of males and females?

c. On a copy of this area model, shade in the squares that represent the event of a female who watches commercials.

d. What is the probability that a person selected at random is a female who watches commercials?

e. What is the probability that a person selected at random is a male who does not watch commercials?

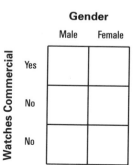

EXPLORE small-group investigation

INVESTIGATION 1 Multiplying Probabilities

The principal idea in this investigation is that if two events *A* and *B* are independent, then we can multiply their probabilities to find the probability that *A* and *B* both occur: $P(A \text{ and } B) = P(A) P(B)$. Equivalently, we can use the area model introduced on page 472 to find $P(A \text{ and } B)$. The area model builds on the model of multiplication that students have used since elementary school. (See the example in the margin below).

Deciding when two events are independent is difficult for students, especially since they tend to confuse independent with mutually exclusive. To avoid this confusion, students should take care to use a correct definition of independence.

There are actually three equivalent definitions of independence:

$$P(A) = P(A|B)$$
$$P(B) = P(B|A)$$
$$P(A \text{ and } B) = P(A) P(B).$$

This unit follows standard practice and uses the first as the definition of independence, points out that the second is the same thing with the events renamed, and says that the third follows as a consequence of the first. (Formally, it follows from the definition of conditional probability: $P(A|B) = \frac{P(A \text{ and } B)}{P(B)}$.

In Activities 6–10, students examine the Multiplication Rule a little further, either applying or extending the newly formulated rule, discovering that very different sequences of events can have the same probability, or finding when you cannot apply this rule. Each activity should be discussed by the whole class after groups have tried them. One way to handle these activities is to have every group complete each activity, but assign each group one particular activity to explain to the whole class. As you circulate among the groups, you can choose your "leading" group appropriately to make sure that correct answers are presented, but also to make sure that surprises (such as the probability of any sequence of 7 tosses of a coin is the same as any other sequence—see Activity 8) or insights (such as that the rule does not apply if the events are not independent—see Activity 9) get addressed.

1. **See Teaching Master 158.**
    a. With the information given, the probability is $\frac{1}{6}$; however, student responses will vary. Having students think about this before looking at it formally will help you and them see what their level of probability understanding already is.
    b. There are two No's under "Watches Commercial," so the area model will have two-thirds of its area devoted to the event of not watching the commercial and one-third of its area devoted to the event of watching the commercial. The model assumes that females are just as likely to watch commercials as are males. If this assumption is not true, the area model will not work.
    c. See the area model at the right.
    d. $\frac{1}{6}$
    e. $\frac{2}{6}$ or $\frac{1}{3}$

Multiplying 2 × 3:

	1	2
1		
2		
3		

Gender

		Male	Female
Watches Commercial	Yes		▓
	No		
	No		

Unit 7

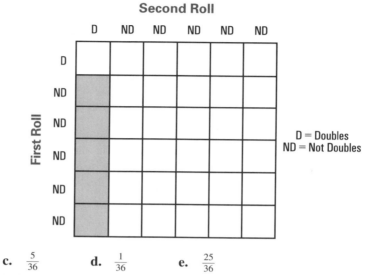

2. See Teaching Master 158.

    a. It makes sense to label the rows as shown because the probability of rolling doubles is $\frac{1}{6}$ and the probability of not rolling doubles is $\frac{5}{6}$. One of the six columns should be labeled "Doubles" and the rest "Not Doubles."

    b. **Rolling a Pair of Dice**

    Second Roll

    D = Doubles
    ND = Not Doubles

    c. $\frac{5}{36}$ d. $\frac{1}{36}$ e. $\frac{25}{36}$

    Before students begin Activity 3, you may wish to discuss further the area model for that activity. There are several questions that can be asked: What do each of the parts of the model represent? What does the vertical dimension represent? Why is it divided into 6 parts? Why should these parts all be equal? What does the horizontal dimension represent? What does each small square represent? What do all the small squares together, the large square, represent?

    Students have used many models: linear models, quadratic models, matrix models, and graph models. In each case, they had to be careful to say what each part of the model represented and how it could be changed if the situation changed. You might ask your students how the area model for Activity 2 would change if they used a different die (for example, a 10-sided die), or if the die were unfair in some way (for example, weighted to generate 6 half of the time). Could they use a similar model to represent the probabilities of the outcomes of rolling 3 dice together?

    When your students understand the implications of the model, they should be successful working in their small groups on Activities 3 and 4. You may want to bring the groups back together as a whole class to discuss Activity 5 and the language immediately following it.

3. a. The probability of a child without freckles is $\frac{1}{4}$.

    b. Responses will vary depending on the class's answer to the "Think About This Situation" question.

Gene from Mother

	Freckles	No-freckles
Freckles (Gene from Father)	Freckles	Freckles
No-freckles (Gene from Father)	Freckles	No-freckles

2. In Lesson 1, you estimated answers to questions like the following one, involving rolling a pair of dice:

What is the probability that it takes exactly two tries to roll doubles?

Now use an area model to analyze this problem.

a. Explain why it makes sense to label the rows of the area model as shown below. On a copy of this area model, label the six columns to represent the possible outcomes on the second roll of a pair of dice.

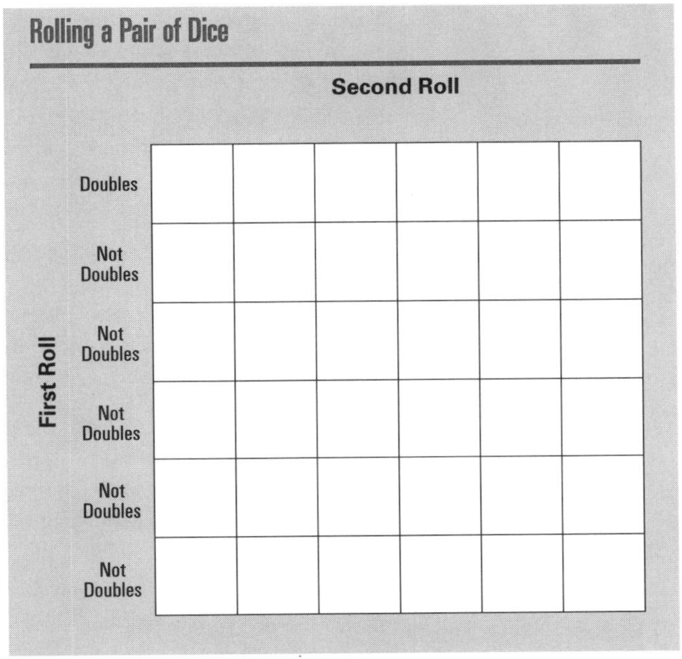

Rolling a Pair of Dice

Second Roll

	First Roll
Doubles	
Not Doubles	
Not Doubles	
Not Doubles	
Not Doubles	
Not Doubles	

b. Find the squares that represent the event of not getting doubles on the first roll and getting doubles on the second roll. Shade those squares on your copy.

c. Use your area model to find the probability of not getting doubles on the first roll and then getting doubles on the second roll.

d. Use your area model to find the probability you will get doubles both times.

e. Use your area model to find the probability you won't get doubles either time.

3. Make an area model to help you determine the probabilities that a child will or will not have freckles, when each parent has one freckles gene and one no-freckles gene.

a. What is the probability that the child will not have freckles?

b. Compare your answer to Part a with your class's answer to Part c of the "Think About This Situation" on page 471.

4. Make and use area models to answer these questions:

   a. About 25% of Americans put catsup directly on their fries, rather than on the plate. What is the best estimate for the probability that *both* your school principal and your favorite celebrity put catsup directly on their fries?

   b. About 84% of Americans pour shampoo into their hand rather than directly onto their hair. What is the best estimate of the probability that *both* your teacher and the President of the United States pour shampoo into their hands before putting it on their hair?

5. Look back at the situations described in Activities 1 through 4. The pairs of events in each of those activities were (or were assumed to be) **independent events**. Knowing whether one of the events occurs does not change the probability that the other event occurs.

   a. For each situation, explain why the events are independent.

   b. For each activity, describe how to compute the probabilities without making an area model.

   c. Describe in words how to find the probability that two independent events both occur.

   d. Suppose A and B are independent events. Express your method in Part c using symbols by completing the following equation:

$$P(A \text{ and } B) = \underline{\hspace{2cm}}$$

   The notation $P(A \text{ and } B)$ is read "the probability of event A and event B."

Often a probability problem is easier to understand if it is written in words that are more specific than the words the original problem uses. For example, you could express and find the probability of taking exactly two tries to roll doubles in the following manner:

$P(\text{don't roll doubles on the first try and do roll doubles on the second try})$

$= P(\text{don't roll doubles on the first try}) \cdot P(\text{do roll doubles on the second try})$

$= \left(\frac{5}{6}\right)\left(\frac{1}{6}\right)$

$= \left(\frac{5}{36}\right)$

This example uses the *Multiplication Rule* you probably discovered in Activity 5 to calculate the probability that two independent events both occur.

6. Suppose Shiomo is playing a game in which he needs to roll a pair of dice and get doubles and then immediately roll the dice again and get a sum of six. He wants to know the probability that this will happen.

   a. Which of the following best describes the probability Shiomo wants to find?

   ■ $P(\text{gets doubles on the first roll or gets a sum of six on the second roll})$

   ■ $P(\text{gets doubles on the first roll and gets a sum of six on the second roll})$

   ■ $P(\text{gets doubles and a sum of six})$

   b. Explain why the Multiplication Rule can be used to find the probability that this sequence of two events will happen. What is the probability?

4. a. We must assume that what the celebrity does is independent of what your principal does.

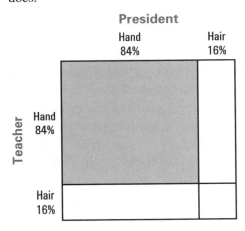

The best estimate of the probability that both your principal and the celebrity put catsup directly on their fries is $\frac{1}{16}$.

b. We must assume that what the President does is independent of what your teacher does.

President

If the students visualize dividing the area into one-percent by one-percent squares, there will be (100)(100) or 10,000 small squares, of which (84)(84) or 7,056 represent the event that both the teacher and the President pour shampoo into their hands. The best estimate of the probability is $\frac{7,056}{10,000}$ or 0.7056.

NOTE: You may wish to use Activity 5 as a class checkpoint before students move on to Activity 6.

---

5. a. In Activity 1, the events are independent because there is no reason to think that the gender of a person will influence whether or not that person will watch commercials. In Activity 3, the events are independent since the gene passed on from one parent has no bearing on the gene passed on from the other parent. In Activity 4, it is safe to assume that the events are independent since the two people involved in each situation probably have nothing in common that would influence how they apply catsup or shampoo.

See additional Teaching Notes on page T533J.

7. **a.** Since the probability of rolling a sum of 11 is $\frac{2}{36}$ and the three events are independent, this probability is $\left(\frac{1}{6}\right)\left(\frac{5}{36}\right)\left(\frac{2}{36}\right)$ or $\frac{5}{3,888}$.

    b. $P(A \text{ and } B \text{ and } C) = P(A) \cdot P(B) \cdot P(C)$ if the events are independent.

    c. $P(A \text{ and } B \text{ and } C \text{ and } D) = P(A) \cdot P(B) \cdot P(C) \cdot P(D)$

8. **a.** $\left(\frac{1}{2}\right)\left(\frac{1}{2}\right)\left(\frac{1}{2}\right)\left(\frac{1}{2}\right)\left(\frac{1}{2}\right)\left(\frac{1}{2}\right)\left(\frac{1}{2}\right) = \left(\frac{1}{2}\right)^7 = 0.0078125$

    b. $\left(\frac{1}{2}\right)\left(\frac{1}{2}\right)\left(\frac{1}{2}\right)\left(\frac{1}{2}\right)\left(\frac{1}{2}\right)\left(\frac{1}{2}\right)\left(\frac{1}{2}\right) = \left(\frac{1}{2}\right)^7 = 0.0078125$

    Students probably will be surprised that the answer to Part b is the same as the answer to Part a. The sequence HTHTTHH looks more random to students than the sequence TTTTTTH, so they think that it is more likely to occur. But, in fact, any *specific* sequence such as HTHTTHH is just as difficult to get when tossing a coin as is TTTTTTH.

    c. $\left(\frac{105}{205}\right)^{10} = (0.512195122)^{10} \approx 0.00124$

    d. The probability of having an older girl and a younger boy is $\left(\frac{1}{2}\right)\left(\frac{1}{2}\right) = \left(\frac{1}{4}\right)$, or, using the proportions in Part c, $\left(\frac{100}{205}\right)\left(\frac{105}{205}\right) \approx 0.25$. Because of the commutative property of multiplication, you can see that the probability of having an older boy and a younger girl is the same.

9. **This is a key activity, which you may want to review with the entire class. In this activity, students see that the Multiplication Rule doesn't always apply. To find P(student is a girl and has long hair), you cannot compute P(is a girl) times P(has long hair) because the events of being a girl and having long hair aren't independent. Although it may vary in different localities, typically if you were told a student was a girl, it would increase the probability that that student has long hair. (In some cultures, it might decrease the probability. But, at any rate, there is no reason to assume that boys and girls are equally likely to have long hair.) Make sure that students apply the same definition of long hair to all students.**

    If you have a single-gender class, you may have to have students get data from outside the classroom. Other examples, which are less visual and thus not as effective as this example, might include events such as *has a pet* and *likes dogs*, or *has siblings* and *has babysat*.

    a. Answers will vary depending on your class. For an example, suppose that a classroom has 16 girls, 10 of whom have long hair, and has 12 boys, 3 of whom have long hair. Then the probability a student has long hair is $\frac{13}{28}$.

    b. Answers will vary depending on your class. For our example, the probability is $\frac{16}{28}$.

    c. Students need to check whether P(girl) P(long hair) $= P$(girl and long hair). This probably won't be the case. For our example, $\left(\frac{16}{28}\right)\left(\frac{13}{28}\right)$ isn't equal to 10/16.

    d. The events in question are not independent. Knowing that a person is a girl changes the probability that the person has long hair. The Multiplication Rule works for independent events only, and so it does not give the correct probability for this situation.

7. A modification of the game in Activity 6 involves rolling a pair of dice three times. In this modified game, Shiomo needs to roll doubles, then a sum of six, and then a sum of eleven.

a. Find the probability that this sequence of three events will happen.

b. Suppose *A*, *B*, and *C* are three independent events. Write a rule for calculating *P*(*A* and *B* and *C*) using the probabilities of each individual event.

c. Write the Multiplication Rule for calculating the probability that each of four independent events occurs.

8. For each of the following questions, explain why the events are independent. Then, use the Multiplication Rule to answer the question.

a. What is the probability that a sequence of seven flips of a fair coin turns out to be exactly HTHTTHH?

b. What is the probability that a sequence of seven flips of a fair coin turns out to be exactly TTTTTTH?

c. In the United States, about 105 boys are born for every 100 girls. What is the probability of a family having 10 boys in a row?

d. What is the probability that a family with two children will have an older girl and a younger boy? Is this probability different than the probability that the family will have an older boy and a younger girl? Explain your reasoning.

9. As a class, decide exactly how long a person's hair must be for it to be considered "long." Count the number of students in your classroom who have long hair. Count the number of girls. Count the number of students who have long hair and are girls. Suppose you select a student at random from your class.

a. What is the probability that the student has long hair?

b. What is the probability that the student is a girl?

c. Does the Multiplication Rule correctly compute the probability that the student has long hair *and* is a girl? Use your answers to Parts a and b in your calculation.

d. How is this situation different from previous situations in which the Multiplication Rule gave the correct probability?

10. Sometimes you want to know the probability of an event occurring when you know that another event occurs.

a. Using the data from Activity 9, find P(student has long hair if the student is a girl). How does this compare to P(student has long hair)? Are the events *having long hair* and *being a girl* independent? Why or why not?

The phrase "the probability event A occurs if event B occurs" is written symbolically as $P(A|B)$. It is sometimes read "the probability of A given B."

b. Refer to your area model for the probabilities of whether a child will have freckles if both parents have one freckles gene and one no-freckles gene. (See Activity 3 on page 473.) Compare the following:

P(freckles gene passed from father)

P(freckles gene passed from father|freckles gene passed from mother)

Are the events *freckles gene passed from father* and *freckles gene passed from mother* independent?

c. Which is greater if you roll a pair of dice once: P(doubles) or P(doubles|sum is 2)? Are the events *getting doubles* and *getting a sum of two* independent?

d. If events A and B are independent, how are $P(A)$ and $P(A|B)$ related?

e. If events A and B are dependent, what, if anything, can you conclude about $P(A)$ and $P(A|B)$?

Checkpoint

a Why does it make sense to multiply the individual probabilities when you want to find the probability that two independent events both happen?

b What is the difference between $P(A)$ and $P(A|B)$?

Be prepared to share your thinking with the entire class.

On Your Own

a. While playing Monopoly, Jenny is sent to jail. She wants to know the probability that she will fail to roll doubles in three tries.

■ Rewrite this probability situation describing the sequence of events that are to occur.

■ Find the probability that Jenny fails to roll doubles in three tries.

■ Explain why you can use the Multiplication Rule for this situation.

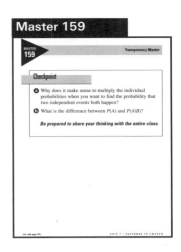

10. The language of Activity 10 is difficult for many students. It will help if you ask them to think of their own examples to illustrate these concepts.

   a. Answers will vary, depending on your class. Our example, P(student has long hair if the student is a girl) $= \frac{10}{16}$ and P(student has long hair) $= \frac{13}{28}$. These aren't equal, so the events aren't independent.

   b. P(freckles gene passed from father) $= \frac{1}{2} = P$(freckles gene passed from father|freckles gene passed from mother). Yes, the events are independent.

   c. P(doubles) $= \frac{6}{36}$ while P(doubles|sum is 2) $= 1$. So P(doubles|sum is 2) is greater. The two events aren't independent since if the sum is 2, then you must have rolled doubles.

   d. If the events are independent, then $P(A) = P(A|B)$.

   e. If the events are dependent, then all that can be said is that $P(A) \neq P(A|B)$.

SHARE AND SUMMARIZE full-class discussion

Checkpoint

See Teaching Master 159.

   ⓐ The student may reason as in the following example: Suppose half of all children are girls, and one-third of all children have freckles. What is the probability that a randomly selected child is a girl with freckles? Assuming gender and freckles are independent, half of all children are girls and $\frac{1}{3}$ of the girls have freckles.

   $\frac{1}{3}$ of $\frac{1}{2}$ is $\frac{1}{3} \cdot \frac{1}{2}$ or $\frac{1}{6}$. Students also may explain using an area model.

   ⓑ $P(A)$ stands for the probability that event A happens when you have no additional information about whether other events happen. $P(A|B)$ stands for the probability that event A happens given the additional information that B happens for sure.

CONSTRUCTING A MATH TOOLKIT: Students should record the Multiplication Rule and an example of its use in their Math Toolkits. Be sure that they include a statement that the events must be independent. An example of when it is inappropriate to use the Multiplication Rule should help students clarify the concept.

Unit 7

APPLY individual task

▶ On Your Own

   a. ■ Jenny needs to find P(doesn't roll doubles on first roll, doesn't roll doubles on second roll, and doesn't roll doubles on third roll).

   ■ $\left(\frac{5}{6}\right)\left(\frac{5}{6}\right)\left(\frac{5}{6}\right) = \frac{125}{216}$

   ■ Each roll is independent from the others. The results of the first roll do not influence the results of the second, and so on.

b. ■ $P(\text{male}) < P(\text{male}|\text{over six feet tall})$ or $P(A) < P(A|B)$

■ $P(\text{female}) = P(\text{female}|\text{brown eyes})$ or $P(A) = P(A|B)$

■ $P(\text{French club}) < P(\text{French club}|\text{French class})$ or $P(A) < P(A|B)$

c. Only the second pair: female and brown eyes. Females are no more or less likely to have brown eyes than are males.

MORE
ASSIGNMENT   *pp. 477–484*

Modeling: 2 and 3
Organizing: 1 and 2
Reflecting: 2 or 3*
Extending: 2, and choice of one*

When choice is indicated, it is important to leave the choice to the student.
NOTE: *It is best if Organizing tasks are discussed as a whole class after they have been assigned as homework.*

MORE   independent assignment

Modeling

1. a. $\left(\frac{1}{12}\right)\left(\frac{1}{12}\right) = \frac{1}{144}$

b. The computation in Part a assumes that the tires rotate independently. To verify this (many people believe otherwise), students could note the position of the valve stems on each of the two tires on one side of a car and see if the valve stems are at the same relative positions after a trip. This should be done many times and with different cars.

c. Responses may vary. Most students probably will think the man should have been issued a ticket. In fact, the judge said that 1 chance in 144 was reasonable doubt, and the man was acquitted.

Unit 7

b. Suppose you pick a high school student at random. For each of the pairs of events below, write the mathematical equality or inequality that applies:

$$P(A) = P(A|B), P(A) > P(A|B), \text{ or } P(A) < P(A|B).$$

■ A is the event that the student is male and B is the event that the student is over six feet tall.

■ A is the event that the student is female and B is the event that the student has brown eyes.

■ A is the event that the student is a member of the French club and B is the event that the student is taking a French class.

c. Which of the pairs of events in Part b is it safe to assume are independent? Explain your reasoning.

MORE
Modeling • Organizing • Reflecting • Extending

Modeling

1. If you completed Extending Task 1 on page 469, you are already familiar with the following famous Swedish trial: A parking officer had noted the position of the valve stems on the tires on one side of a car; upon returning later, the officer noted that the valve stems were still in the same position. The officer noted the position of the valve stems to the nearest "hour." For example, in the following picture, the valve stems are at 3:00 and at 10:00. The officer issued a ticket for overtime parking. However, the owner of the car claimed he had moved the car and returned to the same parking place.

a. Use the Multiplication Rule to estimate the probability that if a vehicle is moved, the valve stems return to the same position they had before the car was moved.

b. What assumption are you making? How can you find out if it is reasonable?

c. Do you think the man should have been issued a ticket? If you previously completed Extending Task 1 on page 469, compare your conclusions.

2. Suppose you are playing Monopoly and have been sent to jail. Recall that in Monopoly you can get out of jail by rolling doubles. If you don't roll doubles in three tries, you must pay $50 to get out of jail or use a "Get Out of Jail Free" card.

   a. What is the probability you will roll doubles and get out of jail on your first try?

   b. What is the probability you will not roll doubles on your first try and will roll doubles on your second try?

   c. What is the probability you will not roll doubles on your first try, will not roll doubles on your second try, and will roll doubles on your third try?

   d. What is the probability that you will get out of jail without having to pay $50 or use a card?

   e. What is the probability that you will have to pay $50 or use a card to get out of jail?

3. About 15.8% of the 97 million households in the United States watched Game 1 of the 1997 National Basketball Association championship between the Chicago Bulls and the Utah Jazz. About 15.1% watched the second game. (Source: *Facts on File* 57 (July 10, 1997):504.)

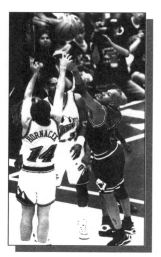

   a. Why isn't it reasonable to estimate that (0.158)(0.151) or approximately 2.4% of the U.S. households watched both Game 1 and Game 2?

   b. What would be a better estimate?

4. Genetics is the study of how characteristics such as freckles or tongue roll are passed from one generation to the next. The laws of inheritance were first understood by Gregor Mendel just over 100 years ago.

   a. How many people in your group can roll their tongues up from the sides into a U-shape?

   b. Each person has two genes, one from each parent, that determine whether he or she can roll his or her tongue. The gene for tongue-rolling dominates the gene for no tongue roll. What is the probability that a child will be able to roll his or her tongue into a U-shape, if each parent has exactly one tongue-rolling gene? Explain your solution method.

   c. Suppose one parent has two tongue-rolling genes and the other parent has exactly one tongue-rolling gene. What is the probability that their child will be able to roll his or her tongue? Explain your solution method.

2. **a.** $\frac{1}{6}$

    b. $\left(\frac{5}{6}\right)\left(\frac{1}{6}\right) = \frac{5}{36}$

    c. $\left(\frac{5}{6}\right)\left(\frac{5}{6}\right)\left(\frac{1}{6}\right) = \frac{25}{216}$

    d. $\frac{1}{6} + \frac{5}{36} + \frac{25}{216} = \frac{91}{216} \approx 0.421$

    e. $1 - 0.421 = 0.579$

3. **a.** It is not reasonable to do this computation because the two events are undoubtedly not independent. If, for example, we knew that a household watched the first game, our estimate of the probability that the household also watched the second game would be greater than 2.4%.

    b. A better, but not perfect, assumption is that it was pretty much the same households that watched both games. The estimate of the percentage of households who watched both games would then be about 15%.

4. **a.** Responses will vary, depending on the group.

    b. The model at the right shows that the child has $\frac{3}{4}$ probability of being able to roll his or her tongue.

    c. Since tongue rolling is a dominant characteristic, this probability will be 1.

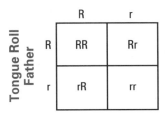

Tongue Roll Mother

Tongue Roll Father

	R	r
R	RR	Rr
r	rR	rr

Unit 7

Organizing

1. **a.** $P(A) = P(\text{doubles}) = \frac{6}{36}$

    $P(A|B) = P(\text{doubles}|\text{sum is 7}) = 0.$

    Not independent. It is impossible to have rolled doubles if the sum of the dice is seven.

   b. $P(A) = P(\text{head on second flip}) = \frac{1}{2}$

    $P(A|B) = P(\text{head on second flip}|\text{head on first flip}) = \frac{1}{2}$

    Independent. The results of the first flip have no influence on the results of the second flip.

   c. $P(A) = P(\text{Sunday}) = \frac{1}{7}$

    $P(A|B) = P(\text{Sunday}|\text{school day}) = 0.$

    Not independent. If the day is a school day, then it is not a Sunday.

2. **a.** The right half of the square represents the event that the first number is greater than 0.5. The upper half represents the event that the second number is greater than 0.5. The upper-right quarter represents the intersection of these two areas, that is, the event that both numbers are greater than 0.5.

   b. $\frac{1}{4}$

   c. $\frac{3}{4}$

3. **a.** $\frac{4}{100}$

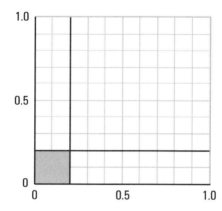

   b. Find the area of the intersection of the inequality $x + y < 1$ and the unit square having vertices (0, 0), (0, 1), (1, 1), and (1, 0). This gives a probability of 0.5. The equations of the lines are $x + y = 1$, $x = 0$, and $y = 0$.

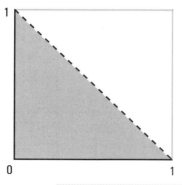

See additional Teaching Notes on page T533J.

Organizing

1. For each experiment below, find $P(A)$ and $P(A|B)$. Which of these pairs of events A and B are independent?

   a. The experiment is rolling a pair of dice once. Event A is getting doubles and event B is getting a sum of 7.

   b. The experiment is flipping a coin twice. Event A is getting a head on the second flip and event B is getting a head on the first flip.

   c. The experiment is picking a day in the year at random. Event A is getting a Sunday and event B is getting a school day.

2. If you select two random numbers that are both between 0 and 1, what is the probability that they are both greater than 0.5? You can think geometrically about this kind of problem, as shown at the right.

   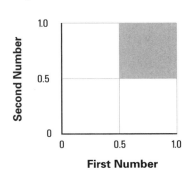

   a. Explain how the shaded region represents the event that both numbers are greater than 0.5.

   b. What is the probability that both numbers are greater than 0.5?

   c. What is the probability that at least one of the numbers is greater than 0.5?

3. Make and analyze an area model to answer the following questions.

   a. If you select two random numbers that are both between 0 and 1, what is the probability that they are both less than 0.2?

   b. If you select two random numbers that are both between 0 and 1, what is the probability that their sum is less than 1? What are the equations of the lines that border the region that represents this event?

   c. If you select two random numbers that are both between 0 and 1, what is the probability that their sum is less than 0.3? What are the equations of the lines that border the region?

   d. Al and Bill will both call Briana at a random time during their lunch hour, from 12:00 until 1:00. Each will talk to Briana for 10 minutes. What is the probability that one of them is talking to Briana when the other calls?

   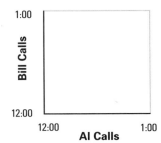

4. Consider the experiment of rolling two dice. Give examples of events *A* and *B* in which the following are true:

a. $P(A) > P(A|B)$

b. $P(A) = P(A|B)$

c. $P(A) < P(A|B)$

5. Look over the probabilities you calculated in Lessons 1 and 2. If the probability that an event *A* will occur is *p* (that is, $P(A) = p$), what is the probability that the event will not occur, $P(\text{not } A)$? Explain why your conclusion makes sense.

Reflecting

1. April and May are playing Monopoly and are both in jail. April has tried twice to roll doubles and failed both times. May has tried only once, and she also was unsuccessful. Who has the better chance of rolling doubles on her next turn? Explain your reasoning.

2. In which of the following examples do you think it is reasonable to assume the events are independent?

a. The experiment is rolling a pair of dice twice in a row. The first event is not getting doubles on the first roll. The second event is getting doubles on the second roll.

b. The experiment is selecting two people at random. The first event is the first person pouring shampoo directly onto his or her hair. The second event is the second person pouring shampoo directly onto his or her hair.

c. The experiment is selecting two people at random. The first event is the first person putting catsup directly on his or her fries. The second event is the second person putting catsup directly on his or her fries.

d. The experiment is selecting a person at random. The first event is getting a person with voice (singing) training. The second event is getting a person who can play a musical instrument.

e. The experiment is waiting for the results of next year's sports championships. The first event is the Celtics winning the NBA championship. The second event is the Reds winning the World Series.

4. Examples may vary. One possibility for each situation is provided here.
    a. Let event A be rolling doubles and event B be getting a sum of seven. Then $P(A) = \frac{6}{36}$ while $P(A|B) = 0$.
    b. Let event A be getting a 1 on the first die and event B be getting a sum of seven. Then $P(A) = \frac{6}{36}$ and $P(A|B) = \frac{1}{6}$.
    c. Let event A be getting a sum of eight and event B be getting doubles. Then $P(A) = \frac{5}{36}$ while $P(A|B) = \frac{1}{6}$.

5. If $P(A) = p$, then $P(\text{not } A) = 1 - p$. This makes sense since either A occurs or it doesn't, and so $P(A) + P(\text{not } A) = 1$. Thus $P(\text{not } A) = 1 - P(A) = 1 - p$.

Reflecting

1. Both April and May have the same probability of rolling doubles: $\frac{6}{36}$ or $\frac{1}{6}$. The rolls of the dice are independent.
2. a. Independent
    b. Independent
    c. Independent
    d. Not independent
        It should seem reasonable to students that someone with musical training in voice would also have training in another instrument.
    e. Independent

Unit 7

2. f. It may not occur to students, but we can't assume the events are independent. It may well be that a person who puts catsup directly on fries just likes to pour liquids on top of things and so may be more likely than other people to put shampoo directly on his or her head.

g. Not independent

Best friends tend to do things together. If we find that the first friend went to the football game, it increases the probability that the second friend went.

3. Whenever events A and B are independent, $P(A) = P(A|B)$. Specific examples will vary but should indicate that students are comparing $P(A)$ and $P(A|B)$.

NOTE: Although the 90% and 72% figures were found from a survey of a random sample of Americans, in Reflecting Task 4 assume these percentages hold for the entire population of married Americans.

---

4. Jesse is not correct. He shouldn't multiply the probabilities. He cannot *assume* that the event that the husband would marry the same wife and the event that the wife would marry the same husband are independent. If, for example, we knew that the husband would marry the same wife, our estimate of the probability that the wife would marry the same husband would be higher than 0.72. Since the husband is happy, it is more likely the wife is too. In symbols, P(wife would marry same husband) $<$ P(wife would marry same husband|husband would marry same wife).

It is not always clear when two events are independent. Students should leave this lesson with a healthy caution for assuming independence. With this activity, students may need to refer to the fact that if two events A and B are independent, then $P(A|B) = P(A)$. We are told that P(wife would marry same husband) $= 0.72$. Ask students if P(wife would marry same husband|husband would marry same wife) $= 0.72$ also. They should see that it is reasonable to think it would be higher than 0.72.

5. Calling the Multiplication Rule the "And Rule" might help students remember that it is used when the events are independent and we want to find the probability that both A **and** B occur. However, some students may prefer the prompt that they should multiply probabilities (as opposed to, for example, adding them).

Unit 7

f. The experiment is selecting a person at random. The first event is getting a person who puts catsup directly on his or her fries. The second event is getting a person who puts shampoo directly on his or her hair.

g. The experiment is selecting a pair of best friends at random from a high school. The first event is the first friend attending the last football game. The second event is the second friend attending the last football game.

3. The idea of independent events can be somewhat difficult to understand. Suppose that someone in your class has asked you to explain it. Write an explanation of the difference between independent events and dependent events. Include examples that would interest students in your high school.

4. Jesse read a survey that said that 90% of American husbands would marry the same woman again, and 72% of American wives would marry the same man again. He computed the probability that a married couple would marry each other again as follows:

P(husband would marry same wife and wife would marry same husband)

  = P(husband would marry same wife) · P(wife would marry same husband)

  = $(0.90)(0.72)$

  = 0.648

Is Jesse correct? Explain your reasoning.

5. Sometimes the Multiplication Rule is called the "And Rule" by students. What do you see as possible advantages and disadvantages of this alternate name?

Extending

1. In Investigation 2 of Lesson 1, three games were described for Activity 2. The rules are reproduced below. To play the games, you will need a bag with one red and one yellow marker in it and some extra red and yellow markers.

In each game, the goal is to draw a red marker. When a red marker is drawn, the game stops and the player's score is the number of draws required. Each player starts a turn with one red and one yellow marker in the bag. The winner of the game is the person with the smallest score.

Game A: Draw until you get a red marker. Replace the marker after each draw. In addition, each time you draw a yellow marker, you must add another yellow marker to the bag before drawing again.

Game B: Draw until you get a red marker. Replace the marker after each draw. In addition, each time you draw a yellow marker, you must add a red marker to the bag before drawing again.

Game C: Draw until you get a red marker. Replace the marker after each draw, but don't add any other markers to the bag. (There are always the original two markers in the bag.)

a. For Game C, complete a probability distribution table like the one below.

Game C

Number of Draws to Get First Red	Probability
1	
2	
3	
4	
5 or more	

b. Complete a similar table for Game A.

c. Finally, complete a similar table for Game B.

d. What is the probability that you will draw a red in two draws or fewer if you are playing Game A? Game B? Game C?

e. Recall that we are considering an event in the upper 5% of a waiting-time distribution to be a rare event. Has a rare event happened if it takes 5 or more draws for Game A? For Game B? For Game C?

f. Write a report giving a complete analysis of the three games.

2. If events A and B are not independent, then the following are true.

$$P(A \text{ and } B) = P(A) \cdot P(B|A)$$
$$\text{and}$$
$$P(A \text{ and } B) = P(B) \cdot P(A|B)$$

a. Show that this rule is true for each of the following cases.

- The experiment is rolling a pair of dice once. Event A is rolling doubles. Event B is getting a sum of 8.

- The experiment is rolling a pair of dice once. Event A is rolling doubles. Event B is getting a sum of 7.

b. Is this rule true even if A and B are independent? Explain.

Extending

1. **a.** Game C

Number of Draws to Get First Red	Probability
1	$\frac{1}{2} = 0.5$
2	$\left(\frac{1}{2}\right)\left(\frac{1}{2}\right) = 0.25$
3	$\left(\frac{1}{2}\right)^2\left(\frac{1}{2}\right) = 0.125$
4	$\left(\frac{1}{2}\right)^3\left(\frac{1}{2}\right) = 0.0625$
5 or more	$1 - (0.5 + 0.25 + 0.125 + 0.0625) = 0.0625$

b. Game A

Number of Draws to Get First Red	Probability
1	$\frac{1}{2} = 0.5$
2	$\left(\frac{1}{2}\right)\left(\frac{1}{3}\right) \approx 0.1667$
3	$\left(\frac{1}{2}\right)\left(\frac{2}{3}\right)\left(\frac{1}{4}\right) \approx 0.0833$
4	$\left(\frac{1}{2}\right)\left(\frac{2}{3}\right)\left(\frac{3}{4}\right)\left(\frac{1}{5}\right) = 0.05$
5 or more	0.20

c. Game B

Number of Draws to Get First Red	Probability
1	$\frac{1}{2} = 0.5$
2	$\left(\frac{1}{2}\right)\left(\frac{2}{3}\right) \approx 0.3333$
3	$\left(\frac{1}{2}\right)\left(\frac{1}{3}\right)\left(\frac{3}{4}\right) = 0.125$
4	$\left(\frac{1}{2}\right)\left(\frac{1}{3}\right)\left(\frac{1}{4}\right)\left(\frac{4}{5}\right) \approx 0.0333$
5 or more	0.0083

d. Game A: 0.6667   Game B: 0.8333   Game C: 0.75

e. A rare event has happened only for Game B.

f. Reports will vary. You may want to ask students to include graphs of the probability distributions for the three games.

2. **a.** ■ $P(\text{doubles and sum 8}) = \frac{1}{36}$

$P(\text{doubles}) \cdot P(\text{sum 8|doubles}) = \frac{6}{36} \cdot \frac{1}{6} = \frac{1}{36}$

$P(\text{sum 8}) \cdot P(\text{doubles|sum 8}) = \frac{5}{36} \cdot \frac{1}{5} = \frac{1}{36}$

■ $P(\text{doubles and sum 7}) = 0$

$P(\text{doubles}) \cdot P(\text{sum 7|doubles}) = \frac{6}{36} \cdot \frac{0}{6} = 0$

$P(\text{sum 7}) \cdot P(\text{doubles|sum 7}) = \frac{6}{36} \cdot \frac{0}{6} = 0$

b. Yes. If A and B are independent, then $P(B|A) = P(B)$; so, $P(A \text{ and } B) = P(A) \cdot P(B|A) = P(A) \cdot P(B)$, which is our Multiplication Rule for independent events. Similarly, $P(A|B) = P(A)$; so, $P(A \text{ and } B) = P(B) \cdot P(A|B) = P(B) \cdot P(A)$.

Unit 7

3. a. There are three paths through the tree that give two girls and a boy: *GGB, GBG,* and *BGG*. Their probabilities are (0.49)(0.49)(0.51), (0.49)(0.51)(0.49), and (0.51)(0.49)(0.49). The probability of two girls and a boy is $3(0.49)^2(0.51)$ or approximately 0.367.

b.

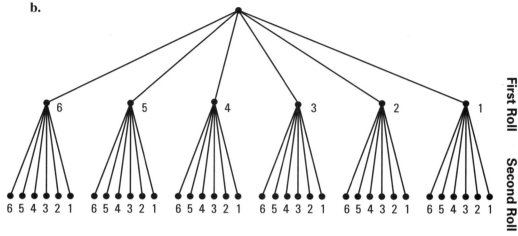

The probability of getting the same number twice is $\frac{6}{36}$.

c.

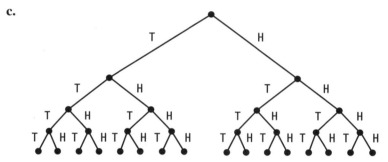

This tree has six paths with exactly two heads: *HHTT, HTHT, HTTH, THHT, THTH,* and *TTHH*. The probability of exactly two heads is $\frac{6}{16}$.

d. This tree has four branches (bird of paradise, tiger, elephant, and crocodile) for each of the three purchases. The probability that all three stickers will be different is $\frac{24}{64}$.

3. Tree graphs are a way of organizing all possible sequences of outcomes. For example, the tree graph below shows all possible families of exactly three children (with no twins or triplets). Each "G" means a girl was born, and each "B" means a boy was born. In the United States, the probability that a girl is born is approximately 49%.

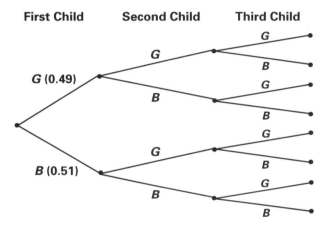

a. Use the graph to find the probability that a family of three children will consist of two girls and a boy (not necessarily born in that order).

b. Make a tree graph that shows all possible outcomes if you roll a die twice and each time read the number on top. What is the probability you will get the same number twice?

c. Make a tree graph that shows all possible outcomes if you flip a coin four times. What is the probability you will get exactly two heads?

d. Make a tree graph that shows all possible outcomes if you buy three boxes of Kellogg's® Cocoa Krispies® cereal, each containing a sticker showing one of the following: a bird of paradise, a tiger, an African elephant, and a crocodile. What is the probability you will get three different stickers?

4. In the Game of LIFE®, there are several PAY DAY spaces throughout the board. On each turn in this game, the player spins a spinner like the one below and moves the indicated number of spaces around the board.

 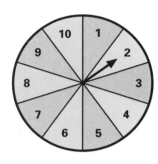

Suppose you are 5 spaces away from the next PAY DAY on the game board. You could land on the space by spinning a 5 on your next turn. Another way to land on the space is by spinning a 1 on your next turn, a 3 on the following turn, and a 1 on the turn after that.

a. Make a tree graph that shows all possible sequences of spins that would get you to this PAY DAY. For example, one sequence of spins would be 1, 3, 1. Another would be 1, 1, 3.

b. What is the probability that you will land on this PAY DAY space on your trip around the board?

4. a.

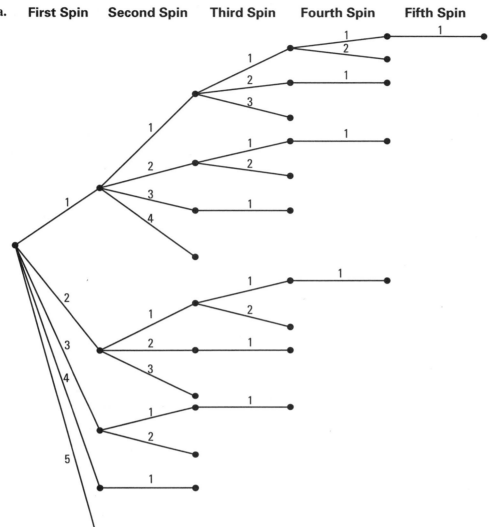

First Spin Second Spin Third Spin Fourth Spin Fifth Spin

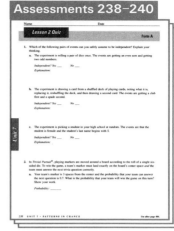
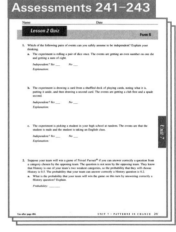
b. In the tree, there is one path that is five segments long, four paths that are four segments long, six paths that are three segments long, four paths that are two segments long, and one path that is one segment long. Each spin is independent of the previous spins, so, for example, any particular path of length 4 has a probability of $(0.1)(0.1)(0.1)(0.1)$ or $(0.1)^4$. To find the overall probability, we need to sum the probabilities of the above paths. Thus the probability of landing on that PAY DAY space is $(0.1)^5 + 4(0.1)^4 + 6(0.1)^3 + 4(0.1)^2 + (0.1)$ or 0.14641.

See Assessment Resources, pages 238–243.

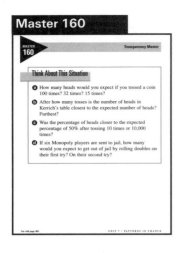

Lesson 3 *Probability Distributions*

LESSON OVERVIEW   In Lesson 1, students constructed frequency distributions by simulation and experimentation. In this lesson, students will construct a waiting-time distribution theoretically.

Students are nearing the culmination of a long development of an important idea, which finally is completed in Lesson 4. Again, it helps if you use the new lesson launch to remind students that the big question in this unit has been "On average, how long do we have to wait until we roll doubles?" In Lesson 2, students found a way to determine the theoretical probability of a triple event, such as *P*(did not get doubles, did not get doubles, and then did get doubles). You may wish to discuss how that is related to finding the probability of different waiting times. Most students are not likely to have a complete answer for this question, but some may begin to see that we can now get theoretical answers for getting doubles for the first time on the second try, or the third try, etc. Focus should remain on the main waiting-time question as students investigate the necessary developmental details along the way.

Correct use of vocabulary in probability is important, yet it may not come naturally to students. In probability, the *expected value* is a single, theoretical number. For example, if you flip a coin 5 times, you might say in ordinary speech that you expect to get 2 or 3 heads, meaning that you think those outcomes are likely to happen. However, in mathematics, you should say that you expect to get 2.5 heads because "on the average" that is the number of heads you will get. In this lesson, the vocabulary words *expectation* and *average* are used interchangeably. (Later *fair* is added.) It is important to emphasize this strict use of the word *expect* in probability. Some students may find this vocabulary awkward. It is helpful if you encourage them to use the words in their explanations.

Lesson Objectives

- To construct the theoretical frequency distribution for a waiting-time situation
- To construct the probability distribution for a waiting-time situation
- To understand how the word *expect* is used in probability

LAUNCH   full-class discussion

Think About This Situation

See Teaching Master 160.

ⓐ 50, 16, and 7.5. We would expect to get heads on half of our tosses, no matter how many times we toss the coin. Some students may say 7 or 8 heads for 15 tosses. Encourage them to settle on the average number of heads as a definition of *expect*.

See additional Teaching Notes on page T533K.

Lesson 3

Probability Distributions

While a prisoner of war during World War II, J. E. Kerrich conducted an experiment in which he flipped a coin 10,000 times and kept a record of the outcomes. A portion of the results is given in the table below.

Number of Tosses	Number of Heads
10	4
50	25
100	44
500	255
1,000	502
5,000	2,533
10,000	5,067

Source: J. F. Kerrich. *An Experimental Introduction to the Theory of Probability*. Copenhagen: J. Jorgenson and Co., 1964.

Think About This Situation

a How many heads would you expect if you tossed a coin 100 times? 32 times? 15 times?

b After how many tosses is the number of heads in Kerrich's table closest to the expected number of heads? Furthest?

c Was the percentage of heads closer to the expected percentage of 50% after tossing 10 times or 10,000 times?

d If six Monopoly players are sent to jail, how many would you expect to get out of jail by rolling doubles on their first try? On their second try?

INVESTIGATION 1 ► Theoretical Waiting-Time Distributions

In Lesson 1 you explored waiting-time distributions by conducting experiments and simulations. As you probably noticed, two different groups could get quite different histograms when they constructed them from simulations. The two groups then would have different estimates of a probability. In this investigation, you will construct waiting-time distributions theoretically, so everyone should get the same answers to the probability questions related to these distributions.

If you flip a fair coin 10 times, you *expect* to get 5 heads. However, you don't get 5 heads each time you flip a fair coin 10 times. Sometimes you get fewer, as Kerrich did; sometimes you get more. In the long run, however, the average number of heads will be 5.

Expectation is another word for the *theoretical average*. For example, if you flip a coin 5 times, you might say in ordinary language that you expect to get 2 or 3 heads. However, in mathematics you should say that you expect to get 2.5 heads, because *on the average* that is the number of heads you will get.

1. Imagine 36 students are playing modified Monopoly in a class tournament. All are sent to jail. A student must roll doubles to get out of jail. (There is no other way out.)

   a. How many of the 36 students do you expect to get out of jail by rolling doubles on the first try? (Remember that the word "expect" has a mathematical meaning.) How many students do you expect to remain in jail?

   b. How many of the remaining students do you expect to get out of jail on the second try? How many students do you expect to remain in jail then?

   c. How many of the remaining students do you expect to get out of jail on the third try? How many students do you expect to remain in jail then?

   d. Complete a table like the one at the top of the next page. Round numbers to the nearest hundredth. The first three lines should agree with your answers to Parts a–c.

INVESTIGATION 1 ▶ Theoretical Waiting-Time Distributions

Master 161

In this investigation, students will learn to construct a histogram of the theoretical frequencies for a waiting-time situation. To do this, students will use the fact that if you perform a binomial experiment n times and the probability of a success is p, then you expect np successes. For example, if you flip a coin 10 times, you expect 10(0.5) or 5 heads. Most people believe this intuitively. However, students may be uncomfortable with the statement that if you flip a coin 15 times, you expect 15(0.5) or 7.5 heads. You may have to remind them several times that "expect" means "on the average."

You may want to start the table in Activity 1 as a large group. (See Teaching Master 161.) In that way, you can be sure that students are all thinking about this theoretically, taking $\frac{1}{6}$ of the current "in jail" number to get doubles on the next try. They also should be recording decimal answers. Students then should be able to complete Activities 1–4 independently.

As you circulate, you might ask students what pattern they see in the table and if they have seen this pattern before. (Some may need help to see that each entry is $\frac{5}{6}$ of the last. Some may realize this is like an exponential decay pattern, which they have seen in Course 2.) Once they identify the pattern, you could ask why the factor $\frac{5}{6}$ makes sense in this situation. If some groups finish earlier than others, you might ask them to take the table a little further and recompute the average wait time.

After all students have completed Activities 1–4, it may be helpful to have a full-class discussion to be sure that everyone has a chance to share insights about the shape of the distribution and the relationship between the heights of the columns. Some students may need to be reminded how to calculate the average of a histogram. Students can then complete Activity 5.

1. **See Teaching Master 161.**

   a. $36\left(\frac{1}{6}\right) = 6$; 6 students get out of jail.

   $36 - 6 = 30$; 30 students are left in jail.

   b. $30\left(\frac{1}{6}\right) = 5$; 5 students get out of jail.

   25 students are left in jail.

   c. $25\left(\frac{1}{6}\right) \approx 4.17$; 4.17 students get out of jail.

   20.83 students are left in jail.

See additional Teaching Notes on page T533K.

Unit 7

1. **e.** In the first column, $NEXT = NOW + 1$.

   In the second column, $NEXT = \frac{5}{6} NOW$.

   In the third column, $NEXT = \frac{5}{6} NOW$.

2. **a.** About 4.04 students

   b. The expected number of students who need 13 or more rolls to be released is 4.04. See table from Activity 1, Part d on page T533K.

   c. About 11.22%

   d. $10,000(0.1122) = 1,122$ people

3.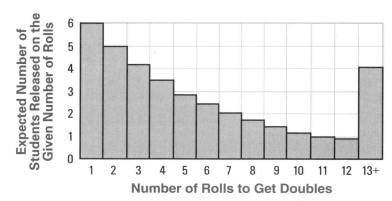

   a. This histogram is probably more "smooth" and less irregular looking than the histogram constructed following the simulation in Lesson 1, but the two histograms should have the same overall shape.

   b. Except for the 13 or more bar, each bar is $\frac{5}{6}$ of the height of the bar to its left. This is a crucial question. You may wish to have the full class discuss why this pattern occurs: with each round, there are $\frac{5}{6}$ as many students because $\frac{1}{6}$ of the students roll doubles in a round.

   c. The average is about 6 rolls.

   d. In a table such as the following,

   $$\text{average number of rolls per plays} = \frac{\text{sum of third column}}{\text{number of players}}.$$

   If students use 13 for the 13 or more row, they will get 5.44 for the average. You may want to discuss how the mean is affected when 13 is used to represent 13 or more. If students take the table further, they will get answers that more closely approximate the theoretical answer of 6.

Number of Rolls to Get Doubles	Expected Number of Students Released on the Given Number of Rolls	Total Number of Rolls to Get Doubles
1	6	6
2	5	10
3	4.17	12.51
⋮	⋮	⋮
13	4.04	52.52

4. The shape of the histogram would be exactly the same. The scale along the vertical axis would be different. The average still would be 6 rolls to get out of jail.

Rolling Dice to Get Doubles

Number of Rolls to Get Doubles	Expected Number of Students Released on the Given Number of Rolls	Expected Number of Students Still in Jail
1		
2		
3		
4		
5		
6		
7		
8		
9		
10		
11		
12		

e. What patterns of change do you see in this table? If possible, describe each pattern using the idea of *NOW* and *NEXT*.

The table you created shows a **theoretical distribution**. The table never really can be completed, however, as the rows should be continued indefinitely.

2. a. How many of the 36 students do you expect to be in jail after 12 tries?

b. Add a "13 or more" row to your table and write the expected number of students in the appropriate place.

c. What percentage of the 36 students do you expect to be in jail after 12 tries to roll doubles?

d. If you had started with 10,000 people instead of 36, how many of them would you expect to remain in jail after 12 tries to roll doubles?

3. Make a histogram of the "expected number of students released on the given number of rolls" from the frequency table you constructed in Activity 1.

a. Compare this histogram to the one you constructed following your class's simulation of this situation in Activity 1 of the first investigation from Lesson 1 (page 457–458).

b. Examine your histogram of the theoretical distribution. The height of each bar is what proportion of the height of the bar to its left?

c. Using your histogram, estimate the average of the distribution.

d. Calculate the average number of rolls of the dice it takes to get doubles. Compare your calculated average to your estimate in Part c.

4. If there were 1,000 people (rather than 36) who had been sent to jail in Activity 1, how would the histogram change? How would the average change?

Unit 7

5. Thirty percent of "M&M's"® Plain Chocolate Candies are brown. Suppose each of 1,000 students removes candies one at a time from a large bag until he or she gets a brown one.

   a. How many students do you expect to get a brown candy on the first try?

   b. Make a table like the one in Activity 1. Give the table 10 rows, and complete each row.

   c. How many of the 1,000 students do you expect to need 11 or more trials to get a brown candy?

   d. Make a histogram of the distribution shown in your table.

   e. The height of each bar of your histogram is what fraction of the height of the bar to its left?

   f. Estimate the average number of draws to get a brown candy from your histogram. Then calculate the average using an appropriate formula.

   ## Checkpoint

   a How is the word "expect" used differently in mathematics than in everyday life?

   b Suppose the probability of an event is p. How many times would you expect this event to happen in a series of n independent trials?

   c Suppose the probability of an event is p and you have made a histogram of the waiting-time distribution for the event. How is the height of each bar of the histogram related to the height of the bar to its left?

   Be prepared to share your group's ideas with the whole class.

   ## ▶On Your Own

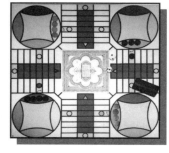

   a. In the game of Parcheesi®, based on the Indian game pachisi, a player cannot move a pawn for the first time until he or she rolls a five with a pair of dice. The five may be on either die, or the five may be the sum of both dice. What is the probability a player can move a pawn on the first roll of the dice?

   b. Approximately half of all high school students are girls. Suppose you select 45 high school students at random.

   - How many do you expect to be girls?
   - How many do you expect to be boys?

Master 162

5. **a.** 300

b.

Number of Candies Drawn to Get a Brown One	Expected Number of Students
1	300
2	210
3	147
4	102.9
5	72.03
6	50.42
7	35.29
8	24.71
9	17.29
10	12.11

c. The table accounts for 971.75 students, so 28.25 will need 11 or more draws.

d.

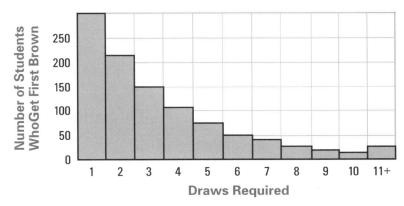

e. 0.7

   This is true for all but the last bar if students include the "11+" bar. The "11+" bar does not follow the same pattern because it is the sum of many different outcomes.

f. A bit more than 3 is a good estimate. The theoretical answer is $3\frac{1}{3}$.

SHARE AND SUMMARIZE   full-class discussion

Checkpoint

See Teaching Master 162.

ⓐ In mathematics, an expected value is an average that might not be attainable in practice. For example, if you ask someone, "If you flip a coin five times, how many heads would you expect?" they would likely say "two or three." A mathematician would say "two and a half."

See additional Teaching Notes on page T533L.

CONSTRUCTING A MATH TOOLKIT: Students should describe in their Math Toolkits how to construct and interpret a histogram for a theoretical waiting-time distribution when given the number of trials and the probability of the event happening.

Unit 7

Modeling: 1, 3, and choice of
             one*
Organizing: 1 and 4
Reflecting: Choose two*
Extending: 2 and 4

*When choice is indicated, it is important
to leave the choice to the student.*
NOTE: *It is best if Organizing tasks are discussed as a whole class after they have
been assigned as homework.*

MORE independent assignment

Modeling

1. **a.** Rain: 14(0.4) = 5.6 days
        No rain: 14(0.6) = 8.4 days or 14 − 5.6 = 8.4 days
    b. Yes. Although we expect 10 days of rain, we know we won't always get exactly that
        many. It's like flipping a fair coin 20 times. We wouldn't be surprised at all to get
        9 heads.

2. To have Tay-Sachs disease, a Jewish baby must inherit one Tay-Sachs gene from the moth-
    er and one from the father. (This problem assumes both parents are Jewish.) The proba-
    bility that the mother is a carrier is $\frac{1}{30}$, and the probability that a carrier passes on the Tay-
    Sachs gene is $\frac{1}{2}$. So the probability the baby that gets a Tay-Sachs gene from the mother
    is $\frac{1}{30} \cdot \frac{1}{2}$ or $\frac{1}{60}$. The probability is the same for the father. The probability that the baby gets
    a Tay-Sachs gene from both parents is $\frac{1}{60} \cdot \frac{1}{60}$ or $\frac{1}{3,600}$.

3. **a.**

Number of Boxes Needed to Get a Tiger Sticker	Expected Number of People
1	9
2	6.75
3	5.06
4	3.80
5	2.85
6	2.14
7	1.60
8	1.20
9	0.90
10	0.68
11	0.51
12 or more	1.51

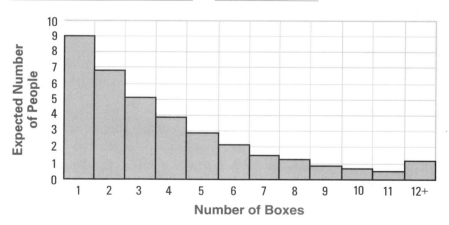

b. We expect 6.4 people will need to purchase more than six boxes.
c. The theoretical average is 4. Students' answers will likely be slightly less than this.

MORE

Modeling

1. If there is a 40% chance of rain today, it means that it rained on 40% of the days in the past that had weather conditions similar to those today.

   a. On 14 different days, the weather report says there is a 40% chance of rain. On how many of these days do you expect it to rain? On how many of these days do you expect it not to rain?

   b. On 20 different days, the weather report says there is a 50% chance of rain. It actually rained on 9 of those days. Do you think the meteorologist did a good job of predicting rain? Explain.

2. Tay-Sachs disease results when a baby inherits the Tay-Sachs gene from both parents. (A person who can pass the gene to the next generation is called a carrier.) Since the disease results in early death, no adults carry two Tay-Sachs genes. A college biology textbook says that "about 1 in 30 American Jews is a carrier, which would result in about 1 Tay-Sachs child in 3600 Jewish births." (Source: Audesirk, G. and T. *Biology: Life on Earth*. New York: Macmillan, 1989.) Explain how the 1 in 3600 figure was computed.

3. In each Kellogg's® Cocoa Krispies® cereal box, there was a sticker of either a bird of paradise, a tiger, an African elephant, or a crocodile. Assume that the stickers were placed randomly into the boxes. Thirty-six people are buying boxes, each trying to get a tiger.

   a. Make a theoretical waiting-time distribution table and histogram of the number of boxes purchased to get a tiger sticker. Place the numbers 1 to 11 in your table followed by a "12 or more" row.

   b. How many of these people do you expect would need to purchase more than six boxes of the cereal?

   c. On the average, how many boxes of cereal need to be purchased to get a tiger sticker?

4. Imagine 1,024 students in a school auditorium all standing up. Each student flips a coin. The students who get heads on this flip sit down. Each student who remains standing flips a coin a second time. The students who get heads on this flip sit down. The coin flips continue until all students are seated.

   a. Make a frequency table that shows what you expect to happen in this experiment.

   b. Make a histogram from your frequency table.

   c. What is the average number of flips required until a student sits down?

   d. What is the probability that it will take two flips or fewer to get a head? What is the probability that it will take more than two flips?

   e. How many times would a student have to toss the coin without getting a head before you would say a rare event has occurred?

   f. How many rare events do you expect to occur among the 1,024 students?

5. The player with the highest field goal percentage in the history of the National Basketball Association (NBA) is Artis Gilmore. In his career in the NBA, Gilmore attempted 9,570 field goals and made 5,732 of them.

   a. What was Gilmore's field goal percentage?

   b. During a typical game, Gilmore might attempt 25 field goals. In a typical game, how many field goals would you expect Gilmore to make?

   The NBA player with the highest lifetime free throw percentage is Rick Barry. Barry had a free throw "percentage" of 0.900. He made a total of 3,818 free throws.

   c. Why do you think the word *percentage* is in quotation marks above?

   d. How many free throws did Barry attempt?

   e. How many free throws would you expect Barry to make in 50 attempts?

   f. Write an equation that relates the number of free throws T expected for a player who makes A attempts and whose free throw percentage is p.

4. a.

Number of Flips to Get First Head	Number of Students	Number of Flips to Get First Head	Number of Students
1	512	7	8
2	256	8	4
3	128	9	2
4	64	10	1
5	32	11 or more	1
6	16		

b.

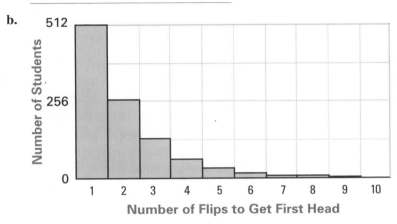

c. 2

d. Two flips or fewer: 0.75; more than two flips: 0.25

e. 6 or more

(In cases like this in which the upper 5% of the distribution falls between two numbers, pick the one so that fewer than 5% of the events will be classified as rare rather than the one in which more than 5% will be classified as rare. When an event is classified as rare, it often means that some future action is to be taken as a result. This may include special study of the event to establish if it belongs to the population described. Thus, it is usually better to identify too few events as rare rather than too many.)

f. We have defined a rare event of a waiting-time distribution as one that lies in the upper 5%. So ideally, expect 5% of the 1,024 students, or 51.2 students, to be in the upper 5% of the distribution.

However, as we saw in Part e, we cannot cut off exactly 5% of the distribution, and so we had to classify "6 or more" as rare. The expected number of students who get "6 or more" is about 32.

5. a. $\frac{5,732}{9,570} \approx 0.599$ or 59.9%

b. $25(0.599) \approx 14.974$ field goals, assuming the attempts are independent.

c. The reported number is a proportion, not a percentage. To get a true percentage, multiply the number by 100%.

d. 4,242 free throws

e. $50(0.900) = 45$ free throws

f. $T = Ap$

Organizing

1. **a.** Note that students may not be able to construct this box plot on their calculators or computer software, so this may be a good time to review constructing box plots by hand from the five-number summary: minimum, first quartile, median, third quartile, and maximum.

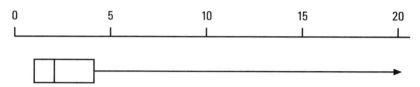

   b. 510 students need only one or two draws. The median number of draws is 2 candies.

   c. Both the box plot and histogram are skewed right. The box plot has no lower whisker and a very long upper whisker, showing how strongly skewed the distribution is.

2. The mean might be used if we were playing a game and wanted to know the average number of games we could expect to play before we won. The median gives different information. It tells us that half the time we will wait longer than the median and half the time we will wait less time than the median for our first win.

3. A waiting-time distribution will not have a line of symmetry because the distribution is skewed right.

4. **a.**

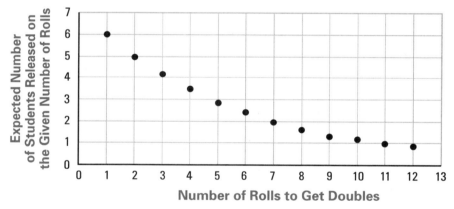

   b. The best algebraic model will be an exponential equation. The exponential equation that passes through these points is $y = 7.2\left(\frac{5}{6}\right)^x$, where $x = 1, 2, 3, \ldots$.

   c. $NEXT = \frac{5}{6} \times NOW$

See additional Teaching Notes on page T533M.

Organizing

1. **a.** Make a box plot for the waiting-time distribution for a brown candy in Activity 5 of Investigation 1 (page 488).

   b. What is the median number of candies drawn to get the first brown one?

   c. How does the shape of the box plot reflect the shape of the histogram? In which direction is the distribution skewed?

2. When would the mean be a good measure of the center of a waiting-time distribution? When would the median be a good measure?

3. Explain why the histogram of a waiting-time distribution does not have line symmetry.

4. Refer to Activity 1 of Investigation 1 for this task.

   a. Make a scatterplot of the (*number of rolls to get doubles, expected number of students who get out of jail on this roll*) data.

   b. Find an algebraic model of the form "$y = \ldots$" that is a good fit for these data.

   c. Let *NOW* be the number of people who are expected to get doubles on a roll, and let *NEXT* be the number of people who are expected to get doubles on the next roll. Write an equation relating *NOW* and *NEXT*.

5. Make a box plot for your distribution from Modeling Task 3 (getting a tiger sticker). Using the same number line, make box plots for the distribution from Modeling Task 4 and for the distribution from Activities 1 and 2 (rolling doubles) of Investigation 1. Write a few sentences about what you can learn about waiting-time distributions from examining these box plots.

Reflecting

1. It is quite common for a person's first guess about a probabilistic situation to be wrong. Part of learning probability is learning to be wary of your first reaction and learning how to check whether your first reaction is correct. What have you found most surprising so far in this unit?

2. List some businesses or jobs in which the manager should be interested in waiting-time distributions.

3. Marina and Jamie are playing a game in which the first person to roll doubles wins. Marina has had 10 turns and hasn't rolled doubles yet. Marina says, "I'm due to get doubles on my next roll."

   a. Explain what Marina means by this statement.

   b. Is Marina correct? Why or why not?

   c. Design an experiment to show Marina that she is no more likely to roll doubles on her 11th roll than she was on her 1st roll.

LESSON 3 • PROBABILITY DISTRIBUTIONS   491

Unit 7

4. Board games involving chance have a long history of providing recreation for people from many different cultures.

   a. Investigate the history of Backgammon, Parcheesi, Senet (an Egyptian game), or a similar game that you have played with your family or friends.

   b. Review the rules of the game.

   c. Write several questions about the probabilities involved in the game.

   d. Answer one of your questions either theoretically or by using a simulation to estimate the probability.

Extending

1. What are some characteristics that theoretical waiting-time distributions for independent trials have in common?

2. In this task you will find the average of another type of frequency distribution. This distribution is called a **binomial distribution**. "Binomial" means "having two names."

   On each flip of a coin, you can describe the outcome using one of two names: "heads" or "tails." In a waiting-time distribution, you might count the *number of trials* until you get the first head. In a binomial distribution, you would count the *number of heads* in a fixed number of independent trials.

   a. Flip eleven coins and count the number of heads. Add the result to a copy of the frequency table below.

Number of Heads	Frequency
0	1
1	0
2	4
3	5
4	16
5	18
6	27
7	15
8	5
9	3
10	1
11	0
Total	

4. One source of information about board games is *Hoyle's Rules of Games*, edited by Albert
   H. Morehead and Geoffrey Mott-Smith (Chicago: Times-Mirror, 1963).

Extending

1. The bars of the histograms get shorter from left to right. Each bar is $(1 - p)$ times the
   height of the previous bar. The curved shape is the same in each distribution. The number of bars is infinite in each waiting-time distribution.

2. **a.** Adjustments to frequency table will vary, depending on students' coin flips.

Unit 7

2. **b.** Frequency tables will vary. It makes no difference if one coin is flipped eleven times and the number of heads counted or if eleven coins are flipped once and the number of heads counted.

c. The histogram for the distribution of the 95 trials given in the student text follows. Students will add the results of their five trials to it.

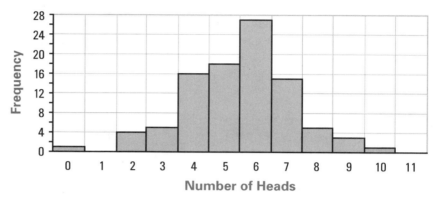

d. The binomial distribution is approximately normal. It is highest in the middle and tapers off at the ends. The waiting-time distribution is tallest on the left and tapers off to the right. The histogram does not have line symmetry but is certainly much closer to having it than the waiting-time distribution is.

e. For the table given in the student text, the average number of heads can be computed like this.

Number of Heads	Frequency	(Number)(Frequency)
0	1	0
1	0	0
2	4	8
3	5	15
4	16	64
5	18	90
6	27	162
7	15	105
8	5	40
9	3	27
10	1	10
11	0	0
Total	95	521

The average number of heads is $\frac{521}{95}$ or approximately 5.48. Your students will get a slightly different number because they have added the results of their own five trials. The theoretical average is (0.5)(11) or 5.5.

See additional Teaching Notes on page T533N.

b. Repeat this experiment four more times until you have a total of 100 frequencies. Does it make a difference if you flip one coin eleven times and count the number of heads or flip eleven coins at one time and count the number of heads?

c. Make a histogram from the frequency distribution.

d. How does the shape of the histogram differ from that of the waiting-time distributions? Does this histogram have line symmetry?

e. What is the average number of heads in the 100 experiments? Theoretically, how many heads would you expect in 11 flips of a coin?

f. Use your frequency table to estimate the probability that if a couple has eleven children, they are either all girls or all boys. What assumptions are you making?

3. According to the National Safety Council, about 25% of all fatal car accidents are due to too fast or unsafe speeds. Suppose that in a certain county, 40 of the last 50 fatal car accidents were due to too fast or unsafe speeds. In this task, you will investigate whether it is reasonable to attribute this result to chance variation or whether this county should look for some other explanation.

a. Assume that the probability is 0.25 that a fatal car accident is due to too fast or unsafe speeds. Design a simulation using random digits to determine the number of fatal car accidents out of 50 that are due to too fast or unsafe speeds.

b. Repeat your simulation enough times so that you feel confident in answering the question whether 40 out of 50 fatal accidents is a result that reasonably could be attributed to chance or whether the county should look for another explanation. What is your conclusion? How many times did you repeat the simulation?

c. Would your conclusion be different if the county had 30 such fatal car accidents out of 50?

Unit 7

4. The formula below gives the probability of getting exactly x heads if a coin is flipped n times.

$$P(x) = \frac{n!}{x!(n-x)!}\left(\frac{1}{2}\right)^n$$

The symbol $n!$, read "n factorial," is defined as follows:

$0! = 1$

$1! = 1$

$2! = 2 \cdot 1 = 2$

$3! = 3 \cdot 2 \cdot 1 = 6$

$4! = 4 \cdot 3 \cdot 2 \cdot 1 = 24$

and so on.

a. If you flip a coin 11 times, what is the probability of getting exactly 4 heads?

b. Use the formula to complete the table below for the experiment of flipping a coin 11 times.

Number of Heads	Probability
0	
1	
2	
3	
4	
5	
6	
7	
8	
9	
10	
11	

c. Make a graph of the distribution in this table. How does the graph compare to your histogram from Extending Task 2?

d. How does the formula appear to incorporate the Multiplication Rule?

4. a. $P(4) = \frac{11!}{4!\,7!} \left(\frac{1}{2}\right)^{11} = 330 \left(\frac{1}{2}\right)^{11} \approx 0.161$

b.

Number of Heads	Probability
0	0.000
1	0.005
2	0.027
3	0.081
4	0.161
5	0.226
6	0.226
7	0.161
8	0.081
9	0.027
10	0.005
11	0.000

c.

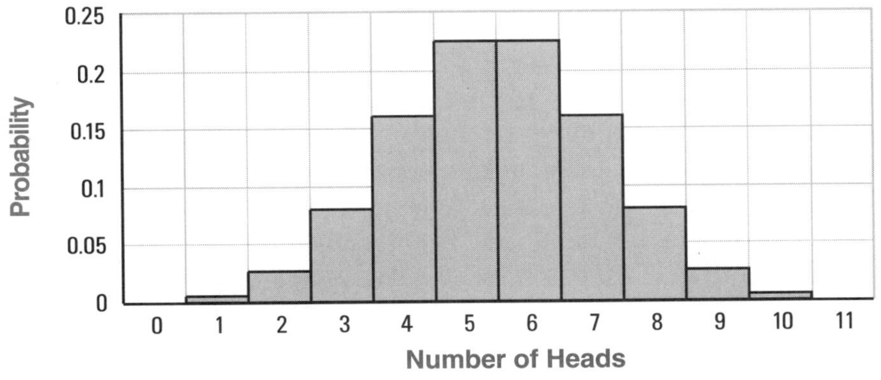

This histogram should be similar to the one from Extending Task 2, but this one will be more symmetrical. This is the theoretical distribution corresponding to the experiment in Extending Task 2.

d. The final factor, $\left(\frac{1}{2}\right)^{n}$, comes from the Multiplication Rule. For example, to get 11 heads, we must have heads on the first flip, second flip, third flip, …, and eleventh flip. The probability can be found using the Multiplication Rule: $\frac{1}{2} \cdot \frac{1}{2} \cdot \frac{1}{2} \cdot \ldots \cdot \frac{1}{2} = \left(\frac{1}{2}\right)^{11}$. To get 10 heads and 1 tail, we could have heads on the first to tenth flips and a tail on the eleventh flip. The probability of this particular outcome is also $\left(\frac{1}{2}\right)^{11}$. However, there are 10 other ways to get 10 heads and 1 tail because the tail can occur on any of the 11 flips.

Unit 7

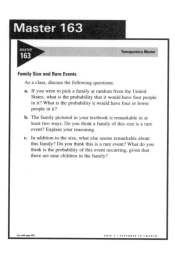

EXPLORE small-group investigation

INVESTIGATION 2 Probability Distributions and Rare Events

Because of the question that has dominated all of this unit ("How many rolls does it take on average to get doubles?"), most of the distributions so far have been waiting-time (geometric) distributions in which each bar of the histogram was theoretically a multiple of the preceding bar. The distributions recorded frequencies of different events. In this investigation, students begin recording probabilities; they see other common distributions, a rectangular and a triangular distribution, so that they can contrast the shapes and the situations that underlie these shapes. In the second part of this investigation, students use the concept of a probability distribution and mathematical notation to consider whether or not an event qualifies as a rare event.

At the beginning of the investigation, you might ask your students about the table and graph on page 495: Why are the probabilities all $\frac{1}{6}$? How is this different from the tables we made about rolling doubles? What does the first column in the histogram tell you? What does the shape of the histogram tell you? How is this different from the situation we have been investigating? It should be clear to students that you have to label the table and histogram with care to make interpretation accurate.

Activity 1 should be discussed as a class. With this discussion, you can be sure your students understand how to read tables such as the one of family sizes. You also can reinforce the idea that a table of proportions can be used to find probabilities, in this case, the probability that a randomly selected family will be a given size.

You may want to bring all students together after they have completed Activity 4 to be sure everyone can correctly use the notation introduced just before the activity.

Many students find Activity 5 challenging. Some can access the problem following the questions asked and using the Multiplication Rule. Some will revert to thinking about frequencies. However, in one case, a student connected the two ideas by drawing diagrams to explain the probabilities. (See the following table.) You may find this a helpful suggestion for students who are not immediately comfortable thinking about the probabilities as a product of fractions.

Number of rolls to get doubles	Fraction out of jail	Fraction still in jail
1		
2		
etc.		

The other difficulty with Activity 5 is that students need to be careful in interpreting $P(2)$, for example. This means "the probability of having to roll twice to get doubles" in this problem, but it may be mistaken for the probability of rolling a sum of 2.

See additional Teaching Notes on page T533N.

INVESTIGATION 2 Probability Distributions and Rare Events

The table and histogram below give the proportion of families in the United States that are a given size.

Size of Family	Proportion
2	0.42
3	0.23
4	0.21
5	0.09
6	0.03
7 or more	0.02
Total	1.00

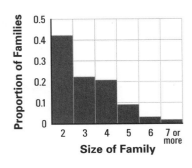

Source: U.S. Bureau of the Census, *Statistical Abstract of the United States: 1996* (116th edition). Washington, DC, 1996.

1. As a class, discuss the following questions.

a. If you were to pick a family at random from the United States, what is the probability that it would have four people in it? What is the probability it would have four or fewer people in it?

b. The family pictured below is remarkable in at least two ways. Do you think a family of this size is a rare event? Explain your reasoning.

c. In addition to the size, what else seems remarkable about this family? Do you think this is a rare event? What do you think is the probability of this event occurring, given that there are nine children in the family?

In the remainder of this investigation, you will learn to construct and use **probability distributions**. A probability distribution tells you at a glance the probabilities associated with all possible events. For example, the table of family sizes on page 495 tells you the probability that a family selected at random in the United States will have exactly five members. It was constructed after a census that tried to count all families in the United States.

Probability distribution tables also can be constructed for theoretical events. Shown below is the probability distribution table and graph for the experiment of rolling a die and reading the number on the top. Note that the shape of the graph of this probability distribution is *rectangular*.

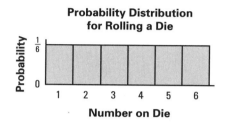

Number on Die	Probability
1	$\frac{1}{6}$
2	$\frac{1}{6}$
3	$\frac{1}{6}$
4	$\frac{1}{6}$
5	$\frac{1}{6}$
6	$\frac{1}{6}$
Total	$\frac{6}{6}$

Probability Distribution for Rolling a Die

2. **a.** Make a probability distribution table and graph for the experiment of rolling a tetrahedral die (with four faces).

   b. What is the shape of your graph?

3. Consider again the experiment of rolling two standard dice and adding the two numbers on the tops of the dice. (See Activity 2 of Investigation 1 in Lesson 1, page 458.)

   a. Complete a probability distribution table like the one at the right. Write the probabilities as fractions.

Sum of Two Dice	Probability
2	
3	
4	
5	
6	
7	
8	
9	
10	
11	
12	
Total	$\frac{36}{36}$

2. **a.**

Number on Die	Probability
1	$\frac{1}{4}$
2	$\frac{1}{4}$
3	$\frac{1}{4}$
4	$\frac{1}{4}$
Total	$\frac{4}{4}$

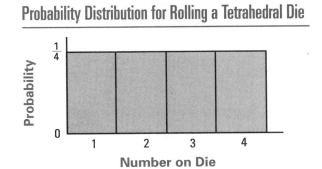

Probability Distribution for Rolling a Tetrahedral Die

b. This graph is also rectangular.

3. **a.**

Sum of Two Dice	Probability
2	$\frac{1}{36}$
3	$\frac{2}{36}$
4	$\frac{3}{36}$
5	$\frac{4}{36}$
6	$\frac{5}{36}$
7	$\frac{6}{36}$
8	$\frac{5}{36}$
9	$\frac{4}{36}$
10	$\frac{3}{36}$
11	$\frac{2}{36}$
12	$\frac{1}{36}$
Total	$\frac{36}{36}$

Unit 7

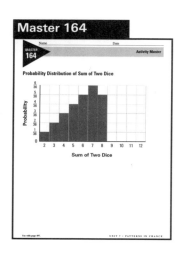

3.   b.   See Teaching Master 164.

Probability Distribution of Sum of Two Dice

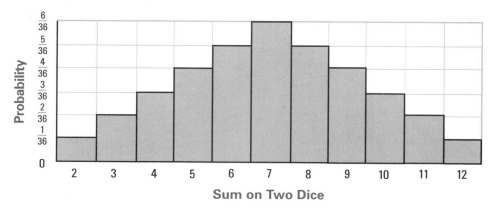

Sum on Two Dice

c.   If all outcomes have the same probability, then the distribution will be rectangular. A triangular probability distribution will occur if, for example, the experiment consists of drawing two numbers from a rectangular distribution and finding their sum.

4.   a.   ■ $P(4) = \frac{3}{36}$

■ $P(\text{sum} > 5) = \frac{26}{36}$

■ $P(\text{sum} \leq 5) = \frac{10}{36}$

■ $P(7 \text{ or } 11) = \frac{8}{36}$

b. Below is a partially-completed graph of the probabilities in your table. Copy and complete the graph.

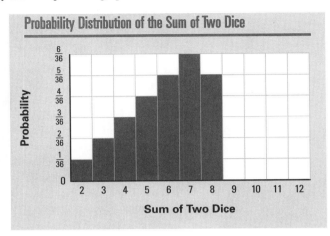

Probability Distribution of the Sum of Two Dice

c. The shape of the distribution in Part b is *triangular*. What kinds of situations or experiments can be expected to give probability distributions that are rectangular? Triangular?

Writing with words about probability distributions such as the one above can get somewhat complicated, so a more compact mathematical notation often is used. For example, the mathematical notation

$$P(\text{sum} \geq 7) = \frac{21}{36}$$

says exactly the same thing as

the probability that the sum of the two dice is seven or greater equals $\frac{21}{36}$.

If it is understood that you are talking about the sum of two dice, you can use the notation

$$P(5) = \frac{4}{36}$$

to mean

the probability that the sum of the two dice is 5 equals $\frac{4}{36}$.

4. This activity will help you become comfortable using this new notation. Refer to the probability distribution in Activity 3.

a. Find each of the following probabilities about the sum of the two dice.

- $P(4)$
- $P(\text{sum} > 5)$
- $P(\text{sum} \leq 5)$
- $P(7 \text{ or } 11)$

b. Rewrite each sentence below using mathematical notation. Then decide if the statement is true or false.

- The probability that the sum is more than 12 equals 0.
- The probability that the sum is 2 equals $\frac{1}{36}$.
- The probability that the sum is an even number equals $\frac{18}{36}$.

5. Now that you are familiar with the idea of a probability distribution, you can construct the theoretical waiting-time distribution for the number of rolls of a pair of dice until doubles appear. Again, imagine that all students in your class are playing modified Monopoly. All are sent to jail. To get out of jail a student must roll doubles.

a. Copy the following waiting-time probability distribution table. You will complete the "Probability" column as you do Parts b–h. Report all probabilities as fractions.

Number of Rolls to Get Doubles	Probability
1	
2	
3	
4	
5	
6	
7	
8	
9	
10	
11	
12	

b. What is the probability of getting doubles on the first roll? Enter your answer as a fraction on the first line of the table.

Master 165

4. **b.** ■ $P(\text{sum} > 12) = 0$; true

   ■ $P(2) = \frac{1}{36}$; true

   ■ $P(2, 4, 6, 8, 10, \text{ or } 12) = \frac{18}{36}$; true

5. **See Teaching Master 165.**

   This is an important task. At this stage, most students will see how to generate the pattern shown in Part f, but some may not understand why this pattern is the correct one. That's OK for now; there will be opportunities later for them to deepen their understanding.

   a. Students will complete the table in Parts b–h.

   b. $\frac{1}{6}$

5. c. ■ The Multiplication Rule: $P(A \text{ and } B) = P(A) \cdot P(B)$

■ $\frac{5}{6} \cdot \frac{1}{6} = \frac{5}{36}$

d. ■ You must not roll doubles on the first try, you must not roll doubles on the second try, and you must roll doubles on the third try.

■ $\frac{5}{6} \cdot \frac{5}{6} \cdot \frac{1}{6} = \frac{25}{216}$

e. ■ Don't roll doubles on the first try, don't roll doubles on the second try, don't roll doubles on the third try, and do roll doubles on the fourth try.

■ $\left(\frac{5}{6}\right)\left(\frac{5}{6}\right)\left(\frac{5}{6}\right)\left(\frac{1}{6}\right) = \left(\frac{5}{6}\right)^3\left(\frac{1}{6}\right) = \frac{125}{1,296}$

f. In each case, use the Multiplication Rule for independent events. There is another way to look at it. For example, the probability a person will roll doubles for the first time on the third roll is $\left(\frac{5}{6}\right)\left(\frac{5}{6}\right)\left(\frac{1}{6}\right)$ or $\left(\frac{5}{6}\right)^2\left(\frac{1}{6}\right)$. We expect that $\frac{5}{6}$ of the people won't roll doubles on their first try and $\frac{5}{6}$ of that $\frac{5}{6}$ won't roll doubles on their second try. So $\frac{5}{6}$ of $\frac{5}{6}$ of the people who started are left to try a third roll. We expect that $\frac{1}{6}$ of them, or $\frac{1}{6}$ of the $\frac{5}{6}$ of the $\frac{5}{6}$, will roll doubles for the first time on their third try.

g. The first answer is $\frac{1}{6}$. With each successive roll of the dice, another factor of $\frac{5}{6}$ is multiplied.

■ $P(5) = \left(\frac{5}{6}\right)^4\left(\frac{1}{6}\right) = \frac{625}{7,776}$

$P(6) = \left(\frac{5}{6}\right)^5\left(\frac{1}{6}\right) = \frac{3\,125}{46,656}$

■ $P(x) = \left(\frac{5}{6}\right)^{x-1}\left(\frac{1}{6}\right)$

h. Waiting Time for Doubles

Number of Rolls to Get Doubles	Probability
1	$\frac{1}{6}$
2	$\left(\frac{5}{6}\right)\left(\frac{1}{6}\right)$
3	$\left(\frac{5}{6}\right)^2\left(\frac{1}{6}\right)$
4	$\left(\frac{5}{6}\right)^3\left(\frac{1}{6}\right)$
5	$\left(\frac{5}{6}\right)^4\left(\frac{1}{6}\right)$
6	$\left(\frac{5}{6}\right)^5\left(\frac{1}{6}\right)$
7	$\left(\frac{5}{6}\right)^6\left(\frac{1}{6}\right)$
8	$\left(\frac{5}{6}\right)^7\left(\frac{1}{6}\right)$
9	$\left(\frac{5}{6}\right)^8\left(\frac{1}{6}\right)$
10	$\left(\frac{5}{6}\right)^9\left(\frac{1}{6}\right)$
11	$\left(\frac{5}{6}\right)^{10}\left(\frac{1}{6}\right)$
12	$\left(\frac{5}{6}\right)^{11}\left(\frac{1}{6}\right)$

Notice that the sequence $\frac{1}{6}$, $\left(\frac{5}{6}\right)\left(\frac{1}{6}\right)$, $\left(\frac{5}{6}\right)^2\left(\frac{1}{6}\right)$, $\left(\frac{5}{6}\right)^3\left(\frac{1}{6}\right)$, ... is a geometric sequence with first term $\frac{1}{6}$ and common ratio $\frac{5}{6}$, which is why this distribution is called a geometric distribution.

See additional Teaching Notes on page T5330.

c. To get out of jail on the second roll, two events must happen. You must not roll doubles on the first roll *and* you must roll doubles on the second roll.

- What rule of probability can you use to compute $P(A \text{ and } B)$ when A and B are independent events?

- What is the probability of not getting doubles on the first roll and getting doubles on the second roll? Write your answer on the second line of the table.

d. To get out of jail on the third roll, three events must happen.

- What are these three events?

- What is the probability all three events will happen? Write your answer on the third row of the table.

e. To get out of jail on the fourth roll, four events must happen.

- What are these four events?

- What is the probability all four events will happen? Write your answer on the fourth row of the table.

f. Explain why your work for Parts b–e can be summarized in the following manner.

$$P(1) = \frac{1}{6}$$
$$P(2) = \left(\frac{5}{6}\right)\left(\frac{1}{6}\right)$$
$$P(3) = \left(\frac{5}{6}\right)^2\left(\frac{1}{6}\right)$$
$$P(4) = \left(\frac{5}{6}\right)^3\left(\frac{1}{6}\right)$$

g. What patterns do you see in the above equations? Compare your patterns with those of other groups.

- What is $P(5)$? $P(6)$?

- What is $P(x)$? That is, what is the probability the first doubles will appear on the xth roll of the dice?

h. Use your general formula in Part g to complete the rest of the probability distribution table. Don't bother multiplying the fractions for now.

i. Express the probabilities as decimals and then make a graph of the probability distribution table.

j. How does this graph of the theoretical waiting-time probability distribution compare with the histogram you produced for Activity 1 of Investigation 1 in Lesson 1 (page 458)?

6. Recall that 30% of "M&M's"® Plain Chocolate Candies are brown. Find the first five entries of the table for the waiting-time probability distribution for drawing a brown candy.

Unit 7

Checkpoint

Examine each of the probability distributions shown below.

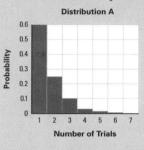

Distribution A

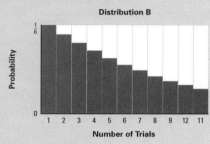

Distribution B

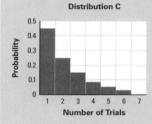

Distribution C

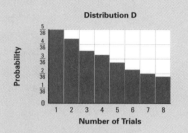

Distribution D

a Match the following descriptions to the probability distributions.

- The experiment is rolling a die until a 6 appears.

- The experiment is rolling two dice until a sum of 6 appears.

- The experiment is counting the days on which the weather report says there is a 60% chance of rain until there is a rainy day.

- The experiment is selecting a person at random until one with type O blood appears. (About 45% of the U.S. population has type O blood.)

b What is the height of the second bar (representing 2 trials) in each case?

Be prepared to explain your description-graph matches to the class.

SHARE AND SUMMARIZE   full-class discussion

When students explain their answers, you may need to urge them to say what clues they see in the histograms. They should mention the initial bar representing the initial probability (or *y*-intercept in the exponential function that models this distribution) and the proportion of the heights of a bar to the bar on its left as the proportion of people who do not succeed (or the decay factor).

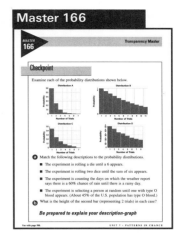

Checkpoint

See Teaching Master 166.

ⓐ ■ Distribution B
   ■ Distribution D
   ■ Distribution A
   ■ Distribution C

ⓑ Distribution A: $(0.4)(0.6) = 0.24$

Distribution B: $\left(\frac{5}{6}\right)\left(\frac{1}{6}\right) = \frac{5}{36}$

Distribution C: $(0.55)(0.45) = 0.2475$

Distribution D: $\left(\frac{31}{36}\right)\left(\frac{5}{36}\right) = \frac{155}{1,296}$

Unit 7

Waiting Time for Doubles

Number of Rolls	Probability
1	0.167
2	0.139
3	0.116
4	0.096
5	0.080
6	0.067
7	0.056
8	0.047
9	0.039
10	0.032
11	0.027
12	0.022
13	0.019
14	0.016
15	0.013
16	0.011
17	0.009
18	0.008
19	0.006
20	0.005
21 or more	0.025

Use with page 502.   UNIT 7 • PATTERNS IN CHANCE

MORE

ASSIGNMENT   *pp. 503–509*

Students now can begin
Modeling Task 3 or Extending
Task 2 or 3 from the MORE
assignment following
Investigation 2.

APPLY   individual task

▶**On Your Own**

a.   0.422

b.   0.578

c.   0.056

EXPLORE   small-group investigation

7.   See Teaching Master 167.

  a.   The probability that it will take 19 rolls or more is $0.006 + 0.005 + 0.025$ or 0.036. So requiring 19 rolls is in the upper 5% of the distribution and is a rare event.

  b.   No. The probability that it will take 9 or more rolls to get out of jail is 0.232. This is greater than 0.05.

NOTE: One of your students may notice that there are three ways to compute the probability it will take 9 rolls or more to get out of jail. The first is to add the probabilities $P(9) + P(10) + P(11) + ... + P(21$ or more$)$. The second is to reason that to require 9 or more means that you must start with 8 failures. The probability is $\left(\frac{5}{6}\right)^8$, or 0.233, that 9 or more rolls will be required. The third method is to find $P(1) + P(2) + P(3) + P(4) + P(5) + P(6) + P(7) + P(8)$ and subtract this sum from 1.

On Your Own

Use your completed probability distribution table in Activity 5, page 498, to find the following probabilities. "Rolls" stands for the number of rolls to get doubles.

a. $P(\text{rolls} \le 3)$

b. $P(\text{rolls} > 3)$

c. $P(\text{rolls} = 7)$

---

7. Shown below is the probability distribution of the waiting time for doubles, with the probabilities expressed as decimals rounded to the nearest thousandth.

Number of Rolls	Probability	Number of Rolls	Probability
1	0.167	12	0.022
2	0.139	13	0.019
3	0.116	14	0.016
4	0.096	15	0.013
5	0.080	16	0.011
6	0.067	17	0.009
7	0.056	18	0.008
8	0.047	19	0.006
9	0.039	20	0.005
10	0.032	21 or more	0.025
11	0.027		

a. What is the probability it will take 19 or more rolls to get out of jail? Is it a rare event to take 19 rolls of the dice to get out of jail? (Recall that we are considering a rare event to be one in the upper 5% of the distribution.)

b. Suppose in playing the modified game of Monopoly, Michael is still in jail after trying 8 times to roll doubles. Has a rare event occurred?

LESSON 3 • PROBABILITY DISTRIBUTIONS 501

8. Complete a probability distribution table like the one below for the experiment of flipping a coin until a head appears. Complete the "Probability" column using decimals rounded to the nearest thousandth.

Number of Flips to Get a Head x	Probability $P(x)$
1	
2	
3	
4	
5	
6	
7	
8	
9	
10	

   a. Make a graph of your distribution.
   b. What is the probability that the first head occurs on the second flip?
   c. What is the formula for $P(x)$, the probability of getting the first head on flip number x?
   d. If Scott requires 5 flips to get a head, has a rare event occurred? Explain.
   e. If Michele flips a coin 8 times before the first head appears, has a rare event occurred? Explain.

Checkpoint

Refer to the table of family sizes and the family pictured at the beginning of this investigation (page 495).

ⓐ What family sizes would qualify as rare events? Explain.

ⓑ Suppose that the family pictured had planned to have children until they had a boy.

   ■ Is a family of nine girls and no boys a rare event? Explain your reasoning.

   ■ If the parents have another child, is it more likely to be a boy or a girl? Justify your answer.

Be prepared to share your thinking with the entire class.

502 UNIT 7 · PATTERNS IN CHANCE

502 UNIT 7 · PATTERNS IN CHANCE

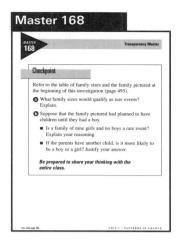
8.

Number of Flips to Get a Head x	Probability P(x)
1	0.5
2	0.25
3	0.125
4	0.063
5	0.031
6	0.016
7	0.008
8	0.004
9	0.002
10	0.001

a.

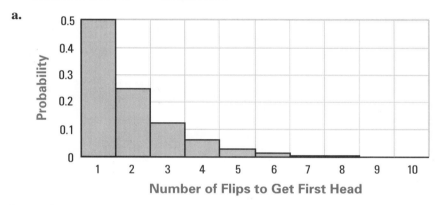

b. $P(2) = 0.25$

c. $P(x) = (0.5)^{x-1}(0.5) = (0.5)^x$

d. No, the probability that it will take 5 or more flips to get heads is about $1 - 0.938$ or 0.062.

e. Yes, the probability that it will take 8 or more flips to get heads is only about $1 - 0.993$ or 0.007.

SHARE AND SUMMARIZE   full-class discussion

Checkpoint

See Teaching Master 168.

ⓐ Family sizes of 6 or more would be rare events, since, from the table, exactly 5% of the families have 6 or more people in them.

ⓑ ■ Yes, a rare event has occurred. The probability of having at least 9 children before getting a boy is $1 - 0.998$ or 0.002.

   ■ It is generally considered equally likely to be a boy or a girl; having children are independent events. However, there may indeed be other factors than chance at work in such families; students should justify any answer they give.

▶ On Your Own

a. **Probability Distribution for Type O Blood**

Number of People	Probability	
1	0.45	
2	(0.55)(0.45)	= 0.2475
3	$(0.55)^2(0.45)$	≈ 0.1361
4	$(0.55)^3(0.45)$	≈ 0.0749
5 or more	$(0.55)^4 \approx 0.0915$	

b. $P(x) = (0.55)^{x-1}(0.45)$

c. If students continue the table, they will get the following probabilities:

$P(5) \approx 0.0412$

$P(6) \approx 0.0227$

Since $P(1) + P(2) + P(3) + P(4) + P(5) + P(6) \approx 0.9724$, a rare event has occurred any time it takes more than 6 people to get the first type O blood. Certainly having to wait until the eighteenth person is a rare event.

MORE

ASSIGNMENT   pp. 503–509

Modeling: 1 and 3
Organizing: 1, 2, and 3
Reflecting: 2
Extending: 1 and choice of one*

*When choice is indicated, it is important to leave the choice to the student.
NOTE: It is best if Organizing tasks are discussed as a whole class after they have been assigned as homework.

MORE independent assignment

Modeling

1. a. **Probability Distribution for Drawing a Red Candy**

Number of Draws to Get First Red Candy	Probability
1	0.2
2	0.16
3	0.128
4	0.102
5	0.082
6	0.066
7	0.052
8	0.042
9	0.034
10 or more	0.134

See additional Teaching Notes on page T533P.

On Your Own

Consider an experiment in which a blood bank is testing people at random until it finds a person with type O blood. About 45% of the U.S. population has type O blood.

a. Make a probability distribution table for this experiment. Number the first four rows in your table and follow them with a row for 5 people or more.

b. Write a formula for $P(x)$, the probability that the xth person tested is the first with type O blood.

c. Suppose the 18th person tested was the first with type O blood. Would this be considered a rare event? Explain your reasoning.

MORE

Modeling • Organizing • Reflecting • Extending

Modeling

1. Twenty percent of plain "M&M's"® Plain Chocolate Candies are red.

   a. Make a probability distribution table for the experiment of drawing a candy until a red one appears. Use the numbers 1 through 9 in your table and end it with a "10 draws or more" row.

   b. Make a graph of your distribution.

   c. Write a formula for $P(x)$, the probability of getting the first red candy on the xth draw.

   d. How many candies would you have to draw before getting the first red in order for a rare event to have occurred?

2. Refer to Modeling Task 3 on page 489.

   a. Write a formula for $P(x)$, the probability of getting a tiger sticker on the xth purchase.

   b. How many boxes of Kellogg's® Cocoa Krispies® cereal would a person have to buy without getting a tiger sticker before a rare event would have occurred?

Unit 7

3. In an episode of a television show, a man receives an anonymous letter that correctly predicts the outcome of a sports event. In the next four weeks, similar letters arrive, each making a prediction that turns out to be correct. The final letter asks the man for money before he receives another prediction. The whole thing turns out to be a scam.

Two versions of the first letter had been sent out, each to a large number of people. Half of the people received letters that predicted Team A would win, and half of the people received letters that predicted Team B would win. Those people who received letters with the correct prediction were sent letters the second week. Again half of the letters predicted Team C and half predicted Team D.

How many letters should have been sent out the first week so that exactly one person would be guaranteed to have all correct predictions at the end of the five weeks?

4. Now that you can describe waiting-time probability distributions with an algebraic formula, you can use a calculator to help analyze situations modeled by these distributions. A helpful calculator procedure to produce a waiting-time probability distribution table makes use of a sequence command found on some graphing calculators. The command is usually of the form seq(*formula, variable, begin, end, increment*). The following keystroke procedure uses A for the variable and 1 for both the beginning value and the increment. (The exact structure of this command and how to access it vary among calculator models. You may need to refer to the manual for your calculator.)

First you need to access the sequence command. For example, from the home screen on a TI-83, press `2nd` `STAT` `▶` 5. (On a TI-82, the arrow is not needed.) Then, complete the command by entering the following example:

Store the result in a data list for easier access. The following are sample display screens for this procedure:

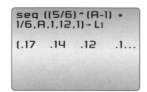

The data list now holds the first 12 table entries of the waiting-time probability distribution for rolling doubles. (Note that the decimal display was set to show only two digits.)

3. 32 letters. This may be easiest to understand if you work backwards: One correct letter was sent on the fifth week, so two correct letters were sent on the fourth week, four on the third week, eight on the second week, and sixteen correct letters on the first week. There would also be sixteen incorrect letters the first week, for a total of 32.

You also can ask your students the total number of letters sent out: 62.

4. **a.** The entries stored in List 1 should be equivalent to those calculated in Activity 5.

   b. The first part of the command uses the formula students wrote in Activity 5 Part g, although the variable used is A instead of x. The command provides only the first 12 entries, whereas the formula can be used to get any one particular entry.

   c. Actual commands may vary.

   $\text{seq}(0.30*(0.70)^{\wedge}(A - 1), A, 1, 10, 1)$

Number of Draws to Get Brown Candy	Probability
1	0.3
2	0.21
3	0.147
4	0.1029
5	0.07203
6	0.05042
7	0.03529
8	0.02471
9	0.01729
10	0.01211

   The first five entries generated by the command should be equal to the five entries in the table in Activity 6.

   d. You need to know the probability that the event you are waiting for will occur on any given trial. In addition, you must decide how many rows you want in the table. If the probability is p, then the formula will be $(1 - p)^{\wedge}(A - 1)*p$ and the command for N rows will be, for example, $\text{seq}((1 - p)^{\wedge}(A - 1)*p, A, 1, N, 1) \to L_1$.

   e. Most calculators will give the sum of the elements in a list. Students could use this procedure to place probabilities into a list and then find the length of the list needed to get the sum to be greater than 0.95.

Organizing

1. **a–e.** The table is given below.

The Number of Trials	Probability
1	p
2	$(1 - p)p$
3	$(1 - p)^2 p$
4	$(1 - p)^3 p$
5	$(1 - p)^4 p$
x	$(1 - p)^{x - 1} p$

   Note again that the sequence p, $(1 - p)p$, $(1 - p)^2 p$, $(1 - p)^3 p$, ... is a geometric sequence with first term p and common ratio $(1 - p)$.

   The probability of not getting the event (Part b) is $1 - p$; the general formula for getting the event on the xth trial (Part e) is $P(x) = (1 - p)^{x - 1} p$, $x = 1, 2, 3, ...$.

a. Compare the entries produced by this procedure with those you calculated in Activity 5 of Investigation 2 (page 498).

b. Compare the sequence command with the general formula you wrote in Activity 5 Part g of Investigation 2. How are they similar and how are they different?

c. Modify the sequence command to produce the first ten table entries of the waiting-time probability distribution for drawing a brown "M&M's"® Chocolate Candy. Compare the first five entries with the entries you calculated in Activity 6 of Investigation 2.

d. Write a summary of what you need to know in order to use this procedure for producing a waiting-time probability distribution. How do you figure out the needed formula?

e. How could this calculator procedure help you analyze questions about rare events associated with waiting-time probability distributions?

Organizing

1. In this task you will use algebraic notation to construct a formula for waiting-time distributions. In this general case, use the letter p to stand for the probability of getting the waited-for event. (In the experiment of waiting for doubles on a pair of dice, $p \approx 0.17$ on each trial. In the experiment of flipping a coin until a head appears, $p = 0.5$ on each trial.)

a. The first row of the table below gives the probability that the waited-for event will occur on the first trial. Make a copy of this table and then fill in the first row.

Number of Trials x	Probability $P(x)$
1	
2	
3	
4	
5	
x	

b. What is the probability of *not* getting the waited-for event on the first trial?

c. What is the probability of not getting the waited-for event on the first trial and then getting it on the second trial? Fill in the second row of the table.

Unit 7

d. What is the probability of not getting the waited-for event on the first trial, not getting it on the second trial, and then getting it on the third trial? Fill in the third row of the table.

e. Finish filling in the rows of the table. Write a general formula for describing waiting-time distributions.

f. How is your general formula for Part a like the equation for an exponential function? How is it different?

2. Use your formula from Organizing Task 1 to answer these questions.

a. The Current Population Survey of the U.S. Census Bureau recently found that 21.1% of adults over the age of 25 in the United States have four or more years of college. If a line of randomly-selected U.S. adults over the age of 25 is walking past you, what is the probability that the fifth person to pass will be the first with four or more years of college?

b. What is the probability that parents would have seven boys in a row before having a girl? (P(boy) = 0.51) Assume births are independent.

3. **a.** Find the median of the waiting-time-for-doubles probability distribution produced in Activity 5 of Investigation 2 (page 498). In this situation, what does the median tell you?

b. Describe how to find the median of any probability distribution.

4. Use *NOW* and *NEXT* to describe the relationship between successive entries in the probability distribution table for waiting for doubles. (See Activity 5 of Investigation 2 on page 498.)

5. In this task you will explore some of the geometry and algebra connected with the probability distribution for the sum of two dice.

a. Plot the points that represent the probability distribution for the sum of two regular dice: $(2, \frac{1}{36})$, $(3, \frac{2}{36})$, $(4, \frac{3}{36})$, ... , $(12, \frac{1}{36})$.

- Write a single equation whose graph fits the pattern of points for $x = 2, 3, 4, 5, 6, 7$.

- Write another single equation whose graph fits the pattern of points for $x = 7, 8, 9, 10, 11, 12$.

- How are the slopes of these two graphs related?

- Use absolute value to write one equation whose graph fits the pattern of all 11 points.

1. **d–e.** **See page T505 for answers.**

    f. The general formula is like an exponential equation in that the variable occurs as an exponent. It is different since the exponent is $x - 1$, not x or ax. The overall shapes of the two functions are the same, but an exponential function always contains the point $(0, a)$ and in this waiting-time situation, only positive integer values of x are in the domain.

2. **a.** $(1 - 0.211)^4(0.211) \approx 0.082$

    b. $(0.51)^7(0.49) \approx 0.0044$

3. **a.** The median is four rolls. This means that about half of the people took fewer than four rolls and about half took more.

    b. To find the median, start with the first row and add probabilities until the sum first exceeds 0.50. The median is the number of the last row added. If the sum should ever become exactly 0.50, the median is the average of the number of the last row added and the number of the next row. Note that the average number of rolls waiting for doubles was six. That the median is less than the mean is characteristic of a distribution that is skewed right.

4. $NEXT = \left(\frac{5}{6}\right) NOW$

5. **a.**

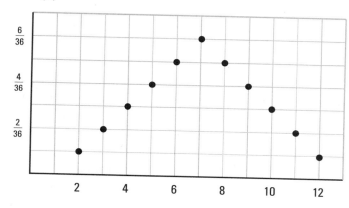

■ $y = \left(\frac{1}{36}\right)x - \frac{1}{36}$

■ $y = -\left(\frac{1}{36}\right)x + \frac{13}{36}$

■ The slopes are $\frac{1}{36}$ and $-\left(\frac{1}{36}\right)$; they are additive inverses.

■ $y = -\left(\frac{1}{36}\right)|7 - x| + \frac{6}{36}$

Unit 7

5. b.

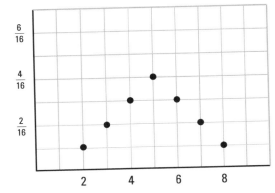

- $y = \left(\frac{1}{16}\right)x - \frac{1}{16}$
- $y = -\left(\frac{1}{16}\right)x + \frac{9}{16}$
- They are additive inverses.
- $y = -\left(\frac{1}{16}\right)|5 - x| + \frac{4}{16}$

c. $y = -\left(\frac{1}{n^2}\right)|(n + 1) - x| + \frac{1}{n}$

Reflecting

1. Adding up the heights of all of the bars, students may find that it appears that there was a total of 100 repetitions. Since 23 of them were successful on the first trial, a good estimate is $p = 0.23$. Alternatively, there were 23 successes on the first trial and 15 on the second trial. The second bar is 0.65 times the first. The estimate of p would then be $1.00 - 0.65$ or 0.35. A third strategy would be to count the total number of trials, which is 479. One hundred of these were successful trials. The estimate of p in this case is $\frac{100}{479}$ or approximately 0.21. Your students may think of other methods. In fact, this distribution was simulated with $p = 0.2$.

2. In general, students should discuss that there is a 0.7 chance of not getting a brown candy, and a 0.3 chance of getting a brown candy on any one draw. Furthermore, the draws are independent of each other. Using the Multiplication Rule to find the probability of non-brown on the first draw, non-brown on the second, ... , non-brown on the fifth, and brown on the sixth draw, we get $(0.7)(0.7)(0.7)(0.7)(0.7)(0.3)$ or $(0.7)^5(0.3)$.

3. Think of a large room of people trying to achieve a success. All try at once and those who were successful sit down. Although the probability of a success remains the same on each trial, there are fewer people trying to achieve a success as time goes on because some people are now sitting.

4. Responses will vary. Look for a waiting-time situation that has independent trials and 50% chance of success on any trial. One obvious example would be waiting to have a girl (or boy).

b. Graph the points that represent the probability distribution for the sum of two tetrahedral dice: $(2, \frac{1}{16})$, $(3, \frac{2}{16})$, $(4, \frac{3}{16})$, ... , $(8, \frac{1}{16})$.

  ■ Write a single equation whose graph fits the pattern of points for $x = 2, 3, 4, 5$.

  ■ Write another single equation whose graph fits the pattern of points for $x = 5, 6, 7, 8$.

  ■ How are the slopes of these two graphs related?

  ■ Use absolute value to write one equation whose graph fits the pattern of all 7 points.

c. Write an equation whose graph fits the pattern of the points that represent the probability distribution for the sum of two dice, each with n sides.

Reflecting

1. The waiting-time distribution below was constructed by a computer simulation. How could you use it to estimate p, the probability of the event occurring on each trial? What is your estimate of p?

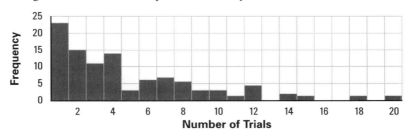

2. You have seen that if the experiment is drawing "M&M's"® Chocolate Candies until a brown one appears, the probability of getting the first brown on the 6th try is $(0.70)^5(0.30)$. Write a paragraph explaining to a friend who has been absent from school why this makes sense.

3. Explain why the heights of the bars are decreasing in a waiting-time probability distribution.

4. What are other situations that could be modeled by the probability distribution you constructed in Activity 8 of Investigation 2 (page 502)?

5. The table below gives the mileage at which each of 191 buses had its first major motor failure.

Mileage before Failure	Number of Buses
0 to 19,999	6
20,000 to 39,999	11
40,000 to 59,999	16
60,000 to 79,999	25
80,000 to 99,999	34
100,000 to 119,999	46
120,000 to 139,999	33
140,000 to 159,999	16
160,000 and up	4
Total	191

Source: Mudholkar, G.S., D.K. Srivastava, and M. Freimer.
"The Exponential Weibull Family: A Reanalysis of the Bus-Motor-Failure Data." *Technometrics* 37 (Nov. 1995): 436–445.

a. Make a histogram of this distribution.

b. Is the shape of the distribution the same as that of other waiting-time distributions you have seen? Explain why this makes sense.

Extending

1. Let *A* be the event of requiring exactly 5 rolls of a pair of dice to get doubles for the first time. Let *B* be the event that the first four rolls of a pair of dice aren't doubles. Find the following probabilities:

a. $P(A)$

b. $P(B)$

c. $P(A|B)$

d. $P(B|A)$

e. $P(A \text{ and } B)$

f. $P(A \text{ or } B)$

2. Make a probability distribution table for the *larger* of the two numbers when two dice are rolled. If both dice show the same number, that number is the larger one.

a. What is $P(5)$?

b. What is $P(\text{larger number} \leq 2)$?

c. Make a graph of the probabilities in your probability distribution table.

d. Describe the shape of this distribution.

5. **a.** In the following histogram, the motor failures that occurred from 160,000 miles and up are represented by the bar to the right of 160,000.

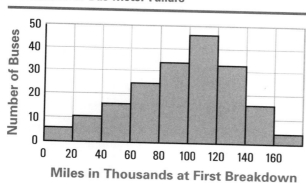

Distribution of Bus Motor Failure

Number of Buses (vertical axis): 0, 10, 20, 30, 40, 50

Miles in Thousands at First Breakdown (horizontal axis): 0, 20, 40, 60, 80, 100, 120, 140, 160

b. It's not the same shape and we wouldn't expect it to be. The probability of a breakdown isn't the same on each mile the bus is driven. The probability of a breakdown increases as the bus gets older. The bars eventually decrease after almost all buses have had their first breakdown.

Extending

1. **a.** $P(A) = \left(\frac{5}{6}\right)^4\left(\frac{1}{6}\right) \approx 0.08$

   b. $P(B) = \left(\frac{5}{6}\right)^4 \approx 0.48$

   c. $P(A|B) = \left(\frac{1}{6}\right) \approx 0.17$

   d. $P(B|A) = 1$

   e. $P(A \text{ and } B) = \left(\frac{5}{6}\right)^4\left(\frac{1}{6}\right) \approx 0.08$

   f. $P(A \text{ or } B) = \left(\frac{5}{6}\right)^4 \approx 0.48$

2. The table on the left below gives all possible outcomes. The probability distribution table is on the right below.

	1	2	3	4	5	6
1	1	2	3	4	5	6
2	2	2	3	4	5	6
3	3	3	3	4	5	6
4	4	4	4	4	5	6
5	5	5	5	5	5	6
6	6	6	6	6	6	6

Larger Number	Probability
1	$\frac{1}{36}$
2	$\frac{3}{36}$
3	$\frac{5}{36}$
4	$\frac{7}{36}$
5	$\frac{9}{36}$
6	$\frac{11}{36}$

   a. $P(5) = \frac{9}{36}$

   b. $P(\text{larger number} \leq 2) = \frac{1}{36} + \frac{3}{36} = \frac{4}{36}$

See additional Teaching Notes on page T533P.

3. The table of possible outcomes and the probability distribution table follow.

	1	2	3	4	5	6
1	0	1	2	3	4	5
2	1	0	1	2	3	4
3	2	1	0	1	2	3
4	3	2	1	0	1	2
5	4	3	2	1	0	1
6	5	4	3	2	1	0

Difference of Numbers	Probability
0	$\frac{6}{36}$
1	$\frac{10}{36}$
2	$\frac{8}{36}$
3	$\frac{6}{36}$
4	$\frac{4}{36}$
5	$\frac{2}{36}$

a. $P(3) = \frac{6}{36}$

b. $P(1, 2, \text{ or } 3) = \frac{24}{36}$

c.

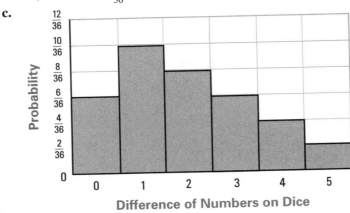

d. The probabilities from 1 to 5 lie on a straight line decreasing $\frac{2}{36}$ each time. $P(0)$ doesn't follow the same pattern.

4. The only possible pair of dice is this pair:

```
      5                    1
  3   8   6            3   2   2
      4                    4
      1                    3
```

See Assessment Resources, pages 244–251.

Unit 7

Assessments 244–247

Lesson 3 Quiz Form A

Assessments 248–251

Lesson 3 Quiz Form B

3. Make a probability distribution table for the absolute value of the difference of the numbers when two dice are rolled.

   a. What is $P(3)$?

   b. What is $P(1, 2, \text{ or } 3)$?

   c. Make a graph of the probabilities in your probability distribution table.

   d. Describe the shape of this distribution.

4. Shown below is the probability distribution table for two six-sided, nonstandard dice. Notice that these nonstandard dice have the same probability distribution as that of two regular dice.

Sum of Two Dice	Probability
2	$\frac{1}{36}$
3	$\frac{2}{36}$
4	$\frac{3}{36}$
5	$\frac{4}{36}$
6	$\frac{5}{36}$
7	$\frac{6}{36}$
8	$\frac{5}{36}$
9	$\frac{4}{36}$
10	$\frac{3}{36}$
11	$\frac{2}{36}$
12	$\frac{1}{36}$
Total	$\frac{36}{36}$

Using positive whole numbers, label the faces of these two nonstandard dice. The two dice may be different from one another and numbers may be repeated on the faces of a die.

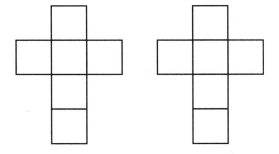

Unit 7

Expected Value of a Probability Distribution

Have you ever watched old gangster movies? If so, you may have heard talk of the "numbers racket." This is an illegal gambling game played in many cities. The player pays $1.00 and picks a number from 000, 001, 002, …, 999. The winning number is one that everyone can check, but no one can control, such as the last three digits of the Dow Jones Industrial Average for the day. Players who select the winning number get about $600 for a $1.00 ticket.

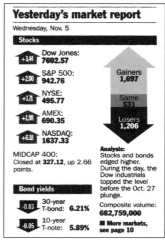

Chicago Tribune, 11/6/97

Think About This Situation

a In the long run, will a player tend to make or lose money?

b For a player to come out even in the long run, how much should a ticket cost?

c Give another impartial way to select the winning number.

Lesson 4 Expected Value of a Probability Distribution

LESSON OVERVIEW   In this lesson, students first learn how to decide if the price charged for a game is a fair price. Eventually they discover the formula for the expected value, $\sum x \cdot P(x)$. You may need to remind students that the order of operations for $\sum x \cdot P(x)$ is multiply $x \cdot P(x)$ for all x before finding the sum.

Students may need help to focus on making sense of the formula. This is just like students' previous work finding an average or expected value, except in this case we do not have to divide by the number of items because all the probabilities add to one. This completes the trio of vocabulary words for closely related ideas: the average (number of rolls to get doubles, for example); the expected value (number of children in the family for example); and the fair price of a game (or insurance or …). Students find the ideas individually manageable, but together a little more challenging. You can expect them to be hesitant about using the vocabulary fluently. The more they talk about the problems and use the vocabulary, the better they will understand the subtle differences.

Lesson Objectives

- ■ To compute the fair price (expected value) of insurance and games of chance
- ■ To compute the expected value of a probability distribution
- ■ To estimate the expected value of a waiting-time distribution from the probability distribution table
- ■ To discover the simple formula for the expected value of a waiting-time distribution
- ■ To understand that some infinite series have a finite sum

LAUNCH   full-class discussion

Think About This Situation

See Teaching Master 169.

ⓐ In the long run, a player tends to lose money. Students may explain this in the following way:

Suppose the player plays 1,000 times. Then we would expect the player to win once since the chance of winning is $\frac{1}{1,000}$. The player will win $600. But the player paid a total of 1,000($1.00) or $1,000 to play the 1,000 games. The player's net loss is $400.

ⓑ To find the cost for a ticket, again imagine that the player plays 1,000 times and so tends to win once. The total winnings will be $600, so the player should be charged $600 to play the 1,000 games, or $\frac{\$600}{1,000} = \$0.60$ each. A fair price for the game is 60 cents. Part d of the Checkpoint on page 512 returns to this question.

ⓒ Other impartial ways to select the winner would be to use the last three digits of some other number listed daily in the newspaper or generate a random number by such schemes as drawing a ball out of a box of 1,000 balls, each with a different number written on it.

Unit 7

INVESTIGATION 1 ▶ What's a Fair Price?

You occasionally may have to remind your students that *fair* now has a mathematical meaning. When they are asked to find a fair price, the question is not asking for their opinion of a fair price, but rather for the mathematical calculation of a fair price.

1. **a.** $\frac{\$400 + \$100 + \$175}{2,000} = \frac{\$675}{2,000} = \$0.3375$

   b. Add up the value of all of the prizes and divide by the number of tickets to be sold.

2. **a.** On each spin, Leroy expects to win $\frac{\$6 + \$7 + \$5 + \$0}{4}$ or \$4.50 in gift certificates. After playing the game 100 times, Leroy can expect to win about \$450, but will pay 100(\$5) or \$500 to play. Thus, his expected loss is \$50.

   b. The fair price for a spin would be \$4.50. The organization charges \$5.00. On each spin, a player expects to lose \$0.50. Leroy should not play the game.

   c. Although Leroy does have two chances of winning, he doesn't win very much (\$1 or \$2) when he wins. However, when he loses, he loses \$5. Students also may suggest that Leroy observe the game for a while before playing.

   d. If the sectors are of equal sizes, the average value on the student's spinner should be \$5. One sample spinner is

3. **a.** No. For every 38 bets on either red or black, we expect 18 winners. The casino would pay us 18(\$2) or \$36. However, we would have paid \$38 to play. A fair price to pay to play would be $\frac{\$36}{38}$ or approximately \$0.947.

   b. The casino expects to have $1,000\left(\frac{18}{38}\right)$ or approximately 473.684 winners, paying 473.684(\$2) or \$947.368. Meanwhile, it has collected \$1,000 from the 1,000 players. The casino's expected profit is \$1,000 − \$947.368 or \$52.632. Alternatively, from Part a, we know that on each bet the casino expects to earn \$1.00 − \$0.947 or \$0.053. On 1,000 bets, it expects to earn (1,000)(\$0.053) or \$53.

INVESTIGATION 1 ▶ What's a Fair Price?

In mathematics, a **fair price** for a game is the price that should be charged so that, in the long run, the players expect to come out even. (That is, the players expect to win as much as they are charged to play.)

1. Suppose your school decides to hold a raffle. The prizes in the raffle will be a microwave that costs $400, a video game that costs $100, and a bicycle that costs $175. Exactly 2,000 tickets will be sold.

   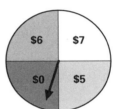

   a. What is a fair price for a ticket?

   b. Write a procedure for finding the fair price of a raffle ticket.

2. At a fund-raising carnival for a service organization, Renee is trying to get Leroy to play a game she has invented. Leroy would spin the spinner shown at the right and get a gift certificate worth the amount indicated. The organization charges $5 to play this game.

   a. How much would Leroy expect to win in 100 games? How much would Leroy have to pay to play 100 games? What is Leroy's expected net earnings?

   b. Explain why Leroy should or should not play this game.

   c. Leroy thinks he should play this game because he has two chances of winning, one chance of coming out even, and only one chance of losing. What would you say to him?

   d. Design a spinner that would make $5 a fair price to charge to play.

3. In roulette, a wheel and ball spin around in opposite directions. When they stop, the ball has an equal chance of landing in any one of the slots. Roulette wheels have 18 red slots, 18 black slots, and 2 green slots. Suppose a player bets on red. If the ball lands in a red slot, the player wins $2. The price to play is $1.

   a. Is $1 a fair price for playing roulette? Why or why not?

   b. On every 1,000 bets of $1 on red in roulette, how much money does a casino expect to make?

4. The National Center for Health Statistics reported that there were 151 deaths in 1994 for every 100,000 males aged 15–24 in the United States. There were 47 deaths per year for every 100,000 females in that age group. (Source: U.S. Bureau of Statistics, *Statistical Abstract of the United States: 1996*, 116th edition. Washington, DC, 1995.) Use these statistics to answer the following.

a. Ignoring all factors other than gender, what would be the fair price for an insurance company to charge to insure the life of a male in that age group for one year for $50,000?

b. Ignoring all factors other than gender, what would be the fair price for an insurance company to charge to insure the life of a female in that age group for one year for $50,000?

c. If the insurance company is not allowed to have different rates for each gender, what would be the fair price for a $50,000 policy for one year? Assume that the same number of insurance policies are sold to males as to females.

d. Compare the procedure you used to get your answer to Parts a and b with your procedure in Part b of Activity 1.

e. In what ways is insurance similar mathematically to a raffle? In what ways is it different?

f. Do you think insurance companies actually charge the fair price for a policy? Explain your thinking.

Checkpoint

a What is the relationship between the fair price of a game and the average winnings of a player?

b Describe a general procedure for finding the fair price of raffle or lottery tickets.

c Describe a general procedure for finding the fair price of an insurance policy.

d What would be a fair price for a ticket in the "numbers racket" game described at the beginning of this lesson?

Be prepared to compare your thinking and procedures with that of other groups.

4. This activity focuses on two characteristics to determine mortality risk: age and gender. Of course, there are many other characteristics that must be considered; some may underlie the gender characteristic, but others will not. Some students may want to do some research about actuaries and insurance calculations.

a. For every 100,000 males, we expect 151 deaths. So the insurance company expects to pay out 151($50,000) = $7,550,000. To break even, it would have to charge $\frac{\$7,550,000}{100,000}$ or $75.50 to insure each person for one year.

Using algebra, let x be the fair price. Then, $151(50,000) = x(100,000)$. Thus, $x = \$75.50$.

b. $47\left(\frac{\$50,000}{100,000}\right) = \$23.50$

c. If 100,000 policies are sold to females and 100,000 to males, we expect a total of $151 + 47 = 198$ deaths out of the 200,000 policyholders. So the insurance company expects to pay 198($50,000) or $9,900,000. A fair price for a policy would be $\frac{\$9,900,000}{200,000}$ or $49.50, the average of the fair price for males and the fair price for females.

d. Responses will vary. The procedures should be very similar to each other: divide the total payout by the number of "players."

e. They are similar in that we can compute the fair price for a ticket or policy in the same way. However, in a raffle, the people running the game know exactly how much they will pay out in prizes. The insurance company is taking a much bigger chance. It never knows exactly how many deaths there will be per 100,000 policyholders.

f. No, they charge more than the fair price. Insurance companies have to cover costs of doing business such as buildings and salaries, and they also want to make a profit.

SHARE AND SUMMARIZE   full-class discussion

This checkpoint is important to clarify the idea of *fair* and to compare it to the idea of *expectation*. It may help if you ask students to give an example of *expected value* from a previous situation (such as the expected number of rolls to get doubles) and to compare this to the fair value found in one of the situations in Investigation 1. It is important that students see the connections.

Checkpoint

See Teaching Master 170.

ⓐ They have the same value.

ⓑ Add the values of the prizes and divide this amount by the number of tickets being sold.

ⓒ Multiply the value of the policy by the expected number of deaths per 100,000 customers and then divide by 100,000. This is the same thing as multiplying the value of the policy by the probability of a death.

ⓓ A fair price would be 60 cents. See the answer to Part b of the "Think About This Situation" on page T510.

CONSTRUCTING A MATH TOOLKIT: Students should write in their Math Toolkits a general procedure for determining the fair price in situations involving chance.

Unit 7

Students now can begin
Modeling Task 1, Organizing
Task 4, or Reflecting Task 3 or 4
from the MORE assignment following Investigation 2.

▶On Your Own

a. The total value of the prizes is 10($10) + $500, or $600. The fair price for a ticket is $\frac{\$600}{1,000} = \$0.60$.

b. If 100 students each buy a policy, the insurance company expects 7 of them to have some property stolen. The company expects to pay 7($30) or $210. A fair price for a policy would be $\frac{\$210}{100}$ or $2.10.

INVESTIGATION 2 Fair Price and Expected Value

1. See Teaching Master 171 for use with Part c.

a. The average winnings will be $3.50, so $3.50 is the fair price.

b.

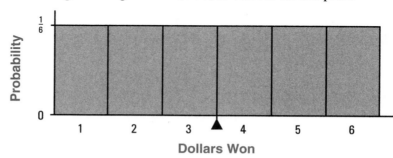

The balance point, or average, of the histogram is 3.5, which is the same as the fair price.

Unit 7

▶ **On Your Own**

a. The prizes in a raffle are ten $10-cassettes and one $500-stereo. If 1,000 raffle tickets will be sold, what is the fair price for a ticket?

b. According to the U.S. Department of Justice, about 7% of high school students reported that they had some property stolen at school within the previous year. (Source: *The World Almanac and Book of Facts 1993*. Mahwah, NJ: World Almanac, 1992.) Suppose the average value of the stolen property in that year was $30. Assuming these statistics stay the same each year, what would be the fair price to charge a student who wanted to be insured against theft for one year of high school?

INVESTIGATION ▶2 Fair Price and Expected Value

You have learned how to construct and analyze probability distributions. In this investigation, you will learn a method of computing the fair price of a game if you are given the probability distribution of the prizes.

1. Examine the probability distribution table below.

Prize Value x	Probability $P(x)$
$1	$\frac{1}{6}$
$2	$\frac{1}{6}$
$3	$\frac{1}{6}$
$4	$\frac{1}{6}$
$5	$\frac{1}{6}$
$6	$\frac{1}{6}$
Total	$\frac{6}{6}$

a. What is the fair price for a game that has this probability distribution?

b. Make a histogram of this probability distribution table. Locate the fair price on the histogram. How does this compare to the mean (balance point) of the distribution?

c. Complete the last column of this table, including the total.

Prize Value x	Probability $P(x)$	$x \cdot P(x)$
1	$\frac{1}{6}$	
2	$\frac{1}{6}$	
3	$\frac{1}{6}$	$\frac{3}{6}$
4	$\frac{1}{6}$	
5	$\frac{1}{6}$	
6	$\frac{1}{6}$	
Total	$\frac{6}{6}$	

d. Compare your total from Part c with the fair price from Part b. What do you notice?

2. The chart below gives the possible outcomes and their probabilities for a version of a scratch-off game played at McDonalds. What is the fair price of one scratch-off card?

Prize	Probability
Win free fries worth 90¢	$\frac{1}{6}$
Win nothing	$\frac{5}{6}$
Total	$\frac{6}{6}$

3. Here is the table for another scratch-off game.

Prize Value	Probability
$1	$\frac{4}{10}$
$2	$\frac{2}{10}$
$3	$\frac{2}{10}$
$5	$\frac{1}{10}$
Win nothing	$\frac{1}{10}$
Total	$\frac{10}{10}$

a. What is the fair price of one scratch-off card?

b. Make a histogram of this probability distribution.

c. Estimate the balance point of the histogram. Compare this answer with the fair price of the card that you computed in Part a. What do you notice?

1. c. See Teaching Master 171.

Price Value *x*	Probability *P*(*x*)	*x* · *P*(*x*)
1	$\frac{1}{6}$	$\frac{1}{6}$
2	$\frac{1}{6}$	$\frac{2}{6}$
3	$\frac{1}{6}$	$\frac{3}{6}$
4	$\frac{1}{6}$	$\frac{4}{6}$
5	$\frac{1}{6}$	$\frac{5}{6}$
6	$\frac{1}{6}$	$\frac{6}{6}$
Total	$\frac{6}{6}$	$\frac{21}{6} = 3.5$

d. The total in Part c and the fair price in Part b are the same. The procedure in Part c is a method of computing the expected value.

2. A fair price (expected value) for a card would be $0.90\left(\frac{1}{6}\right) + 0\left(\frac{5}{6}\right) = 0.15$ or 15¢.

3. a. The fair price is $(\$1)\left(\frac{4}{10}\right) + (\$2)\left(\frac{2}{10}\right) + (\$3)\left(\frac{2}{10}\right) + (\$5)\left(\frac{1}{10}\right) + (\$0)\left(\frac{1}{10}\right)$ or $1.90.

b.

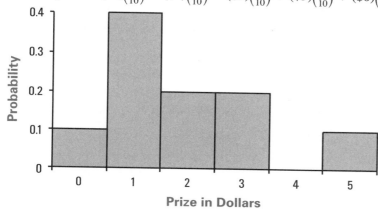

c. The balance point is around $2, which is close to the fair price. This result is no coincidence: the average, or balance point, of a probability distribution is the same as its **expected value** (*E.V.*).

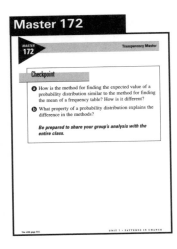

4. a. The expected value of a game is the average amount won on a single play. The fair price is the amount that should be charged to play the game so that in the long run, the players expect to come out even. The fair price and the expected value of a game are equal since the fair price is equal to the total amount expected to be won divided by the number of times the game will be played, which is the average amount won on a single play.

b. $E.V. = 2\left(\frac{1}{36}\right) + 3\left(\frac{2}{36}\right) + 4\left(\frac{3}{36}\right) + 5\left(\frac{4}{36}\right) + 6\left(\frac{5}{36}\right) + 7\left(\frac{6}{36}\right) + 8\left(\frac{5}{36}\right) + 9\left(\frac{4}{36}\right) +$
$10\left(\frac{3}{36}\right) + 11\left(\frac{2}{36}\right) + 12\left(\frac{1}{36}\right) = 7$

5. Responses will vary, but examples follow.

a. One possibility is to make a table with three columns: the first column gives the (numerical) outcome of an event, the second gives the probability of the given event happening, and the third gives the products of the first two columns' entries. In other words, column one has a heading Event Value x, column two is Probability $P(x)$, and column three is $x \cdot P(x)$. The total of column three is the expected value of the probability distribution.

b. Enter the first column of the table in List 1 and the second column in List 2. Define List 3 as the product of Lists 1 and 2 ($L_3 = L_1 \cdot L_2$). Finally, find the sum of List 3.

SHARE AND SUMMARIZE full-class discussion

Checkpoint

See Teaching Master 172.

a In both cases, we multiply the value by how often it occurs (frequency or probability) and add up these products. However, in a probability distribution, you don't need to "divide by the total frequency" because that number, in a sense, is the sum of the probabilities or 1. Compare these two tables:

Amount Won	Frequency	(Outcome)(Frequency)
$1	6	6
$2	4	8
Total	10	14

The average is $\frac{14}{10} = 1.4 = \$1.40$.

Amount Won	Probability	(Outcome)(Probability)
$1	$\frac{6}{10}$	$\frac{6}{10}$
$2	$\frac{4}{10}$	$\frac{8}{10}$
Total	1	$\frac{14}{10}$

The expected value is $\frac{14}{10} = 1.4 = \$1.40$.

b The property of a probability distribution that explains the difference is that the sum of the probabilities is always 1. Dividing by 1 does not change the answer, and so it is not necessary.

CONSTRUCTING A MATH TOOLKIT: Students should summarize in their Math Toolkits the method for finding the expected value of a probability distribution.

See additional Teaching Notes on page T533Q.

4. The mean of a probability distribution is called the **expected value** (*E.V.*).

   a. Explain why the expected value gives the fair price for a game if the probability distribution represents the chances of winning the various prizes in the game.

   b. Find the expected value of the probability distribution table for the sum of two dice. (See Activity 3 of Investigation 2 from Lesson 3, page 496).

5. a. Describe a general procedure for finding the expected value of a probability distribution.

   b. Describe how to implement this procedure in an efficient way on your calculator or computer.

> **Checkpoint**
>
> **a** How is the method for finding the expected value of a probability distribution similar to the method for finding the mean of a frequency table? How is it different?
>
> **b** What property of a probability distribution explains the difference in the methods?
>
> ***Be prepared to share your group's analysis with the entire class.***

▶ **On Your Own**

Find the expected value (fair price) of a ticket from the scratch-off game described in the following table.

Prize/Value	Probability
Free soft drink (89¢)	$\frac{15}{100}$
Free hamburger ($1.29)	$\frac{8}{100}$
T-shirt with restaurant logo ($7.50)	$\frac{3}{100}$
Movie passes ($15.00)	$\frac{1}{100}$
You lose! ($0.00)	$\frac{73}{100}$
Total	$\frac{100}{100}$

Unit 7

MORE

Modeling

1. A Las Vegas Keno ticket has the numbers from 1 to 80 on it. Twenty different numbers are drawn at random. Suppose a player chooses to mark one number on a Keno card. If that number is one of those drawn, the player wins $3.00 for a $1.00 bet.

   a. What is the probability the player wins $3.00?

   b. Is $1.00 a fair price for a ticket? Explain.

   c. What would be a fair price for a bet?

   d. A player also could choose to mark one number and bet $5.00. If that number is one of those drawn, the player wins $15.00. Is this wiser than betting $1.00?

2. Play the game below several times.

   In a game of matching, two people each flip a coin. If both coins match (both heads or both tails), Player B gets a point. If the coins don't match, Player A gets two points.

   a. What is the probability that Player A wins a round? That Player B wins?

   b. Explain why this is or is not a fair game.

3. The table below is copied from the back of a ticket in a scratch-off California lottery game.

Prize	Probability of Winning
$0.75	$\frac{1}{10}$
$2.00	$\frac{1}{14.71}$
$4.00	$\frac{1}{71}$
$10.00	$\frac{1}{50}$
$20.00	$\frac{1}{417}$
$250.00	$\frac{1}{1000}$

   a. What is the probability of winning nothing with one ticket?

   b. What is the expected value of a ticket?

   c. The tickets in this lottery sell for $1.00 each. How much money does the California government expect to make if 1,000,000 tickets are sold?

Modeling

MORE
ASSIGNMENT *pp. 516–520*

Modeling: 1, 3, and 4
Organizing: 3, and 2 or 4*
Reflecting: Choose two*
Extending: 3

*When choice is indicated, it is important to leave the choice to the student.
NOTE: *It is best if Organizing tasks are discussed as a whole class after they have been assigned as homework.*

1. **a.** Since the player selects only one number and 20 are selected out of 80, the probability of winning this game is $\frac{20}{80}$ or $\frac{1}{4}$.

   b. No. If a player plays four times, he or she expects to win once. Thus a fair price is $\frac{\$3}{4} = \$0.75$. Alternatively, the expected value (fair price) is $(\$3)\left(\frac{1}{4}\right) + (\$0)\left(\frac{3}{4}\right)$ or $\$0.75$.

   c. $0.75 would be a fair price.

   d. These are equally bad bets. The expected value on each $1.00 of either bet is the same, only 75 cents.

2. **a.** The probability that Player A wins is $\frac{1}{2}$ since there are four equally likely outcomes (*HH*, *HT*, *TH*, *TT*), and two are wins for Player A. The probability that Player B wins is also $\frac{1}{2}$.

   b. This game is not fair. Since Player A and Player B are equally likely to win, the point rewards should be the same.

3. **a.** Approximately 0.795

   b. $0.765

   c. The California government makes about $0.235 per ticket, or $235,000 for every 1,000,000 tickets sold. From this, the state must pay the costs of running the lottery including printing tickets and paying the stores that sell the tickets.

Unit 7

4. **a.** Game A: $\left(\frac{1}{2}\right)(1) = \frac{1}{2}$

   Game B: $\left(\frac{1}{2}\right)(1)\left(\frac{1}{2}\right) = \frac{1}{4}$

   Game C: $\left(\frac{1}{2}\right)\left(\frac{1}{2}\right)\left(\frac{1}{2}\right) = \frac{1}{8}$

   Game D: $\left(\frac{1}{2}\right)\left(\frac{1}{2}\right)\left(\frac{1}{2}\right)\left(\frac{1}{2}\right) = \frac{1}{16}$

   b. Game A: $(55¢)\left(\frac{1}{2}\right) = 27.5$ cents

   Game B: $(69¢)\left(\frac{1}{4}\right) = 17.25$ cents

   Game C: $(144¢)\left(\frac{1}{8}\right) = 18$ cents

   Game D: $(199¢)\left(\frac{1}{16}\right) = 12.4375$ cents

   c. Game A has the highest probability of winning something.

   d. Game A also has the largest expected value.

Organizing

1. $\sum P(x) = 1$ because the sum of the probabilities of all possible events is always 1.
2. **a.** $0.90; \frac{6}{6}$ or 1; 0.135

   b. $11.00; \frac{10}{10}$ or 1; 5.5

4. A fast-food restaurant once had a scratch-off game in which a player picked just one of the four games on the card to play. In each game, the player stepped along a path, scratching off one of two adjacent boxes at each step. To win, the player had to get from start to finish without scratching off a "lose" box. Here's how the games on one card would have looked. (Of course, the words were covered until the player scratched off the covering.)

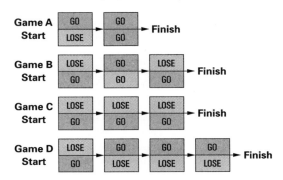

a. What is the probability of winning each game?

The prizes for the games were as follows.

   Game A: free food worth 55¢
   Game B: free food worth 69¢
   Game C: free food worth $1.44
   Game D: free food worth $1.99

b. What is the expected value of each game?

c. Which is the best game to pick if you just want to win something?

d. Which is the best game to pick if you want to have the largest expected value?

Organizing

1. Complete this sentence: In any probability distribution table,
$\sum P(x) =$ _____ because _____ .

2. Using the indicated probability distribution tables from Investigation 2, page 514, find each of the following sums.

   ■ $\sum x$

   ■ $\sum P(x)$

   ■ $\sum x^2 \cdot P(x)$

a. The table from Activity 2

b. The table from Activity 3

3. Write an expression that uses a summation sign and gives the expected value of the probability distribution of a single roll of a die.

4. In a carnival game, players toss quarters onto a table marked with a grid. The length of a side of each square is 10 cm.

It's easy to be sure a quarter lands somewhere on the table, but exactly where is a fairly random event. If a tossed quarter lands entirely inside a square, the player wins a small prize. If the quarter touches a line, the player wins nothing. The game operator keeps the quarter in both cases. What should the prize be worth to make this a fair game? (**Hint:** Think in terms of where the center of the quarter must land so that the quarter does not touch a line.)

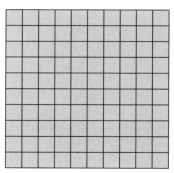

Reflecting

1. If your state has a lottery, investigate the amount of money bet, the amount of money paid in prizes, the operating costs of the lottery, the profit your state makes, and what your state does with the profits of its lottery. Compute the expected value of a ticket. Write a brief report explaining why you support or oppose such lotteries.

2. Why don't gambling games charge the fair price for playing? Why do people gamble when the price of playing a game is more than the expected value of the play?

3. According to the National Center for Health Statistics, in 1993 a newborn male in the United States could expect to live 72.2 years. A 20-year-old male could expect to live to the age of 73.5. A newborn female could expect to live to the age of 78.8, and a 20-year-old female to the age of 79.8. (Source: U.S. Bureau of Statistics, *Statistical Abstract of the United States: 1996,* 116th edition. Washington, DC, 1995.)

   a. What is meant, in this case, by the words "expect to live to the age of"?

   b. Why is the life expectancy for a 20-year-old greater than for a newborn?

   c. Do some research to find some of the reasons scientists give for why females can expect to live longer than males.

3. $E.V. = \sum \frac{1}{6}n$

4. The radius of a quarter is about 1.2 cm. The quarter must land so that its center is farther than 1.2 cm from a side of the square. That is, the center of the quarter must land within the shaded area below.

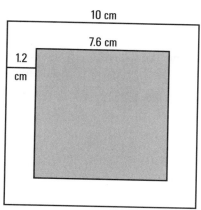

The probability that the center of the quarter will lie within the shaded square is $\frac{7.6^2}{10^2}$ or 0.5776. Since the game costs a quarter, the expected value should be $0.25. If x is the value of the prize, then $0.5776x = 0.25$. Thus $x \approx \$0.433$.

Reflecting

1. Reports will vary. Many state lotteries pay out about 50 cents for every dollar bet.

2. This question is best discussed by the whole class. Gambling games aren't fair because the operator wants to make money. Bring out these points if students do not: it may be the gambler's only chance of ever getting a lot of money, it provides entertainment, a gambler may get addicted, a gambler doesn't understand the probabilities involved and thinks he or she is more likely to win now because he or she has lost in the past.

3. **a.** If we could determine the ages at death for all males who were 20 at the time of this report and average them, that average would be 73.5.

   b. The newborn has a chance of dying before reaching his or her 20th birthday. The 20-year-old already has survived those years.

   c. Responses will vary. Some possible reasons are females tend to have less heart trouble than males, teen violence tends to affect males more than females, and generally women may take fewer life-threatening risks than men.

Unit 7

4. Responses will vary. See answers to Task 3, Part c.

Extending

1. **a.** One way to solve this problem is to reason that we expect one-half of the 5 tosses to be heads, so we expect 2.5 heads.

    Another way to solve the problem is to compute the expected value of the probability distribution by completing the third column in the table and finding its sum.

Number of Heads	Probability	(Number)(Probability)
0	$\frac{1}{32}$	0
1	$\frac{5}{32}$	$\frac{5}{32}$
2	$\frac{10}{32}$	$\frac{20}{32}$
3	$\frac{10}{32}$	$\frac{30}{32}$
4	$\frac{5}{32}$	$\frac{20}{32}$
5	$\frac{1}{32}$	$\frac{5}{32}$
Total	$\frac{32}{32}$	$\frac{80}{32} = 2.5$

    A third way is to make a histogram of the probability distribution and estimate its balance point.

   b. José doesn't understand that the average doesn't have to be one of the possible values because he doesn't understand the mathematical meaning of the word *expect*. He needs to understand that to say the expected value is 2.5 means that if the coin were repeatedly tossed five times, the average of the number of heads that would come up is 2.5.

2. Games and results will vary.

4. Investigate why young adult males have a higher death rate than young adult females. Do you believe it is fair to charge different rates for life insurance for men and for women? Is charging different rates legal in your state? What is the situation for automobile insurance?

Extending

1. This probability distribution table gives the probability of getting a given number of heads if a coin is tossed five times.

Number of Heads	Probability
0	$\frac{1}{32}$
1	$\frac{5}{32}$
2	$\frac{10}{32}$
3	$\frac{10}{32}$
4	$\frac{5}{32}$
5	$\frac{1}{32}$
Total	$\frac{32}{32}$

a. What is the expected number of heads if a person tosses five coins? Find the answer to this question in at least two different ways.

b. José says that the answer to Part a cannot involve half a head. How would you help him understand why it can?

2. Design a simple game that a baby-sitter could play with a young child. Make the game unfair. That is, one player has a better chance of winning than the other. Play your game with a friend and revise it if necessary. Play your game with a child. Did the child notice the game was unfair? In what ways did the child's understanding of probability differ from yours?

3. To help raise money for the local chapter of Big Brothers/Big Sisters, a college service organization decided to run a carnival. In addition to rides, they planned games of skill and games of chance. For one of the booths, a member suggested using a large spinner wheel with the numbers from 1 to 10 on it. The group considered three different games that could be played. The games are described in Parts a–c below. For each game, do the following:

- Make a table showing all possible outcomes and their probabilities.
- Calculate the expected value of the option, and compare that value to the price of playing the game.
- Determine if the game will raise money, lose money, or break even (neither raise nor lose money) in the long run. If the game will not make money, recommend a change that the group might consider.

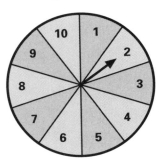

a. **Double Dare** To play this game, the player must pay the booth attendant $1. The player then chooses two numbers from one to ten and gives the wheel a spin. If the wheel stops on either of the two numbers, the attendant gives the player a prize worth $15.

b. **Anything Goes** For this game, the player can choose either one or two numbers. The player again must pay the attendant $1. After paying the attendant and choosing numbers, the player spins the wheel. If the wheel stops on a number the player chose, the attendant gives the player a prize. If the player selected only one number, the prize is worth $10. If the player selected two numbers, the prize is worth $5.

c. **Triple Threat** This game is a little more expensive to play. The player must pay $3 to spin the wheel. If the wheel stops on 1, 2, or 3, the player loses, receiving no prize. If the wheel stops on 4, 5, 6, or 7, the attendant gives the player a prize worth $2. If the wheel stops on 8, 9, or 10, the player gets a prize worth $6.

3. a. ■

Prize Value	Probability	(Outcome)(Probability)
$15	$\frac{2}{10}$	$3.00
$0	$\frac{8}{10}$	$0.00
Total	$\frac{10}{10}$	$3.00

- ■ The expected value for this game is $3, but the price to pay is only $1.
- ■ The game will lose an average of $2 per play in the long run. Either a less expensive prize must be given, or the group must charge more (at least $3). Reducing the probability of winning to $\frac{1}{10}$ will not allow the game to make money.

b. ■ Assume the player selects one number.

Prize Value	Probability	(Outcome)(Probability)
$10	$\frac{1}{10}$	$1.00
$0	$\frac{9}{10}$	$0.00
Total	$\frac{10}{10}$	$1.00

Assume the player splits 1 between two numbers. The table now looks like this:

Prize Value	Probability	(Outcome)(Probability)
$5	$\frac{2}{10}$	$1.00
$0	$\frac{8}{10}$	$0.00
Total	$\frac{10}{10}$	$1.00

- ■ In both cases, the expected value is $1, which is also the price to play the game.
- ■ The game will neither make money nor lose money, since the price to play is the fair price. Changing the prize value or price to play will help.

c. ■

Prize Value	Probability	(Outcome)(Probability)
$0	$\frac{3}{10}$	$0.00
$2	$\frac{4}{10}$	$0.80
$6	$\frac{3}{10}$	$1.80
Total	$\frac{10}{10}$	$2.60

- ■ The expected value for this game is $2.60, and the group will charge $3.00 for each play.
- ■ The group will make an average of $0.40 (in the long run) for each play. This is a good option for them to use without modification.

Unit 7

INVESTIGATION 3 ► Expected Value of a Waiting-Time Distribution

In this investigation, students find a theoretical way to calculate the expected value of a waiting-time distribution. At this point, students know how to calculate the individual probabilities, but they have to repeat their efforts to create a long table (or extensive histogram) representing the situation so that an average can be found. In the case of a waiting-time distribution, the table of possibilities is endless (or the histogram has an infinitely long tail) so that we cannot calculate an exact average or expected value. The strategy in this investigation is for students to cooperate to find good estimates for distributions with different underlying probabilities and to look for a pattern.

Since the answers for each group's contribution to the entire picture are going to be estimates, it is important that the issue of accuracy be discussed and decided at the outset. Therefore, it may be best to do Activity 1 as a full class.

After Activity 1, you have added only one answer to the table, but the method has been reviewed and the issue of accuracy has been decided. Possible shortcuts may have been described. You can assign to each group one or more distributions to make and to find the expected values. This should go quite quickly, and afterwards you can bring everyone back together to share all the data and to make the graph. Discussion should focus on possible models for a graph of this shape. The model that fits best should be $y = \frac{1}{x}$ or $E.V. = \frac{1}{p}$.

1. **a.** Because the table actually has an infinite number of rows and you are using only the first 12 or so, you will underestimate the expected value.
   b. Depending on rounding, the students should get about 3.33.
   c. Larger because the missing rows would add to the sum.
   d. A 26th row would change the expected value by approximately 0.001046.

INVESTIGATION 3 · Expected Value of a Waiting-Time Distribution

One of the waiting-time distributions you have constructed is for the waiting time to draw a brown "M&M's"® Chocolate Candy. The probability of success on a single trial is 0.3. The distribution table is shown below.

Number of Draws to Get First Brown	Probability
1	0.3
2	$(0.7)(0.3)$
3	$(0.7)^2(0.3)$
4	$(0.7)^3(0.3)$
5	$(0.7)^4(0.3)$
6	$(0.7)^5(0.3)$
7	$(0.7)^6(0.3)$
8	$(0.7)^7(0.3)$
9	$(0.7)^8(0.3)$
10	$(0.7)^9(0.3)$
11	$(0.7)^{10}(0.3)$
12	$(0.7)^{11}(0.3)$
⋮	⋮

There should be an *infinite* number of rows in the table. It is possible, although definitely a rare event, that hundreds or thousands of candies would be drawn before the first brown one appeared.

1. In this activity and the next one, you will explore how to find the expected number of draws until a brown "M&M's"® Chocolate Candy appears. In other words, if a large number of people each draw candies until a brown one appears, what is the average number they draw?

   a. What happens if you try to use the $x \cdot P(x)$ procedure from Investigation 2 to find the expected value of this waiting-time distribution?

   b. Make an estimate of the expected value of the distribution by using just the first 25 rows of the table to compute the expected value.

   c. Is the real expected value larger or smaller than your estimate in Part b?

   d. How much would adding the 26th row change your expected value?

Unit 7

2. Place your estimated expected value from Activity 1, Part b in the appropriate space in a copy of the table below.

Expected Value of Waiting Times

Probability of a Success on Each Trial, p	Estimated Average Waiting Time (Expected Value)
0.10	10
0.20	
0.30	
0.40	
0.50	
0.60	
0.70	
0.80	
0.90	

a. Now the students in your class should regroup, if necessary, into seven groups, one for each of the remaining values of p in the table above. Each group should construct a waiting-time probability distribution table for its value of p. Tables should have at least 25 rows. Then estimate the expected waiting time for your value of p.

b. Get the expected values from each of the groups and fill in the rest of the table.

c. Using a copy of this coordinate grid, make a scatterplot of the data from your table.

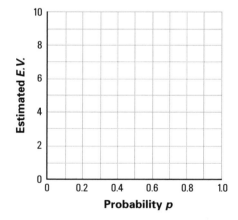

2. **See Teaching Master 173.**

   a–b. The completed table should look similar to this one containing the theoretical expected values:

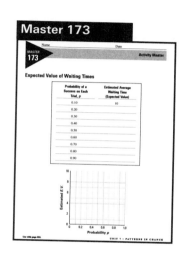

Expected Value of Waiting Times

Probability of a Success on Each Trial p	Estimated Averaged Waiting Time (Expected Value)
0.10	10.00
0.20	5.00
0.30	3.33
0.40	2.50
0.50	2.00
0.60	1.67
0.70	1.43
0.80	1.25
0.90	1.11

c.

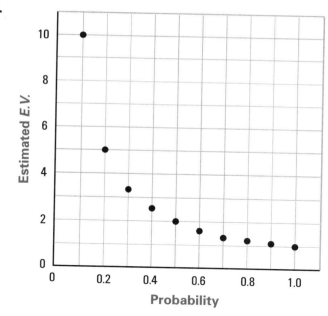

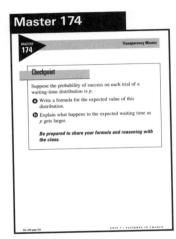

Master 174

2. d. Since the event is sure to happen on the first trial, the expected value is 1.

e. The points appear to lie near the graph of the equation of an inverse power function, $y = \frac{k}{x}$. Specifically, we have $E.V. = \frac{1}{p}$.

A proof of this formula for the case $p = \frac{1}{6}$ appears on page T529, using the sum of an infinite series. Following is another proof that $E.V. = \frac{1}{p}$, although the reasoning will be too difficult for most of your students at this stage.

Let x be the expected waiting time. If you succeed on the first attempt, the actual waiting time is 1. If you fail on the first attempt, the actual waiting time is, on average, $x + 1$. This is because while the expected waiting time is x, we already have one failure. At that point, we are effectively starting over, but we need to add our one failure to the average. Since you must either succeed or fail on the first attempt, you have probability of waiting 1 and probability $(1 - p)$ of waiting an average of $x + 1$ attempts. That is, $x = p(1) + (1 - p)(x + 1)$. Solving for x gives $x = \frac{1}{p}$.

f. $E.V. = \frac{1}{0.3} = 3\frac{1}{3} \approx 3.33$ candies

3. a. The probability of getting a sum of 6 on each roll is $\frac{5}{36}$, so

$$E.V. = \frac{1}{\frac{5}{36}} = \frac{36}{5} = 7.2 \text{ rolls.}$$

b. $E.V. = \frac{1}{0.25} = 4$ adults

c. $E.V. = \frac{1}{\frac{1}{14,000,000}} = 14,000,000$ weeks

This would be $\frac{14,000,000}{52} \approx 269,231$ years or $\frac{269,231}{75} \approx 3,590$ lifetimes.

CONSTRUCTING A MATH TOOLKIT: Students should include the formula for finding the expected value of a waiting-time probability distribution with their previous Toolkit entry. (See page T488.)

SHARE AND SUMMARIZE   full-class discussion

Checkpoint

See Teaching Master 174.

ⓐ $E.V. = \frac{1}{p}$

ⓑ As p gets larger, the expected waiting time gets smaller. If p is large, we have a larger chance of getting a success than if p is small, and so we expect to get a success sooner on the average.

APPLY   individual task

▶On Your Own

a. You need to know the probability of success on each trial.

b. $\frac{1}{0.2} = 5$ candies

d. What is the expected value when $p = 1.00$? Plot the corresponding point on the scatterplot.

e. Describe the overall pattern relating probability p and expected value *E.V.* Find an equation whose graph fits these points well.

f. According to your equation, how many candies would you expect to draw until you get a brown one?

3. Use your equation from Activity 2 to answer the following questions.

a. Suppose you want a sum of 6 on two dice. How many times do you expect to have to roll the dice?

b. About 25% of adults bite their fingernails. How many adults do you expect to have to choose at random until you find a fingernail biter?

c. There is about 1 chance in 14,000,000 of winning the California lottery with a single ticket. If you buy one ticket a week, how many weeks do you expect to pass until you win the lottery? How many years is this? If an average lifetime is 75 years, how many lifetimes is this?

Checkpoint

Suppose the probability of success on each trial of a waiting-time distribution is p.

ⓐ Write a formula for the expected value of this distribution.

ⓑ Explain what happens to the expected waiting time as p gets larger.

Be prepared to share your formula and reasoning with the class.

In Investigation 3, you discovered the formula for the expected value of a waiting-time distribution. It can be proved by twice using the method outlined in Extending Task 3 from the following MORE set.

▶ On Your Own

a. What information do you need about a waiting-time distribution in order to calculate the expected value of the distribution using the formula from the Checkpoint above?

b. Twenty percent of "M&M's"® Plain Chocolate Candies are red. How many candies would you expect to draw from a bag until you got a red one?

MORE

Modeling

1. Two statisticians have estimated that about 6% of all pennies go out of circulation each year. About 10,000,000,000 pennies are minted each year in the United States. Assume that was the number minted the year you were born.

a. Complete this theoretical probability distribution table for the number of those pennies that go out of circulation each year. Add as many rows as you need to get to this year.

Circulation of Pennies from Your Birth Year

Years Since Your Birth	Number of Pennies That Go out of Circulation	Number of Pennies Still Left in Circulation
0	–	10,000,000,000
1	600,000,000	9,400,000,000
2		
3		
4		
5		
⋮		

b. Write a *NOW-NEXT* equation describing the pattern of change in each of the last two columns.

c. Approximately what percentage of the pennies minted the year you were born are still in circulation?

d. Compute the average length of time a penny will stay in circulation using the formula from the Checkpoint on page 523.

e. About how long will it (or did it) take for half of the pennies minted in the year you were born to go out of circulation? (This length of time is called the *half-life* of a penny.)

Modeling

MORE
ASSIGNMENT *pp. 524–529*

Modeling: 1 and 2
Organizing: 1, 2, and 4
Reflecting: Choose two*
Extending: 2

*When choice is indicated, it is important to leave the choice to the student.
NOTE: *It is best if Organizing tasks are discussed as a whole class after they have been assigned as homework.*

1. a. Exact number of rows may vary, depending on students' ages.

Years Since Your Birth	Number of Pennies That Go Out of Circulation	Number of Pennies Still Left in Circulation
0	–	10,000,000,000
1	600,000,000	9,400,000,000
2	564,000,000	8,836,000,000
3	530,160,000	8,305,840,000
4	498,350,400	7,807,489,600
5	468,449,376	7,339,040,224
6	440,342,413	6,898,697,811
7	413,921,869	6,484,775,942
8	389,086,557	6,095,689,385
9	365,741,363	5,729,948,022
10	343,796,881	5,386,151,141
11	323,169,069	5,062,982,072
12	303,778,924	4,759,203,148
13	285,552,189	4,473,650,959
14	268,419,058	4,205,231,902
15	252,313,914	3,952,917,988
16	237,175,079	3,715,742,908
17	222,944,575	3,492,798,334
18	209,567,900	3,283,230,434
19	196,993,826	3,086,236,608

b. Second column: $NEXT = 0.94\ NOW$
Third column: $NEXT = 0.94\ NOW$

c. Responses will vary, depending on students' ages. See the table on the right.

d. Expected (average) length of time until a penny goes out of circulation is $\frac{1}{0.06}$ or approximately 16.667 years.

e. About 11 years

Age	Percentage of Pennies Still in Circulation
12	$(0.94)^{12} \approx 0.476$
13	0.447
14	0.421
15	0.395
16	0.372
17	0.349
18	0.328
19	0.309

Unit 7

2. a.

Hours	Milligrams of Medicine Leaving the Blood	Milligrams of Medicine Left in the Blood
0	0	400
1	140.00	260.00
2	91.00	169.00
3	59.15	109.85
4	38.45	71.40
5	24.99	46.41
6	16.24	30.17

b. The first two columns define a waiting-time distribution that is much like the others we have studied such as the waiting time to get doubles. There is a difference, however. The medicine doesn't leave the blood after the end of 1 hour. This is a continuous process. The medicine leaves gradually throughout the hour. (This is also true of the pennies in Modeling Task 1.)

c. Expected (average) length of time in the blood is $\frac{1}{0.35}$ or 2.857 hours.

d. Between 1 and 2 hours

3. a. The expected time for each strontium-90 atom to decay is $\frac{1}{0.025}$ or 40 years.

b. After 100 years, $(0.975)^{100}$ or about 7.95% of the radioactive strontium-90 will be left.

2. Painkillers often are given as shots to people who have sustained injuries. The time that it takes for a person's body to get the medicine out of his or her system varies from person to person. Suppose one person is given 400 mg of a medicine, and her body metabolizes the medicine so 35% is removed from her bloodstream each hour.

   a. Complete the following chart.

Hours	Milligrams of Medicine Leaving the Blood	Milligrams of Medicine Left in the Blood
0	0	400
1		
2		
3		
4		
5		
6		

   b. Is your table different from the other waiting-time distribution tables you have studied? Explain.

   c. How long does the average milligram of medicine stay in the blood?

   d. What is the approximate half-life of medicine in the blood? That is, how long does it take for half of the medicine to be gone?

3. In the 1986 nuclear reactor disaster at Chernobyl, in the former Soviet Union, radioactive atoms of strontium-90 were released. Strontium-90 decays at the rate of 2.5% a year.

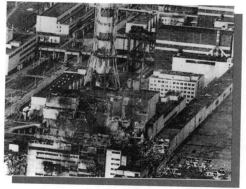

   a. What is the expected time it takes for a strontium-90 atom to decay?

   b. Supposedly it will be safe again for people to live in the area after 100 years. What percentage of the strontium-90 released still will be present after 100 years?

LESSON 4 • EXPECTED VALUE OF A PROBABILITY DISTRIBUTION   525

4. Krypton-91 is a radioactive substance that gradually disintegrates. About 7% of krypton-91 disintegrates every second. Superman® is locked in a room with 5 grams of krypton-91. He can live only 30 seconds if he is near more than a gram of krypton-91.

© 1997 DC Comics

   a. Will Superman make it?

   b. When will half of the krypton-91 be gone? What is the half-life of krypton-91?

Yes, comic fans, we know it's not the same Krypton.

Organizing

1. You have studied many different models for expressing relationships between quantitative variables: linear, exponential, power, quadratic, and trigonometric. When examining the pattern in your scatterplot from Activity 2 of Investigation 3 (page 522), which of these models could you immediately rule out as not reasonable? Explain your reasoning.

2. If the expected value of a waiting-time distribution is 6.5, what is the probability p of success on each trial?

3. James draws marbles one at a time from a bag of green and white marbles. He replaces each marble before drawing the next. If the probability that he gets his first green marble on the second draw is 0.24, what percentage of the marbles in the bag are green?

4. a. Refer to Modeling Task 2, page 525. Write an equation that represents the number of milligrams of medicine left in the blood at any hour x.

   b. Refer to Modeling Task 1, page 524. Write an equation that represents the number of pennies minted in your birth year that are left in circulation x years later.

Reflecting

1. You now have several ways of finding the expected value of a waiting-time distribution. Describe each method. Will one of these methods be easier to remember than the others? Why?

2. Which of the following, if any, are correct interpretations of the expected value of a waiting-time distribution?

   ■ Half of the people wait longer than the *E.V.* and half shorter.

   ■ The *E.V.* is the most likely time to wait.

   ■ More than half of the people will wait longer than the *E.V.*

4. **a.** Students could complete a chart like the one in Modeling Task 2, or they could reason as follows: to find the probability an atom of krypton-91 will be left after 30 seconds, we can use the Multiplication Rule since the atom must survive the first second, survive the second, and so on.

   This probability is $(0.93)^{30}$ or approximately 0.113. We expect a proportion of 0.113 of the atoms to be left after 30 seconds, which is 0.113(5 grams) or 0.567 grams. Superman makes it.

   b. By a little experimentation, we find $(0.93)^9 \approx 0.520$ and $(0.93)^{10} \approx 0.484$. One-half of the krypton-91 is gone in 9 to 10 seconds. The half-life of krypton-91 is between 9 and 10 seconds. You might encourage students to use decimal values of the exponent to find the half-life more exactly and then discuss what rational exponents might mean.

Organizing

1. Since the points follow a curve, we know the relationship is not linear. It cannot be exponential or quadratic because it has a vertical asymptote at $x = 0$. Functions with a vertical asymptote include $y = \tan x$, $y = \frac{1}{x}$, and $y = \frac{1}{x^2}$.

2. We need to solve the equation $6.5 = \frac{1}{p}$ for p. Multiplying both sides by p, we get $6.5p = 1$. Finally, dividing both sides by 6.5 gives $p = \frac{1}{6.5} \approx 0.154$.

3. We need to solve the equation $(1 - p)p = 0.24$ for p. The two solutions are 0.6 and 0.4. So either 60% or 40% of the marbles in the bag are green.

4. **a.** $y = 400(0.65)^x$
   b. $y = 10,000,000,000(0.94)^x$

Reflecting

1. Responses to this will vary, particularly concerning the part asking which is easiest to remember. Students should include finding the balance point of a graph, computing $\sum x \cdot P(x)$, and computing $\frac{1}{p}$.

2. None of the three is a correct interpretation. For example, 100 people are flipping a coin until heads lands face up. Since $p = 0.5$ in this case, the *E.V.* is $\frac{1}{0.5}$ or 2. But we expect 50 people to get heads on the first flip and 25 to get heads on the second flip, for a total of 75 people on or before the *E.V.* Therefore, neither the first nor the third statement holds. The "most likely" time to wait is one flip since more people waited this long than any other time. So the second statement doesn't hold, either.

Unit 7

3. A complete answer would include a summary of the process students completed in Activity 2 of Investigation 2 (page 514), with an explanation of the table and corresponding graph.

4. **a.** $P(x)$ is the probability that success will happen first on the xth trial. p is the probability of a success on any given trial, all of which are independent in a waiting-time distribution. q is the probability of *not* having success on any given trial. Thus, $p + q = 1$.

   b. $\dfrac{1}{p}$

5. **a.** Estimates will vary. Ten billion pennies have a volume of approximately 4300 m^3.

   b. Estimates will vary.

   c. $100,000,000 (one hundred million dollars)

   d. The population of the United States is more than 250,000,000, so each person would get at most $\frac{\$100,000,000}{250,000,000} = \$0.40$. (And it seemed like so many pennies!)

   e. Pennies go out of circulation if they are lost, are put in coin collections, or are put in a drawer or bottle. Some are taken out of circulation when they become bent or worn. Some people actually throw them away.

Extending

1. **a.** Responses may vary. Possibilities include rolling a pair of dice and waiting for doubles, rolling a die and waiting for any particular number to turn up, or rolling a pair of dice and waiting for a sum of 7.

   b. $E.V. = \dfrac{1}{\frac{1}{6}} = 6$

3. In Investigation 3, you discovered a surprisingly simple formula for the expected value of a waiting-time distribution. Write a summary of the methods that led to this discovery.

4. Most of the waiting-time distributions you investigated in this unit could be represented by formulas of the form $P(x) = pq^{x-1}$.

   a. For a given situation, what would the symbols, $P(x)$, p, and q represent? How are p and q related?

   b. What is the expected value of this distribution?

5. Ten billion pennies are minted in the United States every year.

   a. Make an estimate of how many rooms the size of your classroom are needed to hold 10,000,000,000 neatly stacked pennies.

   b. Count the number of pennies that can be found at your home. Make an estimate of the number of pennies in circulation in the United States. Don't forget the pennies in cash registers.

   c. What is the value of 10,000,000,000 pennies in dollars?

   d. If ten billion pennies were distributed equally among all of the people in the United States, how much money would you get?

   e. In what ways could a penny "go out of circulation"?

Extending

1. Examine this typical waiting-time probability distribution table.

Number of Trials x	Probability $P(x)$
1	$\frac{1}{6}$
2	$\left(\frac{5}{6}\right)\left(\frac{1}{6}\right)$
3	$\left(\frac{5}{6}\right)^2\left(\frac{1}{6}\right)$
4	$\left(\frac{5}{6}\right)^3\left(\frac{1}{6}\right)$
5	$\left(\frac{5}{6}\right)^4\left(\frac{1}{6}\right)$
⋮	⋮

   a. What waiting-time experiment could the above table be describing?

   b. Find the expected waiting time.

2. You have seen two ways to compute the expected value of the waiting-time distribution for rolling doubles. The first is to use the formula $\sum x \cdot P(x)$, which gives an **infinite series:**

$$1\left(\tfrac{1}{6}\right) + 2\left(\tfrac{5}{6}\right)\left(\tfrac{1}{6}\right) + 3\left(\tfrac{5}{6}\right)^2\left(\tfrac{1}{6}\right) + 4\left(\tfrac{5}{6}\right)^3\left(\tfrac{1}{6}\right) + 5\left(\tfrac{5}{6}\right)^4\left(\tfrac{1}{6}\right) + \cdots.$$

The ellipsis (…) indicates that the series continues, following the same pattern.

The second way is to use the formula you discovered in this investigation:

$$E.V. = \frac{1}{\tfrac{1}{6}} = 6$$

Since these two methods give the same expected value, you can set them equal. So,

$$6 = 1\left(\tfrac{1}{6}\right) + 2\left(\tfrac{5}{6}\right)\left(\tfrac{1}{6}\right) + 3\left(\tfrac{5}{6}\right)^2\left(\tfrac{1}{6}\right) + 4\left(\tfrac{5}{6}\right)^3\left(\tfrac{1}{6}\right) + 5\left(\tfrac{5}{6}\right)^4\left(\tfrac{1}{6}\right) + \cdots.$$

It's rather amazing that a series can keep going forever and still add up to 6.

a. Write the next three terms of the infinite series above.

b. Here is another example of an infinite series:

Since $\tfrac{1}{3} = 0.333333333\ldots$ (check by dividing 1 by 3), you can write

$$\tfrac{1}{3} = 0.3333333\ldots = \tfrac{3}{10} + \tfrac{3}{100} + \tfrac{3}{1000} + \tfrac{3}{10\,000} + \tfrac{3}{100\,000} + \cdots$$

Multiply both sides of $\tfrac{1}{3} = 0.3333333\ldots$ by 3. What do you conclude?

c. Write $\tfrac{2}{3}$ as an infinite series.

d. The following square is 1 unit on each side.

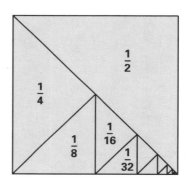

- What is the area of the square?
- Describe its area by adding the areas of the (infinite number of) individual triangles.
- What can you conclude?

2. a. $6\left(\frac{5}{6}\right)^5\left(\frac{1}{6}\right)$; $7\left(\frac{5}{6}\right)^6\left(\frac{1}{6}\right)$; $8\left(\frac{5}{6}\right)^7\left(\frac{1}{6}\right)$

b. $0.999999999 \ldots = 1$

This is particularly difficult for many people to believe, but it is true!

c. $\frac{6}{10} + \frac{6}{100} + \frac{6}{1,000} + \frac{6}{10,000} + \ldots$

d. ■ 1

■ $\frac{1}{2} + \frac{1}{4} + \frac{1}{8} + \frac{1}{16} + \frac{1}{32} + \ldots$

■ $1 = \frac{1}{2} + \frac{1}{4} + \frac{1}{8} + \frac{1}{16} + \frac{1}{32} + \ldots$

Unit 7

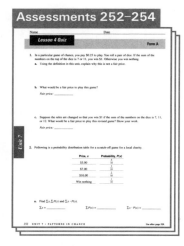
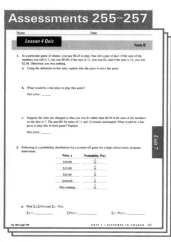
MORE *continued*

3. a. ■ $3S = 3\left(\frac{1}{3} + \frac{1}{9} + \frac{1}{27} + \frac{1}{81} + \ldots\right)$

$3S = \frac{3}{3} + \frac{3}{9} + \frac{3}{27} + \frac{3}{81} + \ldots$

$3S = 1 + \frac{1}{3} + \frac{1}{9} + \frac{1}{27} + \ldots$

Subtract:

$3S = 1 + \frac{1}{3} + \frac{1}{9} + \frac{1}{27} + \ldots$

$-S = \quad -\frac{1}{3} - \frac{1}{9} - \frac{1}{27} - \ldots$

_____

$2S = 1$

$S = \frac{1}{2}$

■ $S = \frac{7}{9}$

This is obtained by multiplying both sides of the equation by 10 and then subtracting to get $9S = 7$.

b. There is no multiplier that results in all of the terms except one canceling during the subtraction. In fact, this is the harmonic series, which grows infinitely large.

c. $S = \frac{1}{6} + \frac{1}{6}\left(\frac{5}{6}\right) + \frac{1}{6}\left(\frac{5}{6}\right)^2 + \frac{1}{6}\left(\frac{5}{6}\right)^3 + \ldots$

$\frac{6}{5}S = \frac{1}{5} + \frac{1}{6} + \frac{1}{6}\left(\frac{5}{6}\right) + \frac{1}{6}\left(\frac{5}{6}\right)^2 + \frac{1}{6}\left(\frac{5}{6}\right)^3 + \ldots$

Subtracting the first equation from the second gives $\frac{1}{5}S = \frac{1}{5}$, so $S = 1$.

See Assessment Resources, pages 252–257.

▶ How to Sum an Infinite Series for the Expected Value of a Waiting-Time Distribution

If your students liked the trick given for summing the infinite series, they will enjoy learning to sum the infinite series for the expected value of a waiting-time distribution. For example, the infinite sum for the expected waiting time to roll doubles is given here:

$$S = 1\left(\frac{1}{6}\right) + 2\left(\frac{5}{6}\right)\left(\frac{1}{6}\right) + 3\left(\frac{5}{6}\right)^2\left(\frac{1}{6}\right) + 4\left(\frac{5}{6}\right)^3\left(\frac{1}{6}\right) + \ldots$$

It is necessary to use the trick twice. First, multiply S by $\frac{6}{5}$.

$$\left(\frac{6}{5}\right)S = \left(\frac{1}{5}\right) + 2\left(\frac{1}{6}\right) + 3\left(\frac{5}{6}\right)\left(\frac{1}{6}\right) + 4\left(\frac{5}{6}\right)^2\left(\frac{1}{6}\right) + 5\left(\frac{5}{6}\right)^3\left(\frac{1}{6}\right) + \ldots$$

Subtracting S gives the following:

$$\left(\frac{6}{5}\right)S = \left(\frac{1}{5}\right) + 2\left(\frac{1}{6}\right) + 3\left(\frac{5}{6}\right)\left(\frac{1}{6}\right) + 4\left(\frac{5}{6}\right)^2\left(\frac{1}{6}\right) + 5\left(\frac{5}{6}\right)^3\left(\frac{1}{6}\right) + \ldots$$

$$-S = \quad -1\left(\frac{1}{6}\right) - 2\left(\frac{5}{6}\right)\left(\frac{1}{6}\right) - 3\left(\frac{5}{6}\right)^2\left(\frac{1}{6}\right) - 4\left(\frac{5}{6}\right)^3\left(\frac{1}{6}\right) - \ldots$$

$$\rule{5cm}{0.4pt}$$

$$\left(\frac{1}{5}\right)S = \left(\frac{1}{5}\right) + \left(\frac{1}{6}\right) + \left(\frac{5}{6}\right)\left(\frac{1}{6}\right) + \left(\frac{5}{6}\right)^2\left(\frac{1}{6}\right) + \left(\frac{5}{6}\right)^3\left(\frac{1}{6}\right) + \ldots$$

Since $\left(\frac{1}{6}\right) + \left(\frac{5}{6}\right)\left(\frac{1}{6}\right) + \left(\frac{5}{6}\right)^2\left(\frac{1}{6}\right) + \left(\frac{5}{6}\right)^3\left(\frac{1}{6}\right) + \ldots$ is an infinite geometric series, which can be summed in the usual way to get 1, we have $\left(\frac{1}{5}\right)S = \left(\frac{1}{5}\right) + 1$ or $S = 6$.

3. Here is a way to find the sum of one kind of an infinite geometric series:

To find the sum of a series like $\frac{1}{2} + \frac{1}{4} + \frac{1}{8} + \frac{1}{16} + \frac{1}{32} + \cdots$, first set the sum of the series equal to S:

$$S = \frac{1}{2} + \frac{1}{4} + \frac{1}{8} + \frac{1}{16} + \frac{1}{32} + \cdots \qquad (*)$$

Multiply both sides by 2:

$$2S = 2\left(\frac{1}{2} + \frac{1}{4} + \frac{1}{8} + \frac{1}{16} + \frac{1}{32} + \cdots\right)$$

$$2S = \frac{2}{2} + \frac{2}{4} + \frac{2}{8} + \frac{2}{16} + \frac{2}{32} + \cdots$$

$$2S = 1 + \frac{1}{2} + \frac{1}{4} + \frac{1}{8} + \frac{1}{16} + \cdots \qquad (**)$$

Finally, subtract each side of equation (*) from the corresponding side of equation (**):

$$\begin{aligned} 2S &= 1 + \frac{1}{2} + \frac{1}{4} + \frac{1}{8} + \frac{1}{16} + \cdots \\ -\,S &= \qquad \left(\frac{1}{2} + \frac{1}{4} + \frac{1}{8} + \frac{1}{16} + \frac{1}{32} + \cdots\right) \\ \hline S &= 1 \end{aligned}$$

In this example, both sides of equation (*) were multiplied by 2. With other infinite sums of this type, other numbers must be used.

a. Use the method above to find the sum of each of the infinite series below. Your first task will be to find the number to use for the multiplication.

- $S = \frac{1}{3} + \frac{1}{9} + \frac{1}{27} + \frac{1}{81} + \cdots$
- $S = \frac{7}{10} + \frac{7}{100} + \frac{7}{1000} + \cdots$

b. Why doesn't the method work with the following infinite series?

$$\frac{1}{2} + \frac{1}{3} + \frac{1}{4} + \frac{1}{5} + \frac{1}{6} + \frac{1}{7} + \cdots$$

c. Show that the sum of the probabilities in the waiting-time distribution for rolling doubles is equal to 1.

Looking Back

In this unit, you have learned about probability distributions, specifically, the waiting-time (or geometric) distribution. You should be able to recognize a waiting-time situation and construct its probability distribution both theoretically and by simulation. You also should know how to find the average waiting time.

Among the concepts you investigated were probability distribution, graph of a probability distribution, expected value, fair price, Multiplication Rule, independent trials, and independent events. In this lesson, you will review and apply many of these ideas in new contexts.

1. In the "Simulation Models" unit in Course 1, one investigation focused on the population issues in China. In 1993, the population of China was more than 1,200,000,000. To control population growth, the government of China has attempted to limit parents to one child each. This decision has been unpopular in the areas of rural China where the culture is such that many parents desire a son.

Suppose that a new policy has been suggested by which parents are allowed to continue having children until they have a boy. You might assume that half of all children born are boys, but the actual percentage is closer to 51%. For the following tasks, assume that the probability that a child born will be a boy is 0.51.

Lesson 5 *Looking Back*

SYNTHESIZE UNIT IDEAS small-group activity

One teacher began by asking students to recall examples of each of the ideas listed in the introduction: probability distribution, expected value, and so on. The first answers were vague. For example, a student said, "A probability distribution is when we saw how long it took to get a brown candy." The teacher responded, "Tell me more." After a few more tries, and input from other students, the initial student was able to say, "We simulated the situation and saw how the probability of getting your first brown candy would decrease from a starting probability in a particular pattern. The graph shows how these probabilities change for different wait times. That's a probability distribution." Saying what you mean is not easy in this unfamiliar and complex context.

A little later, when the class was working on Activity 1, the teacher asked a student what model he would use. His answer was, "Random numbers, 51 and down for a boy." Another student, listening to this, thought that this indicated that the probability of getting a boy was anything less than 51%. Asking the first student to say clearly what he meant by "51 and down" cleared up the problem. Another student copied the table in Activity 1 Part c as the following table on the left, below, instead of the one on the right.

Boys	Probability		Number of Children to Get First Boy	Probability
1	0.51			
2	(0.51)(0.51)			
3				

The teacher asked what 0.51 represented and then what (0.51)(0.51) represented. The student answered, "A boy and another boy" and caught his own error. The error may have stemmed from the inappropriate headings on the tables. As the teacher circulated, she asked a student why the probabilities did not continue to fall after 7 children in the family. The student's answer showed she clearly understood that the probabilities did, in fact, continue to fall but that the last row of the table accumulated the remaining probabilities for larger families. Again, these concepts are not easy for students. One way to cope with the complexity is to have students express themselves, both orally and in writing. Prompts such as the ones this teacher gave could be very helpful.

1. a. One possible simulation: Let the pairs of digits 00, 01, 02, ... , 50 represent a boy and the pairs of digits 51, 52, ..., 99 represent a girl. Enter the table at a random spot and count the number of pairs of digits needed until a "boy" appears.

b. 51; 24.99; 12.2451

c.

Number of Children to Get First Boy	Probability
1	0.510
2	0.250
3	0.122
4	0.060
5	0.029
6	0.014
7	0.007
8 or more	0.008

d. Using the table, an (under)estimate of the average number of children is 1.958. The expected number using the formula is $\frac{1}{0.51}$ or 1.96.

e. The population will decrease if all adults follow the plan of having children until they get a boy. Each pair of adults produces an average of only 1.96 children, not quite replacing themselves.

f. 51% of all children born will be boys. Since the chance of a boy is 0.51 on each birth, the proportion of boys will be 0.51, ignoring differences in mortality rates after birth of boys and girls.

2. The area model for this situation is shown at the right.

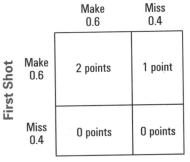

Second Shot

	Make 0.6	Miss 0.4
First Shot — Make 0.6	2 points	1 point
First Shot — Miss 0.4	0 points	0 points

a. ■ P(Teri scores 2 points) $= (0.6)(0.6) = 0.36$
■ P(Teri scores 1 point) $= (0.6)(0.4) = 0.24$
■ P(Teri scores 0 points) $= 0.4$

b. $E.V. = 2(0.36) + 1(0.24) = 0.96$

c. Assuming the two shots are independent and using the Multiplication Rule, we get the following:
■ P(2 points) $= P$(Make and Make)
   $= (0.6)(0.6) = 0.36$
■ P(1 point) $= P$(Make and Miss)
   $= (0.6)(0.4) = 0.24$
■ P(0 points) $= P$(Miss) $= 0.4$

d. In this two-shot situation, we have the following:
P(2 points) $= P$(Make and Make) $= (0.6)(0.6) = 0.36$
P(1 point) $= P$(Make and Miss) $+ P$(Miss and Make)
   $= (0.6)(0.4) + (0.4)(0.6) = 0.48$
P(0 points) $= P$(Miss and Miss) $= (0.4)(0.4) = 0.16$
Thus the expected value is $2(0.36) + 1(0.48)$ or 1.2 points.

a. Describe a method using random digits to simulate the situation of parents having children until they get a boy.

b. Out of every 100 sets of parents, how many would you expect to get the first boy with the first baby? With the second baby? With the third baby?

c. Construct a theoretical probability distribution table for this situation, using a copy of the table below.

Number of Children to Get First Boy	Probability
1	
2	
3	
4	
5	
6	
7	
8 or more	

d. From your table, what is the average number of children two parents will have? From the formula for expected value, what is the expected number of children?

e. Explain whether the population will increase, decrease, or stay the same under this plan.

f. If this new policy were adhered to, what percentage of the population would be boys? Explain your reasoning.

2. Throughout the basketball season, Teri has maintained a 60% free-throw shooting average.

a. Suppose in the first game of the post-season tournament, Teri is in a one-and-one free throw situation. That is, if she makes a basket with her first shot, she gets a second attempt. Use an area model to determine:

- P(Teri scores 2 points)
- P(Teri scores 1 point)
- P(Teri scores 0 points)

b. What is the expected number of points Teri will score?

c. Explain how you could determine the probabilities in Part a without using an area model.

d. Now suppose that later in the game, Teri is in a two-shot foul situation. That is, she gets two attempts regardless of whether she makes the first shot. Determine the expected number of points Teri will score in this situation.

Unit 7

3. The Bonus Lotto game in Michigan is similar to those in many other states. The jackpot starts at $4,000,000. On Saturday, the lottery draws 6 numbers from 1 through 47. A seventh number, called the Bonus Ball, then is drawn from the remaining numbers. A player wins if the numbers he or she selects match the Bonus Ball and at least two of the numbers drawn.

The probabilities of winning various prizes are given in the following table:

Match	Winnings	Probability
6 of 6	$4,000,000	$\frac{1}{10,737,573}$
5 of 6 + bonus ball	$50,000	$\frac{1}{1,789,595}$
4 of 6 + bonus ball	$1,000	$\frac{1}{17,896}$
3 of 6 + bonus ball	$100	$\frac{1}{688}$
2 of 6 + bonus ball	$4	$\frac{1}{72}$
other	0	

a. What is the probability of winning nothing? Write your answer in decimal form.

b. What would be a fair price to pay for a ticket?

c. Bonus Lotto costs $2 to play. How much does the Michigan government expect to earn on every 1,000,000 tickets sold?

d. If the jackpot isn't won on the Saturday drawing, it grows by $4,000,000 for the next week. If you buy one ticket that second week, what is the probability of winning the jackpot?

e. What is a fair price for a ticket the second week?

f. What is the probability that a person who plays Bonus Lotto once this week and once next week will not win anything either week?

g. Suppose a person buys one ticket a week. What is the expected number of weeks he or she will have to wait before winning the jackpot? How many years is this?

h. The above table actually presents a simplified situation. In fact, if there is more than one winner, the $4,000,000 jackpot is shared. Explain why this fact makes the answer to Part b even smaller.

3. **a.** Add the probabilities in the right column to get 0.0154. Since the sum of all probabilities must be 1, the probability of winning nothing is 1 − 0.0154 or 0.9846.

    b. The fair price is about $0.66. See the following table.

Winnings	Probability	(Winnings) · (Probability)
$4,000,000	$\frac{1}{10,737,573}$	0.373
$50,000	$\frac{1}{1,789,595}$	0.028
$1,000	$\frac{1}{17,896}$	0.056
$100	$\frac{1}{688}$	0.145
$4	$\frac{1}{72}$	0.056
0	0.985	0
Total		0.658

    c. $(1,000,000)(2 - 0.66) = \$1,340,000$

    d. Still $\frac{1}{10,737,573}$

    e. The fair price is about $1.03. See the following table.

Winnings	Probability	(Winnings) · (Probability)
$8,000,000	$\frac{1}{10,737,573}$	0.746
$50,000	$\frac{1}{1,789,595}$	0.028
$1,000	$\frac{1}{17,896}$	0.056
$100	$\frac{1}{688}$	0.145
$4	$\frac{1}{72}$	0.056
0	0.985	0
Total		1.031

    f. $(0.985)(0.985) \approx 0.97$

    g. 10,737,573 weeks or almost 206,492 years

    h. One chance in 10,737,573 is actually the probability of matching 6 of 6, not the probability of winning $4,000,000. That is the largest amount you could win. There is a chance you will have to share the prize with others, which brings the expected value down.

Unit 7

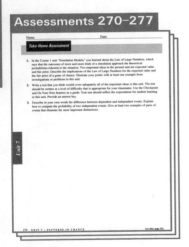

SHARE AND SUMMARIZE full-class discussion

Checkpoint

See Teaching Master 175.

a A waiting-time distribution occurs in situations in which someone is watching a sequence of independent trials and waiting for a certain event to occur. The probability that the event occurs remains the same for each trial. The formula for $P(x)$, the probability that the event first occurs on the xth trial, is $P(x) = (1 - p)^{x-1}p$, where p is the probability that the event occurs on any one trial. The histogram of a waiting-time distribution has the highest bar on the left, and the height of each bar is $(1 - p)$ times the height of the bar to its left. To find the average waiting time, or expected value, one can find the balancing point of the histogram, or evaluate $\sum x \cdot p(x)$, or $\frac{1}{p}$.

b The Multiplication Rule is used when we want to find the probability that two or more *independent* events all occur.

CONSTRUCTING A MATH TOOLKIT: Ask students to reread their toolkit entries from this unit and clarify or augment them following the final Checkpoint discussion.

See Assessment Resources, pages 258–277.

Checkpoint

a Write a general description of a waiting-time distribution. Include how to construct the probability distribution table, what the shape of the distribution looks like, and ways to find the average waiting time.

b For what kinds of problems and under what conditions should you use the Multiplication Rule to calculate probabilities?

Be prepared to compare your descriptions with those of other groups.

Looking Back, Looking Ahead

▶Reflecting on Mathematical Content

In this unit, students learned about the waiting-time, or geometric, distribution. This distribution occurs if we conduct a series of independent trials in which the probability of a "success" is p for each trial and we count the number of trials needed until the first success. Waiting-time distributions have a characteristic shape, shown below, in which the first bar is the tallest (height p), and each succeeding bar is $(1 - p)$ times the height of the bar to its left. The probability that it will take x tries until the first success is

$$P(x) = p(1 - p)^{x-1}$$

since there must be $(x - 1)$ failures followed by a success. The sequence of probabilities is indeed geometric with first term p and common ratio $(1 - p)$:

$$p, p(1 - p), p(1 - p)^2, p(1 - p)^3, \dots$$

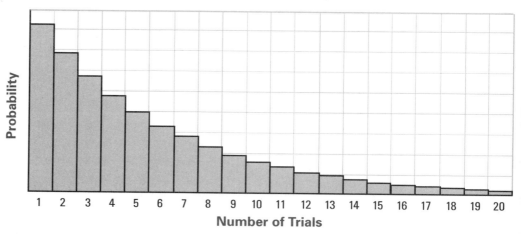

Perhaps the main goal in teaching probability is for students to understand that while we may not know the next outcome in a random process, we have a very good idea of what the distribution of the next ten thousand outcomes will look like. Further, students should understand that the distributions for related random processes have characteristic shapes. Waiting-time distributions are skewed right. Binomial distributions in many cases are symmetrical and mound-shaped. (Students will study the binomial distribution formally in Course 4.) For each of these distributions, we can compute a measure of center such as the mean (expected value) and a measure of spread. (The standard deviation, the most commonly used measure of spread, will be introduced in the Course 3 unit, "Patterns of Variation.") These distributions can be constructed approximately using simulation or constructed exactly using mathematical theory.

The distributions the students have seen so far are discrete. That is, the values on the x-axis are not continuous. It isn't possible to wait 1.273 trials for the first success. No values strictly between 1 and 2 trials are possible. In the Course 3 unit, "Patterns of Variation," students will see examples of probability distributions in which the variable is continuous. For example, height of people is a continuous variable. When the variable is continuous, we represent probabilities by area under a curve. Thus students will get an intuitive introduction to some ideas of calculus in that unit.

Another important goal of this unit was for students to understand why, when *A* and *B* are independent, we multiply to find the probability of *A* and *B* both occurring. This idea was developed through area models and through the intuitive idea that in a waiting-time situation, the proportion of people who have their first success on the *x*th trial is *p* times the proportion of people who were left after the previous trial.

Although it was not made explicit in this unit, students used the Addition Rule for Mutually Exclusive Events. For example, they found the probability that it will take fewer than 3 trials to get a success by adding the probability that it will take 1 trial to the probability that it will take 2 trials. In "Patterns of Variation," the Addition Rule will be presented formally.

The next unit in the probability and statistics strand will be "Modeling Public Opinion" in Course 3. In that unit, students will learn about confidence intervals and margins of error. These are reported, for example, with the results of political surveys. In that unit, students will construct examples of the binomial distribution and learn more about its characteristic shape.

Unit 7 Assessment

Lesson Quizzes	Assessment Resources
Lesson 1 *Waiting Times*	pp. 232–237
Lesson 2 *The Multiplication Rule*	pp. 238–243
Lesson 3 *Probability Distributions*	pp. 244–251
Lesson 4 *Expected Value of a Probability Distribution*	pp. 252–257
In-Class Exams	
Form A	pp. 257–262
Form B	pp. 263–268
Take-Home Assessment	pp. 269–270
Unit 4 Projects	
Probability Distributions	pp. 271–272
Rare, Please	pp. 273–276

Teaching Notes continued

Notes continued from page T457

1. **See Teaching Master 151.**

   a–b. A typical table might look like this:

   ## Rolling Doubles

Event	Number of Rolls	Frequency
Rolled doubles on first try	1	17
Rolled doubles on second try	2	14
Rolled doubles on third try	3	12
Rolled doubles on fourth try	4	10
etc.	etc.	etc.
Total		100

   There are many ways to have the class work together to complete this table. One way that students enjoy is to make a histogram on the wall of the classroom. Assign each student a number of trials to conduct so that the class will total 100 trials. Give each student a removable sticker or sticky note for each trial. Have students put their stickers on the wall of the classroom above stickers already marked with the numbers 1, 2, 3, 4, ... according to how many rolls it took them to get doubles.

Notes continued from page T458

■ **Rolling Two Dice**

	Number on Green Die					
	1	2	3	4	5	6
1	1, 1	1, 2	1, 3	1, 4	1, 5	1, 6
2	2, 1	2, 2	2, 3	2, 4	2, 5	2, 6
3	3, 1	3, 2	3, 3	3, 4	3, 5	3, 6
4	4, 1	4, 2	4, 3	4, 4	4, 5	4, 6
5	5, 1	5, 2	5, 3	5, 4	5, 5	5, 6
6	6, 1	6, 2	6, 3	6, 4	6, 5	6, 6

(Rows labeled: Number on Red Die)

■ There are 36 possible outcomes. One of the first counterintuitive truths in probability that students have to confront is that, for example, both "1, 2" and "2, 1" have to be listed above so all of the outcomes are equally likely. The red die and green die organization convinces some students that there are 36 equally likely outcomes. (Similarly, students must be convinced that if two coins are flipped, there are four equally likely outcomes, and so the probability of getting, for example, two heads is $\frac{1}{4}$. Many students believe it should be $\frac{1}{3}$ as they think there are three equally likely outcomes: two heads, one head and one tail, and two tails. This is a legitimate listing of all possible outcomes, but they are not equally likely.)

■ Yes, the 36 outcomes are equally likely since each number has an equal chance of appearing on each die.

Teaching Notes *continued*

Notes continued
from page T459

Checkpoint

See Teaching Master 153.

ⓐ ■ The histograms most likely will not be exactly the same. They were created by actually rolling dice, and not every class will have the same rolls.

■ The overall pattern in the histograms should be that the bars gradually decrease in height as the number of rolls increases.

ⓑ Be sure that students understand that this question is asking about the probability of getting doubles on any particular roll, not about when the first doubles will be rolled. The probability of getting doubles on any one roll is $\frac{1}{6}$.

This might be a good time to revisit the estimates students made during the launch discussion about what was likely and unlikely. You might ask students if they want to change their estimates. Discussion should include students' new estimates about what is expected and what is unlikely and why they may have changed their minds. By giving students this opportunity to look back, you are encouraging them to reflect and connect. You are also demonstrating that making corrections to their thinking as they learn is appropriate and encouraged. This also keeps the big question present in students' minds. By the end of the unit, they will find a theoretical answer for the question in Part c of the "Think About This Situation" on page 457. It would spoil their discovery if you tell the students the correct answer at this time.

APPLY   individual task

▶On Your Own

a. Tables and histograms will vary. The first bar will be the tallest. (About half of the people get out of jail on their first flip.) The second bar will be about half as high as the first bar. The third bar will be about half as high as the second bar. This general pattern will continue with each bar being about half the height of the bar immediately to its left.

b. Much easier. The probability of getting heads, $\frac{1}{2}$, is quite a bit larger than the probability of getting doubles, $\frac{1}{6}$.

c. The theoretical answer is $\frac{7}{8}$ or 0.875. Students should respond based upon the results of their 24 trials.

MORE

ASSIGNMENT   *pp. 466–470*

Students now can begin Modeling Task 4, Organizing Task 1 or 4, or Extending Task 2 or 3 from the MORE assignment following Investigation 3.

Unit 7

Teaching Notes continued

Notes continued from page T462

1. a. $\frac{22}{5} = 4.4$ candies drawn

   b. Responses will vary. Two good examples are a typical grade point average and average number of children per family.

2. a.

x	f	xf
0	9	0
1	5	5
2	6	12
3	4	12
Σ	24	29

   $$\bar{x} = \frac{\Sigma\, xf}{n}$$

   $$= \frac{29}{24}$$

   $$\approx 1.21$$

   b. Put the x values in List 1 and the corresponding frequencies in List 2. Then set List 3 to be the product (List 1) (List 2). To find the mean evaluate $\frac{\text{sum (List 3)}}{\text{sum (List 2)}}$.

Teaching Notes *continued*

▶ **Notes continued from page T464**

3. f. Since 284 out of 1,000 students removed a brown candy on the first try, a good estimate for the percentage of candies that are brown is 28.4%. Another way to estimate this percentage is to count the total number of browns in the entire experiment and divide by the total number of draws. There were 1,000 browns (each student got exactly one brown candy) out of 3,399 draws. This estimate for the percentage of candies that are brown is equal to $\frac{1,000}{3,399}$ or approximately 29.4%.

    g. Out of 1,000 trials, 11 or more draws were needed $13 + 5 + 6 + 1 + 1 + 1$ or 27 times. The estimated probability is 0.027.

    h. Ninety-five percent of 1,000 trials is 950. Adding the first eight entries, we get $284 + 197 + 163 + 91 + 88 + 52 + 39 + 30$ or 944, which is the closest we can get to 950. These are the number of trials that required 8 draws or fewer. So Marty must have required 9 draws.

    i. The upper 5% of the distribution would be the 50 largest values. The 50 largest values include some of the 9s and larger values. So, drawing 11 candies is a rare event according to the definition given here. But, drawing eight candies is not.

SHARE AND SUMMARIZE   full-class discussion

Checkpoint

See Teaching Master 156.

  ⓐ The first bar was the tallest in all the histograms. In general, each successive bar was slightly shorter than the preceding one.

  ⓑ Using a histogram, students can find an estimate of the average waiting time by estimating the point where the histogram "balances." It is much more difficult to estimate the average from a frequency table, without doing actual calculations. However, some students may be able to visualize the balance point from the table.

  ⓒ Determine the upper 5% of the waiting times. If an event falls in the upper 5%, then it is a rare event.

> **JOURNAL ENTRY:** The probability of picking a brown candy is about 30%. Would you be surprised if you got a brown candy on the first pick? If you had to wait until the 10th pick? How long would you expect to have to wait? If the candy company increased the proportion of brown candies to 40%, how would your answers change? What if $\frac{1}{6}$ of the bag was brown candies? Does this last variation address our initial question about Anita waiting for doubles?

CONSTRUCTING A MATH TOOLKIT: You may wish to have students record the definition of rare event in their Math Toolkits.

NOTE: If you have not yet reviewed setting up a simulation with your students, you may want to do so before they begin the "On Your Own" tasks. See Teaching Master 150.

Unit 7

Notes continued from page T468

4. The tree graph below represents the 36 possible rolls of a pair of dice.

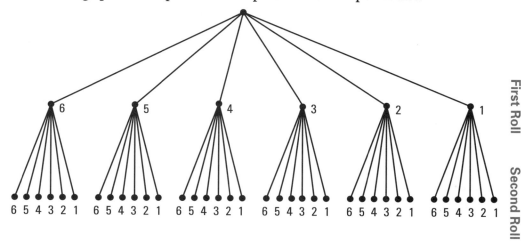

First Roll

Second Roll

The tree graph may be used to answer the questions in Activity 3, Part b by counting the paths that fit each description (*e.g.*, the paths corresponding to doubles) and dividing the count by 36 (the total number of distinct paths).

Reflecting

1. It has already been established that the probability of rolling doubles with one red and one green die is $\frac{1}{6}$. You could take two red dice and have each student in the class roll them 10 times, recording the number of doubles. Compile this data. As the number of trials increases, the empirical probability should approach $\frac{1}{6}$.

Unit 7

Teaching Notes *continued*

► **Notes continued from page T470**

4. a–d. This is not the same kind of waiting-time experiment that we have been doing in which the trials are independent. Answers will vary depending on individual results. A sample table with 20 trials and a sample histogram with 100 trials follow.

NOTE: All odd draws would have a frequency of zero.

Draws Required	Frequency
2	5
3	0
4	4
5	0
6	3
7	0

Draws Required	Frequency
8	2
10	2
14	1
16	1
20	1
30	1

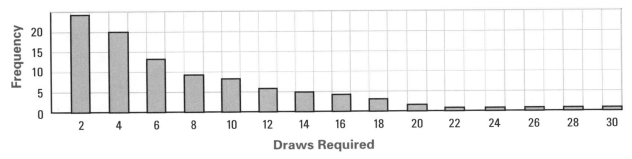

e. Almost. The only difference between this distribution and a waiting-time distribution is that the probability is zero for all odd number of draws. But, this distribution is geometric for all even number of draws. You might come back to this problem after students have learned to construct waiting-time distributions.

f. Responses will vary. For the preceding histogram, the average is probably close to 8.

g. Responses may vary. Using a table of random digits or a random number generator, students could consider the digits 1, 2, 3, and 4. Initially let 1 and 2 represent red markers and 3 and 4 yellow ones. After each draw, the numbers that represent each color will have to be adjusted. For example, if the first random number was 3 (representing a yellow marker), then we need to simulate placing a red marker in the bag. So on the next draw, the digits 1, 2, and 3 will represent red and 4 will represent yellow. This procedure will need to be continued until all four digits represent the same color.

A TI-82 program that runs this simulation and displays the number of draws is provided at the right. R represents the number of red markers in the bag, and K keeps count of how many draws are required.

See Assessment Resources, pages 232–237.

```
MARKERS        • Program
:2 → R
:0 → K
:while R ≠ 0 and R ≠ 4
:K+1→ K
:int 4rand+1→ M
:If M ≤ R
:Then
:R–1→ R
:Else
:R+1→ R
:End
:End
:Disp "NUMBER OF DRAWS"
:Disp K
```

Unit 7

Teaching Notes continued

Notes continued from page T471

c Students may devise several ways of understanding that the probability this child will not have freckles is $\frac{1}{4}$. To analyze this problem, biologists construct a Punnett square:

Gene from Mother

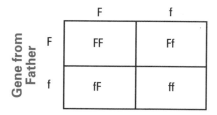

The uppercase *F* stands for a freckles gene, and the lowercase *f* stands for a no-freckles gene. The *F* for freckles is capitalized because it is the dominant gene: a person with *Ff* genes has freckles. From the Punnett square, students can see that there are four equally likely outcomes: *FF* (child has freckles), *Ff* (child has freckles), *fF* (child has freckles), and *ff* (child doesn't have freckles). Thus the probability that the child will not have freckles is $\frac{1}{4}$.

d There is no way to determine the probability that the child of freckled parents will have freckles unless we know whether the parents have two freckles genes or one freckles gene and one gene for no freckles. If both parents are of the type *FF*, then the child is certain to have freckles. If both parents have only one freckles gene, then there is a $\frac{3}{4}$ chance the child will have freckles. If one parent is of the type *Ff* and the other is *FF*, you might ask students to analyze the situation using a Punnett square:

Gene from Mother

		F	f
Gene from Father	F	FF	Ff
	F	FF	Ff

From this we can see that the child will have freckles.

Teaching Notes *continued*

▸ **Notes continued from page T474**

5. b. Students should notice that the probabilities could be multiplied.

For Activity 1: $\left(\frac{1}{2}\right)\left(\frac{1}{3}\right) = \frac{1}{6}$

For Activity 3: The child does not have freckles if he or she gets a no-freckles gene from each parent, each of which happens with probability $\frac{1}{2}$. The probability of a child without freckles is $\left(\frac{1}{2}\right)\left(\frac{1}{2}\right)$ or $\frac{1}{4}$.

For Activity 4a: $(0.25)(0.25) = 0.0625$

For Activity 4b: $(0.84)(0.84) = 0.7056$

c. To find the probability that two independent events both occur, multiply the probability that one event occurs by the probability that the other occurs.

d. $P(A \text{ and } B) = P(A) \cdot P(B)$

6. a. *P*(gets doubles on the first roll and gets a sum of six on the second roll)

b. The probability of rolling doubles is $\frac{1}{6}$, the probability of rolling a sum of six is $\frac{5}{36}$, and the two rolls are independent. So the probability of Shiomo getting what he needs is $\left(\frac{1}{6}\right)\left(\frac{5}{36}\right)$ or $\frac{5}{216}$.

▸ **Notes continued from page T479**

3. c. The probability that their sum is less than 0.3 is 0.045. The equations of the lines that border the region are $x + y = 0.3$, $x = 0$, and $y = 0$.

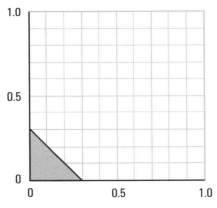

d. In the diagram below, the gray area represents the times when one person would be on the phone to Briana when the other person calls her.

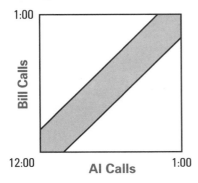

The probability the calls will conflict is $\frac{11}{36}$ or 0.306. Perhaps the easiest way to calculate this is to find the areas of the two unshaded triangles (each is $\frac{1}{2} \cdot \frac{5}{6} \cdot \frac{5}{6}$) and subtract the two from the area of the square.

Teaching Notes *continued*

Notes continued from page T485

b After 50 tosses, exactly half of his tosses were heads. He was farthest away after 10,000 tosses. He had 67 extra heads.

c After 10 tosses, Kerrich had 40% heads. After 10,000 tosses, he had 50.67% heads. His percentage was closer to the expected percentage after 10,000 tosses. (Remind students that the Law of Large Numbers says that as the number of tosses increases, the percentage of heads tends to get closer to 50%. This law was introduced in the "Simulation Models" unit of Course 1.)

d We would expect one player to get out of jail on the first try. This is because the probability of rolling doubles is $\frac{1}{6}$, and $\frac{1}{6}(6) = 1$. On the second try, we would expect $\frac{1}{6}$ of the 5 players left or $\frac{5}{6}$ of a player to get out of jail. Encourage students to use the single theoretical number $\frac{5}{6}$ player rather than rounding.

Notes continued from page T486

1. d. The final row is added in Activity 2, Part b.

Rolling Dice to Get Doubles

Number of Rolls to Get Doubles	Expected Number of Students Released on the Given Number of Rolls	Expected Number of Students Still in Jail
1	6	30
2	5	25
3	4.17	20.83
4	3.47	17.36
5	2.89	14.47
6	2.41	12.06
7	2.01	10.05
8	1.67	8.37
9	1.40	6.98
10	1.16	5.81
11	0.97	4.85
12	0.81	4.04
13 or more	4.04	

Unit 7

Teaching Notes *continued*

Notes continued from page T488

ⓑ Students may well find it easier to think in terms of specific numerical examples instead of the general n and p. If so, encourage them to write down their examples. Then use their examples to get them to generalize that we would expect the event to occur np times.

ⓒ Students may be more comfortable giving a numerical example. For example: If the probability of the initial event is 20%, then each bar is 80% of the last bar. In several classrooms, when asked what shape the distribution looked like, students recognized it as exponential decay. In fact, the decay factor is $1 - p$, and students will make that connection explicitly in Investigation 2. Many students recognized the shape first before they made the connection that the heights of the bars followed the pattern $NEXT = (1 - p)NOW$.

APPLY | individual task

▶On Your Own

a. Students may use the table they constructed for Activity 2 of Investigation 1, Lesson 1 (page 458) to find that this probability is $\frac{15}{36}$.

b. ■ 22.5
   ■ 22.5

Notes continued from page T491

5. The five-number summaries for the three situations are as follows:

Situation	min	Q_1	median	Q_3	max
Tiger Sticker $p = 0.25$	1	1.5	3	5	infinite
Heads on Coin Flip $p = 0.5$	1	1	1.5	2.5	infinite
Rolling Doubles $p = \frac{1}{6} \approx 0.17$	1	2	4	8	infinite

The box plots follow.

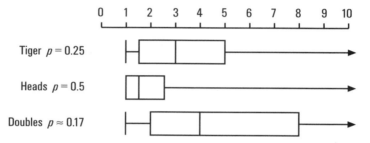

The box plots are all skewed right, and all have a minimum of 1 and a maximum that is infinite. As p becomes smaller, the box plot stretches out more to the right.

Reflecting

1. Student responses will vary. For more information, see the references given in the "Misconceptions about Probability" section on page T455A.

2. Responses will vary. Certainly anyone who is involved in the gambling industry or who runs lotteries would be interested in waiting-time distribution. Managers of sport teams might also be interested in the number of games before a win or the number of at-bats before a hit. A salesperson might be interested in the number of contacts that have to be made before a sale.

3. a. Marina means that the probability that she will roll doubles on her next try is greater than it was on her first few tries. She thinks the probabilities change depending on what has happened in the past.

   b. She is not correct. The probability of rolling doubles stays the same, $\frac{1}{6}$, no matter what has happened with the dice previously.

   c. One student could show Marina that the probability of rolling doubles on her first roll is about $\frac{1}{6}$ by rolling a "first" roll over and over. A second student will have to roll dice until there has been no doubles for 10 times in a row. The proportion of doubles on the 11th row will be close to $\frac{1}{6}$ also.

Teaching Notes *continued*

Notes continued from page T493

2. f. The estimated probability from the table in the student text is $\frac{1}{95}$ or approximately 0.011. This is the number of trials that were either all heads or all tails divided by the total number of trials. The assumptions are that the probability of either gender is 0.5 and that the gender of the children in a family are independent.

3. a. We can use a random digit table and let the digit 0 represent a fatal car accident that is due to too fast or unsafe speed. We will let the digits 1, 2, and 3 represent a fatal car accident that isn't due to these causes. We will ignore all other digits. Start at a random place in the table and look at the first 50 digits that are 0, 1, 2, or 3. Count the number of 0s. Repeat this procedure many times.

b. The following table summarizes a simulation that was repeated 100 times. In this simulation, the largest number of fatal accidents due to too fast or unsafe speed was 20 out of 50. Thus, 40 out of 50 cannot be attributed reasonably to chance. The county should look for another explanation.

Number of Accidents	Frequency
7	2
8	11
9	7
10	13
11	10
12	10
13	15
14	7
15	8
16	8
17	4
18	2
19	2
20	1

c. No, 30 out of 50 cannot be attributed reasonably to chance either.

Notes continued from page T495

1. **See Teaching Master 163.**
  a. Exactly four: 0.21; four or fewer: 0.86
  b. Only 2 percent of families in the United States have 7 or more people. Thus a family with 11 people in it is a rare event. (However, note that, judging by the clothes, this picture was not taken in 1990. So it's possible that when this picture was taken, a family of this size was not a rare event.)
  c. It is remarkable that the family has 9 girls and no boys. This is a rare event. Students' estimates of the probability will probably vary. The theoretical probability is $\left(\frac{1}{2}\right)^9$ or approximately 0.002. If we count the event of getting all boys as equally extreme, the probability of getting a family this extreme is $0.002 + 0.002$ or 0.004.

Notes continued from page T499

5. i. Waiting Time for Doubles

Number of Rolls to Get Doubles	Probability
1	0.167
2	0.139
3	0.116
4	0.096
5	0.080
6	0.067
7	0.056
8	0.047
9	0.039
10	0.032
11	0.027
12	0.022

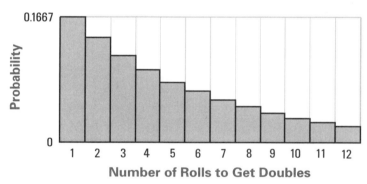

j. The two should have a similar shape although the one from the simulation will be more irregular. The scale on the *y*-axis in the investigation was frequency; here it is probability.

6.

Number of Draws to Get Brown Candy	Probability
1	0.3
2	$(0.7)(0.3) = 0.21$
3	$(0.7)^2(0.3) = 0.147$
4	$(0.7)^3(0.3) = 0.1029$
5	$(0.7)^4(0.3) = 0.07203$

Unit 7

Teaching Notes continued

Notes continued from page T503

1. b.

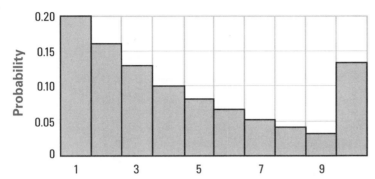

Number of Draws to Get First Red Candy

c. $P(x) = (0.8)^{x-1}(0.2)$

d. The probability of choosing 14 or more candies before you get the first red one is approximately 0.0550, and for 15 or more, the probability is approximately 0.0438. So a rare event would have occurred if someone had chosen at least 15 candies.

2. a. $P(x) = (0.75)^{x-1}(0.25)$

b. A rare event would be having to buy 12 boxes or more.

Notes continued from page T508

c.

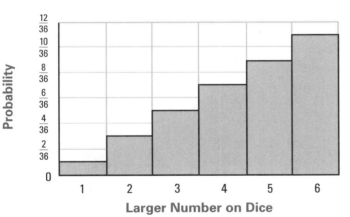

Larger Number on Dice

d. The shape is like a wedge. The probabilities all fall on a straight line, increasing $\frac{2}{36}$ each time.

Teaching Notes continued

Notes continued from page T515

APPLY individual task

▶On Your Own

The expected value of a ticket is $0.6117. See the work in the table below.

Prize Value	Probability	(Value)(Probability)
Free soft drink (89¢)	$\frac{15}{100}$	0.1335
Free hamburger ($1.29)	$\frac{8}{100}$	0.1032
T-shirt with restaurant logo ($7.50)	$\frac{3}{100}$	0.225
Movie passes ($15.00)	$\frac{1}{100}$	0.15
You lose! ($0.00)	$\frac{73}{100}$	0
Total	$\frac{100}{100}$	0.6117

Teaching Notes *continued*

Your notes here:

Capstone

Looking Back at Course 2

CAPSTONE OVERVIEW This capstone unit provides a whole-course review and valuable closure. It should leave students with feelings of accomplishment and satisfaction after learning much powerful mathematics.

▶Approximate Timeline

The Capstone will take one or two weeks, depending on the makeup of your class and how thoroughly students work through the unit and present the oral reports. For example, with only one week, or approximately 5 hours, to spend on the Capstone, you may use 1 hour on the "Think About This Situation" and Investigation 1, setting the scene and clarifying group responsibilities for the remaining investigations. Then groups may choose two, instead of three, of the investigations from 2 through 7. (Some negotiation may be required to ensure that too many groups do not do the same investigations. These investigations make connections among two or more major mathematical concepts, and some are longer than others. Investigation 7 is particularly long. You may want to guide choices with these facts and your time frame in mind.) Three hours should be sufficient for students to complete the two investigations and plan an oral report on one of them. On the last day of this lesson, each group should give a short oral presentation. Students can complete the written report on the other investigation for homework.

With two weeks to spend on the Capstone, groups can complete three investigations. There will be time to read each other's reports. Oral reports will become more elaborate and more thorough because students have seen the work of others on the same subject. There will be time for students to choose an additional "On Your Own" task. Given two weeks, Investigation 8 becomes a viable group option.

One way to assess group presentations and written reports is provided in Teaching Masters 181a–181c. You may wish to have each student evaluate other groups' presentations. You may wish to have each group submit one written report or have each student write an individual report as suggested in the student text. The written report may be included in student portfolios. This comprehensive assessment may replace a final exam or be used along with selected tasks from the bank of assessment items for a final evaluation. See the Course 2 Final Exam assessment masters.

Looking Back
at Course 2

535

Forests, the Environment, and Mathematics

In this course, you have continued your investigation of important mathematics and used it to analyze realistic situations. The mathematics you have studied includes matrices, systems of equations, coordinate models, transformations, correlation, linear regression, direct and inverse power models, quadratic functions, network optimization, the geometry of mechanisms, trigonometric models, and waiting-time probability distributions. In this Capstone, you will pull together and apply much of the mathematics you have learned, in order to analyze issues related to forests and the environment.

Forests are valuable for business and industry, recreation, and the maintenance of a healthy environment. Mathematics is used to help manage forests so that they can serve all these purposes most effectively.

Think About This Situation

A lumber company has submitted a proposal to begin logging operations in a nearby forest. While the owner of the property considers the proposal, the local community is debating its own concerns. The debate centers around three issues: economics, recreation, and the environment.

ⓐ What do you see as the major value of forests?

ⓑ Think of as many economic uses of forests as you can. Make a list.

ⓒ Make a list of recreational uses of forests.

ⓓ List as many environmental issues and benefits related to forests as you can.

Capstone

Forests, the Environment, and Mathematics

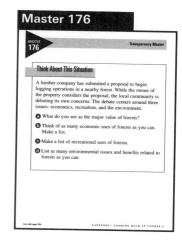

LAUNCH full-class discussion

Think About This Situation

See Teaching Master 176.

The objectives of the "Think About This Situation" and Investigation 1 are to elicit prior student knowledge about forestry issues and to relate these to the mathematics they have learned in this course. You may choose to meet these objectives by following the instructions and answering the questions in the student text. (One hour should be sufficient for both the "Think About This Situation" and Investigation 1.) Or you may wish to conduct the inquiry without formal reference to the text, supplying your own oral and/or written prompts for a discussion that alternates between whole class and small group. Be sure that students have an opportunity to share briefly their individual knowledge about forestry-related issues before proceeding to the mathematical connections. It will be helpful to have some individual reflection time built in so that the large-group discussion is not dominated by a few voices. Some possible sources for student comments include newspaper or TV accounts of controversy and confrontation over environmental and economic uses of forests, forestry programs at local colleges, camping trips to national or state forest campgrounds, and news accounts of forest fires. Ask students to watch and listen for forest-related stories in the media.

The notes for the large-group discussion on general forestry-related issues and on specific mathematical connections should be preserved (perhaps on the board) for later reference. If students do not generate many ideas at this point, you may wish to return to Investigation 1 and the "Think About This Situation" after student reports.

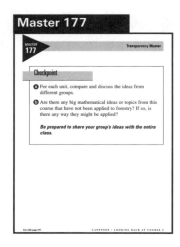

MASTER
177   Transparency Master

Checkpoint

❶ For each unit, compare and discuss the ideas from
   different groups.

❷ Are there any big mathematical ideas or topics from this
   course that have not been applied to forestry? If so, is
   there any way they might be applied?

*Be prepared to share your group's ideas with the entire
class.*

Use with page 537.   CAPSTONE • LOOKING BACK AT COURSE 2

EXPLORE   small-group investigation

INVESTIGATION 1   Forestry and Mathematics

This investigation provides a structure for students to review briefly the units they have studied in Course 2. It may also generate ideas that they may use in Investigation 8, Further Analysis.

SHARE AND SUMMARIZE   full-class discussion

Checkpoint

See Teaching Master 177.

See the suggestions in the "Think About This Situation" box. You may wish to come back to the "Think About This Situation" and this Checkpoint after the group oral reports on Investigations 2–8.

a Briefly discuss students' ideas.

b Try to fill in any gaps, that is, important ideas from the year that could be applied to a mathematical analysis of forests in some way.

If students are having difficulty getting started, suggest some of the major mathematics for consideration, such as systems of equations, the geometry of mechanisms, correlation, etc.

Capstone

INVESTIGATION 1 ▶ Forestry and Mathematics

Mathematics can be used in many different ways to help study and manage forests. Think about the mathematics you have studied in each of the units in this course (listed below). Brainstorm with your group about how the mathematics in each unit might be used in forestry. You may consider economic, recreational, or environmental aspects of forests. Your group should identify at least two ways to use the mathematics in each unit. Be prepared to share your group's thinking with the whole class.

1. *Matrix Models*
2. *Patterns of Location, Shape, and Size*
3. *Patterns of Association*
4. *Power Models*
5. *Network Optimization*
6. *Geometric Form and Its Function*
7. *Patterns in Chance*

Checkpoint

a For each unit, compare and discuss the ideas from different groups.

b Are there any big mathematical ideas or topics from this course that have not been applied to forestry? If so, is there any way they might be applied?

Be prepared to share your group's ideas with the entire class.

Your goal in this Capstone is to use mathematics to analyze certain aspects of forestry. At the end of the Capstone, you will prepare oral and written reports that will provide useful information for the community debate you considered in the "Think About This Situation" at the beginning of the Capstone. (Guidelines for the reports are given on page 554.)

As a group, take a quick look at Investigations 2 through 8 and then choose three to complete. (Investigation 7 counts as two.) Confirm your choices with your teacher before you begin. Investigations 2 through 7 include an optional "On Your Own" task. Individually, each group member should select and complete one of the "On Your Own" tasks from your group's investigations.

Capstone

INVESTIGATION 2 Land Use Change in Rapid-Growth Areas

The United States Department of Agriculture (USDA) keeps track of how many acres of land are used for different purposes around the country. They publish their data regularly so that planners and policymakers can make informed decisions. Examine the following USDA data. These data show how land use changed in U.S. counties that grew rapidly in population during the period 1960 to 1970.

Transition Matrix of Land Use Change for 53 Rapid-Growth Counties, 1960–1970

Land Use in 1970

	1	2	3	4	5	6	7	8	9	10	11	12	Row Totals
1	6315	106	363	2	48	149	4	45	14	55	20	6	7127
2	108	1514	100	0	18	12	0	7	3	5	2	1	1770
3	128	70	1387	2	180	145	3	23	16	58	32	13	2057
4	2	0	2	185	0	1	0	1	0	2	0	0	193
5	26	14	74	2	6309	143	2	34	6	33	9	4	6656
6	0	0	1	0	0	1449	0	2	0	2	0	0	1454
7	0	0	0	0	0	17	49	2	1	12	0	0	81
8	0	0	0	0	0	0	0	780	1	0	0	0	781
9	0	0	0	0	0	0	0	0	113	0	0	0	113
10	0	0	8	0	0	0	0	0	0	391	0	0	399
11	0	0	7	0	0	1	0	0	0	0	645	0	653
12	5	1	14	0	1	2	0	2	0	0	3	435	463
Column Totals	6584	1705	1956	191	6556	1919	58	896	154	558	711	459	21747

Land Use in 1960 (row label)

Numbers in the matrix show land use change from 1960 (row) to 1970 (column), except for the diagonal which shows use remaining unchanged. All numbers given are in 1,000 acres. The rows and columns are labeled with categories of land use according to the codes below.

Codes and Categories of Land Use

1. Cropland
2. Pasture & Range
3. Open/Idle
4. Farmstead
5. Forest
6. Residential
7. Urban idle
8. Transportation
9. Recreation
10. Commercial, Industrial, Institutional
11. Water Bodies > 40 Acres
12. Miscellaneous

Capstone

INVESTIGATION 2 Land Use Change in Rapid-Growth Areas

In this investigation, students will review how to read, interpret, create, and multiply matrices. They probably will have the most difficulty interpreting the percent-change matrix. You may need to assist students in understanding how to compute percent change when the raw change and the "before and after" totals are known.

$$\text{Percent Change} = \frac{\text{Raw Change}}{\text{Original Total}} \times 100$$

Be sure to ask about the purpose of the matrix multiplication in Activity 2, Part c, and to have students interpret the new matrix they have created.

Capstone

1. a. 53 rapid-growth counties are included in the data. Students likely will be interested in seeing if their counties, or nearby ones, are included.

b. The matrix is read using the usual convention of reading from the row to the column. Thus, for example, "18" in the 2nd row, 5th column means that from 1960 to 1970, 18,000 acres of pasture and range were converted to forests. Students might look at the summary column for 1960 (far right) and the summary row for 1970 (bottom) and notice information such as the decrease in total cropland from 7,127,000 acres in 1960 to 6,584,000 acres in 1970.

c. The (5, 3) entry indicates the number of acres of forestland that became open land. The (3, 5) entry gives the number of acres of open land that became forestland. The two entries would not be the same unless both changes in land use were identical in acreage. The *cropland,* and *pasture and range* categories indicate almost identical changes in use as seen by the (1, 2) and (2, 1) entries.

Since more open land became forest than forest became open land, the overall change between open land and forestland was $180,000 - 74,000 = 106,000$ acres more forestland. This indicates that more open land was planted with trees than land left open from deforestation.

d. There are no negative entries because each entry tells the number of acres of one type of land that changed to a new land use. Only positive numbers or a zero would make sense. In this context, a negative number of acres is not meaningful.

e. The row sums are the total acres in 1960 of land in the category indicated by the row number.

The column sums are the total acres in 1970 of land in the category indicated by the column number.

f. The least change in land use is found by subtracting each category's row total from its column total. The smallest change was in farmstead land. Only 2,000 acres of farmstead land were lost from 1960 to 1970.

g. The least percentage change was in the Miscellaneous category $\left(\frac{4,000}{463,000} \approx 0.86\%\right)$.

The Miscellaneous category had only a 0.86% change. All percentage changes could be computed quickly by using lists.

L_1 = Total acres in 1960 (Row totals)

L_2 = Total acres in 1970 (Column totals)

$L_3 = \frac{|L_2 - L_1|}{L_1}$

h. Forestland decreased from 1960 to 1970 by 100,000 acres or –1.5%. The biggest loss was to Residential. The biggest gain was 180,000 acres from the Open/Idle category. Forestland changed into each other category from 1960 to 1970. Cropland, Pasture & Range, Open/Idle, and Miscellaneous were the categories that became forestland by 1970. Other patterns could also be described.

i. Student observations will vary. For example, Recreation is the only category in which no acres were converted to another use from 1960 to 1970. Students may notice that the diagonals represent the acreage for each category that remained in the same category from 1960 to 1970. There are many other trends that could be described. Look for breadth and depth in reports given by students and groups.

Capstone

53 Rapid-Growth Counties

County	State	County	State	County	State
Madison	AL	Howard	MD	Morris	NJ
Santa Clara	CA	Montgomery	MD	Sussex	NJ
Santa Cruz	CA	Prince Georges	MD	Cumberland	NC
Adams	CO	Plymouth	MA	Mecklenburg	NC
Arapahoe	CO	Macomb	MI	Wake	NC
Lee	FL	Washtenaw	MI	Portage	OH
Pasco	FL	Anoka	MN	Cleveland	OK
Sarasota	FL	Dakota	MN	Bucks	PA
Cobb	GA	Washington	MN	Chester	PA
De Kalb	GA	Jackson	MS	Collin	TX
Du Page	IL	Boone	MO	Dallas	TX
Lake	IL	Clay	MO	Denton	TX
Will	IL	Jefferson	MO	Harris	TX
Monroe	IN	St. Charles	MO	Tarrant	TX
Porter	IN	St. Louis	MO	Travis	TX
Johnson	KS	Sarpy	NE	Henrico	VA
Fayette	KY	Burlington	NJ	Waukesha	WI
Harford	MD	Monmouth	NJ		

Source: United States Dept. of Agriculture Economic Research Service, 1988.

1. Examine the transition matrix and the accompanying chart of rapid-growth counties from the USDA report.

   a. Are any of these rapid-growth counties near where you live?

   b. Discuss how to read the matrix. Give and explain two examples.

   c. Notice that the 5-3 (row 5, column 3) entry is not the same number of acres as the 3-5 entry. Explain why this is reasonable. What was the overall change in acreage between open land and forests?

   d. Why are there no negative entries in the matrix?

   e. What do the row and column sums mean in terms of land use? Explain.

   f. Which category of land use had the least change from 1960 to 1970? How can you tell?

   g. Which land use had the least *percentage* change from 1960 to 1970?

   h. Describe the change in land use related to forests from 1960 to 1970.

   i. Describe at least two other trends or patterns you see in this matrix.

Capstone

2. The USDA transition matrix shows land use change in terms of number of acres. Another useful way to describe land use change is in terms of percent change.

Percent Change in Land Use

Land Use in 1970

	1	2	3	4	5	6	7	8	9	10	11	12
1	88.61	1.49	5.09	0.03	0.67	2.09	0.06	0.63	0.20	0.77	0.28	0.08
2	___	85.54	5.65	0	1.02	0.68	0	0.40	0.17	0.28	0.11	0.06
3	6.22	3.40	___	0.10	8.75	7.05	0.15	1.12	0.78	2.82	1.56	0.63
4	1.04	0	1.04	95.85	0	0.52	0	0.52	0	1.04	0	0
5	0.39	0.21	1.11	0.03	94.79	2.15	0.03	___	0.09	0.50	0.14	___
6	0	0	0.07	0	0	99.66	0	0.14	0	0.14	0	0
7	0	___	0	0	0	___	60.49	2.47	1.23	___	0	0
8	0	0	0	0	0	0	0	99.87	0.13	0	0	0
9	0	0	0	0	0	0	0	0	100.00	0	0	0
10	0	0	2.01	0	0	0	0	0	0	97.99	0	0
11	0	0	1.07	0	0	0.15	0	0	0	0	98.77	0
12	1.08	0.22	3.02	0	___	0.43	0	0.43	0	0	0.65	93.95

(*Land Use in 1960* labels the rows.)

a. Examine the matrix above. Verify and explain the 1-5 entry of this matrix.

b. Now, by sharing the workload among members of your group, complete the remaining entries in the matrix.

c. Use the matrix and matrix multiplication to estimate the number of acres of land in each category in 1980, 1990, and 2010. Based on these estimates, describe at least two patterns in land use from 1960 to 2010.

d. Describe any limitations of the predictions you made in Part c. How could your predictions be improved?

3. Make a neat copy of your work on this investigation and file it at the location designated by your teacher. Examine the work filed by other groups in the class and compare their work to what you did. Write a question to at least one group asking them to explain something about their work that you found interesting or that you did not understand. Answer any questions your group receives.

▶ **On Your Own**

Search your library or the Internet to find more recent USDA data on changes in land use. Use the more recent data to make a better estimate of land use for the year 2010.

2. See Teaching Master 178.

a. The (1, 5) entry is $\frac{48}{7{,}127}$ or approximately 0.006735 or 0.67%. From the acreage matrix, the row sum for row 1 is the total cropland in 1960, or 7,127,000 acres. Of this, there were 48,000 acres turned into forest.

b.

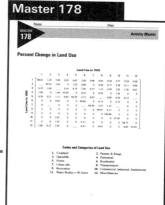

Percent Change in Land Use

Land Type in 1970

	1	2	3	4	5	6	7	8	9	10	11	12
1	88.61	1.49	5.09	0.03	0.67	2.09	0.06	0.63	0.20	0.77	0.28	0.08
2	6.10	85.54	5.65	0	1.02	0.68	0	0.40	0.17	0.28	0.11	0.06
3	6.22	3.40	67.43	0.10	8.75	7.05	0.15	1.12	0.78	2.82	1.56	0.63
4	1.04	0	1.04	95.85	0	0.52	0	0.52	0	1.04	0	0
5	0.39	0.21	1.11	0.03	94.79	2.15	0.03	0.51	0.09	0.50	0.14	0.06
6	0	0	0.07	0	0	99.66	0	0.14	0	0.14	0	0
7	0	0	0	0	0	20.99	60.49	2.47	1.23	14.81	0	0
8	0	0	0	0	0	0	0	99.87	0.13	0	0	0
9	0	0	0	0	0	0	0	0	100	0	0	0
10	0	0	2.01	0	0	0	0	0	0	97.99	0	0
11	0	0	1.07	0	0	0.15	0	0	0	0	98.77	0
12	1.08	0.22	3.02	0	0.22	0.43	0	0.43	0	0	0.65	93.95

(left side label: **Land Type in 1960**)

c. Let the column total row from the Land Use Matrix be matrix *A*. Then multiply the percent change matrix by 0.01 to get the decimal change matrix *B*. To get the 1980 acreage, find the product $[A] \cdot [B]$. In a like manner, the 1990 acreage is represented by $[A] \cdot [B]^2$ and the acreage in 2010 is $[A] \cdot [B]^4$. These products follow.

1980: $[A] \cdot [B] =$

[6,092.2 1,637.7 1,859.4 188.8 6,448.0 2,356.6 43.6 1,005.6 192.8 703.3 765.0 454.0]

1990: $[A] \cdot [B]^2 =$

[5,645.7 1,569.2 1,767.9 186.4 6,333.3 2,769.8 34.4 1,110.2 229.7 836.9 815.1 448.3]

2010: $[A] \cdot [B]^4 =$

[4,869.9 1,432.8 1,600.5 181.3 6,087.5 3,532.0 24.5 1,306.2 298.1 1,074.3 905.0 434.7]

Students may notice a variety of trends in land use. They may notice that the cropland acreage is predicted to go down and quite possibly will be reduced even further by population increases (which could be exponential increases). The forest acreage remains fairly stable. The water acreage is predicted to increase. Students may indicate that these changes will have either positive or negative consequences. Look for students to use sound reasoning in support of their statements.

d. Students must be aware of the big assumption made in Part c (and in all Markov-type processes like this) that the transition percentages remain constant from year to year. This is not a realistic assumption, but it is reasonable in terms of using a simple mathematical model. The predictions could be improved by using more recent data or by building a more complicated model that takes changing transition percentages into account.

> **See additional Teaching Notes on page T555C.**

Capstone

INVESTIGATION 3 Valuing Urban Trees

The mathematical objectives for this investigation are to interpret data tables, search for patterns in data, write these patterns with symbolic expressions, and make predictions. Students will have to use what they know about linear relationships (constant rate of change) to create one equation, they must use a formula from their knowledge of geometry to relate two other variables in a second equation, and then they create a third formula from these two equations.

1. Students should brainstorm about how they think a tree could be assigned a dollar value.

2. **See Teaching Master 179.**

   a. Reading directly from the table, students learn that a tree with a 26-inch diameter has a basic value of $9,556.

   b. $B = 18A$ or $A = \frac{1}{18} B$. This is a linear relationship. The rate of change of B as A increases one square inch is 18. It is not immediately clear from a quick glance at the data in the table that the relationship is, in fact, linear. Students may investigate this by entering some or all of the data in lists and creating a scatterplot, or they may calculate $\dfrac{\text{Change in Basic Value}}{\text{Change in Cross-Section Area}}$ for pairs of data. As the cross-section area increases by one square inch the basic value increases by 18 dollars. The rate of change is shown on the graph by the slope of the line.

   c. There seems to be a nonlinear relationship between the diameter and the cross-sectional area. If students use a power regression on these data, they will get the equation $y = 0.785x^2$.

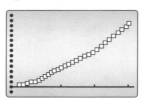
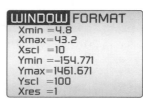

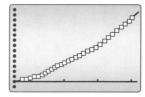

   d. Students might guess the implicit assumption is that the cross section is circular. Push them to confirm this mathematically. One way to do this is to create a Radius column and check that the Area column is indeed πr^2.

INVESTIGATION 3 ▶ Valuing Urban Trees

Trees are an important part of urban landscapes. Whether in parks, in corporate plazas, or on city streets, trees are a valuable natural resource. In particular, they are worth money; and depending on size, location, and other factors, they can be worth a *lot* of money. Determining the dollar value of trees is one part of urban forestry.

1. Think of a tree somewhere near your school. Describe at least two ways that you think could be used to determine the dollar value of the tree.

2. The Council of Tree and Landscape Appraisers (CTLA) and the International Society of Arboriculture developed a method for valuing urban trees that has been used widely. This method uses the formula

$$V = B \times S \times L \times C$$

where V is the dollar value of the tree, B is the basic value based on cross-sectional area, S is the species value, L is the location value, and C is the condition value. Values for S, L, and C require the expert opinion of an urban forester, but the basic value B is computed using a table like the one on page 542. For this activity, only consider the basic value B.

a. Use the table to find the basic value of a tree that has a 26-inch diameter.

b. Let A represent the cross-sectional area and B the basic value of a tree. Write an equation showing the relationship between A and B. Describe the rate of change of the basic value as the cross-sectional area increases. Sketch a graph of the equation and describe how the rate of change is shown in the graph.

c. Let D be the diameter of a tree with cross-sectional area A. Plot the (D, A) data and describe the relationship between D and A. Find and graph an equation that models the data.

d. A key assumption has been made about the shape of a cross section, although the assumption is not explicitly stated in the table. Look at the data and think about trees. What assumption is being made about the shape of the cross section?

Capstone

Basic Formula Value Determinations Taking into Consideration Tree Size and Species

Trunk Caliper or Diameter (in.)	Cross Section Area (in.²)	Basic Value in Dollars (at $18/in.²)	Trunk Caliper or Diameter (in.)	Cross Section Area (in.²)	Basic Value in Dollars (at $18/in.²)
8	50.3	905	25	490.9	8,836
9	63.6	1,145	26	530.9	9,556
10	78.5	1,413	27	572.6	10,307
11	95.0	1,710	28	615.8	11,084
12	113.1	2,036	29	660.5	11,889
13	132.7	2,389	30	706.9	12,724
14	153.9	2,770	31	754.8	13,586
15	176.7	3,181	32	804.2	14,476
16	201.1	3,620	33	855.3	15,395
17	227.0	4,086	34	907.9	16,342
18	254.5	4,581	35	962.1	17,318
19	283.5	5,103	36	1,017.9	18,322
20	314.2	5,656	37	1,075.2	19,354
21	346.4	6,235	38	1,134.1	20,414
22	380.1	6,842	39	1,194.6	21,503
23	415.5	7,479	40	1,256.6	22,619
24	452.5	8,143			

Source: Council of Tree and Landscape Appraisers. *Guide for Establishing Values of Trees and Other Plants,* Revision 4. Savoy, Illinois: International Society of Arboriculture, 1979.

e. Let D be the diameter of a tree with cross-sectional area A. Using the assumption from Part d, write an equation showing the relationship between D and A. Compare this equation to your equation in Part c. Explain similarities and differences.

f. Use your equations from Parts b and e to predict the basic value of a tree that has a diameter of 80 inches. (An 80-inch diameter tree is a very big tree but, for example, it's less than half the diameter of the world's tallest tree. See Investigation 5.)

g. Combine your equation relating D and A from Part e with the equation relating A and B from Part b to get a single equation that shows the relationship between D and B. Use this equation to find the basic value of a tree with diameter 45 inches.

3. Make a neat copy of your work on this investigation and file it at the location designated by your teacher. Examine the work filed by other groups in the class and compare their work to what you did. Write a question to at least one group asking them to explain something about their work that you found interesting or that you did not understand. Answer any questions your group receives.

2. **e.** Using the area of a circle, $A = \pi\left(\frac{D}{2}\right)^2$. Students should use an approximate value for π and find that A is approximately equal to $0.78D^2$, which is close to their equation from Part c. While both results should be power models, coefficients given by students may vary because of variations in curve-fitting and approximations.

    f. For a tree with a diameter of 80 inches, use $A = \pi\left(\frac{D}{2}\right)^2$ to get

        $A = 5{,}026.5$ square inches. Then use $B = 18A$ to get $B = \$90{,}478$.

    g. Students may have difficulty writing this relationship symbolically. One way to help them, without doing too much telling, might be to ask them to write the relationships in words first.

        Basic value $= 18 \cdot$ Cross section

        Cross section $= \pi \cdot \text{radius}^2 = \pi \cdot \left(\frac{D}{2}\right)^2$

        So $B = 18\left(\pi\left(\frac{D}{2}\right)^2\right)$ or $B = 18\pi \, \frac{D^2}{4}$ or $B = 4.5\pi D^2$

        Using this formula for a tree with diameter of 45 inches yields $B = \$28{,}628$.

3. This activity is an important part of each investigation. It provides a mechanism for students to talk with each other about what they have done, to compare answers, to make revisions, and to reflect more deeply upon their work. It also gives you the opportunity to monitor each group's progress and give feedback on any changes or additions that may need to be considered before the group gives its report.

Capstone

▶On Your Own

Responses will depend on the tree.

INVESTIGATION 4▶ Forests, the Greenhouse Effect, and Global Warming

The mathematical objectives of this investigation are to review patterns of change in exponential relationships, to create a linear model to fit data, and to interpret whether or not the model is useful.

1. a. $(NEXT) = 0.973(NOW)$

> ▶ **On Your Own**

Locate a copy of the CTLA *Guide for Establishing Values of Trees and Other Plants* or the *Guide for Plant Appraisal.* Choose a tree near where you live. Use the valuation method described in the guide to estimate the value of the tree.

INVESTIGATION 4 ▶ Forests, the Greenhouse Effect, and Global Warming

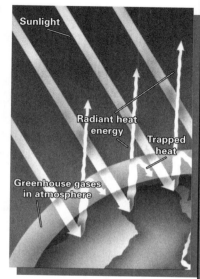

The *greenhouse effect* refers to the warming effect of the Earth's atmosphere. Some gases in the atmosphere act much like the glass walls of a greenhouse, which let in sunlight from the outside but trap the resulting heat inside. In a similar manner, sunlight passes through the atmosphere and is absorbed by the Earth. The energy then radiates away as heat, but some of the heat is trapped by gases in the environment, thereby keeping the Earth's surface warm. It is the greenhouse effect that makes the Earth habitable. Without it, too much heat would escape into space and the Earth would be too cold to sustain life.

The main gases in the atmosphere responsible for the greenhouse effect, called "greenhouse gases," are water vapor, carbon dioxide, methane, nitrous oxide, ozone, and chlorofluorocarbons (CFCs).

1. Among all the greenhouse gases, water vapor and carbon dioxide have the highest levels of concentration in the atmosphere. Forests play a key role in determining the concentration level of carbon dioxide. Trees absorb vast quantities of carbon dioxide through the process of photosynthesis. Along with animals, trees also release carbon dioxide through respiration and decay. However, human activities, like fossil fuel consumption and destruction of forests, have begun to create extra carbon dioxide in the atmosphere. About one-fourth of the extra carbon dioxide resulting from human activity is attributed to deforestation.

   a. To examine the impact of deforestation, consider the case of Ecuador. In 1990, data showed that the annual rate of destruction of forests in Ecuador was 2.7%. Assuming this rate of deforestation remains constant, write an equation using the words *NOW* and *NEXT* that shows how the area of forest land in Ecuador changes from year to year.

Capstone

b. In 1990, Ecuador had 141,666 square kilometers of forests. Use your equation from Part a to estimate the present area of forests in Ecuador.

c. Write an equation that uses the number of years elapsed since 1990 to estimate the area of forests in Ecuador. Use the equation to estimate the area of forests in Ecuador today and 7 years from now.

d. Locate current information giving the area of forests in Ecuador. Use that information to judge the accuracy of your equations from Parts a and c. If necessary, modify your models.

2. Recently, there has been concern that the greenhouse effect is being intensified artificially, resulting in so-called *global warming*. Is there a connection between increased carbon dioxide levels in the atmosphere and rising average temperatures over the whole planet? Is this a potentially serious environmental problem? Scientists have gathered data on carbon dioxide levels and average Earth temperatures over time in order to study these questions. Examine the table below, which shows some of these data.

Global Warming?

Year	Carbon Dioxide Concentration (in parts per million by volume, ppmv)	Temperature Deviation (in °C, compared to mean average temperature from 1950–1980)
1960	317.0	0.05
1965	320.4	−0.05
1970	325.5	0.00
1975	331.0	−0.05
1980	338.0	0.15
1985	345.7	0.18
1990	353.8	0.21

a. Produce three scatterplots, one each for the *(year, carbon dioxide concentration), (year, temperature deviation),* and *(carbon dioxide concentration, temperature deviation)* data. Does there appear to be an association between any pair of variables?

b. Do you think any scatterplot reveals a linear association? Why or why not?

c. What statistical measures do you think would be helpful to compute? Explain your reasoning.

d. Write a brief report that you could submit to a group of concerned citizens. In the report, summarize your analysis of the relationship between carbon dioxide levels and changes in the Earth's climate. Include discussion of the *overall* trend during the period 1960–1990, trends *within* that period, use of the least squares regression lines for prediction, measures of correlation, and possibilities of a cause-and-effect relationship.

1. b. This table includes estimates for 1991–2000.

Year	Area
1991	137,841
1992	134,119
1993	130,498
1994	126,975
1995	123,546
1996	120,211
1997	116,965
1998	113,807
1999	110,734
2000	107,744

c. $F = (141{,}666)(0.973)^x$

Responses will depend on the current year. Approximate area of forests in 1998 was $(141{,}666)(0.973)^8 \approx 113{,}807$ square kilometers.

The approximate area of forests in 2005 is projected to be $(141{,}666)(0.973)^{15} \approx 93{,}963$ square kilometers.

NOTE: Students may have difficulty creating the equation. If so, ask them to explain their work in Part b. They may have used a calculator feature to recursively multiply by 0.973. If so, ask them how many times they multiplied by 0.973. Is there a short way to write this? A general way to write this?

---

d. Current information is available on the Internet.

2. a.

Year and Carbon Dioxide Concentration

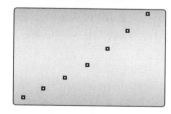

Year and Temperature Deviation

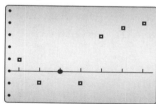

Carbon Dioxide Concentration and Temperature Deviation

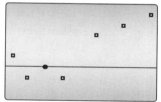

There is an association between year and carbon dioxide concentration. Carbon dioxide concentration is increasing over time, and the pattern appears to be nonlinear.

For year and temperature deviation, there is no association in the data for the first four data points (corresponding to 1960, 1965, 1970, and 1975). In fact, the deviation is so small it may be negligible. However, for the last 3 data points (1980-1990), the temperature deviation becomes greater and positive.

Students may say that the third plot (temperature deviation and carbon dioxide concentration) also has little association or that there appears to be linear association for the last three points of the graph. In the early years, the carbon dioxide increase was not as great as in the later years, and this corresponds with the lack of pattern in temperature deviation in the early years and the steady increase in deviation in the later years.

See additional Teaching Notes on page T555C.

Capstone

3. This activity is an important part of each investigation. It provides a mechanism for students to talk with each other about what they have done, to compare answers, to make revisions, and to reflect more deeply upon their work. It also gives you the opportunity to monitor each group's progress and give feedback on any changes or additions that may need to be considered before the group gives its report.

APPLY **individual task**

▶On Your Own

The two other major greenhouse gases are methane and nitrous oxide. Students should be able to find current information on the Internet.

EXPLORE **small-group investigation**

INVESTIGATION ▶5▶ Measuring Trees

The mathematical objectives for this unit are to review the application of right triangle trigonometry in making indirect measurements and to interpret the meaning of the quadratic relationship between board feet and diameter and the meaning of the linear relationship between board feet and length. Students may be confused by the vocabulary words *roots* and *solutions*.

If you observe this confusion, you may want to spend a few minutes clarifying that a root is a solution to a quadratic equation formed when a quadratic expression is set equal to zero.

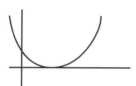

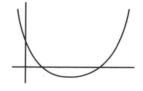

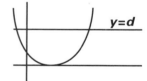

1 root, the value of *x* where *ax²* + *bx* + *c* = 0

2 roots, the values of *x* where *ax²* + *bx* + *c* = 0

2 solutions, the values of *x* where *ax²* + *bx* + *c* = *d*

1. **a.** Students might suggest indirect measurement using trigonometry or some form of direct measurement.

    b. You could use right triangle trigonometry if you measure the distance d from the tree and the angle from horizontal eye level to the top of the tree. Using the tangent of the measured angle A, you could solve for the height: $\tan A = \frac{h}{d}$.

    c. Using the method described in Part b, students will find that the height of the tree, from the forester's eye level, is approximately 151.2 feet. Assuming that the forester's eye level is 5.5 feet, the total height of the tree is 156.7 feet.

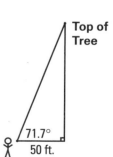

3. Make a neat copy of your work on this investigation and file it at the location designated by your teacher. Examine the work filed by other groups in the class and compare their work to that of your group. Write a question to at least one group asking them to explain something about their work that you found interesting or that you did not understand. Answer any questions your group receives.

▶ **On Your Own**

In this activity, you have examined just one of the greenhouse gases, namely, carbon dioxide. Choose one of the other greenhouse gases, and write a one-page essay describing it and its role in the greenhouse effect. Include in your essay its concentration in the atmosphere, how it is released into and absorbed from the atmosphere, and its particular environmental impact.

INVESTIGATION 5 ▶ Measuring Trees

Often, the first step in forest management is measuring the forest and the trees. For example, a lumber company planning to harvest a particular forest needs to know the height of the trees and the estimated board feet of lumber that the harvest will yield.

1. The tallest known tree in the world was discovered in 1963 by the National Geographic Society in Tall Trees Grove, Redwood National Park, California. The giant redwood tree, similar to the one pictured at the right, is 367.8 feet tall, has a circumference of 44 feet, and is 583 years old.

a. How do you think the height of this tree was measured? List some possible measurement methods.

b. Describe how trigonometry could be used to measure indirectly the height of the tree.

c. Suppose that a forester wants to measure the height of a tree. She stands 50 feet from the base of the tree and uses a surveying instrument to determine that the angle of her line of sight to the top of the tree is 71.7°. Sketch a diagram of this situation and then find the height of the tree.

Capstone

2. A *board foot* is a measure of volume of lumber. One board foot is a piece of lumber 1 foot long by 1 foot wide by 1 inch thick, or its equivalent. It is important to remember that, when measuring with board feet, you may not actually have pieces of lumber 1 ft × 1 ft × 1 in.; instead you have the equivalent of such pieces. Lumber companies need to be able to estimate the number of board feet that a given log will yield. One of the most commonly used formulas for estimating board feet is the *Doyle Log Rule:*

$$B = \frac{L}{16}(D^2 - 8D + 16)$$

where B is board feet; D is the diameter, in inches, of the log inside the bark at the small end; and L is the length of the log in feet. For Parts a–e, only consider logs that are 16 feet long.

a. Rewrite Doyle's formula for the case of logs that are 16 feet long.

b. How many board feet will a 20-inch-diameter log yield (assuming the log is 16 feet long)?

c. Produce a graph and table for the quadratic equation you wrote in Part a. Describe the relationship between board feet and diameter shown by the graph and table. Is the rate of change of board feet with respect to diameter greater for large or small logs? How can you tell from the graph? From the table?

d. How many roots does the quadratic equation in Part a have? Find the roots and explain how you found them. What do the roots tell you about the kinds of logs for which Doyle's rule makes sense?

e. What information will you get if you solve the following quadratic equation?

$$620 = D^2 - 8D + 16$$

Solve the equation. Explain your solution method and the meaning of the answer.

f. So far you have used Doyle's rule for logs with a length of 16 feet and varying diameters. Now, rewrite Doyle's rule for logs that have a diameter of 28 inches and varying lengths. What kind of model do you get? Describe how board feet changes with respect to log length.

g. The equations you wrote in Parts a and f are quite different. They imply different rates of change for board feet as a function of diameter and for board feet as a function of length. Explain in your own words why it makes sense that board feet changes at a different rate with respect to diameter than it does with respect to length.

3. Make a neat copy of your work on this investigation and file it at the location designated by your teacher. Examine the work filed by other groups in the class and compare their work to yours. Write a question to at least one group asking them to explain something about their work that you found interesting or that you did not understand. Answer any questions your group receives.

2. **a.** $B = D^2 - 8D + 16$

   b. A 20-inch diameter log will yield 256 board feet.

   c. The graph is a parabola with vertex at (4, 0). For $D \le 4$, the graph does not apply to this situation, as elaborated in Part d. As diameter increases beyond 4 inches, the number of board feet increases. The rate of change of board feet with respect to diameter is greater for large logs. This can be seen from the increasing rate of change in the table as the diameter increases in one-inch increments, or by the steeper graph for larger values of D.

D	0	1	2	3	4	5
B	16	9	4	1	0	1

D	6	7	8
B	4	9	16

   d. There is one root, $D = 4$, which can be found, for example, by using the table or graph. Given the shape of the curve and the root at $D = 4$, it is seen that Doyle's formula does not apply for logs with diameter of 4 inches or less. In fact, it would be reasonable to assume that the formula applies only for diameters larger than 5 or 6 inches.

   e. Solving this equation gives the diameter size that yields 620 board feet. Solving by table or graph gives $D \approx 29$ inches. So a log with diameter close to 29 inches will yield about 620 board feet. Since Doyle's rule only estimates board feet, it is not very sensible to state an answer with more precision.

   f. For a fixed diameter of 28 inches and varying lengths, Doyle's rule is $B = \left(\frac{L}{16}\right)(576) = 36L$. This is a linear model. There is a constant rate of change of board feet with respect to log length. This constant rate of change is seen in the graph as the constant slope, 36, and is seen in the table as the constant increment in B as L changes by one-foot increments.

   g. Remember that a board foot is a measure of volume of lumber. Think about how volume of lumber changes as length and diameter change. Suppose length changes and diameter is fixed, as in Part f. Then if you increase the length foot by foot, each time you get the same additional volume of wood; thus, rate of change of board feet is constant. Conversely, suppose the diameter changes and the length is fixed, as in Part a. For each inch that you increase diameter, volume increases by an *increasing* amount. An increase in diameter causes a change in area of cross section, which varies quadratically.

3. This activity is an important part of each investigation. It provides a mechanism for students to talk with each other about what they have done, to compare answers, to make revisions, and to reflect more deeply upon their work. It also gives you the opportunity to monitor each group's progress and give feedback on any changes or additions that may need to be considered before the group gives its report.

Capstone

On Your Own

A *Biltmore stick* or adaptation of the same principle can be used to provide rather imprecise measurements. A Biltmore stick is a straight rule specially graduated to read diameters. The scale is not linear. The stick is held horizontally touching the bole of a tree and at a fixed distance from the observer (usually a convenient arm's length). The stick is held so that the end with the origin of the scale (usually the right-hand end) is aligned with the tree profile and the observer's eye. Without moving the head or scale, the observer takes the reading of the opposite edge of the tree on the scale; this is the tree's diameter.

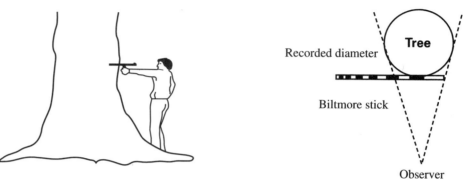

Information on the relascope can be found on the Internet.

INVESTIGATION 6 Producing Wood Products

The mathematical objectives for this investigation are to apply methods for solving a system of two linear equations, to apply the concept of angular velocity and relate this to linear velocity, to create a waiting-time distribution and find its mean, and to interpret an observation as "rare" or not. This investigation makes more connections and may take longer to complete than the others.

1. **a.** The system of linear equations representing this situation is:

$20L + 30P = 11,000$ and

$L + P = 400$

It could be solved using matrices, by substitution, by linear combination, with tables, or with graphs.

b–c. See student methods.

100 units of lumber and 300 units of particle board will cost $11,000 to produce.

d. If this production continues and only 150 units of particle board are sold, the warehouse will contain a lot of extra particle board. Student suggestions for resolution will vary. One suggestion might be to find other buyers for the extra particle board.

► On Your Own

Foresters in the field use a variety of handy and ingenious instruments to measure trees. For example, a *Biltmore stick* can be used to estimate tree diameter and a *relascope* can be used to estimate the sum of the cross-sectional areas of all trees in a particular region. Write a brief research report explaining how either the Biltmore stick or a relascope is used and why it works.

INVESTIGATION 6 Producing Wood Products

In the lumber business, there is a constant tension between harvesting and conserving trees. The profit of a lumber company depends not only on how many trees are harvested but also on the kind of wood products into which trees are converted.

1. Ketchikan Lumber Company in Alaska converts logs into particle board and into lumber such as two-by-fours and two-by-sixes. When the mill is running at peak capacity, it can turn out 400 units of wood products per week. The production cost for a unit of lumber is $30 and for a unit of particle board is $20. The owner wants to keep the mill running at full capacity while keeping production costs at $11,000 per week.

   a. Describe three different methods you could use to determine the number of units of each type of product that should be produced in a week.

   b. Choose one of your methods in Part a to find the number of units of lumber and of particle board that should be produced.

   c. Verify your solution in Part b using a different solution method.

   d. Of course, there are factors other than production costs that should be taken into account when setting production levels. Customer demand and profit per unit are two such factors. For example, suppose the weekly demand is for 100 units of particle board and 250 units of lumber. If the production levels stay as you calculated in Part b, what will happen to the company's inventory of these products? What would you suggest doing to correct this situation?

Capstone

2. One type of saw used to produce lumber in sawmills is a *band saw*. A band saw blade is a long strip of metal, with teeth, that runs between two pulleys, similar to the side-view diagram at the right.

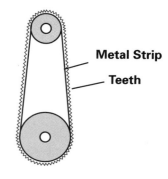

Metal Strip

Teeth

One band saw uses a blade that is 8 feet long in circumference. The larger pulley has a diameter of 12 inches and is attached to the saw motor, which has an angular velocity of 24,000 rpm. The smaller 6-inch pulley is adjusted to keep the blade tight.

a. At what angular velocity does the smaller pulley turn?

b. How many times will the blade revolve through its entire length in one minute?

c. The teeth should be sharpened after "traveling" 100,000 miles. About how often should the teeth be sharpened if the saw runs 6 hours per day?

3. Because of the potential danger in a sawmill, the machinery is tested thoroughly for reliability. Suppose the manufacturer of a band saw motor reports that the motor has about a 0.001 probability of failing each hour it is running.

a. Out of every lot of 10,000 motors produced, how many would you expect to fail in the first hour of operation?

b. Using the reliability estimate provided by the manufacturer, complete the following partial probability distribution table for the hour in which a sample motor fails.

Hour in Which Motor Fails	Probability
1	
2	
3	
500	
1000	
1500	

c. Sketch a graph of the probability distribution.

d. What is the expected number of hours until a motor fails?

e. The probability that a motor selected at random fails within the first 48 hours of operation is 0.046889. Find the probability that a motor fails within the first 49, 50, 51, and 52 hours. Under what time frame would you consider failure of one of these motors to be a rare event?

Capstone

2. **a.** The top pulley turns at 48,000 rpm.

   b. $\frac{(24,000 \text{ rpm})(12 \text{ inches})(\pi)}{(12 \text{ inches})(8 \text{ feet})} \approx 9,425$. Thus, the saw band will revolve through its entire

   length about 9,425 times in one minute.

   c. The distance traveled by any point on the saw band in one minute is $(24,000)(12)(\pi)$
   $\approx 904,778.6842$ inches ≈ 14.27997 miles. So, the time needed to go 100,000 miles
   is $\frac{100,000}{14.27997} \approx 7,002.8175$ minutes ≈ 19.45227 days if the saw runs 6 hours per day.
   Thus, the saw band should be sharpened in about $19\frac{1}{2}$ days.

3. **a.** You would expect $(10,000)(0.001) = 10$ to fail in the first hour.

   b. Following is a partial theoretical probability distribution table for this situation.
   Students should compute these values theoretically. Let h represent the hour the
   motor fails and p represent the probability of failure within an hour. Then the theoretical probability, P, that the motor fails after a given number of hours if found by
   multiplying the probability of no failure up to this number of hours by the probability of failure within the final hour. Therefore, $P = (1 - p)^{h-1} p = (0.999)^{h-1}(0.001)$.

Hour in Which Motor Fails	Probability
1	0.001
2	0.000999
3	0.000998
:	:
500	0.000607
:	:
1000	0.000368
:	:
1500	0.000223

   c.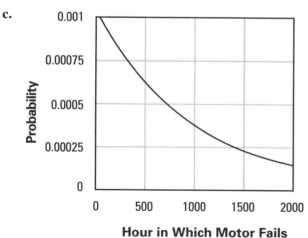

   Hour in Which Motor Fails

   d. The expected number of hours until a motor fails (i.e., the expected value of the distribution) is $\frac{1}{0.001} = 1,000$ hours.

   See additional Teaching Notes on page T555D.

Capstone

3. **f.**   For a given lot of 10,000 motors produced on the same assembly line, you would expect about 5% to fail within 52 hours since the probability of failure within 52 hours is about 0.05. Thus, you would expect 500 to fail within the first 52 hours of operation. Students might argue whether this number of failures is or is not acceptable, but they must discuss it. It seems reasonable to assert that this is too many failures and the manufacturer needs to improve the reliability of the motors.

4. This activity is an important part of each investigation. It provides a mechanism for students to talk with each other about what they have done, to compare answers, to make revisions, and to reflect more deeply upon their work. It also gives you the opportunity to monitor each group's progress and give feedback on any changes or additions that may need to be considered before the group gives its report.

APPLY   individual task

▶On Your Own

To simulate the probability that a motor fails within 50 hours, try the following. Generate a random number between 1 and 1,000 and let a 1 represent a failure. Then repeat this 50 times to represent 50 hours. If 1 does not occur in the 50 trials, then this represents the situation in which the motor did not fail within 50 hours. If 1 occurs, then stop as soon as the 1 appears and conclude that this represents the motor failing within 50 hours. Repeat this entire experiment many times, perhaps 200 times. For each of the 200 experiments, record whether or not a 1 appeared, which corresponds to whether or not the motor failed within 50 hours. Then compute the proportion of experiments in which a 1 appeared. This will give you an estimate of the probability that a motor fails within 50 hours. This estimate should be close to the theoretical probability from Activity 3, Part e, which is about 0.048794. A sample program for the TI-82 is provided here. Execution of this many trials on the TI-82 is slow.

```
Program:Motor
  0 → S
  For (T,1,200)
  0 → F
  For (K,1,50)
  Int 1000rand + 1 → M
  If M = 1
  F + 1 → F
  End
  If F ≠ 0
  S + 1 → S
  End
  DISP "PROB IS,"S/200
```

EXPLORE   small-group investigation

INVESTIGATION ▶7▶ Geographic Information Systems

The mathematical objectives for this investigation are to interpret a matrix and create the associated vertex-edge graph, to recognize when the goal is to find the shortest path and when it is to find a minimum spanning tree, and to compute slope and distance to solve problems.

f. For a given lot of 10,000 motors produced on the same assembly line, how many would you expect to fail within 52 hours of use? Do you think this is an acceptable number? Do you think 0.001 is an acceptable probability level for motor failure?

4. Make a neat copy of your work on this investigation and file it at the location designated by your teacher. Examine the work filed by other groups in the class and compare their work to what you did. Write a question to at least one group asking them to explain something about their work that you found interesting or that you did not understand. Answer any questions your group receives.

▶ **On Your Own**

Referring to the situation in Activity 3, design a simulation model to estimate the probability that a motor fails within 50 hours. Extend the programming skills you developed in Unit 2 to develop a calculator or computer program to implement your simulation model. Run the program and compare your simulation results to the theoretical results you obtained in Part e of Activity 3. Explain any differences.

INVESTIGATION 7 ▶ Geographic Information Systems (GIS)

Many geographic features must be taken into account when studying a forest. *Geographic Information Systems* (GIS) compile all sorts of geographical data and use a variety of mathematical techniques to analyze the data. More and more foresters are using GIS in their analysis and management of forests. For example, Geographic Information Systems are used to locate fire towers, hiking paths, and microwave relay towers.

1. When considering where to locate fire observation towers, it is important to consider the location of key areas that are at-risk in a forest fire, like cabin clusters, lodges, forest service buildings, and logging camps. In a Geographic Information System, these key areas and others are represented as points. Then the region containing the points is subdivided into a grid. One of the most useful ways to subdivide an area so that it can be described and studied systematically is to use a *Triangulated Irregular Network* (TIN). A TIN for a set of points is constructed by first drawing line segments between some of the points to form an outer boundary, and then drawing additional segments to create a triangular network. This network is called a *triangulation*.

Capstone

a. Below is a partial TIN for nine at-risk points in the Atika forest preserve. The outer boundary is completed, forming a polygon, and some of the additional segments needed to create the triangulation have been drawn. The TIN is not finished until all subdivided regions are triangles.

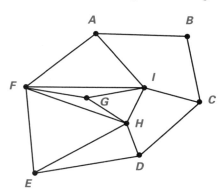

Working in pairs, complete the triangulation by adding more segments between points until the entire polygon is subdivided into triangles.

b. Compare your triangulation with that of other members of your group. Try to construct different triangulations. Is it possible to have two different triangulations for the same set of points?

c. There is a special triangulation, called a *Delaunay triangulation,* that is most useful. It is formed using triangles that are not "extreme." Extreme triangles are long and narrow, like triangles *FGH* or *FGI* in the triangulation from Part a. Brainstorm with your group to devise possible algorithms for producing a Delaunay triangulation from a partial TIN or a non-Delaunay TIN.

d. One way to modify any triangulation to get a Delaunay triangulation is as follows: Look for quadrilaterals formed by two triangles that share a side, where one of the triangles is "extreme." Swap diagonals in that quadrilateral if the result increases the size of the smallest of the six interior angles in the two triangles.

For example, in the triangulation you completed in Part a, consider the quadrilateral *FGHE*. Erase the existing diagonal, $\overline{FH}$, and replace it with $\overline{GE}$. Is the smallest angle of the two new triangles larger than the smallest angle of the original triangles? Does this diagonal swap eliminate the "extreme" triangle?

Continue swapping diagonals in this way until your triangulation in Part a has become a Delaunay triangulation.

1. a. See Teaching Master 180.

Quadrilaterals *ABCI* and *DCIH* need to be subdivided. One possible triangulation follows.

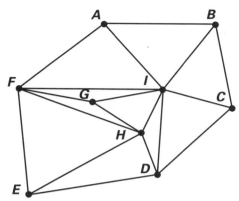

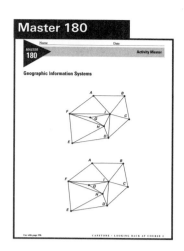

Master 180

b. It is possible to have several different triangulations. For example, in the triangulation given above as a solution to Part a, add $\overline{AC}$ instead of $\overline{BI}$ or add $\overline{CH}$ instead of $\overline{DI}$.

c. Student algorithms might focus on diagonals in quadrilaterals. The key idea here is to think about how the diagonal of a quadrilateral will create two triangles. Students might think about how to add a diagonal of a quadrilateral in a partial TIN in order to create a Delaunay triangulation, or they might think of swapping diagonals in an existing TIN to eliminate "extreme" triangles. Some possible methods follow:

■ Swap diagonals if the result increases the size of the smallest of the six interior angles in the two triangles. This method does produce a Delaunay triangulation. This is explored in Part d.

■ Use the quadrilateral diagonal of shortest length. This is a plausible strategy, but it is not guaranteed to create a Delaunay triangulation.

■ Use the diagonal that goes between the pair of opposite angles with the greatest sum. This strategy will create a Delaunay triangulation. It is possible that some students will use a strategy based on circumscribed circles. See the "On Your Own" option at the end of this investigation.

d. Yes, the two new triangles are closer to being equiangular. The small acute angles at *F* and *H* are eliminated as shown in the Delaunay triangulation below.

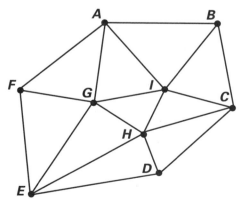

2. **a.** Points *A, B, C,* and *I* are visible from point *B*.

   b. The best places to put a single fire tower are either *G* or *H* since you can see the most points (7) from there. However, you cannot see all the points from any one location.

   c. The row sum for a given point tells you how many points you can see from that point. (The column sums are equivalent to the corresponding row sums.) Thus, the points with the largest row sums are the best candidates for a single fire tower location. Since no row sum is 9, it is not possible to see all 9 points from any single location.

   d. Two fire towers are enough to see all points. For example, if one tower is at point *H*, then the only points not visible are *A,* and *B*. But points *A* and *B* can be seen from point *A*. So towers at points *A* and *H* will allow observation of all nine points. *B* and *G* or *E* and *I* are other possibilities.

   e. The visibility matrix for a smooth bowl-shaped valley would be all 1s, since all points are visible from all other points. A flat terrain could also qualify.

   f. Using a square such as the one below, you get the following visibility matrix.

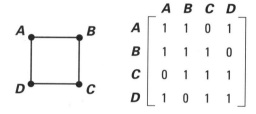

3. **a.** The visibility graph corresponding to the matrix in Activity 2 follows.

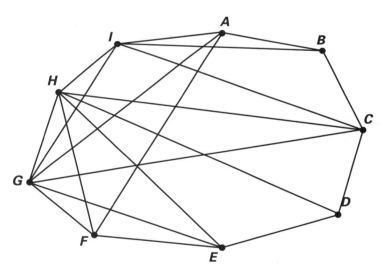

2. Once a region has been triangulated, you can begin to analyze it. Continuing with the fire tower example, it is important to know which points are visible from different potential locations of a fire tower. Using known elevations of all vertices in the grid, you can construct a *visibility matrix* to help you decide where to place the fire tower. Consider the visibility matrix below, in which a "1" in a cell means that the two points are visible to each other.

Visibility Matrix

	A	B	C	D	E	F	G	H	I
A	1	1	0	0	0	1	1	0	1
B	1	1	1	0	0	0	0	0	1
C	0	1	1	1	0	0	1	1	1
D	0	0	1	1	1	0	0	1	0
E	0	0	0	1	1	1	1	1	0
F	1	0	0	0	1	1	1	1	0
G	1	0	1	0	1	1	1	1	1
H	0	0	1	1	1	1	1	1	1
I	1	1	1	0	0	0	1	1	1

a. Which points are visible from point *B?*

b. Assume that a fire tower will be located at one or more of the points *A* through *I*. If you can only build one fire tower, where would you put it? Why? Will one fire tower be enough to observe all nine points?

c. Compute the row sums and explain how they can help you answer the questions in Part b. (The row sums are called *visibility indices.*)

d. Where should fire towers be built so that all nine points can be observed and the fewest number of fire towers are built?

e. Describe the type of terrain that could yield a visibility matrix in which all the entries are 1s.

f. Construct the visibility matrix for a mountain range in the shape of a square-based pyramid, where the vertices in the matrix are the five vertices of the pyramid.

3. Geographic Information Systems also use vertex-edge graphs to represent and analyze geographic data.

a. The vertex-edge graph corresponding to a visibility matrix is called a *visibility graph.* Construct the visibility graph corresponding to the matrix in Activity 2.

Capstone

b. It is necessary to have line-of-sight communication between microwave transceivers for such things as telephone, television, and digital data networks. Referring to your visibility graph in Part a, suppose one transceiver is at vertex *A* and another is at vertex *D*. Since *A* and *D* do not have direct line-of-sight communication between them, relay towers will have to be built. Assume that relay towers will be built only at other vertices.

■ What is the fewest number of relay towers necessary for line-of-sight communication between the transceivers at *D* and *A?* Where should the relay towers be built?

■ Explain how finding a shortest path in the visibility graph between *D* and *A* provides an answer to the above questions.

c. Weighted graphs also are used to represent geographic data. The graph below represents hiking trails between lakes in Atika forest. The weights on the edges represent distances in miles.

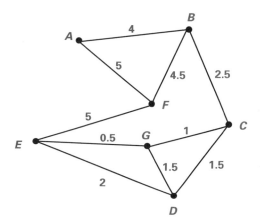

Because of weather and maintenance costs, it is not possible for the Forest Service to keep all trails open for the entire season. However, the Service does want to keep enough trails open so that it is possible to get from every lake to every other lake by some sequence of trails.

■ What is the minimum number of miles of trails that the Forest Service must keep open? Sketch a network of open trails.

■ Explain how you found your network of trails. Is this problem modeled with Euler paths, Hamiltonian paths, shortest paths, or minimal spanning trees?

Capstone

3. b. ■ The lowest number of relay towers necessary for line-of-sight communication between the transceivers at *A* and *D* is 2. You could put relay towers at *B* and *C* or at *F* and *E* or at *I* and *H* or at other possible pairs. (You may wish to ask students to find all possible pairs.)

■ To get line-of-sight communication between *A* and *D*, you need a sequence of relay towers, each of which is visible from the previous. Thus, you need a path from *A* to *D*, and vertices along a shortest possible path will be locations for the lowest number of relay towers.

c. ■ The minimum number of miles of trails that the Forest Service must keep open is 14 miles. See the network shown.

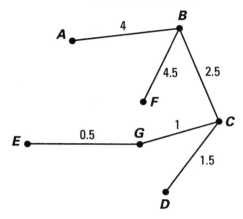

■ This is a minimal spanning tree problem. Students should describe how they found a minimal spanning tree. For example, they might describe the steps of the best-edge (Kruskal's) algorithm or Prim's algorithm.

4. a. Point D would be the best place for a single fire observation tower.

   b. You cannot see point A from point F because the peak at point D blocks the view. This is because points F, D, and A are all on the same line. They are on the same line because the slope between points F and D is the same as the slope between points D and A (slope $= 0.5$). (NOTE: You might allow the answer that point A is "barely" visible from point F if there is good explanation.)

   c. Point B cannot be seen from point D because, for example, if you line up D and B with a straight edge, the line of sight goes through the intervening mountain.

   d. The slope between points D and C is 1.5. The slope between points B and C is 2. Thus, they are not on the same line of sight.

   e. The bear is about 506 feet from you. Distance $= \sqrt{(975 - 700)^2 + (275 - 700)^2}$ That may be in range depending on your weapon and your skill.

5. This activity is an important part of each investigation. It provides a mechanism for students to talk with each other about what they have done, to compare answers, to make revisions, and to reflect more deeply upon their work. It also gives you the opportunity to monitor each group's progress and give feedback on any changes or additions that may need to be considered before the group gives its report.

4. In Activity 2, you were given a visibility matrix. To construct a visibility matrix, you need to figure out which points are visible from where. For example, consider the mountainous terrain represented by the diagram below.

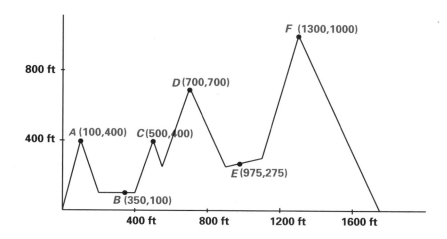

a. At which of the points *A–F* would you place a single fire observation tower so that you could see the most terrain? Explain.

b. Suppose there is an observation tower at point *F.* Can you see point *A* from the tower? Justify your answer. Give an argument supporting the claim that points *F, D,* and *A* lie on the same line of sight.

c. Can you see point *B* from point *D?*

d. Compute the slope of the line containing points *D* and *C.* Then compute the slope of the line containing points *C* and *B.* Explain how to use these slopes to answer the question in Part c.

e. Suppose that you work for the Forest Service and you are sent to point *D* with orders to keep a look-out for a renegade bear that has attacked several campers. In this extreme situation, your instructions are to shoot the bear with a tranquilizer dart if you get an open shot. You see the bear at a small lake located at point *E.* How far away is the bear? Do you think it is within range?

5. Make a neat copy of your work and file it at the location designated by your teacher. Examine the work filed by other groups in the class and compare their work to what you did. Write a question to at least one group asking them to explain something about their work that you found interesting or that you did not understand. Answer any questions your group receives.

Capstone

▶On Your Own

A Delaunay triangulation has the property that no vertices of the graph are enclosed by the circumscribing circle of any triangle. (There may be vertices *on* a circumscribing circle, however. In fact, the three vertices of a triangle *must* be on its circumscribing circle.) Verify this property by circumscribing circles for all the triangles in your triangulation from Part d of Activity 1. You may wish to use some geometry software to help you do this.

INVESTIGATION 8▸ Further Analysis

There are many other aspects of forests and the environment that you might investigate. Choose one of your ideas from Investigation 1 or from the "Think About This Situation" on page 536. Carry out a brief mathematical analysis of the idea. Specifically, you should formulate and answer at least two questions related to your idea.

REPORTS: Putting It All Together

Finish this Capstone by preparing two reports, one group oral report and one individual written report as described below.

1. Your group should prepare a brief oral report that meets the following guidelines:

   ■ Choose one investigation from this Capstone. Confirm your choice with your teacher before beginning to prepare your report.

   ■ Examine the work that other groups have filed on your investigation. Compare your work to theirs, discuss any differences with them, and modify your solutions, if you think you should.

   ■ Begin your presentation with a brief summary of your work in the investigation. Then explain your solutions to the various activities.

   ■ Be prepared to discuss alternative solutions, particularly those proposed by other groups that worked on your investigation.

   ■ Be prepared to answer any questions.

2. Individually, write a two-page report summarizing how the mathematics you have learned in this course can be used to understand issues related to forestry and the environment.

APPLY   individual task

▶On Your Own

See student verifications. If students use geometry software to do this, have them redraw a new diagram that is close to the one in Part d and work with it.

EXPLORE   small-group investigation

INVESTIGATION 8▶ Further Analysis

Here is where students can think about other ways to analyze forests and the environment mathematically.

SYNTHESIZE   share and summarize

Reports: Putting It All Together

See Teaching Masters 181a–181c.

These reports take some time, but are a valuable part of the unit.

If enough time has been available for students to have examined the work of other groups for the investigation they have selected for their oral report, they may wish to make amendments. This kind of collaborative effort mirrors a learning community in which insights are shared, developed, and maximized. Students are encouraged to see the whole course as such a learning community, not just a long exercise in finding predetermined answers. The quality of the oral reports will improve if this time for sharing is available. Encourage groups to give each other credit for ideas that are unique or to say where and how they disagree.

You may want to give specific roles to the listening groups. For example, if two groups, A and B, each selected the same investigation and only group A will do an oral report on that investigation, then encourage group B to think of questions that will force group A to be clear. Why did you choose to … ? Did your answer make sense? We found a particular activity difficult. Did you? Why or why not? and so on.

Activity Masters 181a–181c explain guidelines for possible methods of assessing the oral and written reports.

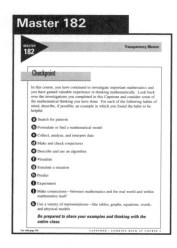

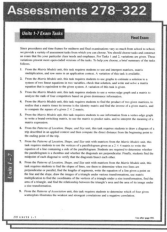

NOTE: In addition to the Capstone, if you wish to administer a written, individual final exam, you may select items from the **Assessment Resources, pages 278–322,** which are appropriate for your students.

Checkpoint

See Teaching Master 182.

This Checkpoint is an important conclusion to the Capstone. Students will be able to reflect upon their development of important mathematical habits of mind. Some examples of when each was executed are given here. Your students may come up with different examples.

ⓐ Students looked for patterns in the Land Use Matrix, in the table of basic values, and in the scatterplots related to global warming.

ⓑ Students found mathematical models for the relationships between diameter of a tree and its basic value, for estimating the area of forests in Ecuador, and for determining production levels for the Ketchikan Lumber Company.

ⓒ Students analyzed and interpreted data in Investigations 2 and 4.

ⓓ Students may have made and checked conjectures at many different points during their work on the Capstone.

ⓔ Students were specifically asked to describe and use algorithms to find the Delaunay triangulation.

ⓕ Many students may have used visualization to help determine where to build fire observation towers.

ⓖ Some students may have developed a simulation to model the failure rate of a band saw motor for the On Your Own on page 549.

ⓗ Students predicted the area of forests in Ecuador and when a randomly chosen motor will fail.

ⓘ Students may have experimented when trying to find modeling equations.

ⓙ This was done throughout all investigations.

ⓚ This was done throughout all investigations.

CONSTRUCTING A MATH TOOLKIT: Students may wish to include their responses to this Checkpoint in their Math Toolkit to remind them of the valuable thinking skills that they are cultivating. Students should retain their Math Toolkits from Course 1 and Course 2 as resources for following courses. This will allow them to access the mathematical tools they have learned thus far in the curriculum. You may wish to store the students' Math Toolkits over the summer break to help prevent misplacement.

Capstone

Checkpoint

In this course, you have continued to investigate important mathematics and you have gained valuable experience in thinking mathematically. Look back over the investigations you completed in this Capstone and consider some of the mathematical thinking you have done. For each of the following habits of mind, describe, if possible, an example in which you found the habit to be helpful.

ⓐ Search for patterns

ⓑ Formulate or find a mathematical model

ⓒ Collect, analyze, and interpret data

ⓓ Make and check conjectures

ⓔ Describe and use an algorithm

ⓕ Visualize

ⓖ Simulate a situation

ⓗ Predict

ⓘ Experiment

ⓙ Make connections—between mathematics and the real world and within mathematics itself

ⓚ Use a variety of representations—like tables, graphs, equations, words, and physical models

Be prepared to share your examples and thinking with the entire class.

Capstone

Looking Back, Looking Ahead

This Capstone brings to conclusion the second course in the *Contemporary Mathematics in Context* curriculum. While enabling students to synthesize and apply some of the important modeling concepts, methods, and skills developed in Course 2, the Capstone once again underscores the pervasive use of mathematics in our world. The final Checkpoint summarized important habits of mind that were introduced in Course 1 and nurtured in Course 2. Course 3 will continue the integrated development of the major strands of the curriculum with increasing attention to reasoning with, and manipulating, symbolic expressions.

■ Algebra and Functions

Algebraic concepts and methods were developed in Courses 1 and 2 from a modeling and a function perspective. The ability to recognize, represent, and solve problems involving relations among quantitative variables was developed across the four strands of the curriculum. Algebraic models and methods will be expanded in Course 3 to include algebraic relations involving more than two variables. Linear models, exponential models, power models, quadratic models, and trigonometric models are explored in new ways and in more complex situations, and then organized and extended as families of functions. Reasoning with symbolic forms to write equivalent expressions, to solve equations and inequalities, and to prove mathematical patterns across strands is highlighted.

■ Geometry and Trigonometry

This strand has focused on developing visual thinking and the ability to construct, reason with, interpret and apply mathematical models of patterns in the visual world. Representations with drawings, coordinates, and physical models have been used to assist this development. The focus on more formal mathematical reasoning characteristic of Course 3, continues in this strand, often with a blend of both algebraic and geometric reasoning. Important geometric relationships and properties of shapes are deduced and organized using local axiomatics. Familiar theorems for triangle similarity (and thus for congruence when the scale factor is 1) are established as consequences of the Law of Cosines and the Law of Sines. Based on a small number of additional assumptions, familiar relations involving parallel lines and angles and properties of special quadrilaterals are proven.

■ Statistics and Probability

The primary goals of this strand have been to enable students to analyze data intelligently, to recognize and measure variation, and to understand probalistic situations. In Course 3, statistics and probability ideas become increasingly intertwined. Variation (and how to both measure and interpret it) continues as a central theme. Making sense of variation in data from measurements leads to the mathematics behind quality control methods in industry. These topics include standard deviation, normal distribution, control charts and the underlying criteria involving application of the multiplication and addition rules for probability. Making sense of data from sample surveys of a population leads to sampling distributions and related probabilistic ideas of confidence intervals and margin of error.

■ Discrete Mathematics

In Courses 1 and 2, the discrete mathematics strand has focused on modeling and solving problems involving decision making in finite settings and relationships among a finite number of elements. Key mathematical models were vertex-edge graphs and matrices. The fundamental idea of recursion introduced in Course 1 in terms of NOW-NEXT equations is formalized in Course 3 and used to extend the study of sequential change. Recursion is used to provide a unified approach to arithmetic and geometric sequences, to finite sums of such sequences, to finite differences, and to function iteration. The latter topic foreshadows the work in function composition that appears in Course 4. In Course 3, discrete mathematics also focuses on how to measure and analyze public opinion through voting as a compliment to survey methods.

Teaching Notes continued

Notes continued from page T540

3. This activity is an important part of each investigation. It provides a mechanism for students to talk with each other about what they have done, to compare answers, to make revisions, and to reflect more deeply upon their work. It also gives you the opportunity to monitor each group's progress and give feedback on any changes or additions that may need to be considered before the group gives its report.

APPLY individual task

▶ **On Your Own**

If you have Internet access, an interesting project is to access the USDA Internet site and try to find and use more recent data.

Notes continued from page T544

2. **b.** Students may say that the plot of data for year and carbon dioxide concentration looks somewhat linear though appears to be increasing at a more rapid rate as time passes. They may conclude that the plot will look less linear later. If students suggest that a linear model is appropriate for these data, you may want to have them find the changes in carbon dioxide concentration from one year to the next. This should help them see that the change is not constant, in fact there appears to be a pattern to the change, and thus a linear model is not the most appropriate. (More current data may reinforce or contradict this conclusion.)

   There is some indication of a linear pattern for the (temperature deviation versus carbon dioxide concentration) data, particularly in the later years. Thus, it makes sense to at least consider a least squares regression line.

   c. For prediction, students may find it helpful to compute the linear regression line and the correlation coefficient for this data. The equation of the regression line is $y = -2.1544 + 0.0067x$. The correlation coefficient for this data is $r = 0.822$. Using this equation to predict temperature deviation for a carbon dioxide concentration of 375 ppmv yields 0.35°C. The linear relationship here is only tentative, so more data are needed before we would feel confident about making predictions based on the linear regression line.

   d. Students should pull together their responses to Parts a–c, along with other analysis they may choose to do, into a brief report.

   We cannot on the basis of these data and this correlation infer that there is a cause-and-effect relationship. There is a strong correlation between these factors, but correlation does not imply causation.

Capstone

Teaching Notes *continued*

Notes continued from page T548

3. e. Note that the given probability for failure within 48 hours is calculated as $1 - $ (probability that it does not fail within 48 hours) $= 1 - 0.999^{48} \approx 0.046889$.

The probability of failure within the first 49 hours $= 1 - 0.999^{49} \approx 0.047842$. Another way to compute the probability is (probability of failure within 48 hours) $+$ (probability of failure in the 49th hour) $\approx (0.046889) + (0.000953)$ or 0.047842.

Similarly, the probabilities for failure within 50, 51, and 52 hours are 0.048794, 0.049746, and 0.050696, respectively. Failure within about 52 hours would be considered a rare event since the probability of that happening is about 0.05.

Capstone

Index of Mathematical Topics

E

Error in prediction, *213*
Euler circuit, 347
    versus Hamiltonian circuit, 347
Events, 457
    dependent, 476
    independent, 474
Expectation, 486
Expected value, 513–515
Explanatory variable, *199*
Exponential models, *244*, 544
    compared to inverse variation, *256–259*
    compared to linear models, 238–249
    compared to power models, tables, and graphs, 238–241, 244
    identifying from a table, 262
Exponents, *238, 301–302*

F

Fair price, 511–515
    and expected value, 513–515
Flag Turn Algorithm, *152*
FLAGTURN Program, *153*
Follower pulley, *370, 413, 425*
4-bar linkage, *370–372*
Frame, *370*
Frequency, 449
Frequency table
    rolling doubles, 457–459

G

Geometric probability, 479
Geometry
    coordinate model of, *90*
Geometry drawing programs, *81*
GEOXPLOR, *81, 99, 129, 149, 164*
Glide reflection, *125*
Grade
    of a pyramid, 409
    of a road, 407–408
Graphics calculators, *81*
    input, *84*
    output, *84*
    perspective, *87*
    processing, *84*
    programming, *84*
Graphs
    bipartite, 357
    complete, 357
    complete bipartite, 357
    to solve quadratic equations, *267, 278*
    weighted, 340

Grashof's principle, 370
Gravity, force of, *268*
Gray Code, 353–354
    using Hamiltonian circuits to find, 353–354, 358

H

Hamilton, Sir William Rowan, 345–346
Hamiltonian circuit, 346
    versus Euler circuit, 347
    existence of, 347
    Gray Codes, using to find, 353–354, 358
    and Traveling Salesperson Problem, 349
Hamiltonian path, 356–357
Hipparchus, *308*
Homogeneous coordinates of a point, *164*
Horizontal line, *94*
    distance between points, *82–83*
Horizontal translation, *110, 111*
Hypotenuse, 396

I

Icosahedron, 468
Identity matrix, 43–44
Images
    of lines, *120–126*
    of polygons, *121–123*
    under reflection rotation, *121*
    of segment under translation, *120*
Inclined plane, 394
Independent, 460
Independent events, 474
Independent trials, 460–461
Infinite geometric series, 528
    sum of, 528, 529
Influential point, *193*
Intercepts, using to graph linear equations, 69
Inverse matrix, 44
    for solving systems of more than two linear equations, 74
Inverse transformations, *146*
Inverse variation functions and models, 250–264
    compared to exponential models, 256–259
    compared to linear models, 259–262
    identifying from a table, 262
    multiplicative inverse and, 256
    patterns in tables and graphs of, 254–255
    rate of change of, *251*
    reciprocal and, 256
    shape of, 256–259
    tables and graphs of, *256–259*

K

Kendall's rank correlation coefficient, *185*
Kruskal, Joseph, 325
Kruskal's algorithm, 325, 357
    versus Prim's algorithm, 338

L

Least squares regression, *211–226*, 544
    "best-fitting" line, *216–219*
    error in prediction, *213*
    regression line, *212, 217–218*
    residual, *214*
    slope and y-intercept formulas, *225–226*
Linear combination, finding intersection coordinates, *100*
Linear data patterns, connections between correlation coefficients and, *192*
Linear equations, systems of
    adding two equations, 98–101
    comparing solution methods, 63–66
    effects of multiplying each term by a constant, 98–99
    and families of lines, 97–101
    graphs, using to solve, 65
    intercepts, using to graph, 69
    inverse matrices for solving more than two, 73–74
    limitations of using matrices to solve, 70
    linear combination, 100
    linear regression procedure to graph, 69–70
    and matrices, 59–78
    matrix equations for solving more than two, 73–74
    matrix representation for, 61
    in modeling polygons, 97
    rewriting, 64
    solving, 61
    substitution method of solving, 73
    sum equations, graphing, 99
    tables of values for, 64
    table, using, 60

Linear models, 244, 546
    compared to exponential models, 238–249
    compared to inverse variation models, *256–258*
    compared to power models, tables, and graphs, 238–249
    identifying from a table, 262
Linear regression procedure, 69–70
Linear velocity, 417, 548
Line reflections, *113*
Lines
    families of, *97–101*
    images of, *121*
    intersect in a point, *104–105*
    parallel, *104–105*
    same, *104–105*
Line segment
    calculating length of, *82*
    medians, *108*
    midpoint of, *85–86*
Linkages
    parallelogram, *371–372, 373*
    using quadrilaterals in, *370–376*
    of rhombuses, *382, 391*
    and similarity, *373–376*
List and Line Plot calculator feature, *122*
Lurking variables, *197*

M

Main diagonal, *8*
Markov, A. A., 55
Markov process, 55
    states, 55
    transition matrix, 55
Mathematical modeling, *75–78*
Matrices
    adding, *10–11, 12, 42*
    analyzing, *6–10*
    and animation, *149–164*
    combining, *10–13*
    degree of difference, *7*
    without inverses, 44
    main diagonal, *8*
    multiplying, *12, 26–58*
    powers of, *36–41, 159*
    properties of, *41–45*
    rank correlation, *178*
    scatterplot, *177*
    square matrix, *8*
    square root of, finding, *58*
    subtracting, *10–11, 12*
    symmetric, *321*
    and systems of linear equations, *59–78*
Matrix addition, *10–11, 12, 42, 158*
    addition of numbers versus, *42*
    commutativity of, *42*

Matrix equation
solving, *61–62*
for solving systems of
more than two linear
equations, *74–75*
Matrix models
building and using,
2–25
columns, *4*
rows, *4*
variables, *22*
Matrix multiplication, *12,
26–58, 159*
commutative property
of multiplication, *43*
distributive property for
matrices, *41, 52*
versus multiplication of
real numbers, *43*
multirow, *34*
one-row, *26*
and zero property of
multiplication, *45*
Mean, *109*
Measurement
direct, 400
indirect, 400, 545
Mechanical advantage, 392
Median, *108, 109*
Method of least squares, 216
Midpoint algorithm, *86*
Midpoint of a segment,
85–86, 93
MIDPT Program, *93*
Minimal spanning tree
best-edge algorithm,
323
clustering detection,
330
nearest-neighbor algo-
rithm, 324
and Traveling Sales-
person Problem, 349
Multiplication Rule, 471–484
for three or four inde-
pendent events, 475
Multiplicative inverse, *44,
256*

N

Nearest-neighbor algorithm,
324
for Traveling Sales-
person Problem, 360
Network, finding the best,
320–339
connected, 322–323
shortest, 322
n factorial (*n*!), 494
Nonsymmetry, *109*
NOW-NEXT, 29, 269, 468,
506

O

Oblique line, *85*
Octahedron, 468
One-row matrix, *28*
Opposite matrix, *42–43*
Optimization, 358
Overlap matrix, *24*

P

P(not *A*), 480
Pantographs, 373–376
and coordinate systems,
379
and distances scale fac-
tor for, 375–376
reducing, 383
and size transforma-
tions, 380
triangle images using,
375
Parabola, *277*
vertex of, *277*
Parallelogram linkage,
371–372, 373
Parameter, 444
Parametric equations, 444
Paths
in adjacency matrices,
37
critical, *51*
of length one, *37*
of length two, *37*
in powers of matrices,
37
Pearson, Karl, *188, 193*
Pearson's correlation coeff-
cient *r, 188–196,
208–209*
versus Spearman's rank
correlation coefficient,
206
Pentagon, regular, *109*
Perimeter, *236*
Period, 441
Periodic change, patterns of,
436–442
Periodic graph, 441
Pixels, *81*
Plane, coordinate model,
80–108
Polygons
determining classifica-
tion, *89*
image of, finding, *121*
modeling, *97*
plotting with computer
graphics, *81–87*
similar, *147*
transforming using List
and Line Plot calcula-
tor feature, *122*
Power models, tables, and
graphs, *238–241,
541–542*
compared to exponential
models, *239–240, 244*
compared to linear
models, *239–240, 244*
rate of change, *247*

Powers, *238,* 300–302
fractional exponents and
rules, 302
negative exponents, *301*
power of, *301*
product of, *300*
of a product, *301*
quotient of, *300*
of a quotient, *301*
Prim's algorithm, 337–338
versus Kruskal's algo-
rithm, 338
Prismoidal formula, *137*
Probability
of complement (not *A*),
480
multiplying, 472–477
Probability distributions,
485–509, 496
expected value of,
510–529
rectangular, 496
triangular, 497
Program-planning algorithm,
84, 93
Project digraphs, *51*
Pyramid
hexagonal, *137*
octagonal, *137*
square, *137*
Pythagorean Theorem, *83,
290*

Q

Quadratic equations, solving,
278–280, 546
number/existence of
solutions, *281*
roots, *278, 281–283*
symbolically, *279*
using graphs, *278*
using tables, *278*
Quadratic functions and
models, *265–288,* 546
parabola, *277*
patterns in graphs and
tables, *270, 274–277*
shape of, *274–277*
solving inequalities, *288*
symbolic rule for, *275*
using tables and graphs
to solve equation, *267*
Quadrilateral, *87–90, 91, 102*
flexible, 368–383
in linkages, 370–376

R

Radian, 421
measure, 441
relationship to degree,
421
relationship to revolu-
tion, 421
Radicals, *289–310*
adding expressions, *298*
Radical symbol, *290*
Rank correlation, *171–185*
matrix, *178*
Rare event, 464
Reciprocal, *256*

Rectangle, drawing with computer graphics, *81*
Rectangular coordinate system, *95*
Reflection Algorithm, 157
Reflection image, *114–116*
Reflection symmetry, *109*
Residual in a regression line,
214
Response variable, *199*
Revolutions
versus degrees, 420
per minute, converting
to degrees per minute,
417
Rhombus linkage, 391
of three, 382
Rigid grid, minimum number
of braces for, 333–334
Rigidity, 333–334
and connected graphs,
334
and spanning trees, 334
and vertex-edge graphs,
333–334
Rigid transformations, *110*
coordinate model, *120*
modeling, *111–126*
versus size transforma-
tions, *135*
Roots, *278, 281–282*
Rotational symmetry, *109,*
412
Rotations, *116–119*
clockwise, *116–119*
counterclockwise,
116–119
not centered at origin,
164
180°, *116–119*
ROT90 Program, *123*
Row reduction, *53*
Rows in a matrix, *4*
rpm, converting to degrees
per minute, 417

S

Scalar multiplication, *12, 50,
160*
Scale drawings versus vertex-
edge drawings, 355
Scale factor of *k*, 408
Scale models, *234–237*
Scatterplots, *171*
matrix, *177*
of trigonometric ratios,
408
Shapes of constant width, 431
SHORTCUT software, 344,
360
row sums computed by,
344
Shortest paths, 340–362
and Traveling Sales-
person Problem, 349
in visibility graphs, 552
in weighted graphs,
341–345
Similar right angles, 408
Similar triangles, 395
Simplest radical form, *292*

Sine, 398
  equations of function, 433–434
  length of cycle of function, 436
  maximum and minimum of function, 436
  relationship to cosine function, 439
  scatterplots and tables of function, 433
  symmetries of function, 446
Size transformations
  area of figures and composition of, *141*
  center at the origin, *128*
  composing with rotations, *142*
  composition of, 380
  distances, to measure indirectly, *134–135*
  of magnitude *k*, *130*, *160*
  of magnitude 3, *127*
  matrix representations for, *154–156*
  modeling, *126–138*
  negative numbers as magnitudes, *132*
  and pantographs, 380
  prismoidal formula, *137*
  versus rigid transformations, *135*
  scale factor, *142*
  similarity transformation, *143*
  similar shapes, *142*
  successively applying two, with center at origin, *140*
  without use of coordinates, *147*
Slope algorithm, 85
Slopes, *81*, 104
Spanning tree, 332
  and rigidity, 334
Spearman, Charles, *173*
Spearman's rank correlation coefficient, *173–175*
  versus Pearson's correlation coefficient, *206*
  sum of squared differences, *175*
Spiral
  drawing, *295*
  edge length, *295–296*
  total length, *296*
Spreadsheets, *18*, 24
Square, drawing with computer graphics, *81*
Square matrix, *8*, 43
  symmetric, *20*
Square root, *290*
  radical symbol, *290*
Square root of a matrix, finding, 58
Steiner, Jacob, 338
Steiner tree, 338
Subscript notation, *94*
Sum of squared errors (SSE), 217, 226
  and relationship to *r*, 226

Surface area, *238*
Symmetry, *20–21*, 109
  reflection, *109*
  rotational, *109*
  translational, *110*

T

Table, using
  to solve quadratic equations, 267, 278
  to solve system of equations, *60*
Tangency, point of, 428
Tangent, 398, 428
Tetrahedron, 468
Theoretical
  average, 486
  distribution, 487
Transformations
  and animation, *149–164*
  composing, *140*, 146
  composition of, *139*
  coordinate models of, *109–148*
  effects of various combinations of, *139–140*
  inverse, *146*
  matrix representation, *159–160*
  modeling combinations of, *138–148*
  rigid, *110*, *111–126*
  shear, *159*
  size, *126–138*
Translation
  components of, *112*
  composing, *139–140*
  image of segment under, *120*
Translational symmetry, *110*
  horizontal, *110*, *111*
  oblique, *112*
  vertical, *112*
Translation image, *111*
TRANSL Program, *113*
Transmission factor, 414
Traveling Salesperson Problem, 348–352, 357, 360
  best-edge algorithm for, 349
  and Hamiltonian circuit, 349
  lack of good algorithm for, 351
  and minimal spanning tree, 349
  and shortest path or circuit, 349
Tree, 323
  minimal spanning, 323
  spanning, 332
  Steiner, 338
  vertex colorings of, 332
Tree graph, 483
  for rolling dice, 468
Tree-growing algorithm. *See Dijkstra's algorithm.*
Trends, 75
Trial, 460

Triangles, *102*
  adjustable, variable length side, 385–388
  altitude of, *108*
  area under reflection and translation, *123*
  congruent, 166
  images using pantographs, 375
  isosceles right, *306*
  rigidity of, 384
  similar, *166*, 395
  30°-60°-90°, *307*
  and trigonometric ratios, 384–411
Triangulation, 549
  Delaunay, 550, 554
Trigonometric ratios
  and calculator to find angle measures, 403
  to find angle measures, 403
  to find lengths of triangle sides, 402
  scatterplots, 408
  and triangles, 384–411
  using calculator to find values for, 398–399
2 × 2 matrix
  inverse, *53*
  and transformations, *159*

U

Union, *106*

V

Variables in a matrix, *22*
Variables in cause-and-effect relationships
  correlated, *199*
  explanatory, *199*
  response, *199*
Velocity, initial upward, 270
Vertex, 277
Vertex colorings of trees, 332
Vertex-edge graph, *38, 56*, 322, 358, 362, 551
  bipartite, 357
  complete, 357
  for dodecahedron, 346
  and rigidity, 333–334
  versus scale drawings, 355
  weighted, 340
Vertical line, *94*
  distance between points, *82–86*
Vertical translation, *112*
Visibility
  graph, 551
  matrix, 551
Volume, *238*

W

Waiting-time distributions, theoretical, 486–488, 498, 548
  algebraic models for, 491, 505
  box plots for, 491
  calculator, using to generate, 504–505
  expected value of, 521–523
  formula for, 499, 502, 527
  histogram for, 491, 499
Waiting times, 456–470
  distribution of, 462–465
  histogram for, 464
  NOW-NEXT equations, 468
Weighted graphs, 340
  and shortest paths, 341–345
Weighted ranking method, 57
Weights, 340

X

x-axis, reflection across, 115, *157*
x-intercept, 69, *98*

Y

y-axis, reflection across, 115, *157*
y = x, reflection across, 115, *157*
y = −x, reflection across, *115*
y-intercept, 69, *98*, 104

Z

Zero matrix, *42*

Index of Contexts

Photo Credits for the Pupil Edition